ENCYCLOPEDIA OF THE ATOMIC AGE

RODNEY P. CARLISLE
Editor

☑® Facts On File, Inc.

For Loretta

❧

Encyclopedia of the Atomic Age

Copyright © 2001 by Rodney P. Carlisle

Facts On File, Inc.
132 West 31st Street
New York NY 10001

Library of Congress Cataloging-in-Publication Data
Encyclopedia of the atomic age / Rodney P. Carlisle, editor.
p.   cm.
Includes bibliographical references and index.
ISBN 0-8160-4029-X
1. Nuclear physics—History—20th century—Encyclopedias. 2. Nuclear weapons—History
20th century—Encyclopedias. I. Carlisle, Rodney P.
QC773 .E49 2001
539.7'09—dc21   00-068129

Facts On File books are available at special discounts when purchased in bulk quantities for businesses, associations, institutions or sales promotions. Please call our Special Sales Department in New York at 212/967-8800 or (800) 322-8755.

You can find Facts On File on the World Wide Web at
http://www.factsonfile.com

Cover and text design by Cathy Rincon

Printed in the United States of America.

VB FOF 10 9 8 7 6 5 4 3 2 1

This book is printed on acid-free paper.

CONTENTS

LIST OF
ILLUSTRATIONS

LIST OF MAPS

PREFACE

This volume is intended to provide the student and the general reader with a guide to the atomic age as it unfolded in the 20th century. By a narrow definition, the period known as "The Atomic Age" covered the years from the development of the concept of nuclear fission in 1938 through the end of atmospheric nuclear testing by the United States and the Soviet Union in 1961. However, the issues surrounding nuclear weapons and peaceful uses of nuclear energy, particularly the generation of electricity from reactors and the problems of dealing with radioactive waste, continue to the end of the 20th century. Furthermore, the scientific groundwork to the discovery of fission was accomplished in the early decades of the 20th century. In deciding what topics to include in this encyclopedia, we have given emphasis to the period from 1938 to 1961, with a focus on the contributions of individuals, decisions of political leaders and administrators, and controversies of that period. However, a number of entries explore the earlier science, and many more provide information about the later policy ramifications of nuclear energy for civilian and military uses and its place in international relations through the end of the 20th century.

The entries for the encyclopedia were prepared in the years 1999–2000. Accidents, episodes of nuclear espionage, international negotiations to limit weapons, threats of nuclear weapons proliferation and operational use, and developments in nuclear science and nuclear technology will all continue into the 21st century, but the reader will need to look elsewhere for coverage of such later ramifications of the broader atomic age.

This work is based entirely on research materials available at the time of writing that were never classified or had been declassified and publicly released. Part of the rich flood of material becoming available to historians are the Venona documents, which are the decrypted communications detailing Soviet espionage in the United States during World War II. Several scholars have used these and recently opened Russian materials to shed new light on Soviet nuclear developments, which have been given some coverage here. Despite the fact that many technical and policy matters remain properly closed from public view, the amount of reliable literature on nuclear matters that is available to researchers, students, and the general reader is both vast and constantly growing. The bibliography presented at the end of this encyclopedia is by no means exhaustive, but it gives some access to the book-length studies (and a few of the thousands of articles) through which interested students of the subject may learn more.

Several contributors helped in the preparation of this volume. Most notably, Professor Sidney Katz of Rutgers University, Camden, New Jersey, assisted by personally developing over 60 entries that explain scientific and technical terms. While this work is not intended as a technical dictionary, we believe that an understanding of some key aspects of nuclear science and technology is essential to exploring the ramifications of policy issues. Other scholars assisted with specific areas, including Edward Rice-Maximin with entries pertaining to France, Scott Bennett regarding antinuclear movements, Jason Krupar on the early years of the Atomic Energy Commission, and J. J.

Ahern on the Philadelphia Navy Yard in World War II. Research assistance and preliminary drafts of another dozen entries were prepared by student assistants at Rutgers, including James Tuvell, Charles Rossano, and Danny O'Brien.

Factual matters have been checked against multiple sources, and we have made concerted efforts to present balanced views of controversial issues. It is our hope that this encyclopedia will serve to provide an accurate basis of facts and a sound starting point for further inquiry into the many continuing issues of the atomic age.

—Rodney P. Carlisle

INTRODUCTION

Early in the 20th century, nuclear physicists in Europe and the United States made a number of spectacular advances in understanding the nature of the atom. Physicists developed new tools, including machines that could accelerate atomic particles to great speed to impact and transform atoms of target materials, and the field of nuclear physics underwent a scientific revolution in just a few years. That revolution would reshape the conduct of war, the hazards of peace, and the possibilities of world prosperity.

By the early 1930s, ideas that had been the fantasies of science fiction authors only a decade before seemed possible. Physicists realized that by unleashing the energy of the atom, as calculated by Albert Einstein, the world might have a source of unlimited power. Men and women working obscurely at the study of the invisible world of the nuclear structure became historic figures whose discoveries reshaped the world. They included Ernest Rutherford, John Cockroft, Madame Marie Curie, Frédéric and Irène Joliot-Curie, Otto Hahn, Werner Heisenberg, J. Robert Oppenheimer, and many others. Step by step, their discoveries took humanity closer to unleashing the power that resulted when matter was transformed into energy at the atomic level.

Just as the developments that ushered in the atomic age took place, World War II broke out in Europe on September 1, 1939. Within a few months, scientists in Great Britain and the United States voluntarily began to stop the publication of their findings. To do so constituted a sharp break with the custom of prompt and open publishing in the rapidly advancing field. Publication had served to bring recognition to individual scientists, and it had stimulated progress throughout the world by the sharing of discovery across international boundaries and fostering further breakthroughs.

With the sudden cutoff of published research, scientists in Germany and the Soviet Union realized that their counterparts in the United States and Great Britain must have turned their talents to the possibility of an atomic bomb. They were right. Behind the walls of secrecy, further great advances took place. In the United States, the U.S. Army established the Manhattan Engineer District and began to fund the pursuit of a nuclear weapon design on a massive scale. Scientists from Britain and Canada, already at work on aspects of the problem, joined the Manhattan Project. Refugee scientists from many European countries also brought their talents to the questions surrounding reactor and weapon design.

One such emigré scientist, Italian Enrico Fermi, designed CP-1, or Chicago Pile #1. The reactor Fermi built was a crucial step toward harnessing the atom, and his colleagues viewed its first operation on December 2, 1942, as the birth of the atomic age. With the reactor, a new element could be created, plutonium, that could fuel nuclear weapons. Furthermore, the reactor promised a means for converting nuclear energy into heat; the heat could be used to generate electricity if connected to a system of steam generation. From that reactor, future designs descended—in one direction, to make the production reactors that would produce plutonium, and in another, to make reactors that could power ships or generate electricity for peaceful purposes.

From these beginnings, the science and technology of nuclear weapons and nuclear power continued to flow for the rest of the 20th century. The weapons made by the Manhattan Engineer District, detonated over the cities of Hiroshima and Nagasaki in Japan, ended World War II and ushered in a worldwide recognition of the devastating potential of nuclear weaponry.

Nuclear weapons soon became the most important part of the arsenal of the United States and the Soviet Union, the two superpowers that emerged after World War II. In the Soviet Union, scientists urged on by premier and Communist Party chairman Joseph Stalin worked feverishly to catch up with the American weapons program, utilizing information derived from espionage and harnessing some of the brightest young minds in the Soviet physics community. In 1949, barely four years after the United States, the Soviets tested their first nuclear weapon.

The principles used in CP-1 soon provided the basis for more sophisticated, more powerful, and larger reactors. Nuclear propulsion of ships, beginning in the 1950s, soon transformed the nature of submarines, allowing them to evade detection by remaining submerged for days, weeks, or months. Nuclear reactors for the generation of electric power were built in the United States, Britain, France, and the Soviet Union, and they were soon exported by those nations to help meet the energy needs of many other countries. Other reactors were used for research, while still others continued to produce the fuel for nuclear weapons.

The world soon faced grotesque threats from this new source of energy. Reactors generated radioactive nuclear waste that was difficult to dispose of safely. As with any mechanical system, human error soon led to accidents—some minor, several very serious—with the reactors themselves. Nuclear weapons became more devastating in their capability of destroying whole cities. Accidents with weapons and with the aircraft and ships that carried them created new hazards and new fears.

To test the weapons, the United States, the Soviet Union, Britain, and later France detonated nuclear devices in the atmosphere, underwater, and underground. Radioactive clouds of dust and debris from some of these detonations spread around the world, generating further hazards from radioactive fallout, often quite far from the test sites. In several cases in the Soviet Union, the United States, and the South Pacific Ocean, civilians were exposed to potentially dangerous amounts of radiation; some suffered serious health effects as a consequence.

As public awareness of the risks associated with reactors and with nuclear weapon testing mounted in the United States, Britain, France, and elsewhere, anti-

nuclear political organizations formed as early as the 1950s to oppose further development of both reactors and nuclear weapons.

The United States and the Soviet Union shaped their cold war rivalry around their nuclear arsenals. Both nations developed even more powerful weapons, based on using an atomic fission weapon as a trigger to ignite a hydrogen-fusion reaction that released energy on a far larger scale than the first weapons used against Japan. Nuclear war–fighting strategies and negotiations toward limitations on nuclear testing, on the deployment of weapons, and finally on reducing nuclear armaments became the measuring points of international diplomacy between the two sides during the cold war.

For a period between the mid-1960s and the mid-1970s, the United States and the Soviet Union entered a period of detente, during which the tensions of the early cold war years appeared to abate. However, in the mid-1970s, with increasing armaments on both sides, and then with the invasion of Afghanistan by the Soviet Union in 1979, an ever more risky rivalry over nuclear weapons heated up. The brief "second cold war," which lasted from 1978 to 1987, saw an intense period of nuclear arms development by both the United States and the Soviet Union coupled with several rounds of arms control negotiations, finally resulting in treaties that brought that arms race to a rather rapid halt in the period 1987 to 1992. The treaties, including the Intermediate Nuclear Forces Treaty (INF) and the Strategic Arms Reduction Treaty (START), coupled with the political dissolution of the Soviet Union in December 1991 marked the end of the cold war. But the atomic age was not over.

As the technology of atomic weapons became more widespread, new nations developed and tested them; the spread of such weapons was called "proliferation." The fear that a nuclear weapon or device might be used by a small group of terrorists or by an irresponsible national government continued to haunt the world in the 1990s.

Almost weekly, a news story or magazine article made reference to one or another of the many continuing issues that derived from the atomic legacy. News reports detailed nuclear proliferation among countries such as India, Pakistan, Iraq, and North Korea. Others explored environmental dangers of nuclear power, revelations of espionage in the nuclear field, pronouncements by nuclear power company officials or nuclear weapons strategists, charges by advocacy groups, the changing nature of nuclear armaments, or the threat of nuclear detonation against a population by terrorists or by an irresponsible or "rogue" state.

There are many fascinating historical works, biographies, and policy analyses that spell out aspects of the history of the atomic age, constituting an ever-growing library of rich information. Some are highly critical, providing arguments and evidence for public-action groups opposed to the spread of nuclear weapons or to use of reactors for nuclear power. Many such works focus only on risk, hazard, expense, and the negative aspects of the technologies. Other more positive or neutral books, while technically accurate, sometimes gloss over the risks and hazards of the atomic age or studiously avoid the more controversial aspects of the subject. Some works focus on particular aspects of weapons, technology, policy, or international relations, or they stress science and technology without reference to sensitive or heated policy issues.

In order to understand those works and to follow nuclear issues, the general reader needs to understand the physics of nuclear weapons, nuclear reactors, and radioactivity. For many students, and for many well-read adults, the task seems daunting. The works are often highly detailed, the terminology unfamiliar, the technology difficult to grasp, the cast of players unfamiliar. For students with historical or policy backgrounds, terms and principles of technology and science often appear obscure. For those trained in science, the by-ways of policy and history may seem clouded with confusing issues, quirky personalities, and almost endless open-ended debate together with the uncertainties that plague the world of politics and human affairs.

The dramatic stories of science breakthroughs, atomic espionage, weapons development, tough policy decisions, and international crises haunted by the threat of nuclear holocaust are often buried deep in works that seem inaccessible and excessively detailed, technically difficult, and even, at times, politically biased. No matter the background of the reader, vocabulary, concepts, ill-defined historical references, frequent acronyms, and cryptic formulas often stand in the way of clear understanding.

We have compiled this encyclopedia to help address the needs of readers confronted with the unfamiliar language and topics of this broad subject. The entries have been chosen to cover the major events of the atomic age and to make the most commonly used technical and scientific terms clear to the general reader. International policy revolves around nuclear issues with treaties such as the Anti-Ballistic Missile Treaty, in which both the United States and the Soviet Union agreed not to construct antimissile systems to protect themselves against each other's intercontinental ballistic missiles, or other treaties limiting weapons and tests. With a balanced approach that describes benefits and risks, successes and accidents, the entries outline some of the moral dilemmas in detail. Entries include brief biographical sketches of major scientists and government officials responsible for aspects of nuclear policy in the major nuclear nations.

The reader may be curious about the role of relatively familiar names, such as Einstein or Oppenheimer, or of those less familiar but no less crucial, such as Lise Meitner, Otto Hahn, and Eugene Wigner. The Russian scientists Igor Kurchatov and Nikolai Dollezhal', who played crucial roles in the development of the Soviet atomic weapon are here, along with the details of programs in India, South Africa, France, and elsewhere.

Our intention was to make the work as clear and as objective as possible. Rather than providing extended essays on individuals, topics, principles, and policies or attempting to argue convincingly for one side or another on controversial questions, we have always kept in mind that the reader needs concise definitions and explanations upon which to build understanding.

For many but not all entries, we provide suggested readings that the reader may locate in most libraries. We have appended a bibliographic guide that will also serve to lead the reader to sources with more information. Cross references may take a reader from one to another entry to pursue more information on related topics. A detailed chronology provides an overview of events that have shaped the atomic age.

As further aids, all the acronyms and abbreviations introduced in the text are defined in two listings that precede the alphabetically arranged entries. Scientific and technical abbreviations as used in nuclear physics and reactor technology are presented in the first list; acronyms used to define reactors, agencies, treaties, strategies, and institutions are presented in the second list.

SCIENTIFIC AND
TECHNICAL ABBREVIATIONS

amu	atomic mass unit	km	kilometer
ATWS	Anticipated Transient Without Scram	Kt	KILOTON
B	BORON*	linac	LINEAR ACCELERATOR
b	barns	LOCA	LOSS OF COOLANT ACCIDENT
Bq	Bequerel	MeV	million electron volts
C	Carbon	Mt	MEGATON
C.	Centigrade	MW	MEGAWATT
Cd	CADMIUM	MWe	Megawatt-electric
CDF	Core Damage Frequency	MWth	Megawatt-thermal
Cf	Californium	N	Atomic Number
Ci	CURIE	n	NEUTRON
cm	centimeter	NAA	NEUTRON ACTIVATION ANALYSIS
Cs	CESIUM	nfcm	neutron fluence per centimeter
d	density	Np	Neptunium
D	DEUTERIUM	O	Oxygen
dps	disintegrations per second	p	proton
D_2O	Deuterium Oxide or Heavy Water	Po	POLONIUM
DU	DEPLETED URANIUM	psi	pounds per square inch
eV	Electron volts	Pu	PLUTONIUM
F.	Fahrenheit	R	ROENTGEN
fis	FISSION	Ra	Radium
g	gram	RAD	Radiation-Absorbed Dose
GeV	giga (billion) electron volts	REM	Radiation-Equivalent Man
GWe	Gigawatts, electric	Sb	Antimony
H	Hydrogen	Sr	STRONTIUM
HEU	Highly Enriched Uranium	Sv	Sievert
HLLW	High Level Liquid Waste	T	TRITIUM
I	Iodine	U	URANIUM
k	MULTIPLICATION FACTOR	Xe	XENON
kg	kilogram		
Kj	Kilojoules		

*Items in SMALL CAPITAL LETTERS above have an entry in this encyclopedia.

ACRONYMS

AAA	Anti-Aircraft Artillery	CNVA	COMMITTEE FOR NON-VIOLENT ACTION
ABC	America-Britain-Canada (agreement)	COs	Conscientious Objectors
ABCC	ATOMIC BOMB CASUALTY COMMISSION*	CP-1	CHICAGO PILE No. 1
ABM	ANTI-BALLISTIC MISSILE	CPC	Combined Policy Committee (U.S.–Britain–Canada)
ACRS	ADVISORY COMMITTEE ON REACTOR SAFE-GUARDS	CPSU	Communist Party of the Soviet Union
ADM	ATOMIC DEMOLITION MUNITIONS	CPUSA	Communist Party of the United States of America
AEC	ATOMIC ENERGY COMMISSION	CTBT	COMPREHENSIVE TEST BAN TREATY
AFRRI	ARMED FORCES RADIOBIOLOGY RESEARCH INSTITUTE	DASA	DEFENSE ATOMIC SUPPORT AGENCY
AFSWP	ARMED FORCES SPECIAL WEAPONS PROJECT	DDR&E	Director of Defense Research and Engineering
AGR	Advanced Gas-Cooled Reactor	DOD	Department of Defense
AIF	ATOMIC INDUSTRIAL FORUM	DOE	DEPARTMENT OF ENERGY
ALARA	As Low As Reasonably Achievable	D-T	Deuterium-Tritium
ALCM	Air Launched CRUISE MISSILE	EBR	EXPERIMENTAL BREEDER REACTOR (I and II)
ANEC	American Nuclear Energy Council	EMP	ELECTROMAGNETIC PULSE
ANL	ARGONNE NATIONAL LABORATORY	EPA	ENVIRONMENTAL PROTECTION AGENCY
ATR	Advanced Test Reactor	ER	ENHANCED RADIATION
BAPL	BETTIS ATOMIC POWER LABORATORY	FAS	FEDERATION OF ATOMIC SCIENTISTS (FATS), FEDERATION OF AMERICAN SCIENTISTS (FAMS)
BMD	Ballistic Missile Defense		
BMI	BATTELLE MEMORIAL INSTITUTE		
BNL	BROOKHAVEN NATIONAL LABORATORY		
BWR	Boiling Water Reactor	FBI	Federal Bureau of Investigation
CANDU	CANADIAN DEUTERIUM-URANIUM REACTOR	FFTF	FAST FLUX TEST FACILITY
CDC	Centers for Disease Control	GAC	GENERAL ADVISORY COMMITTEE
CEA	(French Atomic Energy Commission)	GCR	Gas-Cooled Reactor
CEP	CIRCULAR ERROR PROBABLE	GE	General Electric
CERN	Center for European Nuclear Research	GLCM	Ground-Launched CRUISE MISSILE
CFE	Conventional Forces in Europe (treaty)	GOCO	Government-Owned, Contractor-Operated
CFR	Code of Federal Regulations	GRU	*Glavnue Razvedyvatel'nyi Upravlenie –* Soviet Army Intelligence
CIA	Central Intelligence Agency		
CNO	Chief of Naval Operations		

HEMP	High-Altitude Electromagnetic Pulse		NSG	Nuclear Suppliers Group
HLLW	High-Level Liquid Waste		NSM	National Security Memorandum
HTGR	HIGH-TEMPERATURE GAS-COOLED REACTOR		NTPR	NUCLEAR TEST PERSONNEL REVIEW
IAEA	INTERNATIONAL ATOMIC ENERGY AGENCY		NTS	NEVADA TEST SITE
ICBM	INTERCONTINENTAL BALLISTIC MISSILE		NUMEC	NUclear Materials and Equipment Corporation
INEL	IDAHO NATIONAL ENGINEERING LABORATORY		NUWAX	NUclear Weapons Accident eXercise
INF	INTERMEDIATE-RANGE NUCLEAR FORCES (TREATY)		NWC	Nuclear Weapons Council
INPO	INSTITUTE FOR NUCLEAR POWER OPERATIONS		OCAW	Oil, Chemical, and Atomic Workers (union)
KAPL	KNOLLS ATOMIC POWER LABORATORY		ORINS	Oak Ridge Institute of Nuclear Science
LANL	LOS ALAMOS NATIONAL LABORATORY		ORNL	OAK RIDGE NATIONAL LABORATORY
LLNL	LAWRENCE LIVERMORE NATIONAL LABORATORY		OSIA	ON-SITE INSPECTION AGENCY
LMFBR	LIQUID METAL FAST BREEDER REACTOR		OSRD	Office of Scientific Research and Development
LTBT	LIMITED TEST BAN TREATY (atmospheric test ban)		OSS	Office of Strategic Services
MAD	MUTUALLY ASSURED DESTRUCTION		PAL	PERMISSIVE ACTION LINK
MED	MANHATTAN ENGINEER DISTRICT		PDD 59	PRESIDENTIAL DECISION DIRECTIVE 59
MIRV	MULTIPLE INDEPENDENTLY TARGETABLE REENTRY VEHICLE		PHWR	Pressurized Heavy Water Reactor
MIT	Massachusetts Institute of Technology		PNE	Peaceful Nuclear Explosion
MLC	MILITARY LIAISON COMMITTEE		PNI-91	PRESIDENTIAL NUCLEAR INITIATIVE-1991
MOX	Mixed Oxide Fuel		PRA	PROBABILISTIC RISK ASSESSMENT
MRV	Multiple Reentry Vehicle		PSA	Probabilistic Safety Analysis
MTR	MATERIALS TESTING REACTOR		PSAC	President's Scientific Advisory Committee
NAS	National Academy of Sciences		PWR	PRESSURIZED WATER REACTOR
NATO	NORTH ATLANTIC TREATY ORGANIZATION		RBMK	*Reactory Bolshoi Moshchnosti Kanalynye* or "Channelized Large Power Reactor"; Graphite-moderated water-cooled power reactor (Soviet type)
NBTL	Naval Boiler and Turbine Laboratory			
NDRC	National Defense Research Committee		ROK	Republic of Korea
NEI	Nuclear Energy Institute		RTG	Radioisotope-fueled Thermoelectric Generator
NEPA	National Environmental Protection Act (also, 1946–1961, Nuclear Energy for Propulsion of Aircraft)		RV	REENTRY VEHICLE
			SA	Surface to Air (missile). Also "SAM."
			SAC	Strategic Air Command
NERVA	Nuclear Engine for Rocket Vehicle Application		SACEUR	Supreme Allied Command–Europe
			SALT	STRATEGIC ARMS LIMITATION TREATY (I and II)
NIMBY	Not in My Back Yard			
NKVD	*Narodnyi Komissariat Vnutrennkyh Del* – People's Commissariat for Internal Affairs (Soviet secret police)		SAM	Surface to Air Missile
			SDI	STRATEGIC DEFENSE INITIATIVE
			SDIO	Strategic Defense Initiative Office
NPG	Nuclear Planning Group (of NATO)		SIOP	SINGLE INTEGRATED OPERATIONAL PLAN
NPT	NON-PROLIFERATION TREATY		SL-1	STATIONARY LOW-POWER REACTOR-1
NRC	NUCLEAR REGULATORY COMMISSION		SLBM	SUBMARINE-LAUNCHED BALLISTIC MISSILE
NRL	NAVAL RESEARCH LABORATORY		SLCM	Ship-Launched CRUISE MISSILE
NRTS	National Reactor Test Site (Idaho)		SNAP	Systems for Nuclear Auxiliary Power
NRX	Natural uranium Reactor eXperimental (Canadian)		SRAM	Short-Range Attack Missile
			SRS	SAVANNAH RIVER SITE
NSC	National Security Council		SS	Surface to Surface (missile)

SSBN	Ballistic Missile Submarine-Nuclear
START	STRATEGIC ARMS REDUCTION TREATY (I and II)
TMI	THREE MILE ISLAND
TRIGA	Training, Research, Isotope-General Atomics (reactor)
TTAPS	Turco, Toon, Ackerman, Pollack, and Sagan (authors of NUCLEAR WINTER thesis)
TTBT	THRESHOLD TEST BAN TREATY
TVA	Tennessee Valley Authority
UCS	UNION OF CONCERNED SCIENTISTS
UN	United Nations

UNSCOM	United Nations Special Commission on Iraq
VA	Veterans Administration
VVER	*Vodo-Vodyannoy Energeticheskiy Reactor* or water-cooled and water-moderated reactor, equivalent to the Western Pressurized Water Reactor.
WIPP	WASTE ISOLATION PILOT PLANT
WMD	Weapon of Mass Destruction
WRL	WAR RESISTERS LEAGUE
WTO	WARSAW TREATY ORGANIZATION (Warsaw Pact)

*Items in SMALL CAPITAL LETTERS have an entry in this encyclopedia.

ABC Agreement

During World War II, the United States, Great Britain, and Canada entered into a three-party arrangement to develop the nuclear weapon, informally known as the America-Britain-Canada, or "ABC," Agreement. More formally, the agreement rested on a Combined Policy Committee (CPC) that had been established at a conference in Quebec, Canada, in August 1943.

One of the first actions under the CPC was the transfer to the United States of Klaus FUCHS, a German refugee scientist working in Britain, who was secretly supplying information to the Soviet Union. The Soviets also learned of the work of the CPC through another espionage agent, the British member of the joint secretariat of the committee in Washington, Donald Maclean.

The three countries cooperated rather extensively at first, with Canada providing basic physics research and expertise in heavy water reactor design, much of it at McGill University in Montreal. Britain's scientists also continued to contribute to the American effort, a number coming to work at LOS ALAMOS. The three countries also collaborated on acquiring uranium for the project.

The cooperation under the three-power agreement was never completely comfortable. Some of the Canadian scientists working with their counterparts at the University of Chicago felt themselves isolated from key information, and some felt they were given peripheral assignments. Nevertheless, the agreement among the three countries had several long-range consequences.

One aspect of the agreement came back to haunt the United States after World War II. That was a provision requiring the United States to consult with the partners before using a nuclear weapon. The British agreed at a secret meeting on July 4, 1945, that the nuclear weapon, if successful, should be employed against Japan.

The direct participation of British and Canadian scientists in the Manhattan Project was generally withheld from the public. Thus it came as a surprise to the members of the U.S. congressional JOINT COMMITTEE ON ATOMIC ENERGY in 1948 when they learned that the Quebec agreement required that the United States secure consent of the British for the use of an atomic weapon and that the British possessed sufficient knowledge to build such a weapon themselves.

In several of the postwar meetings to discuss what information should be declassified, both Donald Maclean and Klaus Fuchs, working as Soviet agents, participated as representatives of the British nuclear community. Apparently neither knew the other was working for the Soviets.

The Combined Policy Committee worked out an agreement or modus vivendi early in 1948, in which the British agreed to delay construction of their own nuclear weapon for several years and give up their power to decide if the U.S. weapons could be employed, and in which the United States was permitted to acquire all of the uranium exported from the Belgian Congo over the following two years.

Suggested Reading

Richard Rhodes, The Making of the Atomic Bomb. New York: Simon and Schuster, 1986.

Aboveground Testing   *See* ATMOSPHERIC TESTING.

Acheson, Dean   (1893–1971)   *U.S. secretary of state from 1949 to 1953*

Dean Acheson served as secretary of state during the early years of the nuclear arms race between the United States and the Soviet Union. His influence on nuclear policy began earlier and extended beyond his period of formal service as secretary of state, as he became an elder statesman arguing for a convincing nuclear deterrent policy during the administrations of John F. KENNEDY and Lyndon JOHNSON.

Acheson was born April 11, 1893, in Middletown, Connecticut. His father was Canadian-born and his mother had been born in Britain, perhaps accounting for Acheson's lifelong belief in and support for cooperation between Britain and the United States.

He graduated from Yale University in 1915 and received his law degree from Harvard Law School in 1918. He served as clerk to Supreme Court Justice Louis Brandeis before entering private law practice in Washington, D.C. In 1933, he briefly served in the Franklin ROOSEVELT administration as under secretary of the treasury, but he soon resigned. With the outbreak of World War II in 1939, he was an outspoken advocate of American intervention on the side of Britain. He rejoined the Roosevelt administration as assistant secretary of state in 1941.

During the war, he served as acting secretary of state during the absence of secretaries James BYRNES and George C. Marshall. Truman appointed Acheson as undersecretary of state in 1945. In 1946, he worked with David LILIENTHAL in preparing the Acheson-Lilienthal Report, a predecessor to the BARUCH PLAN that would have turned atomic research and development over to the United Nations. The Acheson-Lilienthal Report differed from the Baruch Plan in that Acheson and Lilienthal believed that members of the United Nations Security Council should retain a veto power over nuclear matters, while Bernard Baruch believed the charter should be amended to prevent such vetoes. The Acheson-Lilienthal Report was made public in March 1946. Acheson resigned from the government in 1947 and then returned when he was appointed by President Harry TRUMAN as secretary of state to replace Marshall in 1949.

In negotiations with the Soviet Union, Acheson advocated developing a position of strength. Thus he believed the United States should maintain its lead in atomic weapons. Following the 1949 detonation of the Soviet's first atomic bomb, he urged Truman to support the development of a hydrogen bomb. During this period, he and George Kennan, the State Department Russian expert who had first articulated the concept of "containment" of the Soviet Union in 1946, disagreed over nuclear weapons, with Acheson urging their development and Kennan arguing for a scaling down of the arms race.

When NORTH KOREA invaded the South in 1950 and launched the KOREAN WAR, some of Acheson's critics blamed him for having delivered a speech that implied Korea was not within the area of strategic concern for the United States.

Acheson retired from the State Department in 1953 with the election of Republican Dwight EISENHOWER. When Eisenhower's secretary of state John Foster DULLES developed the doctrine of "Massive Retaliation," suggesting the use of nuclear weapons to oppose conventional attacks by communist forces, Acheson published a major criticism of the doctrine in the *New York Times Magazine* on March 28, 1954. Soon Acheson became well known as the leading critic of the Dulles policy, regarding it as a reckless brandishing of atomic weapons, an attempt at "defense on the cheap," and a gamble with war and peace.

Instead, Acheson argued that the United States needed to maintain a large defense establishment, without excessive reliance on the nuclear weapon as the single deterrent to Soviet aggression. He also opposed the development of nuclear weapons by the European allies, believing that the Europeans should expend their limited defense budgets on conventional forces. Although working in a private law firm during this period, he devoted much of his time and energy to matters of foreign policy, and he emerged as the major spokesman of the Democratic Party on such issues.

Working with Paul NITZE, Acheson prepared foreign policy statements for the Democratic presidential candidates, and he continued to author pamphlets attacking Republican foreign policy and nuclear policy. One essay he wrote in 1958, entitled "America's Present Danger and What We Must Do about It," was a response to Soviet successes in launching SPUTNIK.

When the Democrats returned to office in 1961, Acheson served as an advisor to John F. Kennedy and later to Lyndon Johnson. In an essay he wrote for Kennedy in March 1961, known as the Acheson Report, he suggested that nuclear retaliation would come from the United States for any nuclear attack on a NORTH ATLANTIC TREATY ORGANIZATION member state. Kennedy adopted the policy in National Security Memorandum #40.

During the Cuban Missile Crisis of October 1962, Acheson, acting as an unofficial advisor to President Kennedy, advocated an air strike to destroy the Soviet missiles on the ground. When that recommendation was rejected, he served as a personal envoy of Kennedy to explain to European allies the maritime "Quarantine" or blockade of Cuba that Kennedy decided upon against Acheson's advice.

Acheson's influence on U.S. nuclear policy and foreign policy was far-reaching, and it went well beyond his tenure as secretary of state. In arguing against the Republican policy of massive retaliation, and then in supporting a policy of raising levels of defense manpower, improved and modernized military equipment, and the retention of U.S. nuclear weapons in Europe, Acheson set the tone for the intensification of the cold war under Kennedy. Advocates for a strong nuclear policy, mostly Republican, borrowed a phrase from his 1958 essay when in 1976 they established the COMMITTEE ON THE PRESENT DANGER, whose members later shaped nuclear and foreign policy under Republican Ronald REAGAN.

Acheson's writing ability, his arguments from conviction, and his style of turning a phrase that others echoed (such as "present danger") accounted for some of his influence. In 1969, he published a volume of his

Dean Acheson. Acheson was one of the architects of American nuclear policy, as coauthor of the Acheson–Lilienthal Report that proposed a system of U.N. control of atomic weapons. He later served as secretary of state under President Harry Truman, helping to develop the concept of nuclear deterrence.
(Library of Congress)

memoirs, entitled *Present at the Creation,* in which he recounted the evolution of cold war policy and the positions he had taken.

Acheson's conservative critics faulted him for his support of Alger Hiss, a State Department employee accused of espionage for the Soviets and convicted of perjury for denying it. Others criticized Acheson's strictly European orientation in his foreign policy concerns, claiming that he tended not to give Asian issues their due importance. Such a bias, they believed, accounted for his crucial oversight regarding Korea and for advice he gave to Lyndon Johnson to pull out of Vietnam. On the other hand, Acheson's critics from the "left" regarded his pro-nuclear armament position and his willingness to confront the Soviets as high-risk policies that tended to worsen U.S.–Soviet relations at crucial turning points.

Acheson died October 12, 1971.

Suggested Reading

David McLellan, *Dean Acheson: The State Department Years.* New York: Dodd, Mead, 1976.
Douglas Brinkley, *Dean Acheson: The Cold War Years, 1953–1971.* New Haven: Yale University Press, 1992.

Advisory Committee on Reactor Safeguards

The Advisory Committee on Reactor Safeguards (ACRS) represented a group of distinguished nuclear scientists who provided the ATOMIC ENERGY COMMISSION (AEC) and later the NUCLEAR REGULATORY COMMISSION (NRC) with independent reviews of the safety of reactor facilities and also commented on the adequacy of proposed safety standards.

The ACRS had its roots in the Reactor Safeguards Committee established in 1947 by the Atomic Energy Commission. In 1950, the AEC set up a committee to investigate problems of where to site future production reactors. After the selection of the SAVANNAH RIVER SITE by the AEC, the two committees were combined in 1953 into the ACRS.

Following the accident to the FERMI REACTOR in 1963, the Atomic Energy Act was amended to establish the ACRS as a committee in the law itself, with statutory functions. When the Nuclear Regulatory Commission was established in 1974, the ACRS was transferred to the NRC.

At first the ACRS and its predecessor committees dealt with reactors constructed by and for the AEC, offering reviews of production and experimental reactors. When the AEC began to license commercial power reactors, the ACRS reviewed the license application and all safety-related items and policy issues.

With the separation of commercial- and government-owned reactors that came with the reorganization in 1974, the ACRS function was restricted to commercial reactors licensed under the NRC. However, the ACRS continued to provide advice to the Defense Nuclear Facilities Safety Board on Energy Research and Development Agency–owned reactors, and, later, Department of Energy–owned reactors.

The ACRS took the lead within the NRC in supporting the move toward PROBABILISTIC RISK ASSESSMENT in the early 1980s. In recent years, the ACRS has been required to prepare an annual report for Congress, providing results of studies on NRC-sponsored reactor safety research.

Advisory Committee on Uranium

Prior to the establishment of the MANHATTAN ENGINEER DISTRICT (MED) under the U.S. Army Corps of Engineers, preliminary work on developing a military use for atomic energy went forward under civilian government organizations. The first of these was the Advisory Committee on Uranium, which had its origins in October 1939.

After President Franklin ROOSEVELT received a letter from Albert EINSTEIN and a note from Leo SZILARD on October 1, 1939, urging federal government support for research into a possible military application of atomic fission, he established the Advisory Committee on Uranium. The committee was headed by Lyman Briggs, chief of the Bureau of Standards, and it was sometimes called the Briggs Committee.

Within three weeks, the committee recommended procuring 4 tons of graphite and 50 tons of uranium oxide to test graphite as a neutron MODERATOR. Scientists in Britain and the United States worked on various aspects of the fission problem. On February 29, 1940, Alfred Nier in Minnesota separated microscopic amounts of URANIUM into the two ISOTOPES, ^{238}U and ^{235}U. In early March 1940, John Dunning at Columbia University demonstrated that the ^{235}U was responsible for slow-neutron fission, using the samples developed in Minnesota. In the same month, British scientists Rudolf PEIERLS and Otto FRISCH estimated that 1 kilogram of ^{235}U would be sufficient to make a nuclear explosion. On May 29, 1940, Louis Turner at Princeton University showed that PLUTONIUM, which could be created in a controlled CHAIN REACTION, would be an even more useful source for a nuclear explosion.

Enrico FERMI reported to the Advisory Committee on Uranium in June 1940 that graphite would be an effective moderator, showing the way to the construction of a reactor for the production of plutonium, using the more plentiful isotope of uranium, ^{238}U, as reactor fuel.

Also in June 1940 Roosevelt ordered that the Advisory Committee on Uranium be reorganized as part of the National Defense Research Committee (NDRC), headed by Vannevar BUSH. The NDRC began to issue contracts to universities and industrial companies to proceed immediately with the work.

Officially a subsection of the NDRC, the Advisory Committee on Uranium continued to coordinate work on the project until the formation of the OFFICE OF SCIENTIFIC RESEARCH AND DEVELOPMENT (OSRD) in December 1941, when the project was transferred to the S-1 section of the OSRD. During the period June 1940 to December 1941, several crucial scientific advances further demonstrated the feasibility of an atomic bomb. Some of the work proceeded in Britain, under the MAUD COMMITTEE, and some of the results of that work were communicated to the groups working under the NDRC.

In early March 1941, American physicists were able to demonstrate that element 94 (plutonium) was the end product of neutron absorption by ^{238}U. Work proceeded in the study of the NEUTRON CROSS SECTION of both plutonium and ^{235}U, and the required CRITICAL MASS of each was recomputed. By September 1941, Fermi had developed a test reactor at Columbia that could be used to demonstrate the moderating properties of graphite. Methods of separating the two isotopes of uranium were demonstrated at the University of California at Berkeley, using electromagnetic techniques, and at Columbia, using a gaseous diffusion method.

CHRONOLOGY OF EARLY ATOMIC BOMB WORK, U.S.A.

Oct. 1, 1939	Einstein letter delivered to Roosevelt, Advisory Committee on Uranium established
June 1940	Advisory Committee on Uranium incorporated in NDRC
Dec. 6, 1941	NDRC work transferred to OSRD, Atomic Bomb project is administered in S-1 section
June 1942	Manhattan Engineer District organized and OSRD work and contracts taken over by MED

Over the first half of 1942, work proceeded under the OSRD, lining up industrial contractors to begin work on production reactors and separation plants, and with universities to better fund the physics research.

Suggested Reading

Richard Rhodes, *The Making of the Atomic Bomb*. New York: Simon and Schuster, 1986.

Aircraft Nuclear Propulsion

In the period 1946 to 1961, one scheme for utilizing nuclear power was to develop a nuclear-powered jet turbine for aircraft propulsion. Supported within the ATOMIC ENERGY COMMISSION (AEC) and advanced by study groups within the commission, the proposal ran into severe criticism from President Dwight EISENHOWER, and it was terminated early in the administration of President John KENNEDY.

In 1944, the concept of Nuclear Energy for Propulsion of Aircraft (NEPA) began with an inquiry from Colonel Donald J. Keirn to Vannevar BUSH. Keirn's suggestion was turned down immediately because of the priority of bomb work. However, in 1946, Keirn was able to secure the approval of General Leslie GROVES for a study by Fairchild Engine and Airplane Corporation, working with OAK RIDGE. A NEPA technical staff was established at Oak Ridge.

Under the leadership of Gordon Simmons, the NEPA group investigated engineering problems associated with using nuclear reactor heat in propeller jets, turbojets, and ramjet engines. The GENERAL ADVISORY COMMITTEE, under the leadership of J. Robert OPPENHEIMER, studied the idea of an aircraft propulsion reactor in 1947–1948. Both James CONANT and Oppenheimer believed the project would be too expensive. The AEC approved a formal study of NEPA in 1948 by a group from the Massachusetts Institute of Technology, to be called the Lexington Report. The Lexington Report spelled out the need for a nuclear aircraft as a means of ensuring that nuclear weapons could be delivered from bases in the United States to targets in the Soviet Union. However, the Lexington Report also stated that it would take 15 years and at least a billion dollars to achieve an aircraft reactor.

Oak Ridge staff continued to support the concept, urging the expenditure of some $200 million over several years to study the possibility. The AEC funded a much smaller study project of NEPA during the period 1949–1950. Oak Ridge engineers began to suggest a design that would include light shielding around the reactor and a long distance between the reactor and the crew quarters on the aircraft.

However in 1950–1951, the Joint Chiefs of Staff refused to endorse the diversion of scarce uranium from bomb manufacture to the reactor program for aircraft. As the AEC considered many alternative reactor development issues in 1950, including reactors for submarine propulsion and the need for more PRODUCTION REACTORS, support for the aircraft reactor faded. One of the reasons was that long-range conventionally fueled jet aircraft became more feasible. Like the PLUTO and Rover projects for rocket development, the NEPA proposals were imaginative suggestions for the utilization of nuclear power that could not be supported for budgetary reasons, especially after the hazards of reactor accidents became publicized. Even more basic, competing technologies using liquid hydrocarbon and solid propellant fuels began to move ahead rapidly in the 1950s, leaving the high cost of nuclear propulsion research as a barrier to further development.

When Dwight Eisenhower took office in 1953, he was immediately skeptical of the idea of an expensive project to develop an aircraft reactor. During the 1950s, increasing awareness of the hazard to the public in the event of a crash of an aircraft with a reactor aboard, coupled with the expense of development, further diminished support for the program. In 1961, it was one of the first nuclear projects terminated by President Kennedy.

Suggested Reading

Richard G. Hewlett and Francis Duncan, *Atomic Shield* (Vol. 2 of *A History of the United States Atomic Energy Commission*). Washington, D.C.: Atomic Energy Commission, 1972.

ALARA–As Low As Reasonably Achievable

The Nuclear Regulatory Commission established the principle in 1973 that radioactive emissions from nuclear facilities should be as low as reasonably achievable (ALARA). The ALARA principle was defined in the Code of Federal Regulations: CFR 20.1101 and CFR 20.1003. The regulation called for "every reasonable effort to maintain exposures to radiation as far below the dose limits" as practical. The NRC set as a limit for annual whole-body DOSE to individuals outside a nuclear power plant to 3 millirems uptake by liquid and 5 millirems by air. The annual total release of radioactive material from a plant should not exceed 5 CURIES. The NRC called for expenditure of reasonable amounts to reduce the exposure and releases even further but made it clear that there was no attempt to reduce risk to absolute zero.

Although NRC regulations do not legally apply to the defense establishment, DOE has attempted to apply ALARA guidelines to reducing hazards at federal nuclear facilities.

See also REM.

Aleksandrov, Anatoly Petrovich (1903–1994)

Ukrainian nuclear physicist who designed the first Soviet nuclear reactors

A. P. Aleksandrov was born in 1903 in Traschi, near Kiev in the Ukraine. He was the designer of early Soviet graphite production reactors, such as those con-

structed at Chelyabinsk-40 and at Tomsk-7. He also designed the RBMK type of reactors, the type at CHERNOBYL. He developed the system of thermal diffusion used for the separation of isotopes.

He graduated from Kiev University in 1930, and he replaced Peter KAPITSA as head of the Institute of Physical Problems when Kapitsa decided not to participate in nuclear weapons development. Aleksandrov worked with Igor KURCHATOV on the construction of the first production reactors. In 1960, Aleksandrov became director of the Kurchatov Institute of Atomic Energy, and he served for 11 years as president of the Soviet Academy of Sciences, from 1975 to 1986. He received several prizes for his contributions to the Soviet nuclear weapons program, including the Lenin Prize in 1959 and three Hero of Socialist Labor prizes. He died in 1994.

Algeria

Briefly in the early 1990s, Western intelligence agencies became concerned that Algeria was attempting to develop a nuclear weapon. Algeria had been the site of French nuclear testing as early as 1960. After Algeria received its independence in 1962, French tests continued at Reggane through 1966. After that, France conducted its nuclear tests in the Pacific.

Algeria had a single small research reactor at Draria on the Mediterranean Sea, subjected to INTERNATIONAL ATOMIC ENERGY AGENCY (IAEA) safeguards and monitoring. However, in 1991, intelligence sources learned that Algeria was secretly building another reactor at Ain Oussera, and experts guessed that the reactor might be intended as a PRODUCTION REACTOR for the manufacture of plutonium.

Under pressure, Algeria agreed to place the new reactor, called Es Salam, under IAEA inspection. At that time Algeria explained that the new heavy-water moderated, highly enriched uranium-fueled 15 megawatt-thermal reactor had been supplied by China. That scale was too small to be used as a production reactor, although protective missiles, large cooling towers, and other factors, such as a nearby plant that appeared to be devoted to reprocessing, had raised suspicions.

In 1993, after disclosing details of the new reactor, Algeria pledged to adhere to the NON-PROLIFERATION TREATY. The nation followed up in 1996 and 1997 with an agreement with the IAEA for full inspection of all of Algeria's nuclear facilities.

Alikhanov, Abram Isaakovich (1904–1970)

Russian engineer who designed an early Soviet heavy-water production reactor

A. I. Alikhanov was one of the leaders in building the first Soviet nuclear reactor that was moderated with heavy water. That reactor at CHELYABINSK-40 went critical in April 1949 with a 500 kilowatt-thermal power output. The small reactor served as a prototype for a large production reactor later built at Chelyabinsk-40.

Alikhanov was born in 1904 in Tbilisi, Georgia, and graduated from Leningrad Polytechnical Institute in 1928. He then worked at the Leningrad Physico-Technical Institute. He joined the weapons program in 1943 at the suggestion of A. F. IOFFE. After work on the heavy-water reactor, he led the project to build a high energy accelerator. He was director of the Institute of Theoretical and Experimental Physics from 1945 to 1968. He received the honor of Hero of Socialist Labor in 1954. He died in 1970.

Allen v. United States

Allen et al. v. United States was the name given to a lawsuit that consolidated the claims for damages from the nuclear testing program of over 1,000 individuals who lived in Nevada, Utah, and Arizona. Sometimes called the "downwinder case," the suit involved claims that fallout from aboveground nuclear testing led to injuries and deaths. The plaintiffs argued that the ATOMIC ENERGY COMMISSION was negligent in the conduct of the tests at the NEVADA TEST SITE and had failed to protect civilians living downwind from the tests.

In 1978, residents of the three states had organized a group called the Committee of Survivors, and, with the assistance of former interior secretary Stewart Udall, the claims were grouped and presented to the Federal District Court in Salt Lake City in 1979. Irene Allen was alphabetically first on the list and her name headed the lawsuit. Attorneys working on the case eventually reduced the number of individual claims to 24 in order to represent the typical, commonly alleged injuries and illnesses resulting from FALLOUT.

The trial ran from September to December 1982. Judge Bruce Jenkins issued his decision in May 1984. Although he denied that the government was negligent in its testing procedures, he agreed that it had been negligent in the protection measures taken. He awarded compensation in 10 cases, including wrongful death or personal injury from diseases that could be linked to radiation exposure, such as leukemia and certain cancers. In the other 14 cases, the judge ruled that the plaintiffs had failed to show that their illnesses were caused by radiation. Although this decision seemed to many outside observers to be objective and fair, it was overturned on appeal in *Allen v. United States* 816 F2d 982 (9th Circuit, 1987).

The government then used the denial of the Irene Allen suit in later cases to demonstrate that health and safety measures were at the government's discretion, leaving the government immune from suit. However, in 1990, President George BUSH signed a law that authorized a $100 million trust fund to which those in downwind areas could apply for an indemnity of $50,000 if they suffered from specific radiation-related diseases. Uranium miners were included, and they were eligible for $100,000. Workers at the nuclear test site could receive compensation of $75,000 for such illnesses if they had been present at the test site during a test. Although the Irene Allen court case was defeated, the establishment of the trust fund by Congress provided a system of relief similar to that set up for the MARSHALL ISLANDERS.

Documents that had been collected and copied at archives across the United States and deposited at the Coordinating Information Center in Las Vegas for use in the original lawsuits were available to members of the public to use in helping to substantiate their claims under the 1990 federal law, the Radiation Exposure Compensation Act. The documents showed the patterns of fallout associated with various tests and included records of radiation counts, protective measures taken, and wind and weather patterns, among other pertinent materials.

Suggested Reading

Howard Ball, *Justice Downwind: America's Atomic Testing Program in the 1950s.* New York: Oxford, 1986.

Barton Hacker, *Elements of Controversy: The Atomic Energy Commission and Radiation Safety in Nuclear Weapons Testing, 1947–1974.* Berkeley: University of California, 1994.

Alsos Project

The Alsos Project or Alsos Mission was the American military effort during World War II to discover and locate the scientists and equipment that had been used by Germany in nuclear research and in the effort to build a GERMAN ATOMIC BOMB.

General Leslie GROVES established the group late in 1943, and the code word, *Alsos*, was Greek for "grove." The general considered changing the term because of the pun on his own name, but he decided to keep it.

General Groves appointed Lt. Col. Boris Pash to head Alsos. Pash was a security officer with the MANHATTAN ENGINEER DISTRICT who had conducted investigations of J. Robert OPPENHEIMER. Pash established his base in London in 1944 and then drove across France as Free French troops liberated Paris in late August. After meeting Frédéric JOLIOT-CURIE in Paris, Pash established his office there and began to follow up on leads to the whereabouts of German supplies of uranium, the secret German nuclear laboratories, and the scientists who had worked on the project.

One of the successes of the Alsos Mission was the capture of several hundred tons of Belgian uranium by Lt. Col. John Lansdale. Operating in a region that would fall in the Russian occupation zone, Lansdale assembled a team that located the uranium supplies at Stassfurt. They had to transfer the material from broken barrels to heavy-duty paper bags, wire the bags shut, and ship the material out to the permanent American zone.

Meanwhile Pash chased down the various German scientists who had worked on the nuclear project. He went first to the town of Haigerloch in the Black Forest region, moving with a small contingent of American troops ahead of the French invasion army into German-controlled areas. The Alsos troops "liberated" Haigerloch, where they located the German "uranium machine," a small model reactor located in a cave. The German reactor used heavy water as a moderator, imported from the NORSK-HYDRO plant. However, the reactor was so small as to constitute only a test or scaling model, and it could not develop or sustain a controlled chain reaction.

Samuel GOUDSMIT took charge of these facilities while Pash went on to the town of Hechingen with a small force of American troops. There they captured many of the German scientists, later locating Otto HAHN at Tailfingen and Werner HEISENBERG at a lake cottage in Bavaria. These prisoners were sent to Farm Hall in Britain where they were held until after the end of the war with Japan.

The major discovery of the Alsos Project was that the Germans had not developed a nuclear weapon, and that their research into it had stalled for lack of funds and from lack of material resources. The Alsos Project staffmembers were doubtful of Heisenberg's later claims that the scientists had intentionally held off making the nuclear weapon because it was too terrible to place at Hitler's disposal. The other major achievement of the project was to capture the German supply of URANIUM, keeping it from falling into the hands of the Soviet Union.

Suggested Reading

Samuel Goudsmit, *Alsos*. New York: Henry Schuman, 1947.
Thomas Powers, *Heisenberg's War*. New York: Knopf, 1993.
Richard Rhodes, *The Making of the Atomic Bomb*. New York: Simon and Schuster, 1986.

Alvarez, Luis W. (1911–1988) *American physicist who participated in the Manhattan Project and who witnessed all three of the first nuclear detonations* Luis Alvarez, a Nobel Prize–winning physicist, was instrumental in the construction of the first atomic bombs, and he accompanied the weapon on the bombing missions over Hiroshima and Nagasaki.

Alvarez was born in San Francisco on June 13, 1911, and he studied at the University of Chicago. In addition to working on the MANHATTAN ENGINEER DISTRICT during the war, he contributed to radar research at the Massachusetts Institute of Technology. He assisted in the design of the plutonium weapon. He was present at the TRINITY test at Alamogordo on July 16, 1945, and he flew aboard one of the observation planes that accompanied the ENOLA GAY that dropped the nuclear weapon on Hiroshima. After the war, he moved to the University of California, and in the period from 1954 to 1959, he worked at the Lawrence Livermore Radiation Laboratory.

Alvarez developed a bubble chamber to study subatomic particles and also developed automatic equipment that could record data directly onto punched cards for computer analysis. He and his fellow researchers discovered a number of short-lived particles, including mesons. He received a NOBEL PRIZE for this work in 1968.

In 1965, Alvarez led an expedition to use high-energy particle beams to look for hidden chambers in a pyramid in Egypt. In 1980, he and his son Walter, then a professor of geology at the University of California, accidentally discovered a band of sedimentary rock in Italy that had an unusually high concentration of the rare metal, iridium. The Alvarezes postulated that the iridium resulted from the impact of a meteorite about 65 million years ago.

Luis and Walter Alvarez developed the idea that the extinction of the dinosaurs at about that time could have been due to the large quantities of dust and smoke that obscured the sun and led to a rapid world-wide chilling, which would have widely extinguished plant life and led to the rapid death of large plant-eating dinosaurs and the meat-eaters who had fed on them. At first this contribution to a field in which neither had specialized was regarded with considerable skepticism. Existing explanations of the extinction of dinosaurs had focused on overpopulation and other more gradual effects. In fact, evolutionary theory had moved away from "catastrophism" to "gradualism" more generally, and the Alvarez theory appeared to represent a return to theories of mass extinction that had been popular before Charles Darwin had first published his theory of evolution in 1859.

Later discovery of an impact crater on the Caribbean coast of the Yucatán Peninsula in Mexico confirmed that a large meteorite had hit the earth at the time. By the late 1980s, the catastrophic explanation for dinosaur extinction became much more widely accepted. This concept was adopted by others in 1983 to suggest that a nuclear war could generate a NUCLEAR WINTER leading to a similar mass extinction of life. In this way, the Alvarez theory contributed to popular efforts to bring about nuclear arms control, the "Ban the Bomb" movement. Later popular fiction that focused on the potential impact of an asteroid or meteor on the earth largely derived from the interest stimulated by the Alvarez theory of the mass extinction of dinosaurs 65 million years ago.

Luis Alvarez died in Berkeley, California, on September 1, 1988.

Suggested Reading

Luis Alvarez, *Alvarez: Adventures of a Physicist*. New York: Basic Books, 1987.

Amchitka

Amchitka Island in the Aleutian Islands in Alaska was the site picked by the ATOMIC ENERGY COMMISSION (AEC) for a series of underground nuclear tests in the 1960s. The island is located in the remote far western section of the Aleutian Islands, in the "Rat Group," approximately 179 degrees east longitude and 52 degrees north latitude. The site was chosen after considering other locations—an island in the Pacific, the Brooks Range on the mainland of Alaska, a new site in

Nevada, and even a cooperative venture with Australia to use a remote site in that country. The Australian site was rejected on political grounds and the Brooks Range site was regarded as too costly to develop.

In developing the *Spartan* ANTI-BALLISTIC MISSILES (ABMs), the AEC sought to test very large-yield, multi-megaton nuclear devices. Although the purpose of tests was not announced, as the AEC did not wish to stimulate further debate over ABM systems, the large projected yields were announced. With the growing concern about damage from high-yield devices set off at the NEVADA TEST SITE, some of which had broken windows and caused minor structural damage in nearby Las Vegas, the AEC chose the spot in Alaska because it was remote from human habitation but could be readily reached by sea. Preparations for the test included the relocation of 350 sea otters to other areas by airplane in 1968.

However, as plans for testing matured in 1968 and 1969, political opposition to holding the tests in Alaska began to mount among members of Congress from Alaska, Hawaii, and eventually from the external affairs minister of Canada. It was feared the test would set off a set of earthquakes in the seismically sensitive region or possibly initiate a tsunami that would endanger coastal regions as far away as the west coast of the United States and Hawaii.

Nevertheless, the AEC went ahead with two underground tests at the site, announcing that they were necessary to the development of the planned ABM systems. The first was "Milrow" on October 2, 1969, a test to establish data points for further tests. The Los Alamos–designed device had a yield of about a megaton. Members of Congress argued that a smaller device should be used and that the test should be delayed, but the AEC rejected the advice and continued with the test as planned. Milrow generated a seismic reading of 6.5 on the Richter scale. There were no resulting earthquakes. After further debate and opposition from a number of U.S. senators, the second test was conducted. "Canniken" was detonated on November 6, 1971, with a yield reported by the AEC as less than five megatons in response to press reports that suggested that the planned yield was 20 megatons or more. There were some seismic aftershocks, but no large earthquake was triggered.

Both Milrow and Canniken at Amchitka attracted national and international attention. The rising concern with the impact of nuclear testing on the environment focused on these two well-publicized tests in a remote and pristine area. Neither test vented radioactive material nor caused an earthquake. In response to the mounting criticism in the press, the AEC decided to make public the purpose of the tests, and the agency also released information about the sea otter relocation effort. However, the AEC recognized as a result of the Amchitka tests that public opinion was far more sensitive to issues surrounding nuclear testing in the period from 1969 to 1971 than it had been in the mid-1960s, and plans for any further tests in Alaska were scrapped. The Amchitka test site was closed down beginning in 1972.

See also UNDERGROUND NUCLEAR TESTING.

Suggested Reading

Glenn T. Seaborg and Benjamin Loeb, *The Atomic Energy Commission under Nixon: Adjusting to Troubled Times.* New York: St. Martins, 1993.

Anti-Ballistic Missiles (ABMs)

Both the United States and the Soviet Union began to develop missiles in the 1960s, armed with nuclear warheads, that would be capable of destroying incoming INTERCONTINENTAL BALLISTIC MISSILES (ICBMs). Such anti-ballistic missiles (ABMs) would be set to detonate outside the atmosphere, destroying incoming missiles with intense radiation.

The development of these systems in the United States resulted in the creation of two missiles: SPRINT and SPARTAN by the late 1960s. Under the Strategic Arms Limitation Treaty (SALT I), both the United States and the U.S.S.R. agreed not to deploy ABMs at more than two sites in each country. Later, both sides agreed to reduce the arming to one site each. In the case of the United States, a *Spartan* defense was constructed as part of the "Safeguard" program near ICBM silos at Grand Forks, North Dakota. However, the system was only tested and then turned off. The *Sprint* and *Spartan* missiles were returned to storage.

A 1972 ANTI-BALLISTIC MISSILE TREATY between the United States and the Soviet Union prohibited ABMs capable of intercepting ICBMs, but it did not prohibit the development of surface-to-air missiles capable of destroying tactical or medium-range ballistic missiles, armed either with nuclear or high explosive warheads. Thus, the United States, the Soviet Union, and Britain proceeded to develop surface-to-air missiles with extremely high altitude capabilities. These ballistic

missile defense (BMD) systems have sometimes been regarded as types of ABMs.

The *Nike-Hercules,* although intended as an anti-aircraft missile, could be loaded with either high-explosive or nuclear warheads, and it proved its efficacy against some ballistic missiles when tested against a Corporal ballistic missile and against another *Nike-Hercules.* The announced altitude limit of the *Nike-Hercules* was 150,000 feet. *Nike-Hercules* missiles were deployed to NATO nations in the 1970s. Since NATO targets could be reached by intermediate-range, rather than intercontinental-range ballistic missiles, such deployment of the *Nike-Hercules* as a BMD system did not represent a violation of SALT I.

The *Nike-Hercules* was succeeded by the *Patriot,* which was primarily designed as an anti-aircraft ground to air missile loaded with s high-explosive warhead. With an announced altitude limit of 78,750 feet, the *Patriot* proved somewhat successful against *Scud* missiles during the Gulf War of 1992.

The Soviets developed in the early 1960s a missile they designated the S-200 *Volga,* referred to in the West as the SA-5 *Gammon* missile. The SA 5B, deployed in 1970 had a nuclear warhead; the SA 5C, deployed in 1975, had the option of either a nuclear or high-explosive warhead. With a potential altitude of 95,000 feet, the missile was thought to be capable of destroying incoming ballistic missiles. Western observers were divided over whether the SA 5B and 5C represented violations of the SALT I treaty.

The Soviet SA-12B *Giant* surface-to-air missile was also capable of extremely high altitudes, over 98,000 feet. Like the SA 5s, it appeared to be in violation of the SALT I agreements when introduced in 1986.

Many other anti-aircraft missiles designed and built in the United States, the Soviet Union, and Great Britain were capable of high altitude performance and might have been capable of intercepting some ballistic missiles.

Suggested Reading

Christopher Chant, *Air Defense Systems and Weapons: World AAA and SAM Systems in the 1990s.* London: Brassey's Defence Publishers, 1989.

Anti-Ballistic Missile Treaty (ABM Treaty)

Formally known as the Treaty on the Limitation of Anti-Ballistic Missiles, the ABM Treaty was negotiated and signed on May 26, 1972, by President

Richard NIXON and Premier Leonid Brezhnev. It was signed at the same time as SALT I, and the two treaties are sometimes (not quite accurately) referred to as the same treaty.

By enshrining an agreement not to build ABM systems, the ABM Treaty formalized acceptance of the principle of assured destruction as the means to prevent nuclear war, and it also represented a step in the direction of limiting the total number of offensive strategic weapons. Together with SALT I, the two treaties represented a major milestone in the policy of DETENTE that characterized the late 1960s and early 1970s. The ABM Treaty was ratified by the U.S. Senate in 1972 and it went into force on October 2, 1972. The ABM Treaty was permanent, or of "unlimited duration." Each country had the right to withdraw from the treaty after giving six-months notice.

By later protocol, signed July 3, 1974, the deployment of ABM systems was limited to one in each country. In the end, only one ABM system was built in the United States, at Grand Forks, North Dakota. After it was activated in 1975, it was then turned off. The missiles and warheads for the defense system were retired from the active stockpile.

An ironic consequence of the SALT I treaty was that it placed limitations for both the United States and the Soviet Union on the delivery vehicles, not the warheads. Thus both nations could increase their weaponry only by developing multiple warheads within the delivery system limits. The United States and the Soviet Union developed smaller, more lethal MIRV systems, eventually reaching the capability to install 10 or more warheads per missile. The pair of treaties, intended to reduce armaments, had led to the channeling of technological talent into a system that would be extremely difficult to defend against with multiple warheads. Mirved weapons became essential parts of the MUTUALLY ASSURED DESTRUCTION strategy that ruled over the uneasy peace of the detente years of the cold war.

See also ARMS CONTROL TREATIES.

Argentina

Argentina began work on developing both nuclear power and nuclear weapons quite early, establishing the National Atomic Energy Commission in 1950. In 1958, Argentina built a research reactor at Constituyentes following a design from the United States.

Over the period from 1958 to 1967, Argentina constructed three more research reactors and, in 1968, purchased a 320 megawatt-electric (MWe) power reactor from Germany.

In the late 1970s, Argentina appeared to be moving in the direction of constructing a nuclear weapon. Observers noted that both a uranium enrichment plant at Pilcaniyeu, begun in 1978, and a laboratory-scale reprocessing plant at Ezeiza were suitable for producing weapons-grade fissile material. Neither was needed for the power reactor program.

In the 1970s and 1980s Argentina began to supply nuclear technology and materials to other countries, including some suspected of attempting to develop a nuclear weapon. In 1974, Argentina provided Libya with mining and reprocessing equipment, and it later assisted Libya in other ways in its nuclear research. During the war with Britain over the Malvinas (Falkland Islands) in 1982, Libya supplied Argentina with anti-aircraft and air-to-air missiles with an estimated value of over $100 million. In 1985, Argentina provided Algeria with a small research reactor. In 1987 the Argentine Atomic Energy Commission joined an international group providing assistance to Iran in the construction of a power reactor at Bushehr, but the work was suspended in 1995. Pressure by the government of the United States brought an end to a planned shipment by Argentina of a fuel-fabrication facility that could be used to acquire weapons-grade material.

The work on nuclear power and the apparent development of nuclear weapons in Argentina stimulated BRAZIL to compete, and, as the Brazilian program stepped up, Argentina responded in turn. However, conditions improved in the 1990s. Argentina's president Carlos Saúl Menem took control of the nuclear program from the military and in 1992 established controls over nuclear exports. The nuclear rivalry cooled off with the achievement of civilian governments in both Argentina and Brazil, culminating in a set of bilateral agreements in the early 1990s. Brazilian president Fernando Collor de Mello worked with Menem to allow mutual inspection of nuclear installations and to set up a special bilateral commission. Under these agreements, Argentina and Brazil allowed inspection of their nuclear facilities and worked with the INTERNATIONAL ATOMIC ENERGY AGENCY (IAEA) in Vienna to demonstrate that neither was pursuing a weapons program. A Quadripartite Agreement including both Argentina and Brazil, together with the IAEA and the bilateral commission, was approved in 1992 by the Argentine Congress.

Argentina joined the TREATY OF TLATELOLCO in 1994, committing the country not to develop nuclear weapons, and, in 1995, Argentina signed the nuclear NON-PROLIFERATION TREATY (NPT).

By the late 1990s, Argentina had two heavy-water moderated, natural-uranium fueled power reactors and another under construction. In addition, the country maintained five operating low-power research reactors, with two more planned. Argentina also maintained a wide range of nuclear fuels facilities. All of the reactors and fuel facilities were opened in the 1990s to inspection by the IAEA and to inspectors from the Argentina-Brazil joint commission. In accord with its commitment to cease work on weapons, Argentina stopped construction on a plutonium extraction reprocessing plant.

With the easing of nuclear rivalry between Argentina and Brazil and with Argentina's agreement to the Treaty of Tlotelolco and the NPT, the nuclear arms race in South America appeared to be over.

See also PROLIFERATION.

Suggested Reading

Rodney Jones et al., *Tracking Nuclear Proliferation.* Washington, D.C.: Carnegie Endowment, 1998.

Leonard S. Spector, *The Undeclared Bomb.* Cambridge, Mass.: Ballinger Books, 1988.

Argonne National Laboratory

Argonne National Laboratory represented the continuation of the research projects of the MANHATTAN ENGINEER DISTRICT at the University of Chicago during World War II. Established under the ATOMIC ENERGY COMMISSION in 1946, Argonne National Laboratory continued as a site for research in nuclear reactor technology, biology and medicine, and material sciences, as well as programs in nuclear physics and high-energy physics. In the 1950s it focused on the development of civilian nuclear power, and then it broadened its scientific and technical base in response to the crisis in confidence following the launch of SPUTNIK.

The main facilities of Argonne were located in a Cook County forest reserve a few miles west of Chicago. Argonne also ran a research facility at the IDAHO NATIONAL ENGINEERING LABORATORY where it operated a materials testing reactor built by Oak Ridge and

constructed an Experimental Breeder Reactor (EBR). EBR-I suffered a fuel meltdown accident on November 29, 1955.

The directors of the laboratory were:

Walter ZINN	1946–1956
Norman Hilberry	1957–1961
Albert Crewe	1961–1967
Robert Duffield	1967–1973
Robert Sachs	1973–1978
Walter Massey	1979–1984
Alan Schriesheim	1984–1996

From a high point of 5,300 employees in 1979, the number of staff dropped to less than 3,700 in the middle years of the administration of Ronald REAGAN (1981–1989). However, by the 1990s, the staff level was back to more than 5,000.

As research priorities of the Atomic Energy Commission and its successor agencies changed, so did the research agenda of Argonne. Operated by a consortium of universities, the institution operated somewhat like LOS ALAMOS, a government-owned, contractor-operated facility with an academic or research orientation. Under Zinn, Argonne focused primarily on reactor design. But under Crew and Duffield, the institution moved in the direction of broader physics research. The energy crisis of the 1970s invigorated the laboratory and provided a new rationale for it to deal with national priorities.

See also CHICAGO, UNIVERSITY OF.

Suggested Reading

Jack Holl, *Argonne National Laboratory, 1946–1996.* Urbana: University of Illinois Press, 1997.

Armed Forces Radiobiology Research Institute (AFRRI)

Secretary of Defense Robert McNamara established the Armed Forces Radiobiology Research Institute (AFRRI) by a Department of Defense directive issued on May 12, 1961. The basic mission of the institute was to carry on research in the field of radiobiology in support of the military services, as well as for the national welfare and for human welfare more generally. The establishment of the institute was part of a wider program under the Kennedy administration to put federal resources into science and technology, especially through the Department of Defense.

Argonne National Laboratory. The Argonne Lab, west of Chicago in a Cook County forest preserve, continued the work of the University of Chicago in reactor development. (Argonne National Laboratory)

The institute was set up at the National Naval Medical Center in Bethesda, Maryland, and for the first three years operated under naval supervision. The other services wanted to ensure that AFRRI did not become entirely a naval operation, and in response to this concern, its management was restructured. After July 1964, AFRRI was supervised by a board of governors that included the three surgeons general of the services and the chief of the DEFENSE ATOMIC SUPPORT AGENCY (DASA), who served as chairman of the board.

The budget of AFRRI ran between $2 and $3 million per year through the 1960s. As DASA was restructured in later years, its successor agencies continued to supervise AFRRI, including the DEFENSE NUCLEAR AGENCY through the 1980s, the DEFENSE SPECIAL WEAPONS AGENCY after 1996, and then the DEFENSE THREAT REDUCTION AGENCY. AFRRI maintained a staff that numbered in the range of 200 to 300 personnel,

including scientists, medical specialists, and support staff. DASA and its successor agencies regarded AFRRI as a subsidiary operation and they included discussion of its activities in their reports and public affairs presentations.

AFRRI developed responsibilities in a number of basic research areas. The Experimental Pathology Department studied the effects of ionizing radiation on organisms; the Behavioral Sciences Department worked on areas of the psychological effects of radiation; the Physical Sciences Department worked with reactors and accelerators; and a Radiation Biology Department worked on both pure and applied research. The Physical Sciences Department expanded into areas of chemical research, theoretical research, and radiological physics.

Studies with animals helped determine the incapacitating doses and effects of radiation through testing the reaction of nerves, blood, and other tissues. The institute generated much research that was both published in the open literature and presented as papers at conferences. AFRRI entered into interagency agreements with universities and colleges in cooperating on research projects related to radiation, exposure rates, and basic medical research, including cancer research.

AFRRI calculations as to the predicted radiation effects on humans provided military strategists with data to incorporate as they developed doctrine regarding the use of nuclear weapons in combat. AFRRI remained the primary resource available to the military services for investigating the incapacitating effects of radiation from nuclear weapons, fallout, reactors, nuclear waste, and accidents at nuclear facilities. Such information could be utilized in both civil defense and defensive military planning, and it could also be used in planning various targeting strategies. AFRRI-generated information and standards were utilized in radiological cleanup operations, such as that managed by DNA at ENEWETAK.

Armed Forces Special Weapons Project (AFSWP)

In the years following World War II, the role of the army in nuclear weapons development was greatly reduced with the creation of the ATOMIC ENERGY COMMISSION (AEC). Nevertheless, certain functions and personnel from the MANHATTAN ENGINEER DISTRICT were retained by the military, and those nuclear activities were concentrated in the Armed Forces Special Weapons Project, set up in 1947. The original charter of AFSWP in January 1947 authorized training for the assembly and employment of atomic weapons. The charter was revised in July 1947 to give the new agency a coordinating role in atomic energy research and oversight over the storage and surveillance of weapons under the custody of the armed forces.

Through 1950, all nuclear weapons remained in the jurisdiction of the AEC. Even so, AFSWP established a training facility in Albuquerque, where instructors from SANDIA Laboratory taught weapons-assembly procedures. AFSWP participated in the fission weapon tests in the SANDSTONE test series at ENEWETAK in 1948, and the agency prepared reports on the effects of the weapons. AFSWP technicians developed instruments to measure weapons blast and shock.

Working with the AEC, AFSWP developed three national stockpile sites under U.S. Air Force jurisdiction in the period 1949–1950. In 1949, the Joint Chiefs of Staff gave AFSWP responsibility for collecting and disseminating data on the effects of atomic weapons. The 1950 publication by Samuel Glasstone, *The Effects of Atomic Weapons,* was jointly sponsored by AEC and AFSWP.

During the Berlin Airlift of 1948, AFSWP participated with the Strategic Air Command in a deception action to convince the Soviets that the United States had transferred nuclear weapons to Britain. Later analysts have concluded that this action prevented the Soviet Union from interfering with the airlift of supplies to Berlin during their ground blockade of that city in 1948 and 1949.

During the KOREAN WAR (1950–1953), AFSWP began training military personnel in great numbers in courses devoted to weapons assembly and maintenance, operational site storage, and technical inspection of weapons. Using information from the 1951 GREENHOUSE test series, AFSWP distributed information to Civil Defense authorities on weapons effects. AFSWP also participated in troop exercises during OPERATION DESERT ROCK in 1951 and OPERATION UPSHOT-KNOTHOLE in 1953 in which military personnel were trained in dealing with precautions that should be taken during battlefield use of nuclear weapons. AFSWP personnel assisted in inspections of nuclear weapons in storage sites through these years.

AFSWP cooperated in forward deployment of nuclear weapons to NATO bases in the mid-1950s, participating directly in the training of military personnel. In 1954–1955, President Dwight EISENHOWER ordered the nuclear stockpile to be dispersed to a number of military sites around the United States, and AFSWP played a key role in training the large numbers of personnel who would take over these custody and inspection responsibilities. As the system for new weapons design became more formalized through these years, AFSWP participated in helping to define the desired military characteristics of new weapons that would be suggested to the weapons design personnel of the AEC weapons laboratories at LOS ALAMOS and LAWRENCE LIVERMORE. AFSWP continued to provide personnel who participated in issues involving weapons effects of nuclear weapons tests through the 1950s.

In 1958, AFSWP established the Joint Nuclear Accident Coordinating Center to deal with BROKEN

ARROW incidents, namely instances in which nuclear weapons were involved in aircraft crashes or accidentally dropped from aircraft.

In 1959, AFSWP was reorganized as the DEFENSE ATOMIC SUPPORT AGENCY (DASA), and the military's participation in the nuclear weapons program of the United States continued under the direction of that successor agency. DASA continued until 1971 when it was reorganized as the DEFENSE NUCLEAR AGENCY (DNA). DNA, in turn, was reorganized as the Defense Special Weapons Agency (DSWA) in 1996 and as the Defense Threat Reduction Agency (DTRA) in 1998.

Armenia

When Armenia was a member of the Union of Soviet Socialist Republics, two nuclear power plants were constructed there. Both were the 440 megawatt, VVER type of pressurized water reactors built by the Soviets. In 1989, both reactors were shut down following the massive earthquake there on December 7, 1988. The government completed a series of improvements and inspections and then restarted one of the reactors in June 1995.

See also POWER REACTORS, WORLD.

Arms Control

Over the period from World War II through 1992 the leaders of the United States and the Soviet Union held many meetings to discuss arms control issues. The meetings in World War II were called "BIG THREE MEETINGS," and they included prime ministers and staff from Great Britain. By the 1950s, conferences held at the level of chiefs of state were called SUMMIT meetings. Lower level meetings of the U.S. secretary of state with the foreign minister of the Soviet Union were called ministerials. At both summits and ministerials, sometimes involving other nations such as Great Britain, many separate issues were discussed and some resolved.

Arms control referred to any international agreement aimed at limiting or reducing forces, regulating armaments, or restricting the deployment of weapons. The Strategic Arms Limitation Treaty I (SALT I) arms control agreement was of five-year duration and it limited weapon delivery systems. The unratified SALT-II would have limited the total number of delivery systems. Later arms control agreements, including the

INTERMEDIATE NUCLEAR FORCES (INF) treaty and the Strategic Arms Reduction Treaties, START I and START II, aimed at the reduction and elimination of some nuclear weapon delivery systems. Other agreements have focused on the spread of nuclear weapons to new states and on the creation of nuclear-free zones.

In addition to the summits, agreements, and treaties designed to maintain peace and to control the numbers of nuclear weapons, the nuclear powers entered several NUCLEAR TEST LIMITATION TREATIES. Other treaties and agreements dealt with creation of nuclear-free zones and with stopping the proliferation of nuclear weapons to other countries. These various nuclear-related treaties are sometimes referred to as arms control treaties.

Arms control treaties include:

SALT I	ratified	1972
SALT II	never ratified	
INF	ratified	1988
START I	ratified	1992
START II	ratified	2000
START III	negotiated	

See also NUCLEAR TEST LIMITATION TREATIES, SUMMIT MEETINGS.

Suggested Reading

Committee on International Security and Arms Control, National Academy of Sciences, *Nuclear Arms Control: Background and Issues.* Washington, D.C.: National Academy Press, 1985.

Julie Dahlitz, *Nuclear Arms Control.* London: George Allen and Unwin, 1983.

Patrick Glynn, *Closing Pandora's Box: Arms Races, Arms Control, and the History of the Cold War.* New York: Basic Books, 1992.

Artsimovich, Lev Andreevich (1909–1973)
Soviet physicist who worked on separation of uranium isotopes

Artsimovich's work focused particularly on the problem of eletromagnetic separation of isotopes, similar to the method developed by E. O. LAWRENCE and realized in the CALUTRONS constructed at OAK RIDGE during World War II.

Born in Moscow in 1909, Lev Andreevich Artsimovich graduated from the University of Byelorussia, in Minsk, in 1938. In the period from 1930 to 1944 he worked at the Leningrad Physico-Technical Institute, heading up the high-voltage laboratory. In 1944 he joined the atomic weapons program under Igor KUR-CHATOV. The Soviet eletromagnetic separation plant was built at Severnaia Tura in the northern Urals, at a location called SVERDLOVSK-45, in the region around Sverdlovsk.

Artsimovich was appointed scientific director for the eletromagnetic plant. He and his colleagues created the first ion source consisting of an electron beam traversing vaporized uranium tetrachloride. Using an electromagnet acquired as part of the war reparations from Germany, they were able to direct a beam of the separated ^{235}U at the collector.

The problems and the solutions to those problems that the Soviets encountered in refining uranium were very similar to those faced by the Americans during the Manhattan Project only a few years before. Artsimovich had great difficulty in obtaining the required purity with the electromagnetic separation method. Using material produced in a gaseous diffusion plant, Artsimovich was then able to enrich it to the required 92% to 98% ^{235}U needed for a weapon. However, the first weapon developed by the Soviets relied on PLUTONIUM, not on URANIUM. Later, one of Artsimovich's group was able to apply electromagnetic methods in the separation of lithium isotopes needed in the construction of the hydrogen bomb. He was elected to the Academy of Sciences in 1953 and earned the Hero of Socialist Labor award for his work in 1969. Artsimovich died in 1973.

Arzamas-16

One of two weapon design laboratories in the Soviet Union, Arzamas-16 is located at Sarov, about 60 kilometers from Arzamas and about 400 kilometers east and slightly south of Moscow. The site was officially known as the All-Russian Scientific Research Institute of Experimental Physics. Arzamas-16 was founded in April 1946, with the original designation of KB-11 or Design Bureau 11, occupying an ancient monastery on site. The installation was informally called Khariton's Institute, after scientific director Yuli Khariton, who served from 1946 until his retirement in 1992; and it was sometimes jokingly called "Los Arzamas," after the original U.S. weapons laboratory at LOS ALAMOS, New Mexico. The existence of the city was concealed until 1990. In 1995, the name of Arzamas-16 was changed back to the traditional name of the community, "Sarov." As in many Soviet industrial and research cities, the central technical enterprise provided most

of the funding for the local civic infrastructure, such as the hospitals, transportation facilities, and sports arenas.

The first Soviet atomic bomb was designed and fabricated at Arzamas-16, closely following the design that had been obtained by the spy Klaus FUCHS. Over the years, Arzamas-16 represented one of four weapons-assembly plants in the Soviet Union, employing some 25,000 to 30,000 people, with a capacity to assemble and disassemble several hundred weapons per year. Altogether some 80,000 people lived in the closed city. However, by the late 1990s, the work force at the nuclear institute had dwindled to about 18,000.

Like Los Alamos in the United States, with the ending of the nuclear arms race in the early 1990s Arzamas-16 increasingly engaged in a variety of energy research projects, some of a non-military character. Work at the Sarov institute included safety studies of reactors, magnetic fields, elimination of chemical weapons, and disposal of hazardous waste.

The institute at Sarov was the center of a controversy in the period from 1996 to 1999, when International Business Machines (IBM) sold 16 computers to Sarov through a Moscow middleman, without securing the required export licenses. Although a U.S. federal grand jury investigated the sale, no charges were brought against IBM for the irregular sale. Washington insisted that the computers be either returned or openly dedicated to nonweapons work. However, Russia initially refused to cooperate.

In October 1999, Russia agreed to establish the computers as part of an open computing center, jointly sponsored by the United States DEPARTMENT OF ENERGY and the Russian agency, Minatom. It was expected that the new computing center would provide jobs to several hundred technicians over its first few years of operation. The United States sponsored such activity in the hope of keeping Russian technicians who had formerly worked on nuclear weapons research from emigrating to nuclear proliferation countries or selling their knowledge to such countries.

By the late 1990s, about 15% of the Sarov institute's personnel worked on civilian projects, and, with U.S. support, it was hoped the percentage would increase.

Suggested Reading

Thomas B. Cochrane, Robert S. Norris, and Oleg A. Bukharin, *Making the Russian Bomb: From Stalin to Yeltsin*. Boulder, Colo.: Westview Press, 1995.

David Holloway. *Stalin and the Bomb*. New Haven: Yale University Press, 1994.

Ashtabula   *See* WEAPONS PRODUCTION COMPLEX.

Assured Destruction   *See* MUTUALLY ASSURED DESTRUCTION.

Aston, Francis (1877–1945)   *British physicist who established that elements have different isotopes*
Francis Aston discovered that atomic elements take more than one form and have more than a single atomic weight. This discovery of what came to be called ISOTOPES became crucial in the development of both peaceful and military uses of atomic energy.

Aston was born in 1877 in Birmingham, England, where he studied at Mason's College. He studied chemistry, and after graduation he became a brewery chemist for three years. He returned to Birmingham University as a research student and in 1909 taught there as an assistant lecturer. In the period 1910 to 1919 he worked at the Cavendish Laboratory at Cambridge, under J. J. Thomson. Thomson and Aston examined the effects of electric and magnetic fields on positive rays in gaseous discharge tubes, known as CROOKES tubes after their inventor. In 1912, Thomson discovered that neon apparently had two distinct atomic weights, of 20 and 22.

Aston studied the problem and built a positive ray spectrograph, or mass spectrograph. Using the device, Aston was able to demonstrate that indeed neon had two isotopes, one with weight 20 and one with weight 22, in a 10 to 1 ratio that would result in the average mass of neon that was 20.2. With the discovery of isotopes, Aston destroyed one of the last premises of the atomic theory of John Dalton, who, in 1808, had stated that all the individual atoms of any given element had the same mass.

Over the next few years, Aston examined the isotopic composition of more than 50 separate elements, and he published his findings in *Isotopes* in 1922. He concluded that the fractional atomic weights of elements were due to the proportions of isotopes in the element. Aston won the NOBEL PRIZE for chemistry in 1922 for his work on isotopes. Constantly updating and reediting the work over the next few years, Aston drew attention to his discoveries and to his forecasts of the power and dangers of harnessing atomic power.

Atlas Missile

The *Atlas* missile was the first effort by the United States to develop an INTERCONTINENTAL BALLISTIC MISSILE (ICBM). Following World War II, Consolidated Vultee Aircraft Corporation (Convair) began work to design a missile capable of long-distance delivery of a payload. Over the years 1946 to 1951, Convair continued to work on rocket motors and flight control systems, with limited success. In 1951, the U.S. Air Force approved the name "Atlas" for the Convair project.

The project was revealed publicly in 1954, and by 1956, Convair was able to ship the first missile to Cape Canaveral in Florida for flight testing. The first launch was on June 11, 1957, and the missile was destroyed less than one minute into its flight.

The *Atlas* A had a planned range of 600 miles, and the *Atlas* B had a range of 6,000 miles. The A model was powered by two North American booster engines,

Atlas Missile. A basic part of the nuclear weapons delivery systems, the Atlas missile was capable of reaching targets deep in the Soviet Union. Atlas missiles were also put to peaceful purposes, as in this launch of a satellite for the National Aeronautics and Space Administration. (NASA)

each delivering 120,000 pounds on takeoff. In November 1958, a two-stage *Atlas* B missile completed its flight down range to target, representing the first successful test of an ICBM by the United States, about one year after the first successful Soviet test of an SS-6 missile.

The *Atlas* missiles were 10 feet in diameter and 75 feet, 10 inches long. The *Atlas*, over a decade in development, was soon superseded by the TITAN missile, deployed first in 1962.

Atmospheric Nuclear Testing

Tests of nuclear weapons aboveground, in the atmosphere, were conducted by all of the first nations to develop nuclear weapons: the United States, the Soviet Union, Great Britain, France, and China. Later, INDIA and PAKISTAN conducted nuclear tests only underground.

The first test of a nuclear weapon was by the United States on July 16, 1945, at the TRINITY site, near Alamogordo, New Mexico, at 5:35 A.M. The device was placed on a tower for detonation. Following World War II, the United States under Operation CROSSROADS conducted a series of tests in the South Pacific at BIKINI Atoll.

Over the period 1946 to 1958, the United States conducted 20 more operations or projects, usually with several different shots or separate detonations, for a total of more than 200 tests. Many of the test devices were set on towers, while others were dropped from aircraft. The tests were conducted at several sites: Bikini Atoll, ENEWETAK Atoll, near Christmas Island or Johnston Island in the Pacific Ocean, at a site in the Atlantic Ocean, and at the NEVADA TEST SITE, north of Las Vegas, Nevada. Following a self-imposed moratorium on atmospheric testing in the period 1959 to 1962, the United States conducted a series of tests, the DOMINIC series, in the Pacific before agreeing to the Limited Test Ban Treaty signed in 1963, under which the signatory countries agreed to no longer test nuclear weapons in the atmosphere, underwater, or in outer space.

After the first tests conducted by the Manhattan Engineer District at Alamogordo and by a Joint Task Force at Operation Crossroads in 1946, the Atomic Energy Commission supervised weapons-related tests and safety experiments, while the ARMED FORCES SPECIAL WEAPONS PROJECT (and its successor agencies) supervised weapons-effects tests. Some tests series, in particular those with double names, incorporated both weapons-effects tests and weapon-design or weapon-proof tests.

ANNOUNCED NUCLEAR TESTS, 1946 TO 1961

SERIES	DATE	LOCATION	NUMBER OF SHOTS
TRINITY	July 16 1945	ALAMOGORDO	1
CROSSROADS	June/Jul 1946	PACIFIC	2
SANDSTONE	Apr/May 1948	PACIFIC	3
RANGER	Jan/Feb 1951	NEVADA	5
GREENHOUSE	Apr/May 1951	PACIFIC	4
BUSTER-JANGLE	Oct/Nov 1951	NEVADA	6+1 U.G.
TUMBLER-SNAPPER	Apr/Jun 1952	NEVADA	8
IVY	Oct/Nov 1952	PACIFIC	2
UPSHOT-KNOTHOLE	Mar/Jun 1953	NEVADA	11
CASTLE	Feb/May 1954	PACIFIC	6
TEAPOT	Feb/May 1955	NEVADA	14
WIGWAM	May 14 1955	PACIFIC	1 U.W.
REDWING	May/Jul 1956	PACIFIC	17
PLUMBBOB	May/Oct 1957	NEVADA	30
HARDTACK I	Apr/Aug 1958	PACIFIC	35
ARGUS	Aug/Sep 1958	SO. ATLANTIC	3
DOMINIC I	Apr/Jun 1962	PACIFIC	36

Note: HARDTACK II series, September–October 1958, was conducted underground in Nevada, as were later test series over the period 1963 to 1993.

The yield and the type of weapon being tested during many of the announced tests remained classified. Several exceptions were widely publicized, such as the Mike shot of the Ivy series, October 31, 1952, which was estimated at 15 megatons, the first thermonuclear explosion.

The Soviet Union began testing in 1949, and the American press designated the tests as Joe 1, Joe 2, and so on, after Joseph Stalin.

EARLY SOVIET ATMOSPHERIC TESTS

Joe 1	August 29, 1949
Joe 2	October 3, 1951 (announced)
Joe 3	October 22, 1951 (announced)
Joe 4	August 12, 1953

The Soviets later claimed that Joe 4 was a hydrogen bomb, and American atmospheric samples appeared to confirm the assertion. However, Joe 4 was later determined to be what the Americans would term a "boosted" fission device. In other words, the Joe 4 detonation was a fission weapon boosted with a small amount of tritium, developing a yield of about 400 kilotons.

Soviet records showed that there was an earlier test in August 1953 that the Americans did not record, making Joe 4 actually the fifth Soviet test. However, the controversy over who first developed the thermonuclear weapon centered around what the American records showed as Joe 4.

After the Joe 4 test, there were an additional 14 tests in the atmosphere through 1955. Most were held at SEMIPALATINSK-21, in Kazakhstan. A 1954 detonation was held at Totskoe in the Ural Mountains, apparently an exercise involving troops. Another was held at NOVAYA ZEMLYA, the island archipelago north of Norway and the Soviet Union. A test held November 22, 1955, involved a two-stage thermonuclear weapon, yielding 1.6 Mt, similar in design to the U.S. hydrogen bombs.

The Soviets stopped testing in 1958, but they broke their self-imposed moratorium, or halt, with more than 100 tests, beginning September 1961. The United States, also engaging in a self-imposed moratorium, rapidly fielded a series of new tests in 1962 in Operation Dominic. When the LIMITED TEST BAN TREATY was signed in 1963, all further testing by the United States, Great Britain, and the Soviet Union was conducted underground. In the early 1990s, as the Soviet Union and the United States negotiated a COMPREHENSIVE TEST BAN TREATY (not ratified by the end of the century),

even underground testing by the Americans and the Russians came to a halt.

Great Britain began testing in 1952 in Australia and at Christmas Island. She joined the atmospheric test ban in 1963. France began its atmospheric testing of nuclear weapons in 1960 in Africa and later in the South Pacific. France and CHINA did not join the atmospheric test ban. France continued atmospheric testing through 1974, and China continued until 1978.

See also ATOMIC VETERANS; BRITISH ATMOSPHERIC TESTING; OPERATION CASTLE; FRANCE–NUCLEAR ARMS; UNDERGROUND TESTING.

Suggested Reading
Barton Hacker, *Elements of Controversy: The Atomic Energy Commission and Radiation Safety in Nuclear Weapons Testing, 1947–1974*. Berkeley: University of California Press, 1994.

Richard G. Hewlett and Francis Duncan, *Atomic Shield* (Vol. 2 of *A History of the United States Atomic Energy Commission*). Washington, D.C.: Atomic Energy Commission, 1972.

David Holloway. *Stalin and the Bomb*. New Haven: Yale University Press, 1994.

Atomic Age

The term "atomic age" was apparently first introduced by the journalist William Laurence, who had been recruited by General Leslie Groves to write public relations material about the Manhattan Project for publication after the dropping of the atomic bombs on Japan. Laurence's stories took the form of press releases widely reproduced in papers throughout the world immediately after the bombs were dropped on August 6 and August 8, 1945. Laurence also may have been the first journalist to use the terms "atomic bomb" and "atomic era."

By 1956, the phrases had entered common usage. In the 1956 presidential election, the Democratic Party platform gave credit to both Franklin ROOSEVELT and Harry TRUMAN for having initiated the atomic era.

In this encyclopedia, the term "atomic age" is used in its broader sense to cover the period from the identification of nuclear fission in 1938 through the end of the 20th century.

Suggested Reading
William Laurence, *Dawn over Zero: The Story of the Atomic Bomb*. New York: Knopf, 1947.

Robert Jay Lifton and Greg Mitchell, *Hiroshima in America: A Half Century of Denial*. New York: Avon, 1996.

Atomic Bomb Casualty Commission

Immediately following the atomic attacks on HIRO-SHIMA and NAGASAKI, Japanese physicians not only provided care for as many survivors as they could, but they began to gather data on the number of people killed and the type and extent of injuries. When American medical teams arrived in September 1945 the Japanese were already preparing reports based on their findings. An American military commission followed up on the Japanese studies with examinations of 7,000 survivors.

Before the end of 1946, the military services recommended a more extensive survey, assisted by the National Academy of Sciences. The ATOMIC ENERGY COMMISSION set aside $100,000 in 1947 to support preliminary surveys. Radiological and medical field teams studied conditions through 1946 and 1947. The first groups in the field worked as a survey team traveling throughout Japan in the 406th Medical General Laboratory, consisting of three railroad cars that provided laboratory space and living quarters for the specialists. By 1948, the preliminary field groups had been reorganized by the National Academy of Sciences as the Atomic Bomb Casualty Commission (ABCC).

This commission spent $450,000 in 1948, and its budget rose in 1949 to $1.4 million and to $1.5 million in 1950. The teams involved included about 50 Americans, several Australians, and about 150 Japanese. Most of the work was centered at Hiroshima.

By 1950, the commission had collected data on over 150,000 victims in the two bombed cities. The studies revealed an increase in the occurrence of leukemia, and 40 cases of eye cataracts among 800 people who were situated within close proximity to the detonations. A genetics group collected data on 20,000 births.

Expenditures were cut to $1 million in 1952, and the Atomic Energy Commission dropped the project in 1953. With some assistance from the National Academy of Sciences, a limited number of studies of the data continued over the next few years. The ABCC continued to make studies through early 1975. Its work was later conducted under the Radiation Effects Research Foundation. That foundation was equally funded by the governments of Japan, through the Ministry of Health and Welfare, and the United States, through the National Academy of Sciences under contract with the U.S. DEPARTMENT OF ENERGY.

Suggested Reading

Richard G. Hewlett and Francis Duncan, *Atomic Shield* (Vol. 2 of *A History of the United States Atomic Energy Commission*). Washington, D.C.: Atomic Energy Commission, 1972.

Atomic Demolition Munitions (ADM)

Atomic Demolition Munitions (ADMs) were developed for the demolition of bridges, buildings, and other structures. Designed with comparatively low yields and highly portable, the weapons typically could be deployed by truck and then hand-carried by one or two individuals for final emplacement. Their ease of portability increased their risk of being diverted or stolen for unauthorized use by terrorists or a military adversary.

Atomic Energy Act of 1946

The Atomic Energy Act of 1946 established the civilian controlled U.S. ATOMIC ENERGY COMMISSION (AEC). The act empowered the commission to supervise the production of nuclear weapons for the nation's atomic arsenal, encourage the research and development of nuclear technology for peaceful purposes, and disseminate scientific and technical information related to atomic energy. The Atomic Energy Act created a five-member board or commission that directed the decision making and operations of the AEC.

The 1946 act authorized the creation of the congressional JOINT COMMITTEE ON ATOMIC ENERGY (JCAE) to monitor the actions of the AEC and oversee the development of the nation's atomic policies. Furthermore, the Atomic Energy Act ordered the formation of the General Advisory Committee to advise the commission on scientific and technical matters and the Military Liaison Committee to permit the participation of the U.S. Department of Defense in military aspects of atomic weapons development and manufacturing.

Senator Brien MCMAHON of Connecticut proposed the Atomic Energy Act, or the McMahon bill as it was sometimes referred to, in 1945 as an alternative to an earlier proposal, the MAY-JOHNSON bill. The Manhattan Project's success in building atomic bombs meant that the United States possessed a nuclear monopoly in 1945. A national debate occurred in the fall of 1945 concerning the future governance of the country's atomic arsenal. Although heavily reliant upon civilian scientists, engineers, and workers, the U.S. Army

Corps of Engineers and the military managed the Manhattan Project during the war.

The War Department sought to retain control of the atomic energy and weapons program and the May-Johnson Bill, introduced by two congressmen, would have established an atomic energy commission or agency within the War Department. However, civilian scientists continued to lobby for civilian control.

While the scientists pressured Congress, Senator Brien McMahon introduced a resolution on October 4 that established a Senate special committee to investigate all atomic energy bills and resolutions. Senator Edward Johnson of Colorado failed in his efforts to capture control of the committee. On October 23, the Senate created the Special Committee on Atomic Energy and appointed McMahon committee chairman. The Special Committee offered a forum for the atomic scientists and other opponents of the May-Johnson Bill to explain their criticisms. By mid-December 1945, Congress recognized that the May-Johnson proposal faced too much opposition and new legislation was needed.

On December 20, Senator McMahon introduced Senate Resolution (S.R.) 1717 that contained a proposal to create a five-member, civilian-controlled agency to supervise the production of nuclear weapons and to promote the development of atomic energy for peaceful uses. The bill contained guarantees for maximizing the free exchange of scientific information and possessed less stringent penalties than the May-Johnson Bill for security violations. The McMahon Bill included a provision that supported the study of the social, political, and economic implications of atomic energy.

The McMahon Bill received widespread support among the scientific community. Although the War Department and Navy Department objected to the exclusion of the military, President Harry TRUMAN and his administration backed the concept of civilian control. However, a spy scandal intervened, which altered the legislation's fate. On February 16, 1946, news broke in the United States concerning the arrest of 22 people in Ottawa, Canada, for passing secret information, including materials related to the atomic bomb, to the Soviet Union.

The Canadian spy scare added fuel to the already tense relations between the United States and the Soviet Union. Caught in the storm of cold war tensions and growing fears of atomic espionage, the McMahon Bill quickly lost support. Several Special Committee members proposed the addition of a mili-

tary presence in the legislation. Senator Arthur Vandenberg of Michigan submitted an amendment which required the civilian commission to consult with a military board on all matters related to national defense. Although McMahon vigorously opposed the amendment, the Special Committee voted in favor of its adoption. In addition, the committee added two other amendments that authorized the formation of a congressional joint committee to supervise the civilian commission and establish a committee to advise the commission on technical and scientific matters.

The McMahon Bill passed the Senate easily on June 1, 1946, but it encountered opposition in the House of Representatives. Opponents criticized the McMahon Bill's stipulations relating to government ownership of fissionable materials and industrial development as an unacceptable expansion of federal power. They also equated the bill's provisions for exchanges of basic scientific information with a lax attitude by the government toward security. Critics exercised enough power to stall the bill in the House. A conference between House and Senate members finally resulted in the approval of the bill on July 26, 1946. President Truman signed the Atomic Energy Act of 1946 on August 1, 1946.

The final version of the McMahon Bill assigned the Atomic Energy Commission the title to source and special materials and it prohibited the private ownership of production facilities. The Act fostered tight government control over atomic energy information and patents relating to industrial and military applications. The early emphasis on the international exchange of information gave way to restrictions that prohibited such interaction and stipulated severe punishments, including the death penalty. As the cold war worsened, the act's civilian aspects became less important. Not long after the 1946 Act created the Atomic Energy Commission, weapons research, development, and production consumed the agency's attention. It would require an entirely new act to refocus the AEC on the peaceful uses of atomic energy.

See also ATOMIC ENERGY ACT OF 1954.

Suggested Reading

Richard Hewlett and Oscar Anderson, *The New World, 1939–1946: A History of the United States Atomic Energy Commission,* Volume I. Berkeley: University of California Press, 1990.

Jessica Wang, *American Science in an Age of Anxiety: Scientists, Anticommunism and the Cold War.* Chapel Hill: University of North Carolina Press, 1999.

Atomic Energy Act of 1954

The Atomic Energy Act of 1954 departed from the civilian governmental management and operations of the nuclear weapons complex, which served as the focus of the Atomic Energy Act of 1946. Instead, the Atomic Energy Act of 1954 encouraged the private development of nuclear reactors and established the formal basis for regulating private operators.

The 1954 Act loosened the monopoly enjoyed by the U.S. ATOMIC ENERGY COMMISSION (AEC) over nuclear fuels, materials, and facilities. By 1954, circumstances had changed both nationally and internationally, which made alterations in the law necessary. Most notably, the United States no longer enjoyed a monopoly in atomic weapons after the Soviet Union successfully tested an atomic bomb in 1949. In addition, considerable progress had been made in research on civilian applications of nuclear energy, particularly in generating electrical power.

Representative Sterling Cole (R-New York) and Senator Bourke Hickenlooper (R-Iowa), chairman and vice chairman, respectively, of the congressional Joint Committee on Atomic Energy (JCAE), sponsored the initial legislation proposing a new direction for the nation's nuclear program. The Joint Committee, under the direction of Cole and Hickenlooper, started to reconsider the Atomic Energy Act of 1946 in June 1953. Committee members wanted to loosen the federal government's control over nuclear technology while still retaining safety and security supervision. By November 1953, AEC chairman Lewis STRAUSS and the other commissioners drafted proposals that broadened the involvement of private industry in atomic energy development and liberalized the commission's information-control provisions.

Although supported by President Dwight EISENHOWER, these legislative alterations encountered resistance from the Joint Committee when the commissioners presented them in January 1954. Representative Cole felt that, instead of amending the 1946 Atomic Energy Act, a new bill needed to be created. Therefore, the Joint Committee assumed responsibility for drafting a new act for the AEC. Cole and Hickenlooper took a personal interest in the bill and spent long sessions laboriously drafting sections of the legislation with Joint Committee staff members. The Joint Committee forwarded a copy of the bill to Strauss and the commissioners in April 1954. The Cole-Hickenlooper Bill, as the legislation became known, formed the basis for the Atomic Energy Act of 1954.

The Cole-Hickenlooper proposal authorized the commission to provide licensing for the private possession and use of nuclear materials, although the federal government retained the ownership of these materials. The bill also empowered the AEC to license industrial firms to build and operate private nuclear reactors. The legislation proposed greater declassification of restricted information for use by private industry.

The commissioners reacted negatively to a number of the suggested changes offered in the Cole-Hickenlooper Bill. Chairman Strauss felt that it was impracticable for the Joint Committee to require the commission to retain government ownership of all fissionable materials, regardless of who produced them. The legislation abolished the special patent provisions incorporated in the 1946 Act and opted instead to eliminate the transition period of compulsory licensing of patents developed under government contract. The commissioners opposed this measure, as did the Eisenhower administration. Cole and Hickenlooper redrafted their bill and introduced it to the House and Senate on June 30, 1954. The legislation retained the government ownership of fissionable materials, recommended the compulsory cross licensing of patents, and gave appropriations authorization powers to the Joint Committee.

A heated congressional debate developed surrounding the proposed bill. By July 15, 20 senators organized to oppose the bill. Opponents objected to the legislation's perceived attempt to give away the nation's atomic energy program to the control of American industrial corporations. By July 22, the opposition coalition in the Senate had enough votes to control the Senate floor and amend the bill on several issues. Senator Edwin Johnson (D-Colo.) presented an amendment granting the commission authority to produce and market electric power generated in its own plants while Senator Guy Gillette (D-Ia.) suggested that public utilities and co-operatives be given preference in purchasing this power.

Majority leader William Knowland (R-Calif.) resorted to tabling any amendment on which debate was not limited to move the bill through the Senate. Knowland also introduced a petition of cloture to end the filibuster tactics of the opposition. Cole and the Republican House leaders were more successful in avoiding any controversies concerning the bill. The Republicans successfully defeated the House equivalent of the Johnson amendment and limited debate on proposed amendments to just five minutes. The House approved the bill 203 to 159 on July 17 with only five amendments added to it. The opposition coalition in the Senate began to collapse when Senate minority leader Lyndon Johnson (D-Texas) and other conservative Democrats grew impatient with the long debates and lack of resolution. The Senate finally voted on the legislation July 26 after more than 180 hours of discussion.

The House and Senate met in conference to reach a compromise between the two proposals. The Democrats opposed the elimination of public power issues and compulsory licensing provisions from the bill. Finally, the two sides agreed to a compromise in which the Republicans kept the sections governing patents in commission-related activities intact and the Democrats secured compulsory licensing for a period of five years. President Eisenhower signed the act into law on August 30, 1954.

In its final form, the Atomic Energy Act of 1954 provided for the following:

1. Private ownership of atomic energy facilities, such as research and power reactors, subject to compliance with AEC licensing requirements.
2. Private leasing of special nuclear materials under license and use-charge arrangements.
3. Private access to certain categories of classified information, including restricted data, subject to compliance with commission procedures.
4. A more liberal patent policy.
5. Broadened international cooperation in the development of peaceful uses of nuclear energy.
6. Exchange with other nations of classified information on certain aspects of military applications of nuclear energy.

The Atomic Energy Act of 1954 remained the basic legislation governing both the nuclear weapons program and the nuclear power program in the United States until the Energy Reorganization Act of 1974 created the ENERGY RESEARCH AND DEVELOPMENT AGENCY.

Suggested Reading

Brian Balogh, *Chain Reaction: Expert Debate and Public Participation in American Commercial Power, 1945–1975* New York: Cambridge University Press, 1991.

Richard Hewlett and Jack M. Holl, *Atoms for Peace and War, 1953–1961: Eisenhower and the Atomic Energy Commission.* Berkeley: University of California Press, 1989.

Atomic Energy Commission

The Atomic Energy Commission (AEC) was created by Congress in 1946 to take over the nuclear research, development, and production facilities established under the MANHATTAN ENGINEER DISTRICT during World War II. The ATOMIC ENERGY ACT OF 1946 that created the commission was amended by the ATOMIC ENERGY ACT OF 1954 in order to foster the development of nuclear power and to allow for the export of nuclear technology for peaceful purposes.

The AEC managed the many properties of the nuclear WEAPONS PRODUCTION COMPLEX, including laboratories, factories, production facilities, and research programs in academia and industry. During the 1950s, the AEC cooperated with the U.S. Navy in the development of NUCLEAR PROPULSION for submarines. In the 1950s and early 1960s, the commission continued to license experimental power reactors rated from a few megawatts of power to a few hundred megawatts. In the late 1960s, the commission licensed much larger power reactors on the scale of 1,000 megawatts or more.

The AEC was the subject of continuing controversies during the 1960s and early 1970s. Several issues brought the agency into the public limelight. Radioactive FALLOUT from ATMOSPHERIC NUCLEAR TESTING of nuclear weapons in the period 1950 to 1962, problems of disposal of nuclear waste, and concern over the safety of the many large nuclear power reactors being constructed in the 1960s all became festering issues in the press and among the public.

A source for criticism of the agency was its general practice of making decisions behind closed doors, a culture inherited from its origins as an agency devoted to a highly sensitive and classified weapons technology. The AEC set policies that could affect public health, safety, worker safety, and the environment. The commission often decided such matters with a degree of confidentiality that tended to exclude proper public discussion and disclosure.

Other criticisms derived from the fact that the Atomic Energy Act of 1946 vested congressional control over the commission in a new and powerful JOINT COMMITTEE ON ATOMIC ENERGY (JCAE). The JCAE, with members from both the House of Representatives and the Senate, worked closely with the AEC, tending to support its positions and policies. Certain long-serving members of the JCAE became extremely strong advocates of atomic power and atomic weaponry, including Chet HOLIFIELD, Craig Hosmer, and Henry JACKSON.

Leslie Groves and David Lilienthal. General Leslie Groves, former officer in charge of the Manhattan Engineer District, confers with David Lilienthal, the first chairman of the Atomic Energy Commission, about the transition from military to civilian control. (Department of Energy)

Political scientists pointed to the alliance between the agency, Congress, and industrial groups as an "iron triangle," allowing decisions to be made and power to be exercised outside of the traditional political constraints on federal activity.

The chairmen of the Atomic Energy Commission tended to be strong-willed advocates for the commission, and, during the 1960s and 1970s, they acted as powerful supporters for the construction and licensing of nuclear power reactors and defenders of nuclear power as a means of addressing the nation's energy needs. Chairs of the commission:

David LILIENTHAL	1946–1950
Sumner PIKE	1950
Gordon DEAN	1950–1953
Lewis STRAUSS	1953–1958
John MCCONE	1958–1961
Glenn SEABORG	1961–1971
James SCHLESINGER	1971–1973
Dixy LEE RAY	1973–1975

The intention of the 1946 act was to ensure that nuclear weaponry be controlled by a civilian agency, not by the military alone. That emphasis had several origins. One was that during the Manhattan Project, many civilian scientists believed that the mindset of military officers precluded creative scientific work. Another concern was to preserve the traditional control over the military exercised by the civilian executive branch of government. The legislation, by placing control of research, development, and production of nuclear weapons in civilian hands and by creating a powerful congressional structure to oversee the commission, helped to guarantee the further development of technologies based upon nuclear science.

Suggested Reading

Richard G. Hewlett and Oscar E. Anderson, *The New World* (Vol. 1 of *A History of the United States Atomic Energy Commission*). Washington, D.C.: Atomic Energy Commission, 1962.

Richard G. Hewlett and Francis Duncan, *Atomic Shield* (Vol. 2 of *A History of the United States Atomic Energy Commission*). Washington, D.C.: Atomic Energy Commission, 1972.

Richard Hewlett and Jack Holl, *Atoms For Peace and War, 1953–1961: Eisenhower and the Atomic Energy Commission*. Berkeley: University of California Press, 1989.

Jack Holl, Roger Anders, and Alice Buck, *The United States Civilian Nuclear Power Policy, 1954–1984: A Summary History*. Washington, D.C.: Department of Energy, 1986.

Atomic Industrial Forum

The Atomic Industrial Forum (AIF) originated as an idea suggested in the fall of 1952 by T. Keith GLENNAN, a commissioner of the U.S. ATOMIC ENERGY COMMISSION (AEC) at the time and president of the Case Institute of Technology. During his term as a commissioner, 1950 to 1952, Glennan spurred American industry to enter the nuclear field. He envisioned a nonprofit association that brought businessmen, scientists, engineers, and educators together as a possible vehicle to educate and attract greater industrial involvement in developing nuclear technology.

In April 1953, Glennan announced the incorporation of the Atomic Industrial Forum. Walker L. Cisler, president and general manager of the Detroit Edison Company, served as the first president of the forum. Several leading educators and industrialists volunteered as directors for the AIF. Executives and presidents from the B. F. Goodrich Company, Purdue University, Case Institute of Technology, the Babcock and Wilcox Company, National Lead Company, the Dow Chemical Company, Phillips Petroleum Company, and the Standard Oil Company of California participated on the board of the AIF.

The forum operated from a main office located in New York City. The AIF intended to act as a clearinghouse for information and a stimulant for private business interest in nuclear energy. The major activities for the forum were fourfold. First, the forum held an annual energy conference that included an industrial exhibit. It also sponsored meetings on specific topics of special interest, such as reactor safety.

Second, the forum used standing committees and ad hoc working groups to study particular problems affecting the American nuclear energy industry. The AIF established standing committees in subject areas such as contract practices, insurance and indemnity, mining and milling, patents, and public understanding. The forum created ad hoc groups that examined the U.S. Atomic Energy Commission's regulatory organization, reactor safety, the space applications of nuclear energy, the private ownership of nuclear fuel, and labor compensation.

Third, the forum published the proceedings of its conferences and the reports of its committees. Additionally, the AIF published an annual report, a periodic tabulation of U.S. nuclear power plant projects, and a monthly news summary and analysis, the *Forum Memo to Members*. The forum also issued occasional special publications that surveyed the growth of the American nuclear industry and worldwide atomic industrial activity. Finally, the Atomic Industrial Forum assembled a library that included a comprehensive collection of unclassified U.S. Atomic Energy Commission literature.

Besides offering information and educational materials, the forum evolved into an informal advising organization to the Atomic Energy Commission as well as an industry lobbyist. The forum supported the commission's efforts to pass legislation, specifically the PRICE-ANDERSON ACT that provided liability insurance for industrial participants in nuclear reactor development in 1957. The AIF's Committee on Reactor Safety assisted the Atomic Energy Commission in reviewing the consequences of a major nuclear reactor accident in 1965. The forum later argued against the commission's regulatory design codes for commercial reactors in 1967. At the same time, the forum co-produced with the AEC numerous films and pamphlets extolling the benefits of nuclear energy.

The Energy Reorganization Act of 1974, which dissolved the U.S. Atomic Energy Commission, brought changes to the forum. The AIF moved its offices from New York to Washington, D.C., in 1975 to engage in greater political advocacy for the industry. The forum initiated a new public relations campaign designed to rehabilitate the image of commercial nuclear reactors. Once in Washington, the forum established close relations with the newly created NUCLEAR REGULATORY COMMISSION.

As a consequence of its move from New York, the AIF changed its formal status from an education organization to a trade association. To handle its lobbying activities, the forum established the American Nuclear Energy Council (ANEC). Approximately 125 firms participating in the nuclear power industry contributed to the funding of the ANEC. The ANEC held weekly legislative workshops in Washington for lobbyists and industry representatives.

Beginning in 1976, the AIF lobbied the Nuclear Regulatory Commission and Congress to standardize reactor designs. A wave of project cancellations shocked the industry in 1974. The AIF believed standardization could make financing nuclear reactors easier by bringing stability and predictability in licensing, design, and construction. For the next five years, the forum worked hard to convince industrialists and government officials about the necessity of standardization. Competition between manufacturers and inconsistent decision making by government officials prevented the industry from adopting a standardized reactor design by 1981.

The forum refocused its energies as the number of orders for new reactors declined in the late 1970s and early 1980s. The AIF became an advocate for the reprocessing and recycling of used uranium and plutonium in response to the public's growing concerns about the environmental effects of nuclear by-products. Forum members attributed the eventual collapse of the reprocessing industry to the interventions of antinuclear and environmental groups.

In 1987, the AIF changed its name to the Nuclear Energy Institute (NEI). The NEI maintained an office in Washington, D.C., to serve the needs of members in the United States and abroad. The NEI continued the forum's advocacy and educational traditions.

See also PRICE-ANDERSON ACT.

Suggested Reading

Robert J. Duffy, *Nuclear Politics in America: A History and Theory of Government Regulation.* Lawrence: University Press of Kansas, 1997.

J. Samuel Walker, *Containing the Atom: Nuclear Regulation in a Changing Environment, 1963–1971.* Berkeley: University of California Press, 1992.

Atomic Mass Unit (amu)

Atomic mass units are based on the atomic weight of the most common isotope of carbon. ^{12}C is exactly 1 atomic mass unit; $1\ amu = 1.6606 \times ^{-27}kg$.

Atomic Veterans

Orville Kelly, a veteran who had observed 22 separate aboveground nuclear explosions, later suffered from cancer. On discovering his cancer, Kelly had first organized a group of cancer victims to assist each other in adjusting to their own imminent death. On concluding that the cancer was a result of his exposure to radiation, Kelly took on the cause of representing other veterans who had similar experiences. Kelly was the founder and first president of the National Association of Atomic Veterans, set up in 1979. Like Paul R. Cooper, another veteran whose claim set off the NUCLEAR TEST PERSONNEL REVIEW, Kelly's claim was first denied by the Veterans Administration but then granted on appeal. Between the denial and the appeal date, as Kelly's cancer advanced, he vigorously campaigned for his own case and for the claims of others.

On being notified that his appeal had succeeded, Kelly responded, "The award will allow me to die in peace. . . . I out-waited them. Maybe that's what kept me alive." Many of the atomic veterans believed that they confronted a conspiracy or government cover-up.

Charges of a conspiracy or cover-up ranged from relatively accurate recognition that the policy of the AEC had long been to downplay the significance of radiation exposure from all tests and sites, to charges based on little more than a general suspicion that an extensive conspiracy had worked to suppress evidence.

The advocates firmly believed that the exposures at the nuclear tests accounted for cancer among the atomic veterans. When the statistics seemed ambiguous, the advocates would interpret the figures to suggest a correlation between the exposure and the illness, even when the epidemiologists were more cautious. Atomic veteran advocates interpreted expert caution as either suspicion on the part of the experts that low-level radiation could have long-term residual effects or as evidence that the scientists were presenting biased information in order to satisfy their employers.

The reasons that atomic veterans came to suspect that the government was not fully truthful with them sprang from several causes:

- An estimated 37,000 of the 250,000 participants in the test series would be expected to die of cancer simply on the basis that about 15 percent of the general U.S. population dies of cancer. Thus many veterans would contract cancer and suspect that exposure at a nuclear test had been a cause, even when their disease had sprung from other factors.

- Public distrust for the government and the Department of Defense in particular increased vastly in the wake of the Vietnam War.
- The fact that much of the government's documentation was contained in classified files contributed to suspicions that information was being suppressed.
- The fact that the information was dispersed and difficult to access further contributed to the sense of delay.
- The logic of epidemiology was particularly unconvincing, not only to the general public but also to the courts. Statistical presentations sometimes seemed confusing, tedious, and couched in terms that suggested concealing rather than conveying information.
- AEC policy in the 1950s had explicitly been designed to prevent public alarm at the tests and the dangers associated with them. Thus historical documentation often supported the veterans' assertions that the government had not been fully truthful about risks, radiation hazards, and weapon FALLOUT.
- The military had urged maximum realism in the exercises, sometimes overriding or opposing civilian scientists' concerns to minimize radiation hazard.
- When troops had participated in exercises during nuclear tests, not every soldier wore a film badge. Exposure records were often estimated, based on selected badges. Furthermore, when records indicated that individuals or groups had not been overexposed, the records were sometimes disposed of or poorly filed.

The very effort of the Nuclear Test Personnel Review in the 1980s to collect information required extensive publicity, which in turn stimulated journalistic interest and public concern. Claims continued to mount, and finally Congress resolved the issue through legislation.

In 1988, President Ronald Reagan signed the Radiation-exposed Veterans Compensation Act, lifting the burden of proof from the veterans. A list of radiation-related diseases was presented, and it was presumed that if a veteran had participated in a nuclear test or related activity, such diseases were service-related. The Court of Veterans Appeals served as the final authority in determining if a particular veteran was eligible for a claim under the act because of his presence at a

Atomic Veterans. Marines get ready to charge during a training exercise at the Nevada Test Site. Some military men who participated in such exercises later contracted cancer and sought compensation from the government. (National Archives and Records Administration)

nuclear test. Atomic veterans who believed they had suffered ill-effects from their exposure to radiation during aboveground testing could make use of records held in a public facility, the Coordinating Information Center, in Las Vegas, to help demonstrate that they had been involved in a nuclear test. Claims continued to come in well into the 1990s.

See also EPIDEMIOLOGICAL STUDY.

Suggested Reading

F. Lincoln Grahlff, *Voices from Ground Zero*. Lanham, Md.: University Press of America, 1991.

Barton Hacker, *Elements of Controversy: The Atomic Energy Commission and Radiation Safety in Nuclear Weapons Testing, 1947–1974*. Berkeley: University of California Press, 1994.

Atoms for Peace

On December 8, 1953, President Dwight EISENHOWER addressed the General Assembly of the United Nations, stating that the United States would devote its efforts to turn "the miraculous inventiveness of man" to life, not to death. This speech, which came to be known as the "Atoms for Peace" speech, initiated a new policy for the United States in the mid-1950s.

Eisenhower wanted to bring international efforts to bear on atomic research, but he recognized that the earlier Baruch Plan and similar proposals would fail because they required inspection of atomic research facilities, a concept that would be rejected by the Soviet Union. In fact, it was difficult to implement specific measures in accord with Eisenhower's concept because of the continued growth of the U.S. nuclear arsenal, the heightened tensions of the cold war between the United States and the Soviet Union, and the suspicions harbored by other countries with nuclear research programs, including European nations and India, that the United States sought to dominate the market for nuclear reactors and prevent other nations from developing nuclear armaments.

In February and March 1954, the U.S. State Department communicated a plan for the creation of an international agency devoted to peaceful uses of atomic energy. When the Soviet Union appeared unwilling to cooperate, the United States proceeded to announce a series of bilateral agreements under which it would share nuclear materials for research and for power reactors with other nations. Meanwhile, negotiations proceeded to work out a basic plan for an international agency that would meet the objections of the Soviet Union and other countries.

At a conference held at the United Nations in September and October 1955, the Atoms for Peace proposal took more concrete shape with agreement on a charter for the INTERNATIONAL ATOMIC ENERGY AGENCY (IAEA).

As another aspect of the Atoms for Peace concept, the Atomic Energy Commission (AEC) sponsored the development of nuclear power reactors, with the first reactor to provide commercial electric power opened at SHIPPINGPORT, Pennsylvania, in December 1957. Gradually at first and then with more success, nuclear power plants were built with encouragement and support from the AEC through the 1960s and 1970s, and American companies began to export reactor technology to other countries.

The IAEA held its organizing meeting and began to hire staff on October 1, 1957, at Geneva, Switzerland. At a second conference, held in 1958, the United States and other nations carried out demonstrations of advances in nuclear technology and arranged for the exchange of nuclear information.

In later years, the IAEA would develop procedures for safeguarding nuclear material and preventing its diversion from peaceful purposes to weapons programs. IAEA safeguards ultimately came to be one of the more practical aspects of the original Eisenhower 1953 initiative, allowing the export of nuclear material, power reactors, and related technology without stimulating the construction of production reactors and other equipment necessary for the development of nuclear weapons.

See also POWER REACTORS, U.S.; PROLIFERATION.

Suggested Reading

Richard Hewlett and Jack Holl, *Atoms for Peace and War, 1953–1961: Eisenhower and the Atomic Energy Commission.* Berkeley: University of California Press, 1989.

Arnold Kramish, *The Peaceful Atom in Foreign Policy.* New York: Dell, 1965.

Babcock and Wilcox

One of four nuclear reactor manufacturing companies in the United States, along with GENERAL ELECTRIC, WESTINGHOUSE, and COMBUSTION ENGINEERING, Babcock and Wilcox had been a long-time vendor of boilers and steam generators for conventional power plants. Babcock and Wilcox had built boilers for electrical power systems since 1881 and it began its nuclear work in providing some components for naval PROPULSION REACTORS. Its first major commercial nuclear power plant was built at Indian Point for Consolidated Edison of New York. That reactor opened in 1962. By the end of the century, Babcock and Wilcox had provided nine of the 104 operating reactors in the United States, but the company never successfully challenged the leadership of Westinghouse and General Electric in the field.

Bacher, Robert F. (1905–) *American physicist who participated in the Manhattan Project and later became an advisor on nuclear policy*

Robert Bacher was a key worker at LOS ALAMOS during work on the MANHATTAN ENGINEER DISTRICT, playing an important part in the design of the first atomic bomb, and he continued to play a role in the making of nuclear weapons policy for several years after World War II.

Bacher was born in 1905, and he received his education in physics from Cornell University. After working on neutron reactions in 1941 at Cornell, Bacher went to the Massachusetts Institute of Technology, where he worked on the radar project. Bacher joined the weapons laboratory at Los Alamos in 1943. In 1944, he was appointed division director of "G-Division" to design the actual plutonium "gadget" or bomb. The use of high-explosive lenses to compact the core of the weapon into a supercritical mass required considerable exploratory work with explosives to determine exactly how to focus the blast effect to achieve IMPLOSION. This feature and many other innovations, including a means of igniting the various high-explosive charges simultaneously, were worked out under Bacher.

With Isidor RABI, Bacher insisted that the scientists retain their civilian status; he announced he would resign the day the laboratory became a military installation. When the test device was delivered to the site near Alamogordo for testing, he insisted on a receipt for it, signifying that the civilian institution running the laboratory, the University of California, had turned over the valuable device to the army "for destruction." After World War II he served as a technical advisor to Bernard BARUCH at the United Nations while remaining on the faculty at Cornell.

Bacher also served on the planning committee which established the Brookhaven National Laboratory at Upton, Long Island. He was appointed a member of the ATOMIC ENERGY COMMISSION (AEC) on its formation in 1946, and he served on the commission until 1949.

Among the first members of the Atomic Energy Commission, Bacher was alone in having scientific and technical background in the subject. On several issues dealt with by members of the commission, Bacher represented the more liberal side, advocating sharing ISO-TOPES with other nations, working to improve scientist morale, and noting that individuals receiving fellowships from the Atomic Energy Commission did not necessarily need security clearances. He was a strong supporter of basic or theoretical research under the AEC. After being asked to stay on an extra year, Bacher resigned from the commission on May 10, 1949. He continued to advise the AEC as a consultant, arguing that, when a second generation of PRODUCTION REAC-TORS were built, they should be capable of producing both plutonium and tritium.

In the summer of 1951, he headed a group working to prepare a report on tactical use of nuclear weapons. In the resulting Vista Report, Bacher stressed the need for small fission weapons that could be delivered in any weather in support of ground troops. Advocates of strategic bombing and of the development of the hydrogen bomb saw the Vista Report as reflecting the influence of J. Robert OPPENHEIMER, who argued along the same lines in a GENERAL ADVISORY COMMITTEE panel report.

Suggested Reading

Richard G. Hewlett and Oscar E. Anderson, *The New World* (Vol. 1 of *A History of the United States Atomic Energy Commission*). Washington, D.C.: Atomic Energy Commission, 1962.

Richard G. Hewlett and Francis Duncan, *Atomic Shield* (Vol. 2 of *A History of the United States Atomic Energy Commission*). Washington, D.C.: Atomic Energy Commission, 1972.

Ballistic Missile Defense *See* ANTI-BALLISTIC MIS-SILE.

Baneberry

Baneberry was the name of a low-yield underground nuclear test conducted on December 18, 1970, at the NEVADA TEST SITE (NTS). The test vented, that is, released a radioactive cloud of dust. The cloud spread over the test site and then over neighboring states, and its FALLOUT received far more publicity than earlier such accidents. Six hundred NTS employees were evacuated and decontaminated.

The radiation count in Salt Lake City was substantially higher than usual, although the Atomic Energy Commission (AEC) determined that no member of the public received a radiation dose higher than permitted standards. There had been a 20-foot-wide fissure at the surface of the ground, about 300 feet long, through which the radioactive dust had escaped.

After investigation, the AEC determined that water in the ground had contributed to the venting problem. Officials at the AEC regarded the fallout from Baneberry as a public relations issue, and they worked to allay public concerns in the United States and elsewhere. A proposed test at AMCHITKA, Alaska—the Cannikan test of an anti-ballistic missile warhead—raised concerns in Canada in the wake of Baneberry. Congressmen and senators from western states, including Hawaii and Alaska, grew concerned about the environmental impact of such a test.

Baneberry and its subsequent publicity contributed strongly to public opposition to continued nuclear testing, helping to bring together environmentalists and nuclear disarmament groups in a common cause. At the same time, public attention was drawn to the Baneberry event because of already increased awareness of environmental issues, and in that regard the AEC was correct in viewing the matter as a public relations issue rather than a radiation hazard problem. Earlier atmospheric testing, which ended in 1962, had accounted for far more radioactive fallout than the 1970 Baneberry event.

Barns *See* CROSS SECTION.

Baruch Plan

Immediately after World War II, the United States developed a proposal for United Nations control of nuclear weapons. Developed first by David LILIENTHAL and Dean ACHESON and expounded in the Acheson-Lilienthal Report, the plan was then further elaborated and presented to the United Nations by U.S. Ambassador Bernard Baruch. As a man who had made a fortune on Wall Street early in the century and as a former advisor to Presidents Woodrow Wilson and Franklin Roosevelt, Baruch was widely regarded as an elder statesman. The proposal became known to the world as the Baruch Plan.

Under the plan, the nations of the world would agree that the UN would set up an agency to control all atomic manufacturing and mining operations, including all possible future nuclear reactors for generating electricity. The international agency would have a team of inspectors to ensure that no nation would pursue the development of nuclear research in a direction that would lead to the creation of atomic weapons. If the authority were established, the United States would agree to dismantle its nuclear weapons facilities and destroy its stockpile of bombs.

The Baruch Plan differed in one crucial respect from the Acheson-Lilienthal Report in that Baruch required that the members of the United Nations Security Council give up their veto power over matters relating to nuclear energy.

The plan, which would have eliminated nuclear weapons before they spread around the world, reflected the advice of prominent scientists such as Niels BOHR, who predicted an expensive and dangerous nuclear arms race if the knowledge were not placed under international control. Bohr had suggested that the invention of the nuclear weapon suddenly made national sovereignty obsolete.

From the point of view of the Soviet Union there were several aspects of the treaty that were unacceptable. First, the provision to allow inspectors to verify compliance with the treaty appeared to be an excuse for espionage. The inspection system would allow potential enemies to learn exactly what strategic facilities could become targets within the Soviet Union, and it would challenge the generally secretive nature of the Soviet state. Second, even if the United States gave up its nuclear weapons, it would retain the knowledge and the trained specialists who could reconstitute a nuclear weapons capability any time they wanted to. Perhaps the most important sticking point for the Soviets was the provision of the Baruch Plan that exempted the new international nuclear agency from control by veto of members of the U.N. Security Council. In effect, the nations of the world would be agreeing to a form of world government in the single area of nuclear research and development, just as Bohr had predicted would be necessary.

Critics suggested that the United States offered the plan with the knowledge that it would be unacceptable to the Soviets and that it represented little more than propaganda or a form of bluff. The Soviets offered a modified version of the plan that would have left the control of the agency under the Security Council (where they would retain a veto power) and would have allowed inspection only of pre-agreed facilities. Both the Baruch Plan and the Soviet response were discussed through 1946 and 1947, but it was clear that an impasse had been reached, and neither was accepted.

Late in the 1950s, an INTERNATIONAL ATOMIC ENERGY AGENCY was established, which took on some of the inspection duties envisioned in the Baruch Plan, in the original Acheson-Lilienthal Report, and in the more limited Soviet plan of inspection of specified facilities.

Suggested Reading
James Grant, *Bernard M. Baruch: The Adventures of a Wall Street Legend.* New York: Simon and Schuster, 1983.
Jordan Schwarz, *The Speculator: Bernard Baruch in Washington, 1917–1965.* Chapel Hill: University of North Carolina Press, 1981.

Battelle Memorial Institute

Battelle Memorial Institute (BMI), a nonprofit research enterprise most noted for work in metallurgy, became involved in the MANHATTAN ENGINEER DISTRICT, assisting in the fabrication of nuclear fuel. Following World War II, Battelle took on a contract to operate a laboratory at HANFORD, the Pacific Northwest National Laboratory (PNNL). BMI continued to be a major contractor at Hanford over the next five decades.

The institute was funded from the inheritance of Gordon Battelle, a steel industry executive who died in 1927. Battelle specified in his will that an institute devoted to doing industrial research should be established, and in its first decade, the institute concentrated in the field of metallurgy. At the time, research done on contract was an innovative concept, and BMI was one among very few such laboratories in the United States. Gradually, the institute branched out into agriculture and health sciences. The institute developed, on contract with the Elgin Watch Company, a special alloy for watch springs that later found use in heart valves.

In 1944, Chester Carlson, a patent attorney, brought an invention to Battelle for further development. His ideas led to the dry photocopier later marketed by Xerox Corporation. Revenue from this development put Battelle in a strong position to take on many other activities in the post–World War II period. It expanded internationally and established a Marine Sciences Laboratory as well as the PNNL at Hanford.

Belgium   *See* POWER REACTORS, WORLD.

Bentonite

Bentonite is a type of clay that swells when in contact with water. It has been recommended as a back fill to be used in emplacing radioactive waste in geologic repositories.

Berg, Morris ("Moe") (1902–1972)   *an American baseball player who served in World War II as an intelligence officer engaged in nuclear espionage*

Moe Berg was a third-string catcher for the Washington Senators and Boston Red Sox professional baseball teams during the 1920s and 1930s. Berg was recruited during World War II because of his command of the German language to work with the Office of Strategic Services (OSS) in an early and bizarre case of nuclear espionage.

In 1943–1944 he traveled to Switzerland under OSS auspices, with instructions to assassinate or kidnap Werner HEISENBERG, the leading German physicist. General Leslie Groves, the commander of the MANHATTAN ENGINEER DISTRICT and head of the U.S. project to build the atomic weapon, suspected that Heisenberg and his team were well advanced in developing a nuclear bomb for the Nazi government. Working through the ALSOS PROJECT mission, Berg interviewed scientists in Italy to try to determine the progress of the German bomb project.

His early reports from Italy provided concrete information as to which German scientists would most likely be working on the atomic bomb project. According to one account by Berg in later years, he attended, with a pistol in his pocket, a talk that Heisenberg gave in Zurich, Switzerland, on December 19, 1944. By his own improbable account, he listened to determine whether Heisenberg had made progress on the atomic bomb. Discovering that the scientist's work on the weapon was nowhere near completion, Berg spared Heisenberg's life.

See also GERMAN ATOMIC BOMB PROJECT; GOUDSMIT, SAMUEL.

Suggested Reading

Luis Kaufman et al. *Moe Berg: Athlete, Scholar, Spy.* Boston: Little Brown, 1974.

Thomas Powers, *Heisenberg's War.* New York: Knopf, 1993.

Beria, Lavrenty (1899–1953)   *head of the Soviet secret police from 1938 to 1953 and head of the program (1945–1953) to build the first Soviet atomic bomb*

Lavrenty Beria was best known as the director of the Soviet secret police, the People's Commissariat of Internal Affairs (NKVD), during and immediately after World War II. His importance to nuclear history is that he personally supervised the program leading to the first Soviet nuclear weapons, chairing the Special Committee on the Atomic Bomb from 1945 to 1953.

Beria let the Soviet scientists working on the project know that, if they failed in their work, they would not only be replaced but they would be imprisoned or executed.

Beria's early career had been in the police apparatus in Georgia and Azerbaijan in the 1920s. He went to Moscow in 1938, appointed by Stalin to serve as deputy to the head of the NKVD. His fellow administrators viewed him as talented but very cruel and ruthless. Beria not only identified individuals to be shot, but he personally supervised the torture and execution of some of his victims. During and after World War II, Beria became widely known and feared as the head of Stalin's secret police, which served as the primary machinery of suppression and state control.

Immediately after the American use of nuclear weapons in Japan in August 1945, Stalin established the Special Committee on the Atomic Bomb and put Beria in charge. The choice was logical as Beria was feared and his orders were regularly carried out. Beria took over the existing nuclear establishment in the Soviet Union, adding not only members of the secret police as administrators but also a number of industrial managers to ensure that the project would move swiftly to fruition. They were able to convert what had been a laboratory project into a nationwide industrial scale operation, just as the MANHATTAN ENGINEER DISTRICT had done a few years before in the United States.

When Beria took charge, B. L. KAPITSA, a senior nuclear physicist in the Soviet Union during the war years, soon urged Stalin to ensure that scientists, not police agents and administrators, run the program. Beria insisted that the scientists take the intelligence information gained from Klaus FUCHS and from other espionage work in Britain, Canada, and the United States and build a nuclear weapon identical to the American device tested at Alamogordo and used at Nagasaki. Kapitsa urged a more scientific approach, developing the knowledge in a less imitative way.

Due to the disagreements between Kapitsa and Beria, Kapitsa was relieved of all responsibilities on the project, but I. V. KURCHATOV, appointed in 1943 as the scientific director of the project, retained his position. Ultimate control remained in Beria's hands. Although he was not arrested, Kapitsa was soon dismissed from all scientific employment. Kurchatov followed the Beria plan of imitating the U.S. design very closely. However, many of the problems encountered in the design of both the weapon and the plutonium production reactors had to be independently solved, as Klaus Fuchs and the other sources had simply not gathered information as to all the American approaches.

At the test of the first nuclear device in the Soviet Union on August 29, 1949, Beria showed up at the project every day, observing the work. He and the scientists were relieved at the resulting explosion, estimated at about 20 kilotons, because their lives literally depended on its success. Beria had already chosen successors to the leading scientists in case of failure. The success of the test gave Kurchatov increased prestige, and Beria briefly considered replacing him. However, Kurchatov was essential to the project as he was able to keep prominent Soviet scientists energized and committed.

Beria continued to oversee the nuclear project for the next four years, as the Soviets worked to improve the nuclear weapon and began development of a thermonuclear bomb. Tests held on September 24, 1951, and October 18, 1951, involved a more original design, utilizing both ^{235}U and ^{239}Pu. The October test was of a true air-dropped bomb, rather than a device mounted on a tower, and it produced an estimated yield of 40 kilotons.

Shortly after the death of Stalin, Beria was arrested by a group of military officers on June 26, 1953, and charged with crimes against the state. A major charge against him was that he decided to test the hydrogen bomb without informing other members of the Soviet leadership. Georgy Malenkov, who first emerged as the most powerful figure in the leadership as chairman of the Council of Ministers, took the lead in denouncing Beria at a meeting of the Central Committee of the Soviet Communist Party in July. Beria was tried in secret and executed on December 23, 1953.

Suggested Reading

David Holloway, *Stalin and the Bomb*. New Haven: Yale University Press, 1994.

Beryllium

Beryllium is a toxic steel-gray metal with a low neutron absorption CROSS SECTION and high melting point. It is used in nuclear reactors as a moderator, reflector, or as a cladding material. In some nuclear weapon designs, beryllium is used to surround the FISSILE MATERIAL to reflect neutrons back into the nuclear reaction. Thus, a beryllium case or container can be used to reduce the amount of fissile material required in the weapon.

Betatron

The betatron was the first device for accelerating electrons to energies greater than a few million electron volts (MeV). Professor Donald Kerst developed the first practical betatron in 1940 at the University of Illinois. It was a doughnut-shaped device in which electrons (ß particles) were accelerated to 2.5 MeV by steadily increasing magnetic induction in an orbit of constant radius, a process similar to the flow of an electrical current through a secondary winding of a transformer. Energies as high as 300 MeV have been achieved in subsequent betatrons. Few if any betatrons remain in operation because synchrotrons and linear accelerators have proved to be superior machines for accelerating electrons.

Bethe, Hans (1906–) *German-born American physicist who participated in the Manhattan Project*

Hans Bethe emigrated to the United States from Germany in the 1930s, and he worked in the Manhattan

Project as head of the theoretical division at LOS ALAMOS. He was born in Strasbourg, then part of Germany, in 1906 and was educated at the Universities of Frankfurt and Munich. With the Nazi ruling that Jews could not hold positions in German higher education, he left Germany in 1933, taking refuge first in Britain and then moving to the United States in 1935. He accepted an appointment as professor of physics at Cornell University. In 1938, he worked out the details of how thermonuclear reactions serve to fuel the sun and stars. He received the NOBEL PRIZE in physics for this work in 1967.

During World War II, he moved to Los Alamos to work on the Manhattan Project, serving there as head of the Theoretical Division. After the war, Bethe became a vocal critic of Werner HEISENBERG, doubting Heisenberg's contention that the German physicists who remained in Germany during World War II sought to delay or obstruct the development of a nuclear weapon there. Bethe continued to argue for the social responsibility of the scientist, and he criticized the STRATEGIC DEFENSE INITIATIVE proposals developed in the period 1983 to 1987.

Suggested Reading

Hans Bethe, *The Road from Los Alamos.* New York: American Institute of Physics, 1991.

Bettis Atomic Power Laboratory (BAPL)

The Bettis Atomic Power Laboratory (BAPL) is a government-owned, contractor-operated facility for power and propulsion reactor design. Operated by Westinghouse, BAPL is located about 10 miles from Pittsburgh, Pennsylvania. Originally supervised by then Captain Hyman RICKOVER, BAPL designed and built the land-based prototype for the reactor for NAUTILUS, the first atomic submarine, launched in 1954. BAPL designed another pressurized water-type reactor for aircraft carriers, modifying that design for the first U.S. power reactor connected to the commercial power network at SHIPPINGPORT, Pennsylvania.

BAPL also operated the NAVAL REACTOR TEST STATION at the IDAHO NATIONAL ENGINEERING LABORATORY.

See also KNOLLS ATOMIC POWER LABORATORY.

Suggested Reading

Richard G. Hewlett and Francis Duncan, *Nuclear Navy, 1946–1962.* Chicago: University of Chicago Press, 1974.

"Big Three" Meetings

During World War II, the leaders of the United States, the Soviet Union, and Great Britain met for several strategic conferences, attempting to resolve questions regarding entry of the Soviet Union into the war against Japan and future plans for the occupation of the defeated enemy nations, particularly Germany, Italy, and Japan. Although these Big Three meetings did not directly bear on the issue of nuclear weapons development, President Harry TRUMAN, at the Potsdam meeting in 1945, did casually inform Joseph STALIN that the United States had developed an extremely powerful weapon.

Some evidence suggests that Truman attempted to get the Potsdam meeting delayed until mid or late July 1945 so that he would know whether or not the test of the first atom bomb at TRINITY in mid-July had been successful. The Big Three conferences during the war were as follows.

Tehran. November 28–December 1, 1943 Roosevelt, Churchill, and Stalin met to plan the invasion of occupied France. They also discussed the plan for the future of Germany and the formation of the United Nations as a permanent organization. The Soviets agreed to enter the war with Japan after the defeat of Germany.

Yalta. February 4–11, 1945 Roosevelt, Churchill, and Stalin agreed on conditions for the Soviet entry into the war against Japan, two to three months after the surrender of Germany. The future of Poland, Germany, and Eastern Europe were discussed.

Potsdam. July 17–August 2, 1945 Truman met with Stalin, and first with Churchill, then Clement Atlee. They discussed German occupation, German war reparations, and Soviet entry into the war against Japan. Truman mentioned to Stalin in very vague terms the nuclear weapon that was tested at Alamogordo on July 16.

Suggested Reading

Gar Alperovitz, *Atomic Diplomacy: Hiroshima and Potsdam.* New York: Penguin, 1985.

Bikini

Bikini is a small atoll, or coral ring of islands, located in the Marshall Island group in the western Pacific Ocean, at 11 degrees 30 minutes north latitude and 165 degrees 30 minutes east longitude. Both Bikini

Bikini. The local people of Bikini evacuated the island in 1946 to make way for the U.S. nuclear weapons testing program. Their island was restored to them later, but it remains too radioactive for permanent residency. (Library of Congress)

and ENEWETAK lie on the northwestern-most reaches of the Marshall Island group and are extremely isolated. Both were home to several hundred MARSHALL ISLANDERS at the end of World War II.

The United States chose Bikini Atoll as the site for nuclear tests because of its isolation. However, weather conditions on the island were not ideal. Frequent tropical storms and unpredictable winds made forecasting of wind direction on test days extremely difficult. Bikini served as the site of 23 nuclear detonations in four series: two shots in OPERATION CROSSROADS in 1946, five shots in OPERATION CASTLE in 1954, six shots of OPERATION REDWING in 1956, and 10 shots of the series OPERATION HARDTACK in 1958.

The BRAVO shot of the CASTLE series at Bikini earned the most public attention of all the Pacific nuclear tests. In 1954, FALLOUT from this 15-megaton detonation blew to the east rather than to the north,

as predicted, contaminating the atolls of Rongelap, Alinginae, and Rongerik. After initial delays, the Marshallese were removed from these islands, but they received dangerous radioactive dosages from this fallout.

Fallout from CASTLE-BRAVO caused serious illness and at least one death in 1954 among the crew of the Japanese fishing boat *Fikuryu Maru* (*Lucky Dragon*). The controversy surrounding the fallout from BRAVO contributed to the worldwide movement for a Comprehensive Test Ban Treaty.

In December 1966, Secretary of the Interior Stewart Udall asked the ATOMIC ENERGY COMMISSION (AEC) if the island was safe for habitation and when the inhabitants might have hazard-free use of the resources of the atoll. Aboveground testing of nuclear weapons had ended in 1962 and maintaining the islands as possible test sites was no longer practicable.

After radiological surveys of the island, in August 1968, President Lyndon Johnson announced that the United States no longer required Bikini for nuclear testing. When the DEFENSE ATOMIC SUPPORT AGENCY (DASA) took on the cleanup of Bikini Atoll in 1969, it was the first such effort in the world to repair a landscape damaged by nuclear tests. DASA worked with the AEC in the first phase of the cleanup of the atoll, dismantling abandoned nuclear test facilities and disposing of radioactive debris. During the cleanup, DASA buried over 40,000 tons of scrap and rubble and dumped about 500 tons of radioactive scrap at sea, a practice allowed at the time but outlawed soon after the conclusion of the work in 1971.

DASA turned over administration of Bikini to the Department of the Interior on October 12, 1969. The Trust Territory government took five more years to prepare for the return of the Bikini natives from Kili island, an isolated spot over 400 miles away, where they lived almost entirely on imported food. Contractor crews laid out housing sites and planted trees. The Trust Territory government preferred that Bikini settlers return in small groups, allowing time for newly established plants and coconut groves to mature.

Between 1974 and 1977, over 100 Bikinians gradually returned to their atoll. In the spring of 1977, however, regular testing revealed an alarming increase in radioactive cesium that the Bikinians had taken into their bodies. Specialists traced the problem to the diet. Since the islanders preferred fresh food to imported supplies, they had relied especially on the coconuts from the new groves. In the summer of 1978, the U.S. government removed the islanders once again.

In later years, Bikinians won a settlement of over $200 million dollars. They did not return to their island to live, but they began to convert it into a tourist destination. Over 2,300 descendants of the original 186 Bikinians removed from the island in 1946 live on Kili, other islands in the Marshall Islands, and in other countries.

See also ATMOSPHERIC NUCLEAR TESTING.

Suggested Reading

Barton Hacker, *Elements of Controversy: The Atomic Energy Commission and Radiation Safety in Nuclear Weapons Testing, 1947–1974.* Berkeley: University of California Press, 1994.

Defense Atomic Support Agency, *Cleanup of Bikini Atoll.* Washington, D.C.: DASA, 1971.

Ralph Lapp, *The Voyage of the Lucky Dragon.* New York: Penguin, 1958.

Bohr, Niels (1885–1962)   *Danish nuclear physicist regarded as the world's most brilliant theoretician in the field in the mid and late 1930s*

Niels H. D. Bohr became noted for his work developing a quantum-based model for the atom and winning the Nobel Prize in 1922. In the interwar years, he was widely regarded as the world's leading nuclear theoretical physicist. In later years, he gained fame for his advocacy of international control of atomic weapons.

He was born in 1885 in Copenhagen, Denmark, and was educated in that city. In 1911, he went to Great Britain to study at the Cambridge atomic research laboratory with J. J. Thomson. In 1912 he moved to Manchester to work with Ernest RUTHERFORD. He studied the atomic model, in which electrons orbited the atomic nucleus in specific rings.

In 1913, he developed his quantum theory of the atom. In Denmark, he was given the rank of professor, and the Danish government built the Institute of Theoretical Physics that he then headed. Physicists from all over the world came to study with Bohr, and Denmark became a leading center of nuclear research. In 1922, his theory of the structure of the atom was validated with the discovery of a new element, hafnium, that he had predicted under his theory. He won the NOBEL PRIZE that year for the quantum model of the atom.

Following the suggestions of Lise Meitner, in 1939, Bohr further developed the theory of fission, with the proposal that a heavy nucleus could undergo FISSION following neutron capture.

After the surrender of Denmark to Germany in World War II, Bohr continued to provide a haven for European scientists fleeing from German persecution. In September 1941, he was visited by Werner HEISENBERG, who had remained in Germany to work on atomic research, and the two discussed whether scientists should support the building of a nuclear weapon. Heisenberg later remembered that he had argued that scientists should not do so, but Bohr's memory of the meeting was somewhat different. He apparently believed Heisenberg was trying to determine the extent of progress toward a nuclear weapon among the Allies. Eventually, in September 1943, Bohr escaped in a motor launch to Sweden. From there, the Allies arranged for Bohr to be flown out, and he made a dangerous crossing to Britain from Sweden in a wooden aircraft, unable to hear instructions over the airplane intercom on how to don an oxygen mask.

After arrival in Britain, Bohr then moved to the United States to become a consultant to the MANHATTAN ENGINEER DISTRICT, with the code name of "Nicholas Baker." He was so well known among physicists, however, that he was immediately recognized throughout the project.

He asked President Franklin ROOSEVELT to consider sharing the nuclear weapon with the Soviet Union at the earliest possible date. He visited both Roosevelt and Churchill and sent them several memoranda outlining his suggestion for sharing of nuclear weapon design. Without sharing, he argued, the world would soon enter a nuclear arms race.

Peter KAPITSA invited Bohr to come to the Soviet Union, but Bohr declined. However, he continued to try to persuade the leaders of the Manhattan Engineer District that the nuclear secret be shared. His ideas later became embodied in the plan developed by David LILIENTHAL and advanced as the BARUCH PLAN.

After the war, Bohr remained an advocate of nuclear disarmament and openness in the scientific community. He was instrumental in establishing a European nuclear research organization, the Center for European Nuclear Research, in Geneva, Switzerland. He developed the concept of "complementarity" by which he described basic particles as having complementary features of waves and particles. He died in 1962.

Suggested Reading

Thomas Powers, *Heisenberg's War.* New York: Knopf, 1993.
Richard Rhodes, *The Making of the Atomic Bomb.* New York: Simon and Schuster, 1988.

Boiling Water Reactor

A boiling water reactor (BWR) is a nuclear reactor in which water, used as both the coolant and the moderator, is allowed to boil in the core. The resulting steam passes through a HEAT EXCHANGER to produce lower temperature and to pressure steam to turn turbines for the generation of electricity. In a 500 megawatt BWR, 550 degree F. steam is produced in a 20-foot diameter × 70-foot-high reactor vessel at a pressure of 1,000 psi. Of the approximately 500 nuclear reactors in operation worldwide, some 98, nearly 20%, are boiling, light-water–cooled, and moderated reactors. The BWRs are concentrated in 10 countries, as shown in the following list.

COUNTRY	COMMERCIAL REACTORS, TOTAL	BWRs
Finland	4	2
Germany	20	6
India	18	2
Japan	57	32
Mexico	2	2
Spain	9	2
Sweden	12	9
Switzerland	5	2
Taiwan	8	6
USA	109	35
World Total BWRs		98

In the United States, the 35 BWRs were all manufactured by General Electric (GE). That company also exported models to INDIA, JAPAN, SPAIN, Taiwan, and Mexico. In Japan, Toshiba and Hitachi companies worked with GE on some designs and then developed their own models. In Finland, Germany, Switzerland, and SWEDEN, European firms built the reactors.

See also POWER REACTORS, U.S.

Boosted Weapons

A boosted weapon is a fission device containing a small amount of deuterium-tritium (D-T) gas at the center. As the CHAIN REACTION proceeds, the temperature of the fissile material and the adjacent gas in the middle become intense. At a high enough temperature, a thermonuclear reaction will be initiated, which proceeds very rapidly. Since they are introduced independently of the chain reaction in the PLUTONIUM and in a near-instantaneous pulse, the neutrons from the fusion reaction increase the rate of fissions very sharply, with the result that the ultimate yield may be several-fold larger than it would have been without the boosting. The neutrons react with the still unfissioned plutonium, thus using up more of the plutonium. Almost all weapons since about 1960 have been boosted to make more efficient use of plutonium. Boosting allows weapons designers to achieve a fuller degree of FISSION of a given amount of plutonium, thus achieving greater weapons effect in a smaller, lighter, and more efficient design. The first test involving the boosting principle was during OPERATION GREENHOUSE on May 24, 1951.

Borden, William L. (1920–1985) *American attorney, executive director of the Joint Committee on Atomic Energy (1946–1953), and author of work predicting long-range nuclear-armed missiles*

William Borden played a significant part in the development of nuclear policy in the United States in the period 1946 to 1953, serving as executive director to the JOINT COMMITTEE ON ATOMIC ENERGY (JCAE). Borden had served in the U.S. Army Air Force in World War II, where he had witnessed the flight of a German *V-2* missile. This experience would haunt him in later years.

While Borden was still attending Yale Law School, he published a book urging the modernization of the U.S. military, warning of the dangers that arose from the future combination of nuclear weapons with long-range missiles. Borden's 1946 vision was correct in that, by the early 1970s, INTERCONTINENTAL BALLISTIC MISSILES with thermonuclear warheads would become the leading strategic armament of both the Soviet Union and the United States. He pointed out that in both World War I and World War II, the United States had two or more years to build up the military while the war was fought in Europe. However, a sudden nuclear "Pearl Harbor" type attack could initiate the next war, leaving the United States not only ill prepared but at least partially devastated.

His work, *There Will Be No Time*, attracted the attention of Brien MCMAHON, chair of the JCAE. McMahon sought out Borden for the administrative post of executive director of the joint congressional committee established under the ATOMIC ENERGY ACT OF 1946 to provide legislative oversight over the ATOMIC ENERGY COMMISSION.

Over the next few years, Borden worked with others to stress the need for more scientists at LOS ALAMOS and to advocate a faster rate of production of nuclear weapons. Borden and some members of the joint committee supported Edward TELLER in arguing for a thermonuclear weapon. In the nuclear politics of the era, Borden was widely recognized as a force behind the scenes for vigorous pursuit of more-powerful nuclear weapons and for a larger and more productive weapons complex. In particular, through the early 1950s, he sided with those who believed that the thermonuclear weapon had to be built to offset the Soviet achievement of a nuclear weapon in 1949.

Borden's influence declined in the mid-1950s for several reasons. After the death of Brien McMahon in 1952, he lost his patron on the Joint Committee on Atomic Energy. More especially, after the loss in January 1953 by scientist John A. Wheeler of a highly sensitive document that Borden had ordered prepared, describing the development of the thermonuclear weapon, Borden's standing with the Atomic Energy Commission sharply declined. Nevertheless, he worked closely with Lewis STRAUSS, the new JCAE chair, and, in many ways, Borden's views coincided with those of Strauss.

In Borden's last months as executive director of the joint committee, he actively supported the effort to revoke the security clearance of J. R. OPPENHEIMER. Supporters of Oppenheimer viewed Borden as a sinister behind-the-scenes influence. On the other hand, Oppenheimer's critics sided with Borden in regarding Oppenheimer's opposition to the thermonuclear weapon as based on excessive sympathy for the Soviet viewpoint. In 1953, Borden resigned his post to return to private life.

Suggested Reading

Richard G. Hewlett and Francis Duncan, *Atomic Shield* (Vol. 2 of *A History of the United States Atomic Energy Commission*). Washington, D.C.: Atomic Energy Commission, 1972.

Richard G. Hewlett and Jack M. Holl, *Atoms for Peace and War: 1953–1961*. Berkeley: University of California Press, 1989.

Boron

Boron, the element with atomic number 5, has six ISOTOPES ranging in mass number from 8 to 13. Two isotopes of boron, ^{10}B and ^{11}B, are stable. The capture CROSS SECTION of the less-abundant (20%) ^{10}B is 3,837 barns, making it useful as a neutron absorber.

Brazil

Brazil began a nuclear program in 1953, pursuing both nuclear power development and a program to develop a nuclear weapon. The military program was stimulated by the development of a nuclear capability in neighboring ARGENTINA in the same period. In 1971, Brazil obtained a light waterpower reactor built by Westinghouse, Angra I. This 676-megawatt reactor began commercial operation on January 1, 1985.

During the 1970s, Brazil began a nuclear weapons program code-named the Solimoes Project. The army, air force, and navy each pursued a different pathway to the development of fissile material for a nuclear weapon. Only the navy's program, using an ultracentrifuge method of uranium enrichment, with a plant in São Paulo, reached the point of being able to enrich uranium to the level needed for nuclear weapons. The navy also constructed an industrial-scale plant for uranium enrichment at the Aramar Research Center in Ipéro. A nuclear test site, with underground facilities for detonating a weapon, was started at Cachimbo, in the Amazon Forest.

The military continued to advocate nuclear weapons development, but by the late 1980s civilian political leaders worked to diminish tensions with Argentina and reduce the commitment of Brazilian resources to the weapons program. In 1990, the president of Brazil, Fernando Collor de Mello, announced that the country was ending its military program. The Cachimbo test site was closed.

In 1991, Brazil and Argentina signed a bilateral agreement to allow joint inspection of nuclear facilities. They also established an Argentine-Brazilian Accounting and Control Commission to handle the inspections. Later, both countries and the bilateral commission they had established made an agreement with the INTERNATIONAL ATOMIC ENERGY AGENCY (IAEA) in Vienna to inventory and inspect nuclear facilities. That four-way agreement between Argentina, Brazil, the bilateral commission, and the IAEA was ratified in 1994.

By the 1990s, Brazil had one operating nuclear power plant, the Westinghouse-provided pressurized water reactor Angra I, near Rio de Janeiro, at 626 megawatts-electric (MWe). The German-built Angra II and Angra III, both under construction, were designed to operate at 1,245 MWe. Angra II was to begin operation in 1999 and Angra III in 2006. All three reactors were at the Itaorna power station near Rio. In addition, Brazil maintained six research reactors. Although the weapons program was discontinued, enrichment plants in São Paulo and at Aramar continued to operate. Also indefinitely postponed or shut down were facilities for reprocessing, that is, for the extraction of plutonium from reactor fuel.

Brazil began planning for a nuclear-powered submarine, but in 1996 the Brazilian navy announced that it had suspended or postponed such plans. Reportedly one of the activities at the Aramar research center had been to use the ultracentrifuges there to provide enriched uranium fuel for submarines, rather than weapons-grade enriched uranium. About half of the center's 2,000 employees left. In the late 1990s, the navy planned to supply centrifuges from the Aramar facility for use at Resende to provide enriched uranium for the commercial reactors.

Brazil had been correctly regarded by proliferation experts as a "threshold" nation, about to develop nuclear weapons. But the agreements of the early 1990s to eliminate the program in Brazil and Argentina under civilian governments in both countries appeared to have ended, or at least suspended, nuclear rivalry in South America.

See also PROLIFERATION; TREATY OF TLOTELOLCO.

Suggested Reading

Rodney Jones et al., *Tracking Nuclear Proliferation.* Washington, D.C.: Carnegie Endowment for International Peace, 1998.

Leonard S. Spector, *The Undeclared Bomb.* Cambridge, Mass.: Ballinger Books, 1988.

Breeder Reactor

The concept of a breeder reactor derives from a design that would make best use of the neutrons resulting from FISSION of the fuel in a reactor by converting ^{238}U to produce more fissionable fuel than has been burned up in the process. The objective is to have the maximum amount of ^{238}U converted into fissionable plutonium. Furthermore, the breeder reactor itself would be used to produce electric power. In order to perform both functions efficiently and for the system to operate at a profit, the fuel has to be concentrated in a relatively small volume. Therefore the reactor produces much more heat than a regular light waterpower reactor. For this reason, breeder reactors are sometimes designed using a liquid metal, such as molten sodium, as a coolant, which is capable of transporting greater amounts of heat than is water or pressurized steam. Thus, one breeder reactor design was a LIQUID METAL FAST BREEDER REACTOR (LMFBR).

ARGONNE NATIONAL LABORATORY built an experimental breeder reactor (EBR I) that suffered a severe accident on November 29, 1955, which destroyed the reactor. News of the accident was not released publicly for several months. Argonne then built EBR II at its installation at the IDAHO NATIONAL ENGINEERING LABORATORY, which operated successfully for over 10 years beginning in 1963. The EBR II, which at full power would run at about 16.5 megawatt-electrical, demonstrated that such a reactor could be operated safely. Another, full-scale breeder reactor, the Enrico FERMI REACTOR was built a few miles south of Detroit. Started up in August 1963, Fermi Reactor had to be shut down in October of that year after a serious accident.

The British planned a breeder reactor, and they began operating a demonstration Prototype Fast Reactor in 1974. The French also began operating the Phénix fast breeder reactor at Marcoule in 1974.

The concept of constructing more breeder reactors along the LMFBR design line was appealing in the United States as the country faced an energy shortage in the 1970s. However, liquid sodium is itself an unfamiliar material and is extremely hazardous. Furthermore, one of the attractive, and at the same time, dangerous aspects of a breeder reactor is that it produces great amounts of plutonium to be used to fuel other reactors. As a consequence, a whole "plutonium economy" would need to develop, with plutonium-fueled reactors and the transportation of plutonium from breeder reactors to power reactors. Since only a few pounds of plutonium would be sufficient to use in the design of a nuclear weapon, the procedures and expense of protecting the plutonium in transit and storage against theft would be extremely high.

The use of plutonium to fuel a class of power reactors would blur the distinction or boundary between nuclear power for peaceful purposes and the use of nuclear energy for defense. The questions of both safeguarding the material and disposing the waste from a plutonium-fueled reactor caused planners to hesitate. Still another consideration with breeder reactors was the cost and the technical difficulty of building large-scale reprocessing plants to extract the plutonium from the fuel. In the United States, such a plant operated briefly from 1966 to 1972 at WEST VALLEY, New York, and another was planned for Barnwell, South Carolina.

Despite the hazards and concerns, breeder reactors seemed like an attractive pathway to follow, as it was conceivable that a reactor would not only produce electricity but would also produce more fuel than it consumed, providing an answer to any foreseeable energy shortage. Atomic energy enthusiasts saw the breeder reactor as the ultimate solution to the world's need for energy, while atomic energy opponents emphasized the hazards, the tie-in to weapons proliferation, and the high cost and technical difficulty of developing the new fuel cycle.

During the 1970s, the United States embarked on a breeder reactor program and began constructing one at Clinch River, Tennessee. The cost of building the Clinch River breeder reactor climbed astronomically from about $400 million to over $2 billion. The program was canceled early in the administration of Jimmy Carter due to the policy implications of combining defense and peaceful uses of atomic energy. Under President Reagan, the Clinch River project was briefly revived, but the Senate refused to endorse expenditures for the reactor in 1983, putting the project to a final end. Opponents of the use of nuclear reactors for generating electricity frequently recounted the costs and dangers associated with the concept of a breeder reactor. The accident at the Fermi reactor near Detroit appeared to discredit the concept in the United States for decades, although other nations, notably India and the Soviet Union, have pursued the breeder concept.

Brinkmanship

The term "brinkmanship" appeared in the news media after the confrontation between U.S. president John KENNEDY and Soviet premier Nikita KHRUSHCHEV in 1961 regarding the emplacement of Soviet missiles in Cuba. It appeared that both leaders had gone to the "brink," or edge, of war, testing each other's will. Later, as other presidents and premiers confronted international crises that could bring both nations to the brink of war, they sought to avoid mutual threats or escalation of the crises. In general, later leaders tried to avoid practicing brinkmanship.

During the 1961 crisis, Khrushchev decided that one way to offset increased U.S. military presence in Europe was to emplace intermediate-range missiles, armed with nuclear warheads, in Cuba. Under Fidel Castro, the Cuban people had risen in a revolution against the oppressive and corrupt regime of Fulgencio Batista, overthrowing that government in January 1959. Over the period 1959–1960, Castro's government became increasingly aligned with the Soviet bloc, and members of the Cuban Communist Party took many of the senior positions in his government. In effect, by 1961, Cuba represented a pro-Soviet outpost in the Western Hemisphere.

American intelligence learned of the construction of the Soviet missile sites in Cuba through rumors collected by American and French agents in Cuba. The emplacements were confirmed in 1961 by overflights of high-flying U-2 reconnaissance aircraft.

The United States demanded the removal of the missiles, and Kennedy placed the U.S. armed forces on high alert, an indication of preparation for nuclear war. He also ordered the U.S. Navy to intercept and, if necessary, stop by armed force Soviet ships bringing missiles and equipment to the bases in Cuba. After an exchange of messages between Khrushchev and Kennedy in which the United States agreed to remove some aging *Jupiter* missiles from Turkey, Khrushchev ordered the Soviet ships to return to base, and the armed confrontation was avoided at the last minute. Thus, both nations had gone to the "brink."

British Atmospheric Nuclear Tests

Like the United States, the British government conducted a series of aboveground or atmospheric nuclear detonations to test the weapons they had developed in their independent nuclear program. The decision of the British cabinet to build nuclear weapons was taken in January 1947, and the first test was held in 1952.

Altogether the British detonated 21 devices between 1952 and 1958, 12 in or near Australia, and nine at Christmas Island.

In addition to these announced tests, the British conducted many tests of weapons components at the Australian test range of Maralinga.

As in the United States, initial public support for or indifference to the tests gradually switched to growing concern over risk to the environment and to public health, even though the tests were conducted in remote areas. Eventually, the British government decided to recompense aboriginal peoples in Australia for disruption of their homelands. Also, some of those individuals who participated in the tests, like the American ATOMIC VETERANS, later filed suit for damages, believing that exposure to radiation led to incidents of cancer in some 400 cases. Like the Americans, the British set up a panel to review the cases, and they granted pensions in a number of them.

See also ATMOSPHERIC NUCLEAR TESTING; NUCLEAR TEST PERSONNEL REVIEW; UNITED KINGDOM.

Suggested Reading
Lorna Arnold, *A Very Special Relationship*. London: Her Majesty's Stationery Office, 1987.
Denys Blakeway and Sue Lloyd-Roberts. *Fields of Thunder: Testing Britain's Bomb*. London: Allen and Unwin, 1985.

Broken Arrow

The term "Broken Arrow" was adopted by the nuclear weapons community in the United States to describe accidents in which aircraft carrying nuclear weapons crashed, or in which a weapon accidentally fell to the ground, or in which an aircraft crashed into a nuclear weapons storage facility. Although the Department of Defense announced over 30 such accidents during the period 1950 to 1980, none of the episodes resulted in a nuclear detonation. In several cases, however, the release of radioactive material from the weapon required extensive cleanup and decontamination. In some of the cases, the weapon was recovered free of damage.

When nuclear weapons were carried aboard aircraft, whether to be transported, used in training, or as part of maintaining the arsenal on alert status, such accidents were almost inevitable. Operation Chrome

BRITISH ATMOSPHERIC NUCLEAR TESTS			
NAME OF SERIES	DATE	LOCATION	YIELD
Operation Hurricane	Mar. 10 '52	Monte Bello Is. Australia	25 Kt
Operation Totem	Oct. 14 '53	Emu Field South Australia	10 Kt
	Oct. 26 '53	Emu Field South Australia	8 Kt
Operation Mosaic	May 16 '56	Monte Bello Is. Australia	15 Kt
	Jun. 19 '56	Monte Bello Is. Australia	98 Kt
Operation Buffalo	Sep.–Oct. '56	Maralinga Range South Australia series of 4 tests	1.5–15 Kt
Operation Antler	Sep.–Oct. '57	Maralinga Range series of 3 tests	1, 6, 25Kt
Grappie Series	May 57–Sep. '58	Christmas Island series of 7 H-bomb tests, 2 fission device tests	yields classified

Dome, which required at least 12 Strategic Air Command bombers to be armed and in the air at all times, increased the likelihood of aircraft accidents involving weapons. Several of the better-known broken arrow incidents of the 1960s, including CUMBERLAND, PALOMARES, and THULE, occurred during those operations. However, even the early design of weapons and the procedures involved in not arming weapons for detonation combined to limit the damage and the danger.

Since nuclear weapons were designed with high explosives to compress the nuclear material, there was danger that the high explosive would detonate if there were a fire or impact as a result of an air crash. Considerable care went into improving the weapons designs in order to minimize the risk of detonation of the high explosives because even though no nuclear explosion would take place, a blast of high explosive could spread radioactive material over quite a wide area. Of the announced broken arrows between 1950 and 1980, several were at or near airfields in the United States.

LOCATIONS AND NUMBER OF ANNOUNCED BROKEN ARROW ACCIDENTS, 1950–1980

Ocean/water	7	New Mexico	2
Ohio	2	California	2
Texas	2	Louisiana	2
Overseas Base	2	Florida	1
Georgia	1	S. Carolina	1
Washington	1	Kentucky	1
New Jersey	1	N. Carolina	1
Maryland	1	S. Dakota	1
Indiana	1	Spain	1
Greenland	1	Arkansas	1

The broken arrow accidents attracting the most public attention were those near Cumberland, Maryland, on January 13, 1964; in Palomares, Spain, on January 17, 1966; in Thule, Greenland, on January 21, 1968; and the explosion of a fuel tank on a *Titan* II INTERCONTINENTAL BALLISTIC MISSILE in its silo at DAMASCUS, Arkansas, on September 19, 1980.

The death of General Robert F. Travis in an early broken arrow accident in California on August 5, 1950, was the cause for renaming a nearby air base Travis Air Base.

Other episodes in the 1950s included a crash of a plane on Manzano mountain at Kirtland Air Force Base, New Mexico, on April 11, 1950, and the accidental release of a heavy hydrogen bomb near the same base on May 22, 1957. Cleanup crews from the ARMED FORCES SPECIAL WEAPONS PROJECT determined that the radiation release from the latter drop was confined to the 25-foot diameter impact crater in a pasture area. That bomb had come loose from its rack and smashed through the bomb bay doors. A similar loss occurred on March 11, 1958, near Florence, South Carolina, when a bomb destroyed a home and garage in a residential neighborhood. Two announced broken arrows resulted in 1962 during attempts to detonate a nuclear weapon at a high altitude aboard a Thor ICBM rocket. As the rockets failed, the weapons were destroyed, their remains falling into the ocean. The loss of the nuclear submarine THRESHER at sea in April 1963, with a nuclear-tipped Subroc weapon aboard is sometimes included in listings of broken arrow events.

Suggested Reading

Shaun Gregory, *The Hidden Cost of Deterrence: Nuclear Weapons Accidents*. London: Brassey's, 1990.

Brookhaven National Laboratory (BNL)

In 1947, Brookhaven National Laboratory (BNL) was started on the former site of the U.S. Army's Camp Upton about 60 miles east of New York City in Suffolk County, Long Island. A group of colleges and universities, the Associated Universities, Incorporated, operated BNL under a contract with the ATOMIC ENERGY COMMISSION (AEC). With AEC funding, the universities utilized the Brookhaven Graphite Research Reactor (1950–1968). In 1952, the AEC added the Cosmotron, a particle accelerator which ran until 1966. In 1960, BNL acquired the Alternating Gradient Synchrotron, and in 1970, the Tandem Van de Graff accelerator. In 1999, the institution planned to add Relativistic Heavy Ion Collider.

BNL has acquired other equipment, including the Brookhaven Medical Research Reactor in 1959, a High Flux Beam Reactor in 1965, and a number of smaller pieces of equipment. Research ranged from the fields of medical research and nuclear medicine to solid state physics, solar phenomena, and microbiology.

In 1989, a number of environmental problems at Brookhaven came to light with pockets of radioactive contamination on the 5,300-acre site. A further problem was discovered in 1997 when a tritium leak from the High Flux Beam Reactor was identified. In 1997,

Brookhaven National Laboratory. Located on Long Island, New York, the Brookhaven National Laboratory houses research in basic physics, including the work of several Nobel Prize winners. (Brookhaven National Laboratory)

the Department of Energy terminated the contract with Associated Universities and, beginning in March 1998, Brookhaven Science Associates took over BNL, representing a partnership between BATTELLE MEMORIAL INSTITUTE and the State University of New York at Stony Brook.

Using the Alternating Gradient Synchrotron at Brookhaven, scientists won Nobel Prizes for studies of subatomic particles, including mesons, neutrinos, and muons.

BNL NOBEL PRIZE RESEARCH

1976: Burton Richter and Samuel Ting
1980: James W. Cronin and Val Fitch
1988: Leon Lederman, Melvin Schwartz,
and Jack Steinberger

Brown, Harold (1927–) *American physicist and science administrator who served as U.S. secretary of defense under President Jimmy Carter (1977–1981)* Some of the policies initiated under Brown, particularly the plan to develop and deploy CRUISE MISSILES, contributed to the heightened arms race with the Soviet Union. Brown's policies have been regarded as initiating the second cold war, after the lull or "thaw" of detente during the period of the Johnson, Nixon, and Ford administrations. Brown was viewed as a "hawk" by his contemporaries in regard to his nuclear

policies, although he was a strong advocate of arms control as well.

Harold Brown was born in New York City on September 19, 1927. After graduating from the Bronx High School of Science at the age of 15 with extremely high grades, he studied physics at Columbia University under Nobel Laureate I. I. RABI. He earned a doctorate in physics at the age of 22 and then took a research post at the Lawrence Radiation Laboratory in 1950. In 1952, he accepted an appointment at the Livermore Laboratory (later Lawrence Livermore National Laboratory), under Herbert York. York credited Brown with contributing more ideas to the thermonuclear weapon than anyone besides Edward TELLER.

Brown worked on the PLOWSHARE PROGRAM, and he also directed work on the warhead for the Polaris class of missiles. He served on the delegation to the Geneva Conference on Nuclear Tests in 1958–1959, and he then recommended to the congressional JOINT COMMITTEE ON ATOMIC ENERGY that the test ban treaty should be rejected until development of more sophisticated test-detection technology.

In the administration of John KENNEDY, Brown succeeded Herbert York as director of defense research and engineering (DDR&E), working closely with Secretary of Defense Robert MCNAMARA. At DDR&E, Brown developed a reputation for skepticism about new weapons and for a degree of self-assurance that often irritated members of congress when he testified before committees. Brown opposed the development of the B-70 strategic bomber and also supported the nuclear test ban treaty in 1963.

President Lyndon JOHNSON appointed Brown to serve as secretary of the air force. In that position he argued for greater use of bombing in the Vietnam War.

With the inauguration of Republican president Richard NIXON in 1968, Brown left the government to accept appointment as president of the California Institute of Technology. In that position, he continued to advocate more extensive control of nuclear weapons. President Nixon appointed Brown to serve on a five-man commission to prepare for the Strategic Arms Limitation Talks, which eventually resulted in SALT I, signed in 1972.

President-elect Jimmy CARTER selected Brown as secretary of defense in December 1976, and Brown was sworn into office on January 21, 1977. As secretary of defense, Brown argued against production of the B-1 bomber, favoring instead the remodeling of the B-52, armed with cruise missiles. He supported the development of the mobile MX missile and the *Trident* submarine. Brown supported deployment of "Euromissiles," that is, ground-launched cruise missiles and *Pershing* II missiles in order to restore equivalence in the missile balance of power in Europe. He also supported PRESIDENTIAL DECISION DIRECTIVE 59 (PDD59), issued in 1980 that many observers viewed as a more aggressive policy toward the Soviet Union in matters of nuclear weapons strategy.

He was a proponent of SALT II, the abortive arms limitation treaty President Carter withdrew from Senate consideration. After the election and inauguration of Ronald REAGAN, Brown left government to take a position with The Johns Hopkins University in Baltimore. He criticized the STRATEGIC DEFENSE INITIATIVE proposed under the Reagan administration.

Suggested Reading

Harold Brown, *Thinking about National Security*. Boulder, Colo.: Westview Press, 1983.

Browns Ferry Accident

On March 22, 1975, a severe accident took place at the Browns Ferry power reactor of the Tennessee Valley Authority (TVA) system. Located near Decatur, Alabama, two 1,000 megawatt-electrical reactors, Unit 1 and 2, incorporated a design flaw not discovered until the accident. Both reactors had all electrical cables for the controls, both primary and backup safety cables, running through a cable-spreading room beneath the control room. In order to prevent any possible radioactive materials from escaping by air, the reactor buildings were held at low pressure, depending on a flow of air through the walls.

During a safety check to ensure that the air flow did not leak through the cable connection passage, workers would insert polyurethane foam around the cables if an air leak was discovered. In order to check if there was an air flow, a worker held a lit candle near the opening, checking to see if the flame moved. The flow of air carried the flame into the wall, igniting the polyurethane foam. Trying to extinguish the fire, workers first used carbon-dioxide fire extinguishers. However, the fire continued to progress into the foam and the cable connection trays.

Engineers hesitated to authorize the use of water to extinguish an electrical fire, but finally, after more than five hours, the electrical current was shut down and the fire extinguished with water. However, with the

power off and many control cables burned through, pumps sending cooling water to Unit 1 did not work properly and the danger of the reactor overheating and melting began to mount. Operators rigged an emergency water flow system, and finally, after nearly four more hours of nerve-wracking work, they were able to establish normal cooling and to bring the reactor to a shutdown.

Evaluating the accident, it was clear that the procedure of using a candle near flammable material to check air flow was inappropriate. But all cables, both the primary system and the backup safety systems, ran through the same spreader area, which constituted a more serious design flaw. Altogether over 1,600 cables were damaged, with over 600 of them related to one or another safety system. Repairs to the control room cabling system cost over $10 million, and the TVA had to purchase another $10 million worth of electrical power from outside the system to make up for the power lost during the shutdown period of Browns Ferry Unit 1.

Bulgaria

Bulgaria had four VVER-440 nuclear reactors, imported from the Soviet Union, in operation in 1986. In 1988 and 1992, the country added two new 953 megawatt-electrical reactors of Soviet design. By 1994, the total electrical output of the six reactors was 1.8 gigawatts, representing about 46% of the nation's electrical consumption. In its efforts to join the European Union and NATO, Bulgaria began a program of updating the reactors to modern safety standards.

Bulgaria signed the NON-PROLIFERATION TREATY on July 1, 1968, and the country has accepted comprehensive INTERNATIONAL ATOMIC ENERGY AGENCY inspection.

Bulletin of the Atomic Scientists

In 1945, several of the scientists who had participated in the MANHATTAN ENGINEER DISTRICT organized the publication of a magazine to discuss nuclear policy questions. Eugene Rabinowitch was co-founder and first editor of the magazine, the *Bulletin of the Atomic Scientists*.

A Russian-born scientist, Rabinowitch had been educated at the University of Berlin and emigrated to Great Britain in 1933 and then to the United States. During the war he left his post at the Massachusetts

Institute of Technology to work at the Chicago Metallurgical Laboratory at the University of CHICAGO. While there, he worked with James Franck and members of the committee preparing the various petitions regarding the moral and social implications of the new weapon.

Scientists who had worked on the FRANCK REPORT established a group in September 1945 called the Atomic Scientists of Chicago. John Simpson and Rabinowitch from Chicago met with colleagues from Oak Ridge, LOS ALAMOS, and Columbia University on October 31, 1945, to form the Federation of Atomic Scientists (FAS), later superseded by the FEDERATION OF AMERICAN SCIENTISTS.

In December 1945, Rabinowitch and a few colleagues from the Atomic Scientists of Chicago met in Stineway's Drugstore on 57th Street in Chicago to establish the *Bulletin of the Atomic Scientists*. They set as a goal the establishment of international control over atomic weapons. The magazine served as a channel for opinion, often challenging the official AEC positions over the coming years. In May 1946, the *Bulletin* published the full text of the Franck Report, and in February 1948 it published the details of a poll taken among Chicago scientists in July 1945, opposing the dropping of a nuclear weapon on civilians.

In the June 1947 issue, the editors printed on the cover of the magazine the "Doomsday Clock," set at seven minutes to midnight, indicating the imminent danger of nuclear holocaust. By 1999, the hands of the clock had been moved forward or back 16 times to indicate the ebb and flow of risk.

Organizationally, the *Bulletin* became independent of the Atomic Scientists of Chicago in 1948, and it never became an official organ of either the Federation of Atomic Scientists or the Federation of American Scientists. It continued to operate with its own independent editorial board for the rest of the century.

Suggested Reading

Alice Kimball Smith, *A Peril and a Hope: The Scientists' Movement in America, 1945–1947*. Cambridge, Mass.: MIT Press, 1971.

Bush, George Herbert Walker (1924–) *president of the United States 1989–1993*

During the presidential administration of George H.W. Bush, the cold war with the Soviet Union came to an

George H.W. Bush. President of the United States, 1989–1993, during the breakup of the Soviet Union, Bush was responsible for a series of arms reductions and confidence-building measures with Russia that reduced the threat of nuclear war. (Library of Congress)

end, Germany was reunited, the START I treaty was signed, the Soviet Union dissolved, and the United States and Russia began a series of confidence-building measures in the reduction of nuclear arms and weapon delivery systems.

Bush was born on June 12, 1924, into a wealthy Connecticut family and educated at private schools. When World War II broke out, he enlisted in the naval reserve, and he was commissioned as an ensign in 1943, becoming the navy's youngest pilot. He served in the Pacific theater of war, and he returned to finish a degree in economics at Yale at the end of the war. He then moved to Texas and entered the oil business, becoming quite successful. He ran for the U.S. Senate in 1964 but lost. In 1966, he was elected to a term in the House of Representatives as a Republican.

Through the 1970s, Bush served in a series of diplomatic and national security positions. He was ambassador to the United Nations (1971–1973); he served as head of mission to China for Gerald FORD; he then served as director of the Central Intelligence Agency (1976–1977).

In 1980, he sought the presidential nomination of the Republican Party, but he lost to Ronald REAGAN. Reagan selected Bush as his vice-presidential candidate, and Bush served two terms as vice president (1981–1989). When he ran for president in 1988, he brought more experience in foreign affairs and national security matters than most candidates.

His presidency was marked by a series of world changes that brought the cold war to an end and with it a decline in tension over nuclear weapons. After signing START I, with Mikhail GORBACHEV, Bush announced a set of measures collectively called PRESIDENTIAL NUCLEAR INITIATIVE-91. The initiative effectively ended the role of the U.S. Army in nuclear weapons delivery, reduced naval nuclear armaments, and cut back on orders of aircraft and other systems.

Under START I, the ON-SITE INSPECTION AGENCY (OSIA) continued to expand its responsibilities. In particular, after the brief Gulf War in January and February 1991, OSIA inspectors worked with UNSCOM in conducting inspections of the nuclear weapons program of IRAQ.

During Bush's administration, the Nunn-Lugar program of COOPERATIVE THREAT REDUCTION was enacted, providing for funding and other direct aid to those former member-states of the Soviet Union (RUSSIA, Belarus, UKRAINE, and Kazakhstan) that possessed nuclear weapons to assist them in providing security and dismantling of such weapons.

With the end of the cold war in 1989 and the breakup of the Soviet Union in December 1991, a "New World Order" began to emerge. However, that order was filled with many signs of disorder. The breakdown of authority in the states of the former Soviet Union could lead to a black market in nuclear weapons and materials for their construction and to the possible emigration of experts to countries hoping to develop nuclear capability. Thus PROLIFERATION of nuclear weapons in the post–cold war world was a greater threat than earlier.

Other crises added to international instability. In particular, the breakup of Yugoslavia into constituent republics led to more than a decade of civil war there.

President Bush was noted for his conservative, yet decisive response to several of the new developments on the world scene. However, with the end of the cold war, American voters gave greater emphasis to domestic issues. Bush was perceived as taking little interest in domestic affairs, and partly for this reason, he was defeated for reelection by William CLINTON in 1992.

Bush, Vannevar (1890–1974) *American electrical engineer and science administrator in the period during and immediately following World War II*
Vannevar Bush was a leading science administrator during World War II, and he headed the OFFICE OF SCIENTIFIC RESEARCH AND DEVELOPMENT (OSRD) that carried forward the atomic bomb research already developed by the ADVISORY COMMITTEE ON URANIUM, work later taken over and operated by the MANHATTAN ENGINEER DISTRICT.

Bush was born in 1890 in Everett, Massachusetts, and he studied at Tufts College. He earned his doctorate in electrical engineering at the Massachusetts Institute of Technology (MIT). At MIT he developed an early form of the computer, the product integraph, in 1925. He perfected the differential analyzer, which formed the basis for later computers, in 1931. He joined the faculty of MIT in 1932.

Prior to the entry of the United States in World War II, he headed the National Defense Research Committee (NDRC), which funneled federal funds to academic and private laboratories to pursue defense-related research. President ROOSEVELT then appointed Bush to head the Office of Scientific Research and Development. The OSRD sponsored a wide variety of research at academic and private laboratories through contract arrangements. Some of the early research into nuclear reactors and fission by Leo SZILARD, Enrico FERMI, Eugene WIGNER, and others was conducted under NDRC funding and then under OSRD contracts.

In 1942, when the Manhattan Engineer District was established, Bush remained in touch with nuclear developments, and he served in an advisory capacity. He helped to bring together specialists for related tasks, such as the ALSOS PROJECT, which provided intelligence about progress by the Germans on developing a nuclear weapon. Bush advocated cooperation with the British, but only if it advanced the war effort.

In 1945–1946, Bush worked on a study of the role of the federal government in research, publishing both a government report and a popular edition of the report entitled *Science, the Endless Frontier*. In this work he advocated federal support for theoretical, or "pure," research. His work and his ideas contributed to the eventual formation of the National Science Foundation. In 1948, he published a plea for federal support of scientific research for defense purposes, *Modern Arms and Free Men*. Bush's arguments for support for scientific research influenced the management of such research in the United States over the following decades.

Bush believed that scientists working on theoretical research problems provided the foundation on which later technological developments would take place. This approach would provide a basis for federal support for scientific research, in that such fundamental work would be necessary in order to provide knowledge from which technological applications for national defense would be developed. Such theoretical research, he argued, was also required to lay the groundwork for other technical applications to meet national objectives, such as improved health and agricultural production. The arguments of Vannevar Bush lay behind both the burgeoning of research and development under federal funding in the 1950s and the formalization of the research and development concept in Defense Department planning in the 1960s under Secretary of Defense Robert MCNAMARA.

Suggested Readings

Vannevar Bush, *Science, the Endless Frontier.* Washington, D.C.: Government Printing Office, 1946.

Richard G. Hewlett and Oscar E. Anderson, *The New World* (Vol. 1 of *A History of the United States Atomic Energy Commission*). Washington, D.C.: Atomic Energy Commission, 1962.

Richard Rhodes, *The Making of the Atomic Bomb.* New York: Simon and Schuster, 1986.

Byrnes, James F. (1879–1972) *presidential advisor and U.S. secretary of state 1945–1947*

James (Jimmy) Byrnes played an important role in establishing early atomic weapons policy under President Harry TRUMAN. Truman took Byrnes with him as foreign policy advisor to the POTSDAM CONFERENCE, and he shared with Byrnes a belief that the nuclear weapon would provide the United States with a means to manage its relationship with the Soviet Union more easily. The early views of Byrnes and Truman on this issue help account for the central role played by nuclear weapons strategy in the evolution of the cold war.

Byrnes was born in Charleston, South Carolina, on May 2, 1879. He studied law while serving as a court reporter, and he started his political career with election to the House of Representatives from South Car-

olina in 1911. He served in the House for 14 years and then in the U.S. Senate for 10 years. President Franklin ROOSEVELT appointed Byrnes to the Supreme Court in 1941. Byrnes resigned the Court position in 1942 to serve as a special assistant to Roosevelt (1942–1945), in which capacity he was often called "assistant president." He believed he should have been selected as Roosevelt's vice-presidential candidate in 1944.

When Truman became president on Roosevelt's death on April 12, 1945, Byrnes immediately became one of Truman's most valuable advisors. Truman appointed him secretary of state early in July 1945.

Truman and Byrnes attended the Potsdam Conference in July 1945, and while there they heard of the successful test of the first nuclear weapon at TRINITY. Byrnes urged Truman to keep the development of the weapon secret from the Soviets. He hoped that Truman would utilize the nuclear weapon in Japan in order to prevent the Soviets from entering the war in its final days to seize territory from the defeated Japanese. Byrnes assisted in the drafting of the Japanese surrender document.

Perhaps because of his extensive experience in Congress, Byrnes was a great believer in personal negotiation, and his method of face-to-face discussions contributed to the significant role played by summit conferences in the cold war period. After Truman appointed Byrnes to serve as secretary of state in 1945, Byrnes at first sought to use the nuclear weapon to argue from a position of strength in negotiations with the Soviets. However, when he offered the Soviets conciliatory positions, such as recognition of their regimes in Eastern Europe, conservative Republican critics in the United States accused him of attempting to appease the Soviets.

Soon Truman decided that Byrnes had acted too independently as secretary of state and replaced him with George Marshall on January 8, 1947. Byrnes returned to private life and wrote his memoirs *Speaking Frankly.* In this work he advocated a firm but fair approach to the Soviet Union. In 1948, he finalized his split with Truman by breaking with him over civil rights. He went on to serve as governor of South Carolina (1951–1955), defending racial segregation. Byrnes died January 24, 1972.

Suggested Reading

Robert Messer, *The End of an Alliance: James F. Byrnes, Roosevelt, Truman, and the Origins of the Cold War.* Chapel Hill: University of North Carolina Press, 1982.

Cadmium

Cadmium, the element with atomic number 48, has eight naturally occurring isotopes and at least 10 radioactive isotopes ranging in mass number from 103 to 119. The capture cross section for the ^{113}Cd (n, γ) ^{114}Cd is 1.98×10^4 barns (b), and the weighted average CROSS SECTION for all of the stable isotopes is 2450 ± 20 barns, making cadmium very useful as a neutron absorber. For this reason, control rods are often fabricated from cadmium. The high toxicity of cadmium and cadmium compounds demand that special precautions be taken to prevent exposure and release.

Calder Hall

The British developed the first reactor that produced electricity regularly for commercial consumption. Constructed at Calder Hall, two 50 megawatt-electrical (MWe) reactors went on line October 17, 1956, when Queen Elizabeth II threw the switch. The Calder Hall reactors preceded the U.S. reactor at SHIPPINGPORT by more than a year. The two Calder Hall units were planned as the first step of a 12-reactor plan that would supply a large percentage of British power needs.

Both reactors were dual purpose; that is, they were production reactors for making plutonium and also power reactors for supplying electric power. The high cost of conventional power in Great Britain and the production of plutonium would put the Calder Hall reactors on a paying basis from the beginning. The Soviets disputed the claim that Calder Hall was the first reactor to produce electricity for commercial use. They had put in operation a 5 MWe reactor in Obinsk in June 1954.

Calutrons

The term "Calutron" was developed by Ernest O. LAWRENCE late in 1941 to refer to the machine invented at the University of California to use the principle of electromagnetic separation to obtain ^{235}U from pure uranium ore. Since the fissionable ISOTOPE ^{235}U represented less than 1% of URANIUM, separation of that isotope for construction of the first nuclear weapon was essential.

As early as 1918, Francis ASTON had developed the principle of electromagnetic separation. He had found that when ions of two isotopes of the same element in the same charge state are accelerated through the same magnetic field, the energy is the same, but the radius of the curvature is proportional to the square root of the mass of the isotopes. Using this principle, it was possible to separate a lighter isotope from a heavier one. With the Calutron, the ^{235}U could be separated from the heavier ^{238}U. The device developed by Lawrence and his team, however, separated the isotopes one atom at a time, making the accumulation of enough material for a nuclear weapon an extremely time-consuming and tedious process.

Using the design developed at California, General Leslie GROVES of the MANHATTAN ENGINEER DISTRICT ordered that large-scale Calutrons be constructed at Oak Ridge. The building they occupied was designated Y-12 at Oak Ridge, and the construction employed thousands of workers. The massive Calutrons built there required vast amounts of electric winding. Copper was in short supply during the war, so Groves obtained from the U.S. Treasury department some 395 million troy ounces of silver (over 13,500 tons) to make into wire for the windings of the magnets. At the end of the war, the silver was returned to the Treasury reserve.

The Calutrons presented many technical problems and the production rate from them was minuscule. Each magnetic system had to be mounted inside a vacuum, and maintaining the vacuum in a large chamber proved difficult. The magnets were so powerful that they tended to shift the steel housings in which they were mounted. Impurities in the oil that was circulated to cool the windings led to many electrical shorts. At a crucial period over the winter of 1943–1944, the Calutrons had to be shut down for major repairs, idling many of the technical workers at Oak Ridge.

By late 1944, however, one set of Calutrons produced a steady flow of uranium enriched to 10% ^{235}U. That material was then sent through another set of Calutrons and enriched to 80%. When the uranium bomb was constructed in mid-1945, all of the fissionable material in it had passed through one or more Calutrons.

Although the method was slow and expensive in the electricity consumed, it had the advantage of being relatively simple and straightforward. After the war, the windings were removed from the Calutrons, and the United States utilized other methods of uranium separation, including GASEOUS DIFFUSION and centrifugal separation.

The story of the Calutrons had an ironic twist many years later. Although most information regarding the technology of the weapons program had been highly classified and kept secret, the DEPARTMENT OF ENERGY deemed the design information and related documents regarding the Calutron as so outdated as to declassify them for historic purposes in the 1980s. After the brief Gulf War in 1991, inspectors from the INTERNATIONAL ATOMIC ENERGY AGENCY and from the United Nations Special Commission on IRAQ (UNSCOM) evaluated the Iraqi nuclear weapons program. Working on a tip from an Iraqi defector, UNSCOM discovered that the Iraqis had obtained thousands of pages of U.S. documentation regarding Calutron designs and had constructed several prototype devices to begin isotope separation. The Iraqis had improved on the design, using modern microprocessors and fiber optic and computer-assisted manufacturing controls to achieve improvements in the reliability and productivity of the machines. Iraq is thought to be unique among the possible nuclear proliferation states in having used the electromagnetic separation method.

See also IRAQ.

Suggested Reading

Richard Rhodes, *The Making of the Atomic Bomb*. New York: Simon and Schuster, 1986.

Calvert Cliffs Case

In a historic case decided on July 23, 1971, the U.S. District Court of Appeals for the District of Columbia ruled that the provisions of the National Environmental Protection Act (NEPA) of 1969 applied to power reactors licensed under the ATOMIC ENERGY COMMISSION (AEC). The case was filed by the Calvert Cliffs Coordinating Committee, Inc., against the AEC and the U.S government and became popularly known as the Calvert Cliffs case.

NEPA had gone into force on January 1, 1970, with the creation of a new agency to implement its provisions, the Environmental Protection Agency (EPA). In the Calvert Cliffs case, protesters in Maryland argued that, although the AEC had licensed reactors, the agency was not absolved from filing an environmental impact statement, such as those required by EPA. The court case hinged on whether the AEC, by permitting a reactor to be built before the filing of an environmental impact statement, might create a situation in which the power company could claim that it had spent an irreversible and irretrievable amount of resources. In effect, the companies would be able to claim that once they had spent the money in good faith and in accordance with permission from the AEC, the federal government could not come back and argue that they were not in compliance with federal rules. Once the government had given the companies permission to proceed along certain lines, they claimed, it would be wrong for the government to withdraw or qualify that permission with new rules.

Attorneys for the coordinating committee argued that the AEC practice of issuing the license after the plant had been completed could be used to circumvent the requirement for an impact statement prior to beginning of construction. The final issuance of a license could be contingent upon environmental compliance. The AEC argued that the regulatory power of the EPA was so vague and broad that the AEC already met the requirement for regulation with its licensing provisions. The NEPA legislation had left unresolved the effect of the new agency in dealing with industries already regulated by other federal agencies and especially had left vague the status of projects already underway.

The court ordered that the AEC require the filing of impact statements, even for projects that had begun construction before the environmental act came into operation, and that as full an environmental review as possible be carried out. This decision followed the logic of the coordinating committee and used the licensing provision as a means of imposing NEPA-like controls on projects started under the AEC and prior to the passage of NEPA.

Antinuclear advocates hailed the Calvert Cliffs case as an early victory in their opposition to the expansion of nuclear power. Until that time, the government, through the AEC, had both advocated nuclear power and exercised regulation of the industry. With the EPA and the Calvert Cliffs case, opponents believed that they had made progress in winning over governmental support for their position requiring a more independent regulatory process. The later creation of a separate NUCLEAR REGULATORY COMMISSION (NRC) represented the culmination of this effort. NRC would handle licensing and regulation of power reactors and the management of nuclear research and development would remain the province of the AEC and its successor agencies, the ENERGY RESEARCH AND DEVELOPMENT ADMINISTRATION, and later the DEPARTMENT OF ENERGY.

Suggested Reading

Federal Reporter Series. 449 F.2d 1109 (1971) (case report).

J. Samuel Walker and George Mazuzan, *Containing the Atom: Nuclear Regulation in a Changing Environment, 1963–1971.* Berkeley: University of California Press, 1992.

Canada

During the MANHATTAN ENGINEER DISTRICT work in World War II, Canadian universities and scientists cooperated with the United States and Great Britain in the development of the nuclear weapon. Despite concerns about security on the part of General Leslie GROVES, Canadian scientists were closely engaged, particularly in reactor development. They concentrated on development of a heavy-water reactor and on a plant to produce heavy water. Canada built an experimental natural uranium reactor, NRX, during the war. Scientists from McGill University in Montreal participated in reactor work at the University of CHICAGO.

The September 1945 defection of Igor Gouzenko, a cipher specialist from the Soviet Embassy in Ottawa, to the Canadians yielded extensive information about Soviet espionage in both Canada and the United States. In particular, Gouzenko's revelations pointed to Alan Nunn May, a Canadian scientist who quickly defected to the Soviet Union, and to others in both Canadian government and scientific circles. One member of the Canadian Parliament, Fred Rose, was identified, along with three members of the Canadian National Research Council. Altogether, the Royal Canadian Mounted Police arrested 22 Canadian citizens on the basis of Gouzenko's revelations.

When the U.S. ATOMIC ENERGY COMMISSION took over Manhattan Project facilities in 1946 and 1947, cooperation between the U.S. and Canadian nuclear programs tapered off.

Canadian scientists concentrated on further developing reactors that would operate with natural uranium, that is, uranium that had not been enriched in U-235 content. They continued to use heavy water as the reactor moderator. In the mid-1950s, Canada proceeded with the development of POWER REACTORS along these lines, collectively called CANDU, or CANadian Deuterium-Uranium reactors.

Beginning in 1971, Canada began to install these reactors, first in Ontario, completing 22 reactors by the end of the century. At Pickering, Ontario, eight reactors, eventually rated at 515 and 516 megawatts-electric (MWe) were built between 1971 and 1986.

Another four reactors, rated at 769 MWe, were constructed between 1977 and 1979 at Bruce, Ontario, on the shores of Lake Huron, followed by four more rated at 785 MWe between 1984 and 1987. At Darlington, Ontario, four reactors rated at 881 MWe were built between 1990 and 1994. All 20 of these reactors were operated by the Ontario Hydro electric utility service. One reactor at Point LePreau Bay, New Brunswick, built in 1983, was rated at 650 MWe and operated by the New Brunswick Power Company. One other power reactor, the Gentilly plant, at Becancour, Quebec in 1983, operated by Hydro Quebec was rated at 635 MWe.

Canada exported small CANDU reactors to INDIA and PAKISTAN, a 630 MWe reactor to South Korea, and a 648 MWe reactor to Embalse, ARGENTINA. ROMANIA completed one CANDU unit. Each of these nations found the CANDU reactors useful because they did not require enriched uranium; the developing countries could produce or buy natural uranium at lower cost and without appearing to be working toward a weapons capability. However, since the CANDU reactors used heavy water as both a moderator and a coolant, a regular supply of heavy water was required. Since heavy-water–moderated reactors could be constructed as PRODUCTION REACTORS, proliferation experts have been concerned that the diversion of heavy water from the commercial reactor program in India, Pakistan, and Argentina could have assisted in weapons development in those countries.

Canada joined the NON-PROLIFERATION TREATY on July 23, 1968, among the first group of signatories. As a member of the NORTH ATLANTIC TREATY ORGANIZATION, Canada relied on the nuclear armaments of both the United States and Britain to provide a deterrent during the cold war. Like several nations in Western Europe and elsewhere with a strong commercial nuclear power base, a large industrial capability, and a sophisticated community of nuclear physicists and research institutions, Canada was quite capable of developing nuclear weapons but voluntarily refrained from doing so.

CANDU (CANadian Deuterium-Uranium) Reactors

During World War II, CANADA had participated with the United States and Great Britain in helping to develop the nuclear weapon in the MANHATTAN ENGINEER DISTRICT. Canada's primary contribution had been in the production of HEAVY WATER, or water with a high proportion of the deuterium isotope of hydrogen. During the war years, Canada built an experimental natural URANIUM reactor moderated with heavy water, known as NRX.

Following the war, Canadian scientists further experimented with developing reactors that would operate with natural uranium that had not been enriched in U-235 content and which would be moderated using heavy water. In the mid-1950s, Canada proceeded with the development of POWER REACTORS along these lines, collectively called CANadian Deuterium-Uranium reactors (CANDU).

In 1971, two CANDU reactors, originally rated at 508 megawatts-electric (MWe), were put in operation at Pickering, outside of Toronto. Eventually the Pickering station included eight CANDU units. Another power production station was built at Bruce, on Lake Huron, eventually with eight CANDU units, with a total rating over 750 MWe each.

Canada exported smaller CANDU units to INDIA and PAKISTAN and a medium-sized 630 MWe reactor to South Korea; at Embalse, ARGENTINA, the Canadians supplied a 648 MWe reactor. ROMANIA ordered five such reactors but only completed one of them. The CANDU reactors prove quite useful in developing nations as they can use natural uranium, not requiring an enrichment plant.

The CANDU reactors can be refueled continuously while the plant is in operation. The fuel tubes run inside larger pipes through which the heavy water circulates; the fuel is pushed through the reactor, with the spent fuel dropping out the back as fresh fuel is inserted at the front, in a refueling system very similar to the first PRODUCTION REACTORS constructed at HANFORD, Washington. The heated heavy water is piped out to steam generators where it heats light water to produce the steam to turn the power turbines. Thus the heavy water serves as both a MODERATOR and a coolant in this type of reactor.

Carbon 14

Carbon 14 (^{14}C) is a radioactive ISOTOPE of carbon the nucleus of which contains six protons and eight neutrons. ^{14}C decays by beta emission ($E_{max} = 150$ keV) and demonstrates a half-life of 5,730 years. ^{14}C is formed in the outer atmosphere by an (n,p) reaction with ^{14}N. Subsequent equilibration of ^{14}C with the nonradioactive isotopes of carbon, 98.90% ^{12}C and 1.10% ^{13}C, in all living things is the basis for radiocarbon dating.

All living things are in equilibrium with ^{14}C. Hence, all living things contain the same percentage of ^{14}C in their carbon composition. Upon death, metabolic carbon uptake ceases, and the ^{14}C decreases by radioactive decay. Knowing that this decrease takes place at a rate corresponding to a half-life of 5,730 years allows the date of death to be approximated. Thus by examining wood, vegetable matter, or animal remains and determining the ^{14}C content, the approximate date when the material was harvested or died can be established, allowing archeologists to tell roughly when certain structures were built or when certain human settlements were established.

See also WILLARD, LIBBY.

Carter, James Earl (1924–   ) *president of the United States 1977–1981*

During the presidential administration of James (Jimmy) Carter, the move toward DETENTE with the Soviet Union evaporated, and the two nations intensified their hostility in what some have called a "second cold war." Part of that change was reflected as Carter ordered the development of new nuclear weapons, approved a DUAL-TRACK STRATEGY toward nuclear weapons in Europe, and issued PRESIDENTIAL DECISION DIRECTIVE 59, calling for a change in weapon targeting policy toward the Soviet Union. Although perceived by the press as a president largely motivated by humanitarian concerns and criticized for his inability to secure the release of American hostages held in Iran during the last year of his presidency, Carter's policy decisions in the area of nuclear weaponry and nuclear weapons production demonstrated his commitment to a very strong and modernized nuclear arsenal.

Carter was born on October 1, 1924, in Plains, Georgia. He graduated from the U.S. Naval Academy in 1946 and entered the nuclear navy as an aide to Hyman RICKOVER in 1952. He studied physics at Union College. Following his father's death in 1953, Carter left the navy to operate the family business. He was elected to the Georgia state senate (1963–1967) and then was elected governor of Georgia, serving from 1971 to 1975. In 1976, Carter won the nomination of the Democratic Party for the presidency and defeated Gerald FORD.

During his first year in office, he promulgated Presidential Decision Directive 59 (PDD 5), which spelled out his principle of "countervailing power." Under this strategy, the United States would target highly valued assets in the Soviet Union, including the leadership centers. As a consequence, the accuracy of nuclear-tipped missiles would need to be improved. The *Trident* II was delivered and installed during his administration. The already-developed *Minuteman* III missiles also were suited to this strategy, requiring greater accuracy or lower circular-error-probable numbers.

PDD-59, when publicly discussed, struck both American and Soviet observers as representing a more aggressive policy. Part of the Soviet response over the next few years was further development of ground-based missiles, with many capable of hitting precise targets in Western Europe.

In 1979, the United States and its NATO allies announced a dual track strategy that called for the development and deployment in Europe of intermediate-range nuclear missiles to offset the Soviet developments. The strategy, announced during the last year of the Carter administration, led to the development and emplacement of ground-launched mobile CRUISE MISSILES in Europe and to deployment of PERSHING II missiles as well. These deployments during the administration of Ronald REAGAN had been planned and the weapons developed during the Carter administration.

President Carter signed the SALT II treaty at a SUMMIT in Vienna, Austria, on June 18, 1979. The treaty, first sketched out by President Gerald FORD at VLADIVOSTOK, would have limited the number of nuclear weapons delivery systems to 2,400 strategic launch vehicles, to be cut to 2,250 launch vehicles in 1985. The treaty involved a series of complex compromises and sublimits that had been arranged only after years of negotiation. Carter submitted the treaty to the Senate for ratification, but the treaty encountered strong opposition there. After the Soviet Union invaded Afghanistan in late 1979, Carter recalled the treaty from the ratification process. He announced that the United States would abide by the limits of the signed but unratified treaty.

On the domestic side, the ENERGY RESEARCH AND DEVELOPMENT ADMINISTRATION was replaced by the DEPARTMENT OF ENERGY (DOE) under a law enacted, on August 4, 1977. The new DOE opened for business October 1, 1977, and Carter appointed as the first secretary of energy James R. SCHLESINGER, former director of the Central Intelligence Agency and former secretary of defense in the administration of Gerald Ford. Schlesinger initiated cleanup of the islands of BIKINI and ENEWETAK. Under Schlesinger's successor, Charles DUNCAN, the Carter administration worked to increase plutonium and tritium production, initiating the movement to restart L reactor at the SAVANNAH RIVER SITE.

The greatest setback to the country's civilian nuclear power program came during Carter's administration with the accident at THREE MILE ISLAND in March 1979. Due to increased concern over reactor risk that had already developed, and due to heightened public awareness following that accident, the NUCLEAR REGULATORY COMMISSION placed a two-year moratorium on the issuance of new licenses for reactors.

Under Duncan, the Department of Energy sponsored a wide variety of investigations into alternate energy sources, including solar energy.

On the whole, the Carter administration was characterized by an increased reliance on nuclear weaponry as part of the foreign policy posture of the nation. At the same time, presidential and public support for nuclear-generated electric power in the United States saw a rapid decline.

Carter ran for reelection but was defeated by Ronald REAGAN, who took office on January 20, 1981.

Cerenkov (Cherenkov) Radiation

When high-energy, charged particles moving at the speed of light pass from one transparent medium of low refractive index to another transparent medium of higher refractive index, they must decelerate to the speed of light in the second medium. The decrease in kinetic energy appears as electromagnetic radiation. Pavel Cerenkov used this idea to explain this radiation. The blue glow in the water around the core of a SWIMMING POOL REACTOR is attributed to Cerenkov radiation. For his contribution, Cerenkov shared the 1958 Nobel Prize in physics with Ilya Frank and Igor TAMM.

See also SWIMMING POOL REACTORS.

Cesium

Cesium, the element with atomic number 55, is monoisotopic in nature as ^{133}Cs, but it has at least a dozen and a half radioactive ISOTOPES ranging in mass number from 123 to 144. ^{137}Cs is a long-lived FISSION product with a half-life of 30 years. The chemical and physical properties of cesium compounds make them highly mobile in biological and environmental systems. Hence, compounds containing ^{137}Cs are of special concern; ingestion of small amounts of such compounds can produce cancers or fatality in humans since cesium is a biological analog of potassium and is treated as such in the body.

Chadwick, James (1891–1974)   *British physicist noted as the discoverer of the neutron and a participant in the development of the first atomic bomb*

James Chadwick headed the British team of scientists who worked on the MANHATTAN ENGINEER DISTRICT in the United States in developing the atomic bomb during World War II, and he is recognized as the discoverer of the neutron.

Chadwick was born in Cheshire, England, in 1891 and studied at Manchester University under Ernest RUTHERFORD. In 1913, he went to Germany to work with the German physicist Hans GEIGER, and during World War I Chadwick was interned as an enemy alien. Following the war he returned to Cambridge to work with Rutherford and in 1932 discovered the particle later known as the neutron, one of the two nucleons of the atom. He received the Nobel Prize in physics for this work.

In 1935 he took an appointment as professor of physics at Liverpool University, where he established a cyclotron and a research school devoted to nuclear physics. He took a leave from Liverpool to work on the Manhattan Project, returning there after World War II.

On the Manhattan Project, he worked through the Combined Policy Committee to hammer out the regulations for both the exchange of information between the scientists at the University of Chicago and those at Montreal University and the sharing of information concerning larger issues among the British, Canadians, and Americans. He worked closely with General Leslie Groves, advising him on what information should be shared with French scientists.

Chadwick was knighted in 1945. In 1948, he became a master of Gonville and Caius College at Cambridge University. He died in 1974.

Chain Reaction

A chain reaction is a reaction in which one of the products of the reaction is also one of the agents necessary to cause a like reaction. For example, in uranium-235 fission, the reaction is as follows: neutron + uranium-235——>fission fragments + 2 or 3 neutrons. The production of more than one neutron leads to the possibility of a chain reaction in the fissionable material, in this case, U-235. Since uranium-235 fission also produces energy release, the chain reaction is key to the production of atomic energy for reactors and weapons.

The concept of a nuclear chain reaction is said to have occurred to Leo SZILARD in 1933 while he waited for a street light to change in London. He patented the concept, requesting the patent and its contents be kept secret. It was not until 1938, hearing of the work of STRASSMAN, HAHN, and MEITNER, that he recognized that his concept of a chain reaction explained fission process in URANIUM.

Chelyabinsk-40

Near Kyshtym in the Soviet Union, the first Soviet PRODUCTION REACTOR was built at the site called Chelyabinsk-40, renamed Chelyabinsk-65 about 1990. Chelyabinsk-40 was built about 15 kilometers east of the city of Kyshtym on the eastern side of the southern Ural Mountains. Construction began in 1946, and assembly of the reactor began in March 1948. The reactor was called A, or sometimes "Annushka," and it began operations in June 1948. This A reactor suffered many of the problems encountered by the Americans in operating their World War II reactors at HANFORD with swelling and leakage of fuel slugs. The first Chelyabinsk-40 reactor was decommissioned in 1987.

Igor KURCHATOV supervised the construction of the early production reactors at Chelyabinsk. The building of the reactors and related facilities reputedly required 70,000 prison camp slave laborers.

Later reactors at Chelyabinsk-40 included a second uranium-graphite production reactor in 1950, a third in 1951, and a fourth in 1952. In January 1952, a smaller research reactor for work on isotopes went into operation, and a heavy-water moderated reactor was opened at Chelyabinsk-40 in about 1952–1953. The four newer graphite reactors built in 1951 and 1952 were all decommissioned in the period 1988 to 1990.

Chelyabinsk also housed many other facilities related to nuclear weapons production, including several chemical separations plants, plutonium processing facilities, component manufacturing, and related industrial activities. Several mixed oxide (MOX) fuel fabrication facilities produced uranium and plutonium oxide fuel elements for reactors throughout the Soviet Union. Chelyabinsk was very similar to the American facility at Hanford in its function within the Soviet nuclear weapons complex.

After the passage of the COOPERATIVE THREAT REDUCTION Act in the United States in 1991, the United States provided funds for equipment to be installed at Chelyabinsk for the disassembly of weapons and the long-term storage of parts.

CHELYABINSK PRODUCTION REACTORS

REACTOR	POWER	YEAR	TYPE	COMMENT
A Reactor	500MWth	1948	Graphite	nickname: Annushka hazardous operation
IR Reactor	65MWth	1951	Graphite	Pu production & Fuel Rod research
AV1	250MWth	1950	Graphite	Power ratings AVs probably upgraded
AV2	250MWth	1951	Graphite	
AV3	250MWth	1952	Graphite	
LF2	1000MWth	1952	Heavy Water	nickname: Lyudmila probably converted to LWR in 1980s
Ruslan	1000MWth	1953?	Light Water	tritium and isotope production

See also KRASNOYARSK-26; KURCHATOV, IGOR; PRODUCTION REACTORS; TOMSK-7.

Suggested Reading

Thomas B. Cochrane, Robert S. Norris, and Oleg A. Bukharin, *Making the Russian Bomb: From Stalin to Yeltsin.* Boulder, Colo.: Westview Press, 1995.

David Holloway, *Stalin and the Bomb.* Hew Haven: Yale University Press, 1994.

Chernobyl

The Chernobyl power reactor complex is located near Pripyat, about 80 miles north of the major city of Kiev in UKRAINE, a republic of the former Soviet Union. The 1986 accident at that reactor was the largest and most severe accident to date. Although the reactor followed a design not commonly used outside of the former Soviet Union and some of the former satellite states of Eastern Europe, the accident intensified public concern about the risks of nuclear reactors.

The reactor was a Soviet RBMK-1000 type. The RBMK was a *Reactory Bolshoi Moshchnosti Kanalynye* or "Channelized Large Power Reactor." This design was graphite-moderated and water cooled, similar to the early production reactors in the United States. It was rated at 1,000 megawatt-electric (MWe), later downgraded to 925 MWe. In 1986, there were four RBMK reactors at the Chernobyl site with Units 3 and 4 in the same building. The accident occurred on April 26, 1986, in Unit 4, about 1:20 A.M.

The accident itself resulted from a mixture of deficiencies in the design, operator misjudgments, and a test procedure that was unwise and poorly carried out. A safety feature included standby diesel generators to provide power in cases when there was a failure of outside power and when the reactor itself was shut down. In order to test whether the diesel generators would start up after a reactor shutdown, while the reactor-driven steam turbogenerators were still coasting down from high speed, the operators would start by cutting back the reactor power by one half and disconnecting the emergency core-cooling system and other safety systems.

In conducting this procedure, the reactor dropped well below half power to about 30 megawatts-thermal on the night of April 25. Operating at low power led to a XENON buildup, which poisoned the reaction. Operators attempted to raise the reactor power by removing control rods. At 1:23 in the morning, the operators attempted to scram the reactor, or conduct an emergency shutdown. However, the control rods were too far removed from the reactor to have immediate effect, and suddenly there were two explosions. Apparently one was a steam-pressure explosion and the other was a reaction of hydrogen and carbon monoxide. These explosions blew a section off the building's roof, starting a series of fires.

Local firefighters arrived and extinguished the building fires, but the graphite in the reactor itself caught fire. The firefighters worked in extremely dangerous conditions of intense heat and radiation exposure. The internal graphite fire was not extinguished until May 6. The reactor was doused with boron carbide to retard the reaction and then encased in limestone. Lead, clay, sand, and concrete were added and Unit 4 was entombed in a so-called sarcophagus.

During the 10-day fire, the reactor released a cloud of radioactive materials, including iodine-131 and cesium-137, that spread to the north and west. Two days after the reactor accident, detectors in Sweden and then in Finland began to monitor the increase in radiation.

Soon the Soviet government ordered evacuation from the region nearby, eventually moving some 135,000 people from a zone of about a 20-mile radius from the reactor. Immediate casualties among firefighters and other workers totaled 31, and within a few months, an additional 11 died.

Calculating the effect of the FALLOUT from Chernobyl not only within the former Soviet Union, but in northern and western Europe, was difficult. Different groups of experts came to different conclusions. Some responsible estimates suggested that the results of the radiation exposure would eventually produce about 50,000 deaths from cancer. Other estimates suggested that the average annual exposure from the fallout would be minuscule, amounting to 1% or less of the usual background rate.

Even accepting the very low estimate, however, the accident was the most serious to have occurred at any nuclear reactor, resulting in at least 40 deaths immediately or shortly after the accident.

Suggested Reading

International Atomic Energy Agency, *The International Chernobyl Project, An Overview.* Vienna: International Atomic Energy Agency, 1991.

Lynn R. Anspaugh et al., "The Global Impact of the Chernobyl Accident," *Science* 242 (1988): 1513–1519.

Chevalier, Haakon (1901–1985) *Norwegian-born American linguist and specialist in French literature, member of the Communist Party of the United States in the period from 1938 to 1942*

Haakon Chevalier taught French at the University of California, where he met and became friends with J. R. OPPENHEIMER in 1937. Chevalier's father was French and his mother Norwegian, and he had grown up in both France and Norway. He ran away to sea at age 18, and he settled eventually in the United States. He became a college teacher, specializing in modern French literature. Chevalier headed the Teacher's Union at the University of California. Chevalier was a member of the United States Communist Party from 1938 to 1942.

In 1943, when Oppenheimer was visiting in Berkeley from LOS ALAMOS, Chevalier and Oppenheimer met at a party and had a conversation in the kitchen. During the conversation, Chevalier mentioned that he knew George Eltenton, who could get information to the Soviets if Oppenheimer wanted to provide it. Oppenheimer cut off the conversation. Although Oppenheimer did not report the episode immediately, as regulations required, he later informed the security staff at Los Alamos that three scientists had been approached by Eltenton about transmission of secret information. When he would not reveal the names of the scientists, he later admitted that it had been Chevalier who approached him.

In 1946, agents from the Federal Bureau of Investigation questioned Chevalier about the episode, and he revealed the details of the kitchen conversation. Later, when Chevalier wrote his memoirs, he affirmed that both he and Oppenheimer had been members of a unit of the Communist Party. Oppenheimer objected to that assertion, stating that he had never officially belonged to the party.

Chevalier moved to France, and Oppenheimer visited him there just before Christmas in 1953. This visit, combined with the earlier contacts with Chevalier, all became part of the security case presented at OPPENHEIMER'S SECURITY HEARING. At that hearing, he admitted that when questioned about the Chevalier "kitchen meeting" in 1943 he had made up a "tissue of lies" about the incident. Perhaps more than any other part of his testimony at the 1954 Hearing, Oppenheimer's memory of how he handled his conversation with Chevalier led to his loss of security clearance. Leslie GROVES was charitable about Oppenheimer's position, claiming that he simply obeyed the ethic of not wanting to tell on a friend. Even so, Groves admitted that, given the security rules of the mid-1950s, he probably would not clear Oppenheimer. Oppenheimer made it clear at the hearing that the reason he had made up lies about the kitchen meeting was that Chevalier was a friend and that he did not want to implicate him.

Thus, Haakon Chevalier is remembered in nuclear history as the man whose friendship with Oppenheimer was the primary cause of Oppenheimer's loss of clearance in 1954.

Suggested Reading

Haakon Chevalier, *Oppenheimer, The Story of a Friendship*. New York: George Braziller, 1965.

Peter Goodchild, *J. Robert Oppenheimer: Shatterer of Worlds*. Boston: Houghton Mifflin, 1981.

Chicago Pile-1 (CP-1)

The successful operation of Chicago Pile-1 or CP-1 on December 2, 1942, marked the first demonstrated, sustained, and controlled nuclear chain reaction. For this reason, the date is sometimes taken as the beginning of the atomic age. Many of the principles and terms developed on CP-1 became standard parts of nuclear reactor design in later years. For this reason, CP-1 can be considered an "invention," like the first light bulb by Thomas Edison or the first aircraft by the Wright brothers.

The reactor was designed and built under the leadership of Enrico FERMI at the University of Chicago. The university had abandoned its football field, Stagg Field, and the reactor was built in a squash court underneath the football field stands. Fermi's design utilized graphite bricks to slow down neutrons emitted from fissioning natural uranium, thereby increasing their chances of collision with nuclei of other URANIUM atoms. This use of an element low on the atomic table, in this case carbon in the form of graphite, to slow neutrons was essential to all controlled nuclear reactions.

As the terminology soon developed, graphite was known as a "moderator." Fermi originally planned to stack the four-inch thick graphite blocks in 76 layers. As the stack was raised, certain blocks would be hollowed out to contain spheres of natural uranium. By carefully arranging the internal geometry of the stack in a large flattened sphere configuration, the uranium could be so spaced as to maximize the chance of neu-

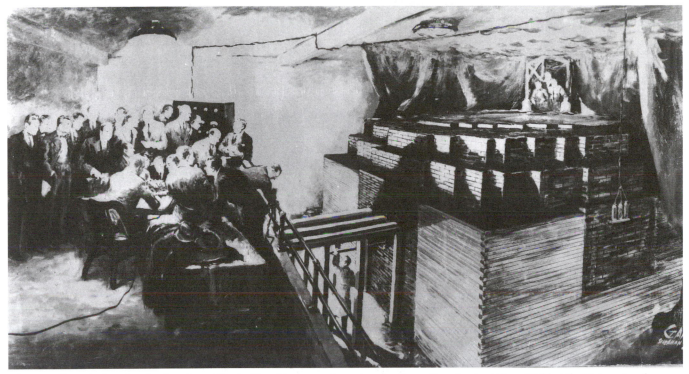

Chicago Pile 1. Built under the direction of Enrico Fermi in a squash court under the seating stands at Stagg Field at the University of Chicago, the first nuclear reactor in the world went critical on December 2, 1942. No photograph was taken and this later painting was an attempt to recreate the scene. (National Archives and Record Administration)

tron collision and nuclear FISSION. With improved quality of both graphite and uranium, Fermi was able to complete the pile at 56 layers. At the University of Iowa at Ames, physicist Frank Spedding produced 2.25-inch spheres of high-purity uranium metal that the team dubbed "Spedding's eggs."

To control the reaction, wooden rails were inserted into open slots in the stack from above. Nailed to the rails were 13-foot-long strips of cadmium metal. The cadmium strips would absorb neutrons and thus prevent the reaction from progressing. By removing the strips, the reaction would get under way. The principle of control through such inserted "control rods," invented or developed on this first reactor or atomic pile, became standard on later nuclear reactors.

Fermi used graduate students in the physics program at the University of Chicago to engage in the difficult job of stacking the blocks. A few local teenagers were also recruited to assist in the work. Over the last two weeks of November 1942, the layers of graphite brick steadily increased. As winter progressed, the unheated squash court became bitterly cold. Those stacking the heavy blocks were warmed by the exer-

cise, but the guards nearly froze. The university supplied them with surplus raccoon coats from storage since the school had discontinued football playing.

On the day of the experiment, one of the control rods was arranged so that it could be released by an electrical switch to drop into the reactor, in case of an emergency or run-away nuclear reaction. As a joke, the red button to throw the emergency control rod was labeled "Scram," and that term has since become reactor jargon for an emergency shutdown of a reactor.

Another control rod was tied off, and, rather dramatically, Norris Hilberry stood by with an axe to cut the rope so the rod could drop into the reactor if needed. As a further precaution, three young physicists stood on a platform over the reactor with large jugs of cadmium sulfate solution that could be dumped over the reactor to stop the reaction.

A crowd of some 40 witnesses gathered on the morning of December 2 to watch the first reaction. Fermi ordered the control rods removed gradually, as a GEIGER COUNTER ticked off the rising rate of radiation, a measure of the reaction. After a lunch break, the witnesses waited as Fermi ordered the process to continue. At 3:49 in the afternoon, he announced that the reaction was self-sustaining. A few minutes later, he ordered the control rods reinserted.

The group realized that the moment was historic, and they shared a bottle of Italian wine, signing the straw covering as a memento. Later, Arthur H. COMPTON called James B. CONANT at Harvard to announce that the reaction had worked, encoding his message in a set of phrases later remembered as historic. "The Italian navigator has just landed in the New World," he said. Conant got the idea and went along. "Were the natives friendly?" he asked. "Everyone landed safe and happy," said Compton.

Among those attending the demonstration on December 2 was Crawford GREENEWALT, representing Du Pont Corporation. Relaying his observations to the company, he felt confident in recommending that Du Pont take over design and construction of an industrial-scale model of the reactor to produce plutonium. Du Pont, with Greenewalt in charge, managed the construction and operation of the facilities at HANFORD.

At first the squash-court reactor was dubbed "Fermi's pile." But as the group working at Chicago built later reactors, the first one came to be known as Chicago Pile-1. Further reactors, including reactors built in the forest preserves outside of Chicago, later established as ARGONNE NATIONAL LABORATORY, were known as CP-2 through CP-5.

Suggested Reading

Arthur Holly Compton, *Atomic Quest*. New York: Oxford University Press, 1956.

Richard Rhodes, *The Making of the Atomic Bomb*. New York: Simon and Schuster, 1986.

Chicago Scientists' Petition   See FRANCK, JAMES.

Chicago, University of

Like a number of other major universities in the United States, the University of Chicago had hosted a strong and expanding nuclear physics department during the 1930s. During World War II the university acquired a relatively unique status because it took on major research tasks for the U.S. nuclear weapons program under the OFFICE OF SCIENTIFIC RESEARCH AND DEVELOPMENT (OSRD); these tasks were then transferred to the MANHATTAN ENGINEER DISTRICT (MED) in 1942 when that organization was established.

Other projects at Princeton, the Berkeley campus of the University of California, and Columbia University in New York also contributed to the wartime project and became parts of the emerging postwar nuclear weapons complex. The laboratories at Chicago and Berkeley were the most far reaching and hosted the most significant work of all the university projects that contributed to the MED during the war.

The OSRD and MED contracts at the University of Chicago were administered through the innocuous-sounding Metallurgical Laboratory or "Met Lab." The director of the Met Lab, Arthur Holly COMPTON, worked with Vannevar BUSH of the OSRD and then later with General Leslie GROVES of the MED. Compton was largely responsible for recruiting a group of leading physicists from around the United States, including several recent emigrés from Europe. Among the emigré scientists he brought to the project were Eugene WIGNER, Leo SZILARD, and Enrico FERMI. Among the younger American scientists whose early work at the Met Lab helped launch their careers in nuclear physics were Glenn SEABORG, later chairman of the ATOMIC ENERGY COMMISSION, and Walter ZINN, later director of the ARGONNE NATIONAL LABORATORY.

Working through the Met Lab, Fermi developed CHICAGO PILE-1 or CP-1. Fermi had first worked on piles that would determine the moderating effect of graphite on the neutron radiation from uranium, or "exponential piles," at Columbia University. Compton invited Fermi to Chicago to continue his work. Fermi demonstrated the first self-sustained CHAIN REACTION on the Chicago Pile, the first full-scale nuclear reactor. Robert M. Hutchins, president of the University of Chicago, had closed down the college football program, and the first reactor was built in a squash court under the stands of the abandoned Stagg Field.

CP-1 was graphite-moderated and was fueled with natural uranium. Later reactors built by Fermi and the Met Lab staff included CP-3, the first heavy-water reactor in the United States, and others designed to further explore the production of PLUTONIUM and reactor physics. For the sake of safety, later reactors were constructed outside downtown Chicago in forest preserve land a few miles from the city limits.

The preliminary work done on CP-1, and the design work of various groups at the Met Lab was crucial to the design of the first three PRODUCTION REACTORS built at HANFORD. Using the same principle of graphite moderation and using a system of water cooling, the production reactors were much larger than CP-1, and they were designed to allow the URANIUM fuel to be pushed through from one side of the reactor to the other. After irradiation in the reactor, some small amount of the ^{238}U would be transformed into ^{239}Pu. The work of Fermi, Wigner, Zinn, and Seaborg was crucial to the later production reactor design and the processing systems for separating the plutonium from the uranium after irradiation.

After World War II, the Met Lab's equipment and staff were reorganized into the ARGONNE NATIONAL LABORATORY. Facilities that the Met Lab had built to the west of Chicago became the core of the Argonne structure.

The collection of brilliant men and women at the University of Chicago under the leadership of Robert Hutchins and Arthur Holly Compton was extremely difficult to control and manage in a structured environment such as demanded by the Manhattan Engineer District. The independent thinking, strong personalities, and individualism of the scientists presented the MED leadership with a number of difficulties and left a mark on the future of nuclear politics. Even before information about nuclear weapons became publicly known, the internal debates at Chicago would foreshadow the debates and issues that would characterize atomic age history for the next 50 years.

University of Chicago scientists engaged in the MED work were among the first to recognize some of the moral and political implications of the new weapon and began to express their opinions through internal channels. Leo Szilard and James Franck (author of the FRANCK REPORT) took the lead in asking that the weapon be demonstrated to the Japanese rather than detonated over a populated area. Their opinion, although it reached the Interim Committee making the recommendation that shaped TRUMAN'S DECISION, was not relayed forward because of fear that, without the element of surprise, the impact of the weapon would be diminished.

The Chicago scientists became the core group in the later formation of the Federation of Atomic Scientists that published the BULLETIN OF THE ATOMIC SCIENTISTS. For decades, this magazine became the outlet for well-informed but often highly independent views on matters related to nuclear weapons policy.

Policies of the wartime MED that some of the Met Lab scientists found inappropriate included the military concept of compartmentalization. Under this principle, knowledge of secret information was shared only with those with a direct need to know. Although J. R. OPPENHEIMER had succeeded in modifying that principle at LOS ALAMOS, the scientists at Chicago, particularly those who had come from Europe, such as Szilard, Wigner, and Fermi, were excluded from much confidential work concerning the atomic bomb project. Szilard, in particular, refused to sign a commitment to keep information classified, even though he had succeeded in his claim to have invented the nuclear reactor and had urged scientists not to publish their findings for fear that Germany would obtain crucial information. General Groves never fully trusted Wigner, Szilard, or Fermi, even though all of them had contributed important knowledge and findings to the weapons program.

Other Chicago nuclear scientists visualized the future that nuclear energy would bring. Farrington Daniels headed a group that designed a gas-cooled reactor, and he produced a report anticipating the growth of a nuclear power engineering field that he dubbed "nucleonics."

Suggested Reading

Leslie Groves, *Now It Can Be Told: The Story of the Manhattan Project.* New York: Harper and Row, 1962.

Richard Rhodes, *The Making of the Atomic Bomb.* New York: Simon and Schuster, 1986.

Alice Kimball Smith, *A Peril and a Hope: The Scientists' Movement in America, 1945–1947.* Cambridge, Mass.: MIT Press, 1971.

China

China first became an announced nuclear power on October 16, 1964, with an atmospheric test of a nuclear device. On June 17, 1967, China conducted a thermonuclear test. Since the 1970s, when China began a more aggressive policy of international trade, it began to export arms and sensitive nuclear technology to other states. With these exports, Chinese technology began to threaten the non-proliferation regime. In the period 1970 to 1983, China explicitly promoted nuclear proliferation.

Applying diplomatic pressure, other states encouraged China to join the INTERNATIONAL ATOMIC ENERGY AGENCY (IAEA). Even so, China continued to export weapons technology to several threshold nuclear states, including PAKISTAN, that received special magnets from China used in a process to enrich URANIUM to weapons grade. Although China joined the IAEA in

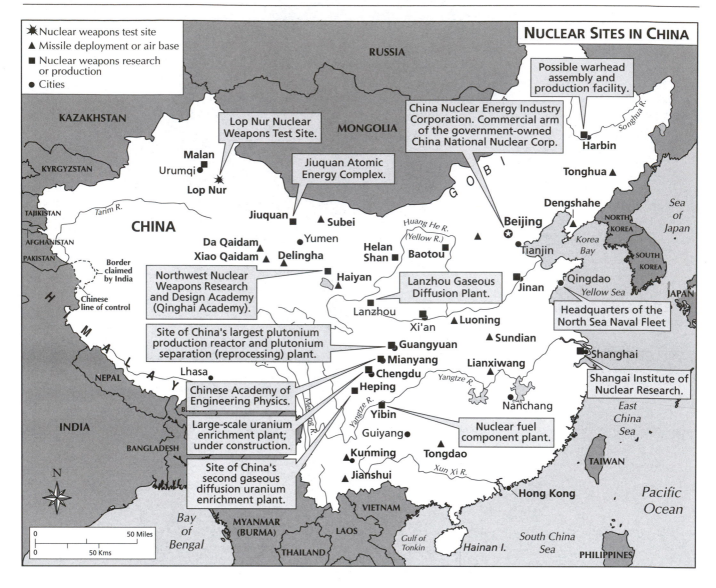

NUCLEAR SITES IN CHINA

Nuclear weapons test site
Missile deployment or air base
Nuclear weapons research or production
Cities

Possible warhead assembly and production facility.

China Nuclear Energy Industry Corporation. Commercial arm of the government-owned China National Nuclear Corp.

Lop Nur Nuclear Weapons Test Site.

Jiuquan Atomic Energy Complex.

Northwest Nuclear Weapons Research and Design Academy (Qinghai Academy).

Lanzhou Gaseous Diffusion Plant.

Headquarters of the North Sea Naval Fleet.

Site of China's largest plutonium production reactor and plutonium separation (reprocessing) plant.

Chinese Academy of Engineering Physics.

Shangai Institute of Nuclear Research.

Large-scale uranium enrichment plant; under construction.

Nuclear fuel component plant.

Site of China's second gaseous diffusion uranium enrichment plant.

1984, it did not join the NON-PROLIFERATION TREATY until 1992.

In addition to the sale of ring magnets to Pakistan, China planned to sell two 300 megawatt-electric pressurized water reactors to Iran, a plan canceled on U.S. insistence. China had a nuclear cooperation agreement with ALGERIA, and it supplied missiles to Pakistan, IRAN, SYRIA, IRAQ, and Saudi Arabia.

During the Cultural Revolution (1966–1976) China's nuclear scientists were shielded to a degree from the persecution of intellectuals characteristic of the period because of their enforced isolation in the country's remote research establishments.

China's nuclear establishment is shrouded in security, but some details are known. From 1964 to 1987, China produced weapons-grade uranium at two sites,

Lanzhou and Heping. From 1969 until 1991, China produced plutonium at two other locations, Jiuquan and Guangyuan. Outside experts estimate that China has detonated 45 nuclear explosions. Its weapons stockpile is estimated at about 300 strategic weapons and 150 tactical weapons. Estimates of special nuclear material stockpiled suggest that it has enough to manufacture about 2,700 weapons.

By the late 1990s, China had some 10 to 20 INTERCONTINENTAL BALLISTIC MISSILES and one submarine capable of launching 12 ballistic missiles. A second submarine under development, to be launched about 2005, is expected to carry 16 missiles.

China is known to have two production reactors. Both are light-water cooled, graphite moderated reactors. The larger, 1,000 megawatt (MW) reactor is located in Guangyuan, Sichuan province, while the smaller, estimated at 400 to 500 MW, is located at the Jiuquan Atomic Energy Complex at Subei, in Gansu province. In addition, China is known to have at least 12 research reactors. The main research facility, the "Los Alamos of China," consists of 11 separate institutes, mostly located in Mianyang, in Sichuan province. Most production is believed to be centered in Guangyuan, the location of the larger production reactor. A weapons-testing site is operated at Lop Nor, in the western province of Xinjiang. Together with URANIUM enrichment and processing facilities, a major gaseous diffusion plant at Lanzhou, PLUTONIUM reprocessing plants, and TRITIUM and lithium-6 DEUTERIUM production plants, China maintains an active weapons research and manufacturing complex.

CHRONOLOGY OF EVENTS, CHINA'S NUCLEAR WEAPONRY

1953	Chinese Atomic Energy Committee established
1956	Mao Zedong sets atom bomb goal
1960	November 5: First successful flight, short-range ballistic missile
1964	October 15: First nuclear detonation
1966	October 27: First missile-delivered nuclear test
1966	December: First test intermediate range ballistic missile (IRBM)
1967	June 17: First test of hydrogen bomb
1970	January: First launch ICBM
	April 24: First satellite in orbit
	May: Deployment of IRBM
1976	November 17: 4MT thermonuclear warhead, delivered by ICBM tested
1982	October 12: First SLBM launch
1985	September 28: First sub-launched cruise missile

In the 1990s, China, like other nuclear powers, has encountered difficulties in recruiting technical and scientific talent for its weapons program in the face of competition for personnel from the more lucrative commercial sector. In addition, the traditional "Brain Drain," in which bright young graduates study abroad and sometimes emigrate permanently, has presented a problem for staffing the research and development facilities.

In 1999, revelations that China appeared to have developed a miniaturized thermonuclear warhead similar to an American design led to publicized accusations that China had relied upon espionage to get details of the system. China denied the charges, noting that its scientists and engineers were quite capable of developing advanced nuclear weapons without relying on espionage or stolen materials. The Chinese production of a small warhead capable of being mounted as a multiple independently targetable warhead, together with the introduction of new missile systems, provided arguments for constructing a ballistic missile defense system in the United States in the late 1990s.

In May 1999, a congressional investigating committee, headed by Congressman Christopher Cox (R-Calif.), released an unclassified version of its report, accusing the Chinese of having conducted extensive espionage. In particular, the Cox Report specified that the Chinese had obtained data on every currently deployed thermonuclear warhead in the American arsenal, design information on the enhanced radiation weapon (neutron bomb), electromagnetic technology for attack on satellites and missiles, and improved submarine-detection techniques. The committee further concluded that the 45 nuclear tests conducted by China between 1964 and 1996 were insufficient to have developed the modern weapons they possessed without the assistance of espionage. Critics suggested that the Cox Report was alarmist and that some of its conclusions were crafted to discredit the administration of President Bill CLINTON. The Chinese government denied all charges of espionage.

See also NUCLEAR PROLIFERATION.

Suggested Reading

Rodney W. Jones et al., *Tracking Nuclear Proliferation: A Guide in Maps and Charts, 1998.* Washington, D.C.: Carnegie Endowment for International Peace, 1998.

Chong-Pin Lin, *China's Nuclear Weapons Strategy: Tradition within Evolution.* Lexington, Mass.: D.C. Heath, 1988.

Church Rock

In one of the largest environmental accidents to come out of the American nuclear experience, a mill tailings dam collapsed at Church Rock, New Mexico, on July 16, 1979. The dam contained waste from a uranium ore processing mill operated by United Nuclear Corporation. The NUCLEAR REGULATORY COMMISSION categorized the spill as the worst case of radiation contamination in the history of the United States.

The breakage spilled nearly 100 million gallons of chemical and radioactive liquid milling waste, containing some 1,100 tons of solid waste into a nearby stream, the Puerco River. Later investigation showed high levels of radioactivity miles downstream from the dam. Wells in Gallup, New Mexico, revealed the presence of radioactivity and heavy-metal contamination in groundwater 30 to 40 feet below the surface.

See also NUCLEAR WASTE POLICY ACT.

Circular Error Probable (CEP)

Circular Error Probable (CEP) referred to the degree of accuracy of a long-range missile. Specifically, the CEP number was the radius of a circle around a target such that a weapon aimed at the target had a 50% probability of hitting within the circle. Thus a lower CEP number, usually measured in hundreds of meters or fractions of a nautical mile, would indicate a more accurate weapon, and a higher number would describe a less accurate one. In general, submarine-launched missiles had higher CEP numbers than late-generation intercontinental ballistic missiles.

See also MINUTEMAN; INTERCONTINENTAL BALLISTIC MISSILE.

Cisler, Walker L.   *See* ATOMIC INDUSTRIAL FORUM.

Cladding

Cladding is the outer jacket on a nuclear fuel element. Its function is to prevent corrosion of the fuel element and the subsequent release of fission products into the coolant. Common cladding materials include aluminum and its alloys, zirconium alloys, and stainless steel. The former are often used as cladding for the fuel elements in SWIMMING POOL research reactors. A zirconium alloy cladding such as ZIRCALLOY-2 is needed to withstand the high temperatures in the cores of power reactors.

Clinton Laboratory   *See* OAK RIDGE NATIONAL LABORATORY.

Clinton, William Jefferson (1946–) *president of the United States from January 20, 1993, until January 20, 2001*

William Clinton campaigned against incumbent president George H. W. BUSH in 1992 on domestic issues, claiming that Bush had devoted too much attention to foreign affairs. His own administration was characterized by an emphasis on social and economic policy, and in his second term, he was confronted with a major scandal surrounding a sexual liaison he conducted while in office with a young White House aide. He was impeached for lying under oath, but he was not removed from office under a trial before the Senate.

In the conduct of nuclear affairs, Clinton maintained the moratorium on underground nuclear testing that began during the Bush administration, and he worked to secure approval of both the COMPREHENSIVE TEST BAN TREATY and START II.

Clinton was born in Hope, Arkansas, on August 19, 1946. He graduated from Georgetown University in 1968 and from law school at Yale in 1973. He attended Oxford University as a Rhodes Scholar in the period 1968 to 1970. He entered politics in Arkansas and was elected governor of the state in 1978. He was reelected four times before running for the presidency in 1992.

In relations with Russia and the other states of the former Soviet Union, Clinton at first acted to support President Boris YELTSIN, but he was unable to secure congressional support for a financial aid package for Russia. The COOPERATIVE THREAT REDUCTION agreement and the Nunn-Lugar legislation enacted during the Bush administration continued to provide funding and personnel to assist the governments of RUSSIA, UKRAINE, Belarus, and KAZAKHSTAN in their efforts to eliminate older nuclear weapons and handle the waste management issues stemming from their aging nuclear weapons complex.

In 1995, Clinton supported an expansion of the NORTH ATLANTIC TREATY ORGANIZATION to include some of the nations that had previously been members of the WARSAW TREATY ORGANIZATION. Poland, Hungary, and the Czech Republic subsequently joined the organization.

The Clinton administration continued the process of converting the American Nuclear Weapons Complex into a set of institutions devoted to the dismantling of nuclear weapons and the handling of nuclear waste and environmental issues. His first secretary of energy, Hazel O'Leary, stressed in her public positions the environmental restoration work of the department.

Late in Clinton's second administration, revelations of nuclear espionage and related matters regarding the security of nuclear weapons information brought public focus on Secretary of Energy Bill Richardson. Investigations into supposed security leaks from LOS ALAMOS proceeded but with little public release of information about the extent of the damage.

Closely Spaced Basing *See* DENSE-PACK BASING.

Cloud Chamber

The (Wilson) cloud chamber is a device containing a supersaturated vapor the condensation of which is initiated along the paths taken by ionizing radiation. This allows visualization of the motions of and interactions between subatomic particles. The "nuclear tracks" resemble the vapor trails of high-flying aircraft. The cloud chamber was perfected for this purpose by British physicist Charles T. R. Wilson in 1911. His work was recognized with the award of 1927 Nobel Prize in physics.

Cockroft, John D. (1897–1967) *Nobel Prize–winning British physicist who worked in Canada in World War II in cooperation with the Manhattan Project and later served as director of the Harwell Research Establishment in Great Britain (1946–1959)*

John Cockroft's early career in nuclear physics prepared him for a leadership role in the joint American-Canadian atomic weapons development project in World War II and in the development of a major Canadian nuclear reactor. He became widely recognized as one of the leaders in developing particle accelerators, and he established a reputation as a proponent of international cooperation in the realm of nuclear physics.

Cockroft was born in Yorkshire, England, on May 27, 1897, and he attended public schools in the town of his birth, Todmorden. He entered the University of Manchester in 1914, but his college career was interrupted by World War I, during which he served in the artillery as a signaler. At the end of the war, he took up the study of electrical engineering and worked as a college apprentice at Metropolitan Vickers Company. He earned an M.S. degree in technology in 1922 and went on to Cambridge University, where he earned a B.A. in 1924.

Cockroft joined the team headed by Ernest RUTHERFORD at Cavendish Laboratory in Britain in 1924. Through the 1920s, he concentrated his research on magnets, working briefly with the Russian experimenter Peter KAPITSA. Cockroft developed several advanced magnet designs and made contributions in the field of vacuum technology. With his strong background in these two areas, Cockroft helped design and build a proton accelerator, a "voltage multiplier," and, with E. T. S. Walton, used it to produce one of the first artificial nuclear transformations by bombarding a lithium target with protons.

The work of Cockroft was soon confirmed at Berkeley, California, by E. O. Lawrence on the more powerful cyclotron there. Cockroft's work with the proton accelerator, including the production of radioactivity by artificial means and the transmutation of atomic nuclei, won him international recognition in the physics community. Beginning in 1935, Cockroft built a cyclotron at Cavendish.

During World War II, Cockroft worked on radar and served on the MAUD COMMITTEE in Britain, investigating the possibility of a nuclear weapon. In 1944, Cockroft went to Montreal, Quebec, to serve as director of the Anglo-Canadian atomic energy research laboratory there. Under his direction, the heavy-water moderated reactor, NRX, was built at Chalk River, Canada. The later Canadian development of natural-uranium fueled, heavy-water reactors for power production can be traced to the wartime NRX reactor built under the leadership of Cockroft.

In 1946, Cockroft returned to Britain to head the HARWELL ATOMIC ENERGY RESEARCH ESTABLISHMENT. In 1951, he was awarded a Nobel Prize for physics, which he shared with Ernest T. S. Walton. The award was for the earlier work in transmutation of atomic nuclei by means of accelerated subatomic particles. Cockroft served as director at Harwell until 1959.

Cockroft's contributions in particle accelerators for basic research and his service as a science administrator during the years of cooperation between the United States, Canada, and Britain put him at the center of the scientific revolution that harnessed the power of the atom for war and peace.

In the postwar years, he remained active in international scientific leadership circles, and he was elected president of the PUGWASH CONFERENCES on Science and World Affairs, just before his death on September 18, 1967.

See also CANDU REACTOR.

Combustion Engineering

Combustion Engineering was a small nuclear reactor construction company specializing in PRESSURIZED WATER REACTORS. The company got its start in nuclear work by providing components for submarine PROPULSION REACTORS. In the mid-1950s, Combustion Engineering bought General Nuclear Engineering Corporation, a small business established by engineers from ARGONNE NATIONAL LABORATORY. Its first commercial reactor sale was to Consumers Power Company of Michigan in 1966 for the Palisades nuclear power plant. By the end of the century, Combustion Engineering had supplied 14 of the 104 operating commercial power reactors in the United States.

Committee for Nonviolent Action (CNVA)

Responding to nuclear fear and anxiety, the established peace movement and several antiwar liberals created two ad hoc groups in spring 1957 to spearhead an American campaign to abolish nuclear testing and nuclear weapons. Despite different memberships and methods, the National Committee for a SANE Nuclear Policy (SANE) and Committee for Nonviolent Action (CNVA) shared the same goals and often cooperated.

SANE appealed to nuclear pacifists and antiwar activists and functioned as a broad, liberal, conventional organization devoted to political education; CNVA remained a small, disciplined group of from 60 to 70 radical pacifists who championed direct action and civil disobedience. Dubbed "the pragmatists and visionaries" of the peace movement by their historians, SANE and CNVA contributed to the birth of the postwar peace movement.

Lawrence Scott, a Quaker and radical pacifist activist, was the person most responsible for both SANE and CNVA. Convinced that words were not enough to abolish radiation poisoning and nuclear arsenals, Scott resigned as peace education director of the Chicago American Friends Service Committee in 1957 to promote a program of nonviolent civil disobedience. Scott invited some 20 radical pacifist, nuclear pacifist, and liberal antiwar leaders to a meeting in Philadelphia, Pennsylvania, on April 22, 1957, to discuss his proposal for a campaign to abolish nuclear testing and nuclear weapons. Both SANE and CNVA emerged from this meeting. Robert Gilmore led SANE, while Scott led the more radical CNVA, which until

Antinuclear Demonstration. In the 1950s, members of the Catholic Workers group joined with Quakers and others in protesting the development of the hydrogen bomb. (Library of Congress)

1959 was known as Nonviolent Action against Nuclear Weapons (NVAANW).

At Scott's initiative, in mid-May 20 representatives from various peace organizations met in Washington, D.C., and decided to organize a civil disobedience project to protest against the upcoming nuclear tests in Nevada. Nearly two weeks later, representatives of the WAR RESISTERS LEAGUE (WRL), Fellowship of Reconciliation, Catholic Worker Movement, Women's League for Peace and Freedom, and other groups met in New York City and formed NVAANW.

In its first action, NVAANW protested the ATOMIC ENERGY COMMISSION (AEC) decision to conduct a nuclear test explosion in Operation Plumbbob, on August 6, 1957, the 12th anniversary of Hiroshima. On August 6, 11 NVAANW members stepped past AEC guards to illegally enter the NEVADA TEST SITE, and they were arrested. Reporters observed and publicized this act of civil disobedience.

In 1958, CNVA sponsored the voyage of the GOLDEN RULE, probably the best known of all the CNVA actions.

The next CNVA project, Omaha Action (1959), attempted to focus attention on disarmament by blocking construction of the *Atlas* ICBM base near Mead, southwest of Omaha, Nebraska. Protesters made camp on a knoll near the base entrance, maintained a vigil, and after a week commenced civil disobedience and nonviolent obstruction. Led by A. J. Muste, over two dozen pacifists, in repeated acts of civil disobedience over three weeks, climbed over Camp Mead's wooden fence and were arrested for trespassing. Two pacifists lay in the road to block trucks from carrying construction materials into the base. Omaha Action generated much local publicity and some national and international attention.

Within months after Omaha Action, CNVA cosponsored its first international civil disobedience action, the Sahara Protest Project, which brought together issues of nonviolent revolution, support for decolonization, and nuclear disarmament. In response to French plans to perform a nuclear test in the Algerian Sahara in January 1960, CNVA participated in an international Sahara protest.

Proposed by the British-based Direct Action Committee against Nuclear War, a pacifist group with views similar to CNVA, the project aimed to place a team of pacifists inside or near the Algerian Sahara test site of El Hammoudia (near Reggane) to prevent or challenge the French test, arouse the conscience of French citizens and those of other nuclear powers, and stir Africans to intensify their protests. In addition, the project offered a direct link between the campaign to abolish nuclear weapons and African colonies' movements for independence.

Independent African nations and an United Nations resolution urged the French to cancel the scheduled January 1960 nuclear test. Despite French attempts to portray El Hammoudia as a desolate and uninhabited empty quarter, the region was home to 200,000 people. Critics charged that the test explosion would threaten this thriving desert civilization and warned that the prevailing winds would carry radioactive fallout beyond the Reggane area and contaminate the air, water, and food supply of nearby countries.

Comprised of a half-dozen pacifists from Europe and the United States and a dozen African volunteers, the protest team included American pacifists Bayard Rustin and William Sutherland. In December 1959,

the Sahara team departed Accra for a 2,000 mile overland trip to the nuclear test site. Sixteen miles into French Upper Volta, French officials stopped the team. The Sahara protest team condemned imperialism and appealed to African nationalism; however, it disavowed the revolutionary violence common to independence struggles, including the Algerian war for independence then being fought between the French and Algerians. Despite its failure to reach El Hammoudia, the team prompted much publicity and numerous demonstrations of solidarity in Europe, America, and Africa.

From 1960 to 1968, CNVA continued to organize direct action and civil disobedience peace actions, many of which received wide publicity. Major CNVA projects included Polaris Action (1961), in which protesters sought to prevent the construction and operation of *Polaris* missile-carrying submarines in New London, Connecticut; the San Francisco to Moscow Walk for Peace (1960–1961); sailings of *Everyman* I/II into the Pacific nuclear testing zone and *Everyman* III to the Soviet Union to demand an end to nuclear testing (1962); the Quebec-Washington-Guantanamo Walk (1963–1964), designed to protest the United States naval base at Guantanamo and provide a model of nonviolent resistance for the Cuban people; and the Saigon Project (1966), which sent six pacifists to Saigon to meet with antiwar Buddhist and Catholic leaders.

By 1968, as direct action within the peace and civil rights movements became commonplace and the rationale for a separate organization waned, CNVA, which increasingly duplicated the War Resisters League efforts and experienced financial difficulties, no longer served a "unique" role in the pacifist movement. Consequently, CNVA merged with the WRL, whose program most resembled its own and with which it had a close relationship and shared overlapping membership.

Suggested Reading

Maurice Isserman, *If I Had a Hammer: The Death of the Old Left and the Birth of the New Left*. Chicago: University of Illinois Press, 1993.

Milton S. Katz and Neil H. Katz, "Pragmatists and Visionaries in the Post–World War II American Peace Movement," in Solomon Wanks, ed., *Doves and Diplomats: Foreign Offices and Peace Movements in Europe and America in the Twentieth Century*. Westport, Conn.: Greenwood Press, 1978.

Lawrence S. Wittner, *Resisting the Bomb: A History of the World Nuclear Disarmament Movement, 1954–1970*. Stanford, Calif.: Stanford University Press, 1997.

Committee on the Present Danger

The Committee on the Present Danger was a conservative group of foreign policy and nuclear policy specialists formed in November 1976 to attempt to influence the administration and Congress. An earlier, lesser-known Committee on the Present Danger had been organized by James CONANT in 1950 to advocate the strengthening of U.S. troop presence in Europe. One of the first objectives of the new group in 1976 was to attempt to prevent the ratification of the Strategic Arms Limitation Treaty II (SALT II), which they believed was injurious to the strategic position of the United States.

Ronald REAGAN was a member of the Committee on the Present Danger, and, when he was elected president, he placed many of his fellow members in important positions in foreign policy, defense, intelligence, and arms control. Among committee members who served in the Reagan administration were Jeane Kirkpatrick (U.S. ambassador to the United Nations), Paul Nitze (negotiator on Theater Nuclear Forces), Walter Rostow (head of the Arms Control and Disarmament Agency), George Schultz (secretary of state after June 1982), Richard Pipes (Soviet expert on the National Security Council), Richard Perle (assistant secretary of defense for international security policy), William Casey (director of the Central Intelligence Agency), and John Lehman (secretary of the navy). Other, lesser-known members of the committee were appointed to other positions.

The leaders of the Committee for the Present Danger were known for their strong opposition to the Soviet Union and to their distrust of the policy of DETENTE that had developed during the Johnson and Nixon administrations.

Suggested Reading

Robert Scheer, *With Enough Shovels: Reagan, Bush and Nuclear War.* New York: Random House, 1982.

Comprehensive Test Ban Treaty

The Comprehensive Test Ban Treaty (CTBT) is designed to put a final halt to the testing by detonation of all nuclear weapons by all nations in the world. The CTBT had been a goal of arms control advocates since the 1950s, but it was not until September 24, 1996, that the treaty was completed and signed by Great Britain, China, France, Russia, and the United States.

Britain and France soon ratified the treaty and over 150 other nations signed the document. However, on October 13, 1999, the United States Senate voted to reject the treaty.

After the election of Vladimir Putin as president of Russia in 1999, the Russian parliament took up the START II treaty and the CTBT, ratifying both in April 2000.

From a practical point of view, the United States ceased all testing of nuclear weapons by detonation. The CTBT, if implemented, would go far toward achieving two goals: preventing proliferation of nuclear weapons to nations not already possessing them by preventing testing, and preventing the development of more sophisticated or advanced weapons by nations already possessing them. Despite these benefits, the CTBT would not be able to prevent the development of effective smaller nuclear weapons. For example, the United States developed and deployed the URANIUM weapon dropped on Hiroshima without first testing it. Pakistan, ISRAEL, and SOUTH AFRICA all developed nuclear weapons without any known tests by detonation.

It is somewhat ironic that the CTBT was first proposed by India, following the Bravo test on March 1, 1954, that led to the contamination of the *Lucky Dragon* Japanese fishing vessel. In 1998, in defiance of the growing world consensus around the CTBT, India set off a series of nuclear tests, soon followed by Pakistan.

Under the provisions of the treaty, 44 nations, including the United States, must ratify it for it to come into force. As of the end of 1999, 23 of the 44 nations had ratified the treaty; INDIA, PAKISTAN, and NORTH KOREA had not yet signed the treaty. Although the United States and China have signed the treaty, neither had ratified it by the end of 2000.

Compton, Arthur Holly (1892–1962) *American physicist and science administrator who headed the University of Chicago Metallurgical Laboratory during World War II*

Arthur Holly Compton was central to the administration of the Manhattan Project in World War II, directing the laboratory at the University of Chicago where the first controlled chain reaction took place and bringing together as a science administrator a brilliant team to work on the atomic bomb project.

A. H. Compton was born on September 10, 1892, the son of a professor of philosophy at Wooster College in Ohio. Compton graduated from Wooster College in 1913 and then attended graduate school at Princeton where he earned a Ph.D. in 1916. He taught physics at the University of Minnesota and then spent two years as a research engineer at Westinghouse Company in East Pittsburgh, Pennsylvania. His work there included a patent on a design for a sodium vapor lamp. He worked on X-rays at Westinghouse, and he developed the concept of a wavelength for the electron and other particles. In other work, later confirmed, he determined the relationship between electron spin and magnetism in ferrous metals.

Following World War I, he spent a year on a National Research Council fellowship at the Cavendish Laboratory in Cambridge, England, where he worked under Ernest RUTHERFORD and J. J. Thompson. In 1920 he returned to the United States and took a position as professor and head of the physics department at Washington University in St. Louis, Missouri. He continued his work on X-ray scattering and soon developed a theory, based on Einstein's general theory of relativity, that explained X-ray scattering. He published his quantum theory of scattering in 1922, and the concept gradually gained acceptance and came to be known as the Compton Effect.

In 1923, he moved to the University of CHICAGO, where he continued his work on X-rays. In the early 1930s, he turned his interest to cosmic rays. He led a number of expeditions around the world to measure variances in cosmic rays in different locations. Variation in cosmic ray intensity due to altitude and latitude suggested the interaction of the earth's magnetic field and cosmic rays.

In World War II, Compton, like many physicists who had worked on other problems, turned his energies to the atomic bomb project. In November 1941, serving as head of the National Academy of Sciences Committee on Uranium, he presented a report that outlined the military potential of atomic energy. Compton had heard from E. O. LAWRENCE of the discovery of plutonium and immediately recognized the potential of the new element as a fissionable material for nuclear weapons.

Compton's career next took him to developments at the center of nuclear progress. The activities he managed led directly to the atomic bomb and to future generations of nuclear reactors. Compton was chosen to direct the Metallurgical Laboratory at the University of Chicago, which housed the construction of the first reactor designed by Enrico FERMI in 1942. Compton was responsible for recruiting to the "Met Lab" Fermi as well as other scientists, including Walter ZINN, Glenn SEABORG, and Eugene WIGNER.

As director of the laboratory, Compton arranged for Crawford GREENEWALT of Du Pont Corporation to be present at the successful demonstration of CHICAGO PILE No. 1 on December 2, 1942. Greenewalt and Du Pont then agreed to take up the project of constructing the first production reactors at HANFORD, Washington. Compton was instrumental in helping to organize several laboratories and facilities that became part of the American nuclear establishment, including the Palos Park laboratory (later ARGONNE NATIONAL LABORATORY), the facilities at OAK RIDGE, Tennessee, and the production reactor complex at Hanford.

After World War II, Compton retired from active research and scientific administration and returned to Washington University where he served as chancellor of the University. He authored his memoirs, *Atomic Quest,* in 1956 and died on March 15, 1962.

Compton, Karl T. (1887–1954) *president of the Massachusetts Institute of Technology (1930–1948) and influential policy advisor on scientific issues*
Karl Compton, the older brother of Arthur Holly COMPTON, was a noted physicist and science administrator of the 1930s and 1940s. Born in Wooster, Ohio, on September 14, 1887, he attended the College of Wooster, earning a master's degree in 1909. He earned a doctorate in physics at Princeton in 1912, publishing papers on electron physics based on his student work. He taught for three years at Reed College in Portland, Oregon, and then he returned to Princeton as an assistant professor in 1915.

During the period 1918 to 1930, while on the Princeton faculty, he published nearly 100 scientific papers on topics in electron physics and the properties of excited atoms. During the decade, he built the graduate physics department at Princeton. He was recruited in 1930 to become president of the Massachusetts Institute of Technology (MIT), leading it over the next decade to become an internationally recognized center for graduate work in the physical sciences.

In 1933, President Franklin ROOSEVELT appointed Karl Compton to the Science Advisory Board and then in 1940 to the National Defense Research Committee. He headed a division of the committee devoted to developing radar and other electronic devices.

In 1948, he resigned his position as president of MIT to succeed Vannevar BUSH as chairman of the Research and Development Board of the National Military Establishment. He died June 22, 1954, in New York.

Unlike his brother, Arthur Holly Compton, Karl Compton did not work directly with the MANHATTAN ENGINEER DISTRICT. However, his influence on nuclear events as a major leader in the scientific community was felt in several ways. He supported David LILIENTHAL as first chairman of the ATOMIC ENERGY COMMISSION, and he later endorsed the concept of development of the hydrogen bomb.

Conant, James (1893–1978)   *president of Harvard University (1933–1950) and during World War II served as deputy director of the Office of Scientific Research and Development (OSRD) in charge of the development of the atomic bomb*

James Conant worked with Vannevar BUSH on both the National Defense Research Committee (NDRC) and the OFFICE OF SCIENTIFIC RESEARCH AND DEVELOPMENT. As a Republican and a scientist, he was often associated in later years with the internationalist wing of the Republican Party in matters dealing with strategic policy and nuclear weaponry.

Conant was born March 26, 1893, in Dorchester, Massachusetts. He earned a doctorate at Harvard University in 1916 and worked during World War I on the development of mustard gas in the Chemical Warfare Service. Following the war, Conant joined the chemistry department at Harvard, and he was selected as president of the university in 1933.

Working with Bush through the NDRC (which Conant chaired) and the OSRD during the war, Conant played an important part in setting policy for the first use of the atomic bomb. He advocated dropping the first weapons on industrial cities in Japan. Following World War II, he returned to the university as president and served on the GENERAL ADVISORY COMMITTEE along with J. R. OPPENHEIMER in the first years after the war. Conant agreed with Oppenheimer that it was not necessary to develop a thermonuclear weapon, arguing that fission weapons provided a sufficient DETERRENCE and defense.

However, with the invasion of South Korea by NORTH KOREA in 1950, Conant became an advocate of a more rigorous national defense. He was an organizer and chairman of a COMMITTEE ON THE PRESENT DANGER (1950–1952), advocating the stationing of more troops in Europe and supporting the classified document, National Security Council Paper 68 (NSC 68). Later recognized as a formative document of the cold war, NSC 68 called for a massive U.S. defense buildup to counteract communist expansion around the globe. Partly for Conant's internationalist orientation, President Eisenhower appointed him to serve as U.S. high commissioner to Germany (1953–1955). When the Federal Republic of Germany was established, Eisenhower appointed Conant to serve as U.S. ambassador. Conant held the post through 1957. He died February 11, 1978.

Suggested Reading

James Hershberg, *James B. Conant: Harvard to Hiroshima and the Making of the Nuclear Age.* New York: Knopf, 1993.

Confidence-Building Measures   *See* START 1.

Containment

Containment is the provision for a gas-tight shell or other enclosure around a nuclear reactor to confine FISSION products that might otherwise escape in the event of an accident.

Control Rod(s)

The control rod is a device for controlling the rate of nuclear FISSION by controlling the neutron population in the reactor core. Rods, tubes, and plates containing a material that absorbs neutrons have been used for this purpose. Cadmium is often used for the fabrication of the control rod; Boron is sometimes used for this purpose. The respective (n, γ) CROSS SECTIONS for thermal neutron capture are $^{113}Cd = 1.98 \times 10^4$ barns (b) and $^{10}B = 3837$ b.

Cooperative Threat Reduction

Following the passage of the INF and START I treaties, together with the Lisbon Protocol which pledged

Dismantling a Soviet Submarine. Under the Cooperative Threat Reduction agreements, the United States provided aid to Russia, Ukraine, and other former Soviet republics to assist in eliminating nuclear weapons and weapon-delivery systems. (On Site Inspection Agency.)

UKRAINE, Belarus, and KAZAKHSTAN to ship their nuclear weapons to Russia, Congress passed a bill sponsored by Senators Sam Nunn (D-Georgia) and Richard Lugar (R-Indiana). Known as the Nunn-Lugar Act or the Safe, Secure-Dismantlement Program, the legislation provided for a large budget to assist those countries to dismantle or transport their nuclear weapons to safety in Russia.

The goals of the Nunn-Lugar program, enacted in 1991 and begun in 1992, were to help the states of the former Soviet Union to become non-nuclear nations; to accelerate the rate of weapons reductions under START I; to enhance nuclear safety, security, and control; to begin the dismantlement of chemical weapons; to encourage demilitarization of the societies through retraining and relocation; and to build contacts between the nuclear and military establishments of the former Soviet states and the United States.

This overall program of Cooperative Threat Reduction was administered through the DEFENSE SPECIAL WEAPONS AGENCY, later combined with the ON-SITE INSPECTION AGENCY in the Defense Threat Reduction Agency. These defense agencies were staffed by military officers from all three services and with a permanent staff of scientific, technical, and support civilian personnel. The agencies also worked through established civilian contractors to accomplish the goals.

By 1996, the Defense Special Weapons Agency conducted over 50 separate Cooperative Threat Reduction projects, ranging from supplying containers for the safe transport of fissile material to the removal of over 1,200 warheads from deployed weapon systems in Russia. Other projects included purchase of emergency response equipment and elimination of ICBMs and their launchers. Belarus, Ukraine, and Kazakhstan all became nuclear-free nations by 1997.

Core

The core of a nuclear reactor is its central part containing the assembly of FISSILE MATERIAL in the fuel elements as well as any moderator and control materials.

Counterforce Strategy

The term "counterforce strategy" was developed by nuclear strategic weapons policy analysts to describe a plan for targeting nuclear weapons against an opponent's nuclear and general military resources. To be credible or believable and therefore effective as a deterrent policy, a counterforce strategy requires large numbers of very accurate nuclear weapon delivery systems.

See also SECOND-STRIKE CAPABILITY.

Countervalue Strategy

The term "countervalue strategy" was used by nuclear weapons policy analysts to describe a targeting plan in which nuclear weapons would be targeted against an opponent's population and industrial centers. Unlike a COUNTERFORCE STRATEGY, a countervalue strategy relies less on highly accurate placement of nuclear weapons than on less accurate and more powerful weapons capable of destroying larger areas.

See also SECOND-STRIKE CAPABILITY.

Critical

An assembly of FISSILE MATERIAL is critical when it is capable of supporting a self-sustaining CHAIN REACTION.

Critical Mass

The critical mass is the smallest quantity of FISSILE MATERIAL that will support a self-sustaining CHAIN REACTION under appropriate conditions of size and shape.

Crookes, William (1832–1919) *British inventor of glass vacuum tubes used for the study of the nature of gases*

William Crookes was a 19th-century British scientist who developed a method of examining the nature of gases by bombarding them in an evacuated glass tube with an electric current. Known as "Crookes tubes," these devices became crucial in nuclear research in the early 1920s, when they were used by Frederick Soddy and Francis ASTON in the discovery of ISOTOPES.

Crookes was born in 1832 in London. He studied at the University of London, and his research and development work was carried on in his own private laboratory. He was knighted in 1897, and he died in 1919.

Cross Section

Cross section is the probability that a nuclear reaction will occur. Cross sections are usually expressed in barns (b) where $1b = 1 \times 10^{-24}$ cm². The cross section is analogous to the apparent cross-sectional area exposed as a target for the bombarding particle for a particular nuclear reaction, but it does not reflect the geometrical cross section (πr^2). A target nuclide has characteristic cross sections for the various nuclear reactions, i.e., (n, γ), (n,p), (n,fis), and so on. The fission cross section refers to the probability that a neutron will initiate a nuclear FISSION. The slow (thermal) neutron fission cross section for ^{235}U is 580 ± 2 b and the fast neutron fission cross section for ^{235}U is 1.44 b. The corresponding fission cross sections for ^{239}Pu are 742 ± 3 b and 1.78 b, respectively. The larger cross section of PLUTONIUM means that it fissions much more rapidly, necessitating a different weapon design from URANIUM-based weapons.

See also GUN-TYPE; IMPLOSION; NUCLEAR REACTIONS.

Cruise Missile

The term "cruise missile" refers to an air-breathing missile that can carry a weapon of mass destruction such as a nuclear warhead for an intermediate range of a few score to several hundred miles. The weapons are regarded as "autonomous"; that is, once they are launched, they do not require remote guidance, but automatically home in on their preassigned targets. Modern cruise missiles developed in the 1980s can be extremely accurate when coupled with radar, land-tracking, or video-homing devices.

Air-launched cruise missiles (ALCMs), ground-launched cruise missiles (GLCMs), and ship-launched cruise missiles (SLCMs) have entered into the arsenals of the major nations. Some commentators have observed that the German *V-1* or "buzz-bomb" operated in World War II propelled with a ram-jet, air-breathing engine was the first GLCM.

Among the best known types of modern cruise missiles are the French-built ALCM, the *Exocet;* the American-built SLCM, the *Tomahawk;* and the Chinese-built anti-ship ALCM, the *Silkworm.* Cruise missiles are distinguished from intermediate-range ballistic missiles (IRBMs) in that the cruise missiles have an internal system of targeting, and they are air-breathing, whereas IRBMs are fired in a ballistic arc, utilizing either solid or liquid rocket fuel together with oxygen to sustain the rocket at extremely high altitude. IRBMs leave the atmosphere in exo-atmospheric flight. Since cruise missiles fly low and are air-breathing, they can be built lighter than IRBMS, which must carry an oxidizer, taking up weight.

Cruise missiles have been employed with high-explosive warheads in several wars of the 1980s and 1990s. Particularly effective was the use of the French *Exocet* during the Argentine-British war over the Malvinas Islands in 1982 and the use of *Tomahawk* missiles in both the Gulf War in 1991 and in the NATO air campaign against Yugoslavia in 1999.

Cruise missiles may carry either conventional high explosives, with a capacity of a half-ton or more, or a nuclear, chemical, or biological weapon. Since cruise missiles are capable of carrying nuclear weapons, experts in nuclear proliferation usually examine whether a nuclear state or a potential nuclear state, such as ISRAEL, IRAQ, or PAKISTAN, possesses either domestically constructed cruise missiles or imported ones from suppliers in France, RUSSIA, CHINA, or NORTH KOREA. For example, China has provided Silkworm missiles and SLCMs to Iran.

The *Tomahawk* Land Attack Missile (TLAM) was originally designed to be able to fit in a submarine's torpedo tube. In effect, by arming TLAM missiles with nuclear warheads, attack submarines could be converted into nuclear-missile launching platforms. The *Tomahawk* Anti-Ship Missile (TASM) was another type of cruise missile. Since such a missile would carry 1,000 pounds of high explosive, it would take very few such missiles to disable a major warship. The TASM had a much longer reach than a torpedo, although a torpedo would have an advantage over a TASM in that it would detonate under the sea, loading the target ship with greater shock and stress.

Some cruise missiles use a system of terrain-following, which requires that they incorporate into an onboard computer a map of the route they will fly from launch to target. Such sophisticated systems have made cruise missiles capable of reaching precise targets at distant locations.

When cruise missiles were first under development, in the early 1980s, there was considerable uncertainty about their Circular Error Probable (CEP), with estimates predicted to run from under 100 feet to over 600 feet. In any case, such a weapon, carrying a nuclear device, would be far more accurate than an intercontinental SUBMARINE-LAUNCHED BALLISTIC MISSILE or than most ICBMs. However, with the development of terrain-following and then laser-guided ALCMs, extremely accurate cruise missiles were developed that could be aimed at a particular airshaft, window, or door of a target building.

As part of the Dual Strategy announced by NATO in 1979, 464 cruise missiles were stationed in Germany, Great Britain, Belgium, the Netherlands, and Italy in the period 1983 to 1985. These highly accurate and long-range ground-launched cruise missiles (GLCMs) could reach targets deep in the Soviet Union. Thus, when the Soviets discussed strategic arms limitation or reduction, they wished to include the GLCMs since they could reach strategic targets. However, the United States insisted that the GLCMs were long-range Theater Nuclear Force weapons, and should be covered in the treaty dealing with intermediate-range nuclear forces. The issue was difficult to resolve, but the GLCMs were included in the INF treaty negotiated in 1987 and signed in 1988. They were removed from Europe under that treaty.

In light of the proliferation of modern anti-aircraft missiles around the world, cruise missiles armed with conventional high explosives rather than nuclear weapons have become increasingly valuable. Since cruise missiles can be launched from aircraft or ships many miles from their targets, they are classed as "stand-off" weapons. The launching platform, either ship or airplane, need not come within range of the defenses of the target. For this reason, they were extensively employed by the United States, carrying conventional high-explosive warheads, in the Gulf War of 1991 and the Kosovo conflict of 1999.

See also INTERMEDIATE NUCLEAR FORCES TREATY; PRESIDENTIAL INITIATIVE 1991; PROLIFERATION; START I.

Suggested Reading

Richard K. Betts, ed., *Cruise Missiles: Technology, Strategy, Politics.* Washington, D.C.: The Brookings Institution, 1981.

Rodney Jones et al., *Tracking Nuclear Proliferation.* Washington, D.C.: Carnegie Endowment for International Peace, 1998.

Cuban Missile Crisis *See* BRINKMANSHIP.

Cumberland Broken Arrow

On January 13, 1964, a B-52 carrying two thermonuclear bombs broke apart in a storm over southern Pennsylvania, crashing just over the state line near the village of Grantsville, Maryland. The nearest large town is Cumberland, Maryland, and this episode is usually referred to as the Cumberland accident or BROKEN ARROW. The seven-year-old B-52 aircraft, B14 or "Buzz One Four," had just returned from a Chrome Dome flight to Turkey. It was being ferried from Westover Air Force Base in western Massachusetts to Turner Air Force Base, near Albany, Georgia.

Like other B-52s of the period, the aircraft suffered a defect in the bolts holding the tail section to a rear bulkhead. Although the problem had been reported several times, the air force had hesitated to pull the planes from the constant Chrome Dome exercises, which required several bomb-carrying aircraft to be in the air near the Soviet borders at all times.

At about 31,000 feet, the aircraft encountered severe turbulence, and the pilot planned first to try to fly down out of the weather and then to climb above it. In the storm, the tail wrenched off, and four of the five crewmen were able to eject from the plane as it broke apart. The fifth could not strap himself into his ejection seat in time and died on impact as the plane crashed.

Of the four who parachuted, two died from injuries and exposure in the bitter cold, and the other two were rescued by local volunteers on the ground on the morning after the crash.

The two thermonuclear weapons on the plane were recovered intact from the crash site. Local residents placed markers at the site of the three deaths, treating them as casualties of the cold war.

Curie

The Curie (Ci) is a unit of radioactive material producing the same activity as one gram of ^{226}Radium. One Ci of any radioactive material produces 3.7×10^{10} disintegrations per second (dps). The Curie has been replaced by the Becquerel (Bq), where one Bq of any radioactive material produces one dps. The Becquerel is named to honor Antoine Henri Becquerel, the co-discoverer of RADIOACTIVITY. The Curie honors the other co-discoverers, Marie Sklodowska Curie and Pierre Curie, who shared the 1903 NOBEL PRIZE with Becquerel.

See also CURIE, MARIE.

Curie, Marie (1867–1934) *Polish-born Nobel Prize–winning physicist who was the co-discoverer of radium, and the first woman professor of physics at the Sorbonne University in Paris*

Marie Curie's work early in the 20th century with X-rays, radium, and other radioactive elements lay the groundwork for further research that opened new insights into atomic structure and eventually led to atomic fission and the use of nuclear energy.

Marie Curie was born Manya Sklodowska in Warsaw, Poland, then ruled by Russia, on November 7,

Marie Curie. The discoverer of radium and a Nobel Prize–winning physicist, Marie Curie later died from cancer developed while working with radioactive materials. (Library of Congress)

1867. Both of her parents were educators, and her father taught physics and mathematics at the secondary level in Warsaw. After a difficult childhood and youth, she became a governess and worked in an "underground university" in Warsaw. She studied in Paris and married Pierre Curie there in 1895. She and her husband worked on radioactivity, following up on discoveries by William Roentgen and Antoine Henri Becquerel. Marie and Pierre had a daughter, Irène, born in 1897. In 1898, Marie and her husband discovered two new elements, both of them radioactive, found in pitchblende. They discovered polonium, which they named after her native Poland, in July of that year, and radium in December. They were able to isolate the two new elements in 1902, and they jointly received the Nobel Prize for physics in 1903 with Becquerel.

In 1906 Pierre Curie died, and Marie Curie succeeded him as professor of Physics at the Sorbonne, the first woman to hold that rank there. In 1910, working with André Debierne, Marie Curie was able to isolate pure radium metal. She published a *Treatise on Radioactivity* in 1910 and won the Nobel Prize for physics in 1911 for that and her earlier work. With the outbreak of World War I in 1914, she helped to set up ambulances with X-ray equipment, and she personally worked in the ambulance corps as a driver and X-ray technician. The Red Cross appointed her head of the radiological service in recognition of her contributions. She gave courses to medical orderlies and taught doctors how to locate shrapnel or other foreign objects in the human body. In 1920, she published an account of her work during the war.

Her daughter Irène followed in her footsteps, marrying a physicist, Frédéric Joliot. Together, Joliot and Irène Curie made further contributions to the understanding of radioactive elements.

Marie Curie refused to patent her discovery of radium, believing that discoveries of physics should be openly published and that it would be wrong to take any profit from a substance that could be used in the treatment of disease. As little was known about the dangerous effects of radiation, neither Marie nor Pierre Curie took precautions against exposure. She died July 4, 1934, as a consequence of radiation poisoning.

As the best-known woman scientist of her time, Marie Curie was often held out as an example to young women studying physics and chemistry, and her high principles in refusing to make money from her discoveries and her tragic death as a consequence of her researches only added to the international respect she had gained from her work.

See also FRANCE—NUCLEAR POWER; JOLIOT-CURIE, FRÉDÉRIC; POLONIUM.

Cyclotron

A cyclotron is a particle accelerator in which charged particles, usually β but possibly protons, receive repeated synchronized accelerations by electrical fields as the particles spiral outward from their source. The particles are kept in the spiral by a powerful magnetic field.

Czech Republic   *See* POWER REACTORS, WORLD.

Daghlian, Harry (1919–1945) *American physicist who was the first to die from an accident with nuclear materials*

Harry Daghlian was a 24-year-old instructor from Purdue University who joined the Manhattan Project at LOS ALAMOS in 1943. In August 1945, he was working at Omega Site there, where PLUTONIUM cores were tested to measure the point at which they would reach criticality or initiate a CHAIN REACTION. On August 21, Daghlian discovered that a plutonium core was undergoing a chain reaction, and he attempted to stop it by physically separating the two hemispheres of radioactive metal. He tipped over the table with a small housing of tungsten bricks surrounding the core, stopping the reaction, but he received a lethal dose of radiation in doing so.

He was rushed to a hospital and suffered severe radiation burns. He died 24 days later. News of the event was not released publicly, and when Louis SLOTIN died from a similar accident on May 21, 1946, that case was erroneously reported as the first fatality resulting from an accident with a weapon core.

Suggested Reading
Richard Miller, *Under the Cloud*. New York: Free Press, 1986.

Damascus, Arkansas

On September 19, 1980, a TITAN II missile exploded in its SILO as a result of an accident that had punctured the fuel tank. The nuclear warhead was thrown several hundred feet from the silo.

A team of eight maintenance men were engaged in a routine procedure of pressurizing the oxidizer tank on the missile. At about 6:30 in the evening, one of the workers dropped a large wrench socket weighing over 15 pounds, which bounced and fell about 70 feet. He was wearing a bulky protective suit that hampered his movements. The tool bounced off a rocket mounting and struck the fuel tank, tearing a three- to four-inch gash in the thin-walled aluminum pressurized tank. The fuel began to spray out, and an automatic washdown system carried the fuel to drains below, releasing some 100,000 gallons of water. However, vapor from the fuel tank accumulated, and when two men entered the silo to investigate the fume level, a violent explosion occurred. One man, David Livingston, was killed, and 21 other workers were injured.

The explosion blew off the silo door and sent the 5,000-pound reentry vehicle into the air. The warhead contained a 9-megaton hydrogen warhead that flew some 600 feet into the air. Although the warhead created a large crater on impact, it was only slightly dented, and it did not detonate or leak radiation. Flames leaped out of the silo and could be seen for miles.

The Damascus accident was the last major BROKEN ARROW event in the United States in the 20th century.

Dean, Gordon (1905–1958)   *served as chairman of the Atomic Energy Commission (AEC) from 1950 through 1953*

Gordon Dean was first appointed a member of the commission May 24, 1949, to serve out the term of William Waymack, who had resigned. Dean was appointed by President Harry TRUMAN to serve as chairman on July 11, 1950. He served a full three-year term until June 30, 1953.

Dean was born on December 28, 1905, and grew up in California. He had studied law at Redlands University in southern California and had been admitted to the bar in 1930. In that year, he moved to North Carolina, joining the faculty of Duke University Law School. In 1934, Dean joined the U.S. Justice Department in the Criminal Division. From 1937 to 1940, he served as a special assistant to the attorney general. In 1940, he resigned to work with Brien MCMAHON in private law practice. During World War II, he served in the U.S. Navy as a lieutenant in the Intelligence Branch. On May 16, 1945, Dean was appointed to assist Justice Robert Jackson, U.S. chief counsel for the prosecution of the major Nazi war criminals at Nuremberg.

After the war crimes trial, he returned to civilian life, teaching law at the University of Southern California. In 1949, he was appointed to the AEC. When David LILIENTHAL resigned as chairman in the wake of the controversies over Klaus FUCHS and over whether to push for the development of a thermonuclear weapon, the post of chairman of the commission was first temporarily filled by Sumner PIKE.

Dean's appointment represented a shift in the make-up of the AEC, as four of the five commissioners who had served with Lilienthal resigned or their terms were not renewed. Thus Dean came in with a new team, including H. D. SMYTH, Thomas E. Murray, and T. Keith GLENNAN, together with Pike, who served as a commissioner but no longer as chair. Under Dean's leadership, the AEC established better relations with a conservative Congress, concerned with maintaining a

Gordon Dean, T. Keith Glennan, and Marion Boyer. Gordon Dean (center), chair of the Atomic Energy Commission (1950–1953), meets with T. Keith Glennan (left), who was just appointed a member of the commission, and with the new general manager of the AEC, Marion Boyer, in November 1950. (Department of Energy)

strong lead over the Soviet Union in nuclear matters and with improving security against espionage at U.S. nuclear facilities. Dean's liaison with Congress improved partly because Brien MCMAHON, his former associate in private law practice, served as head of the JOINT COMMITTEE ON ATOMIC ENERGY. Dean was concerned with tightening the management of the commission over the widespread nuclear production complex. Dean secured from McMahon agreement to the principle that the commission should hire its own general manager. Caroll WILSON, who had served as manager under Lilienthal, resigned and was replaced by Marion Boyer, a former Standard Oil executive who worked well with Dean.

Dean's service as chair of the AEC coincided with the duration of the KOREAN WAR, a period during which the United States greatly expanded its nuclear weapons production facilities. During Dean's chairmanship, new PRODUCTION REACTORS were planned and built, and a second weapons laboratory, LAWRENCE LIVERMORE NATIONAL LABORATORY, was built to supplement LOS ALAMOS. Continued disclosures regarding previous Soviet espionage at Los Alamos, including the arrest and conviction of Julius and Ethel ROSENBERG, added to the sense of urgency regarding both security and the need to develop the hydrogen bomb in order to maintain a lead over the Soviet Union during Dean's chairmanship.

Suggested Reading

Richard G. Hewlett and Francis Duncan, *Atomic Shield* (Vol. 2 of *A History of the United States Atomic Energy Commission*). Washington, D.C.: Atomic Energy Commission, 1972.

Decapitation *See* PRESIDENTIAL DECISION DIRECTIVE 59.

Decision to Bomb Hiroshima *See* TRUMAN'S DECISION.

Decoupling

The term "decoupling" has two completely different meanings in reference to nuclear matters, one technical and one strategic.

1. Meaning in a technical context. Interpreting the first fully contained underground nuclear test conducted in 1957, the Rainier test held at the NEVADA TEST SITE, scientists concluded that a detonation conducted in a large underground cavern in certain soils could be decoupled from contact with the earth. Such decoupling would reduce the seismic signal sent by underground tests and would make verification of the yield of underground tests very difficult. This consideration became important when President Kennedy entered the final negotiations for the LIMITED TEST BAN TREATY of 1963. Since verification of underground tests in the event of decoupling would be difficult by national technical means, the United States negotiated only for a ban on atmospheric nuclear tests.

See also ATMOSPHERIC NUCLEAR TESTING; NATIONAL TECHNICAL MEANS; UNDERGROUND NUCLEAR TESTING.

2. Meaning in a strategic context. The term "decoupling" was also used to refer to the concept that the United States might have been willing to commit conventional and nuclear forces in Europe in the event of a war between the NORTH ATLANTIC TREATY ORGANIZATION and the nations of the WARSAW TREATY ORGANIZATION, but would not put the United States at risk by using strategic nuclear weapons against the Soviet Union. Under this scenario, the United States would be said to have "decoupled" its nuclear deterrent from European defense.

See also COUNTERVALUE STRATEGY; DETERRENCE.

Defense Atomic Support Agency (DASA)

The Defense Atomic Support Agency (DASA) was organized in 1959 to replace the ARMED FORCES SPECIAL WEAPONS PROJECT (AFSWP), which had inherited the military side of the United States atomic weapons program from the MANHATTAN ENGINEER DISTRICT. DASA continued as the military's agency for nuclear matters during the height of the early cold war, from 1959 through 1971. During this period, intense development of INTERCONTINENTAL BALLISTIC MISSILES required that the agency enhance its scientific capabilities.

DASA reported directly to the Joint Chiefs of Staff and to the secretary of defense, raising the level of the agency and its significance within the Department of Defense. The Joint Strategic Target Planning Staff began to consult with DASA experts, and DASA personnel provided advice to the Strategic Air Command as well as for the planning of an underground national military command center at Fort Ritchie, Maryland, in 1961.

DASA personnel were closely involved in the development and deployment of PERMISSIVE ACTION LINKS (PALs) and in the development of better protective igloos for the storage of nuclear weapons in the early 1960s. Following the 1962 atmospheric test series and the imposition of the 1963 LIMITED TEST BAN TREATY, which prohibited atmospheric tests, DASA reorganized to raise the level of expertise and to attract more highly trained and experienced scientists and engineers. DASA began to work closely with other scientists and engineers in the national laboratories and in academia, setting up peer-review processes to ensure unbiased and independent research into weapons effects.

A panel of scientists headed by William G. McMillan urged survivability tests for nuclear weapons, and DASA designed and fielded a series of such tests in the period 1964 to 1970. In particular, the tests examined whether the *Minuteman* missile could survive the intense radiation that might be expected during a full exchange of nuclear weapons. The vulnerability of such weapons to FRATRICIDE and to ELECTROMAGNETIC PULSE became of great interest as MULTIPLE INDEPENDENTLY TARGETED REENTRY VEHICLES came to characterize both U.S. and Soviet weapons. With the restriction on atmospheric testing, DASA worked out a number of procedures for conducting weapons effects tests in underground shafts and tunnels. DASA specialists developed line-of-sight tunnels in which radiation effects on weapons, materials, and weapons components could be tested independently of blast effects.

DASA managed the ARMED FORCES RADIOBIOLOGY RESEARCH INSTITUTE and established an information center that would ensure the collection and preservation of high altitude test data and, later, technical information related to all types of nuclear weapons effects. DASA also began to develop a variety of weapons effects SIMULATORS, which could develop intense bursts of radiation similar to those generated during a weapon detonation. Similarly, DASA operated a program of high-explosive tests of high magnitude (at a half kiloton or more) to measure the effect of airblast and ground shock without the necessity of an atmospheric test of a nuclear weapon. OPERATION SNOWBALL, in 1964, mounted a 500-ton high-explosive detonation at a site near Alberta, Canada. Subsequent tests at the Canadian site helped the air force assess and improve the survivability of the SILOS in which *Minuteman* missiles were mounted.

DASA specialists participated in the cleanup of the two major BROKEN ARROW incidents of the 1960s, the loss of hydrogen bombs at PALOMARES, Spain, in 1966, and at THULE, Greenland, in 1968.

DASA also continued with more routine stockpile management and surveillance, as had begun to develop under AFSWP. In the late 1960s, the military services obtained direct control over the weapons in the stockpile, and the number of DASA personnel engaged in stockpile stewardship declined.

DASA cooperated with the Atomic Energy Commission in many underground nuclear tests, including tests of potential ANTI-BALLISTIC MISSILE weapons, before the deployment of such weapons was canceled as a result of the 1972 SALT I treaty.

On March 29, 1971, Secretary of Defense David Packard announced the reorganization of DASA as the DEFENSE NUCLEAR AGENCY.

Defense Nuclear Agency (DNA)

The Defense Nuclear Agency(DNA) was established in March 1971 to replace the DEFENSE ATOMIC SUPPORT AGENCY (DASA) as the Defense Department agency to house the military's technical expertise regarding nuclear weapons. DNA continued to perform this function until it was replaced in 1996 by the DEFENSE SPECIAL WEAPONS AGENCY.

During its 25-year period, DNA managed the military's participation in nuclear weaponry. Moving from a period of detente into the second cold war of the late 1970s and early 1980s and then into the period of the collapse of the Soviet Union and the Warsaw Pact, the agency faced many drastic changes. In 1971, DNA became the sole agency concerned with nuclear weapons effects. Like DASA before it, DNA at first focused on means of testing radiation effects on objects while protecting them from blast and debris. Among other objects tested, DNA worked with high-altitude satellites and components to develop means of protecting them from the heavy radiation effects expected if a nuclear weapon were detonated at very high altitudes in a near-vacuum.

A classified and then unclassified volume of information on weapons effects was published to provide planning data for both U.S. and allied military officials and civil defense authorities. DNA continued the work on SIMULATORS that had begun under DASA and developed handheld calculators that could be used by battlefield officers to determine the effects of various types of nuclear weapons at various ranges.

As the United States deployed PERSHING II and ground-launched CRUISE MISSILES in the early 1980s to offset Soviet weapons emplacements in Eastern Europe, DNA provided support to NATO headquarters in Europe, both in hardening the facility against possible attack and in providing training and expertise in weapons storage and handling.

DNA became involved in two of the activities taken on by the Defense Department in response to the political pressures of the era; that is, after complaints by ATOMIC VETERANS that their exposure to earlier weapons tests had led to cases of cancer among them, the Defense Department established the NUCLEAR TEST PER-

SONNEL REVIEW, which was managed by DNA. In response to complaints by MARSHALL ISLANDERS that their homelands at BIKINI and ENEWETAK had been destroyed by earlier nuclear testing there, DNA led the effort to clean up and restore the islands. In particular, the effort to clean up Enewetak, by constructing a large dome to contain radioactive waste and to rebuild and replant the island chain to make it habitable, was ultimately successful, and the islands were returned to their original inhabitants in 1986.

DNA also conducted massive exercises to help various agencies coordinate their efforts in the event of a major nuclear accident. NUWAX-79 was the first of several such exercises held every two years, simulating an aircraft accident, short-lived radio-isotope scattering for realistic effects, and training and hazard assessment in nuclear weapons and nuclear materials recovery operations.

With its experience in weapons effects, DNA continued to be called upon to provide help in a number of related areas. These included increased hardening and protection of command centers and weapons silos; analysis of the effects of radiation on a wide variety of new electronic devices, computers, and electronic components; and effects of nuclear weapons on conventional munitions and communication equipment. The knowledge gained in studying nuclear weapons delivery systems and weapons effects proved useful in a number of non-nuclear areas, such as helping to support precision strike operations in the Persian Gulf War (1990–1991). When the Kuwaiti oil fields were set afire during that war by Iraqi forces, DNA studies of the smoke and dust effects of a major nuclear exchange became useful in providing computer models of the smoke effect and dispersal to be expected from the oil field fires.

Other uses of DNA expertise came with assistance to the UKRAINE and RUSSIA after the 1986 fire at CHERNOBYL and in the implementation of the terms of the 1987 INTERMEDIATE NUCLEAR FORCES (INF) treaty. Under both the INF and START I treaties, inspectors from the United States had to visit the Soviet Union and Warsaw Pact countries to verify the destruction of weapons. DNA personnel participated in these ARMS CONTROL verification activities.

In the early 1990s, DNA began to develop expertise in related areas, including other weapons of mass destruction, such as chemical and biological weapons, and in dealing with terrorist detonations of large, high-explosive weapons. DNA's computer modeling and technical experience provided a base for further work. Since DNA had a structure for funding research and the development of data bases through contracting with private firms and academia, it was relatively easy for the agency to move into new areas by developing new tasks and new contracts. As the COOPERATIVE THREAT REDUCTION effort between the United States and the former Soviet Union moved forward in the mid-1990s, DNA was able to provide experts, both military and contracted civilian specialists, to assist in the work.

In 1996, the Defense Nuclear Agency was reorganized as the DEFENSE SPECIAL WEAPONS AGENCY to recognize its expanded role in non-nuclear weapons of mass destruction and its activities in support of arms control and threat reduction.

Defense Threat Reduction Agency

Established October 1, 1998, the Defense Threat Reduction Agency (DTRA) replaced the existing DEFENSE SPECIAL WEAPONS AGENCY and combined the functions of several other agencies. The organization could trace its ancestry back to the MANHATTAN ENGINEER DISTRICT and to the postwar ARMED FORCES SPECIAL WEAPONS PROJECT and its successors. These prior agencies had consolidated the Defense Department's nuclear expertise, including staff concerned with conducting nuclear tests to determine weapons effects on military equipment. With the ending of nuclear testing in 1992, the agency had focused on developing SIMULATORS that could be used to test various types of weapons effects on materials, equipment, and other weapons. With the development of the Nunn-Lugar COOPERATIVE THREAT REDUCTION effort, military personnel with nuclear expertise increasingly began to participate in new sorts of efforts to assist the nations of the former Soviet Union and the former Warsaw Pact to dismantle their nuclear weapons.

With these new sorts of emphases, and to coordinate and consolidate the efforts of defense offices working on matters of nuclear weaponry, Secretary of Defense William S. Cohen established the new agency. The agency incorporated the work of the Defense Special Weapons Agency, the personnel and mission of the ON-SITE INSPECTION AGENCY, as well as elements of the staff of the Office of the Secretary of Defense, and the Defense Technology Security Administration. In its consolidated mission, DTRA was responsible for cooperative threat reduction programs, arms control treaty monitoring and on-site inspection, force protection, and nuclear biological and chemical defense and counterproliferation. The agency provided technical support on all matters related to weapons of mass destruction.

Dr. Jay Davis was appointed director of DTRA. In the agency's first fiscal year, beginning October 1, 1998, its projected budget was $1.9 billion.

Delayed Neutrons

Delayed neutrons are those neutrons emitted from the FISSION fragments within a few seconds or minutes after a controlled fission of ^{235}U occurs. The majority of the neutrons produced in a fission process are prompt neutrons; they are released within 1×10^{-13} seconds of the fission event. Less than 1% are delayed. Delayed neutrons are important considerations in the design and control of nuclear reactors. Many of the delayed neutron emitters are clustered just above the N = 50 and N = 82 closed nuclear shells. The following isotopes, with their half-lives shown in seconds (s), are among the most prominent delayed neutron emitters observed in the thermal neutron-induced fission of ^{235}U: 1.7s ^{135}Sb, 2.8s ^{94}Rb, 4.4s ^{09}Br, 24.5s ^{137}I, and 55.6s ^{07}Br.

See also SHELL MODEL OF THE NUCLEUS.

Delta Class Submarines

Upon completion in 1972, the Delta class Soviet nuclear ballistic missile submarine (SSBN) was the largest in the world. The Deltas became the backbone of the Soviet SSBN force over the next decade. Throughout its life, the Delta design was modified four times, keeping it in the forefront of the Soviet navy. Only one submarine class, the TYPHOON, could claim superiority in technology and design.

The original design of the Delta class (Delta 1) constituted a modification of the YANKEE class, fundamentally just an increase in size. The Delta class design differed from Yankee in several particulars. The Delta was longer, wider, and taller than Yankee class ships. The second major modification involved the weaponry. The Delta ships carried 12 SS-N-8 missiles, the first Soviet two-stage missile launched from a submarine.

The SS-N-8 was larger than the SS-N-4 and had an increased range. All other elements of the Yankee and Delta were the same, including the machinery inside the ships. They were built with the same propulsion systems and the same reactors. Other modifications to the basic Yankee/Delta design were made during the years Delta was under production.

Delta II modifications consisted of lengthening the ship and increasing its complement of missiles to 16. The missiles in Delta II were still SS-N-8s. The next generation of missile was first used in the Delta III class. Delta III submarines kept the same basic dimensions as Delta II, but they were armed with the new SS-N-18 missile. The SS-N-18 (*Stingray*) was the first Soviet MULTIPLE INDEPENDENTLY TARGETABLE REENTRY VEHICLE (MIRV) warhead. The MIRV allowed greater accuracy and flexibility in target planning.

After Delta III was introduced, the Soviet navy rolled out its first new submarine design since it began production of ballistic missile submarines. The Typhoon class was a truly modern ship, with modern design, weaponry, and technology. The Delta class ships were thrust into a secondary, yet important role.

Deltas continued to account for a large percentage of the Soviet SSBN fleet. Deltas also accounted for a major part of the Soviet seaborne missile arsenal. The mission for some of the earlier Deltas changed. A few units were moved onto forward positions to counter belligerent political moves by the United States. In perspective though, the advent of the Typhoon class had little if any effect on the Delta class as a whole. Typhoon even precipitated another modification to the Delta class, the Delta IV.

The Delta IV class was built concurrently with some of the Typhoon class and was called the poor man's Typhoon. Delta IV was armed by the most advanced submarine-launched missile to date, the SS-N-23 (*Skiff*). The *Skiff* was a three-stage missile with more accuracy than the SS-N-18 that armed most of the other members of Delta class. Delta IV was even bigger than the Yankee class and was armed with missiles more advanced than those on board the Typhoon. Nevertheless, the same design limitations that plagued early members of the Yankee/Delta class continued.

Creation of the Delta IV class did not reduce the Soviet navy's use of Yankee, its immediate predecessor in design. The Deltas were used, but a change in Soviet doctrine kept them in a protected bastion, meaning that the Yankees would be on the front line on patrol while the Deltas were held in reserve. In the event of conflict with the United States and the West, the Yankees would absorb the brunt of the first wave of attack, leaving the modern and more powerful Deltas IVs for a strategic response.

The Delta class was an important intermediary, leading the Soviet navy from an old design to a new one. An important fact about the Deltas was that they never outlived their usefulness. The Soviet navy always modified the design to meet current need and to incorporate technological improvements.

With the end of the Soviet Union, RUSSIA inherited the Soviet submarine fleet. By the mid and late 1990s, much of the fleet fell into disrepair as crews and maintenance personnel went unpaid.

Suggested Reading

Jan Breemer, *Soviet Submarines: Design Development and Tactics.* Coulsdon, Surrey, United Kingdom: Janes Information Group, 1989.

Dense-Pack Basing

Also referred to as closely spaced basing mode, dense-pack basing was a suggested means of defending INTER-CONTINENTAL BALLISTIC MISSILES (ICBMs), utilizing the concept of FRATRICIDE. In a dense-pack or close-basing mode, ICBM SILOS would be placed near each other, with each heavily hardened under concrete lids. If the silos were attacked in a first strike, the detonation of the first nuclear weapon intended to destroy a silo would create weapons effects, including dust, heat, and radiation that would be so intense that simultaneously arriving weapons would be either destroyed or rendered ineffective. The presumption was that the detonation of the first weapon over a silo would provide time for the attacked party to launch an effective second strike, thus enhancing the deterrent effect. Although discussed in the early 1980s as a basing mode for the PEACEKEEPER MX missile, the United States did not implement the concept.

Department of Energy (DOE)

In 1977, the ENERGY RESEARCH AND DEVELOPMENT AGENCY (ERDA), successor to the ATOMIC ENERGY COMMISSION (AEC), was replaced by the cabinet-level Department of Energy (DOE). The organization act was signed on August 4, 1977, and James R. SCHLESINGER was appointed first secretary of energy August 5. The new department was officially activated on October 1.

The department consolidated into one administration the nuclear research work that had proceeded under the AEC and ERDA, together with activities from other agencies and departments connected with energy matters. Work in petroleum and fossil fuels (primarily coal) was transferred from the Bureau of Mines, and various research projects in alternate energy sources such as solar energy, wind power, and geothermal power were consolidated in DOE.

One of the earliest crises faced by the new department was the accident at THREE MILE ISLAND on March 28, 1979. Although private nuclear power reactors were regulated by the NUCLEAR REGULATORY COMMISSION, DOE was concerned that the accident might have a negative effect on the promotion of nuclear power. DOE representatives and contractors helped track the radiation releases from the accident and participated in the investigation of the causes of the accident.

Like the AEC and ERDA, the new department worked closely with the military in the design and construction of nuclear weapons. DOE inherited the weapons manufacturing complex, including the weapons research laboratories at Los Alamos and Livermore California, and other research facilities at ARGONNE NATIONAL LABORATORY near Chicago, OAK RIDGE, Tennessee, and BROOKHAVEN, on Long Island, New York. Manufacturing facilities connected with the weapons program at Sandia (Albuquerque, N.Mex.), PANTEX (near Amarillo, Tex.), ROCKY FLATS (Colo.), Mound (Ind.), HANFORD (Wash.), SAVANNAH RIVER SITE (S.C.), and PINELLAS (Fla.) were all operated by contractors. The laboratories were usually operated by universities or consortiums of universities, while the manufacturing facilities were operated by industrial firms. DOE retained ownership while the contractors carried out the work. Such facilities were referred to as government-owned, contractor-operated enterprises or GOCOs. Under the GOCO arrangement, the department directly employed only some 50,000 staff members, but the contractors employed another 200,000 to build and test the weapons and conduct related nuclear research.

DOE had a complex role as it sought to support energy conservation through changing petroleum and electrical consumption habits of Americans, sponsored alternate energy sources and traditional fossil fuel source research, and continued the nuclear weapons program. Non-nuclear work included the administration of the Strategic Petroleum Reserve, support for new research facilities in the basic sciences, such as the

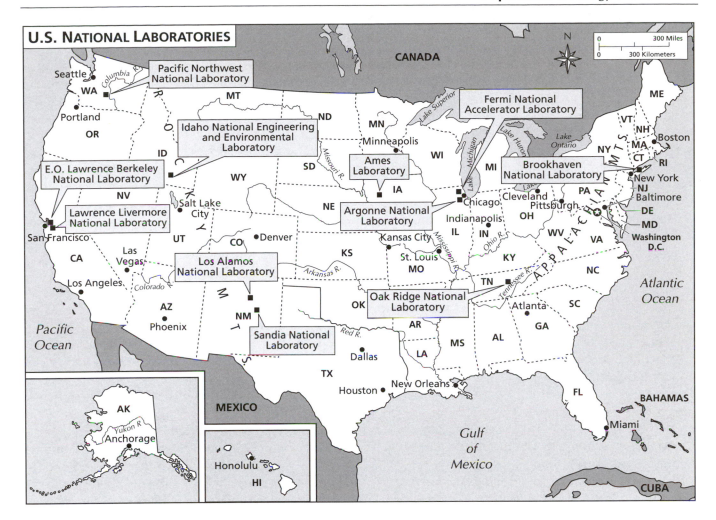

U.S. NATIONAL LABORATORIES

---

planned but terminated Super-Conducting Super-Collider, and research in a variety of areas, including biological sciences, supercomputers, and theoretical physics.

U.S. SECRETARIES OF ENERGY

SECRETARY	TERM OF OFFICE BEGAN
James R. SCHLESINGER	August 5, 1977
Charles W. DUNCAN, Jr.	August 24, 1979
James B. EDWARDS	January 23, 1981
Donald P. HODEL	November 11, 1982
John S. HERRINGTON	February 7, 1985
James WATKINS	March 9, 1989
Hazel O'LEARY	January 22, 1993
Francisco PEÑA	March 13, 1997
Bill RICHARDSON	August 18, 1998

Secretaries of energy were appointed by the president. The early secretaries generally served fairly short terms, averaging two or three years, but three later sec-

retaries, under Presidents Ronald REAGAN, George BUSH, and William CLINTON, served longer terms.

The department remained in charge of the development and testing of nuclear weapons. Working through liaison with the Department of Defense, the DOE would transmit to the laboratories and research facilities requirements for weapons improvements. In the period 1977 to 1993, Los Alamos, Livermore, and Sandia representatives would work with contractors at the NEVADA TEST SITE to test alternate weapons designs and modified weapons underground. After preliminary design and testing, the weapons components would be produced and assembled in the GOCO facilities and then transferred to the using military service for active stockpile storage. Following a moratorium imposed by President George H.W. Bush in 1992 and its extension and a Comprehensive Test Ban Treaty approved by President William Clinton in 1993 (but unratified by the end of the century), underground testing of nuclear weapons was terminated. In 1992, Secretary Watkins announced that for the first time since World War II, the United States was no longer building any atomic weapons.

With the INTERMEDIATE-RANGE NUCLEAR FORCES TREATY and the STRATEGIC ARMS LIMITATION TREATY, thousands of nuclear weapons were retired from the active stockpile. During this period of nuclear disarmament, DOE facilities, especially Pantex, that had been formerly devoted to the construction of weapons were turned over to the disassembly of weapons and the disposal of their components.

DOE remained in charge of the vast facilities, most of them dating back to the period 1942–1946, when they were built under the auspices of the MANHATTAN ENGINEER DISTRICT. Thus by the 1980s and 1990s, some of the facilities had developed serious environmental problems due to aging equipment, and to practices and systems created in an earlier era that did not conform to modern environmental standards. Radioactive contamination and chemical-release problems plagued DOE facilities, most notably at Rocky Flats, Colorado, Mound, Indiana, and Oak Ridge, Tennessee. Repeated exposés by news media of current and past practices, some of which put public safety or health at risk, drew the attention of the public to DOE and its contractors.

Secretaries Herrington, Watkins, and O'Leary, during the period from the mid-1980s through the mid-1990s, devoted much of their administrative effort to conducting cleanups, investigating accidents, and dealing with legal claims of injury or illness resulting from earlier nuclear practices. An abiding problem was the question of locating and constructing a facility for the long-term storage of nuclear waste materials generated from the federally owned nuclear weapons program.

Suggested Reading
Internet sites maintained by the Department of Energy.

Depleted Uranium
Depleted uranium (DU) is URANIUM containing less that the normal 0.71% ^{235}U. DU is the by-product of uranium enrichment processes, and it has found use as material for projectiles for armor-piercing munitions.

Detente
The change in American popular values in the late 1960s and early 1970s had an effect in producing what

the press came to call a period of detente or "cold war thaw." The arms control talks and arms limitation treaties over the period 1968 to 1979 showed that detente was a two-sided easing of tensions, with the Soviet Union reciprocating American gestures in offering concessions and negotiation. Great Britain joined in the spirit of negotiating nuclear arms settlements.

The NON-PROLIFERATION TREATY (NPT) was opened for signature on July 1, 1968, and it entered into force on March 5, 1970. This treaty prohibited announced nuclear weapons states from transferring or assisting in the acquisition or manufacture of nuclear weapons among non-nuclear weapon countries. The treaty also prohibited non-nuclear states from manufacturing or acquiring nuclear devices.

The United States and the Soviet Union agreed to two more treaties on September 30, 1971. One improved the existing hot-line telephone link between the two countries, with a satellite phone connection. The second treaty, an agreement to reduce the risk of nuclear war through accidents, required each party to give immediate notification of any unauthorized incident that might seem to be a detonation of a nuclear weapon. It required immediate notification of the detection of an unidentified object by either country's missile warning system. Both countries agreed to notify each other in case of any planned missile launches beyond their own borders in the direction of the other country.

Such relatively minor treaties helped reduce tensions. President Richard Nixon achieved a major step with the Strategic Arms Limitation Treaty and with the ANTI BALLISTIC MISSILES Treaty (ABM treaty) that limited permissible ABM systems to the defense of the capital of both the United States and the Soviet Union, together with a system at one other site housing ICBMs. Both treaties were signed in May 1972. By prohibiting ABM systems around population centers and by protecting weapons instead of people, the threat of population destruction would serve to deter each country from embarking on a nuclear first strike. The ABM treaty officially established the concept of "MUTUALLY ASSURED DESTRUCTION" as the policy of both the United States and the USSR. The treaty stipulated protection of the capital cities to allow leaders to make decisions in the unlikely event of an accidental war, with the hope that escalation might be limited.

A protocol added to the ABM treaty in 1974 went into force in 1976, reducing the sites to be protected by ABMs to one in each country. The United States developed one ABM system, turned it on and off immediately, and thereafter never deployed or maintained the system. The Soviets deployed a system around Moscow.

Part of the first SALT treaty limited the number of offensive missiles each country would mount for a period of five years as an interim measure while the two countries worked out further details. Several other treaties later in the 1970s continued to reflect the spirit of detente.

U.S.-SOVIET TREATIES AND AGREEMENTS, 1973–1979

Basic Principles of Negotiation	Signed June 1973
Agreement on Prevention Nuclear War	In Force June 1973
THRESHOLD TEST BAN TREATY	Signed July 1974
VLADIVOSTOK ACCORD	Signed Nov. 1974
PEACEFUL NUCLEAR EXPLOSIONS TREATY	Signed May 1976
SALT II	Signed June 1979

Underground testing was particularly governed by the Threshold Test Ban Treaty (TTBT) of 1974. That treaty prohibited underground nuclear tests over 150 Kt yield, and it specified the sites at which the tests would be conducted. For the U.S. test program, this limitation did not change policy, as the vast majority of weapons tests were well under the limit. The Defense Nuclear Agency took official responsibility for monitoring Soviet compliance with the treaty through national technical means, that is, through remote sensing of seismic shock and other nonintrusive detection systems.

Henry KISSINGER, who served as secretary of state and national security advisor under Presidents NIXON and FORD, was closely identified with the policy of detente and with the negotiation of most of the U.S.–Soviet treaties and agreements in the period 1972 to 1976.

President Jimmy CARTER was the first president since John KENNEDY to make a serious effort to negotiate a Comprehensive Test Ban (CTB). In two speeches, in January and March 1977, Carter announced that he would seek an end to all nuclear testing. Secretary of State Cyrus Vance and Soviet Foreign Minister Andrey Gromyko met in March 1977 and agreed to work toward a treaty that would involve Great Britain in a comprehensive treaty to ban all nuclear tests, includ-

ing those underground. Negotiations began in earnest in October 1977 at Geneva.

With the Soviet deployment in 1977 of SS-20 missiles, which possessed with the ability to target Western Europe accurately, and with the Soviet invasion of Afghanistan in 1978, the policy of the Carter administration toward the Soviet Union hardened. The negotiations toward a CTB broke down. The failure to ratify the SALT II treaty marked the end of the period of detente.

Suggested Reading

Julie Dahlitz, *Nuclear Arms Control*. London: George Allen and Unwin, 1983.

Patrick Glynn, *Closing Pandora's Box: Arms Races, Arms Control, and the History of the Cold War.* New York: Basic Books, 1992.

Deterministic Risk Assessment

Under deterministic risk assessment of reactor safety, a set of strict criteria for design and construction are established. Then the system is analyzed for behavior under condition of various types of failures. The most serious of these types of failures, such as a major feed water-pipe rupture, is called a design basis accident. Considering such serious design basis accidents, the total system is closely evaluated to determine if it is adequate to deal with that type of accident.

While this approach is clear and easy to understand, it does not deal with probabilities of minor accidents compounding into major problems. If several minor problems, which are not considered under the heading of design basis accidents, are fairly likely to occur, and if two or more such problems coincide to produce a catastrophe, deterministic risk assessment would not provide an estimate of how likely such an occurrence is. Since major accidents at WINDSCALE (Britain), THREE MILE ISLAND (U.S.), and CHERNOBYL (UKRAINE, U.S.S.R.) all developed from relatively minor errors of equipment and procedure, a method called PROBABILISTIC RISK ASSESSMENT was developed to predict the likelihood and to pinpoint such weaknesses.

Deterrence

Deterrence refers to the basic concept that a nation that possesses a devastating weapon system and demonstrates its ability to employ it will deter actual or potential enemies from using a similar weapon. The Soviet Union developed the nuclear weapon so rapidly, largely so as to deter the United States from employing a nuclear weapon against it.

As the cold war developed, deterrence became a cornerstone of U.S. nuclear weapons policy. A "credible" or believable deterrent had to include sufficient weapons and delivery systems to survive a surprise first strike by a potential enemy and to hit back with a second strike. Such SECOND-STRIKE CAPABILITY, to ensure a credible deterrent, required large numbers of weapons and led to the construction of thousands of weapons and eventually to the TRIAD concept of land-based missiles, submarine-launched missiles, and airplane-delivered nuclear bombs.

The principle of deterrence has also led to PROLIFERATION of nuclear weapons in other countries. China sought nuclear weapons to deter both the United States and the Soviet Union. India developed nuclear weapons partially to deter CHINA, and PAKISTAN followed to deter INDIA. A similar possibility of an arms race built on mutual deterrence led both ARGENTINA and BRAZIL to begin nuclear programs, later discontinued.

The principle of deterrence made ARMS CONTROL negotiations extremely difficult. No nuclear armed nation was willing to unilaterally disarm, as such an action would immediately place its nuclear-armed adversary or adversaries in a strongly advantaged position. Yet the logic of deterrence meant that to maintain a strong second-strike capability, each nuclear armed nation had to develop a massive stockpile. Thus, in 1949, the United States had a very small stockpile of nuclear weapons, estimated to be less than 50. However, with the Soviet development of nuclear weapons in that year, the United States immediately began to produce much larger numbers and newer types of weapons. The stockpile of both the United States and the Soviet Union increased in a nuclear arms race as each sought to develop a deterrent to the other, involving a second-strike capability.

Without a system of verification through on-site inspection, neither the United States nor the Soviet Union believed that it could maintain a sufficient deterrent to the other. The Soviets regarded inspection by air surveillance or on-site inspection as a ruse to permit espionage and gathering of target information. In effect, the principle of deterrence tended to prevent a workable arms-control agreement until both sides began to develop NATIONAL TECHNICAL MEANS, such as satellite observation, to ensure that the other complied with agreements.

Detroit Edison *See* FERMI REACTOR ACCIDENT.

Deuterium

An ISOTOPE of hydrogen, deuterium has the atomic number 1 and a mass of 2. Deuterium makes up about 0.015 % of natural hydrogen on this planet. Deuterium oxide (D_2O) is HEAVY WATER. Heavy water has been utilized as a moderator in reactors. Deuterium, mixed with tritium, has been used as a booster in FISSION weapons.

See also BOOSTED WEAPONS; HEAVY-WATER REACTORS.

Dollezhal', Nikolai Antonovich (1899–   )

Nikolai Antonovich Dollezhal' was a Ukrainian scientist crucial to the development of the nuclear weapon in the Soviet Union in the years immediately after World War II. His most important work corresponded to that of Enrico FERMI, which entailed designing and developing early nuclear reactors that could both demonstrate the harnessing of nuclear energy and produce PLUTONIUM for use in nuclear weapons. He designed most of the Soviet PRODUCTION REACTORS.

Dollezhal' was born in Omel'nik, in the UKRAINE in 1899. He graduated from the Moscow Higher Technical School in 1923. Beginning in World War II, Dollezhal' directed the All-Union Design, Planning and Scientific Research Institute of Chemical-Mechanical Engineering in Moscow. He was asked by the experimental physicist I. V. KURCHATOV to help with the design of a production reactor, after the successful experiments on December 25, 1946, with an experimental graphite-uranium reactor, F-1. The first reactor of his design was built at Kyshtym, near Chelyabinsk, the site designated CHELYABINSK-40. Many of the features incorporated in Dollezhal's design were similar to the reactors built at HANFORD, including the use of canned uranium slugs, pass-through cooling with water, and the use of graphite as moderator. For his work on the production reactor, he was awarded the high honor of Hero of Socialist Labor in 1949.

Through the 1940s and 1950s, Dollezhal' designed more production reactors. He assisted in addressing technical problems with the Soviet Union's first power reactor at Obninsk in 1954. He designed a dual-purpose production and power generating reactor opened in 1958 at TOMSK-7, known as the Siberian reactor.

Dose

Dose refers to the quantity of radiation to which an individual is exposed or which an individual may absorb. The former is the exposure dose; the latter is the absorbed dose.

Double-Key System

As the United States developed systems to prevent the accidental launch of a nuclear weapon, a double-key system was put aboard U.S. submarines that carried missiles with nuclear warheads. The system required that two separate officers would each have to use their own key to initiate a launch sequence, thus preventing an irrational or ill-informed judgment by a single officer. Since security aboard submarines was such that there was virtually no chance of seizure of the weapons by terrorists or enemy forces, naval nuclear weapons aboard ships did not have PERMISSIVE ACTION LINKS (PALs). In effect, the double-key system provided security against accidental or erroneous launch and substituted for the PAL approach utilized on land-based weapons.

See also SUBMARINE-LAUNCHED BALLISTIC MISSILES.

Dounreay

Dounreay is a site in Scotland, near Caithness on the North Sea, devoted to nuclear reactor development. The site was opened in 1955 for the development of fast reactors. Three were built at the site, including the Dounreay Fast Reactor, the Prototype Fast Reactor, and the Dounreay Materials Test Reactor. By the 1990s, all of these reactors were closed, and most of the work at the site consisted of decommissioning the Prototype Fast Reactor. The site is the main employer in the region, with some 1,200 people and about 30 million pounds per year payroll.

Over the years, the mission of Dounreay has changed from reactor research to a decommissioning

and nuclear environmental legacy site. In 1957, an intermediate level waste site was opened and operated until 1977, when it was closed after a chemical explosion. Sodium-contaminated materials reacted with water in the disposal shaft. In 1998, the British government accepted the advice of the United Kingdom Atomic Energy Authority to remove the waste from the storage shaft for treatment and safer long-term storage.

Ground adjacent to the 16th-century Dounreay Castle was decontaminated, and cleanup and freeing of ground for use proceeded in the 1990s. Since the 1950s, authorities conducted routine monitoring of RADIOACTIVITY in the area, up to 40 kilometers from the site.

Downwinders   *See* FALLOUT.

Dual-Track Strategy

The dual-track strategy originated during the Carter administration. It had been originally announced on December 12, 1979, in a communiqué issued following a special meeting of foreign and defense ministers of the NORTH ATLANTIC TREATY ORGANIZATION (NATO) held in Brussels. The NATO ministers referred to the same concept as the "double track" decision on Theater Nuclear Force Modernization and Arms Control. The strategy was amplified at a 1983 meeting of NATO held at Montebello, Nova Scotia, Canada, at which the organization agreed to simultaneously continue to modernize its weapons, draw down the total number of weapons, and continue to engage in arms-control negotiations.

When the foreign ministers announced their strategy, they pointed to the large and growing capability of the Warsaw Pact in the area of nuclear weapons. In particular, they pointed to the Soviet SS-20 missile, which was more mobile, more accurate, and had greater range than prior Soviet missiles. In addition, they drew attention to the introduction of the new Soviet Backfire bomber, which had better performance statistics than other Soviet aircraft. While the Soviet long-range theater nuclear forces had been quantitatively and qualitatively improving, the similar forces of the NATO powers had remained static. Continued growth of Soviet forces would undermine the stability achieved in intercontinental systems and cast doubt on the ability of NATO to deter the Soviets. Such growth would highlight the gap in NATO's available nuclear response to aggression.

Under the dual-track strategy, the United States supplied European NATO allies with 104 PERSHING II missiles and 464 ground-launched cruise missiles to offset the threat of Soviet SS-20 missiles installed in western Russia in 1977. The NATO foreign ministers stated that they had decided to pursue these parallel and complementary approaches in order to avert an arms race in Europe caused by the Soviet buildup while preserving the viability of NATO's strategy of DETERRENCE and defense.

Over the following years, the United States pursued arms control discussions with the Soviets toward achieving both a strategic weapons treaty and an INF Treaty. At first the proposed strategic weapons treaty was negotiated as "SALT III," but by the mid-1980s negotiators and the press referred to the proposed treaty as the Strategic Arms Reduction Treaty or "START." Discussions over both the START and INF treaties bogged down repeatedly over Soviet reluctance to allow on-site inspection and over the issues of how to count British and French weapons and whether to regard the GLCMs and Pershing missiles as strategic or theater weapons. Since both GLCMs and Pershings were based in Europe and had long range, they could reach strategic targets deep inside the Soviet Union. Thus from the Soviet point of view, these so-called intermediate range or long-range theater nuclear forces could target the same cities and military installations targeted by U.S.–based intercontinental ballistic missiles. Coupled with a tough negotiating stance maintained by Soviet and American diplomats in the period 1980 to 1985, these factors made it appear that the negotiating side of the dual-track strategy was not going to produce agreement.

However, with a new policy toward the West emerging under Soviet premier Mikhail Gorbachev in 1985–1986, negotiators finally made progress. Discussions focused on the "zero option," or complete removal of nuclear weapons from European soil.

The new missiles were deployed in the period 1983 to 1985, and the INF treaty was agreed to in 1987 and formally signed in 1988. When President George H. W. Bush's secretary of defense Frank Carlucci reported to Congress on the 1990–1991 defense budget, he provided an explanation of the dual-track strategy that had been in effect for more than a decade. Carlucci stated that the INTERMEDIATE NUCLEAR FORCE TREATY, which had gone into effect in June 1988, showed the wisdom of pressing for a ban while developing a system. He noted that simultaneously developing a weapon system and negotiating for a ban of the same system was "not contradictory, but complementary." The United States continued to fund major missile improvements while continuing to negotiate for START.

In one sense, the dual-track strategy announced in 1979 provided the underpinning for U.S. nuclear weapons strategy for the whole decade from 1979 through the end of the 1980s. GLCMs and Pershing II missiles deployed in Europe in the period 1983 to 1985 were among the first removed when the negotiating logjam broke in 1987–1988. The START I treaty, signed in July 1991, came only after the most massive buildup of intercontinental strategic weaponry in U.S. history.

See also: PRESIDENTIAL NUCLEAR INITIATIVE-91; START I; ZERO OPTION.

Suggested Reading

NATO Information Service, *The North Atlantic Treaty Organisation: Facts and Figures.* Brussels, Belgium: NATO Information Service, 1989.

Report of the Secretary of Defense, Frank C. Carlucci, to the Congress on the FY 1990/FY 1991 Biennial Budget. Washington, D.C.: USGPO, 1989, pp. 74–75.

Dulles, John Foster (1888–1959)   *U.S. secretary of state, 1953–1959*

John Foster Dulles served as secretary of state under President Dwight D. EISENHOWER. As the cold war between the United States and the U.S.S.R. reached a higher pitch during this period, Dulles announced the policy of MASSIVE RETALIATION, which implied that a nuclear weapon would be used against communist-supported conventional-force aggression.

Born in Washington, D.C., in 1888, Dulles was educated at Princeton, the University of Paris, and George Washington University. He served as a prominent attorney specializing in international law with the firm of Sullivan and Cromwell in New York. He was a senior U.S. advisor in negotiations to establish the founding of the United Nations, and he was largely responsible for drafting the peace treaty with Japan, signed in 1951. His strong ties to the Republican Party and his prominence in international relations made him a natural choice for secretary of state when the

John Foster Dulles and Allen Dulles. John Foster Dulles (right), U.S. Secretary of State during the Eisenhower administration, meets with his brother, Allen Dulles, director of the Central Intelligence Agency. (Library of Congress)

Republicans took over the national administration after a 20-year period of Democratic Party rule.

Allen Dulles, the brother of John Foster Dulles, had served in the Office of Strategic Services in World War II, and he was director of the Central Intelligence Agency during the Eisenhower administration. The presence of the two brothers in high positions in the government struck some critics as putting excessive power in the hands of a single family.

Although John Foster Dulles was a strong advocate of going beyond the containment policy to achieve a reduction in the size of the Soviet sphere of influence, he was unable to accomplish such a rollback during his tenure in office.

In a speech on January 4, 1954, he reiterated the principle that the United States might choose to respond to communist-led aggression by means of conventional forces with any means at its disposal. This broad hint that the United States was prepared to use nuclear weapons to offset aggression by army or guerrilla units became known as the doctrine of massive retaliation. By 1956, Dulles recognized that Soviet nuclear armaments and means of delivering them to the United States were increasing to a point at which the United States could no longer rely on massive retaliation. The development of long-range missiles, as demonstrated by the Soviet launch of the artificial satellite SPUTNIK in 1957, brought the doctrine of massive retaliation under review. Dulles began to advocate some form of nuclear disarmament, arranged through the United Nations.

Dulles supported the nuclear test moratorium in discussions with Eisenhower and other advisors. However, he did not support a comprehensive test ban, as his experts advised him that it would be too difficult to distinguish underground nuclear tests from earthquakes. He supported the concept of a limited test ban that would prohibit atmospheric nuclear tests while allowing underground testing to continue. A treaty based on that position was finally negotiated during the Kennedy administration. Even though Dulles shifted his position during the last years of his life, he remained associated with the doctrine of massive retaliation in the public eye.

See also ATMOSPHERIC NUCLEAR TESTING; DECOUPLING; LIMITED TEST BAN TREATY.

Suggested Reading

John Foster Dulles, "Policy for Security and Peace," *Foreign Affairs* 36 (April 1954).

Richard Hewlett and Jack Holl, *Atoms for Peace and War, 1953–1961: Eisenhower and the Atomic Energy Commission.* Berkeley: University of California Press, 1989.

Duncan, Charles (1926–) *American governmental administrator who served as secretary of energy 1979–1981*

Charles Duncan was the second secretary of energy, succeeding James SCHLESINGER on August 24, 1979. President Jimmy CARTER appointed Duncan five months after the THREE MILE ISLAND accident.

During Duncan's administration, the Department of Energy (DOE) continued to advance non-nuclear alternate energy sources and to stress energy conservation. For example, in October 1979, DOE selected the Bonneville Power Administration for a two-year demonstration project using large-scale wind turbines that would generate power to be sold on the commercial power grid. The department also sponsored projects to reduce home energy bills through conservation, developed a stand-by gasoline rationing plan, and undertook research into the conversion of coal into synthetic liquid fuel.

In April 1980, the DOE participated actively in the celebration of "Earth Day," stressing the promotion of environmental, conservation, and non-nuclear energy sources. In June, the department set aside 13,000 acres at its OAK RIDGE facility as a National Environmental Park. A series of six bills developed at the department were signed into law in June 1980. They dealt with synthetic fuels, biomass and alcohol fuels, renewable energy resources, solar energy, geothermal, and ocean-thermal sources of power. The department assisted in securing international cooperation in funding work on synthetic fuels at a new plant in West Virginia.

Other energy initiatives during Duncan's administration included support for a major solar power plant in California and heightened support for magnetic fusion energy technologies. The shift away from the department's emphasis on nuclear power that had begun during the administration of James Schlesinger continued under Duncan.

On the weapons side, however, the department responded to a shift in policy toward increased weapons production and an increase in the size of the nuclear stockpile. As the United States undertook to match the Soviet buildup of missiles in Eastern Europe, the department's increased production of strategic nuclear materials and new weapons signaled the end of nuclear detente and the beginning of the second cold war.

In July 1980, a DOE–Department of Defense Long-Range Resource Planning Group concluded that one or two new production reactors would be required by the year 2000, and it recommended moving ahead immediately to undertake construction of a new production reactor. Meanwhile, the department advocated increased PLUTONIUM production, requesting and receiving funds from Congress to restart PRODUCTION REACTORS that had been closed during the administration of President Lyndon JOHNSON more than a decade previously.

With the end of the Carter administration in January 1981, Duncan's term as secretary of energy also came to an end. His successor, appointed by President Ronald REAGAN, was James B. Edwards.

See also CARTER, JIMMY; PRODUCTION REACTORS.

Edwards, James B. (1927–) *American dentist who served as secretary of energy from 1981 to 1982*
President Ronald REAGAN appointed James B. Edwards as secretary of energy, and Edwards was sworn in on January 23, 1981. During the presidential campaign, Reagan had suggested that he would eliminate the DEPARTMENT OF ENERGY (DOE) if elected. Popular concerns with energy shortages and conservative criticism of the department for its emphasis on environmental issues contributed to support for this position. Therefore, observers assumed that the main responsibility of secretary Edwards would be to oversee the dismantling of the department. That impression was supported among critics, who doubted Edwards's qualifications as a former dentist to take on the operation of the department with its many technical, scientific, and industrial functions. In May 1982, Reagan proposed legislation that would have transferred most of the responsibilities of DOE to the Department of Commerce.

However, as President Reagan continued the nuclear weapons buildup initiated during the Carter administration, it soon became clear that the department's massive weapons research and production facilities were essential to national defense and to the president's program. The plan to close or dismantle the department was quietly abandoned.

Undersecretary Edwards, several energy policies of the prior administration were reversed. Price controls on oil were lifted in January 1981, a ban on reprocessing nuclear fuel was removed, and a plan for the establishment of a facility for the storage of high-level radioactive waste was announced. Secretary Edwards was replaced by Donald P. HODEL on November 11, 1982.

Einstein, Albert (1879–1955) *German-American physicist internationally known for his special theory of relativity published in 1905 and his general theory of relativity published in 1915*
Einstein was born in 1879 in Ulm in the province of Württemberg in Germany. He lived in Munich and Italy before moving to Switzerland, where he served as an inspector of patents. He earned a doctorate in physics at Zurich and taught physics there and in Prague in the period 1909 to 1913. He returned to Germany and served as the director of the Kaiser Wilhelm Institute for Physics in Berlin. He received the NOBEL PRIZE for physics in 1921.

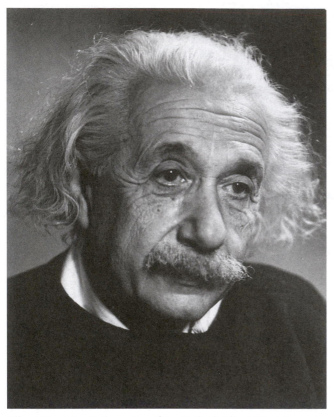

Albert Einstein. At the urging of Leo Szilard, Albert Einstein wrote to President Franklin Roosevelt in October 1939 suggesting that the discovery of nuclear fission could lead to a nuclear weapon. The Einstein letter prompted Roosevelt to initiate the development of the atomic bomb. (Library of Congress)

When the Nazis took power in Germany in 1933, he lost his position and emigrated to the United States. During the 1930s, he was widely regarded, along with Niels BOHR, as the most brilliant elder scientist in the field of theoretical physics. Due to his fame, rather than to any special work in the burgeoning nuclear field in the 1930s, he was approached in 1939 by Hungarian physicist Leo SZILARD to warn president Franklin ROOSEVELT of the danger of a German development of a nuclear weapon. In October 1939, Einstein sent a letter, drafted by Szilard, warning the president that the Germans might use the recent discovery of nuclear fission to produce a bomb of terrible power. It was Einstein's letter that prompted Roosevelt to begin federal assistance to nuclear research, which eventually led to the U.S. weapon program in the MANHATTAN ENGINEER DISTRICT.

Einstein continued his life at Princeton, New Jersey, and he did not join in the Manhattan Project. He died in 1955.

Eisenhower, Dwight David (1890–1969)   *the 34th president of the United States (1953–1961)*

During Eisenhower's administration, the nuclear arms race advanced, with both the United States and the Soviet Union increasing their nuclear arsenals and developing thermonuclear weapons. At the same time, Eisenhower worked toward arms control and advocated use of the advances of nuclear physics for international development known as the ATOMS FOR PEACE plan.

Born in Denison, Texas, on October 14, 1890, Eisenhower graduated from West Point in 1915. He served in various staff and command posts in the U.S. Army, and during World War II he became commander in chief of the combined U.S. and British forces in the invasion of North Africa in November 1942. In December 1943, he became commander of the Allied Expeditionary Force that attacked German forces through Normandy. After the war he served as president of Columbia University and as chair of the Joint Chiefs of Staff between 1949 and 1950. He resigned from the army in 1952 to run for the presidency as a Republican. He was elected by a wide margin in 1952 and reelected in 1956. He was the only president between Franklin ROOSEVELT (1933–1945) and Ronald REAGAN (1981–1989) to serve two full terms.

During Eisenhower's administration, the security clearance of J. Robert OPPENHEIMER was revoked in a 1954 hearing that later was viewed by many as a victory of hysterical anti-communism. Eisenhower himself refrained from interfering in the hearing, accepting the judgment of advisors that Oppenheimer represented a security risk. The ATOMIC ENERGY COMMISSION sustained the denial of the clearance.

On December 8, 1953, Eisenhower spoke before the General Assembly of the United Nations, declaring that the United States would work to turn "the miraculous inventiveness of man" to life, not to death. The address, known as the "Atoms for Peace" speech, established a policy that later led to the creation of the International Atomic Energy Agency.

Meanwhile, in the United States, the Atomic Energy Commission (AEC) moved ahead with its expansion of production facilities and continued the development of the hydrogen bomb. The AEC also continued its vigorous program of atmospheric testing of weapons during the Eisenhower administration. During the period 1953 to 1960, the United States conducted 100 announced tests at the NEVADA TEST SITE and a further 62 tests at locations in the Pacific and Atlantic Oceans.

Five heavy-water moderated production reactors were opened at Savannah River, South Carolina, together with two new graphite-moderated reactors, KE and KW, at HANFORD. By 1955, the United States had 14 production reactors in operation, producing both plutonium and tritium for its nuclear arsenal. Other weapons complex facilities opened during the Eisenhower administration included the uranium processing plant at Fernald, Ohio (1953), the PUREX chemical separation plant at Hanford (1956), and a weapons parts production facility at Pinellas, Florida (1957). During Eisenhower's administration, the size of the nuclear weapon stockpile increased vastly in both total number of weapons and total yield of the weapons.

Both the United States and the Soviet Union entered into a voluntary moratorium on atmospheric testing of nuclear weapons in 1958, but the Soviet Union broke the moratorium with new testing in 1960 at NOVAYA ZEMLYA. The United States responded with a new series of tests while continuing to negotiate for a ban on nuclear weapons testing in the atmosphere.

During Eisenhower's administration, the first nuclear-powered submarine, NAUTILUS, was launched in 1954, and the United States continued the development of nuclear-powered submarines.

Eisenhower's emphasis on Atoms for Peace was not entirely without results, however. Under its chairman Lewis Strauss, the Atomic Energy Commission fostered work on nuclear power, developing the first U.S. power reactor at SHIPPINGPORT in 1957 under the leadership of Hyman RICKOVER, who also headed the nuclear submarine project. During the Eisenhower administration about 14 power reactors were constructed, some experimental. Most of the reactors were of the pressurized water type, following the ship propulsion model or the boiling water variety that was first designed by the ARGONNE NATIONAL LABORATORY outside of Chicago and then developed by the Bettis and Knolls atomic power laboratories. By the end of Eisenhower's administration, American utility companies were actively ordering new reactors, while reactor manufacturers hoped to expand into foreign markets.

Eisenhower's commitment to atomic energy for both peace and weapons of war marked a major departure or turning point in American nuclear history. Before his administration, the atomic weapon program had floundered and little work was done to convert nuclear energy to the production of electricity. When he took office in 1953, work was just beginning on the

Eisenhower and Truman. Shortly after the 1952 presidential elections, Harry S. Truman and Dwight D. Eisenhower confer about national security issues. (Library of Congress)

development of nuclear submarines and the thermonuclear weapon. When he left office in 1961, the United States had a small and growing fleet of nuclear-propelled submarines, a much improved nuclear materials production capacity with the operation of new reactors at Savannah River, and a growing arsenal of thermonuclear weapons. In addition, nuclear power was being delivered onto the U.S. commercial network, and American companies were beginning to develop power reactors for export abroad.

At the Geneva Summit meeting held on July 21, 1955, Eisenhower made his "Open Skies" proposal. Under this concept, the United States and the Soviet Union would allow overflights of their territories so that the extent of their nuclear weapon delivery systems, such as bombers and missile SILOS, would no longer be secret. Under the proposal, the two nations would exchange blueprints of military facilities as well as make practical arrangements for aerial photography and reconnaissance. Premier Khrushchev rejected the Open Skies idea as little more than a guise for espionage or a propaganda ploy.

Both the Open Skies proposal and the Atoms for Peace plan were readily understood and appeared simple. But in order to implement either idea, many complex technical details would have had to be worked out. Over the next few years, the United States did establish a system of exporting nuclear technology, but the means of prohibiting its use for weapons programs involved complex systems of safeguards, inspections, and export controls. A proposal similar to Eisenhower's Open Skies was finally adopted by President George H.W. BUSH and President Yeltsin of Russia in 1991, in which each nation could overfly the other to count the number of bomber aircraft destroyed, the number of nuclear submarines with missile launchers, and the number of missiles in opened silos.

The cold war moved into a new phase of intensity during the Eisenhower administration. With the Soviet detonation of thermonuclear weapons and with their launch of an earth-orbiting satellite, *SPUTNIK*, in 1957, nuclear strategists believed the United States was vulnerable to attack. When the United States conducted clandestine overflights of the Soviet Union with the U-2 aircraft, in an attempt to determine the extent of Soviet weapons delivery capability, the Soviets responded by shooting down one of the flights on May 1, 1960, and putting the pilot on trial for espionage. Following that incident, the United States stopped its overflights.

Thus, in some regards, 1960 represented the beginning of an intensified phase of the cold war. With no reconnaissance by aircraft, and before the deployment by the United States of satellites that could take photographs, the United States had no direct knowledge of the number or capability of Soviet intercontinental ballistic missiles (ICBMs). John F. KENNEDY ran against Eisenhower's vice president Richard NIXON in the presidential election of 1960 and Kennedy used the issue of a supposed "missile gap" as a campaign charge against the Eisenhower administration. That issue was later proven to be nonexistent, as the Soviets had no real lead over the United States in the capability to deliver nuclear weaponry.

One of the ironies of nuclear history is that despite Eisenhower's well-meaning and genuine attempt to establish nuclear energy as a positive force for peace and for the advancement of humanity, events in the competition between the United States and the Soviet Union for supremacy in atomic weapons and in means to deliver them plunged the two nations into an intense period of hostile, armed competition. The arms race with both thermonuclear weapons and ICBMs that lasted until the late 1980s can be traced to the Eisenhower years.

After his retirement, Eisenhower resided at his farm near Gettysburg, Pennsylvania. He died on March 28, 1969.

See also ATMOSPHERIC NUCLEAR TESTING; NUCLEAR PROPULSION; POWER REACTORS, U.S.; PRODUCTION REACTORS.

Suggested Reading
Richard Hewlett and Jack Holl, *Atoms for Peace and War, 1953–1961: Eisenhower and the Atomic Energy Commission.* Berkeley: University of California Press, 1989.

Electromagnetic Pulse (EMP)

Electromagnetic pulse (EMP) is an effect of nuclear weapons that began to receive considerable attention in the 1960s and later. One of the last ATMOSPHERIC NUCLEAR TESTS conducted by the United States prior to the agreement in the LIMITED TEST BAN TREATY (LTBT) of 1962 to halt tests above ground, in the atmosphere, or in outer space was the test called STARFISH PRIME, conducted in the South Pacific near Johnston Island. The last tests in the DOMINIC series of atmospheric tests in 1962 showed that when nuclear weapons detonated at extremely high altitudes, the released energy took the form of an intense radiation burst.

The electromagnetic pulse was like a giant lightning bolt, caused by the ionization of the atmosphere by gamma rays emitted during the nuclear explosion. The accelerating electrons are deflected when they hit the earth's magnetic field and produce a series of pulses of electromagnetic energy. In general, the higher the burst, the greater the intensity of the pulse. Although not hazardous to humans, the pulses cripple electrical and electronic equipment. Exposed cable and wiring will provide a connection to transport the pulse to susceptible equipment, including transistors and printed circuits.

The EMP is capable of damaging electronic devices over thousands of square miles. The STARFISH PRIME explosion in the DOMINIC series, exploded more than 800 miles from Hawaii, appeared to have had the effect of putting the streetlight system of Honolulu out of commission and to have interfered with radio communications for a short period throughout the South Pacific. Without the opportunity to conduct further high-altitude tests because of the LTBT, the nuclear weapons program faced the challenge of how to measure the full dimensions of EMP effects and other radiation effects.

In planning possible nuclear warfare scenarios, weapons experts soon came to realize that the detonation of a large nuclear weapon high over the atmosphere could virtually close down many electronic systems over thousands of square miles. Thus a single burst could destroy computers, computer chip–regulated automobile and aircraft engines, and electronic communication systems, including telephone, radio, and television in a targeted country. "Hardening" U.S. weapons, communication systems, and artificial satellites against both X-ray and EMP damaging effects became high priorities in the 1970s and later.

The DEFENSE ATOMIC SUPPORT AGENCY and its successor military agencies concerned with weapons effects on military equipment developed a series of means of testing EMP in both underground tests, by evacuating the air from line-of-sight vertical shafts or horizontal tubes. A burst of EMP and other radiation through the near-vacuum would simulate the effect of a high-altitude burst. Later, weapons effects SIMULATORS were designed to generate radiation bursts that could be used to evaluate the effect of radiation on test materials.

High-Altitude EMP or HEMP remained a concern into the 1990s. In investigating various scenarios in which the United States might be attacked by a nation or group with access to only a few nuclear weapons, planners recognized that a single weapon, detonated at sufficient altitude, could effectively cause widespread havoc. Since modern internal-combustion engines incorporated computer chips in their carburetor and ignition systems, HEMP would cause aircraft crashes or collisions and automobile and rail accidents. Similarly EMP would shut down vast numbers of computers in many applications. Hardening such civilian systems became a priority in planning civil defense against terrorist and state-supported terrorist attacks.

Energy Research and Development Administration (ERDA)

In 1975, the Energy Research and Development Administration (ERDA) replaced the ATOMIC ENERGY COMMISSION (AEC) in its research and production capacity. In the early 1970s, concern that the Atomic Energy Commission was responsible for both promoting nuclear energy and regulating it led Congress to separate the functions. The last chair of the AEC, Dr. Dixy Lee Ray, was an advocate of the separation of the functions.

President Richard NIXON had been an advocate of creating a cabinet-level department to take over energy-related matters. However, with the scandal surrounding the Watergate break-in that weakened his presidency in 1973–1974 and his resignation in August 1974, he was incapable of promoting such a major reorganization measure. The creation of ERDA during the administration of Gerald FORD was seen as partly meeting the objective of consolidating energy matters in a single agency.

By a reorganization act passed in October 1974, the Nuclear Regulatory Commission was established to conduct the regulatory functions and ERDA was created to carry on the research and development functions. ERDA took over the weapons laboratories and the weapons production facilities that had been established under the AEC. ERDA was administered by Robert C. Seamans.

ERDA was reorganized in 1977 into the DEPARTMENT OF ENERGY (DOE) absorbing a number of energy-related activities from other independent agencies and commissions within the government. The petroleum and coal energy research activities of the Bureau of Mines as well as the Solar Research Institute were merged into the new cabinet-level department, along with the Federal Energy Administration. James SCHLESINGER, former director of the Central Intelligence Agency, was named as the first secretary of energy.

Enewetak

Enewetak is an atoll, consisting of a ring of small islands in the western Marshall Islands. The atoll had been overrun by troops during World War II. The native people of Enewetak, the dri-Enewetak and dri-

CHRONOLOGY OF ERDA EVENTS

DATE	ACT	RESULT
October 11, 1974	Energy Reorganization Act	Abolishes AEC, Creates ERDA and NRC
January 19, 1975	ERDA activated	Robert Seamans appointed administrator
August 4, 1977	Department of Energy Act	Abolishes ERDA; Federal Energy Admin. shifts functions to DOE
October 1, 1977	DOE activated	James Schlesinger named secretary of energy

Enewetak. The United States tested 43 nuclear devices at Enewetak island, including the 1951 Ivy-Mike shot. (Library of Congress)

Engebi, were evacuated during the first Pacific nuclear tests of the OPERATION CROSSROADS series at BIKINI in 1946. The ATOMIC ENERGY COMMISSION established the Enewetak Proving Ground in 1947.

After a brief return following the CROSSROADS tests, the islanders were again evacuated to Ujelang in December 1947, where they remained for over 30 years. Ujelang is smaller than Enewetak, and 136 evacuees and their descendants wanted to return to their homeland.

Over the decade 1948 to 1958, the United States detonated 43 nuclear and thermonuclear devices on the islands of the Enewetak Atoll, in the atoll lagoon, on barges, on towers, and in the craters left by prior tests. Of the 43 nuclear and thermonuclear detonations at Enewetak, more than half were in the 1958 HARDTACK series:

ENEWETAK TESTS

YEAR	SERIES	NUMBER OF SHOTS
1948	OPERATION SANDSTONE	3
1951	OPERATION GREENHOUSE	4
1951	Operation IVY	2
1954	OPERATION CASTLE	1
1956	OPERATION REDWING	11
1958	OPERATION HARDTACK	22
	total	43

As a result of the tests, two islands, Elugelab and Lidibut, completely vanished along with most of two others, Bokaidrikdrik and Eleleron. Large craters marked the spots of the destroyed islands, and many craters remained on Runit and Boken islands. The surface-emplaced Cactus shot of May 6, 1958, in the HARDTACK series created a wide crater at the northern tip of Runit island, into which the sea flowed. Other atoll damage included leveling the ground and destruction of coconut palms and other vegetation. Construction had further marred the landscape. Semipermanent buildings, tons of concrete, metal debris, miles of cable, and abandoned and rusting landing craft littered the islands. Even on island areas with slight radiological damage, ruined habitat and waste scarred the few livable acres of land.

During a 1971 review of the agreement between the Department of Defense (DOD) and the Department of the Interior, the DOD agreed to end the use of Enewetak and recognized a moral obligation to restore the atoll to a more habitable condition.

Planning, funding, and the actual cleanup and disposal operation took a total of seven years. President Gerald FORD signed the final bill approving the cleanup, Public Law 94–367, on July 16, 1976. The expenditure of $18.1 million appropriated by Congress represented less than 25% of the total estimated expenses, including labor and materials provided by military services and government agencies.

Cleanup operations on the atoll began in early 1977 and continued over the next three years. The DEFENSE NUCLEAR AGENCY, charged with the cleanup, supervised the entombment or burial of radioactive waste at the atoll. Under this plan, radiological debris was taken to the large crater on Runit caused by the Cactus shot of the HARDTACK Series. Workers mixed the debris and contaminated soil with concrete, and they pumped the mix into the crater. Then crews covered the mass with a thick concrete dome. Nonradiological debris was sold as scrap or dumped in the lagoon in deepwater sites.

The project involved not only cleanup but also extensive preparation of home sites, agricultural plantings, and installation of roads, utilities, and common areas. Churches, meeting halls, and other community use buildings were converted from barracks to breeze-cooled structures.

With the completion of the job, the military returned the island to the Enewetak people, now numbering about 400, in a ceremony on April 8, 1980. The full population returned from Ujelang by several trips aboard the Marshall Island government ship *Micro Pilot* in early October 1980.

The islanders declared some contaminated islands off-limits entirely. Their settlements on Medren and Enewetak islands, declared radiation-safe, became permanent residences, and those islands most targeted during the testing were simply not resettled.

The MARSHALL ISLANDERS sued in U.S. federal courts for compensation but eventually accepted a negotiated compact that included compensation for both physical damage to their environment and the risk to their health.

See also ATMOSPHERIC NUCLEAR TESTING.

Enhanced Radiation (ER) Weapon

Enhanced Radiation (ER) weapons are nuclear weapons designed to emit most of their energy in the form of radiation rather than blast or heat. Thus, they would lead to lethal doses of radiation to concentrations of enemy forces without destroying structures or equipment. Development of ER weapons, popularly known as "the neutron bomb," was canceled under the administration of Jimmy CARTER but was revived during the Ronald REAGAN administration.

Enola Gay

The *Enola Gay* was the name of the B-29 aircraft that carried the atomic bomb dropped on HIROSHIMA on August 6, 1945. The aircraft was manufactured by Boeing Aircraft Company and assembled by the Glenn L. Martin Company of Omaha, Nebraska. It was propelled by four Wright cyclone engines, each rated at 2,200 horsepower. The plane had a wingspan of 141 feet, 3 inches. Its maximum speed was 360 miles per hour at 25,000 feet.

The aircraft that were designated part of the atomic bombing raids on Japan had been assigned to a specially trained air force unit, the 509th Composite Group, commanded by Lieutenant Colonel Paul TIBBETS. After training at Wendover Army Air Field, in Utah, the 509th Composite Group moved piecemeal to Tinian Island in the Marshall Islands. The *Enola Gay* arrived at North Field, Tinian, on July 2, 1945.

The *Enola Gay* was named after the mother of Tibbets, who piloted the plane on its Hiroshima mission. He decided on the name in honor of his mother who had always assured him that he would survive the war as a pilot. Tibbets had the name painted on the fuselage the day before the bombing mission.

The atomic bombs were too large to be loaded into the aircraft from the surface of the runway, and specially built pits had to be dug by navy civilian battalion workers (Seabees) for loading the weapons. The aircraft themselves had to be modified to accept Fat Man, the large plutonium-loaded weapon destined for Nagasaki.

The Little Boy uranium bomb intended for Hiroshima weighed four tons. With that bomb loaded, the *Enola Gay* weighed 65 tons, including 70,000 gallons of fuel, or about 35 tons empty. Final assembly of the weapon was conducted inside the airplane after it lifted off on August 6, 1945, under Operations Order #35. Once the airplane was in the air, Tibbets informed the members of the crew that the weapon they carried was an atomic bomb. The *Enola Gay* made rendezvous with two escort planes near Iwo Jima. After dropping the bomb over the target city, Tibbets turned the plane and flew away. When the shock wave from the blast reached the aircraft, they were over 11 miles from the detonation, but the plane bounced with the force of the explosion. The plane turned again, to survey the city under a pall of smoke and fire, and then flew back to Tinian Island safely, the mission of the *Enola Gay* completed.

On August 9, 1945, another pilot, George Marquardt, flew the *Enola Gay* as a weather observation aircraft to Kokura, Japan, in support of the mission to bomb NAGASAKI. In November 1945, the plane was flown back to the United States.

The aircraft was utilized as part of Task Force T5, for OPERATION CROSSROADS, the nuclear tests at BIKINI in 1946. In 1949, Tibbets flew the aircraft from Arizona to O'Hare Airport (then known as Park Ridge, Illinois), outside of Chicago, where it was accepted by the Smithsonian Institution for restoration and eventual display. In 1953, the plane was flown to Andrews Air Force Base in Maryland, and then in 1960 it was disassembled and moved to the Smithsonian's Garber facility for preservation and restoration of aircraft in Suitland, Maryland.

The plane became controversial in 1994–1995, when the Smithsonian Museum planned a display centered around the aircraft at the National Air and Space Museum in Washington, D.C. Although the aircraft *Bock's Car,* which had carried the bomb dropped on Nagasaki, had been displayed without controversy for years at the United States Air Force Museum in Dayton, Ohio, the display that was planned around part of the *Enola Gay* fuselage became a national issue.

Instead of focusing only on the aircraft and its mission in dropping the atomic bomb, the museum planned an exhibit that would deal with the larger issue of the end of World War II and the relationship of the bombing of Hiroshima to the Japanese surrender. Historians had written a good deal about TRUMAN'S DECISION to drop the nuclear weapon on Japan and whether that action had been needed or was decisive in forcing the surrender of the Japanese.

As the plans for the exhibit developed, veteran's groups heard of the proposal and protested against the idea of presenting the moral, ethical, and psychological questions surrounding the decision to drop the weapon. After an intense barrage of criticism from some veterans' organizations, the media, and members of Congress, the officials at the museum altered the script to present simply the aircraft and the role of the atomic weapon in ending the war, without reviewing the scholarly debate over the decision itself or any of the larger issues surrounding the decision.

The forward section of the *Enola Gay* was on exhibit at the Smithsonian from June 28, 1995, through May 18, 1998, when the exhibit was closed and the pieces returned to the Paul Garber Preservation, Restoration and Storage Facility in Suitland, Maryland.

Suggested Reading

Robert Jay Lifton and Greg Mitchell, *Hiroshima in America: A Half Century of Denial.* New York: Avon, 1996.

Richard Rhodes, *The Making of the Atomic Bomb.* New York: Simon and Schuster, 1986.

Enriched Uranium

Enriched uranium is uranium the ^{235}U contents of which have been augmented to increase the ^{235}U presence to more than the naturally occurring 0.71%. Such enriched uranium is more likely to undergo a CHAIN REACTION. Enrichment is on the order of 3.5 to 20% for uranium used as fuel in nuclear reactors. In weapons-grade uranium, the ^{235}U enrichment is greater than 90%, and such material is called highly enriched uranium (HEU).

Epidemiological Study

In the field of health physics, which is defined as the study of the effects of radiation and radiation hazard on humans, epidemiological studies have become a method of determining whether there is a correlation between a particular hazard and ill-effects in a designated population. Epidemiological study is a study of the correlation between the radiation exposure of a particular group or population and selected illnesses (such as certain types of cancers) or the death rate in the population.

For example, in a study of military and civilian personnel exposed to aboveground nuclear weapons testing, the number of various cancers among those exposed has been compared to the rate of specific cancers among the general population of the same age range.

See also ATOMIC VETERANS; NUCLEAR TEST PERSONNEL REVIEW.

EURATOM

Following President Dwight EISENHOWER'S "ATOMS FOR PEACE" speech in 1953, several steps were taken in Europe to develop a collaborative approach to peaceful uses of atomic energy. The Council of Ministers of the European Coal and Steel Community agreed in 1954 to work toward establishing a common market and to make plans for EURATOM. EURATOM would be a multilateral organization to integrate Europe's nuclear power development.

In 1956, EURATOM was formed by West Germany, France, Italy, Belgium, the Netherlands, and Luxembourg. It was created to finance and coordinate research and development, providing a domestic source of electric energy to replace Europe's declining coal reserves. The United States looked forward to cooperating with the organization in providing equipment and uranium to fuel the reactors.

President Eisenhower warmly supported the formation of EURATOM, as did his secretary of state, John Foster DULLES. Lewis STRAUSS, head of the Atomic Energy Commission, was more cool to the idea, fearing that cooperation would entail sharing classified information as well as valuable special nuclear materials.

In October 1956, the closure of the Suez Canal and the Soviet suppression of the Hungarian uprising reawakened Western European concerns over the reliability of oil supplies from the Middle East. France and Germany agreed to the basic principle that EURATOM would control the purchase of nuclear fuel. With agreement underway, the European nations began planning research and development focused on nuclear reactors for power.

EURATOM was formally organized in the Treaty of Rome on January 1, 1958, and the United States cooperated with the organization in providing financial loans and grants, nuclear materials, and equipment.

In working out the procedures that EURATOM would employ to ensure that no nuclear materials would be diverted to weapons programs, the organization found itself working at cross purposes with the INTERNATIONAL ATOMIC ENERGY AGENCY (IAEA), established at the same time in Vienna. The IAEA insisted on establishing systems of inspection, but EURATOM successfully arranged to conduct its own inspections and establish its own guarantees.

Suggested Reading

Richard Hewlett and Jack Holl, *Atoms for Peace and War, 1953–1961: Eisenhower and the Atomic Energy Commission.* Berkeley: University of California Press, 1989.

Fail-Safe

The term "fail-safe" was introduced to represent the last point at which a nuclear attack could be recalled. During the 1950s and 1960s, when much of the United States nuclear arsenal was designed to be delivered by bomber aircraft of the Strategic Air Command (SAC), the fail-safe point was the point at which SAC aircraft could be recalled from their mission without having invaded Soviet air space. A 1962 novel by Eugene Burdick and Harvey Wheeler, entitled *Fail-Safe,* describing an accidental launch of a nuclear war, was made into a film by the same name.

Fallout

Fallout refers to the return to earth of radioactive matter which has been lifted up into the atmosphere by the detonation of a nuclear device or weapon. The term also refers to the material once it is deposited on the ground, vegetation, buildings, or a body of water.

The amount of fallout from any particular device or bomb depends on several factors, including the weather, the exact nature and yield of the device, and where the device was detonated. Fission weapons produce FISSION PRODUCTS that make up most of the fallout,

Fallout. Radioactive debris from atmospheric and underwater nuclear tests became a public policy issue in the mid- and late 1950s, leading to pressure to end such weapons testing. (U.S. Army)

but fusion weapons produce little radioactive material and are sometimes referred to as clean weapons.

98

Nuclear devices detonated underground or high in the atmosphere produce little fallout, whereas detonations at or near the surface result in much material thrown up and much greater fallout, as dirt, dust, and flammable materials are lifted aloft.

Depending on wind conditions, the fallout pattern or "footprint" from a surface detonation can be shaped like a cigar or a broad wedge. Rain or snow can bring down particular hot spots within the extensive footprint, which may extend hundreds of miles in length. Early calculations of fallout suggested that for every megaton of fission yield, there would be about 110 pounds of intensely radioactive fallout material.

Certain radioactive ISOTOPES in fallout are more dangerous to human health than others. Within the first month, iodine-131 and strontium-89 represent great threats. On a longer-range basis, strontium-90 and cesium-137 are among the more dangerous fission and decay products from the point of view of internal hazard to the human body. Radioactive isotopes of iodine and cesium are treated by the body in the same way it treats iodine, often lodging in internal organs. In a similar fashion, the body processes radioactive isotopes of strontium as if they were calcium, passing the material to the bone and marrow structure. In both cases, the presence of radioactive isotopes lodged in the body can lead to cancers.

In the United States, the footprint of fallout from aboveground tests and from vented or leaking underground tests at the NEVADA TEST SITE extended in a generally eastward and northeastward direction. A serious venting occurred on the BANEBERRY test in 1970, for example. Thus residents of Nevada and Utah were particularly concerned about the long-term hazard that might result from fallout in their areas. The so-called downwinders came to represent a considerable political pressure group by the early 1970s.

Increasing awareness of the hazards of fallout following atmospheric nuclear tests in the 1950s led to an international movement to pressure governments into stopping nuclear testing. By international agreement, signed in 1963, the United States, Great Britain, and the Soviet Union agreed to end atmospheric and underwater nuclear testing. Within a few years, the level of background radiation that could be attributed to ATMOSPHERIC NUCLEAR TESTING sharply declined.

During the height of the cold war, tens of thousands of private citizens in the United States constructed underground fallout shelters in their basements or in the ground outside their homes. In many cities, civil defense authorities established communal fallout shelters in the basements of major buildings or in storage areas connected with subway systems. In later years, with the increasing power of thermonuclear weapons to destroy whole cities rather than sections of them, these fallout shelters were discontinued. In certain European countries and in the Soviet Union, extensive programs to construct fallout shelters involved storage of food and water supplies as well as protection from radiation.

People who lived in regions within the fallout footprints from the Nevada Test Site brought legal action. Residents in Nevada, Utah, and Arizona organized a Committee of Survivors. Former interior secretary Stewart Udall provided legal assistance. More than 1,000 separate claims were consolidated into one case, ALLEN V. UNITED STATES. The claimants argued that the AEC had been negligent in failing to protect civilians, and their attorneys focused on 24 typical cases to represent the alleged deaths and injuries from the fallout. Between September and December 1982 the case was argued in the Federal District Court in Salt Lake City. The judge ruled that 10 of the plaintiffs should win compensation. Although widely praised as a victory for the plaintiffs, the case was overturned in 1987 by the Tenth Circuit Court. In another case brought by sheep owners claiming damages, *Bulloch v. United States,* the Tenth Circuit Court overturned a lower court ruling that the government had committed fraud in withholding evidence. By the mid-1980s, court claims brought by U.S. citizens over nuclear fallout appeared quashed.

President George BUSH signed on October 15, 1990, the Radiation Exposure Compensation Act, authorizing a $100 million trust fund to cover claims by members of the public, test-site workers, and uranium miners. Thus congressional action, rather than court cases, brought the issue to conclusion.

See also ATOMIC VETERANS.

Suggested Reading

Howard Ball, *Justice Downwind: America's Atomic Testing Program in the 1950s.* New York: Oxford, 1986.

Barton Hacker, *The Dragon's Tail: Radiation Safety in the Manhattan Project, 1942–1946.* Berkeley: University of California Press, 1987.

Barton Hacker, *Elements of Controversy: The Atomic Energy Commission and Radiation Safety in Nuclear Weapons Testing, 1947–1974.* Berkeley: University of California Press, 1994.

Farm Hall   *See* HEISENBERG, WERNER.

Fast Breeder Reactor

The chain reaction in a fast breeder reactor is maintained by neutrons with energies well above those of thermal neutrons (1×10^5 electron volts [eV] versus 2.5×10^{-5} eV), and the neutron population is controlled so that the ^{238}U (n,γ) ^{239}U reaction can be used to produce ^{239}Pu; that is, $^{238}U + {}^1n \longrightarrow {}^{239}U \longrightarrow {}^{239}Np + \beta \longrightarrow {}^{239}Pu + \beta$. ^{239}Pu decays by α emission with a half-life of 24,400 years. ^{239}Pu is a fissile material. Since ^{239}Pu could be used either as a strategic nuclear material for weapons or as a reactor fuel, the possibility of developing fast breeder reactors appealed to some nuclear planners. Others objected that it would be inappropriate to produce materials for peaceful purposes in generating electricity that would be so ideally suitable for military purposes.

See also BREEDER REACTOR; LIQUID METAL FAST BREEDER REACTORS; NUCLEAR REACTIONS.

Fast Flux Test Facility (FFTF)

The Fast Flux Test Facility (FFTF) was planned as a facility to test various reactor fuels and configurations as part of the research and development to lead to a breeder reactor. Planning on the FFTF began in the mid-1960s for the test reactor to be built at HANFORD. The design power level was 400 megawatts-thermal, with a high density of neutron output, making it a test facility that would be unmatched in scale and versatility anywhere in the world.

The construction of the reactor was handled by Pacific Northwest Laboratory, a division of BATTELLE MEMORIAL INSTITUTE, located in Ohio. Management of development was in the hands of the Division of Reactor Development and Technology at the ATOMIC ENERGY COMMISSION, headed at that time by Milton Shaw. Shaw exercised direct control over the project, and soon Pacific Northwest Laboratory personnel found it difficult to conduct the work without more independence from headquarters control. As a consequence of such management disputes and many technical problems, the FFTF went over budget and took far longer to complete than originally planned. After years of disputes, contracting for the project was transferred in 1970 from Battelle to Westinghouse Corporation.

Even with this change, the final cost of the project approached $600 million, although original estimates had set the budget at $87.5 million. The FFTF was completed in 1980. Soon the original plan to build a Liquid Metal Fast Breeder Reactor was canceled, and the need for the FFTF was diminished. However, the FFTF continued to be used to test reactor fuels for both experimental reactors in the United States and reactors in other countries.

The Department of Energy sought to close the reactor in 1990, but Congress insisted on continuing its funding. Finally, in April 1992, the FFTF was placed on standby status. Alternate plans for its use continued to be put forward through the 1990s, but it was not reactivated.

See also BREEDER REACTOR.

Fat Man

Fat Man was the code name adopted for the PLUTONIUM weapon designed at LOS ALAMOS. A test version of Fat Man was detonated at the Trinity test, Alamogordo, New Mexico, on July 16, 1945. The Fat Man weapon itself was dropped on August 9, 1945, on the city of Nagasaki, Japan, three days after the dropping of the uranium-fueled weapon, LITTLE BOY, on Hiroshima.

The design of the plutonium weapon, relying on IMPLOSION to compress the plutonium into a critical mass, required a large sphere of high-explosive wedges or lenses surrounding a pit of plutonium. The outside casing sphere, nearly six feet in diameter, was fat, compared to the slim gun-type design of the uranium weapon.

Plutonium, because of its high nuclear CROSS SECTION, would fission more rapidly than ^{235}U. Unless the pit were compressed very rapidly through the implosion process, the release of energy could blow the remaining plutonium apart before it had fully fissioned. To avoid such a partial detonation, the spherical implosion design was required.

Federation of American Scientists

Formed late in 1945, the Federation of American Scientists represented an effort to broaden the base of support for the positions taken by the scientists working on the MANHATTAN ENGINEER DISTRICT in their opposition to military control of atomic energy.

Fat Man. The plutonium implosion atomic bomb developed at Los Alamos being lowered to a special trailer cradle for transport to aircraft. (National Archives and Records Administration)

For a period through late 1945 and 1946, the Federation of American Scientists and the FEDERATION OF ATOMIC SCIENTISTS competed for membership among the same groups. Physicists at both CHICAGO and OAK RIDGE were at first reluctant to join the larger, national organization. The fact that both organizations used the same acronym "FAS" led to confusion, and in internal debates they were distinguished as FAmS and FAtS.

Both organizations stood for international control of atomic energy, world peace, and scientific freedom. The dispute apparently centered around whether the movement should be dominated exclusively by atomic scientists or should be open to, and led by, a broader community of scientists. With the dissolution of the FAtS by 1947, the Federation of American Scientists emerged as a voice of the scientific community on political and social positions.

Based in Washington, D.C., the organization has been active in a wide variety of scientific and social issues, including population control, energy, agriculture, medical care, and ethnic conflict. The organization has sought to bring into the open information of a classified nature in order that the public and governments may reach more informed decisions. Along these lines, in the 1990s, the FAS published photographs, taken from earth-orbiting satellites, of nuclear installations in ISRAEL, PAKISTAN, and INDIA to demonstrate the degree to which these nations engaged in nuclear weapons development.

The organization was quick to adapt to the use of the Internet, making many of its findings widely available by electronic means. In this way, it carried on, through new media, a 50-year tradition of publishing information that would help educate and inform the public of the dangers of nuclear war.

By the end of the 20th century, FAS could claim that it was the oldest organization dedicated to ending the worldwide arms race.

Suggested Reading

Donald Strickland, *Scientists in Politics: The Atomic Scientists Movement, 1945–1946*. West Lafayette, Ind.: Purdue University Press, 1968.

Federation of Atomic Scientists

The Federation of Atomic Scientists (FAtS) was founded in 1945. It emerged out of the group of scientists who had worked for the MANHATTAN ENGINEER DISTRICT in developing the atomic bomb. Originating with the groups at the University of CHICAGO, the group was dedicated to preventing and, later, to ending the nuclear arms race. Its goals were to achieve complete nuclear disarmament, avoid the use of nuclear weapons, and work toward ARMS CONTROL and disarmament.

As the organization took on other issues and projects, the organization was superseded by the FEDERATION OF AMERICAN SCIENTISTS. To distinguish the two organizations, Federation of American Scientists has sometimes been abbreviated FAmS, although both used the abbreviation FAS.

The two organizations competed for leadership of the scientists involved in the Manhattan Project and for scientists in America more generally. In a period of conflict from late 1945 through 1946, the scientists at Chicago and at OAK RIDGE tended to adhere to the FAtS, whereas other atomic scientists supported the FAmS.

Suggested Reading

Donald Strickland, *Scientists in Politics: The Atomic Scientists Movement, 1945–1946*. West Lafayette, Ind.: Purdue University Press, 1968.

Fermi, Enrico (1901–1954) *an Italian-born physicist who developed the first atomic pile in 1942 and made other contributions to the development of the American atomic bomb*

Enrico Fermi played a central role in the harnessing of atomic energy as a participant in the MANHATTAN ENGINEER DISTRICT. He designed and operated the first nuclear reactor that demonstrated that nuclear energy

Enrico Fermi. The Italian physicist designed Chicago Pile 1 and was crucial to the success of the Manhattan Project. (National Archives and Records Administration)

could be released and controlled, and he was instrumental in the design of reactors that produced PLUTONIUM used in nuclear weapons.

Fermi was born in Rome on September 29, 1901, the son of a railroad administrator. He attended public schools and then studied at Pisa, where he received his doctorate in 1922, and in Göttingen, Germany. He was a professor of theoretical physics at Rome from 1926 to 1938. In 1928, he married Laura Capon, the daughter of an admiral in the Italian navy. The Capons were Jewish and soon suffered from discrimination under the fascist regime.

While in Rome, Fermi worked on questions of subatomic particles. Building on the work of Joliot, Fermi bombarded atoms with neutrons, inducing artificial RADIOACTIVITY in many elements. His chain of research eventually led to the bombardment of heavy elements THORIUM and URANIUM. In 1935, Fermi discovered the fact that neutrons passed through substances containing hydrogen become more efficient for producing artificial radioactivity, and he identified this effect as due to the slowing down or moderating of the speed of the neutrons by elastic collisions with the hydrogen atoms. He was widely recognized as the most accomplished physicist in Italy while still in his early thirties, and he attracted brilliant students from Italy and abroad to study under him.

Under the fascist regime, a set of racial laws passed in 1938 disturbed both Fermi and his wife. After traveling to Stockholm to accept the NOBEL PRIZE for physics in December 1938, he moved to New York where he had arranged to accept an appointment at Columbia University.

On receiving news of nuclear fission as identified by Lise MEITNER, Fermi began work on this new area at Columbia. Through 1938 and 1939 Fermi and others followed up on the question of developing a controlled CHAIN REACTION of fission. With the outbreak of war, Fermi, Leo SZILARD, and others agreed to impose a degree of secrecy on their work as they realized that fission might have a military application.

When the Manhattan Engineer District was formed in 1942, Fermi soon accepted an appointment to work at the Metallurgical Laboratory in Chicago to develop a reactor that would allow for a controlled chain reaction, using uranium as a fuel and graphite bricks as a moderator. He successfully designed and supervised the construction of CHICAGO PILE No. 1, which went critical on December 2, 1942. During the construction of the pile, he made many adjustments to take into account the varying quality of the uranium oxide that he had to work with, very accurately predicting when there would be a sufficient mass of uranium to achieve a sustained chain reaction.

He later participated in the design and assisted in the start-up of the first production reactor at HANFORD. Although Fermi made a great many contributions to the field of nuclear physics in the areas of elementary particles, the use of accelerators, and cosmic rays, the central role he played in developing the first practical nuclear reactor was perhaps his most important contribution.

After the war, Fermi accepted a position in the new Institute for Nuclear Studies at the University of CHICAGO, and he remained at that University for the remainder of his life. He died in Chicago on November 28, 1954.

Fermi Reactor Accident

The Enrico Fermi Reactor, located about 18 miles south of Detroit, Michigan, suffered an early and extremely serious accident that required it be shut down immediately after opening.

Even before the reactor went operational, it was controversial. The ADVISORY COMMITTEE ON REACTOR SAFEGUARDS, officially reporting to the ATOMIC ENERGY COMMISSION (AEC), had indicated that such a reactor could not be safely operated near an urban area. The United Auto Workers demanded a public hearing to consider the reactor's construction, but the AEC decided to proceed over objections.

The reactor incorporated a liquid-metal design, using molten sodium as the moderator and coolant, with a very dense core containing over 14,000 uranium fuel pins in a cylindrical configuration about three feet in diameter.

Started up in August 1963, the reactor experienced many difficulties over the next two months, including fuel swelling and distortion, sodium corrosion in the core, and problems with the fuel-handling equipment and the steam generators. On October 4, as the reactor control rods were being removed, the temperature of the sodium coolant began to rise. After several pauses to check conditions, the next day operators found that a neutron monitor began to send erratic signals. It was soon discovered that radioactive material had found its way into the coolant—indicating that part of the core had melted. Operators shut down the reactor in fear that the melting could cause chemical or even nuclear explosions.

Investigation revealed that the late addition of a zirconium pyramid at the base of the reactor, which would divide the core materials in case of a meltdown, was the cause of the accident. The liquid sodium lifted a panel from the pyramid and shifted its position so that it partially blocked the coolant flow, creating the overheating and melting of some of the reactor fuel.

Along with other difficulties with breeder reactor design and the concept of a liquid-metal coolant such as sodium, the Fermi accident contributed to the arguments that eventually led to the suspension of U.S. plans to build breeder reactors. The Fermi accident was frequently cited by critics who argued against the expansion of power reactors.

See also BREEDER REACTORS.

Suggested Reading

John G. Fuller, *We Almost Lost Detroit*. New York: Crowell, 1975.

Fermilab

Fermilab was built at the village of Weston, Illinois, beginning in December 1968, as a site to conduct experimentation with particle acceleration. The largest accelerator at the site was the Tevatron, which can beam protons and antiprotons at 0.950 trillion electron volts, or 0.95 TeV. When the particles collide the combined energy is 1.9 TeV. Built at a cost of about $120 million, the Tevatron is designed to explore subatomic particles. The total capital cost of the laboratory was less than $250 million. The 6,800-acre site, purchased by the state and donated to the federal government, housed facilities that employed about 2,000 people by the late 1990s.

The laboratory was operated by a consortium of 86 research universities, combined in Universities Research Association, Inc. The laboratory was named after Enrico Fermi at its dedication in 1969.

Fernald   *See* WEAPONS PRODUCTION COMPLEX.

Finland   *See* POWER REACTORS, WORLD.

Fissile Material

Fissile material is a material that is easily subjected to nuclear fission and suitable for use in the core or pit of a nuclear weapon. PLUTONIUM-239 and URANIUM-235 are particularly fissionable and are the most common fissile materials used in nuclear weapons. Fissile materials, when used in controlled chain reactions, provide the fuel for nuclear reactors.

See also THORIUM.

Fission

Nuclear fission is the splitting of an atomic nucleus into two new nuclei. The split is asymmetrical.

Some radioactive nuclides decay by spontaneous fission. Such highly unstable nuclides usually have very short half-lives. A few nuclides undergo induced fission with slow or thermal neutrons. They are ^{235}U, ^{233}U, and ^{239}Pu. Only ^{235}U occurs in nature.

See also FRISCH, OTTO; MEITNER, LISE.

Fission Fragments

Fission fragments are those radioactive nuclides formed in a fission process.

Fission Products

Fission products are those radioactive nuclides formed in a fission process as well as those radioactive nuclides formed by their decay. Second- and later-generation nuclides are sometimes referred to as daughter products. The half-lives of some of the major fission products from nuclear reactors are shown in the table on the facing page, in seconds (s), minutes (m), hours (h), days (d), or years (y).

See also CESIUM; STRONTIUM; XENON POISONING.

Flexible Response

The term "flexible response" referred to the strategy adopted by NORTH ATLANTIC TREATY ORGANIZATION (NATO) policy makers when planning a possible full-scale war against the Soviet Union and the WARSAW TREATY ORGANIZATION (WTO) or "Warsaw Pact" states. Flexible response as a planning strategy was introduced in the early 1960s as Western leaders recog-

NUCLIDE	HALF-LIFE	NUCLIDE	HALF-LIFE	NUCLIDE	HALF-LIFE
^{85}Kr	4.4h	^{89}Sr	54d	^{90}Sr	25y
^{95}Zr	65d	^{95}Nb	35d*	^{99}Tc	5×10^5y*
^{103}Ru	40d	^{106}Ru	1y	^{103}Rh	57m
^{106}Rh	30s	^{129}Te	34d	^{130}I	1.7 X10^7y
^{131}I	8d	^{133}Xe	2.3d	^{137}Cs	33y
^{140}Ba	13d	^{140}La	40h	^{141}Ce	33d
^{144}Ce	590d	^{143}Pr	14d	^{144}Pr	17m
^{147}Pm	2.3y				

*long-lived nuclide formed by isomeric transition

nized that the earlier doctrine of MASSIVE RETALIATION could lead to a devastating nuclear war initiated by NATO or by the United States in response to an act of aggression with conventional forces by the Soviet Union. Under flexible response, NATO commanders would have a variety of options, including nuclear, non-nuclear, or conventional weapons that could be used in response to a nuclear or conventional attack by the other side.

In November 1984, NATO's Defense Planning Committee approved a policy known as Follow-On Forces Attack that aimed at spelling out the flexible response policy more fully, allowing coordination and better use of information technology to prevent WTO forces from achieving their military objectives.

Suggested Reading

NATO Information Service, *The North Atlantic Treaty Organisation: Facts and Figures.* Brussels, Belgium: NATO Information Service, 1989.

Ford, Gerald (1913–   ) *president of the United States for 29 months, August 9, 1974, to January 20, 1977*

Under his presidential administration, Gerald Ford continued the efforts begun under Lyndon JOHNSON and Richard NIXON to achieve better relations with the Soviet Union in the area of nuclear policy. In particular, he hoped to move negotiations forward toward SALT II.

Ford was born July 14, 1913, in Omaha, Nebraska, with the name of Leslie King Jr. His parents divorced when he was two years old, and his mother remarried. He was formally adopted by his stepfather and given the name of Gerald R. Ford Jr. He was educated at the University of Michigan and graduated from Yale Law School in 1941. He joined the navy during World War II, leaving as a lieutenant commander in 1946.

Ford was elected to the House of Representatives from Michigan in 1949, and he spent the next 25 years as a congressman. He was the only president never to have been elected to the post of either president or vice president. That came about because Richard Nixon's vice president, Spiro Agnew, resigned in October 1973 due to financial scandals. Nixon appointed Ford as vice president, following procedures established under the 25th Amendment to the U.S. Constitution. Then, when Richard Nixon resigned in 1974, Ford became president.

Ford met Soviet premier Leonid Brezhnev in the city of Vladivostok in the Soviet Union in November 1974, where they signed a broad agreement on several policy matters. Initialed on November 24, 1974, the Vladivostok Accord affirmed the two countries' intention to work toward strategic arms control. The accord set as its goal the achievement of SALT II, laying out the treaty's general terms. The positive outcome of the meeting led to the press subsequently referring to the "spirit of Vladivostok" to describe a mood change toward warmer relations between the superpowers.

Following up, the two powers signed the Peaceful Nuclear Explosions (PNE) Treaty in 1976, which limited peaceful nuclear detonations to a 150-kiloton yield. Such a limitation would prevent either country from using the excuse that a larger-scale underground weapons test (that would have violated the LIMITED TEST BAN TREATY limitation to the same yield) had been intended for a peaceful purpose. Ford did not send the PNE Treaty for ratification by the U.S. Senate. However, both nations, following a practice common in such situations, continued to obey the terms of the unratified treaty.

The Vladivostok Accord of 1974 and the PNE Treaty of 1976 represented the last major diplomatic achievements of the period of DETENTE that had begun under President Johnson. Gerald Ford ran for reelection in 1976 and was defeated by Jimmy CARTER. SALT II was never ratified, and no further significant steps toward arms control were achieved until late in the administration of Ronald REAGAN.

Forward-Based Systems

Forward-based systems include nuclear-capable weapons deployed or pre-positioned near possible areas of conflict. Thus, the United States positioned ground-launched CRUISE MISSILES (GLCMs) and *PERSHING* II missiles in Europe during the 1980s to offset modernization of Soviet missile systems. Earlier forward-based systems comprised nuclear-capable artillery, including mobile howitzers, and other missile systems such as the Honest John rocket.

Forward-based systems helped convince the European NORTH ATLANTIC TREATY ORGANIZATION (NATO) partners of the United States that the United States was ready to deter a conventional force invasion of Western Europe by the Soviet Union. Most of the forward-based systems were either tactical weapons systems, such as artillery and short-range missiles, or theater nuclear forces, such as the GLCMs and *Pershing* II missiles.

France—Nuclear Arms

France began its nuclear weapons program during the later years of the Fourth Republic (1946–1958); Charles De Gaulle, as president of the Fifth Republic (1958–1969), greatly accelerated it, and the socialist governments of the 1980s and 1990s have adhered to it, though more conservatively. Even before World War II, Frédéric and Irène JOLIOT-CURIE, daughter of Marie and Pierre CURIE, had discovered the principles of nuclear fission. But their studies were interrupted by World War II, during which other French atomic scientists went to the United States to work on the Manhattan Project. In July 1944 the latter informed Charles De Gaulle, as leader of the wartime Free French, and he, in October 1945, created an Atomic Energy Commission (CEA), directed by Frédéric Joliot-Curie.

The initial French focus was on developing nuclear energy for civilian use, not weaponry. The postwar French economy was too weak; the military was bogged down in an unconventional guerrilla war in Indochina; the politically unstable Fourth Republic lacked a parliamentary majority to support a nuclear weapons program; and certain left-wing scientists, including Joliot-Curie, did not want to develop a bomb that might be used against the Soviet Union. A large percentage of the French population favored the international control of atomic energy, and tens of thousands of French people signed the Stockholm Appeal of 1950 to outlaw all atomic weapons.

Only in 1952–1953, after the purging of Joliot-Curie and other left-wing scientists from the CEA and with the diminished political influence of the pro-Soviet French communists, was the Paris government able to propose the first five-year atomic energy program, which included plans for a plutonium PRODUCTION REACTOR. With sharply reduced coal deposits and absolutely no sources of petroleum, France was then importing 30% of its energy needs and wanted to become energy independent.

By the end of 1954, Premier Pierre Mendés-France, having negotiated an end to the Indochina War and having blocked an American plan to create a European Defense Community (EDC), approved nuclear weapons research to give France some independent military leverage, especially in the face of West German rearmament. A small circle of scientists and military and government officials made the decision in secret, circumventing any parliamentary debate. To save money and strengthen the growing European Union vis-à-vis the Anglo-American powers, France, Germany, and Italy secretly agreed in early 1958 to build their own isotopic separation facility. The French and Germans would each provide 45% of the funding. At the same time, Paris laid its own plans to explode an atomic device no later than in 1960 and to design bomb-carrying planes and missiles.

The unilateral weapons decision hindered rapprochement with Germany, which had pledged not to develop its own program, risked a revival of German militarism, and jeopardized European integration. It also threatened the Atlantic alliance and undercut American plans to stockpile nuclear arms, construct launching pads on French soil, and sell their own enriched URANIUM to Western European nations. Hence, leaders in Washington were clearly hostile because they knew they could not control French use of nuclear weapons as easily as they had the British. Certain French leaders later abetted American fears by boasting

REACTORS IN FRANCE

Legend:
- ■ Pressurized water reactor
- ▲ Gas-cooled reactor
- ⊠ Fast breeder reactor
- ◉ Gas-cooled heavy-water reactor

that their missiles were deployed *tous azimuts*, that is, "in both directions," though few knowledgeable observers took the challenge very seriously.

In May 1958 Charles De Gaulle became president of the Fifth Republic. Fearing that policy makers in

Washington would unilaterally decide on the use of nuclear weapons in Europe, De Gaulle wanted France alone to decide if and how it would involve itself in a major war. He believed the very national independence of France was at stake. The American failure to support the Anglo-French expedition in 1956 to recapture the Suez Canal aggravated his concerns as did fears, following the Soviet launching of SPUTNIK in 1957 that the United States would prefer to defend its own territory more than Europe. Hence De Gaulle believed France had to have its own nuclear bomb, and most French parliamentarians and opinion leaders agreed.

France exploded its first nuclear device, yielding 60-70 kilotons, on February 13, 1960, at Reggane in the Algerian Sahara. France conducted several more atmospheric and underground tests there and in the Hoggar part of the desert before switching in 1966 to Mururoa in French Polynesia in the Southwest Pacific. In 1965, France orbited its first satellite and began developing tactical nuclear weapons. President De Gaulle then withdrew French forces from the NORTH ATLANTIC TREATY ORGANIZATION (NATO) and expelled American troops from French soil. In 1967 France launched its first nuclear-powered submarine and, in 1968, exploded its first thermonuclear device in the South Pacific. By the early 1970s the French military was equipped with surface-to-surface and submarine-launched missiles with nuclear warheads. In the early 1980s France began research on an ENHANCED RADIATION weapon.

By 1974, the United States and Great Britain had formally accepted an independent French nuclear deterrent or, as the French preferred to call it, a *force de frappe,* (literally, a "strike force"). Equally significantly, François Mitterrand and the French socialists who came to power in 1981 reversed long-standing left-wing opposition to possessing nuclear weapons.

However, the American decision to deploy through NATO medium-range ground-launched CRUISE MISSILES in Germany, Italy, Belgium, and Britain greatly irked the Mitterrand government, as did Ronald Reagan's 1983 decision to launch the Strategic Defense Initiative. President Mitterrand responded by proposing general nuclear disarmament and signing treaties with the Soviet Union to prevent accidental use of nuclear weapons, as well as the NON-PROLIFERATION TREATY with the major powers to regulate the export of nuclear materials. However, the NPT did not stop Paris from selling nuclear materials or reactors to other countries, notably PAKISTAN.

By 1991 France had conducted 41 atmospheric explosions and 134 underground tests in the South Pacific. Mitterrand suspended testing in 1992, partly to appease a growing environmentalist electorate; but his Gaullist successor in 1995, Jacques Chirac, re-

sumed testing immediately. However, following the spring of 1998 Chirac was forced to "co-habitate" with a socialist-dominated parliament with strong communist and environmentalist support; therefore, the future of testing remained in doubt. Nevertheless, the French explosions, coming long after most major powers—with the notable exception of China—had agreed to terminate atmospheric nuclear testing, greatly provoked the ire of New Zealand and Australia and other Southwest Pacific nations, to say nothing of the GREENPEACE antinuclear group that tried several times unsuccessfully to sail boats into the waters surrounding the tests.

By 1994 the French military was equipped with some 34 missile-launching naval vessels (10 fitted with long-range missiles), 65 missile-launching planes (18 with long-range missiles), and about 150 long-range, land-based missiles. The total number of French nuclear warheads in 1991 was 538, to be reduced to about 450 by the year 2000, with about 400 to be marine borne. By comparison, Britain had 300 nuclear warheads in 1991, to be reduced to about 200 or less by 2000. The French nuclear arsenal complicated strategic arms limitation treaty (SALT) and strategic arms reduction treaty (START) negotiations between the Soviet Union and the United States, with the former at first insisting that French armament be included in figures for NATO, until Mikhail Gorbachev dropped that demand. The French military emphasized that its essential nuclear strategy was "pre-strategic," that is, to serve as a deterrent or at most to give a warning, not to engage in an all-out nuclear war.

Beginning in 1987, France worked on a new warhead, the TN 75, a miniaturized, hardened, thermonuclear warhead, with a computer-designed shape. In June 1995, President Chirac announced that the weapon needed a final test. Between September 5, 1995, and January 27, 1996, France conducted six nuclear tests at its South Pacific site. The TN 75 was deployed among the French fleet of ballistic submarines in 1996. Finally, on September 24, 1996, France signed the COMPREHENSIVE TEST BAN TREATY and ratified it on April 6, 1998.

There has been relatively little public protest in France toward nuclear weapons, compared to other countries, partly because there is no great tradition of grass-roots agitation in France. Opposition has been traditionally channeled through the political parties, the most antinuclear of which was traditionally the Communist Party (PCF). The PCF dominated the

Mouvement de la Paix, the main organization of the peace movement, and this discouraged many noncommunists from joining. The PCF's opposition to the *force de frappe* waned with the years, particularly when it became a partner with, or supportive of, the socialist governments. The socialists, for their part, firmly opposed French nuclear weapons until the late 1970s when they were about to regain power, recognizing that the electorate generally supported an independent nuclear deterrent. Hence, whatever antinuclear protest there has been belongs to the environmentalists or "Greens," who represent little more than 5% of the vote, or a smattering of isolated groups.

See also INTERMEDIATE NUCLEAR FORCES TREATY.

Suggested Reading

Bertrand Goldschmidt, *The Atomic Adventure*. New York: Macmillan, 1964.

Jolyon Howorth and Patricia Chilton, eds., *Defence and Dissent in Contemporary France*. London: Croom Helm, 1984.

Bruce D. Larkin, *Nuclear Designs: Great Britain, France, and China in the Global Governance of Nuclear Arms*. New Brunswick, N.J.: Transaction Publishers, 1996.

Maurice Vaisse, ed., *La France et l'atome: Études d'histoire nucléaire*. Brussels, Belgium: Bruyant, 1994.

France—Nuclear Energy Program

Immediately after the end of World War II, Charles De Gaulle, as provisional president of the French Republic, established an Atomic Energy Commission (CEA) under Frédéric JOLIOT-CURIE, who, with his wife Irène, daughter of Marie and Pierre CURIE, had discovered the principles of nuclear fission in the late 1930s. Initially the CEA concentrated on developing nuclear energy for civilian use, not weaponry.

France lacked any sources of petroleum, and its once vast coal deposits were becoming rapidly depleted. By the early 1950s it was importing 30% of its energy needs and wanted to become energy independent. The French nuclear program benefited from centralized political and economic control.

In the early 1950s Joliot-Curie and other leftist scientists were purged from the CEA and replaced by engineer/bureaucrats. The CEA then concentrated on building a nuclear reactor based on natural uranium, because of the unavailability of enriched uranium, together with a gas coolant and graphite moderator. France's first reactor at Marcoule began operations in May 1956. Soon there were six more reactors, each

French Physicists. Irène Joliot-Curie is at the control panel of a nuclear reactor at Châtillon, in the suburbs of Paris, observed by Maurice Surdin (left) and Jean Perrin (center). (Library of Congress)

generating 80-500 MW, at Chinon, Saint-Laurent-des Eaux, and Bugey, and one was even exported to Vandellos in Spain.

The reactors in France were operated by the state-owned utility Electricité de France (EDF) with strong support from France's largest trade union federation, the communist-dominated CGT. Overseeing the process was the Production d'Electricité d'Origine Nucléaire commission. However, attitudes toward construction and safety, as in the United States, were at first casual. In the late 1960s, EDF decided, with support from heavy industry and despite opposition from the CEA—which did not want France to become dependent upon American technology and enriched uranium—to produce the less expensive and more exportable American-style light-water reactors while maintaining the gas-graphite ones.

President De Gaulle had been reluctant to surrender French technological independence; however, his successors in the 1970s, Georges Pompidou and Giscard D'Estaing, favored the light-water projects. In

1973, France constructed its first breeder reactor, the Phénix, at Marcoule, which generated 250 MW. This was followed by the Super-Phénix breeder reactor at Creys-Malville along the Rhone River. Built by an European consortium, NERSA, with EDF providing 51% of the funding, the Italian ENEL 33%, and the German SBK 16%, the Super-Phénix became fully operational in December 1986, generating 1200 MW.

Framatome oversaw the production of French-made light-water nuclear reactors. For the first two decades, France had only a modest nuclear program, and the antinuclear movement was limited.

The oil crisis of 1973 changed the situation. France was suddenly forced to import 75% of its energy needs. The government adopted the Messmer Plan calling for extensive nuclear construction, some 13 new reactors by 1975, designed to produce 13,000 MWe, or 50% of France's electricity needs, by the year 2000. In reaction, a number of scientists, technologists, and economists joined the antinuclear forces, as did many environmentalist groups; the CFDT, a leading Catholic-inspired trade union federation; and the PSU, a small socialist party. Small, local protest demonstrations, sometimes violent or involving acts of sabotage, occurred regularly at the proposed reactor sites.

Antinuclear agitation peaked in the late 1970s with the construction of the Super-Phénix, drawing thousands of demonstrators. The government determined to repress these demonstrations vigorously, sending in the CRS (special riot police); they used tear gas, grenades, and clubs on the mostly peaceful protestors, one of whom died. This only increased public sympathy for the antinuclear movement. In 1977 only 37% of French people polled, down from 56% in 1975, approved of the nuclear energy program.

However, grass-roots opposition could accomplish little without the assistance of the leading left-wing political parties, and neither the Communist Party nor the main Socialist Party, despite some strong internal dissent, opposed nuclear energy programs in principle.

They criticized only the government's heavy-handedness in withholding information, stifling public debate, and favoring large private enterprises. Hence, the conservative Gaullist government, with only slight retreats, was able to go ahead with its projects. The socialists, when they took power in 1981 with communist support, continued most of these programs, effectively curtailing the antinuclear movements.

Except for the panic created by the CHERNOBYL disaster of 1986, whose lingering effects on France's envi-

ronment still worry many people, most French citizens by the early 1990s seemed to have resigned themselves to nuclear energy, although 65% opposed any new construction and 17% wanted to shut down all the plants entirely.

Electoral support for the environmentalists or "Greens," however, kept increasing, and in 1998 they became junior partners together with the Communist Party in a socialist-dominated government that then decided to shut down the Super-Phénix and halt construction of new plants. In addition, France was then overproducing nuclear-generated electricity.

By 1999 France had 58 nuclear power plants in operation, each one producing between 900 and 1,450 MW of electricity, with three more facilities planned, which would bring the total nuclear power generated to over 64,000 MW. Nuclear energy now satisfied 75% of France's electricity needs, and the country had even become a major exporter of energy (61.4 TWh) to each of its neighbors, especially Great Britain, Italy, and Germany. If the socialist-environmentalist government in Germany succeeded in shutting down its nuclear power facilities, France's contribution would probably increase. France also reprocesses most of the spent nuclear fuel of its neighbors.

Suggested Reading

Remy Carle, *L'électricité nucléaire.* Paris: Presses Universitaires de France, 1994.

James N. Jasper, *Nuclear Politics: Energy and the State in the United States, Sweden, and France.* Princeton, N.J.: Princeton University Press, 1990.

Franck Report

The Franck Report was a significant document issued in June 1945, written by scientists at the Chicago Metallurgical Laboratory, arguing that the atomic bomb should not be used in a surprise attack on Japan.

In June 1945, the wartime administration of President Harry TRUMAN was making its final decisions as to how to use the atomic bombs that would soon be ready in order to assist in the defeat of Japan. On June 6, the group called the "Interim Committee" reported that a surprise attack on Japan would be the best method to get maximum effect from the weapon. That committee, chaired by Secretary of War Henry Stimson, included Vannevar BUSH, James CONANT, Karl T. COMPTON, J. Robert OPPENHEIMER, Arthur COMPTON, Ernest LAWRENCE, and Truman's friend and later secretary of state James F. BYRNES. On June 6, the Interim Committee filed its recommendations.

Word of the decision reached the scientists working at the Chicago Metallurgical Laboratory through Leo SZILARD. The scientists there wanted to make their opinions known. Accordingly, Arthur Compton organized six different committees to study and report on the policy issues surrounding the use of the atomic weapon. The most significant committee was that chaired by physicist James Franck, called the Committee on Social and Political Implications.

Franck had been born in Germany in 1882 and educated at Heidelberg and Berlin. He had contributed early in the century to studies of colliding electrons, showing that the transfer of energy was governed by quantum theory, winning a NOBEL PRIZE in physics for his work in 1918. Franck had emigrated to the United States in 1933 after protesting against the Nazis' racial policies. He was a professor of physics at the University of CHICAGO (1938–1949).

On June 11, the Franck committee issued its report, known as the Franck Report or the Franck petition. Visualizing the future world in which atomic weapons would be extremely important, the report argued for some system of international control of the weapons. Most important, the Franck Report argued against the use of the atomic bomb in a surprise attack on Japan. The report pointed out that such a use of the weapon would immediately make other nations suspicious, particularly Russia and many neutral nations.

The Franck Report predicted that such use would stimulate a furious postwar arms race. Franck traveled to Washington in an attempt to present the report to Secretary of War Stimson. Stimson referred the matter to the Scientific Panel, chaired by Robert Oppenheimer at LOS ALAMOS. That panel recommended that the original plan to use the atomic bomb in a surprise attack be adhered to. The Scientific Panel and the Interim Committee had earlier reviewed and rejected the concept of a demonstration or warning detonation. They continued to believe that, given the fact that there would be only two bombs ready in early August and there was no assurance both would work, neither should be wasted in a harmless demonstration. Furthermore, they believed that the shock value of an attack on Japanese cities would bring the war to a speedy end.

However, the Interim Committee did accept one aspect of the Franck Report, urging that the Allies be informed of the nuclear weapons. The British had already been informed. Truman adhered to the letter, if not the spirit, of this recommendation, when he spoke to Stalin about the bomb at the POTSDAM CONFERENCE.

At the Chicago Metallurgical Laboratory, other groups organized letters and petitions arguing against the use of the weapon. These documents were forwarded through channels, including a petition gathered by Leo Szilard and a poll of the scientists taken by Farrington Daniels. An earlier report, "The Prospectus on Nucleonics," also known as the Jeffries Report, had urged public disclosure of the work on the atomic bomb and a system of international control.

In later years, the moral implications of the decision to drop the weapon were reconsidered, and the predictions of the Franck Report about the surprise use leading to an international arms race were borne out. Historians and others viewed the dissent expressed by some of the scientists at Chicago through the Franck Report and through other reports and petitions as early stages of a half-century debate over nuclear weapons.

See also BULLETIN OF ATOMIC SCIENTISTS.

Suggested Reading

Martin Sherwin, *A World Destroyed.* New York: Vintage, 1987.
Alice Kimball Smith, *A Peril and a Hope: The Scientists' Movement in America, 1945–1947.* Cambridge, Mass.: MIT Press, 1971.

Fratricide

Fratricide literally means the killing of a brother by a brother, as in the biblical story of Cain and Abel. In nuclear strategic thinking, the term refers to the concept that the detonation of one nuclear weapon over a target would create weapons effects that would interfere with the accuracy or effectiveness of another incoming weapon launched by the same side. Thus, radiation, blast, heat, smoke, and dust created by one warhead could prevent other warheads from reaching their targets or properly detonating. Suggestions that fratricide could be used as a defensive measure led to the DENSE-PACK BASING plan proposed in the 1980s.

See also CIRCULAR ERROR PROBABLE; INTERCONTINENTAL BALLISTIC MISSILE.

Frisch, Otto R. (1904–1979) *Austrian-born physicist known for co-developing the concept of "fission" to describe the splitting of the nucleus of the atom*

Otto Frisch was born in Austria in 1904. He was the nephew of physicist Lise MEITNER (his mother and Lise were sisters) and, like Meitner, he was a refugee from Nazi Germany. He was born and educated in Vienna and was engaged in research in Hamburg when the Nazis took power in 1933. He moved first to Great Britain and then to the Institute of Theoretical Physics in Copenhagen in 1934 after the Nazi takeover.

In 1938, Meitner and Frisch met in the Swedish village of Kungalv over the Christmas holidays, and they discussed a problem presented by Otto HAHN: How had barium apparently been formed from uranium in a reaction? Thinking of a liquid-drop model of the atom proposed by Niels BOHR, Meitner and Hahn discussed the question. She suggested the concept of fission, and after Frisch returned to Copenhagen, they jointly discussed by telephone a proposed paper explaining their concept.

With the German occupation of Denmark, Frisch moved to Britain. While there, he cooperated with another German emigré scientist, Rudolf PEIERLS, in suggesting to the British government that a weapon could be made using the principle of atomic fission. In the period 1943 to 1945, he worked at LOS ALAMOS on the design of the atomic bomb.

In his work for the MANHATTAN ENGINEER DISTRICT, Frisch focused on methods of separating uranium 235 from the more plentiful uranium 238. He also worked on calculating the critical mass that would be required to produce a CHAIN REACTION. At the TRINITY test, Frisch conducted observations from a position some 25 miles from ground zero.

After World War II, Frisch taught at Cambridge University in Britain, retiring in 1971. He died in 1979.

Suggested Reading
Richard Rhodes, *The Making of the Atomic Bomb*. New York: Simon and Schuster, 1988.

Fuchs, Klaus (1911–1988)   *German-born nuclear physicist who worked on the Manhattan Project, who was later revealed as probably the most important nuclear spy for the Soviet Union*
Klaus Fuchs was born in Rüsselsheim, near Frankfurt, Germany, on December 29, 1911. His parents were Emil Fuchs (1874–1971), a Lutheran minister, and Else Wagner. Klaus Fuchs studied mathematics and

Klaus Fuchs. Of all the Soviet spies working inside the Manhattan Project, Klaus Fuchs probably provided the most crucial information, later used by the Soviets in constructing their first atomic bomb four years after the Americans. (National Archives and Records Administration)

physics at Leipzig University, and he continued his undergraduate studies in physics at Kiel University. At Kiel, Fuchs joined the German Communist Party in 1932. Following Nazi attacks on the political left, Fuchs emigrated to Great Britain on September 24, 1933. He continued work in physics at Bristol University, where he completed the Ph. D. in 1937. He began teaching at Edinburgh University in 1937.

By 1939 he joined the Soviet Union's espionage network operated by the GRU (Army Intelligence), establishing contact through Jürgen Kuczynsky, a Polish communist resident in Britain since 1936. In June 1940, the British took Fuchs into custody as a German citizen and sent him to internment camps, first on the Isle of Man and then at Quebec City, Canada, where he worked with others in the Communist Party network. After several months, he returned to Edinburgh to resume his teaching position, cleared of suspicion of pro-Nazi sentiments.

In 1941, he was invited by Rudolf PEIERLS to Birmingham, where Peierls was engaged in the British nuclear project code-named "MAUD." Fuchs was cleared by British internal security (MI-5) for this post. He immediately began to pass information about the classified project to the Soviets through Kuczynsky. Fuchs obtained British citizenship on August 7, 1942. As a member of the Peierls team, Fuchs moved to the United States in November 1943.

As a senior scientist, Fuchs had full access to information, and he actively engaged in espionage for the Soviets while at LOS ALAMOS, New Mexico, transmitting detailed reports on the atomic bomb work through Harry GOLD, whom he knew by the code name "Raymond." Fuchs stayed at Los Alamos after the war and then transferred to HARWELL RESEARCH ESTABLISHMENT, Britain, in August 1946. In 1949, based on information in the VENONA DECRYPTS, the American FBI requested the British interview Fuchs to find out if he had spied while at Los Alamos. After questioning, Fuchs confessed to his espionage work and was convicted in Britain of violation of the Official Secrets Act. He received the maximum prison term of 14 years in 1950.

In June 1959 he was repatriated to Germany, and he accepted an appointment at the Institute for Nuclear Research in East Berlin, in the German Democratic Republic. He continued his work in theoretical physics, retiring from active research in 1979. In retirement he resided near Dresden.

Fuchs is most remembered for his espionage work, which advanced Soviet progress toward nuclear weaponry. The first Soviet nuclear weapon was based on detailed plans that Fuchs and other spies had relayed to them. He died in the German Democratic Republic at the age of 76 on January 28, 1988.

Suggested Reading

Norman Moss, *Klaus Fuchs, a Biography*. New York: St. Martins, 1987.

Robert Chadwell Williams, *Klaus Fuchs: Atom Spy*. Cambridge, Mass.: Harvard University Press, 1987.

Fuel

Nuclear fuel is the fissile (fissionable) material used or usable to produce energy in a nuclear reactor. Most of the power reactors rely on enriched uranium as a fuel.

Fusion Power

Fusion power is based on the energy released when heavier nuclei are formed from lighter nuclei, that is, when lighter atoms fuse together. When a triton is bombarded with a deuteron, a hellion and a neutron are formed, and energy in excess of 17 million electron volts (MeV) is released.

$$^3H + {}^2H \longrightarrow {}^4He + {}^1n, \text{ or } {}^3H(d,n)\,{}^4He$$

The energy released in fission of ^{235}U is just under 200 MeV. However, on a mass-for-mass basis, the fusion reaction produces vastly more energy. In addition, the fuel supply for possible future fusion reactors operating on deuterium fusion (D + D $\longrightarrow$ ^3He + ^1n, or D + D $\longrightarrow$ T + H) is much greater than that available for reactors based on ^{235}U fission. Self-sustained nuclear fusion has not yet been realized, although energy released by fusion is the basis for thermonuclear weapons or hydrogen bombs.

G

Gamma Radiation (γ)

Gamma radiations are high-energy, short-wavelength electromagnetic radiation. Gamma radiations often accompany α or β emissions and always accompany nuclear fission. Gamma radiations are highly penetrating. They are absorbed or shielded by thick layers of dense materials, such as lead (d = 11.35 g/cm³ at 25 degrees C.) or depleted URANIUM (d = 18.95 g/cm³ at 25 degrees C.).

Gamow, George (1904–1968) *Russian-born American physicist who worked on the development of the hydrogen bomb and also gained fame as a science popularizer*

Gamow was born in Odessa, Russia, on March 4, 1904, the son of a teacher of languages. In 1922, he entered Novorossysky University and then transferred to the University of Leningrad. He continued his studies there, finishing a doctorate in physics in 1928.

He then moved to Göttingen, Germany, where he studied the principles of nuclear decay and alpha emission. His research soon led to an appointment under Niels BOHR at the Copenhagen Institute of Theoretical Physics in 1928. There Gamow made contributions to the explanation of thermonuclear reactions in the interiors of stars and the sun. In 1929 he went to the Cavendish Laboratory at Cambridge, England, where his measurements of the energy required to split the nucleus of an atom by accelerated protons led John COCKROFT to build the first accelerator. Gamow returned briefly to the Soviet Union in 1931, and then he was not permitted to leave. He spent two years lecturing at the University of Leningrad and then attended a conference in Brussels, Belgium.

He and his wife, Lyubov Vokminzeva, decided to leave the Soviet Union for good, taking the chance to emigrate to the United States during the visit to the conference in Belgium. After short stays at several laboratories, he took a position at George Washington University in Washington, D.C. He held that post from 1934 to 1956.

Over those decades, Gamow enhanced his already well-established international reputation. Working with Edward TELLER, in 1936, he developed a rule explaining beta decay. He continued his work in the study of the evolution of stars, and he began to develop the concept of an expanding universe. In the late 1930s, he started to write children's books explaining science, and he became known as one of the best popularizers of science while at the same time continuing his scientific work. Overall, he published more than 40 books for the general reader.

During World War II, he conducted research for the U.S. Navy Bureau of Ordnance, and in 1946 he served as an observer at the OPERATION CROSSROADS nuclear test at BIKINI. After 1948, he worked with Stanislaw ULAM and Edward Teller on the project to develop a thermonuclear bomb at LOS ALAMOS. Some writers credit him as one of the co-inventors of the H-bomb as a consequence of this research.

He continued his theoretical work on the origins of the universe, making several contributions to the "big bang" theory. In 1954, after reading of the discovery of the structure of DNA by J.D. Watson and Francis Crick, Gamow, with no experience in this unfamiliar field, made a basic contribution to the understanding of the formation of protein molecules. Gamow's accomplishments in understanding stellar physics, nuclear energy, and the new field of DNA research marked him as a brilliant theoretical scientist. Through both his theoretical work and his popular books, Gamow became one of the best-known nuclear scientists among the general public in the 1940s and 1950s. He moved to the University of Colorado, Boulder, in 1956. He continued his work in Colorado, dying there on August 20, 1968.

Gaseous Diffusion

Gaseous diffusion is a method for the separation of ^{235}U from ^{238}U. Kinetic molecular theory proposes that atoms or molecules of different masses will diffuse at different rates. Actually, the rate of diffusion of a gaseous atom or molecule is inversely proportional to the square root of its molar mass (the preferred usage for the concept of molecular weight); that is, $r = k/(molar\ mass)^{1/2}$. $^{235}U_6$ is separated from $^{238}UF_6$ by passage through many spongy, metallic barriers with very fine pores under the influence of pressure gradients created by many stainless steel pumps in huge and very expensive gaseous diffusion plants. The first U.S. gaseous diffusion plant, designated K-25, was built in OAK RIDGE, Tennessee. Subsequent plants were located in Paducah, Kentucky, and Portsmouth, Ohio.

Geiger Counter

The Geiger (Geiger-Müller) counter is an instrument for detecting and measuring nuclear radiations. It consists of a gas-filled tube containing electrodes between which is a potential difference of several hundred volts but no current flow. When ionizing radiation, usually β, passes through the tube, a short, intense pulse of current passes from the negative to the positive electrode and is registered as a click in an earphone or as a count on a meter. The number of pulses per second is a measure of the intensity of the radiation. This instrument was developed by Hans GEIGER and Wilhelm Müller in 1928.

Geiger, Hans (1882–1945) *German physicist and co-inventor of devices for the measurement of radioactivity, still known as Geiger counters*

Geiger was born in Neustadt an der Weinstrasse, Germany, on September 30, 1882, the son of a professor of languages at Erlangen. Geiger received a doctorate in physics in 1906, and he then took a position in Manchester, England. Ernest RUTHERFORD moved there from McGill University in 1907, and Rutherford convinced Geiger to stay on to work on radioactivity. Geiger continued to work with Rutherford over the years 1908 to 1912, when he returned to Germany to take up a position as director of a laboratory for radium research in Berlin. Both in Manchester and in his post in Berlin, he worked on means to identify alpha and beta particles and to measure them.

After World War I, Geiger continued working on techniques to measure the effects of radiation in experimental studies. In 1925, he took up a teaching position at the University of Kiel. It was there, in 1928, working with Walter Müller, that the two men developed the Geiger-Müller counter.

This device became central to further work in the field of nuclear physics and was crucial in the discovery of radioactive emissions; it was later used as a device to monitor the dangerous effects of radiation in industry and, with the development of the nuclear weapon, in military situations.

Following 1928, more and more of these very practical devices were manufactured. Geiger counters were made increasingly reliable and portable. Using several of the instruments, Geiger made one of the first detections of cosmic rays. In 1936, he took up a position as chair of physics at the Technical Huchschule (a university-level institution) in Berlin, directing a research team studying radioactivity. At the same time, he continued using his instrument to study cosmic rays.

During World War II, he did not work on the German nuclear weapon project, and he fell quite ill. He continued to edit a journal in physics and to do research on cosmic rays on an intermittent basis. At the end of the war he moved to Potsdam, and he died there on September 24, 1945.

General Advisory Committee

Established under the ATOMIC ENERGY ACT OF 1946, the General Advisory Committee (GAC) helped set atomic energy policy on questions such as the number and nature of weapons to be produced, expansion of production facilities, and international sharing of nuclear information. Members of the early GAC included many of the nationally and internationally known scientists who had served on the MANHATTAN ENGINEER DISTRICT, including J. Robert OPPENHEIMER, James CONANT, Enrico FERMI, and Glenn T. SEABORG.

The General Advisory Committee, under the leadership of Oppenheimer in the period 1946 to 1952, opposed the development of the hydrogen bomb. Oppenheimer stepped down from the chairmanship and was relieved of his security clearance. His successor was Nobel Prize winner Isidor I. RABI, who served from 1952 to 1956. In 1950, the GAC began to include some science administrators and men with experience in business.

Warren C. Johnson chaired the GAC (1956–1959), and Kenneth Pitzer chaired the group in 1960–1961.

General Atomics

General Atomics was founded in 1955 as a division of General Dynamics and later became an independent company in the field of nonmilitary applications of atomic energy. The company has been known as a developer and advocate of HIGH-TEMPERATURE GAS-COOLED REACTORS (HTGRs), and it has actively promoted them for both power applications and an alternative NEW PRODUCTION REACTOR, with very limited success in both areas.

By the 1990s, there were no HTGRs in use for either purpose in the United States. However, General Atomics has had greater success in developing and selling the Training, Research, and Isotopes–General Atomics reactor (TRIGA reactor) to universities and research institutions around the world. The company maintained its headquarters in San Diego, California, with branch offices in Washington, D.C., LOS ALAMOS, and Denver, as well as in RUSSIA, Japan, and Australia.

General Atomics sometimes bid jointly with another small nuclear reactor company, COMBUSTION ENGINEERING, in a consortium called CEGA.

General Electric

General Electric Company (GE) was a major participant in the development of nuclear reactors, along with WESTINGHOUSE, BABCOCK AND WILCOX, and COMBUSTION ENGINEERING. Among the four companies, General Electric and Westinghouse captured the majority of the market in the 1960s. Both GE and Westinghouse gained experience under government contracts following World War II. In 1946, Harry Winne, the vice president of General Electric in charge of engineering, developed an interest in the nuclear industry after serving on a panel reporting to Secretary of State James F. BYRNES on peaceful uses of nuclear energy. General Electric moved into reactor work when it took over the PRODUCTION REACTORS at HANFORD that year. In exchange, the ATOMIC ENERGY COMMISSION (AEC) agreed to provide a nuclear development center that would be operated by GE near its Schenectady, New York, headquarters. The GE research plant was called the KNOLLS ATOMIC POWER LABORATORY and was established at West Milton, New York.

In 1953, GE developed a BOILING WATER REACTOR (BWR) and installed one at its own power generating plant at Vallecitos, California. In the mid-1950s, GE also sold reactors to several utilities, including Pacific Gas and Electric in California and Commonwealth Edison Company of Chicago. By 1959, GE had some 14,000 employees devoted to nuclear work, and it had invested approximately $20 million in nuclear research.

Along with Westinghouse, GE dominated the U.S. reactor industry. By the end of the century, some 35 of the 104 power reactors in the United States were of the GE BWR design.

Suggested Reading
George Mazuzan and J. Samuel Walker, *Controlling the Atom: The Beginnings of Nuclear Regulation, 1946–1962*. Berkeley: University of California Press, 1984.

Geologic Waste Disposal

Various plans to dispose of radioactive waste by burial in deep natural or human-made caverns has been termed "geologic" disposal, and it has been widely favored around the world. The different methods involve the use of multiple barriers to protect against the escape of radionuclides into the environment. These barriers include those that are engineered and those that are natural.

The actual repository and its contents are the engineered system, consisting of spent fuel assemblies or resolidified products of reprocessing and their containers, usually concentric cylinders made of materials that resist corrosion and prevent water from reaching the waste. In some of the designs, concrete or other backfill provides additional protection against the intrusion of water.

The natural system is the geologic strata. Usually the strata most sought is rock that prevents or limits the entry of water or that would slow the flow of any water out to the rest of the environment. Other desirable factors are low risk of earthquake and chemical composition of the rock that does not lead to corrosion of the containers.

By the 1970s, alternate methods of nuclear waste disposal, such as dumping at sea, were abandoned and outlawed in the United States. Metal drums previously dumped in the ocean were believed to have collapsed or rusted, spreading radioactive contaminants. Suggestions that radioactive waste could be launched into space, perhaps to fall into the sun eventually, were discounted as impractical, expensive, and extremely dangerous in case of a launch-vehicle failure.

Some early designs for geologic disposal were based on the use of bedded salt deposits, such as those found at a location near Lyons, Kansas, because it was believed that such salt deposits had not experienced water seepage for many thousands of years. By the 1980s, engineers began to move away from preference for salt because of the corrosive nature of salt brines on container materials and on backfill such as concrete.

In Germany, a salt dome provided a waste site near Gorleben. In Sweden and Canada, granite deposits were sought out, while in the United States, basalt formations near HANFORD and the IDAHO NATIONAL ENGINEERING LABORATORY were considered. The site at YUCCA MOUNTAIN in Nevada was chosen because of the tuff formation, consisting of volcanic ash that has been blown and then welded together under extreme heat.

Although tuff is relatively impermeable to water, the fact that it can be fractured and have fissures that admit water led to extensive controversy about the ultimate safety of that site.

While alternate plans for geologic waste disposal were considered in the United States for the back end of the NUCLEAR FUEL CYCLE, much reactor waste continued to be stored in pools of water at the various commercial reactor sites. Some waste from DEPARTMENT OF ENERGY reactors and facilities was stored on site at Hanford and SAVANNAH RIVER, while LOW-LEVEL WASTE began to be transported to the WASTE ISOLATION PILOT PLANT (WIPP) near Carlsbad, New Mexico.

Suggested Reading
David Bodansky, *Nuclear Energy: Principles, Practices, and Prospects.* Woodbury, N.Y.: American Institute of Physics, 1996.

German Atomic Bomb Project

American and British nuclear physicists believed that Germany would be capable of building a nuclear weapon during World War II. As early as 1939, they knew that many of the world's leading scientists and engineers were German and that Germany had the industrial and technical capability to develop a weapon if one could be designed. For this reason, British, American, and continental European scientists who had fled Nazism believed it was essential to develop an atomic bomb before the Germans did in the 1940s.

As the Allies conquered Germany in the early months of 1945, General Leslie GROVES of the MANHATTAN ENGINEER DISTRICT ordered members of the ALSOS PROJECT to uncover the exact extent of the German program. At first, the teams under Samuel GOUDSMIT and Boris Pash could not believe how little progress had been achieved by the German scientists.

Soon a controversy developed in which the German nuclear scientists, led by Werner HEISENBERG, claimed that their lack of progress was due to a more or less conscious decision not to advocate too strongly the development of such a terrible weapon. They implied that they had held back in pushing for the weapon because they understood that, if available, it would have been used in a catastrophic fashion by Hitler. Western scientists, led by Goudsmit, continued to argue after the war that the Germans had not developed the weapon because of a series of fundamental scientific miscalculations, they had stripped the country of many of its leading scientists by the expulsion of all Jews from academic positions in 1933, and some of the essential resources for the weapons program had been destroyed by Allied air raids. There is evidence for all of these arguments.

For historians as well as for those who participated in the weapons programs, the issue has been one of emphasis. Germany did indeed have a nuclear weapons program. It was hampered partly by the exodus or "brain drain" of Jewish and other scientists, not only from Germany but also from Hungary and Italy. The Hungarians Leo SZILARD and Eugene WIGNER and the Italian Enrico FERMI (whose wife was Jewish) emigrated to the United States where they contributed vital expertise in the U.S. project. Physicists in conquered France, such Frédéric JOLIOT-CURIE, continued their research but refused to cooperate with the Nazis. In Denmark, Niels BOHR at first continued his research under German occupation, but he soon fled to Great Britain and then the United States. So the exodus of leading physicists no doubt hampered the German effort.

Heisenberg met once with Niels Bohr in September 1941 in Copenhagen before Bohr fled to the West. Heisenberg later claimed that in that meeting, he sought to hint to Bohr that scientists on both sides should refrain from working on a nuclear weapon. Bohr interpreted the conversation differently, however, assuming that Heisenberg sought to find out how much progress toward producing a weapon had been made by the Allied scientists. The exact nature of the conversation remained in dispute over the following decades.

Early in the war, the Allies soon learned that the Germans had increased production of heavy water at the NORSK HYDRO plant in Norway. This material would be useful in the design of nuclear reactors that could be used to produce radioactive ISOTOPES and PLUTONIUM. In several concerted attempts both through commando raids and bombing, the Allies finally succeeded in closing down that facility by early 1944.

As a consequence of the destruction at Norsk Hydro, Heisenberg's efforts to develop a nuclear reactor were limited to one small heavy-water moderated scale model or test reactor that Pash's Alsos team finally discovered in a mine near Haigerloch in the Black Forest region of Germany. The "uranium machine" that the Germans had developed was a pot containing heavy water sunk into a 10-foot concrete pit. There were 1.5 tons of heavy water, with URANIUM suspended by chains into the water. Heisenberg had calculated that with a 50% increase in the size of the machine, he could have achieved a sustained CHAIN REACTION.

Heisenberg and his fellow scientists were arrested by the Alsos teams and taken as prisoners to Britain where they were held until the end of the war at Farm Hall, a country estate. The British planted microphones in the rooms and lounge areas so that they could listen in on German discussions, and the transcripts were translated into English and finally published in 1992.

From these transcripts it was possible to detect how surprised the German scientists were when news reached them of the American detonation of nuclear weapons over HIROSHIMA and NAGASAKI. A close analysis of the discussion suggested that the Germans had not been very close at all to designing the weapon and that at first they did not understand how it could have been achieved. Some believed that the Americans must have dropped a small reactor as a bomb. Heisenberg himself believed that several tons, rather than a few pounds, of purified uranium-235 would be required for a nuclear detonation.

Some scholars have argued that the Germans focused more on the possible use of nuclear energy for ship propulsion and electrical power than for the design of a bomb. That may have been true, as Heisenberg's team concentrated their efforts on the development of a reactor or uranium machine.

Others have attributed their blocked efforts to the decision to utilize heavy water for reactors rather than graphite or to their gross miscalculation of the quantity of uranium required to achieve critical mass. The decision to use heavy water may have resulted from poor calculations or from the fact that German natural graphite was so full of impurities, compared to American synthetic-produced graphite, that it served as a very poor moderator.

It is also evident that in Nazi Germany it was very difficult to advocate a long-range weapons program in the face of Hitler's expectations that the war would be won quickly. The German *V-2* rocket program, for example, was at first discouraged by the Nazi command on the grounds that it would cost too much and take too long. The leader of the project, Walter Dornenberg, received funding only after an arduous and hard-fought dispute with the Nazi bureaucracy. Other factors no doubt contributed to the failure of the Germans to develop the weapon. Many of the most talented physicists had fled the country after the Nazis took power, and several of the remaining physicists refused to cooperate at all with the German project.

Furthermore, two conflicting programs in Germany sought to develop nuclear research, creating rivalry over scarce resources. Heisenberg himself, some observers noted, was not good at mathematics, although he was a brilliant theoretician. In contrast to Enrico FERMI, who was both a good theorist and a practical, mathematically inclined experimentalist, Heisenberg was a poor choice to head the German program.

With all of these factors, the exact nature of the German atomic bomb project and the reasons for its failure have remained the subject of controversy ever since the Alsos team first apprehended Heisenberg and his associates.

Suggested Reading

Jeremy Bernstein, *Hitler's Uranium Club*. New York: American Institute of Physics, 1996.

David Irving, *The German Atomic Bomb*. New York: Simon and Schuster, 1967.

Jonathan Logan, "The Critical Mass," *American Scientist*, May–June 1996.

Thomas Powers, *Heisenberg's War*. New York: Knopf, 1993.

Richard Rhodes, *The Making of the Atomic Bomb*. New York: Simon and Schuster, 1986.

Mark Walker, *Uranium Machines, Nuclear Explosives, and National Socialism: The German Quest for Nuclear Power, 1939–1949*. New York: Cambridge University Press, 1991.

Germany in International Atomic Affairs

During the atomic age, Germany played a crucial role in several ways in different periods. Germany's capabilities in the nuclear field stimulated the development of the nuclear weapon in the United States and Great Britain, and the division of Germany following World War II contributed to the nuclear arms race between the Soviet Union and the United States.

Prior to the 1930s, Germany was a leading nation in the field of nuclear physics. Göttingen University was a center that attracted many brilliant physicists in the 1920s, including J. Robert OPPENHEIMER from the United States and Enrico FERMI from Italy. However, soon after the Nazi Party took power in 1933, the new government issued a decree banning all Jews from academic positions. When Germany absorbed Austria on March 12, 1938, the policy extended to universities and colleges there. As a result, Jewish scientists and many others who opposed the Nazi regime for political reasons fled the country for Britain, the United States, or other countries. Among those departing were Lise MEITNER. A core of dedicated German physicists remained, however, including Werner HEISENBERG.

Germany's acquisition of Czech territory and subsequent dissolution of the Czechoslovak Republic and its absorption by the German Reich in 1938–1939 attracted the attention of nuclear physicists. The primary source of URANIUM in Europe was in a mining zone at Jáchymov, Czechoslovakia, in the Erzgebirge mountains bordering Germany.

After Germany invaded Poland on September 1, 1939, Britain and France declared war on Germany, launching World War II. Nuclear scientists in Germany, Britain, the United States, and elsewhere recognized that recent discoveries in the release of energy through nuclear fission could lead to an atomic bomb. In the United States, Leo SZILARD urged Albert EINSTEIN to write to President Franklin ROOSEVELT, warning the president of the possibility that Germany might develop a nuclear weapon. In response to Einstein's letter and warning about the potential in Germany, Roosevelt initiated federal support for nuclear weapons work.

The GERMAN ATOMIC BOMB project moved relatively slowly when compared to the British MAUD COMMITTEE studies and the project under the OFFICE OF SCIENTIFIC RESEARCH AND DEVELOPMENT and the MANHATTAN ENGINEER DISTRICT, established following Roosevelt's orders in the United States. Heisenberg and his fellow German scientists began to develop a nuclear reactor, using heavy water from the NORSK HYDRO plant in Norway.

At the end of the war, experts from the United States in the ALSOS PROJECT captured German scientists and studied the progress that had been made there toward creating a nuclear weapon. Later, Heisenberg and his associates claimed that they had not pushed the weapon's development because they feared that it would be used horribly by the Hitler regime. Western scientists, such as Samuel GOUDSMIT, continued to believe that the German project had been slowed through German mistakes, bad policy, and concerted Allied bombing raids on the needed resources.

Following the defeat of Germany on May 8, 1945, the Allied powers occupied the country, dividing it into four zones, each administered separately by the United States, Britain, France, and the Soviet Union.

Berlin, the capital, fell inside the boundaries of the eastern zone that was occupied by the Soviets. Since it had been the capital of the German Reich, that city itself was in turn divided into four zones. This awkward division of the defeated nation left a legacy of problems that became focal points for conflict between the Western Allies (United States, Britain, and France) on the one side and the Soviet Union on the other.

In 1947, the Western Allies united their three zones into a single administration, and the Soviets took this to be a violation of the agreement dividing Germany. The Soviets retaliated with a blockade of the land routes into Berlin beginning on June 18, 1948, effectively isolating the Western-occupied zones of that city from supplies. The United States responded with a "nuclear bluff," flying to Britain a number of bomber aircraft that had been converted to carry the early, large models of the nuclear weapons similar to those that had been dropped on Japan in 1945.

However, the United States had very few nuclear weapons, and none were shipped to supply the aircraft in Britain. The extensive espionage network that the Soviets had maintained in the United States was in disarray during this period, and the Soviets may have believed that the United States intended a nuclear attack if any of its aircraft were shot down. American aircraft supplied Berlin through the winter of 1948 by flying in coal for fuel, food, and other supplies in the so-called Berlin Airlift. This crisis, with its implied nuclear threat, passed when the Soviets lifted the blockade and allowed ground transport back into Berlin in 1949. The blockade in East Germany stimulated the formation of the NORTH ATLANTIC TREATY ORGANIZATION (NATO), which was formally established on April 4, 1949. The Soviets established the German Democratic Republic in their zone of Germany on October 7, 1949.

Germany and Berlin remained flash points in the cold war. In 1955, the western zone of Germany, organized as the Federal Republic of Germany, was admitted to NATO. The Soviet Union responded by the formation of the WARSAW TREATY ORGANIZATION (WTO), which included the Soviet Union and communist-dominated nations of Eastern Europe, including the communist-ruled German Democratic Republic. Other members of WTO included HUNGARY, Poland, Czechoslovakia, ROMANIA, BULGARIA, and Albania. Thus the cold war had become converted into a confrontation between two armed camps, the 14-member NATO alliance, and the eight-member WTO or Warsaw Pact alliance.

Communist rule in the German Democratic Republic became oppressive, and large-scale riots broke out in several East German cities on June 17, 1953. In West Germany, the pro-Western Christian Democratic Union Party under Konrad Adenauer continued to rule following 1949, and he was reaffirmed in his position in a landslide election in 1957. Adenauer served as chancellor from 1949 through 1963.

On August 13, 1961, in response to the exodus of East German citizens to the West, many of whom escaped the communist regime through the divided city of Berlin, the East German government erected the Berlin Wall. The wall itself became a symbol of the cold war and the tensions between the two nations. Confrontations over the wall in 1961 contributed to the heightened danger of nuclear conflict between the United States (and its allies) and the Soviet Union.

During the period of DETENTE, relations briefly improved between the two Germanies, with a treaty of friendly and equal recognition signed on December 21, 1972.

The United States based aircraft carrying nuclear weapons in some NATO countries, and by the 1970s, it had stationed nuclear-tipped short-range missiles in Germany. In the late 1970s, in response to the Soviet emplacement of more powerful and longer-range missiles, NATO developed the DUAL-TRACK STRATEGY of placing new missiles in Europe, including at German locations, while at the same time negotiating for the reduction of intermediate-range nuclear forces. NATO announced the policy of emplacing longer-range intermediate missiles in Germany and Britain on October 7, 1979, an action that represented an end of the detente period.

The Federal Republic of Germany, meanwhile, developed a nuclear power capability. However, the nation decided not to develop nuclear weapons and signed the NON-PROLIFERATION TREATY on November 28, 1969. The nation joined the EURATOM treaty and participated in the various agreements limiting the export of nuclear technology, such as the ZANGGER COMMITTEE in 1975. Seven power reactors went into operation in the 1970s and another 12 in the 1980s.

With the ending of the cold war in the period 1988–1990, Germany reunited. In a dramatic celebration, the Berlin Wall was torn down in November 9–10, 1989. Germany was formally reunited on October 3, 1990, and the united country was recognized as a member of NATO.

Germany–Nuclear Power

By the late 1990s, Germany had 19 power reactors at 14 different power stations, all located in the former western zone or territory of the German Federal Republic. Two of the reactors were built by Siemens, and the rest were built by Kraftwerk Union AG. The total output of the reactors was in the range of 15 gigawatts. As in Britain and the United States, the construction of reactors met political opposition in Germany, focused there in the Green Party that had been established in January 1980. As a consequence, reactor development has remained in abeyance since the early 1990s and several older reactors have been shut.

See also GERMANY IN INTERNATIONAL ATOMIC AFFAIRS.

Glassboro Summit

The Glassboro Summit conference of 1967 is sometimes taken as a high-water mark in the period of DETENTE between the United States and the Soviet Union. In June 1967, Soviet premier Aleksey Kosygin visited the United Nations in New York City. After arguing over whether President Lyndon JOHNSON would visit New York to meet Kosygin or whether Kosygin would go to Johnson in Washington, the two settled on a halfway point, in Hollybush Hall at Glassboro College in southern New Jersey (later named Rowan University). Both sides hoped for the "spirit of Hollybush" to represent a step toward detente.

At their June 23, 1967, meeting at Glassboro, President Johnson tried to explain the U.S. opposition to building an ANTI-BALLISTIC MISSILE system. Finally, Johnson called on Secretary of Defense Robert MCNAMARA to explain the position of the United States to the Soviet representatives.

McNamara spelled out the American logic. The United States believed that a correct response to any Soviet ABM force would be to expand American offensive forces. "If we had the right number of offensive weapons to maintain a deterrent before you put your defenses in," said McNamara, "then to maintain the same degree of deterrence, in the face of your defense, we must strengthen our offense." By this logic, if the Soviets built an anti-ballistic missile force, it would only speed up the arms race, McNamara claimed. "That's not good for either one of us," explained McNamara.

He expected Kosygin to understand the concept immediately, but the Soviet premier could not believe what he had just heard. He saw weapons in much more traditional military terms, and the thought that building a purely defensive weapon would be seen as aggression was foreign to him.

"Defense is moral," said Kosygin angrily. "Offense is immoral."

Following the meeting, McNamara returned to Washington, and he discussed nuclear weapons policy with the Joint Chiefs of Staff. He then decided to go ahead and build a new class of missiles, with MULTIPLE INDEPENDENTLY TARGETABLE REENTRY VEHICLES (MIRVs). The United States did not plan to deploy MIRVed weapons unless attempts to negotiate a treaty prohibiting ABMs failed. By the time such an agreement had been worked out later, with the strategic arms limitation treaty (SALT I), the United States and the Soviets both had MIRV warheads. The chance to outlaw ABMs and perhaps to prevent multiple-warhead weapons at Glassboro had been missed. In this sense, the Glassboro conference represented a lost opportunity, in McNamara's own view.

The effort to discuss arms control and understand each other's positions regarding nuclear armaments was seen by optimists as a step toward the more fruitful arms control discussions later on. However, the arms race intensified through the early 1970s with the development of MIRVs by both sides, improved Soviet long-range bombers, and the deployment of more accurate and longer-range Soviet missiles. Detente began its decline after Glassboro (or "Hollybush") and the cold war intensified through the following 15 to 18 years.

Suggested Reading

Robert McNamara, *Blundering into Disaster: Surviving the First Century of the Nuclear Age.* New York: Pantheon, 1986.

Glennan, T. Keith (1905–1995) *American electrical engineer and advocate of nuclear power who served as president of Case Western Reserve University 1948–1950, member of the U.S. Atomic Energy Commission 1950–1952, and advisor to the federal government on nuclear matters*

T. Keith Glennan was appointed to the ATOMIC ENERGY COMMISSION (AEC) in 1950 and served until November 1, 1952. Glennan later served on a number of advisory commissions for the AEC and its successor agencies, including a Concept and Site Selection Board for a NEW

REACTORS IN GERMANY

- ■ Boiling water reactor
- ▨ Pressurized water reactor

North Sea

Flensburg

Kiel

Rostock

Brunsbüttel

Brokdorf   Lübeck

Cuxhaven   Hamburg

Wilhelmshaven   **Stade** **Krümmel**

Unterweser

Bremen

NETHERLANDS   *Weser R.*   *Elbe R.*   *Oder R.*   POLAND

Emsland   Hannover   Wolfsburg   Brandenburg **Berlin** ✪

Osnabrück   Potsdam

Grohnde

Münster   Bielefeld Hameln   Magdeburg   Cottbus

Hamm

Essen   Dortmund   **GERMANY**

Ruhr R.   Kassel   Halle   Leipzig   *Elbe R.*

Düsseldorf   *Weser R.*   Dresden

Cologne   Weimar

Aachen   Bonn   Siegen   Erfurt   Jena   Chemnitz

Rhine R.   *Lahn R.*

BELGIUM

Koblenz   *Main R.*   CZECH REPUBLIC

Frankfurt   Bayreuth
am Main

LUX.   Wiesbaden   **Grafenrheinfeld**

Trier   Mainz   Darmstadt   Bamberg

Moselle R.   **Biblis**   Würzburg

Mannheim   Heidelberg   Nuremberg

Obrigheim **Neckarwestheim**

Philippsburg

Regensburg

Stuttgart   **Isar**

FRANCE   *Danube R.*   Passau

Gundremmingen

Ulm   Dachau

Augsburg   Munich

AUSTRIA

Rhine R.

Freiburg   *Lake
Constance*   N

SWITZERLAND

| 0 | | 100 Miles |
| 0 | | 100 Kms |

PRODUCTION REACTOR in 1982. Glennan advised that a new reactor for the manufacture of PLUTONIUM and TRITIUM should be based on a heavy-water moderator design.

Glennan was born on September 8, 1905, in a small town in southeastern North Dakota. He attended Yale University, earning the B.S. in electrical engineering in 1927. Over the next few years, he supervised the conversion of motion picture theaters in the United States and Great Britain so that they could show movies with sound, heading a large team of engineers and technicians. After work in New York with the successors to the Edison film studios, he moved to Hollywood, where he worked with Paramount and the Samuel Goldwyn studios as a manager.

During World War II, he worked with the Underwater Sound Laboratory of the U.S. Navy at New London, Connecticut. The laboratory was operated for the Office of Scientific Research and Development, improving means of submarine detection and location. Under Glennan's leadership, the laboratory developed an expendable radio sonobuoy that was credited with playing an important part in tracking German submarines. In 1947, Glennan was appointed the new president of Case School of Applied Science in Cleveland, Ohio. Under his presidency, the school became the Case Institute of Technology and developed a national reputation.

He was selected to serve as a commissioner on the Atomic Energy Commission because of his extensive and varied experience in scientific and technical administration. His nomination was approved by the JOINT COMMITTEE ON ATOMIC ENERGY and by the Senate in August 1950, and he was sworn in on October 2, 1950.

As commissioner, Glennan urged private industry to enter the nuclear field. On his retirement from the commission on November 1, 1952, he became active in founding the ATOMIC INDUSTRIAL FORUM, an industry group that continued to lobby for nuclear power development. He died in 1995.

Glomar Explorer

The ship *Glomar Explorer,* built by Howard Hughes for the Central Intelligence Agency (CIA), engaged in a secret mission, known as Project Jennifer, to recover a sunken Soviet submarine from the floor of the Pacific Ocean. A Soviet submarine had been tracked by U.S.

surveillance from its port in Vladivostok, and American technical systems had identified the submarine as belonging to the Golf class, a diesel-driven submarine with three nuclear missiles aboard. During a routine maneuver in April 1968, the submarine suffered a chemical explosion, thought to have resulted from hydrogen gas leaking from the batteries. The submarine sank before any of the crew of 86 could escape.

American surveillance pinpointed the sinking to a spot northwest of Hawaii, in an area where the ocean is over 15,000 feet deep. The United States sent to the area an intelligence-gathering submarine, *Halibut,* which was able to locate and photograph the sunken Soviet submarine. When American authorities realized, from observing Soviet searches, that they did not know the exact location of the lost submarine, a security panel headed by Henry Kissinger decided that the United States should try to raise the submarine. Experts sought to examine the missiles aboard to determine whether the Soviets would be capable of upgrading them. Such information would be useful to know in advance of the Strategic Arms Limitation Talks (SALT I). In addition, if the submarine could be recovered intact with its code books and equipment, a great deal could be learned about Soviet nuclear submarine capabilities. Navy experts, however, argued that the Golf-class submarine was already dated, that it would be too fragile after being crushed by the sea pressure to lift, and that its sensitive material could be recovered with less expense and more quickly by cutting through the hull and removing the items.

The operation was conducted in great secrecy and was not revealed until February 1975. By some estimates it was the most expensive intelligence effort ever mounted by the United States, costing over $500 million and engaging some 4,000 civilian and military personnel.

Howard Hughes constructed the *Glomar Explorer* especially for the effort. Ostensibly designed to perform seabed drilling and exploration, the ship was built so that it could maintain station in a specific spot and could lower a rig that contained massive claws to encircle the submarine and raise it into the body of the ship on the surface. To construct the derrick system, a completely separate submarine barge was constructed where the lifting system could be built in secret and transferred to the interior of the *Glomar Explorer.* The construction of the two ships and the lifting equipment took nearly five years. By mid-July 1974, the system was in place over the submarine, north of Hawaii.

The whole submarine was grasped by the clawlike system and slowly raised toward the surface. However, when the submarine was only partly lifted, it broke into two pieces, and three of the arms of the claw broke off, dropping the section of the submarine with the missiles aboard to the bottom. The other, much smaller section was raised and recovered. Aboard were the bodies of six crew members. The CIA conducted a funeral service in both English and Russian, filming the ceremony for later documentation. A journal found in the ship was preserved and sent to Washington for preservation and translation.

The information about Project Jennifer leaked in a bizarre fashion, in 1975, when burglars seeking cash found records of the operation in the Hughes headquarters in Hollywood, California. They sought to blackmail the company, and the story soon came out in the press.

The amount of information recovered by the CIA was disputed, and some writers on intelligence have claimed that valuable information about Soviet codes and missiles was retrieved. Others have contended that the project was a serious waste of valuable resources and that little of value was aboard the submarine to begin with.

The *Glomar Explorer* was placed in mothballs and much later was used to assist in underwater exploration.

See also NUCLEAR SUBMARINES.

Suggested Reading

Jeffrey Richelson and Desmond Ball, *The Ties That Bind*. Winchester, Mass.: Allen and Unwyn, 1985.

Sherry Sontag and Christopher Drew, *Blind Man's Bluff: The Untold Story of American Submarine Espionage*. New York: Public Affairs, 1998.

R. Varner and W. Collier, *A Matter of Risk*. London: Hodder and Stoughton, 1979.

Gold, Harry (1910–1972) *Swiss-born American chemist who worked as a courier for the Soviet espionage apparatus in the United States during World War II*

Harry Gold played an important role in the Soviet espionage ring during World War II that succeeded in obtaining secrets regarding the nuclear weapon design. Gold served as a courier, picking up material from Klaus FUCHS, who worked as a scientist at LOS ALAMOS and from David Greenglass, who served as an army technician working on the weapons there. Greenglass was Julius ROSENBERG's brother-in-law.

Harry Gold had been born to Sam and Celia Golodnotsky, Russian Jewish emigrés living in Berne, Switzerland, on December 12, 1910. On immigrating to America, they changed their name to Gold and settled in Little Rock, Arkansas, then Chicago, and finally Philadelphia in 1915. Harry grew up in South Philadelphia, attended public schools, and worked at a sugar factory to save money for college. He worked in industrial jobs, attended Drexel University to study chemical engineering, and began industrial spying for the Russians during the mid-1930s.

During the war, Gold continued his work of taking industrial information to his Soviet contact in New York City. In the winter of 1943–1944, he was given the mission of contacting the nuclear scientist, Klaus Fuchs. Meeting in New York at least three times with Fuchs, Gold relayed information through Anatoli Yatzcov (also known as Yakovlev), his espionage control. The information was routed to Russia, where Igor KURCHATOV, working on the Soviet bomb design, found it very helpful. Gold assisted in maintaining contact with Fuchs, and he reached him again in Cambridge, Massachusetts, at the home of Fuchs's sister.

After Fuchs began work at Los Alamos, Gold was instructed to go to Santa Fe, New Mexico, to meet him and, while on the trip, to make a second contact in Albuquerque with technician David Greenglass. Although he thought it bad espionage practice to combine the two missions, the Soviets needed the information rapidly and did not have enough people to serve as couriers of such information. The original courier planned for the contact was Ann Sidorovich, but she was unable to make the trip and Gold went instead.

During that trip, on June 2, 1945, Gold met Fuchs at the Castillo Bridge in Santa Fe, and Fuchs passed in a thick packet of written material on many details of the FAT MAN design, to be tested in July. The next morning, he went to the home of David Greenglass, saying "I come from Julius." Gold exchanged with Greenglass half of a Jell-O box, the means by which the two men identified each other. Later, Greenglass provided Gold with a sketch of the bomb design as he understood it. Gold took both packets back to New York, which included the information from Fuchs and that from Greenglass.

After Klaus Fuchs was arrested in Great Britain in 1949, the FBI began to suspect that his contact had been Harry Gold, although Fuchs only knew Gold by his code name, Raymond. After Fuchs tentatively identified Gold from a motion picture supplied by the FBI, Gold was arrested and questioned. When his apartment was searched and a map of Santa Fe was discovered, Gold became rattled and then admitted he was the contact for Klaus Fuchs.

Gold was tried for espionage in December of 1950 and sentenced to 30 years in prison.

Suggested Reading

Richard Rhodes, *Dark Sun*. New York: Simon and Schuster, 1995.

Golden Rule

The *Golden Rule* was a 30-foot sailing ketch that participated in a major antiwar protest action organized by the COMMITTEE FOR NON-VIOLENT ACTION (CNVA) in 1958. Of all of the CNVA actions, it may have been the most widely publicized.

On February 10, 1958, the *Golden Rule,* with a crew of four pacifists captained by Albert Bigelow, set sail from California to protest United States nuclear weapons tests in OPERATION HARDTACK, scheduled for April through August off ENEWETAK Island. The organization also sought to send a pacifist delegation to the Soviet Union to appeal for an end to Soviet nuclear testing. Soviet officials thwarted those plans by refusing to grant visas to the five-person group.

Bigelow proved a dashing media figure. A Harvard graduate, he had worked for the election of President Dwight EISENHOWER, and he had earlier served as a World War II naval officer in command of three combat vessels. Shocked by the atomic bomb, the Bigelow family hosted two young women from Hiroshima, survivors of the atomic bomb who were brought to America for cosmetic surgery, and the experience influenced his pilgrimage to pacifism. Like the other *Golden Rule* crew, Bigelow had participated in the earlier Nonviolent Action against Nuclear Weapons group's NEVADA TEST SITE protest the summer before. Bigelow announced his decision to skipper the *Golden Rule* into the prohibited Pacific testing zone on grounds that he wanted to do something about peace, not just talk about it. Ignoring a federal injunction, the crew set sail for the Enewetak testing area; however, the coast guard quickly stopped the ketch and towed it back to Honolulu. Jailed for one week, the crew made a second attempt to reach the test site but again was halted,

arrested, convicted, and sentenced to 30 days in prison.

By coincidence, as the crew of the *Golden Rule* awaited trial, the *Phoenix of Hiroshima* arrived in Honolulu with Earle Reynolds, an anthropologist who had spent three years in Japan studying the effects of radiation, and his wife and two children. The Reynoldses decided to continue the *Golden Rule*'s protest; the *Phoenix* sailed into the nuclear test zone and the Reynoldses were arrested. Both the *Golden Rule* and *Phoenix* garnered enormous publicity for the antinuclear weapons movement.

Gorbachev, Mikhail (1931–) *leader of the Soviet Union as general secretary of the Communist Party (1985–1988) and president of the Supreme Soviet (1988–1991)*

On March 11, 1985, Konstantin Chernenko, general secretary of the Communist Party of the Soviet Union died, and his post passed to a much younger man, Mikhail Gorbachev, whose leadership profoundly affected the international nuclear arms race. From 1985 through November 1988, Gorbachev served as general secretary of the party while Andrey Gromyko was president of the Supreme Soviet of the U.S.S.R. Gorbachev took the position of president of the Supreme Soviet in November 1988, serving through 1991.

Gorbachev was born on March 2, 1931, in the village of Privolynoye in Stavropol region in the north Caucasus Mountains. His parents were from peasant ancestry, and his father was an agricultural machine operator. Mikhail Gorbachev graduated from Moscow State University in 1955 with a law degree. After graduation, he rose quickly through party posts and was elected to the Central Committee of the Communist Party in March 1971 and to the position of agricultural secretary of the Central Committee in 1978. In 1980, he was selected to be a member of the Politburo. When Chernenko died in 1985, the selection of Gorbachev on March 11, 1985, as general secretary of the Communist Party Central Committee represented a sharp change from the pre–World War II generation.

In 1986, Gorbachev announced the planned withdrawal of Soviet troops from WARSAW TREATY ORGANIZATION countries, leading to a series of political changes in those countries over the period 1986 to 1988, culminating in 1989 with the establishment of democratic regimes in most of them.

Meanwhile, Gorbachev continued arms control negotiations, focused on reducing nuclear armaments in Europe. Meeting with President Ronald REAGAN in REYKJAVIK in October 1986, both leaders agreed to a plan for eventual elimination of all nuclear weapons. Later, this plan appeared to form the basis for both the INTERMEDIATE NUCLEAR FORCES (INF) agreement of 1988 and for the Strategic Arms Reduction Treaty (START I), signed by Gorbachev and George BUSH in June 1991. In 1989, Gorbachev announced unilateral deep cuts in the Soviet defense budget, and he completed withdrawal of Soviet forces from Afghanistan.

On August 19, 1991, Gorbachev was taken prisoner by a group of Soviet hard-line leaders. However, the attempted coup failed within two days, and he was released unharmed. The effort to overthrow the government was foiled by the position of the leadership of the Russian Republic, particularly its president, Boris YELTSIN. Nevertheless, the prestige and standing of the Soviet Union had been severely compromised.

In the late summer and fall of 1991, Gorbachev and Bush agreed to a number of "confidence-building measures," by which they meant that each side would unilaterally announce a number of disarmament steps that were not necessarily subject to independent verification. Bush's steps were known as PRESIDENTIAL NUCLEAR INITIATIVE 91, and his first steps were taken in September 1991. Gorbachev announced the elimination of almost half of the nuclear-tipped surface-to-air missiles (SAMs), and he initiated withdrawal of ground-launched CRUISE MISSILES. Planning for these actions and Gorbachev's strained relations with his own internal security forces appeared to have contributed to the decision by the hard-line plotters to attempt the coup against him in August.

Gorbachev announced the dissolution of the Soviet Union and the organization of the Commonwealth of Independent States on December 8, 1991, and on December 25, 1991, he retired from his position as president, turning control of the nuclear weaponry of the Soviet Union over to Boris Yeltsin, the Russian president. He continued to write memoirs and political essays over the next few years. In 1996, he mounted an unsuccessful campaign for the Russian presidency. He served as president of the International Fund of Socioeconomic and Political Studies.

Suggested Reading

Mikhail Gorbachev, *At the Summit.* New York: Richardson, Steirman and Black, 1988.

Gore, Oklahoma   *See* KERR-MCGEE.

Goudsmit, Samuel Abraham (1901–1978)

Dutch-born American physicist who made several contributions to the theory of atomic structure in the 1920s and who, during World War II, headed a secret organization devoted to investigating and locating the extent of the German effort to build a nuclear weapon

Goudsmit was born in The Hague, Netherlands, on July 11, 1901, and studied theoretical physics at the University of Leiden. He was able to demonstrate that electrons spin as they orbit the nucleus of atoms. Working with a fellow student, George Uhlenbeck, Goudsmit's spin theory accounted for fine lines in the spectroscopic images of the elements and helped advance the general theory of the behavior of the electron. Goudsmit received his doctorate in physics from that university, and then, in 1927, he went to the University of Michigan, where he taught until 1941. In 1930, he collaborated with Linus PAULING on *The Structure of Line Spectra,* and in 1932, he published with Robert F. BACHER a technical work, *Atomic Energy States.* During the war, Goudsmit worked first on radar problems at the Massachusetts Institute of Technology and then, in 1944, he headed the ALSOS PROJECT that questioned Werner HEISENBERG.

He became involved in studying German progress on nuclear questions, and he was selected by Vannevar BUSH in 1943 for the job of finding out how close the Germans had come to building an atomic bomb. One of Goudsmit's first tasks was to interview Frédéric JOLIOT-CURIE in Paris about German work on nuclear subjects. Goudsmit identified the facilities to be visited in Germany and the individuals to be captured and interrogated if possible. He soon concluded, correctly, that the Germans had not organized nuclear research very well and that they had bungled the science. Goudsmit concluded that the German scientists had decided that a nuclear weapon was not feasible and instead had turned their attention to the effort to build a reactor for power generation or ship propulsion. Hampered by lack of materials and severe U.S. bombing of facilities, they made little progress toward that goal, building only a test-stage reactor that had never achieved controlled fission.

Heisenberg later disagreed with Goudsmit's conclusions, arguing that the German scientists had not pursued the atomic weapon largely because of the difficulty in obtaining funding and for moral reasons rather than because of any scientific or technical errors on their part.

For his work in heading up the Alsos mission, Goudsmit received the Medal of Freedom from the United States and the Order of the British Empire from Great Britain. He was later elected to the U.S. National Academy of Sciences.

After the war, Goudsmit taught first at Northwestern University and then accepted a position as senior scientist at BROOKHAVEN NATIONAL LABORATORY. In 1948 he was appointed chairman of the Physics Department there. When Senator Joseph McCarthy investigated the issue of the penetration of communist sympathizers in the U.S. Army and sensationalized his charges, Goudsmit became a vocal opponent, indicating that such investigations not only wasted taxpayer money but also damaged morale at scientific institutions.

In addition to his scientific work, he published an account of his experiences during the war. Goudsmit died on December 4, 1978, in Reno, Nevada.

See also GERMAN ATOMIC BOMB PROJECT.

Suggested Reading
Samuel Goudsmit, *Alsos.* New York: Henry Schuman, 1947.
Thomas Powers, *Heisenberg's War.* New York: Knopf, 1993.

Graphite

Graphite is one of the allotropic forms of carbon. Enrico FERMI used graphite in the form of bricks as the neutron moderator in the original CHICAGO PILE-1, and graphite has been used subsequently as the neutron moderator in some other kinds of nuclear reactors. Allotropes are different forms of the same element, that is, graphite and diamond (both are C), oxygen and ozone (O_2 and O_3, respectively), et cetera. During the work on the atomic bomb in World War II, American scientists made use of synthetically produced graphite with a high degree of purity as a moderator. In Germany, naturally mined graphite had many impurities that tended to poison nuclear chain reactions, and this was one reason German scientists chose to use DEUTERIUM or heavy water for their experimental reactors.

Greenpeace

The ship *Greenpeace* was built in 1959 in the Netherlands as a salvage vessel and oceangoing tug. In 1977,

the ship was converted to a pilot ship, and, in 1985, it was acquired by the Greenpeace organization. The organization modified the ship and began to use it to conduct environmental voyages and to attempt, by crossing into prohibited zones, the prevention of nuclear weapons and missile testing.

Modifications to the ship included the addition of a helicopter pad and supplementary passenger space. The ship is 58 meters long, 11 meters wide, and has a gross tonnage of 905 tons. The ship has a crew of 15 and can accommodate up to 38 people.

Although most of the voyages of the *Greenpeace* have been devoted to interruption of whaling by Japanese fleets and to Antarctic exploration, the ship has also been involved in several protest actions against radioactive pollution, nuclear energy, and nuclear weapons. In 1989, while protesting the testing of TRIDENT missiles by the United States, the ship was damaged in collisions with two U.S. Navy vessels. After repairs in port, the ship made a voyage to NOVAYA ZEMLYA in 1990, the Soviet weapons testing area. The ship put ashore a team to measure local radioactivity. The ship was boarded by armed Soviet agents, who destroyed equipment and then released the ship.

In 1993, the ship observed Russian dumping of radioactive waste in the Sea of Japan. In 1995, *Greenpeace* and other ships joined in a protest against the resumption of nuclear testing by France in Polynesia. French police boarded the vessel and destroyed navigation and communications equipment. The ship was held and not released for six months.

Following the mid-1990s, the ship was used to publicize campaigns against nuclear testing and in actions to oppose the shipment of nuclear materials by sea. Other activities included protests against wasteful fishing methods and participation in other environmental campaigns.

Since its founding in 1981, the Greenpeace organization has operated a number of other vessels. Ships have included *Rainbow Warrior,* sunk by the French in 1985, and a replacement *Rainbow Warrior,* a three-masted schooner launched in 1989. *Sirius* was a converted pilot ship that operated mostly in European waters. *Arctic Sunrise* was used primarily in protesting pollution from oil rigs and in Antarctic exploration. Smaller vessels have included *Moby Dick,* which operated mainly in the Baltic and North Sea regions, and *Beluga,* which sailed on inland waterways in Europe.

Gromyko, Andrey Andreyevich (1904–1989)
served as foreign minister of the Soviet Union from 1957 to 1985

Andrey Gromyko, as Soviet foreign minister, was generally regarded as an advocate of peaceful coexistence with the United States and the other Western powers.

Gromyko was born on July 18, 1904, in Belarus to a poor peasant family. He rose through the Soviet bureaucracy and served as the youngest Soviet ambassador to the United States during and immediately after World War II (1943–1946). After serving as Soviet representative to the United Nations (1946–1948), he was appointed foreign minister of the Soviet Union in 1957 and served until 1985. A member of the Politburo from 1973 to 1988, he was briefly chairman of the Supreme Soviet of the U.S.S.R., 1985–1988.

Gromyko tended to work toward DETENTE with the United States, actively supporting the ANTI-BALLISTIC MISSILE TREATY of 1972, and SALT I and SALT II. Convinced that efforts toward better relations with the United States were stalled in 1979, he supported the Soviet invasion of Afghanistan. His efforts to improve relations with the United States during the REAGAN administration were unsuccessful. He left the Foreign Ministry in 1985. Western diplomats regarded Gromyko as a highly professional member of the Soviet foreign service, and he won their respect for his efforts to maintain world recognition of the Soviet Union as a major power. Gromyko died on July 2, 1989.

Suggested Reading
Raymond Garthoff, *Detente and Confrontation: American-Soviet Relations from Nixon to Reagan.* Washington, D.C.: Brookings Institution, 1994.

Groves, Leslie (1896–1970) *served during World War II as the general in charge of the Manhattan Project*

Known as a driving engineer-officer, Groves successfully managed the MANHATTAN ENGINEER DISTRICT from 1942 through 1946 and then served as a member of the MILITARY LIAISON COMMITTEE to the ATOMIC ENERGY COMMISSION.

Groves was born on August 17, 1896, in Albany, New York, the son of a Presbyterian minister. Groves was educated at West Point, graduating fourth in his

Leslie Groves. General Leslie Groves headed up the construction of the Pentagon building before being selected to command the Manhattan Engineer District that developed the American atomic bomb. (National Archives and Records Administration)

class in November 1918. In the 1920s and 1930s, he took on several engineering assignments with the army, including the development of a proposed Nicaraguan transisthmian canal to supplement the Panama Canal. He was in charge of the construction of the Pentagon building, the largest office building in the world. Groves established a reputation as an uncompromising problem solver who avoided army politics and focused on getting results. Secretary of War Henry L. Stimson and President Franklin ROOSEVELT appointed Groves to head the Manhattan Engineer District (MED). Groves was promoted to the temporary rank of brigadier general and assumed formal control on September 7, 1942.

MED expanded rapidly during the war to encompass at least 13 research projects at university laboratories and 37 separate facilities around the United States, employing more than 100,000 persons. This vast operation was conducted in the utmost secrecy, including the construction of three entirely secret facilities whose existence was not announced until after the detonation of the first weapons over HIROSHIMA and NAGASAKI. LOS ALAMOS, New Mexico, became the site of research and development, while HANFORD, Washington, and OAK RIDGE, Tennessee, focused on production of fissile materials for the weapons. Groves personally participated in the selection of the sites.

Groves brought the same determination and drive to the MED that he had to the construction of the Pentagon. His military methods and style, particularly his insistence on compartmentalization of information, rankled some of the scientists who were more used to free exchange of ideas. Groves placed limits on the sharing of information with Canadian and British scientists. He followed developments closely, making many key decisions regarding weapon design, production facility construction, ISOTOPE separation plants, and URANIUM supply.

Groves was unimpressed by arguments from scientists on the project who advocated that the weapon not be used against population centers. He was well aware that the expenditure of $2 billion for a weapon system never employed would be extremely difficult to justify in any postwar review. He was particularly suspicious of the motives and arguments of some of the scientists who he regarded as prima donnas, including Leo SZILARD. However, he was supportive of J. Robert OPPENHEIMER, retaining him as scientific director of the project in the face of charges that Oppenheimer was a security risk because of his former association with members of the Communist Party and because of his failure to properly report security violations.

Groves continued to administer the Manhattan Engineer District immediately after the war. With the establishment of the Atomic Energy Commission, he served as a member of the first Military Liaison Committee, which provided a link between the military services and the civilian agency. Groves worked with Secretary of State Dean ACHESON in hammering out the details of the report prepared by David LILIENTHAL on international control of atomic energy. When the BARUCH PLAN failed to win support at the United Nations, Groves was a firm advocate of maintaining the American monopoly on the nuclear weapon.

Groves retired from the Army in March 1948. He died on July 13, 1970, in Washington, D.C.

Suggested Reading

Leslie Groves, *Now It Can Be Told.* New York: Harper and Row, 1962.

Gun-Type Design

In 1945, during the Manhattan Project, two designs were developed for the nuclear weapon at LOS ALAMOS. The simpler type was the "gun type," in which a subcritical piece of active material was fired down a gun barrel to mate with another subcritical piece of material, so that the two together would constitute more than one critical mass. The weapon dropped on HIROSHIMA used a gun-type design with uranium-235 as the active material.

See also IMPLOSION.

H

Hahn,   Otto (1879–1968) *German   scientist whose   work   in   the   1930s   led   to   the   discovery   of nuclear fission*

Otto Hahn's work in the 1930s in the field of radioactive elements soon led to crucial problems resulting from the bombardment of URANIUM with neutrons. The understanding of what occurred was crucial to the development of atomic fission, leading directly to the possibility of nuclear power and nuclear weapons.

Hahn was born in Frankfurt, Germany, on March 8, 1879, the son of a businessman. He grew interested in chemistry during high school and attended Marburg University beginning in 1897. He completed a doctorate in chemistry in 1901, with a specialty in biochemistry. For two years, he took an appointment as an assistant to a professor at Marburg in anticipation of going into industry as a chemist.

In industry, he would need a foreign language, so he decided to study in Great Britain, moving there in 1904. He took up a position in the laboratory of Sir William Ramsay at University College in London. Ramsay at that time was working on radioactivity, and he asked Hahn to assist him in extracting minute particles of radium from a sample of barium salt. Hahn, who had no experience in the field of radiochemistry,

followed a method established by Marie Curie. His careful work for Ramsay led to the discovery of a new element, radiothorium. He continued further experiments in radiochemistry, impressing Ramsay with his skill as an experimental chemist. Ramsay secured Hahn a position in a chemical institute at the University of Berlin, convincing him not to go into industry.

Hahn agreed, but before taking up his new post, he wanted to improve his knowledge in the field of radioactive elements. Ramsay recommend Hahn to work under Ernest RUTHERFORD, at McGill University in Montreal, Canada. At McGill, Hahn convinced Rutherford of his capability in his adopted field, discovering another element, radio-actinium.

Returning to Berlin, Hahn soon became a recognized expert in radioactive elements. In 1912, he headed a small unit within the Kaiser Wilhelm Research Institute for Chemistry, and he was joined there by Lise MEITNER. Hahn and Meitner continued working on the discovery of new radioactive elements. Their researches were interrupted by World War I, but in the 1920s Hahn and Meitner returned to the subject.

Their field of radiochemistry became nuclear chemistry, with James CHADWICK's discovery of the neutron and other work in the field in the early 1930s. Hahn,

Meitner, and others turned their attention to the possibility of transuranic elements, that is, heavy elements such as uranium that had been bombarded with neutrons that gained in mass and changed into new, heavier elements.

Hahn and Fritz Strassman worked in 1938 to identify the elements that resulted from a bombardment of uranium, as they found radioactivity in the resulting material. Assuming the radioactivity to come from radium, they were puzzled, as radium has a lower mass than uranium, whereas they had expected a new element with a higher mass. They sent a sample of the material to Lise Meitner, who had moved to Sweden to avoid Nazi persecution.

Meitner correctly identified the resulting material as barium with a much lower atomic weight. Meitner identified Hahn and Strassman's work as nuclear fission. Her 1938 discovery of fission as the means to unleash atomic energy was immediately noted with interest in Britain and the United States.

During World War II, Hahn continued his work on the study of fission fragments, and he did not become involved in the German project to study the military applications of splitting the atom. Nevertheless at the end of the war, he was interned with other German nuclear scientists at Farm Hall in Britain. He was there when HIROSHIMA and NAGASAKI were bombed and learned then that his earlier discoveries had led to a weapon made by the Americans.

In 1946 he returned to Germany and took up the leadership of the his old institute, now renamed the Max Planck Institute. Over the next decade he continued to warn against misuse of atomic energy, and he worked to resist German development of an independent nuclear weapons capability. Hahn died in Göttingen, Germany, on July 28, 1968.

See also GERMAN ATOMIC BOMB PROJECT.

Suggested reading
Hans G. Graetzer and David L. Anderson, *The Discovery of Nuclear Fission.* New York: Van Nostrand Reinhold, 1971.

Half-Life

Half-life is the time required for one-half of the radioactive nuclides present to undergo radioactive decay. The half-life is a characteristic of the radioactive nuclide. Half-lives can be as short as a few seconds to as long as thousands of years. After a duration of time equivalent to one half-life has elapsed, one-half of the amount of radioactive material originally present remains. After a second half-life has elapsed, half of the half remains.

Hanford

Hanford, Washington, became the site of one of the most important parts of the American nuclear weapons complex. Before World War II, the region around the small village of Hanford on the Columbia River in eastern Washington State was largely desert. Nearby were some irrigated fields, with orchards and some livestock raising. General Leslie GROVES, after receiving reports from a team looking at several sites, chose the spot early in 1943 as the place to build the production reactors to produce PLUTONIUM for the MANHATTAN ENGINEER DISTRICT.

After purchase of the land, about 1,500 people were moved out and construction began on PRODUCTION REACTORS, a plutonium separation plant, and housing for the workers. The site had been chosen for its remoteness, helping to keep the project secret. Furthermore, in case of an accident, very few people would be exposed. In addition, the Columbia River could provide cold water to cool the reactors. All of the reactors were built close to the river in order to have easy access to cooling water.

The reactors at Hanford began to produce plutonium in 1944, and, by July 1945, enough plutonium had been made to fuel the first nuclear device, tested at Alamogordo, New Mexico, on July 16, 1945. Plutonium from Hanford also was used in the heart of the weapon exploded over Nagasaki on August 8, 1945.

The pass-through cooling system that used Columbia River water was risky. The cooling water ran directly over and through the tin-coated URANIUM fuel slugs in the reactors. Sometimes the coating would rupture and radioactive materials would be washed out of the reactor in the cooling water. To prevent the dangerous material from going directly into the river, engineers had built cooling ponds where the sediments could settle out before the water was pumped back into the river. Nevertheless, radioactive materials would collect in the ponds, to be gathered and stored in large underground metal tanks that caused problems in later years. Despite the settling process, plutonium and chemicals used in the reactors washed through the ponds into the river.

Hanford. The first production reactors were built along the Columbia River in the Hanford reservation in Washington State. The river supplied cold water for cooling the reactors, and the isolated location provided for both security and minimal risk to population in the event of an accident. (Library of Congress)

Immediately after World War II, the Hanford facilities were slightly neglected. However, as the cold war increased in tempo in the late 1940s and the 1950s, new reactors were built at Hanford and the ATOMIC ENERGY COMMISSION worked to improve working and safety conditions. Together with separation plants to refine the plutonium from the reactors, the new reactors employed thousands of people, who lived mostly in nearby Richland, a city that expanded at the southeastern corner of the large Hanford reservation.

Soon Hanford became a major employer, and the thriving support businesses in the local community brought still more people. By the early 1950s, the population of the local area had grown to over 65,000. Even as the reactors and processing plants expanded production during the height of the cold war in the late 1950s, problems continued to mount. Local people grew concerned over radioactive releases to both the river and the atmosphere. Some residents traced unusual cases of cancer to such airborne emissions, and during the 1970s and 1980s the DEPARTMENT OF ENERGY faced rising criticism from activists and journalists over the issue of how safe the Hanford facilities had become. Even so, many local people employed at the reactors were opposed to closing reactors and other facilities, and they fought to keep the federal nuclear facilities operating with one or another form of nuclear work. Reactors for the production of electricity were built in the complex, and the laboratories took up a range of research work, including environmental studies.

All of the production reactors at Hanford were closed by 1988. Nevertheless, the reserve continued to be major part of the Department of Energy's nuclear complex.

Suggested Reading

Rodney Carlisle, *Supplying the Nuclear Arsenal.* Baltimore, Md.: Johns Hopkins University Press, 1996.

Michele Stenhejm Gerber, *On the Home Front: The Cold War Legacy of the Hanford Nuclear Site.* Lincoln: University of Nebraska Press, 1992.

Harwell Atomic Energy Research Establishment

Harwell, in Oxfordshire, Great Britain, is the headquarters and the largest site of the United Kingdom Atomic Energy Authority. The location is about a one hour drive from Heathrow Airport. Harwell is the British equivalent of America's LOS ALAMOS.

The facility is a former Royal Air Force base, transferred to the Ministry of Supply in 1946. Nobel Prize winner John D. COCKCROFT was appointed the first director of the Research Establishment and served until 1959. Early researchers at the facility included Klaus FUCHS, who confessed in 1950 to espionage for the Soviet Union during and after World War II.

Harwell is located on about 500 acres within a fenced site, with adjoining properties for related work.

The government facility hosts some private corporations engaged in scientific work for customers around the world.

The government-owned facilities include partially decommissioned reactors, laboratories, and a storage vault for radioactive waste, built at a cost of 50 million pounds in 1999.

As the British government decreases its commitment to nuclear research, Harwell has been redeveloped for tenant occupation to bring businesses and jobs to the relatively remote location.

Heat Exchanger

A heat exchanger is any device that transfers heat from one fluid (liquid or gas) to another or to the environment. An everyday example of a heat exchanger is the cooling system in an automobile. Heat from the combustion of a petroleum fuel is transferred to the air by way of the circulating coolant and the radiator. In power generators, heat exchangers transfer heat from a primary reactor coolant (such as pressurized water or boiling water) to a secondary loop to generate steam to drive turbines.

Heavy Water   *See* DEUTERIUM.

Heavy-Water Reactor

Heavy water, D_2O, is an expensive alternative to light water, H_2O, for neutron moderation. Heavy-water reactors usually employ a tube-type design in which the fuel elements are positioned inside process tubes that pass through a tank of the heavy-water moderator. Coolant circulates around the fuel elements in the process tubes. In some reactor configurations, the heavy water does not circulate. The tube-type design minimizes the quantity of this expensive moderator.

The Canadian CANDU reactors utilize heavy water as both the moderator and the coolant. The advantages of the heavy-water moderated reactor are its ability to utilize natural uranium rather than enriched uranium as a fuel, and its low fuel consumption. This is due in part to the low neutron capture CROSS SECTION of DEUTERIUM. One of the consequences of heavy-water moderation and cooling is the special care needed to attend to TRITIUM produced in the moderator. Of the approximately 500 nuclear power reactors worldwide, some

BRITISH NUCLEAR SITES

two dozen are of the pressurized heavy-water moderated and cooled type.

The PRODUCTION REACTORS constructed during the 1950s at the SAVANNAH RIVER SITE all utilized heavy water as moderator and coolant.

During World War II, the main source of heavy water for the German nuclear weapon-design effort was a plant in Norway, the NORSK HYDRO facility. Allied raids on this production plant were intended to cripple the German effort to build a nuclear weapon.

Heisenberg, Werner (1901–1976) *leading German physicist and developer of the "uncertainty principle," who headed the abortive attempt to develop a German nuclear weapon*

By World War II, Werner Heisenberg was already famous for discovering the principle that many nuclear events could not be predicted with certainty, but only in terms of probability, known as the Heisenberg principle. Since Heisenberg was well known to the international scientific community, physicists in the United States and Great Britain assumed that the Nazis would be able to develop a nuclear weapon under his able leadership and were surprised to learn at the end of the war that little research toward that end had been accomplished in Germany.

Heisenberg was born in 1901 in Würzburg, Germany, and studied in Munich. He assisted Max Born at Göttingen University and then worked with Niels BOHR in Copenhagen in the period 1924 to 1926. Heisenberg accepted a post as professor at Leipzig and remained at that position until 1941.

In his work in the 1920s and 1930s, Heisenberg worked on a system he called matrix mechanics, developing a mathematical model for the atom and making contributions to the development of quantum theory. He was most famous for developing the uncertainty principle, which stated that there were limits to the achievable accuracy of measurement of the position and momentum of an atomic particle. As one was measured accurately, it became less possible to measure the other accurately. He concluded that for many atomic actions, one could express the outcome not with certainty but only with a probability that an effect would occur. In 1932, he won a Nobel Prize for work he had achieved when only 24 years old.

He became director of the Max Planck Institute for Physics from 1942 to 1970. During World War II, Heisenberg worked for the Nazi government on problems connected with nuclear fission. He visited with Niels Bohr in 1941, apparently trying to determine whether the Allies were having any success with the development of a nuclear weapon. According to his own later account of the meeting, he attempted to encourage Bohr to join with him in agreeing that scientists should not work on developing a nuclear weapon during the war.

Heisenberg's team were not convinced a nuclear weapon could be developed within the time and resources available to Germany during the war, and the project achieved little. Whether the lack of success was due to the unwillingness of Heisenberg and other scientists to provide Hitler with such a terrible weapon as he later claimed or whether it was due to the many financial and technical obstacles that stood in the way of producing a weapon before Germany was defeated has remained a major controversy surrounding Heisenberg's wartime project.

With the defeat of Germany, Heisenberg and fellow German physicists were detained by the British at Farm Hall, in Britain, where they received news of the American success with the nuclear weapon for the first time after the detonation of the weapon over HIROSHIMA. Their stunned reactions and discussion were recorded through secret microphones planted to listen in on their comments.

Analysis of the transcripts, published in 1993, has led some historians to conclude that the German scientists had not been capable of mounting the effort to develop a nuclear weapon during the war. Others have found in the transcripts evidence to support Heisenberg's own contention that he and other German scientists chose not to develop the weapon.

Suggested Reading

David Cassidy, *Uncertainty: The Life and Science of Werner Heisenberg.* New York: Freeman, 1992.

Thomas Powers, *Heisenberg's War: The Secret History of the German Bomb.* New York: Knopf, 1993.

Richard Rhodes, *The Making of the Atomic Bomb.* New York: Simon and Schuster, 1988.

Mark Walker, *Uranium Machines, Nuclear Explosives, and National Socialism: The German Quest for Nuclear Power, 1939–1949.* New York: Cambridge University Press, 1991.

Herrington, John S. (1939–) *American administrator who served as the fifth secretary of energy from 1985 to 1989, the third to serve under President Ronald Reagan*

John Herrington. Herrington served as secretary of energy during the second term of Ronald Reagan, as the Department of Energy faced public outcry regarding environmental and safety issues. (Department of Energy)

John Herrington served as secretary of energy from February 1985 until after the inauguration of President George H.W. BUSH in January 1989, when he was replaced by James WATKINS.

Although much of Herrington's administration was focused on issues of energy supply and oil price regulation, he initiated several projects with the goal of improving the nation's nuclear weapons capability. He announced the development of an Advanced Vapor Laser Isotope Separate process to separate PLUTONIUM from PRODUCTION REACTOR output in 1985 and 1986. He began characterization of the YUCCA MOUNTAIN waste disposal site under the Nuclear Waste Policy Act as amended in 1987. Under his administration, N reactor at HANFORD was closed in response to a study by the National Academy of Sciences following the CHERNOBYL reactor accident in 1986. He requested a similar review of five of the department's large research reactors: the Experimental Breeder Reactor and the Advanced Test Reactor at the IDAHO NATIONAL ENGINEERING LABORATORY, the FAST FLUX TEST FACILITY at Hanford, the High Flux Isotope Reactor at OAK RIDGE, and the High Flux Beam Reactor at BROOKHAVEN NATIONAL LABORATORY.

In 1988, Herrington chartered a Nuclear Weapons Complex Modernization Study Steering Committee to develop a 20-year plan to review the overall size, production capacity, and research and development base of the weapons complex.

Meanwhile, he sponsored programs of international cooperation, especially in the area of developing controlled thermonuclear reactions. On July 2, 1988, Herrington endorsed export of plutonium for use in the Beznau power reactor in Switzerland. Most notably in the area of cooperation, the U.S./Soviet Joint Verification Experiment opened the August 17, 1988, nuclear test KEARSAGE to visits by 43 Soviet experts. This exchange of information was designed to measure each nation's ability to monitor the size of nuclear tests in the other nation. A similar test, with U.S. representatives, took place at SEMIPALATINSK in Kazakhstan on September 14, 1988.

In November 1988, Herrington established the Office of NEW PRODUCTION REACTORS to conduct research and development, site and technology selection for a new reactor to produce TRITIUM and PLUTONIUM.

Hexafluoride Conversion

In processing uranium ore into nuclear fuel, the material goes through several stages, in which hexafluoride conversion is a crucial step prior to separation of the ISOTOPES of URANIUM from uranium hexafluoride or UF_6.

The ore mined in the United States typically contains about 0.2 of 1% uranium. In order to concentrate the pure uranium, first steps usually consist of grinding, washing, flotation, and settling out to remove the waste clay and sandstone from the uranium. These physical processes conducted at the mine can concentrate the uranium but only to less than 50%.

The ore is then treated at a mill, using either a carbonate leach or an acid leach, leading to a precipitate, usually of ammonium diuranate that is dried into a powdered oxide. This material is then taken to a conversion facility where a solvent extraction method produces a solution of uranium that is dried and calcined to form U_3O_8. It is after this stage that conversion to hexaflouride takes place.

Purified U_3O_8 is reduced to uranium oxide (UO_2) and then converted to UF_4 by gaseous hydrogen fluoride in a fluidized-bed reactor. Different firms use different processes and reactors to combine pure fluorine with the uranium oxide and to distill out the uranium hexafluoride or UF_6. The uranium hexafluoride is then taken for isotope separation, in which the proportion of fissile ^{235}U is increased to more than 3% for use in commercial power reactors or to more than 90% for use in small research reactors or ship propulsion reactors as highly enriched uranium (HEU). HEU is also sufficiently concentrated to be used as a special nuclear material in nuclear weapons.

Hickenlooper, Bourke   *See* ATOMIC ENERGY ACT OF 1954.

High-Level Waste

In the nuclear field, high-level waste refers to radioactive waste generated from used FISSILE MATERIALS. REPROCESSING of spent nuclear fuel rods from reactors or target materials from PRODUCTION REACTORS removes about 98% of the URANIUM and PLUTONIUM. After the reprocessing, the remaining material is high-level waste. It is usually produced as a highly radioactive liquid. In order to dispose of it in the United States, it must be converted to solid form. At HANFORD and some other sites, high-level waste was transported to underground storage tanks. Plans call for moving the waste to transport containers and shipping them to a permanent high-level waste site such as YUCCA MOUNTAIN.

High-Temperature Gas-Cooled Reactors (HTGRs)

An alternative to reactors cooled with regular, or "light," water (LWRs) or cooled with DEUTERIUM, or "heavy" water (HWRs), is a high-temperature gascooled reactor (HTGR). The original idea was proposed in 1944 by MANHATTAN ENGINEER DISTRICT scientist Farrington Daniels, who proposed a graphite-moderated, helium gas-cooled reactor. The X reactor constructed to produce sample amounts of PLUTONIUM for a pilot plant at OAK RIDGE during the war was air-cooled.

However, the first HTGR for electrical utility purposes was designed in Great Britain. At the British Harwell Research Establishment, a gas-cooled reactor was proposed and designed using magnesium-oxide

canning of fuel slugs with carbon-dioxide cooling. This reactor was dubbed "MAGNOX" in 1953 and was first built at Calder Hall, operational in 1956, and at Chapelcross, operational in 1959. In 1958, the French developed both air-cooled and carbon-dioxide cooled reactors at Marcoule. Altogether there were 37 MAGNOX reactors built around the world, including 26 in Britain, eight in France, and one each in Italy, Spain, and Japan.

Further British and French reactors continued to use the HTGR designs, whereas most power reactors built in the United States followed a light-water cooling design. Britain exported a Magnox design to Italy in the reactor at Latina, which first went critical in 1962. A helium-cooled reactor, built in Britain as part of a European consortium called the Dragon Project, opened in 1964. Japan opened its Magnox type reactor, Tokai-1, in 1966. Germany developed an advanced gas-cooled reactor using helium gas in 1967. The Swiss developed a heavy-water moderated gas-cooled reactor at LUCENS in 1956, which was closed after a fire on January 21, 1969. The French built nine of the carbon dioxide–cooled reactors, including one in 1972 in Vandellos, Spain. With the spread of HTGRs in Europe, American advocates continued to argue that the reactor would be safer than the water-moderated and water-cooled reactors built for the U.S. commercial power industry. Some claimed that the U.S. preference for pressurized water reactors (PWRs) in particular sprang from the use of that design aboard nuclear submarines.

Only two commercial reactors in the United States ever followed the gas-cooled design. In 1957, the U.S. company General Atomics began planning a gas-cooled reactor, later built at Peach Bottom, Pennsylvania, in 1962. It became operational in 1967 but was decommissioned in 1974.

Public Service Corporation of Colorado entered into a contract with General Atomics Corporation to build a gas-cooled reactor at Ft. St. Vrain as a demonstration plant. This 330 megawatt-electrical reactor went operational in 1976. In 1984, the plant was temporarily closed for environmental modification, opening again in April 1986. In 1987, the plant suffered a fire in a hydraulic system and the reactor was shut down.

In the United States, General Atomics continued to promote the gas-cooled reactor as a safer alternative to water-cooled reactors. However, aside from experimental and demonstration gas-cooled reactors, American power companies have relied almost entirely on water-cooled and pressurized water-cooled reactors. Gas-cooled reactor advocates have claimed that the wider public acceptance of nuclear power in Europe than in the United States has been due to the prevalence of the safer designs there.

See also POWER REACTORS, U.S.; POWER REACTORS, WORLD.

Hiroshima

Hiroshima was the first of two cities attacked with atomic bombs in 1945. Following the test of the weapon at TRINITY in the United States, and following TRUMAN'S DECISION to use the weapon in the war against Japan, Hiroshima was targeted at 8:16 A.M. local time on August 6, 1945.

Piloted by Paul TIBBETS, the B-29 aircraft that he had named ENOLA GAY after his mother carried the bomb that morning. The bomb detonated 1,900 feet above Shima Hospital, with a yield of about 12,500 tons of high-explosive TNT, or 12.5 kilotons.

The number of casualties from the detonation remained a matter of uncertainty and some controversy. Although before the war the city had a population of about 400,000, on the morning of the attack there were about 280,000 civilians and another 43,000 soldiers in the city. Early estimates placed the death toll at about 100,000, while estimates that included those dying by the end of 1945 as a result of the bomb ran to about 140,000. Over the next five years, the total reached 200,000. By contrast with fire bomb raids on Tokyo that had killed 100,000 of the 1 million residents, the proportion of the people in Hiroshima killed by the atomic weapon was very high.

Many of the injured were terribly burned. Memories of the survivors were vivid, horrifying, and often grotesque. The fact that most of the buildings in the city were made of wood contributed to the firestorm that swept the city.

The physical destruction of the buildings was easier to measure numerically. The city had about 76,000 structures, of which 48,000 were totally destroyed and another 22,000 partially damaged. In effect, the city was ruined instantly. All fire departments, police stations, post offices, telephone and telegraph exchanges, schools, and the broadcasting station were demolished. All that remained were a few reinforced concrete buildings and piles of rubble. The destruction of the city was so thorough that it was cut off from communication with the rest of Japan for at least a day.

In the light of President Truman's later claim that the dropping of the atomic bombs saved lives and shortened the war, the destruction of Hiroshima and NAGASAKI three days later have been the subject of much ethical review, historical study, and detailed examination. Debates over the issues remained alive for the rest of the century. The issues surfaced in the public press when the Smithsonian Institution in Washington, D.C., arranged an exhibit of part of the *Enola Gay* aircraft to commemorate the 50th anniversary of the end of the war. Veteran's groups tended to defend the attack, remembering how the bombing of Hiroshima was greeted as the action that brought an end to the war.

Suggested Reading

Gar Alperovitz, *Atomic Diplomacy: Hiroshima and Potsdam.* New York: Penguin, 1985.

Gar Alperovitz, *The Decision to Use the Atomic Bomb and the Architecture of an American Myth.* New York: Knopf, 1995.

Herbert Feis, *The Atomic Bomb and the End of World War II.* Princeton, N.J.: Princeton University Press, 1966.

Gregg Herken, *The Winning Weapon: The Atomic Bomb in the Cold War, 1945–1950.* Santa Rosa, Calif.: Vintage, 1981.

Robert Jay Lifton and Greg Mitchell, *Hiroshima in America: A Half Century of Denial.* New York: Avon, 1996.

Douglas MacEachin, *The Final Months of the War with Japan: Signals Intelligence, U.S. Invasion Planning, and the A-Bomb Decision.* Washington D.C.: Central Intelligence Agency Center for the Study of Intelligence, 1998.

Richard Rhodes, *The Making of the Atomic Bomb.* New York: Simon and Schuster, 1986.

Martin Sherwin, *A World Destroyed.* New York: Vintage, 1987.

Hodel, Donald (1935–) *American attorney who served as secretary of energy and as secretary of interior under President Ronald Reagan*

Hodel was born in Portland, Oregon, on May 23, 1935, and attended Harvard University and the University of Oregon Law School. He served as deputy administrator of the Bonneville Power Administration. Hodel was sworn in as secretary of energy on November 11, 1982, and served until February 1985 when President REAGAN appointed Hodel to serve as secretary of the interior. The president appointed John HERRINGTON to the post of secretary of energy.

As secretary of energy, Hodel faced several major controversies and actions related to nuclear energy and nuclear weapons. His appointment had been opposed by environmentalists, but as someone with former experience in the energy field, he hoped to raise the

Donald Hodel. Hodel served as United States secretary of energy, 1982–1985. (Department of Energy)

department's morale by turning from plans to dismantle the department to plans for future energy needs. Implementing the Nuclear Waste Policy Act of 1982, the department began planning for a high-level waste site at YUCCA MOUNTAIN, Nevada. Hodel and Reagan supported the Clinch River Breeder Reactor project, but in 1983 the Senate refused to continue funding for the breeder, effectively terminating it. Hodel sought to stimulate the acceptance of nuclear power plants, and he urged support for a proposed nuclear plant licensing reform bill in 1984.

Meanwhile, several nuclear weapons projects came to fruition during Hodel's administration, as the department constructed the warheads of weapons to be fielded in Europe, the ground-launched CRUISE MISSILE (GLCM), and the PERSHING II missile. These weapons, originally planned during the Carter administration, were designed to offset the deployment of new and more accurate Soviet missiles. The stationing of GLCMs in Britain, Germany, Italy, Belgium, and the Netherlands and the shipment of Pershing II missiles with relatively long range to Germany were met with considerable opposition from antinuclear demonstrators in the European countries concerned.

The construction of the GLCMs, Pershings, and other new nuclear weapons placed a strain on the aging weapons production complex. Under Hodel, L reactor at SAVANNAH RIVER SITE, closed since 1968, was reopened in 1985 for the production of plutonium. Hodel found that the department could not focus on energy planning for the future but rather had to concentrate on expanding the nuclear weapons program and increasing the production of nuclear power.

Hudson Institute

One of a number of independent "think tanks" devoted to matters of nuclear policy, the Hudson Institute later published a series of studies on a wide variety of policy issues. Founded in 1961 by physicist Herman Kahn, the institute initially provided a non-profit vehicle for the publication of Kahn's own studies. His books *On Thermonuclear War* and *Thinking about the Unthinkable,* which explored the possible scenarios of a full-scale nuclear war, were best-sellers and were distributed through the Hudson Institute.

Kahn continued to write on issues related to nuclear war and other analyses of possible future problems, including a focus on the growth of Japan as an economic power. The institute also published works by other scholars, including studies of the ANTI-BALLISTIC MISSILE, reports on future work force issues, and other economic and technical futurist problems.

Herman Kahn died at the age of 61 on July 7, 1983. The institute continued to publish works, often reflecting a "contrarian" or conservative viewpoint. With the passing of Kahn and the decline of funding available to explore defense topics, the institute's focus moved away from issues of nuclear war to broader international, educational, and policy topics, some of which Kahn had begun to examine prior to his death. In 1990, the institute supported the transition to a market economy by the former Soviet states of Latvia, Lithuania, and Estonia.

Hungary

By the 1990s, the Hungarian government had no plans to expand its nuclear power program. The nation had four VVER-440 type pressurized water reactors in operation, imported from the former Soviet Union. These water-cooled, water-moderated reactors were the counterpart of pressurized water reactors in the

West. An estimated 44% of the nation's electric power derived from these four reactors, with a total 1.5 gigawatts of electricity per year.

See also POWER REACTORS, WORLD.

Hydrogen Bomb Designs

Several designs of hydrogen bombs or thermonuclear bombs were considered in the period 1946 to 1955 by both the United States and the Soviet Union. Because of confusion over the fact that a tritium reaction is used in BOOSTED WEAPONS, some historical treatments have been ambiguous or confusing as to whether the United States or the Soviet Union first detonated a thermonuclear weapon. Further confusion derived from the terminology involved because at first American scientists called one design the "Super," and later the term came to be applied to all thermonuclear weapons. In addition, both the Americans and the Soviets adopted several nicknames for their designs.

In the late 1940s, American weapons designers thought through and abandoned a design that would contain URANIUM as well as hydrogen. The device would be large and difficult to assemble, and it would have an upper limit to its yield in the range of several hundred kilotons. Instead, the United States pursued first an experimental design that required a large structure to keep the hydrogen cooled to a liquid state, which was only tested once in the Ivy/Mike test of October 26, 1952. Edward Teller and some others called this design, which was tested in 1952, the "Super" or the "Classical Super."

The Soviets pursued a weapon similar to the design abandoned by the United States, worked out first by Yakov ZEL'DOVICH as the "First Idea" and improved by Andrey SAKHAROV. Sakharov's "Second Idea" involved adding uranium. In a Russian pun, colleagues referred to the original design as having been "sugarized," as the name "Sakharov" means "of sugar." As part of the Second Idea, Vitali Ginzburg proposed including a solid compound that included a hydrogen isotope in the weapon. The weapon was workable, but it represented a complex idea that would only result in a partial fusion effect.

The Soviet scientists tested the Second Idea with Joe 4. Joe 4 had an upper limit of several hundred kilotons and in fact the Joe 4 test of August 12, 1953, yielded 400 Kt. The United States already had larger boosted weapons, and it appeared that the Joe 4 test comprised a variation on the concept of such a device. However, at the Russian weapons museum at ARZAMAS, the Joe 4 weapon is described as the world's first hydrogen bomb. Outsiders have continued to regard it as a variant on the concept of boosting.

The United States tested a new design that could be delivered as a weapon, with the Teller-Ulam design in the Bravo test in OPERATION CASTLE held in 1954. That device had a yield initially estimated at 15 megatons. The Teller-Ulam design encompassed a two-stage weapon that could be made small enough to be delivered by a long-range bomber aircraft.

Like the Teller-Ulam device, the Third Idea, developed by Igor TAMM and Sakharov, could go much higher in yield than the limits imposed by the Russian Second Idea, and the later Soviet tests of hydrogen bombs followed the Third Idea, with true, two-stage detonations. The first Soviet test of the Third Idea weapon came on November 22, 1955, with a yield estimated at 1.6 megatons. Later, standardized versions of this weapon had a yield of 3 megatons. Apparently the Soviets independently developed the Third Idea, rather than gaining access to U.S. classified information regarding the Teller-Ulam design, which it resembled.

HYDROGEN BOMB DESIGNS

DESIGN NAME	TESTED		
(Hydrogen/Uranium type)	not tested	1946–1949	U.S.
Boosted Fission	Greenhouse/Item	5-24-51	U.S. 45.5 Kt
Classical Super	Ivy/Mike	10-26-52	U.S. 10.4 Mt
First Idea modified to Second Idea	Zel'dovich, Khariton, Ginzburg, Sakharov (Joe 4)	8-12-53	U.S.S.R. 400 Kt
Two Stage Design	Teller-Ulam (Castle/Bravo)	3-1-54	U.S. 15 Mt.
Third Idea	Tamm and Sakharov	11-22-55	U.S.S.R. 1.6 Mt.

Some American journalists and observers assumed that Joe 4 represented a thermonuclear weapon, just as the Soviets asserted. If that had been true, it would appear that the Soviets developed a deliverable nuclear weapon about six months before the United States, which did so with the Castle/Bravo test of 1954 using the huge Classical Super that was too large to deliver as a weapon. However, more careful evaluation of the Joe 4 test revealed that it should be more properly regarded as a boosted fission weapon, along the lines of the weapon detonated in the Greenhouse/Item test by the United States in 1952. Following this reasoning, American scientists could claim that the Classical Super test of Ivy/Mike in 1952 was the first true thermonuclear detonation and that the Castle/Bravo Teller-Ulam weapon tested in 1954 was the world's first thermonuclear weapon.

See also MALENKOV, GEORGY.

Suggested Reading

Thomas B. Cochrane et al. *Making the Russian Bomb: From Stalin to Yeltsin.* Boulder, Colo.: Westview Press, 1995.

David Holloway, *Stalin and the Bomb.* New Haven: Yale University Press, 1994.

Richard Rhodes, *Dark Sun.* New York: Simon and Schuster: 1995.

Idaho National Engineering Laboratory (INEL)

Idaho National Engineering Laboratory (INEL) occupies a land reserve nearly 900 square miles in area, about two-thirds the size of the state of Rhode Island. Located in south-central Idaho, the reservation at its longest and widest points is 39 miles north to south by 36 miles east to west. First established in 1949 as the National Reactor Testing Station, the facility was redesignated as Idaho National Engineering Laboratory in 1975. Since its origins, the facility has housed work on experimental nuclear reactors and related areas of research.

In the post–World War II years ATOMIC ENERGY COMMISSION (AEC) planners sought sites for work on nuclear reactors that would be more remote than those near Chicago established by the University of CHICAGO under the MANHATTAN ENGINEER DISTRICT. One of the early experimental reactors was the Experimental Breeder Reactor (EBR) constructed as part of the breeder reactor development program.

EBR-1 was built at the Idaho site and produced its first electricity in 1951, the first reactor to produce usable amounts of electricity. In 1955, power for nearby Arco, Idaho, was produced on the reservation.

It was four years later that SHIPPINGPORT reactor in Pennsylvania provided the first power sold into the regular commercial network in the United States. ARGONNE NATIONAL LABORATORY administered EBR-1, and parts of INEL continued to be called "Argonne West" by Argonne staff.

When the United States developed the first nuclear-powered submarines in the 1950s, Hyman RICKOVER established a facility at INEL for the training of officers to operate the submarine power plants. The Naval Reactor Test Station at INEL continued as a training school, with rigorous courses first established by Rickover for both officers and enlisted men. The courses included college-level work in engineering and physics in classroom settings, coupled with practical work on the reactors. Instructors would create crisis situations through the reactor controls and students would resolve them, learning to deal with a wide variety of possible nuclear reactor accidents.

By the year 2000, the various facilities at INEL employed over 8,000 people, more than 2% of all the people employed in the state of Idaho. Some are employees of the federal Department of Energy, while others work for the U.S. Navy or for contractors, such as the Associated University group that operates

EBR II. At the Idaho National Engineering Laboratory, more than 50 experimental and test reactors were built. The Experimental Breeder Reactor II operated for a decade following 1963 in an effort to show how reactors could be used to produce plutonium as a fuel for other reactors. (Department of Energy)

Argonne West. Idaho State University economists estimated that the impact of INEL was even larger, with another 8,000 jobs created in businesses to support the 8,000 people who worked at INEL. There are less than 500 direct federal employees on the reserve.

Some 52 different reactors of different kinds were built at INEL over the years, representing about one-third of all experimental and test reactors owned by the federal government. Of the 52 reactors, 11 were built by Argonne, 11 by General Electric, 11 by Aerojet General, and 11 by Phillips Petroleum. Smaller numbers were built by General Atomics, Westinghouse, and Combustion Engineering. Most of them were operated for a period of several years and then either dismantled or shut down. One that continued to operate in the 1990s was the Advanced Test Reactor (ATR).

It produced a heavy flux of neutrons to simulate radiation effects on equipment, materials, and fuels. The ATR was useful in the design of other reactors, allowing engineers to test theoretical models. The ATR was also used to produce radioactive isotopes useful in research and medicine, as well as in industrial applications.

During the late 1980s, as the Department of Energy considered three alternative designs and sites for a NEW PRODUCTION REACTOR, representatives and senators from Idaho, together with lobbyists for the various corporations serving INEL, worked to advocate a HIGH-TEMPERATURE GAS-COOLED REACTOR to be built there. However, with the end of the cold war, the need for strategic materials and for TRITIUM was less pressing, and the decision regarding a production reactor was postponed for nearly a decade.

INEL changed its name in the 1990s to the Idaho National Engineering and Environmental Laboratory to reflect the new emphasis on the environment. The lab continued work on reactor engineering and naval training while moving into areas of radioactive hazards and waste management.

See also SL-1 ACCIDENT.

Suggested Reading

Rodney Carlisle, *Supplying the Nuclear Arsenal: American Production Reactors, 1942–1992*. Baltimore: Johns Hopkins University Press, 1996.

Implosion

In 1945, two types of designs were developed for nuclear weapons. In the implosion design, a near-critical assembly of fissile material is surrounded by a layer of high explosive. When the explosive is detonated, it causes a shock wave that "implodes," compressing the fissile material by a factor of two, making it supercritical. The device tested at Alamogordo and the weapon dropped on NAGASAKI used an implosion design with PLUTONIUM as the fissile material. The higher CROSS SECTION of plutonium than that of URANIUM required the implosion design.

See also GUN-TYPE DESIGN.

India

India demonstrated a nuclear weapons capability in May 1974 by detonating a nuclear device in a so-called peaceful nuclear experiment. Over the following years, until 1998, India claimed that it did not have plans for nuclear weapons, although evidence continued to mount that it developed facilities for weapons manufacture. On May 11 and May 13, 1998, by testing a series of nuclear devices, India made it clear that it had joined the world's nuclear weapon states.

India had been an original sponsor of the NON-PROLIFERATION TREATY (NPT), but the country refused to sign the treaty that emerged from the negotiations in 1968. Along the same lines, India long advocated a COMPREHENSIVE TEST BAN TREATY, but when such a treaty was negotiated and signed in 1996, India refused to join. Since India refused to join the NPT, it was not subject to the various safeguards and prohibitions that such agreement would have imposed. By the mid-1990s, experts estimated that India had sufficient separated PLUTONIUM for at least 65 nuclear weapons, with a production rate that could add sufficient plutonium to the stockpile for an additional 85 or 90 weapons by the year 2000.

Nuclear development in India has a long history. India was one of the first nations to benefit from the United States ATOMS FOR PEACE program started in the 1950s. Canada provided India in 1955 with the Cirus 40 megawatt-thermal (MWth) heavy-water moderated reactor, for research purposes. European-educated scientist Homi Bhabha headed India's Atomic Energy Commission from 1948 until his death in an accident in 1966. Bhabha began preparations for India's first nuclear test. Indian scientists used the Canadian reactor to produce the plutonium used in its 1974 test. Both the United States and Canada provided heavy water to India with assurances that the reactor would not be used for military purposes. India maintained a second 100 Mwth production reactor, Dhruva, located at the Bhabha Atomic Research Center.

In 1964, India constructed at Trombay a plutonium-reprocessing plant on the grounds that it was part of a plan to construct a breeder-reactor cycle that would use plutonium as a reactor fuel. By 1974, it had become clear that the plutonium from Trombay was destined for use in explosive devices, not in reactors.

In addition to the Cirus and Dhruva reactors that produce plutonium, India operated several other reactors not subject to any international safeguards, including Madras I and II, Narora I and II, and Kakrapar I. Kakrapar II opened in 1995 as a power reactor, but it could also be used to generate spent fuel to be put through the reprocessing center at Trombay. In addition, India built a fast breeder test reactor with French cooperation, using the French Phenix design. That reactor, constructed at Kalpakkam in south India, went operational in 1987. India also planned a much larger breeder reactor to be operational in the year 2007. India also has two URANIUM enrichment plants, which could be used to produce weapons-grade uranium. Its reactors operate on natural uranium and the country has no peaceful need for enriched uranium. For the most part, as shown in the accompanying table, India's nuclear facilities have been constructed outside of agreements with the INTERNATIONAL ATOMIC ENERGY AGENCY (IAEA) and outside of the NPT, which would require adherence to the IAEA safeguards.

After the 1974 detonation of a nuclear device by India, both the United States and Canada stopped cooperating with India's nuclear power program.

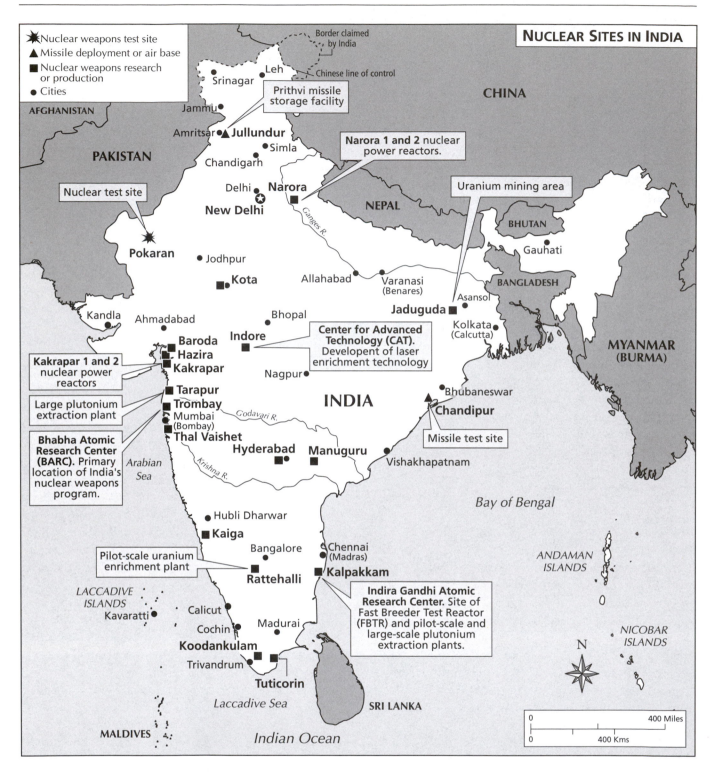

NUCLEAR SITES IN INDIA

* Nuclear weapons test site
▲ Missile deployment or air base
■ Nuclear weapons research or production
● Cities

Border claimed by India

Chinese line of control

CHINA

Prithvi missile storage facility

Narora 1 and 2 nuclear power reactors.

Uranium mining area

Nuclear test site

Center for Advanced Technology (CAT). Development of laser enrichment technology

Kakrapar 1 and 2 nuclear power reactors

Large plutonium extraction plant

Bhabha Atomic Research Center (BARC). Primary location of India's nuclear weapons program.

Missile test site

Pilot-scale uranium enrichment plant

Indira Gandhi Atomic Research Center. Site of Fast Breeder Test Reactor (FBTR) and pilot-scale and large-scale plutonium extraction plants.

AFGHANISTAN
PAKISTAN
Srinagar
Leh
Jammu
Amritsar ● ▲ Jullundur
Simla
Chandigarh
Delhi ● ■ Narora
New Delhi
Pokaran
Jodhpur
Kota
Allahabad
Varanasi (Benares)
NEPAL
BHUTAN
Gauhati
Asansol
Jaduguda
BANGLADESH
Kolkata (Calcutta)
Kandla
Ahmadabad
Bhopal
Indore
Baroda
Hazira
Kakrapar
Nagpur
INDIA
Tarapur
Trombay
Mumbai (Bombay)
Thal Vaishet
Hyderabad
Manuguru
Bhubaneswar
Chandipur
Vishakhapatnam
MYANMAR (BURMA)
Arabian Sea
Godavari R.
Krishna R.
Ganges R.
Bay of Bengal
Hubli Dharwar
Kaiga
Bangalore
Chennai (Madras)
Rattehalli
Kalpakkam
ANDAMAN ISLANDS
LACCADIVE ISLANDS
Kavaratti
Calicut
Cochin
Madurai
Koodankulam
Trivandrum
Tuticorin
Laccadive Sea
SRI LANKA
NICOBAR ISLANDS
N
MALDIVES
Indian Ocean

0   400 Miles
0   400 Kms

Together with technical problems in the power reactors that India built for itself, the power program got off to a slow start. By the mid-1990s, India had achieved only a small fraction of the nuclear power it had earlier planned. Some estimates suggested that only about 2% of India's power needs were supplied by nuclear reactors, instead of the 10% to 15% originally planned.

International tensions with CHINA and PAKISTAN and a long-simmering dispute with Pakistan over jurisdiction of the Kashmir province to the north of India have contributed to the country's commitment to a nuclear weapon program.

On May 11, 1998, India claimed to conduct three simultaneous nuclear explosive tests. Officials claimed that one was about equivalent to the HIROSHIMA weapon, a second was a high-yield thermonuclear device, and the third was a small, tactical nuclear weapon. Indian officials further claimed that on May 13, they detonated two low-yield devices. Analysis of the ground shock of the May 11 test by outside observers suggested a total yield of between 25 and 30 kilotons. This total yield did not indicate that a true thermonuclear weapon had been included in the test series but perhaps a boosted plutonium weapon.

POWER REACTORS

LOCATION/NAME	TYPE AND NET MWE RATING	YEAR OPERATIONAL
Tarapur I	Light Water 150 MWe	1969
Tarapur II	Light Water 160 MWe	1969
Rajasthan, RAPS-1	Heavy Water 90 MWe	1972
Rajasthan, RAPS-2	Heavy Water 187 MWe	1980

(following power reactors not subject to IAEA safeguards:)

Kalpakkam, MAPS-1	Heavy Water 170 MWe	1983
Kalpakkam, MAPS-1	Heavy Water 170 MWe	1985
Narora 1	Heavy Water 202 MWe	1989
Narora 2	Heavy Water 202 MWe	1991
Kakrapar 1	Heavy Water 170 MWe	1992
Kakrapar 2	Heavy Water 202 MWe	1995
Kaiga 1	Heavy Water 202 MWe	1998
Kaiga 2	Heavy Water 202 MWe	1998
Rajasthan, RAPS-3	Heavy Water 202 MWe	1999
Rajasthan, RAPS-3	Heavy Water 202 MWe	1999

(12 more power reactors planned for construction in 2004 and later, all outside IAEA safeguards)

Weapons potential facilities wholly or partially outside IAEA inspection or safeguard agreements:

Two Breeder Reactors
Four Uranium Enrichment Plants
Four Plutonium Reprocessing Plants
10 Heavy-Water Production facilities

Suggested Reading

Shyam Bhatia, *India's Nuclear Bomb*. Ghazibad, India: Vikas, 1979.
Rodney Jones et al., *Tracking Nuclear Proliferation*. Washington, D.C.: Carnegie Endowment for International Peace, 1998.
Leonard S. Spector, *The Undeclared Bomb*. Cambridge, Mass.: Ballinger Books, 1988.

Institute of Nuclear Power Operations (INPO)

Established in the wake of the THREE MILE ISLAND incident in 1979, the Institute of Nuclear Power Operations (INPO) has been devoted to safety and training for the nuclear power industry. In 1982 INPO first established procedures for accrediting industry training programs. The organization established the National Academy for Nuclear Training in 1985, which since published the journal *The Nuclear Professional*. Personnel from the nuclear power industry served as "loaned employees" to INPO. During these periods, they toured nuclear power plants and studied the safety and training methods employed by other companies. Over 500 personnel served on such loan programs in the period 1979 to 1999.

The articles published in *The Nuclear Professional* almost always provided telephone numbers of contact persons, stimulating exchange of information. In addition, nuclear engineers from other countries worked temporarily at INPO on liaison status, allowing for international exchanges of ideas and systems for safety. Since reactors in such widely dispersed countries as BRAZIL and Slovenia sometimes had identical design, the international exchange of information could assist in improving safety and reducing outage time. Similarly, U.S. reactors owned by different companies but manufactured at the same time by the same manufacturers had very similar records.

The organization took some credit for the increased safety performance of the U.S. nuclear power industry since its formation. INPO pointed to the decrease in the number of significant "transients" and other events that raised a risk of damage to reactor cores at nuclear power reactors from an average of more than two per year per reactor to about two such episodes per year for the more than 100 reactors in the nuclear power industry in the United States by 1998. Training, safety programs, and exchange of information, the organization claimed, led to this decrease in the risk of an accident or event that could damage a reactor core.

See also POWER REACTORS, U.S.

Suggested Reading

"Twenty Years Later: People of Three Mile Island Exemplify Changes in Nuclear Industry," *The Nuclear Professional* 14, no. 1 (1999).

Intercontinental Ballistic Missile (ICBM)

During the 1960s, the United States and the Soviet Union began to develop and deploy intercontinental ballistic missiles (ICBMs). The efficiency and long range of these missiles derived from the fact that they required fuel only to be launched up through the atmosphere and directed toward the target. They used virtually no fuel traveling through near outer space. They were "ballistic" rather than guided in that they fell at their target, after a ballistic arc, like a bullet.

During the cold war, the U.S. Air Force deployed more than 10 different ICBMs, if the various models or types of the missiles are counted. Occasionally the same warhead would be employed on different missiles, so confusion among sources sometimes derived from an inability to determine whether the missile or the warhead was referenced in a particular source. The U.S. Air Force ICBMs, in order of introduction, were as follows.

Thor	1957–1975
Atlas	1950s–1975
Jupiter C	1950s–1960s
Titan I	1950s–1960s
Minuteman I	1962–1969
Titan II	1963–1987
Minuteman II	1965–
Minuteman III	1970–
Peacekeeper	1986–
Midgetman	canceled

The *Thor*, ATLAS, *Jupiter C,* and *Titan* missiles were liquid fueled, which represented a serious hazard and also required considerable advance notice for fueling time. The MINUTEMAN and PEACEKEEPER missiles, by contrast, were solid fueled, safer, and could be kept on alert at all times. The *Titan* II, although liquid fueled, could be maintained in a ready state. The explosion of a *Titan* II missile in its SILO near DAMASCUS, ARKANSAS, in 1980 demonstrated the hazards associated with that type of missile.

Precise aiming was important, and a measure of the accuracy of ICBMs was the CIRCULAR ERROR PROBABLE (CEP). Weapons with low CEP, or high accuracy, could have a lower yield to achieve destruction of a target.

By the mid-1980s, both the United States and the Soviet Union each had over 1,000 such missiles, some with MULTIPLE INDEPENDENTLY TARGETABLE REENTRY VEHICLES (MIRVs) on them. A 1985 estimate indicated that the United States had 2,130 warheads on ICBMs, while the Soviets had 6,420 warheads on similar missiles.

The Soviet SS-20 was an intermediate-range nuclear missile introduced in 1978 that could threaten targets all across Western Europe. The United States responded by the deployment to Europe of PERSHING II and ground-launched CRUISE MISSILES in 1983–1984 that could reach targets well inside the Soviet Union.

1985 DEPLOYMENTS

	NUMBER OF LAUNCHERS	WARHEADS PER MISSILE	TOTAL WARHEADS
United States			
TITAN II	30	1	30
MINUTEMAN II	450	1	450
Minuteman III			
Mark 12	250	3	750
Mark 12a	300	3	900
totals		1030	2130
U.S.S.R.			
SS-11	520	1	520
SS-13	60	1	60
SS-17	150	4	600
SS-18	308	10	3080
SS-19	360	6	2160
totals		1398	6420

These "Euromissiles," although they could hold at risk strategic targets, were regarded by the United States as long-range Theater Nuclear Forces rather than as strategic weapons. With ranges of 1,000 to 1,500 miles, they were not intercontinental in range. The Pershing II and the SS-20 were sometimes referred to as medium-range ballistic missiles (MRBMs) to distinguish them from ICBMs.

Since the U.S. MRBMs stationed in Europe could reach Soviet targets, the Soviets argued that they should be considered in any treaty limiting the deployment of ICBMs. This issue, among others, became a stumbling block in negotiations toward SALT II.

Suggested Reading

John M. Collins, *U.S.–Soviet Military Balance, 1980–1985.* Washington, D.C.: Pergamon-Brassey's, 1985.

Intermediate-Range Nuclear Forces (INF) Treaty

The Intermediate-Range Nuclear Forces (INF) Treaty was signed at a summit meeting in Washington on December 8, 1987, and entered into force between the United States and the Soviet Union on June 1, 1988. Under the provisions of the treaty, all ground-launched intermediate and shorter-range nuclear missiles held by the United States and the U.S.S.R in Europe were eliminated over the three-year period ending in May 1991. A key element of the treaty was a provision for on-site inspection, and in the United States, the ON-SITE INSPECTION AGENCY was established in January 1988 to provide expert staff to carry out the inspections. U.S. teams of inspectors examined 130 facilities at 115 locations in the Soviet Union and in Eastern Europe in 1988–1989, establishing the basic numbers of weapons to be destroyed and verifying that elimination of weapons proceeded on schedule. The INF treaty allowed for 13 years of inspection to continue to monitor the destruction of weapons.

The INF treaty emerged from a long series of on-again, off-again negotiations that first began when the United States and the NORTH ATLANTIC TREATY ORGANIZATION (NATO) allies planned to modernize long-range Theater Nuclear Forces in 1979, in response to earlier Soviet deployment of long-range and accurate missiles capable of targeting all of Western Europe. At that time NATO decided to deploy 464 ground-launched CRUISE MISSILES and 108 PERSHING II ballistic missiles in 1983. The Pershing II was highly accurate and could reach ranges up to 1,800 kilometers (km), putting much of the western Soviet Union within a 10-minute flight of missiles based in Europe. The ground-launched cruise missile had an even longer range, up to 2,500 km. NATO planned a DUAL-TRACK STRATEGY of simultaneously upgrading its missile forces and seeking an arms control agreement with the Soviets to limit Theater Nuclear Forces.

As NATO was planning these developments, President Brezhnev of the Soviet Union indicated that his country would limit deployment of the new SS-20 missiles if NATO would hold off on its deployment. Negotiations were interrupted by the Soviet invasion of Afghanistan in late 1979. However, in 1980, INF negotiations began again. The negotiations went through several phases over the following years. President Ronald REAGAN advanced the ZERO OPTION in 1981, under which all intermediate weapons would be removed. A more intricate formula for an agreement

was developed between negotiators Paul NITZE for the United States and Yuli Kvitsinsky for the Soviet Union in 1982, sometimes called the "Walk in the Woods" agreement. The complex terms of an agreement discussed during this walk were rejected by the Soviet leadership in 1983. The development of the concept of a STRATEGIC DEFENSE INITIATIVE (SDI) over the years 1983 to 1987 further delayed progress on the INF treaty, as the Soviet Union "linked" a resolution to the intermediate-range force agreement to U.S. abandonment of SDI. However, President Gorbachev abandoned the linkage in 1987, and the final agreement signed in December 1987 reflected the zero option approach, with a "double-zero" feature that also eliminated shorter-range as well as intermediate-range missiles. For the purposes of the treaty, "shorter range" meant missiles in the range of 500 to 1,000 kilometers.

The issue was complicated by many factors, including the development of accurate cruise missiles by the United States, the large number of weapons that could be carried by U.S. fighter-bomber aircraft, the presence of intermediate range missiles in the possession of France and Great Britain and in place in West Germany, and the existence of British and French submarine-launched missiles. Similarly, the United States viewed the large number of Soviet fighter bombers as part of the intermediate-range nuclear force question. The final INF treaty did not address all of these questions but simply eliminated the intermediate range missiles of both the United States and the Soviet Union that were based in Europe, together with Pershing Ia missiles in Germany. However, when coupled with the STRATEGIC ARMS REDUCTION TREATY (START) in 1991 and with unilateral arms reductions by both the United States and Russia in the following years, the threat of nuclear war beginning in Europe was vastly reduced.

See also INTERCONTINENTAL BALLISTIC MISSILES.

Suggested Reading

Committee on International Security and Arms Control, National Academy of Sciences, *Nuclear Arms Control: Background and Issues*. Washington, D.C.: National Academy Press, 1985.

Patrick Glynn, *Closing Pandora's Box: Arms Races, Arms Control, and the History of the Cold War*. New York: Basic Books, 1992.

International Atomic Energy Agency (IAEA)

The International Atomic Energy Agency (IAEA) was founded in 1957, partly in response to the initiative of

President Dwight EISENHOWER in his 1954 ATOMS FOR PEACE proposal. Established in Vienna, the IAEA mission has been to promote the peaceful uses of nuclear energy. That mission evolved to include the administration of a program of on-site inspections to ensure that nuclear material was not being diverted to weapons programs. The inspections have also included administrative investigations, such as audits and inventory controls. Collectively the physical and administrative inspections constituted a system of safeguards.

With the formation in the mid-1950s of EURATOM, the European states established their own inspection agreements and regulations regarding the sharing of nuclear information. Although the IAEA sought to exercise control there through a series of compromises, the IAEA has accepted Euratom's standards and controls. Thus the IAEA's primary focus has been on the prevention of the spread of nuclear weaponry to nations beyond Europe.

By the late 1990s, the organization had expanded and its budget increased so that it had become an essential part of the international enforcement of the NON-PROLIFERATION TREATY (NPT) to prevent the spread of nuclear weapons beyond the original five nuclear-armed states. With more than 110 nations belonging to the agency and with a board of governors consisting of 35 members, the organization had a staff of more than 2,000 and a budget totaling over $200 million, including a safeguards budget running over $80 million.

The agency operates by agreements with member nations allowing for inspection of nuclear facilities to ensure that nuclear materials are not being diverted to weapons programs. Reactors and fuel processing and research equipment imported from the major nuclear supplying states are usually provided on condition that the receiving country accepts IAEA safeguards. Thus, for example, two of the Tarapur reactors and two of the Rajasthan reactors in INDIA were built subject to IAEA safeguards, but others, built with domestic resources, had no such restrictions. Similarly, one power reactor and two research reactors in PAKISTAN were subject to IAEA inspection and safeguards, whereas all the rest of the Pakistani nuclear establishment was outside of the IAEA system. Neither India nor Pakistan were signatories to the Non-Proliferation Treaty, and both became announced nuclear weapons states in May 1998.

Other nations that had signed the NPT agreed that all their nuclear activities would be declared to the IAEA and open to safeguards. However, after the Gulf War in 1991, it was discovered that IRAQ, a member of the NPT regime, had been developing nuclear weapons in violation of its agreement. IAEA director Hans Blix proposed in 1991 that the agency adopt a more forceful policy to ensure more access to information and better physical access in countries that claimed to be adhering to the NPT. The board of governors of the IAEA adopted a policy in 1992 that reaffirmed the agency's right to conduct special inspections and that also required more information about imports and production of nuclear material.

In 1993, the IAEA went further, developing "Program 93+2" that would help the agency discover clandestine nuclear projects in NPT–signatory countries, such as that developed in secret in Iraq. The new program allowed for audit of preexisting nuclear facilities, that is, facilities that the nation had built prior to joining the NPT treaty. This provision would apply particularly to ARGENTINA, BRAZIL, Belarus, KAZAKHSTAN, and UKRAINE. Each of these countries had extensive nuclear facilities constructed prior to membership in the NPT.

Other features of the new policy in Program 93+2 included increased environmental sampling, increased no-notice inspections of known facilities, and possible increased use of unattended and remote monitoring capabilities such as video monitoring and radiation detection using data relay by satellite and phone lines.

The agency also proposed inspection of support facilities located at nuclear sites that were not directly engaged in nuclear work, such as workshops, warehouses, or administrative offices. Protocols with individual states that would allow such inspection were proposed in 1997. It was envisioned that these inspections would allow the agency to gain a better picture of the nation's future plans and the possible kinds of nuclear activities that could be conducted. Furthermore, no-notice inspections and the inspection of offices and shops would allow the agency to verify or confirm the nation's claims and to monitor the dissemination of information that might be useful in development of weapons.

In effect, the IAEA has had to work as an intelligence-gathering agency with the permission of host countries. The expansion of its powers through agreements in advance to conduct no-notice inspections not only of listed sites but also of related facilities represents an effort to balance national sovereignty against international concerns for control.

The loss of sovereignty implicit in the methods has not always been acceptable to the inspected countries, and such reactions were anticipated as early as the 1940s by Niels BOHR, Leo SZILARD, and other pioneers of nuclear science and policy. They anticipated that the weapons that could be built based on nuclear fission would be so powerful that they would make certain aspects of national sovereignty obsolete. Those predictions were becoming realized in the 1990s, as the international community sought to prevent the spread of nuclear weaponry to new nations, rogue states, and terrorist organizations.

Despite the gradually increased administrative and inspection tools of the IAEA, it is actually powerless to prevent a non-nuclear state from developing one or more nuclear weapons. At best, the IAEA can provide the world community with advanced notice that such a development is possible or likely. When the agency comes to such a conclusion, it can notify members of the United Nation's Security Council, and the council can impose various sanctions on the potential proliferation state. Such sanctions were imposed as a result of IAEA evidence in the case of Iraq in 1991 and NORTH KOREA in 1994.

Suggested Reading

Rodney W. Jones et al., *Tracking Nuclear Proliferation: A Guide in Maps and Charts, 1998*. Washington, D.C.: Carnegie Endowment for International Peace, 1998.

IAEA webpage at: http://www.iaea.org/worldatom

Ioffe, Abram Fedorovich (1880–1960) *served as director of the Leningrad Physico-Technical Institute from 1923 to 1950, during the whole period of the expansion of Soviet nuclear physics and the development of the atomic bomb*

During the 1920s and 1930s, Ioffe worked to bring science and technology to Russian industry, with particular emphasis on using physics as a basis for technological advances. Ioffe's continued emphasis on finding practical applications for physics was well-received by party and government officials through the purges and crises of the 1930s. Ioffe's institute in the 1930s was the Russian center for nuclear research. He anticipated the time when atomic energy would provide power to meet the world's energy needs.

Abram Ioffe was born in the Ukraine in 1880. After graduating from St. Petersburg Technological Institute in 1902, Ioffe went to Munich, Germany, where he worked under Wilhelm Roentgen, the discoverer of X-rays. Ioffe earned his doctorate in physics in 1905. In 1906, Ioffe returned to St. Petersburg where he worked in the Polytechnical Institute.

Several times he demonstrated his loyalty to Russia by turning down offers of academic positions in Munich and later, in Berkeley, California. He briefly left Russia during the Bolshevik Revolution in 1918, but he soon returned and helped build up the Physico-Technical Institute. He traveled to Western Europe in 1921, collecting books, journals, and equipment for the institute. He served as director of the Physico-Technical Institute from 1923 to 1953.

Igor V. KURCHATOV, who was later put in charge of the project to build the Soviet atomic bomb, studied at Ioffe's institute during the 1930s, and Ioffe recommended Kurchatov for the position to head the nuclear project. He urged others to join the project, including A. I. ALIKHANOV.

During World War II, Ioffe's institute turned its attention to practical problems of radar, armor, and demagnetizing ships while many of the researchers either were drafted or volunteered for military service. In 1942, as the Soviets learned through their espionage network of progress toward a nuclear weapon in Great Britain and the United States, Ioffe was called to Moscow to consult on the possibility of developing such a weapon. Ioffe was offered the position to head the effort, but he declined on the grounds that, at age 63, he was too old to take on such a formidable task. Instead, Ioffe supported Kurchatov, who was put in charge.

Ioffe continued to administer his institute and received the Hero of Socialist Labor award in 1955. He died in 1960.

Ionizing Radiation

Ionizing radiation is any radiation that displaces electrons from, or forms ion pairs in, the atoms or molecules of the medium it transverses. In addition to the nuclear radiations, α, β, and γ, X-rays and short-wavelength ultraviolet radiation are capable of ion pair formation.

Iran

Iran joined the Nuclear NON-PROLIFERATION TREATY in 1970, but Western intelligence sources have long suspected that Iran has been trying to develop a nuclear weapons capability, together with long-range missiles. CHINA and RUSSIA provided nuclear technology to Iran, although China agreed in 1997 to terminate assistance in this area while maintaining its transfer of missile technology. Russia worked on civilian nuclear power in Iran, assisting in repair of a two-reactor nuclear power plant at Bushehr, on the Persian Gulf. The two 1,000 MWth (or more) power reactors were restored with Russian assistance after being damaged during the Iran-Iraq war. Russia agreed in the 1990s not to provide Iran with URANIUM-enrichment technology, which would have been crucial in developing the capability to make uranium-fueled weapons.

The revolutionary and fundamentalist regime of Ayatollah Khomeini came to power in 1979, taking over two completed nuclear reactors provided by Germany. In addition there was a small American-supplied research reactor under INTERNATIONAL ATOMIC ENERGY AGENCY safeguards. During its decade-long war with Iraq, Iran began to develop weapons of mass destruction.

In 1995 information reached Western media that Iran was secretly engaged in a gas-centrifuge uranium-enrichment program. Iran had sought help from German, British, and Swiss companies to purchase equipment and machinery suitable for the enrichment technology. Under pressure from the United States, firms from Russia, China, and Europe restricted their sale of materials that would assist in the development of uranium separation and other aspects of a weapons program.

Iran maintained civilian nuclear research facilities, first inspected by the International Atomic Energy Agency in 1997, at Bonab and Ramsar, in the northwestern section of the country. In the capital, the University of Tehran maintained a 5 megawatt-thermal (MWth) research reactor provided by the United States and fueled by ARGENTINA. Also in Tehran, at the Sharif University of Technology, the alleged experimentation with centrifuge separation was conducted. At the Esfahan Nuclear Research center, small reactors provided by the Chinese appeared linked to the possibility that nuclear weapons design research took place there. Initial work on separation under Chinese help was conducted at that location. However, International Atomic Energy Agency inspectors agreed that the small CA-LUTRONS observed there, supplied by the Chinese, appear to have been used for stable ISOTOPE production rather than for uranium-enrichment purposes that would aid in a weapons program.

Iran announced in 1990 that it had made discoveries of uranium deposits in Yazd province, near the center of the country.

Experts suspect that if Iran attempted to develop a clandestine nuclear weapons capacity, it would not have that capability before 2008 or 2009. Meanwhile, the country clearly concentrated on acquiring missile technology and chemical and biological weapons of mass destruction.

Like PAKISTAN and INDIA, Iran and IRAQ may attempt to join the "nuclear club" with one or more announced nuclear detonations. Although Iraq had to sacrifice much of its nuclear capability at the end of the 1990–1991 Gulf War, Iran appeared ready to move ahead to nuclear weapons status. Along with several other nations, Iran was technically capable of making this move early in the 21st century.

Iraq

Although not a nuclear-weapon state, Iraq has made considerable progress toward developing a nuclear weapon.

Following Iraq's defeat in the 1990–1991 Persian Gulf War, the United Nations established a Special Commission on Iraq (UNSCOM) to conduct the inspection and dismantling of that nation's weapons of mass destruction (WMDs). This category included not only the facilities for the production of nuclear weapons but also medium- and long-range ballistic missiles and chemical and biological warfare weapons.

UNSCOM found that Iraq had made great clandestine progress in the development of WMDs and that it had particularly been able to conceal an extensive nuclear weapons program. The Iraqi code name for the nuclear weapons project was Petrochemical-3. Under this secret development program, Iraq had worked on developing a nuclear-implosion device, used a variety of methods to develop enriched URANIUM, had organized secret attempts to produce and separate small quantities of PLUTONIUM, and sought to purchase both nuclear FISSILE MATERIAL and nuclear technology from the countries of the former Soviet Union and China.

UNSCOM discovered that one of the Iraqi methods of uranium separation had been based on an outmoded technology employed during the MANHATTAN ENGINEER DISTRICT—the electromagnetic separation method. The United States had long ago abandoned the CALUTRONS that had been built at OAK RIDGE as a useful means of separation because the method was expensive, wasteful, and fairly primitive. The U.S. DEPARTMENT OF ENERGY had declassified documents pertaining to the method. UNSCOM inspectors found thousands of pages of detailed information regarding the Calutrons and also discovered that Iraqi technicians had sought to improve on the system with modern microprocessors and magnet manufacture methods, building several prototype electromagnetic separation systems.

When Lt. Gen Hussein Kamel, minister of industry and military industrialization, defected in August 1995, UNSCOM and the INTERNATIONAL ATOMIC ENERGY AGENCY (IAEA) learned a great deal more about the Iraqi nuclear program. Some of the information was provided voluntarily when the Iraqi government invited UNSCOM and IAEA inspectors to learn more about their program. Immediately after Iraq's invasion of Kuwait in August 1990, Iraq had started a crash program to develop a nuclear device by extracting weapons-grade uranium from research reactor fuel, as well as working on a number of highly dangerous biological weapons systems, including anthrax and other toxins.

Under the crash nuclear program, Iraq sought to develop enough enriched uranium from several sources. These included diversion of some material from IAEA–safeguarded reactors that had been supplied by Russia and France. Under the plans to extract highly enriched uranium from the reactor fuel, Iraq would have had enough material for at least one weapon by late 1991. However, the bombing campaign during the Persian Gulf War interrupted the nuclear crash program.

When the IAEA obtained this information in 1995, it reevaluated the Iraqi nuclear program. Although the Iraqis had provided much information, inspectors were still dissatisfied. It appeared that, despite Iraq's claim that it had made full disclosure of all of its nuclear programs, research and facilities continued to be devoted to the project, and equipment had not all been accounted for. This was true not only of the nuclear work but also of other WMDs.

For example, it became clear that Iraq was continuing to import such items as missile guidance system components. Earlier imports of Chinese *Silkworm* missiles, *Scud* missiles from Russia, and local production

of *Scud*-type missiles indicated to the United States and Great Britain that Iraq was not fully cooperating with UNSCOM. A brief raid in "Operation Desert Fox" in November 1998 was intended to target some of the suspected sites at which various WMD projects were being developed.

Major nuclear facilities in Iraq included several complexes. At the Al Tuwaitha Nuclear Research Center, there were two reactors. One, Tammuz I or Osiraq, a 40 megawatt-thermal (MWth) light-water reactor was destroyed by a raid by Israeli aircraft in 1981. Tammuz II, or Isis, and a 5 MWth research reactor were the core of a research and development program for weapons. Isis and the research reactor were destroyed by coalition bombing during the Gulf War. The Calutron-type separation facilities and other uranium separation equipment were located at Al Tuwaitha, as were hot cells for working with plutonium. Although not destroyed in Gulf War bombing, the hot cells were destroyed later by IAEA inspectors. Further, a lithium-6 production facility, a necessary step in the production of TRITIUM for boosted or enhanced plutonium weapons was located at Al Tuwaitha.

Al Atheer appeared to be the leading development and testing site for nuclear weapon design and fabrication. It was here that experiments were conducted on an IMPLOSION design.

Operations at the Al Qa Qaa High Explosives and Propellant Facility concentrated on the detonating system and the high explosives necessary in an implosion-type design. Rashidya was the site of Iraq's centrifuge research and development, another system for uranium separation. Al Tarmiya was the site of the construction of at least eight Calutron type separators. Al Furat was the location for a uranium centrifuge cascade system, while Al Jesira was a large-scale facility for the production of uranium feed materials for the electromagnetic separation plant, as well as uranium hexafluoride to feed the centrifuge program.

The extensive network of reactors, research facilities, and manufacturing facilities demonstrated clearly that Iraq was close to the development of a nuclear weapon when the Gulf War intervened and that it retained much of the capability in the period after the war.

See also PROLIFERATION.

Isotope

Two nuclides are isotopes when they have the same numbers of protons but different numbers of neutrons.

Isotopes will have the same atomic number, but their mass numbers will be different. Some examples are ^{1}H (Hydrogen), ^{2}H (Deuterium or D) and ^{3}H (Tritium or T), or ^{235}U and ^{238}U. Not all isotopes are radioactive.

Israel

Since its formation as a nation in 1948 to serve as a homeland for the Jewish people, Israel has maintained a strong modern defense establishment to protect itself from possible destruction by hostile neighboring states. Although its nuclear weapon program has been kept secret, published work in other countries has detailed Israel's growth as a nuclear power since the late 1950s.

Israel has not signed the nuclear NON-PROLIFERATION TREATY, and it has conducted its nuclear weapons program in deep secrecy. For these reasons, information about the Israeli program derives from several nonofficial sources. These include journalists' investigative reports, some of which have been very thorough. Detailed reports issued periodically by the Carnegie Endowment for International Peace survey the issue of nuclear proliferation, including the development of the weapon in countries that have not declared their weapons program publicly, such as Israel. A series of books, compiled by Leonard Spector at that institution over the period 1985 to 1995, contained compilations and analyses of documented information and assessments of various unsubstantiated rumors very effectively.

Another source was the information released by Mordechai Vanunu, an Israeli technician who had worked from 1977 to 1985 at Israel's secret facility at Dimona in the Negev desert. In October 1986, while in Great Britain, he gave much detailed information to the *London Sunday Times*. He was later lured to Italy, where he was kidnapped by Israeli agents and taken back to Israel for trial. He was convicted in 1988 of treason and espionage and sentenced to 18 years in prison.

Israel began work in 1958 on the reactor at Dimona, officially claiming that the reactor would be an experimental one based on a French design. However, investigators claimed that the reactor was much larger and served as a production reactor to produce PLUTONIUM. If outside estimates of the size of the reactor were accurate, it would be capable of producing enough plutonium for two or three weapons a year. It would have approximately the output of the French production reactor at Marcoule.

According to Vanunu, Israel also constructed a large underground factory at Dimona, which included a reprocessing plant. Reputedly eight stories deep into the ground, the plant was kept hidden from outside visitors. When American inspectors came to check on the use of American technology, the doors to the lower levels were bricked up, and a false control room was displayed to suggest the reactor was operating at a lower level than the Israelis admitted.

There are a number of unsubstantiated stories as to the means Israel used to obtain URANIUM to fuel the reactor and heavy water for the reactor moderator. Some of the heavy water was obtained from Norway, and still more from France, through an illegally diverted ship. The source of uranium is even more shrouded in secrecy. According to one account, some 220 pounds of uranium were stolen between 1962 and 1965 from NUMEC, the Nuclear Materials and Equipment Corporation, at its plant in Apollo, Pennsylvania. The story of the NUMEC theft, however, has been vigorously denied as a journalists' fabrication by such individuals as Glenn Seaborg, former chair of the U.S. ATOMIC ENERGY COMMISSION. Investigations by the AEC of the episode revealed only that NUMEC had not fully accounted for amounts of material lost in processing.

Although both SOUTH AFRICA and Israel denied the stories, some observers believed that Israel worked jointly with the Republic of South Africa in developing and perhaps in testing a nuclear device. A U.S. satellite observed a double flash, characteristic of a nuclear detonation, in September 1979 over the South Atlantic Ocean, which many assumed was an Israeli–South African jointly sponsored test of a small nuclear device.

Estimates of the number of weapons by outside experts have varied. For the mid- and late 1990s, the guesses have ranged from as low as 50 weapons to over 200 weapons. However, if the information provided by Vanunu is roughly accurate, the higher estimates are credible.

The scale of the reactor at Dimona is not publicly announced, but estimates put it between 40 and 150 megawatts-thermal (MWth). A smaller 5 MWth research reactor is located at Nahal Soreq, on the Mediterranean coast. The Dimona reactor is heavy-water moderated; the Nahal Soreq reactor is a light-water reactor. Other parts of the Israeli nuclear weapons complex are located at Yodefat, near the Syrian border. Yodefat is reputedly the nuclear weapons assembly facility. A pilot-scale heavy-water production facility is located at Rehovat. A uranium phosphate mine in the Negev region near Beersheba provides a domestic source of uranium. The only part of the Israeli nuclear complex that is subject to INTERNATIONAL ATOMIC ENERGY AGENCY inspection and safeguards is the 5 MWth research reactor at Nahal Soreq.

In 1981, Israeli aircraft bombed and destroyed an Iraqi reactor at Osiraq, the 40 MWth Tammuz I reactor. As Iraq and other nations in the region develop various weapons of mass destruction, including chemical weapons and missiles to deliver them, the deterrent effect of the "undeclared" nuclear weapons held by Israel grows in significance.

See also PRODUCTION REACTORS; PROLIFERATION.

Suggested Readings

Avner Cohen, *Israel and the Bomb*. New York: Columbia University Press, 1998.

Seymour Hersh, *The Samson Option*. New York: Random House, 1991.

Rodney Jones et al., *Tracking Nuclear Proliferation*. Washington: Carnegie Endowment for International Peace, 1998.

Gary Milhollin, "Heavy Water Cheaters," *Foreign Affairs* (Winter 1987–1988): p. 100.

Leonard S. Spector, *The Undeclared Bomb*. Cambridge, Mass.: Ballinger Books, 1988.

J

Jackson, Henry M. (1912–1983)   *a member of the U.S. Congress (1941–1953) and then senator (1953–1983) from the state of Washington, always supporting a strong defense*

Henry "Scoop" Jackson, after 1945, became known as a leading advocate of nuclear weapons as part of the nation's defense.

Jackson was born in Everett, Washington, on May 31, 1912. He attended public schools and then Stanford University. He graduated from the law school of the University of Washington at Seattle, and he was admitted to the bar in 1935. He served as a prosecuting attorney and then entered politics in 1941, serving in Congress and the Senate for the rest of his life.

Jackson was a member of the Senate Armed Services Committee from 1955, and he became extremely influential in defense and foreign policy matters. In 1956, based on conversations with high ranking military officers, he suggested in a public speech that the Soviet Union was ahead of the United States in nuclear missile development. He introduced the phrase "nuclear blackmail" in this speech. Again, in time for the 1960 presidential election, he complained of the development of a MISSILE GAP.

Jackson later objected to the terms of the 1972 SALT I treaty that gave the Soviet Union a numerical advantage in nuclear weapons. He proposed and secured the passage of the "Jackson Amendment," which required that all future nuclear agreements between the United States and the Soviet Union would require numerical parity. In 1974, he supported the Jackson-Vanik amendment to the Trade Act, which allowed the United States to grant most-favored-nation status to communist states only if the state would guarantee free emigration. The Jackson-Vanik amendment was particularly directed at the Soviet Union, which had been limiting the emigration of Jews to Israel.

Jackson sought the nomination of the Democratic Party for the presidency, losing to George McGovern in 1972 and to Jimmy CARTER in 1976. In both cases, he stood for a stronger defense policy than the party's chosen candidate. A number of his supporters left the party to work with Ronald REAGAN, including Richard PERLE, Paul NITZE, and Jeane Kirkpatrick. His support of the Jackson-Vanik amendment was designed to strengthen his following among Jewish voters and among unionized labor, both of whom opposed Soviet policies.

Suggested Reading

William W. Prochnau and Richard W. Larsen, *A Certain Democrat: Senator Henry M. Jackson, A Political Biography.* Englewood Cliffs, N.J.: Prentice Hall, 1972.

Senator Henry Jackson. As senator from Washington State, "Scoop" Jackson was one of the strongest advocates of a powerful nuclear deterrent within the Democratic Party in the 1960s and 1970s. (Department of Energy)

Japan

Despite being the only nation in the 20th century to ever experience attack by atomic weapons, Japan developed an extensive nuclear industry. The number of casualties from the two nuclear weapons dropped on the cities of HIROSHIMA and NAGASAKI in August 1945 has been subject to considerable dispute. If those dying within a few weeks of the detonations from radiation sickness and from wounds are included, the death toll for the two cities mounted to over 200,000. During the United States's tests of thermonuclear weapons in the Pacific, the 1954 exposure of Japanese fishermen aboard the LUCKY DRAGON served to heighten public concern in Japan about the dangers of nuclear weapons and technology. Even though these experiences led to a broadly shared antinuclear sentiment among the Japanese public, as Japan modernized its industry and as its demands for energy increased in later decades, the country turned to nuclear power as a solution.

Japan's first power reactor was a small Magnox-style reactor imported from Great Britain in the 1950s, installed at Tokai Mura. The spent fuel was returned to Britain for reprocessing, and the recovered PLUTONIUM returned to Japan to fabricate the core of a breeder reactor.

Nearly all of the nation's energy resources were imported in the form of oil and coal, although there was a small hydroelectric program. By the 1990s, nuclear energy provided some 29% of all electricity. In 1990, the Japanese government approved a plan to construct some 40 nuclear power plants by the year 2010, which would raise the proportion of electricity generated by nuclear reactors to about 43%. Many of the new reactors in Japan were large, BOILING WATER REACTORS, rated at over 1300 megawatts-electric (MWe) each. If the plans were fully implemented, Japan would exceed the United States in total nuclear power generated by the year 2010.

Japan also began to experiment with a nuclear fuel breeder cycle. The 280 MWe Liquid Metal Fast Breeder Reactor at Monju, together with a reprocessing plant and an enrichment plant at Rokkashomura, were intended to decrease the country's dependence on imported nuclear fuel. As in other countries, there have been public protests against the nuclear power program, but over the decade from the late 1980s through the late 1990s, nuclear power in Japan as a proportion of the energy generated in the country continued to increase at a fairly steady rate.

In a controversial move in the 1990s, Japan began to import more plutonium from several sources, most notably Russia. The plan was to make MIXED OXIDE FUEL, a combination of plutonium and uranium fuels, for use in commercial reactors. Accidents at nuclear facilities, including the 1999 loss of radioactive cooling water at a power plant at Tsuruga, some 200 miles west of Tokyo, increased public concern. Another 1999 accident at a processing facility at Tokai Mura, in which an accidental criticality exposed two workers to an estimated 800 rads (usually a fatal dose), was compared to the criticality events that killed Louis SLOTIN and Harry DAGHLIAN in the early U.S. weapons program.

Japan adhered to the NON-PROLIFERATION TREATY and joined in international efforts to control the export of nuclear technology, such as membership in the ZANGGER COMMITTEE and the Nuclear Suppliers Group, organizations that monitor the export of nuclear technology with the potential for use in weapons. Japan is also a member of a group agreeing to prohibit the export of rockets suitable for conversion to military purposes, the Missile Technology Control Regime.

See also BREEDER; POWER REACTORS, WORLD; TRUMAN'S DECISION.

Suggested Reading

David Bodansky, *Nuclear Energy: Principles, Practices, and Prospects.* Woodbury, N.Y.: American Institute of Physics, 1996.

Rodney W. Jones et al., *Tracking Nuclear Proliferation: A Guide in Maps and Charts, 1998.* Washington, D.C.: Carnegie Endowment for International Peace, 1998.

Johnson, Lyndon (1908–1973)   *president of the United States from November 22, 1963, to January 20, 1969*

Lyndon Johnson had been elected vice president in 1960, and on the assassination of President John KENNEDY, he took office. He was elected president in 1964 and chose not to run for reelection in 1968.

During Johnson's presidency, relations between the United States and the Soviet Union over nuclear weapons matters improved somewhat, and the cold war entered a period of detente. On the domestic side, the ATOMIC ENERGY COMMISSION (AEC) continued to sponsor the development of nuclear reactors for electric power generating purposes, leading to a boom in reactor construction.

Johnson was born August 27, 1908, near Stonewall, Texas. He grew up in Texas and graduated from Southwest Texas State Teachers College in 1930. He taught briefly in Houston and then served as secretary to Congressman R. M. Kieberg. He was appointed to serve out a term of a deceased member of Congress and then was elected in 1938. He served four terms and during World War II also served in the U.S. Navy. He was elected to the U.S. Senate in 1948 and reelected in 1954. In 1960, he had strong support for the nomination to the presidency, and Kennedy chose him as his running mate in that year.

As vice president, Johnson took a special interest in scientific matters. As president, after Kennedy's death in 1963, much of Johnson's focus was on civil rights, on social programs collectively known as the War on Poverty, and then, following 1964, on the conduct of the war in Vietnam. Partly because of the Vietnam War, the Johnson administration sought to reduce tensions with the Soviet Union.

Lyndon Johnson Although remembered for presiding over the escalation of the war in Vietnam, Johnson worked as U.S. president, 1963–1969, to reduce tension with the Soviet Union over nuclear arms. (Library of Congress)

During the period 1964 to 1969, Johnson approved the shutdown of eight production reactors at HANFORD and at the SAVANNAH RIVER SITE. The reactors, some of which had been built during and immediately after World War II, were aging. Plutonium supply seemed sufficient for the immediate future. The closure of the reactors could be presented as part of a series of tension-reducing gestures toward the Soviets. The only new production reactor to come on line during his administration was N reactor at Hanford, the only dual-purpose production reactor and electrical power reactor in the United States.

During the period of Johnson's administration, the number of power reactors licensed to operate steadily increased. When he took office there were 15 on line, and when he left office there were more than 30, with more in construction and on order. The total megawattage of the power reactors steadily climbed, and in the year he left office it met and began to exceed the total megawattage of production reactors, providing a somewhat simplified measure of the degree of peaceful, civilian use of atomic power as contrasted to military use.

In 1967, Philip Sporn, past president of the American Electric Power Service Corporation, described the market for nuclear power stations as the "Great Bandwagon Market," as General Electric and Westinghouse competed for reactor orders. In 1963, General Electric sold its first "turnkey" reactor to Jersey Central Power and Light Company for a reactor at Oyster Creek. Soon Westinghouse offered similar arrangements, delivering a complete reactor and power station, ready to start. During the late 1960s, orders for power reactors grew from the 500 megawatt size to 1000 megawatts and more, even though the reactors already in operation were mostly in the 200 megawatt range. In other words, new reactor designs were built based on extrapolations from current experience, leading to great jumps in size without intermediate experience. With the early growth of the environmental movement in the 1960s, nuclear power appeared to offer a clean alternative to coal-fired electric plants.

The bandwagon market was reflected in orders for new reactor plants:

Year	Number Ordered	Percentage of Power Capacity Purchased
1965	4	17
1966	20	36
1967	31	49
1968	17	47

The flood of construction applications to the AEC meant that staff there had to be increased, but even so, a backlog of paperwork developed. The backlog of applications and the increasing complexity of the safety issues at the AEC contributed to support for creation of a separate regulatory agency, finally achieved with the establishment of the NUCLEAR REGULATORY COMMISSION in 1975.

The only significant summit meeting regarding nuclear policy held by Johnson was in 1967, with Prime Minister Kosygin, at GLASSBORO, New Jersey. The meeting did not result in any specific results, but the tone of the meeting was positive. At this meeting, Johnson suggested that limits be placed on ANTI-BALLISTIC MISSILES, a proposal rejected by Kosygin but eventually embodied in an agreement signed during the administration of Richard NIXON.

One minor and one major arms control agreement were signed by Johnson. In 1967, he approved a treaty banning nuclear weapons in outer space, and, in 1968, he signed the NON-PROLIFERATION TREATY.

Johnston Island

Johnston Island, located in relative isolation in the Pacific Ocean some 800 miles southwest of Hawaii, was utilized by the ATOMIC ENERGY COMMISSION as a launch site for missiles during the OPERATION HARDTACK and OPERATION DOMINIC atmospheric nuclear test series. The atoll is located about 170 degrees east Longitude and about 16 degrees north Latitude.

Johnston Island was selected as the launch site for the high altitude tests Teak and Orange during the HARDTACK series because it was more than 540 miles from the nearest populated island. The high-altitude detonation could possibly cause eye damage or blindness, and the atomic energy commission sought to isolate the tests as much as possible. Teak and Orange were both launched aboard ground-based missiles from Johnston Island.

In the Operation DOMINIC series, five missiles were launched from Johnston Island. This group of five tests were referred to as the Fishbowl tests, and they demonstrated the weapons effect of ELECTROMAGNETIC PULSE. Three of the shots during the DOMINIC series were launched aboard *Thor* missiles from the island, one from a specially designed rocket, and another aboard a *Nike-Hercules* rocket. Another five shots in the series were conducted near the island, with the weapons dropped from aircraft.

Jurisdiction over the island shifted between the Air Force and the DEFENSE NUCLEAR AGENCY (DNA). The island was used in the 1970s as a storage site for hazardous wastes, including Agent Orange, a chemical defoliant that had been used during the Vietnam War. DNA staff and contractors successfully destroyed the material by burning it at sea.

Joint Committee on Atomic Energy

Under the ATOMIC ENERGY ACT OF 1946, a special joint committee of Congress, with members from both the Senate and the House of Representatives, was established to secure congressional oversight over the ATOMIC ENERGY COMMISSION, consider its budget, and deal with policy matters. At first, the Joint Committee on Atomic Energy (JCAE) relied heavily on reports and advice from the GENERAL ADVISORY COMMITTEE, made up of scientists and administrators with close knowledge of atomic research. However, as time went on, the JCAE developed both staff and long-term members with considerable knowledge of the subject.

The committee had unusual powers, including the power to initiate legislation. The committee endorsed the concept of a nuclear-powered aircraft despite criticisms from many in the technical community.

The JCAE continued in operation until August 7, 1977, when it was disbanded with the establishment of the DEPARTMENT OF ENERGY.

PERIOD	CHAIR OF JCAE	PARTY
1947–1948	Sen. Bourke Hickenlooper	Republican
1948–1952	Sen. Brien MCMAHON	Democrat
1953–1954	Rep. Sterling Cole	Republican
1954–1960	Sen. Clinton Anderson	Democrat

Joliot-Curie, Frédéric (1900–1958)   *the leading nuclear physicist in France during World War II, who was instrumental in preventing German progress on the nuclear weapon*

Frédéric Joliot was born in Paris in 1900 and studied at the Ecole Superièure de Physique et de Chimie Industrielle. In 1925, he joined the Radium Institute, and in 1937 he became a professor of nuclear physics at the Collège de France. Together with his wife, Irène Curie, he discovered artificial radioactivity. Irène was the daughter of Marie and Pierre CURIE, who had founded the Radium Institute, and Irène had started work at the institute in 1921. Frederic met Irène at the institute and they were married in 1926. After their marriage, they both followed the French custom of adopting their joint name: Joliot-Curie.

Through the 1930s, M. and Mme. Joliot-Curie worked on radioactivity and the transmutation of elements, producing a radioactive isotope of phosphorous by bombardment with alpha particles. For this work in developing the first artificial ISOTOPE, they won the Nobel Prize in chemistry in 1935.

When World War II broke out, Joliot-Curie was instrumental in ensuring that the French supply of heavy water, useful in possible reactors for the production of PLUTONIUM, was sent out of the country to Great Britain. A large supply of URANIUM was shipped to Algeria to conceal it from the Germans. During the war, Joliot-Curie remained secretly active as a member of the Communist Party in the French underground, and he was able to maintain his work in his laboratory independent of German control. Denying the use of his laboratory to the GERMAN ATOMIC BOMB PROJECT may have been partially responsible for the lack of German progress toward the construction of a nuclear weapon.

After the war, he remained with the Radium Institute, succeeding his wife as director on her death in 1956. He died in 1958.

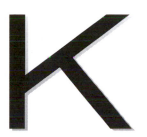

Kahn, Herman   *See* HUDSON INSTITUTE.

Kapitsa, Peter Leonidovich (1894–1984)   *a
Nobel Prize–winning nuclear physicist in the Soviet
Union who worked on the Soviet nuclear weapon proj-
ect in World War II*

Peter Kapitsa was known for his outspoken and often
contrary views on nuclear weaponry.

Kapitsa was born in 1894 at Kronstadt, Russia. In
1918, he graduated from the Petrograd Polytechnical
University and in 1921 he moved to Great Britain.
There he worked in the Cavendish Laboratory at Cambridge University from 1921 to 1934. He returned to the
Soviet Union and was not allowed to leave again. He established the Institute of Physical Problems in Moscow.

When the nuclear project was taken over by
Lavrenty BERIA, Kapitsa asked Joseph STALIN to be
allowed to resign from the project. He objected to the
idea of imitating the American research path, and he
suggested that it would be both cheaper and wiser to
start fresh on a separate Soviet path to the weapon.
He recommended to Stalin that, for two years, the
Soviets should build the industrial base necessary
and build up the scientific base as well. He disagreed
with Beria's crash approach to the project, and he

rankled under Beria's disdainful attitude toward scientists.

Kapitsa also had doubts about the effectiveness of
nuclear weapons. He pointed out that at HIROSHIMA and
NAGASAKI the Japanese had been taken by surprise and
that the cities were largely constructed of wood rather
than modern steel and concrete. Furthermore, most of
the energy released by the nuclear weapon took the
form of radiation, rather than blast. With proper planning and modern cities, he argued, nuclear weapons
would be far less devastating than generally assumed
as a result of the Japanese bombings.

Although Kapitsa was removed from further participation in Soviet nuclear weapon work in August 1946,
his demand that scientists be given a larger voice in the
Soviet project was implemented with the appointment
of Igor KURCHATOV as the technical director. Beria
wanted to arrest Kapitsa, but Stalin prohibited it.
Kapitsa was removed from the directorship of the Institute of Physical Problems for the period 1946 to 1955.

Kapitsa won the award of Hero of Socialist Labor in
1945 and the Nobel Prize in physics in 1978. Kapitsa
was one of only two Soviet physicists to earn both the
Hero of Socialist Labor and the Nobel Prize in physics.
The other was Igor TAMM, the co-discoverer of the
CERENKOV EFFECT. Kapitsa died in 1984.

Kazakhstan

Kazakhstan was the second-largest republic in land area of the Union of Soviet Socialist Republics, after RUSSIA. During the Soviet development of nuclear weapons, Kazakhstan hosted several crucial nuclear facilities, including the test site at SEMIPALATINSK, and several research and production facilities. In addition, Kazakhstan had a number of ICBM launching facilities and long-range bomber airfields that housed nuclear weaponry.

After the dissolution of the Soviet Union in December 1991, Kazakhstan became a member of the Commonwealth of Independent States. Although the country was party to the Lisbon convention, which committed the nuclear-armed countries of the former Soviet Union to abide by the terms of the Strategic Arms Reduction Treaty (START I), it was not clear whether Kazakhstan would become a nuclear power. Together with Belarus, UKRAINE, and Russia, it at first appeared that the dissolution of the Soviet Union could replace one former nuclear power with four such countries, leading to a net increase of three countries with nuclear weapons capabilities. Kazakhstan was estimated to have more than 1,400 strategic nuclear weapons, including some 1,040 warheads on ICBMs and about 370 air-launched CRUISE MISSILES deliverable by Bear-H bombers.

However, in 1995–1996, the Kazakhstan parliament agreed to ship its nuclear weapons to Russia and to accept funding from the United States under the COOPERATIVE THREAT REDUCTION program (the Nunn-Lugar program) to assist in the process of nuclear disarmament. After removing the weapons, the nation destroyed the SS-18 ICBM SILOS on its territory and closed down the Semipalatinsk facility. Kazakhstan was the first of the four nuclear-armed republics of the former Soviet Union to sign the nuclear NON-PROLIFERATION TREATY.

Kazakhstan utilized funding from the Cooperative Threat Reduction program to seal the tunnels that had been used for nuclear testing at Semipalatinsk, destroy ICBM rockets, and destroy the silos. One undetonated weapon that had been put in place for testing was destroyed by conventional explosives in 1995. By 1997, the United States had provided a total of $172 million for these purposes.

Weapons facilities in Kazakhstan had included an ICBM base with SS-18 missiles at Dershavinsk and Zhangis Tobe and the test range and a strategic bomber base for Bear-H bombers at Semipalatinsk. With the closing of the facility at Semipalatinsk, the Bear-H bombers and the air-launched cruise missiles were sent to Russia. At Kurchatov (named after the father of the Soviet atomic bomb), located near Semipalatinsk, the Institute of Atomic Energy maintained three research reactors. Almost all of the low-enriched uranium fuel pellets for nuclear reactors in the Soviet Union were produced at the Ulba Metallurgy Plant at Ust-Kamenogorsk. At Almaty, the Institute of Atomic Energy maintained another research reactor. In Aktau, on the Caspian Sea in the western part of the country, a fast breeder reactor was maintained at the Mangyshlak Atomic Energy Complex. This reactor generated 335 megawatts of electrical power.

The research reactors at Almaty and Semipalatinsk continued to operate after the termination of the weapons program in Kazakhstan. All of the research reactors and the breeder reactor at Aktau were open to inspection and safeguards by the INTERNATIONAL ATOMIC ENERGY AGENCY.

See also PROLIFERATION.

Suggested Reading

Rodney W. Jones et al., *Tracking Nuclear Proliferation: A Guide in Maps and Charts, 1998*. Washington, D.C.: Carnegie Endowment for International Peace, 1998.

William Potter, *Nuclear Profiles of the Soviet Successor States*. Monterey, Calif.: Monterey Institute of International Studies, 1993.

Kennedy, John F. (1917–1963) *president of the United States from January 20, 1961, until his death by assassination on November 22, 1963*

During the period of John Kennedy's presidency, the cold war intensified, centered around several crisis areas, especially Berlin, Cuba, and Vietnam. In the area of nuclear weaponry, the arms race shifted to more emphasis on weapon delivery systems, with the United States launching Polaris submarines, deploying *Atlas* and then *Titan* models of INTERCONTINENTAL BALLISTIC MISSILES, and launching an earth-orbiting satellite to match the Soviet achievement of SPUTNIK in 1957. At the same time, the United States and the Soviet Union were able to move forward in the area of NUCLEAR TEST LIMITATION TREATIES, with the signing of the LIMITED TEST BAN TREATY in 1963. Kennedy held only one rather unsuccessful summit meeting with his counterpart in the Soviet Union, Nikita KHRUSHCHEV, in Vienna in 1961.

Kennedy was born into a large and wealthy family on May 29, 1917, in Brookline, Massachusetts. His father Joseph Kennedy, who had made a fortune in the liquor business and as a financier, was appointed by President Franklin ROOSEVELT as ambassador to Great Britain, serving in the period 1937 to 1940. The senior Kennedy groomed his sons for political careers, but his oldest son Joseph Jr. was killed while serving in the air force in World War II.

John F. Kennedy was educated at Harvard and then served in the U.S. Navy during World War II. Upon his return, he was elected as a Democrat to the U.S. House of Representatives in 1946. He was elected to the U.S. Senate in 1952, and in 1953 he married Jacqueline Lee Bouvier. In 1960, he narrowly defeated Republican candidate Richard NIXON for the presidency. His administration was marked by his efforts to bring many academics, intellectuals, and energetic administrators into the government. Among the appointees who affected nuclear policy were Robert MCNAMARA as secretary of defense and Dean Rusk as secretary of state. Kennedy selected Glenn SEABORG as chair of the ATOMIC ENERGY COMMISSION.

Negotiations between the United States, Britain, and France on the one hand and the Soviets on the other over a peace treaty with Germany broke down in July 1961. On August 13, the East German government closed the border between the eastern and western sectors of Berlin and began construction of the Berlin Wall. That wall became a symbol of the cold war and the division between the pro-Soviet states aligned in the WARSAW TREATY ORGANIZATION and the Western powers aligned in the NORTH ATLANTIC TREATY ORGANIZATION.

The United States and the Soviet Union had entered a voluntary moratorium on atmospheric nuclear testing in 1960 before Kennedy's election. However, when the Soviets broke the moratorium in September 1961, Kennedy ordered a series of atmospheric tests in OPERATION DOMINIC in 1962. Among those tests were several that determined that high altitude nuclear bursts would generate ELECTROMAGNETIC PULSE, capable of damaging or destroying electronic equipment over vast areas.

A buildup of Soviet missiles in Cuba, first revealed by agents on the ground, was confirmed by U-2 aircraft overflights of the island. Kennedy announced the presence of the missile sites on October 22. Over the next week, both the United States and the Soviet Union increased their state of alert, regarded by most observers as the closest the two nations ever came to a full-scale exchange of nuclear weapons. On October 28, Khrushchev and Kennedy reached an agreement in

John F. Kennedy. President John F. Kennedy meets here with Premier Nikita Khrushchev (left) and Foreign Minister Andrey Gromyko, of the Soviet Union. (Library of Congress)

which the Soviets dismantled and removed the missiles from Cuba and the United States removed some older missiles from Turkey. By November 2, Kennedy could announce that the Cuban missiles were being removed.

As a result of the crisis, it was learned that telephone communication between the leaders had been quite slow, with coding, decoding, and translation leading to an average transmission time of about four hours. Earlier, the Soviets had proposed a direct phone link between the Soviet headquarters in the Kremlin and the American White House. At an 18-member disarmament conference held in Geneva in 1962, Dean Rusk proposed a plan to prevent war by accident or miscalculation. Part of the plan was a direct communication link along the lines of the earlier Soviet proposal. By the end of the summer of 1963, the so-called hot line had been installed.

Another indication of the slightly improving relations between the Soviets and Americans over nuclear matters came with the final acceptance by both sides of the Limited Test Ban Treaty. Between July 15, 1963, and August 5, 1963, negotiations proceeded on the treaty prohibiting atmospheric, underwater, and outer-space testing. Representatives of the United States, Great Britain, and the Soviet Union initialed the treaty, and Kennedy signed it on October 7, 1963. He secured a U.S. Senate vote of 80 to 19 in favor of ratification. The treaty entered into force on October 10, 1963.

With the sudden death of Kennedy on November 22, 1963, in Dallas, Texas, the presidency passed to Vice President Lyndon JOHNSON.

Kerr-McGee

Kerr-McGee is a major nuclear contractor with dispersed holdings. One of its plants, owned by subsidiary Sequoyah Fuels, was located in Gore, Oklahoma. A fatal accident there in 1986 contributed to public concern about the nuclear weapons complex in the late 1980s.

The facility processed URANIUM hexafluoride from yellowcake as part of the procedure for refining uranium ore into uranium metal for use as reactor fuel. On January 5, 1986, a tank filled with uranium hexafluoride had been weighed and found 2,000 pounds overweight at 29,500 pounds. In order to reduce the weight, an unsafe plant procedure called for heating the tank.

At about 11:30 A.M., the tank ruptured, spraying a nearby worker, James N. Harrison, with its contents. As the uranium hexafluoride reacted with moisture in the air, it created hydrofluoric acid, which severely burned his lungs. Co-workers immediately attempted to take him for medical care, but no clear plant evacuation or medical procedure existed. After driving him to a nearby facility to get an oxygen tank, they took him to a community hospital. From there, he was transferred to the Regional Medical Center in Fort Smith, Arkansas, where he died.

More than 100 people were treated for inhalation. Uranyl fluoride particles were carried off in the gas cloud. Although a heavy product, nearby communities showed contamination with trace amounts of uranium.

The plant had operated for three years without a license, allowed because its application for a license was pending. Because of leaks and other problems of contamination since the opening of the plant in 1969, the NUCLEAR REGULATORY COMMISSION had requested a detailed report on cylinder handling procedures. That report was still pending when the accident occurred.

See also URANIUM MINING AND MILLING; YELLOWCAKE.

Khlopin, Vitali (1890–1950) *Russian radiochemist who contributed to the Soviet atomic bomb project by developing a method of chemical separation of plutonium from reactor products*
Vitali Grigor'evich Khlopin was born in 1890 in Perm in Russia and graduated from St. Petersburg University in 1912. In 1915 he began work at the Academy of Sciences' Radiological Laboratory. In 1921, he devised a process for extracting radium from URANIUM ore. In 1922, he assisted in the establishment of the Radium Institute in Leningrad with Vladimir VERNADSKII, and in 1939 he became director of that institute.

During World War II, he was chairman of the Uranium Commission. In 1946, as the Soviet effort to construct an atomic bomb moved forward, Igor KURCHATOV called on Khlopin for assistance. Although Khlopin and Kurchatov had difficult personal relations, Kurchatov asked Khlopin, as a leading radiochemist, to assist in finding a separation process to refine element 94 (PLUTONIUM, as it was called in the United States) from production reactor fuel slugs. A large centrifuge that had been tried for separation would break at high speeds, and Khlopin worked on the alternative method of gaseous diffusion. While Khlopin worked on that process, Anatoly ALEKSANDROV worked on thermal diffusion.

Although the Soviets studied the SMYTH Report for clues to the process and asked their leading espionage source, Klaus FUCHS, for information, these sources provided little help. Soviet scientists had to work out many of the industrial processes on their own, and Khlopin developed the chemical method of separating plutonium. He was awarded the Hero of Socialist Labor for this work in 1949, and he died in 1950.

Khrushchev, Nikita S. (1894–1971) *leader of the Soviet Union as first secretary of the Central Committee of the Communist Party in the early and mid-1950s and then as premier (1958–1964)*
During his leadership, Nikita Khrushchev increasingly relied on nuclear diplomacy and explicit or implicit

threats to use nuclear weapons to achieve his objectives in foreign policy.

Khrushchev was born in a small Ukrainian village on April 17, 1894, dropping out of school at the age of 14 to become a metal worker. He joined the Bolshevik Party during the Russian Civil War in 1918 and rose through the party machinery during the next two decades. He took an active part in the purges of the late 1930s, continuing to advance his career through the party apparatus.

After the death of Joseph STALIN in 1953, Khrushchev soon emerged as the party leader and was selected by the Politburo as premier in 1958. In the period 1955 to 1958, although Nikolay Bulganin was premier, Khrushchev, as party leader, dominated Soviet policy. At first, his policies led to a "thaw" in relations with the United States and the West, with Soviet withdrawal of troops from Austria and a summit conference in Geneva in 1955 at which U.S. president Dwight EISENHOWER proposed an "Open Skies" arrangement. The Soviets rejected the concept, which would have endorsed U.S. and Soviet use of aircraft over each other's territories to monitor arms development. Khrushchev continued a program of domestic de-Stalinization, releasing political prisoners and denouncing some of the excesses of the Stalin period in a secret speech later published by Italian communists. The de-Stalinization suggested to Western communist parties and to many independent observers that the Soviet regime was undergoing fundamental reform.

Soon however, relations with the West worsened under Khrushchev. Brutal suppression of an uprising in Hungary in 1956 showed that the Soviet regime would not tolerate fundamental change in the communist regimes in Eastern Europe. After the launch of the satellite SPUTNIK in 1957, Khrushchev increasingly used the supposed advantage in INTERCONTINENTAL BALLISTIC MISSILES over the United States as a threat.

As the East Germany economy fell behind that of West Germany, an exodus of East Germans to the more prosperous western zone of Berlin and through it to the Federal Republic of Germany threatened to undermine the promise of a communist society. Khrushchev attempted to force the United States to recognize East Germany by threatening to sign an independent treaty with East Germany. Negotiations at Camp David in Maryland in 1959 seemed to suggest that Eisenhower would agree, but the "spirit of Camp David" soon evaporated.

Nikita Khrushchev (right) and Leonid Brezhnev (left). Leaders of the Soviet Union during the height of the cold war. (Library of Congress)

A proposed SUMMIT MEETING in May 1960 was spoiled when an American U-2 surveillance aircraft was shot down over the Soviet Union. Khrushchev used the episode to accuse Eisenhower of duplicity. In 1961, Khrushchev ordered the construction of the Berlin Wall, dividing the city between East and West to help slow down the exodus of East Germans for the more prosperous West.

The supposed Soviet lead in capability to deliver nuclear weapons by MISSILES, the so-called MISSILE GAP, did not exist. The United States possessed great numbers of aircraft capable of reaching Soviet targets. By late 1961, the United States knew the limited numbers of Soviet missiles, determined from satellites that could return detailed photographs of Soviet missile sites. Khrushchev continued to threaten the United States by claiming that Soviet arms factories were mass producing nuclear weapons.

When Khrushchev could not achieve nuclear parity or equivalence with missiles or achieve the appearance of parity with assertions or threats, he sought to do so by placing intermediate-range missiles close to American shores in Cuba. When in 1962, he placed the missiles in Cuba, the action resulted in a major crisis, bringing the United States and the Soviet Union close to a nuclear exchange. Khrushchev's Cuban bases had apparently seemed to him a simple way to achieve a nuclear balance between the two states. After tense negotiations, the Soviets agreed to remove the missiles in exchange for the removal of U.S. missiles from Turkey.

In a turn-around, Khrushchev then sought to defuse nuclear tensions by agreeing to the LIMITED TEST BAN TREATY in 1963. In 1964, he began to reduce military spending in the Soviet Union and began further negotiations regarding Germany. He was ousted from power in October 1964, partly due to his unsuccessful nuclear diplomacy over Berlin and Cuba and partly due to his domestic reforms. He was replaced by Leonid Brezhnev as first secretary of the Communist Party and by Aleksei Kosygin as premier.

Suggested Reading

James Richter, *Khrushchev's Double Bind; International Pressures and Domestic Coalition Politics.* Baltimore: Johns Hopkins University Press, 1994.

Killian, James R. (1904–1988)   *American science administrator who served as chairman of the Presidential Science Advisory Committee (PSAC) from 1957 to 1961 and as scientific advisor to the president (1957–1959)*

James R. Killian was instrumental in helping to create the National Aeronautics and Space Administration, in urging the Open Skies proposal to President Dwight EISENHOWER, and then in supporting the secret development of the U-2 reconnaissance aircraft to detect advances in Soviet nuclear weapons delivery capability in the form of INTERCONTINENTAL BALLISTIC MISSILES (ICBMs) and long-range aircraft.

Killian was born on July 24, 1904, in Blacksburg, South Carolina, and earned a B.S. in engineering and business administration from the Massachusetts Institute of Technology (MIT). Over the next 14 years, he served on the staff of *Technology Review,* a journal published by the MIT alumni association. He served as vice president of MIT (1945–1948) and as president of the institute (1948–1959).

In 1954, Killian chaired a panel to study the issue of possible surprise nuclear attack. The report assured President Eisenhower that the United States held su-

periority in nuclear weapons for the time being but warned that by the early 1960s, the lead held by the Soviet Union in rocketry could put the Soviets ahead in the nuclear arms race. The report, National Intelligence Estimate 11-6-54, *Soviet Capabilities and Probable Programs in the Guided Missile Field,* was based on the limited amount of information available in the West about Soviet plans. The report concluded that the Soviets would probably not be able to field an operational ICBM until 1963. In fact, they tested their first ICBM in 1957 and had deployed four by 1960.

Killian's panel recommended the construction of a distant early warning system of radar stations across the Alaskan and Canadian arctic to detect incoming aircraft and a series of other measures to improve American intelligence gathering. The panel's suggestions contributed to Eisenhower's plea for "open skies," or mutual high-altitude surveillance by both the Soviet Union and the United States. With the rejection of this proposal by the Soviets, the United States proceeded with the development of the U-2, a high-altitude aircraft capable of evading Soviet anti-aircraft missiles and conducting aerial photography of Soviet ground installations.

Following the launch of an ICBM and then SPUTNIK by the Soviet Union in 1957, President Eisenhower selected Killian to chair the PSAC and to serve as his personal science advisor. In these roles he continued to argue for greater use of technical means to obtain intelligence about the Soviet nuclear weapons delivery capability.

Killian left the PSAC in 1961. He continued to serve as chair of the MIT Corporation in the years 1959 to 1971. In the period 1965 to 1967, he also served as chair of the Carnegie Commission on Educational Television, and he later chaired the Corporation for Public Broadcasting (1973–1974). Killian died on January 29, 1988, in Cambridge, Massachusetts.

Kiloton

A kiloton (Kt) is a unit of measure of the yield of nuclear devices, equivalent to the energy released from the explosion of 1,000 tons of TNT or trinitrotoluene. The atomic bomb detonated over HIROSHIMA was estimated to have a yield under 20 Kt. A yield of 1,000 Kt is designated a "megaton."

See also MEGATON.

Kissinger, Henry A. (1923–) *German-born American statesman who served as national security advisor and secretary of state under Presidents Richard Nixon and Gerald Ford*

Henry Kissinger was known for his style of personal diplomacy, through which he worked to establish verifiable nuclear weapons agreements and to bring an end to the Vietnam War.

Kissinger was born in Fürth, Germany, in 1923, and he emigrated with his parents to the United States in 1938. He became a U.S. citizen in 1943 and served in the U.S. Army, 1943–1946. He studied at Harvard, earning the doctorate in government in 1954. His first book, *Nuclear Weapons and Foreign Policy,* published in 1958, drew him recognition as an advocate of flexibility in foreign affairs.

Through the 1950s and 1960s, he served as an advisor on foreign policy issues to Presidents EISENHOWER, KENNEDY, and JOHNSON. In 1969, Richard NIXON selected Kissinger to serve as his national security advisor. He was most noted for his participation in opening contacts with CHINA, for working toward a negotiated settlement of the Vietnam War, and for engaging in shuttle diplomacy to help resolve the Israeli-Egyptian conflict.

Nixon appointed Kissinger to serve as secretary of state as well as national security advisor in 1973, the only person to serve in both positions simultaneously in the 20th century. Kissinger, like Nixon, believed in personal diplomacy and in working out realistic bargains through back-channel negotiation, based upon and backed up by powerful force. He was instrumental in establishing SALT I and the ANTI-BALLISTIC MISSILE TREATY signed at the same time.

After leaving government service in 1977, Kissinger took an appointment at Georgetown University, and he wrote memoirs of his experience, *The White House Years* and *Years of Upheaval.*

Henry Kissinger (right) and Andrey Gromyko (left). Henry Kissinger, national security advisor and secretary of state to President Richard Nixon, was noted for his personal, one-on-one negotiating style. Here he chats with his Soviet counterpart, Foreign Minister Andrey Gromyko, in February 1975. (Library of Congress)

Kistiakowsky, George (1900–1982) *Ukrainian-born American physicist who served on the high explosives division of the Manhattan Project*

George Kistiakowsky worked on the MANHATTAN ENGINEER PROJECT during World War II and, after the war, he remained a leading consultant to the American nuclear project.

Kistiakowsky was born in Kiev, in the UKRAINE. His father was a professor of sociology. When the Russian Revolution and Civil War swept through the Ukraine, young Kistiakowsky joined the anti-Bolshevik forces, the White Russian army in 1918. He escaped to Germany and earned his doctorate in chemistry in Berlin in 1925. He emigrated to the United States, taking a fellowship at Princeton University, then moving to Harvard, becoming a professor of chemistry there in 1938.

In 1940, he and Harold Urey investigated the possibility of using a Corning glass material as a barrier in the process of gaseous diffusion to separate ^{235}U from ^{238}U. When Vannevar BUSH started early plans to construct a nuclear weapon in 1941, he sought out Kistiakowsky to serve as an advisor to the National Defense Research Committee as head of the Explosives Committee because of his reputation as an expert on explosives.

In 1943 he served as a consultant to LOS ALAMOS and joined the staff there in February 1944. He worked with Robert BACHER on the design of the *implosion* device that would occupy the core of the plutonium-fueled weapon. Kistiakowsky headed up a new division, "X-Division," devoted to the high-explosive components and the design of the lenses of explosives, while Bacher headed up "G-Division," to design the gadget. Kistiakowsky worked closely with Hans BETHE to learn how the material would behave when imploded. Rudolf PEIERLS explained how the issue of explosive lenses had been studied in England, and Kistiakowsky worked out the precise geometric design and the actual technique of manufacture. Luis ALVAREZ assisted Kistiakowsky in testing implosion methods with high-explosive charges, using army tanks as observation posts during the detonations.

Kistiakowsky had to make peace between different groups working on the problem at Los Alamos, trying to reconcile the conservative style of Captain Deke Parsons with the creative Seth Neddermeyer who had conceived the idea of implosion. Neddermeyer's early experiments with implosion had shown irregularities in the implosive force of high explosives, and Kistiakowsky's background as well as his willingness to work with various personalities helped solve the problem.

Kistiakowsky found that one of the causes of the irregular detonations with the high-explosive lenses was the presence of air cavities inside the materials. They could be detected by X-ray, but when found, the lens material had to be rejected as there was no way to repair the lenses. Kistiakowsky's work on the high-explosive lenses played a crucial part in the design of the plutonium weapon, as no one had ever used explosives before to "assemble" a device. It was information related to Neddermeyer's work and Kistiakowsky's contributions that David GREENGLASS provided to Harry GOLD as part of the Soviet espionage into the design of the nuclear weapon.

At the TRINITY test, Kistiakowsky bet a month's salary against $10 that the detonation of the device using his explosive lenses would work. He won the bet.

Suggested Reading
Richard G. Hewlett and Oscar E. Anderson, *The New World* (Vol. 1 of *A History of the United States Atomic Energy Commission*). Washington, D.C.: Atomic Energy Commission, 1962.
Richard Rhodes, *The Making of the Atomic Bomb*. New York: Simon and Schuster, 1986.

Kiwi   *See* PROJECT ROVER.

Knolls Atomic Power Laboratory (KAPL)

Operated by General Electric (GE) Company, the Knolls Atomic Power Laboratory (KAPL) at GE's headquarters in Schenectady, New York, is one of two propulsion and power laboratories operated by private companies and owned by the federal government. Along with BETTIS ATOMIC POWER LABORATORY, Knolls provided the reactors for the U.S. submarine fleet.

Knolls operates land-based prototype reactors at West Milton, New York, and Windsor, Connecticut. KAPL developed the sodium-cooled reactor for *Seawolf,* a design path later abandoned by the U.S. Navy as the reactor developed many technical problems. Knolls continued to develop light-water reactors for the surface and submarine fleets.

See also IDAHO NATIONAL ENGINEERING LABORATORY; RICKOVER, HYMAN; SHIPPINGPORT.

Suggested Reading
Richard G. Hewlett and Francis Duncan, *Nuclear Navy, 1946–1962.* Chicago: University of Chicago Press, 1974.

Korea, North   *See* NORTH KOREA.

Korean War

The Korean War began on June 25, 1950, and ended with a truce signed in July 1953. The pro-Soviet North Koreans invaded South Korea, and the United States came to the defense of South Korea. The defending forces were empowered under a United Nations resolution introduced by the United States to the Security Council on June 27, 1950.

The war was fought with conventional weapons, but the issue of nuclear weapons haunted the conflict. At the time and later, many analysts believed that NORTH KOREA was emboldened to invade partly because the Soviets had detonated a nuclear weapon in August 1949, ending the American "monopoly" on the weapon. The United States, it was believed, would be reluctant to utilize a nuclear weapon because the Soviets could now retaliate.

Furthermore, the United States and the United Nations placed limits on the war. When Chinese volunteers in great numbers came to the aid of North Korea in October and November of 1950, the U.S. forces were restricted from attacking targets over the border into CHINA to interdict the Chinese supply lines. Again, this restriction was imposed in order to prevent the war from escalating into a confrontation between the nuclear-armed powers. The Chinese supported the

North Koreans not only with troops but also with Soviet-built MiG-15 jet aircraft and Chinese pilots.

After an intense year of battles that swept up and down the Korean peninsula, the war settled into one of attrition. Truce talks began in July 1951 and ran for two years, with the most difficult issue that of repatriation of prisoners. Altogether, the United States forces suffered over 33,000 deaths, and South Korean forces had over 400,000 deaths.

The Korean War was the first armed confrontation between Soviet-supported forces and Western-supported forces in the nuclear age. It demonstrated that, although one side possessed a nuclear arsenal, it would hesitate to use it for fear of igniting a larger conflict.

In the United States, the Korean War led the administration of Harry TRUMAN to increase nuclear production capabilities with construction of new PRODUCTION REACTORS. Furthermore, the war helped convince Truman and his advisors of the need to develop a HYDROGEN BOMB. In the case against atomic spies Julius and Ethel ROSENBERG, Judge Irving Kaufman stated that because of their participation in providing the Soviets with information on atomic bomb design, they had helped precipitate the Korean War. He argued that the North Koreans would not have attacked had the United States still maintained its nuclear monopoly, and it was their actions that had contributed to the end of that monopoly. Although his reasoning seemed simplistic, it appeared to contribute to his willingness to impose the death sentence on them.

Krasnoyarsk-26

In 1950, Soviet premier Joseph STALIN ordered the construction of a major PLUTONIUM production and nuclear weapons facility about 50 kilometers from Krasnoyarsk (also spelled Krasnoiarsk) in Siberia. The earlier facilities built at CHELYABINSK and TOMSK had been above ground, but the facilities at Krasnoyarsk were mostly built below ground.

At Krasnoyarsk-26, Soviet engineers constructed three underground plutonium production reactors, a reactor coolant preparation plant, a chemical separation plant that was opened in 1964, waste treatment and waste storage facilities, and several laboratories. The fenced-off area comprised more than 17 square kilometers. Nearby was a closed city of about 90,000 population, Zheleznogorsk, of whom about 11,000 were employed in production of plutonium.

The underground complex was built by prison labor, supplemented after 1953 by some 100,000 military personnel. The vast underground areas included not only production facilities and laboratories but also shops and some residential quarters.

The first production reactor, AD, began operation in 1958, located some 20 to 25 stories below ground. It was a graphite-moderated, water-cooled reactor, with 2,832 channels, operating much like the D, F, and G reactors at HANFORD, Washington. The second reactor, ADE-1, operated from July 1961 through September 1992, when it was shut down for environmental reasons. Both AD and ADE-1 used the river water as once-through cooling; that is, both returned the cooling water to the Yenisey River. ADE-2 began operating in 1964. It constituted a dual-purpose reactor, somewhat along the lines of N reactor at Hanford. ADE-2 operated with a closed cycle and produced not only plutonium but also about 200 megawatts of electrical power, as well as steam for area heating of the underground facilities.

The location of the facilities in deep underground levels aided in maintaining secrecy about the extent of the effort from American satellite observation. At the same time, the deeply emplaced reactors were quite safe from attack by bombing.

See also PRODUCTION REACTORS.

Suggested Reading

Thomas B. Cochrane, Robert S. Norris, and Oleg A. Bukharin, *Making the Russian Bomb: From Stalin to Yeltsin.* Boulder, Colo.: Westview Press, 1995.

Kurchatov, Igor Vasil'evich (1903–1960) *Russian physicist known as the father of the Soviet atom bomb*

I. V. Kurchatov was the scientific director of the Soviet Union's equivalent of the MANHATTAN ENGINEER DISTRICT, playing a role similar to that of J. Robert OPPENHEIMER. Kurchatov was born in 1903 in the southern Ural Mountains and graduated from the Crimean University in 1923. In 1925, he joined the Leningrad Polytechnic Institute.

During World War II, Kurchatov was appointed scientific director of the nuclear project, and he held that position until the year of his death, 1960.

When Kurchatov was appointed to head the nuclear project in 1943, he was unaware of the state of nuclear research in the United States. Molotov, then in

Igor Kurchatov. Father of the Soviet atomic bomb, Kurchatov was known as "the beard" because he pledged not to shave until the weapon was completed. (Library of Congress)

charge of the project for the government as foreign secretary of the Soviet Union, decided to provide Kurchatov with information gained from espionage into British work on the project.

Kurchatov was impressed and wrote a report, detailing what would be needed for the Soviets to catch up with the West. He recognized that some of the initial work could be bypassed drawing on knowledge of British progress. Kurchatov understood immediately that a practical reactor could be built along the lines of the one Enrico FERMI had built in December 1942, even though he only had seen reports of British experiments with a URANIUM heavy-water reactor.

Within a few weeks, Kurchatov had decided that the most practical pathway to constructing an atomic bomb would be to use PLUTONIUM, then referred to in the literature as "eka-osmium." His insights were to

be proven out as the British and American scientists worked toward just such a weapon.

Kurchatov's positive reaction to the espionage material convinced Molotov and Joseph STALIN to continue to support the project. Further espionage-derived details from Klaus FUCHS and David GREENGLASS, sent via Harry GOLD and the Soviet's New York consulate out of which the espionage apparatus worked, provided Kurchatov with specific information about the design of the American plutonium weapon. When American weapons were detonated over HIROSHIMA and NAGASAKI, Stalin ordered the project to proceed at a faster pace, placing Lavrenty BERIA in charge.

Kurchatov continued to work as scientific director. Legend has it that he started to grow a beard, pledging to shave it off only when the project was a success. His colleagues often called him "the beard."

Kurchatov successfully supervised the construction of the first Soviet nuclear device detonated in August 1949, and he remained in charge of the project during development of the first hydrogen bombs through the 1950s. Under Beria's orders, the first Soviet weapon followed closely the design of the American FAT MAN that had been obtained through the spy operations. Kurchatov also supervised the construction of the first reactors, used for production of plutonium and for power generation. As he turned to the problem of the HYDROGEN BOMB DESIGN in the 1950s, he transferred control of the electrical power generation project to others.

For his work on the nuclear weapon project, Kurchatov was awarded the Hero of Socialist Labor prize three times.

Suggested Reading

David Holloway, *Stalin and the Bomb*. New Haven: Yale University Press, 1994.
Richard Rhodes, *Dark Sun*. New York: Simon and Schuster, 1995.

Kyshtym Accident

Late in 1957, a mysterious accident occurred in the Soviet Union, near the nuclear facilities at CHELYABINSK-40, a few miles from the village of Kyshtym. For years, no official information regarding the event was released. In 1976, a Russian emigré scientist, Zhores Medvedev, referred to the accident. His remarks stimulated such interest that he began researching the event to discover more about it.

Visitors to the region had commented that hundreds of square miles had been evacuated and that road signs indicated that no one was to stop their car while traveling through the region. Soviet maps of the region were studied, and later editions of maps had the names of many villages removed, indicating that a vast area had been evacuated. Soviet officials continued to maintain secrecy about what had happened.

Several theories developed. Medvedev himself believed that radioactive waste stored in a well had heated and exploded, sending steam and radioactive material into the atmosphere. Other theories suggested that ammonium nitrate, produced in a waste-reduction process, had led to a massive explosion.

In January 1982, the U.S. DEPARTMENT OF ENERGY issued a report, which suggested that instead of an accident the radioactively contaminated area may have resulted from radiation from reactors leaking into the Techa river complex or that nuclear waste ponds had evaporated and that winds had blown radioactive dust downwind. A third possibility was that acid rain and possibly radioactive stack emissions had spread airborne contaminants over the region.

Many publications dated in the period 1976 to 1986 contained speculative material regarding the Kyshtym accident. However, in 1986, the Soviet government confirmed that a severe accident had taken place from tanks of radioactive waste on September 29, 1957. A large-scale chemical explosion, with a force equivalent to 70 to 100 tons of TNT, had discharged radioactive contaminants into the atmosphere, spreading a plume or "footprint" of radiation some 65 miles long and five or six miles wide from the plant. Although some 80% of the contaminated region had been rehabilitated, large areas remained uninhabitable and some water supplies were still unusable. About 10,700 people had been evacuated from areas having contamination levels greater than 2 Curies per square kilometer.

Radiation levels near the explosion crater remained high for years. After 36 years, measurements indicated 400 Roentgen (R) per hour within 100 meters of the crater, whereas a kilometer away the rate was 20R per hour. Although many radioactive nuclides were released, the dominant nuclide in the 1990s remained ^{90}Sr, with less than 1% ^{137}Ce. Both radioactive ISOTOPES, strontium and cesium, are particularly dangerous to humans as they are readily taken up into the body.

Although estimates vary, a combined population of 270,000 people lived within the 6,000 to 9,000 square mile area that was contaminated. Although over 10,000 people were evacuated, some studies have suggested that as many as 1,000 additional cancers may result from the exposures. By the end of the century, the Kyshtym accident ranked as the most serious known accident resulting from the handling or disposal of nuclear waste materials.

Suggested Reading

Thomas B. Cochrane, Robert S. Norris, and Oleg A. Bukharin, *Making the Russian Bomb: From Stalin to Yeltsin*. Boulder, Colo.: Westview Press, 1995.

Zhores Medvedev, *Nuclear Disaster in the Urals*. New York: Vintage, 1980.

Lawrence, Ernest O. (1901–1958) *American Nobel Prize–winning physicist who developed the first particle accelerators*

During the 1930s, E. O. Lawrence directed the radiation laboratory of the University of California. There he constructed the first cyclotron, only a few centimeters in diameter. He built larger and larger cyclotrons, and, with a 27-inch model, he was able to create artificial radioisotopes and to synthesize new transuranic elements. By 1939 he had developed a 60-inch machine that became a much-imitated research instrument at many universities after the war. He earned the 1939 NOBEL PRIZE in physics for his work with the cyclotrons.

Lawrence was born in 1901 in South Dakota. He had studied in South Dakota and then at the Universities of Minnesota and CHICAGO and at Yale University. He was appointed to the faculty of the University of California physics department in 1930, and he became director of the radiation laboratory there in 1936.

In 1941, Lawrence anticipated that fast fission could occur in element 94, soon to be named PLUTONIUM. During work for the MANHATTAN ENGINEER DISTRICT, he developed the electromagnetic method of separation of ^{235}U from ^{238}U, which led to the construction of CALUTRONS at the Y-12 site at OAK RIDGE. He continued to advocate the electromagnetic method and worked to improve the Calutrons to produce sufficient ^{235}U to make an atomic weapon. With other scientists who had worked on the project, Lawrence attended the first test at TRINITY, near Alamogordo, New Mexico, on July 16, 1945.

In the postwar period, Lawrence continued to work on particle accelerators, and he became an advocate of the thermonuclear weapon. At Livermore, California, he directed the construction of a massive particle accelerator that could be used to produce plutonium. In 1952 that plan was abandoned, but the laboratory at Livermore began to move more directly into weapons development work.

Lawrence died in 1958, and after his death, the Livermore National Laboratory was renamed the LAWRENCE LIVERMORE NATIONAL LABORATORY.

See also LINEAR ACCELERATORS; TELLER, EDWARD.

Lawrence Livermore National Laboratory (LLNL)

Lawrence Livermore National Laboratory (LLNL), located in Livermore, California, is the second of the

E.O. Lawrence. Lawrence, standing to the right of M. Stanley Livingston, poses in front of an early 27-inch cyclotron developed at the University of California Radiation Laboratory. (National Archives and Records Administration)

nuclear weapon design laboratories, supplementing the first laboratory at LOS ALAMOS. At the University of California, Ernest O. LAWRENCE, who directed the radiation laboratory there, was a leading figure among the group of academic physicists designing the atomic bomb during World War II. After the war, research continued at the Radiation Laboratory, and at Livermore, California, a nuclear accelerator was built with the assistance of the ATOMIC ENERGY COMMISSION (AEC) to assist in the research.

In 1952, Lawrence worked with Edward TELLER to convince the AEC that a second weapons development laboratory to parallel the efforts of Los Alamos should be constructed in California, building on the facilities already established at Livermore. Lawrence asked Teller if he would agree to come to California from the University of CHICAGO to help start the new laboratory. Teller sought a guarantee that the new laboratory could focus on the construction of the hydrogen bomb, a project he had long advocated during the MANHATTAN ENGINEER DISTRICT work.

At Los Alamos, where several concepts for the development of the hydrogen bomb had already been thought through, many opposed the concept of a second weapons laboratory. Even so, the AEC decided to have two laboratories competing in the area. Competition might spur more rapid development. Another motive was that a different group of scientists might be attracted by a laboratory located in California rather than in the mountains of New Mexico.

Herbert York, a former student of Ernest Lawrence, was appointed as the first director of the Livermore National Laboratory in 1952, resigning in 1958 to become the director of defense research and engineering. In 1958, Teller was appointed as director, continuing until 1960. He was followed by Harold BROWN, who later took the same position that Herbert York had held in the Department of Defense.

In 1969, John Nuckolls and Lowell Wood at Livermore began working on a project that would use laser beams to compress the fuel for hydrogen fusion into a pellet, which would release fusion energy in a controlled fashion. This concept led to over $2 billion in federal funds to study laser fusion at Livermore.

When President Ronald REAGAN announced the STRATEGIC DEFENSE INITIATIVE (SDI), which the press labeled the "Star Wars" program, he appeared to have developed the concept out of discussions with Edward Teller about the possibilities opened up by Livermore research. Many SDI experiments went to Livermore during the 1980s, as work on the various alternative defense systems went forward. By the late 1980s, the laboratory employed some 8,000 scientists and other employees with over a $1 billion budget per year. LLNL projects included particle beams, X-ray lasers, and kinetic energy weapons.

During the 1990s, when SDI was scaled back, the X-ray laser approach to missile defense was dropped. But the work of researchers at Livermore on SDI associated the laboratory in the public eye with the "Star Wars" weaponry.

Besides defense work, Livermore continued environmental and biomedical research, examining such questions as how atmospheric pollutants affected plants and how chemical discharges would affect marine life. Of the $1 billion per year spent at Livermore in the late 1980s and early 1990s, about 25% went for weapons research and some 15% went to studies of hydrogen fusion.

Suggested Reading

Stanley Blumberg and Louis Panos, *Edward Teller: Giant of the Golden Age of Physics*. New York: Scribners, 1990.

Richard Hewlett and Francis Duncan, *Atomic Shield* (Vol. 2, *A History of the United States Atomic Energy Commission*). Philadelphia: University of Pennsylvania Press, 1969.

Herbert York, *Making Weapons, Talking Peace*. New York: Basic Books, 1987.

LeMay, Curtis (1906–1990)   *commander of the United States Strategic Air Command (SAC) from 1948 to 1957*

Curtis LeMay was a believer in, and outspoken advocate of, the usefulness of strategic bombing in warfare. During the early years of the cold war, he commanded the bomber force, the only means of delivery of nuclear weapons. His forceful advocacy of the concept of strategic bombing earned him the enmity of many who believed that the United States should take a more conciliatory stand with the Soviet Union.

LeMay was born in Columbus, Ohio, on November 15, 1906. He hoped to attend the U.S. Military Academy at West Point. However, he was not selected for the academy and instead became a member of the Reserve Officers Training Corps as he attended college at the School of Engineering at Ohio State University. He was commissioned a second lieutenant in 1928 and finished his bachelor's degree in 1932. During this period, he was commissioned a second lieutenant in the air corps in the regular army in 1930.

He remained active with the air corps through the 1930s, advancing in rank, attending training courses,

Curtis E. LeMay. As commander of the United States Strategic Air Command at the height of the early cold war, Curtis LeMay was a strong advocate of nuclear weapons. (Library of Congress)

and navigating on long-distance good-will flights. In 1940, LeMay was promoted to the rank of captain and, in 1941, to the rank of major. His experience in transoceanic flights and landings in foreign airports earned him the Distinguished Flying Cross in 1941.

In 1942, with the rank of colonel, he assumed command of the 305th Bombardment Group that flew to England and was part of the Eighth Air Force that engaged in strategic bombing of targets in occupied Europe and Germany. He served as pilot on five combat missions over Europe, receiving the Air Medal and the Silver Star for his work. He personally led a flight of B-17s in an attack on the German-held French port of Saint-Nazaire. From this attack, he changed bombing approach tactics from zig-zagging evasive maneuvers to direct, straight-in runs on the target. He also developed the tactic of assembling 18 bombers in a group so as to concentrate their defensive firepower against attacking fighters. That method became standard operating procedure in European bombing.

LeMay was promoted to the rank of brigadier general in 1943 and to major general in 1944, at the age of 37 one of the youngest men in the Army to hold that rank. In August 1944 he was assigned to the China-India-Burma theater of the war to head the 20th Bomber Command. He directed the bombing by Superfortress B-29s of targets in Manchuria. Early in 1945, he took command of the 21st Bomber Command, engaged in strategic bombing of Japan. In that role, he directed a massive bombing raid on Tokyo, and he also assisted in the planning of the nuclear bombing attacks on HIROSHIMA and NAGASAKI. He developed a tactic of stripping bombers of defensive armaments, loading them heavily with bombs, and making night raids against city targets. Prior to the use of the nuclear weapon, many Japanese cities and strategic areas were devastated by this method. He firmly believed that strategic bombing, including the nuclear weapons, brought an early end to the war and saved the lives of many American soldiers who would otherwise have died in an invasion of Japan.

With the Japanese surrender, LeMay was offered an appointment to serve out a term in the U.S. Senate from Ohio, but he declined in order to stay in the air force. With the creation of an independent U.S. Air Force as a third service along with the army and navy, LeMay commanded the U.S. Air Force in Europe. In that role, he directing the formation of the Berlin Airlift in mid-1948. As relations with the Soviets worsened in that year, the U.S. military underwent a shake-up to strengthen command.

Accordingly, in October 1948, Lemay was appointed as commanding general of the Strategic Air Command, and he stayed in that role until 1957, the longest-serving commander of the branch. He was responsible for building SAC into a massive force during the period before long-range submarine-launched ballistic missiles or INTERCONTINENTAL BALLISTIC MISSILES had been developed. The air force's strategic bombers provided the only means of delivering nuclear weapons to any potential adversary until the successful development of the ATLAS and TITAN missiles in 1960–1961 and deployment of Polaris submarine-launched missiles beginning in 1961.

In 1957 LeMay was named vice chief of staff and then appointed as chief of staff of the U.S. Air Force in 1961. As chief of staff of the air force during the period 1961 to 1965, he waged constant disputes with Secretary of Defense Robert MCNAMARA over McNamara's management style and over the newly developing strategy of FLEXIBLE RESPONSE. LeMay continued to argue strongly for new air weapons such as the B-70 bomber and against new fighter aircraft, the F-111. Furthermore, he disagreed with McNamara over the gradual escalation of the war in Vietnam.

LeMay's abrasive personality in these disputes earned him the reputation of being the strongest of "hawks" in the debates over the conduct of the war. LeMay was quoted as having said that he would "bomb Vietnam back into the Stone Age," although his supporters denied he ever used that expression. His emphasis on strategic over tactical use of airpower, however, may have contributed to the lack of preparedness of the air force for the role it was called upon to play in the Vietnam War. LeMay retired from the air force in 1965, but he continued his advocacy work as a civilian. He died in 1990.

Suggested Reading

Thomas Coffey, *Iron Eagle: The Turbulent Life of General Curtis LeMay.* New York: Crown Publishers, 1986.
Curtis LeMay with McKinlay Kantor, *Mission with LeMay: My Story.* Garden City, N.Y.: Doubleday, 1965.

Libby, Willard F. (1908–1980)   *member of the General Advisory Committee (GAC) of the Atomic Energy Commission (AEC) (1950–1954 and 1960–1962) and member of the AEC itself from 1954 to 1959*

As a chemist, Libby developed the method of CARBON-14 dating, detailed in a work published in 1952, *Radiocarbon Dating* (University of Chicago Press).

Libby was born on December 17, 1908, in Grand Valley, Colorado. When he was about five years old, the family moved to Santa Rosa, California. He attended the University of California at Berkeley, earning the B.S. degree in 1931 and the Ph.D. in 1933. He remained at the university, teaching until 1941 when he joined the division of war research at Columbia University. He assisted in the development of the GASEOUS-DIFFUSION technique for the separation of URANIUM isotopes. Following the war, Libby joined the University of CHICAGO as a professor of chemistry and worked with the Institute of Nuclear Studies established there.

In the period 1946–1947, he developed the method of carbon-14 dating, based on the fact that all living things absorb an amount of this ISOTOPE of carbon during their lifetimes. Since the absorption stops on death, and since carbon-14 has a half-life of 5,730 years, the proportion of the isotope remaining in dead organic matter can tell, with approximate accuracy, the date at which the organic matter died. He tested the hypothesis on objects for which the date was known, such as items from Egyptian tombs. The dating procedure was accurate to within a few percent, and it has since been widely adopted for work with prehistoric objects.

During Libby's tenure on the GENERAL ADVISORY COMMITTEE and the ATOMIC ENERGY COMMISSION from 1950 to 1962, he participated in planning the great expansion of the nuclear weapons production complex and the development of nuclear power. Known as a conservative, Libby opposed the reappointment of J. Robert OPPENHEIMER. As an expert on radioactivity, he was often called upon to be the spokesman of the AEC on questions of testing safety, FALLOUT, and radiation effects. He estimated that the total hazard from all nuclear tests held by the United States was far less than the exposure to cosmic rays and to other natural radiation. He believed that nuclear testing could be conducted safely and that "clean" weapons with reduced fallout could be developed. He warmly endorsed the idea of confining nuclear weapons testing underground as a solution to the popular concern with fallout and radiation hazard from ATMOSPHERIC NUCLEAR TESTING.

Suggested Reading

Richard Hewlett and Jack Holl, *Atoms for Peace and War, 1953–1961: Eisenhower and the Atomic Energy Commission.* Berkeley: University of California Press, 1989.

Libya

Libya has been regarded as a potential nuclear state, or "threshold proliferator," since 1970, when the nation first attempted to purchase nuclear weapons directly from CHINA. The country's flamboyant leader, Colonel Muammar Qadhaffi, has explicitly stated that, to protect the Arab world from Israel, Libya needs weapons of mass destruction, including nuclear weapons. Libya developed a group of technical specialists in the nuclear field. However, the director of the U.S. Central Intelligence Agency, John Deutsch, reported in 1996 that it seemed unlikely that the country could develop a nuclear weapon without significant foreign assistance.

The status of Libya as a "rogue state" in the eyes of the West was confirmed when the United States imposed trade restrictions on Libya in 1986 for its support of terrorist activities. In 1992, the United Nations placed sanctions on the country for the same reason.

Libya signed the NON-PROLIFERATION TREATY in 1975 but did not agree to safeguards through the INTERNATIONAL ATOMIC ENERGY AGENCY until 1980. The country maintains a 10 megawatt-thermal research reactor at Tajoura and plans a 440 megawatt-electrical light-water, low-enriched URANIUM power reactor on the Gulf of Sidra.

According to press and intelligence reports, Libya developed a chemical facility with poison-gas capability early in the 1990s, although construction on the plant at Tarhuna, southeast of Tripoli, was reportedly stopped in 1996. In addition, Libya sought to develop or purchase ballistic MISSILES. Neither China nor RUSSIA sold long-range missiles to Libya, although experts in the United States remained concerned that Libya might seek to acquire them from NORTH KOREA.

Light-Water Reactor

A light-water reactor is a nuclear reactor in which light water, H_2O, serves as the moderator. All of the BOILING WATER REACTORS and most of the PRESSURIZED WATER REACTORS currently operating worldwide are light-water reactors. The term "light water" is used to designate the use of common water, rather than water in which the hydrogen atom is replaced with the hydrogen ISOTOPE, DEUTERIUM, known as heavy water.

Lilienthal, David Eli (1899–1981) *American attorney and government agency administrator who was the first director of the Tennessee Valley Authority and later the first chair of the Atomic Energy Commission*

Lilienthal was born on July 8, 1899, in Morton, Illinois, the son of Czech immigrants. He graduated from DePauw University in 1920 and from Harvard Law School in 1923. He was admitted to the Illinois State Bar, where he practiced labor law and utility law. After winning cases in which he challenged utility company rates, he was appointed by Wisconsin governor Philip La Follette to the Wisconsin State Utility Commission in 1931. In 1933, President Franklin ROOSEVELT appointed Lilienthal as director of the newly established Tennessee Valley Authority (TVA).

As director of the TVA, Lilienthal vastly increased the production of electric power, a major reason for the establishment of the OAK RIDGE facility in Tennessee by the MANHATTAN ENGINEER DISTRICT. The availability of federally produced electric power in a remote region in the interior of the nation met several of the site-selection criteria for nuclear facilities during World War II. Lilienthal served as chair of the TVA from 1941 to 1945, and he was reappointed for another four-year term by President Harry TRUMAN in 1946.

He accepted an appointment to serve as chair of an advisory board of consultants on international control of atomic energy that reported to Secretary of State Dean ACHESON. The product of the board of consultants came to be known as the Acheson-Lilienthal Report, which formed the basis for the BARUCH PLAN. Under that plan, research, production, and custody of nuclear weapons would be under control of an international agency.

In 1946, Truman appointed Lilienthal to be chair of the ATOMIC ENERGY COMMISSION (AEC). His confirmation hearings were extensive, having to face charges of communist sympathy and suspicions from several congressmen that the Tennessee Valley Authority represented a socialist experiment. Lilienthal was confirmed in April 1947 and served as chair of the AEC through mid-February 1950.

David Lilienthal. First chair of the Atomic Energy Commission, Lilienthal (in bow tie, testifying) had an often stormy relationship with the congressional committee overseeing the commission's work. (Library of Congress)

During his term of office, he brought his TVA experience to bear. He believed that local facilities should be relatively free from central control from Washington, leaving a mark on the AEC and its successor agencies. The nuclear industrial facilities and laboratories, operated by contractors, appeared to reflect the decentralized management ideas that Lilienthal had established during the agency's first few years.

Lilienthal found himself at the center of several controversies because of his liberal views. In particular, he opposed the development of the hydrogen bomb on the grounds that it would place too great a strain on the limited weapons capabilities of the AEC. He supported the export of radioactive isotopes for research purposes. In both areas, he ran into stiff opposition from more conservative commissioners. When President Truman supported the development of the hydrogen bomb, Lilienthal resigned the commission to return to private life.

He was the author of several books, including *TVA: Democracy on the March* (1944), *Change, Hope, and the Bomb* (1963), and *Atomic Energy: A New Start* (1980). His six-volume *Journals of David E. Lilienthal* (1964–1976) provide a valuable resource for the history of both the TVA and the early AEC. He died on January 15, 1981, in New York City.

Suggested Reading

Richard G. Hewlett and Francis Duncan, *Atomic Shield* (Vol. 2 of *A History of the United States Atomic Energy Commission*). Washington, D.C.: Atomic Energy Commission, 1972.

Limited Test Ban Treaty (LTBT)

Signed in 1963 by the United States, Great Britain, and the Soviet Union, the Limited or Partial Test Ban Treaty represented an agreement not to test nuclear weapons in the atmosphere, in the ocean, or in outer space. The treaty was first signed on August 5, 1963, and went into force on October 10, 1963. There was no provision for verification of the treaty, although each party agreed that no underground test would release radioactivity beyond the borders of its own territory. Sometimes unofficially referred to as the "Atmospheric Test Ban Treaty," the treaty is officially known as the Treaty Banning Nuclear Weapons Tests in the Atmosphere, in Outer Space, and Under Water. The treaty implicitly endorsed the principle of underground testing.

The treaty followed upon the establishment by both the Soviet Union and the United States of unilateral atmospheric nuclear test moratoriums in the period 1958 to 1962. In this context, a "moratorium" meant that a nation would voluntarily suspend testing with the right to resume at its own discretion. Both nations briefly resumed atmospheric testing prior to the signing of the treaty. International concern with FALLOUT from atmospheric weapons testing contributed to pressures for either self-imposed moratoriums or a more formal treaty banning such tests.

On August 22, 1958, President Dwight EISENHOWER announced that the United States would suspend atmospheric nuclear testing as of October 31, 1958, for an indefinite period, pending an international agreement on inspection and on arms control. The American unilateral nuclear test moratorium on tests in the atmosphere lasted over three years. The Soviets also imposed a moratorium, although they tested in the atmosphere on November 1 and November 3, 1958.

A conference convened at Geneva on October 31, 1958, began discussion of the technical issues involved in verifying that no atmospheric tests were conducted, and on related issues. The negotiations proceeded with much disagreement, and they were finally broken off on August 30, 1960. French atmospheric testing, begun in February 1960, provided the Soviets with an excuse to stop the negotiations and to prepare their own test series. The Soviet Union began testing on September 10, 1961, and conducted altogether over 100 more atmospheric tests, including the largest thermonuclear detonation in the atmosphere ever conducted, estimated at 57 or 58 megatons in yield on October 30, 1961, at NOVAYA ZEMLYA. The Soviets continued testing into 1963.

The United States responded with a series of tests, OPERATION DOMINIC, including 36 atmospheric tests over a period of six months in the South Pacific in mid-1962. Negotiations began on July 15, 1963, and by August 5, 1963, the draft treaty prohibiting atmospheric, underwater, and outer-space testing was initialed by representatives of the United States, Great Britain, and the Soviet Union. President John F. KENNEDY formally signed the treaty on October 7, 1963, after a U.S. Senate vote of 80 to 19 in favor of ratification. With Kennedy's formal signature, the treaty entered into force on October 10, 1963.

Neither France nor China signed the treaty, and both countries continued atmospheric testing, France through 1974 and China through 1978. Over 100 other nations signed the treaty, mostly states without a nuclear weapons capability.

The treaty did not prohibit underground nuclear testing, which continued into the 1990s in both the Soviet Union and the United States.

See also ARMS CONTROL; ATMOSPHERIC NUCLEAR TESTING; THRESHOLD TEST BAN TREATY; UNDERGROUND NUCLEAR TESTING.

Suggested Reading

National Academy of Sciences, *Nuclear Arms Control: Background and Issues.* Washington, D.C.: National Academy Press, 1985.

Linear Accelerator

A linear accelerator (linac) is a straight-line tube in which charged particles gain energy by the action of oscillating electromagnetic fields. The linear accelerator at Stanford University is two miles long and accelerates electrons to energies of 20 billion (20 GeV). The accelerator, like all linacs, operated in short-duration pulses. The burst of high-energy electrons is directed to target materials for studying the microstructure of matter.

Liquid Metal Fast Breeder Reactor

A liquid metal, fast breeder reactor (LMFBR) operates with fast rather than thermal neutrons. Its core contains 20% $^{239}PuO_2$, and 80% $^{238}UO_2$, and little if any moderator. A liquid metal, such as molten sodium, serves as the coolant. An average fast neutron FISSION of ^{239}Pu releases 2.4 neutrons. Only 1.9 neutrons are released in an average ^{239}Pu fission with thermal neutrons. The higher release makes more neutrons available for producing more ^{239}Pu from fertile ^{238}U contained in the reactor core.

The heat produced in the LMFBR raises the temperature of the liquid metal coolant to 1,000 degrees F. The coolant leaves the reactor at this temperature and passes through a heat exchanger where it heats the liquid metal in the secondary loop to 1,000 degrees F. The liquid metal in the secondary loop then heats water in the power generation loop and produces 900 degree F. steam.

Of the 2.4 neutrons released in an average ^{239}Pu fast neutron fission, one is needed to maintain criticality.

The remaining neutrons are available to "breed" ^{239}Pu from the ^{238}U present in the reactor core.

See also BREEDER; HEAT EXCHANGER.

Lithuania

The nuclear power program in Lithuania is notable for the fact that although there are only two reactors in the country, they produced the highest proportion of electricity consumed in any country by the 1990s. The two Soviet 1380 MWe RBMK reactors, Ignalina 1 and 2, went into operation in 1985 and 1987, respectively. Together, they produced more than 75% of the nation's power.

See also POWER REACTORS, WORLD.

Little Boy

The GUN-TYPE DESIGN of the URANIUM weapon dropped on HIROSHIMA was relatively simple. A fraction of CRITICAL MASS of ^{235}U was fired down a tube to compress into a second fraction of critical mass. This tube or gun assembly allowed for a relatively long and thin weapon design, compared to the PLUTONIUM bomb design, which was spherical in shape. Thus the two weapons dropped on Japan were Little Boy on Hiroshima on August 6, 1945, and FAT MAN on NAGASAKI on August 9, 1945.

See also CROSS SECTION.

Los Alamos

Located a few miles north of Santa Fe, New Mexico, Los Alamos sits high on a mesa, overlooking the wide valley of the northern Rio Grande. General Leslie GROVES, head of the MANHATTAN ENGINEER DISTRICT, selected J. Robert OPPENHEIMER to head up the team of scientists and engineers who would design the atomic bomb in 1942. In seeking a secluded spot where scientists could gather to work on the weapon design, Oppenheimer suggested the Boy Scout ranch at Los Alamos that he had visited on horseback years before.

Although the army operated the facility for the Manhattan Engineer District, the civilian scientists and technicians were employed through a contract with the University of California. The University of California continued to be the contractor operating the laboratory, which in later years was renamed the Los

Little Boy. The atomic weapon dropped on Hiroshima, Little Boy rests in a trailer cradle, beneath a bomber. (National Archives and Records Administration)

Alamos National Laboratory (LANL). The laboratory was taken over by the ATOMIC ENERGY COMMISSION (AEC) on its formation in 1946.

Even though close secrecy was maintained, at least two scientists leaked information from Los Alamos to the Soviets during World War II. One was Klaus FUCHS, a young physicist who had been a refugee from Germany before studying in Great Britain. Another was code-named "MLAD" by the Russians and later turned out to be Theodore Hall, an American graduate student. Retired Soviet espionage officials claimed that the network was much more extensive than ever publicly uncovered. David Greenglass, brother-in-law of Julius ROSENBERG, was convicted of espionage conducted when he had served as a technician at Los Alamos.

By early 1945, researchers at Los Alamos had perfected the design of two weapons. The more complicated plutonium-fueled device, they agreed, should be tested prior to any attempt to use it as a weapon. On July 16, 1945, scientists from Los Alamos drove to southern New Mexico to set off the world's first nuclear explosion, in a test code-named Trinity.

When the Soviet Union exploded their first nuclear device in August 1949, the tempo of research at Los Alamos picked up again. Plans to develop a thermonuclear weapon were developed first at Los Alamos by Edward TELLER and Stanislaw ULAM.

The AEC removed the gates that controlled access to the community. Small shopping centers, restaurants, churches, and recreational facilities soon sprang up, allowing the community to resemble more ordinary towns. Fences and guards continued to control access to the laboratories and research facilities. The original Boy Scout lodge became a small museum, displaying the history of the community and the Manhattan Project.

Los Alamos scientists continued to design weapons and to attend the atmospheric tests and underground tests and to measure the nature of the explosions the devices yielded. By the 1980s and 1990s, over 8,000 people lived and worked in Los Alamos. In addition to work on nuclear weapons, by the 1990s, LANL housed research on energy, astrophysics, biological and health research, use of computers, and evaluation methods for the cleanup of hazardous nuclear waste and the environment. Low-level tests during the 1950s involving the detonation of minute quantities of PLUTONIUM caused some local contamination at test sites in the canyons near Los Alamos.

In later years, espionage at Los Alamos again became important, with congressional investigation of possible spying by Chinese agents in the 1980s and 1990s.

See also CHINA; HYDROGEN BOMB DESIGNS.

Suggested Reading

Leslie Groves, *Now It Can Be Told: The Story of the Manhattan Project.* New York: Harper, 1962.

Richard Hewlett and Francis Duncan, *Atomic Shield* (Vol. 2, *A History of the United States Atomic Energy Commission*). Philadelphia: University of Pennsylvania Press, 1969.

Loss of Coolant Accident (LOCA)

As the name implies, a loss of coolant accident could result in overheating the core of a nuclear reactor and possible meltdown of the fuel. A LOCA is potentially a very serious accident, although many minor LOCAs are detected and remedial action is taken immediately before a catastrophic failure of the reactor occurs.

Low-Level Waste

Low-level radioactive waste is produced in a wide variety of industrial and medical situations. The greatest amount comes from electrical power generation facilities and weapons programs. Some low-level waste requires SHIELDING, although most low-level waste contains material with short half-lives (measured in tens of years, rather than thousands of years) and often includes contaminated tools, garments, gloves, and containers. Low-level waste contains little or no URANIUM or PLUTONIUM, such as found in transuranic waste. Despite the limited hazard from low-level waste, it must be stored safely for periods of several decades. Thus the WASTE ISOLATION PILOT PLANT in New Mexico was designed for relatively isolated storage of such wastes as their radioactivity declines.

In one sense, the low-level waste problem was the most pressing of nuclear waste problems to resolve because of the great quantities produced and the wide variety of activities producing them. Low-level waste came from nuclear power reactors, nuclear medicine and research, military programs, and industrial uses of tracers and sterilizing materials. By the 1980s, the accumulated volume of low-level waste was over 2 million cubic meters, and it was growing at over 150,000 cubic meters per year, most of it generated by activities of the DEPARTMENT OF ENERGY, including weapons production and the production of reactor fuel.

Typically low-level waste was originally disposed of by placing it in metal drums and then dumping the drums into open trenches that would be covered with soil. In addition to the hazards this presented to groundwater, the inclusion of MIXED WASTES, such as organic chemicals and toxic agents from industrial and medical activities, created further problems at such dumps. Some low-level wastes were dumped at sea prior to 1970, when such practices were forbidden.

In 1980, Congress passed the Low-Level RADIOACTIVE WASTE POLICY ACT, requiring states to provide facilities or to enter into compacts with other states to share sites for low-level waste disposal.

Lucens

A gas-cooled nuclear power reactor, built in a cavern at Lucens, Switzerland, went critical in December 1966 and operated for only a little more than two years. It first reached its nominal power of 30 megawatts-thermal (MWth) on September 9, 1968. Operators ran it at less than 10 MWth until October 24 and then shut it down for routine maintenance. Then, on January 21, 1969, a severe problem developed.

At a power level of 12 MWth, alarms sounded, the reactor scrammed, and air locks to that section of the cavern automatically closed. It turned out that the carbon dioxide coolant had escaped from the reactor, reducing the pressure and raising the radioactivity in the cavern to hundreds of rem per hour. A pressure tube had burst, releasing radioactive coolant and heavy water into the containment.

Although the reactor had suffered a LOSS OF COOLANT ACCIDENT, the low power rating and the fact that some gas coolant remained prevented a core meltdown. Radiation that leaked from the reactor remained confined in the underground cavern, although some leaked into a machine room and access halls. Radiation safety teams monitored the leakage outside the cavern and found no serious increase in radioactive levels. The cavern chamber was automatically sealed.

After evacuating the air from the chambers, crews entered cautiously and began to examine the reactor. Using a periscope, they found that the problem could be traced to one pressure tube that had ruptured suddenly, crushing other tubes and causing the heavy-water moderator to spill out of the reactor. Dismantling the reactor required the development of special tools, and work proceeded very slowly. Crews could not gain access to the core until 21 months after the accident. The cleanup teams finally decided to store the broken remains of the reactor, including the cooling pipe and shielding in a specially constructed 60-ton steel container; other parts were stored near the cavern.

The Lucens accident was the most serious in the history of the Swiss nuclear program. By the end of the century, Switzerland successfully operated five power reactors, three in Aargau canton, one in Bern, and one in Solothurn canton. The five reactors, with a total output of about 3,100 Megawatts-electric, supplied more than a third of the electric power consumed in Switzerland.

The cavern at Lucens was later used for the storage of radioactive waste.

Lucky Dragon (Fukuryu Maru)

The *Lucky Dragon* was a Japanese fishing boat that was severely contaminated during the U.S. thermonuclear weapon test conducted on BIKINI, the Bravo shot of the CASTLE series, on March 1, 1954.

The episode attracted worldwide attention, worsened Japanese-American relations, and led to international panic over the possibility that tuna caught during the testing operation might be radioactive.

The captain and crew of the *Daigo Fukuryu Maru* (Number 5 Fortunate Dragon—usually translated as *Lucky Dragon*) were unaware that a nuclear test was to be conducted, and they were sailing about 100 miles east of Bikini. The exclusion zone that had been established ran to the north of the island, and unexpected change in the winds took FALLOUT from the test due east, hitting the islands of Rongelap, Alinginae, and Rongerik, where Bikinians had been settled. On discovery of fallout in this area, the MARSHALL ISLANDERS were evacuated.

Meanwhile, the crew of the *Lucky Dragon* saw the flash from the detonation and noted the climbing mushroom cloud across the western horizon. The captain decided to head for home. About three hours later, as the crew hauled in fishing lines in preparation for leaving, white flakes began to fall on the boat. The ashes continued to fall for four hours, covering the ship like a snow shower.

The 23 members of the crew soon showed symptoms of radiation poisoning, including discolored and blistered skin, swelling hands, loosening hair, and oozing eyes and ears. It took nearly two weeks for the ship to reach home port, Yaizu, and some of the crew immediately checked into a local hospital. Two traveled to Tokyo and entered a hospital there. The news story of their contamination came out on March 16, 1954.

American experts in Japan offered to help, and at first their assistance was welcomed. However, as the crisis worsened, Japanese doctors and hospital authorities began to insist that the crew be treated by Japanese specialists. Both the Japanese patients and their doctors suspected, with some justification, that the U.S. doctors would be more concerned with studying the effects of the radiation than in providing therapy and patient care. Word soon spread that the shark and tuna aboard the fishing boat had been sold, and buyers panicked, causing fish prices to fall in both Japan and the United States.

In the United States, ATOMIC ENERGY COMMISSION Chairman Lewis STRAUSS announced that the fishing boat must have been within the exclusion zone, and he continued to suspect that it had been a spy ship set up by the Soviets. Even though all the evidence showed that the ship had not been in the exclusion zone and instead that the fallout had headed in an unexpected direction, the statement by Strauss only fueled Japanese-American tensions over the incident.

The Japanese doctors estimated that the crew members had received very high doses of radiation, in the range of 130 to 450 Roentgens.

During the summer of 1954, most of the crew began to recover from their symptoms. However, radioman Aikichi Kuboyama became very sick. Frequent blood transfusions may have contributed to his problems. He died on September 23, 1954. The official cause of death was from the hepatitis virus. Although the virus may have come from the transfusions, he was obviously weakened by the radiation sickness and would never have needed the transfusion had it not been for the fallout contamination. Thus the press was somewhat justified in claiming that he was the first victim of the hydrogen bomb.

The U.S. government compensated his widow with a payment of 1 million yen (under $3,000 at the time) and provided another $151,000 to the surviving crew members. The U.S. government also made a payment of $2 million to the Japanese government to offset losses to the tuna industry. All of the payments were made without admission of legal liability.

See also ATMOSPHERIC NUCLEAR TESTING; CASTLE-BRAVO.

Suggested Reading

Barton Hacker, *Elements of Controversy: The Atomic Energy Commission and Radiation Safety in Nuclear Weapons Testing, 1947–1974.* Berkeley: University of California Press, 1994.

Ralph Lapp, *The Voyage of the Lucky Dragon.* New York: Penguin, 1958.

M

Magnox Reactors *See* HIGH-TEMPERATURE GAS-COOLED REACTORS.

Malenkov, Georgy M. (1902–1988) *Soviet leader who served for two years as prime minister (1953–1955) following the death of Joseph Stalin*
Born on January 8, 1902, in Orenberg, Russia, Georgy Malenkov served as a member of the State Defense Committee of the Soviet Union (1941–1945) and as deputy prime minister in 1946. On Joseph STALIN's death in 1953, he served for nearly two years as prime minister of the Soviet Union, but he lost out in the struggle for power with Nikita KHRUSHCHEV.

When Stalin died, Malenkov emerged as the leader of the Soviet Union. At that time, he was unaware of the plans of Igor KURCHATOV and his colleagues to develop the hydrogen bomb. With the arrest and subsequent execution of Lavrenty BERIA, Malenkov gave the nuclear weapons scientists a freer hand in managing the program. After Kurchatov briefed Malenkov about the upcoming Joe 4 test in August 1953, Malenkov gave the go-ahead.

During the controversy over HYDROGEN BOMB DESIGN, Malenkov claimed that the Soviets had broken the United States monopoly on a thermonuclear weapon with their design of Joe 4, a design that outside observers did not regard as a true hydrogen bomb. Just before the detonation of Joe 4 on August 12, 1953, Malenkov led the way in a Soviet propaganda barrage claiming they had developed a deliverable thermonuclear weapon. The Soviet press followed up with reiteration of the concept, leading many in the West to assume the Soviets had not only broken the U.S. monopoly but had pulled ahead by developing a deliverable H-bomb.

As Khrushchev emerged as the leader of the Soviet Union, Malenkov fell from favor. He was removed from the Politburo in 1957 and expelled from the Communist Party in 1961. He died in 1988.

Manhattan Engineer District (MED)

During World War II, the development of the atomic bomb was organized from 1942 to 1946 under the Army Corps of Engineers, with the code name Manhattan Engineer District (MED). The preliminary sci-

Enrico Fermi. The Manhattan Engineer District developed the nuclear weapon with the aid of many refugee scientists from Europe. The Italian physicist Enrico Fermi, whose wife was Jewish, decided not to return to fascist Italy after receiving the Nobel Prize in 1938. (Department of Energy)

entific work had been organized on contracts through the ADVISORY COMMITTEE ON URANIUM and the OFFICE OF SCIENTIFIC RESEARCH AND DEVELOPMENT (OSRD). The OSRD, headed by Vannevar BUSH, could not assemble the massive numbers of people and the vast amounts of contract management that would be required to see the project through to completion.

General Leslie GROVES was appointed in 1942 to direct the MED, and he selected J. Robert OPPENHEIMER to be scientific director of the project. The project required not only an engineering task but extensive scientific research and as well as industrial scale facilities to convert the concept of the release of atomic energy through FISSION of atoms from a laboratory demonstration to a usable weapon of war. That was the mission of the MED.

However, the massive effort had to be conducted in secrecy, as it was important not to let the German government know that the United States was even engaged in the problem. German scientists had discovered nuclear fission before the war, and, under Werner

HEISENBERG, they were thought to be making progress toward assembling a weapon. If they became aware of the U.S. effort, it would only encourage them to redouble their efforts and perhaps to achieve the weapon first.

The technical problems facing General Groves as he organized the MED were immense. At the core of a weapon there had to be created a sufficient critical mass of fissionable material to sustain an instantaneous CHAIN REACTION. Fissionable material had to be obtained and a device or "gadget" designed that would assemble the critical mass in an instant. At the beginning of the project, only ^{235}U was known to be fissionable. This ISOTOPE of URANIUM existed in extremely small quantities, representing only 0.7 of 1% of natural uranium. The only known deposits of uranium were in the Belgian Congo and Czechoslovakia. Obtaining control of the ore from the Congo was one of Groves's first objectives.

Then the uranium isotopes had to be separated, a process that had been achieved only on the laboratory scale in the past. Electromagnetic separation could only yield minute amounts of the fissionable isotope. Another method, gaseous diffusion would require a massive factory in order to obtain slightly more.

Another fissionable material, ^{239}Pu, could be manufactured in nuclear reactors from the more plentiful isotope of uranium, ^{238}U. The reactors could be made similar to the one demonstrated by Enrico FERMI at Chicago in December 1942 but on a much larger scale. To get reactors on sufficient scale to produce small amounts of PLUTONIUM would require that those machines would need to be constructed during the war, when materials and labor were scarce.

The Manhattan Engineer District, operating in secrecy, had to assemble manpower and materials to mount major industrial efforts to acquire the fissionable materials during these times of scarcity. Designing the weapons that would make use of the machinery would require a dedicated research and development effort.

For all these reasons, the management of the MED was an extremely difficult task, full of contradictions and near-impossible challenges. The technical difficulties of obtaining fissionable material were barely known. A whole massive industry, involving thousands of workers and hundreds of millions of dollars, had to be started, without those workers knowing exactly what they were engaged in producing. Laboratory processes had to be converted into industrial-scale processes. Completely new weapons had to be designed, and the parts fabricated, assembled, and tested. Pilots and crews would need to be trained in use of the weapons, even before those weapons were completed. A strategy or doctrine of employing the weapons had to be established. Not the least of the problems were the human and personnel issues of assembling teams from the military, academia, and industry and getting them to work together toward common objectives under conditions of urgency, secrecy, and isolation.

The field of nuclear engineering did not exist; that is, although nuclear physicists had discovered fission and they understood the structure of the atom, the nature of the fissionable isotopes, and how to create and isolate them, the scientists had only operated at the laboratory level or thought through the issues in theoretical calculations. No one had designed large-scale machines to create sufficient material for weapon use. Furthermore, no professional group existed with knowledge of how to construct a weapon based on the principles.

Accordingly, nuclear physicists were recruited to play the role of nuclear engineers in designing the weapon while large scale chemical processing firms were offered contracts to construct the necessary industrial equipment and produce the fissionable isotopes. Out of these two disparate groups—academic nuclear physicists and industrial chemical engineers—the field of nuclear engineering was born.

The MED established three entirely secret communities, building the facilities from the ground up. At HANFORD, Washington, the MED contracted with DuPont Corporation to construct three production reactors, together with chemical separation facilities to produce plutonium for the weapons. At OAK RIDGE, Tennessee, the MED contracted with Kellex Corporation to built a massive GASEOUS-DIFFUSION plant to separate ^{235}U from ^{238}U, along with other facilities, including an experimental reactor and electromagnetic isotope separation facilities. Later, Monsanto Company took over operation of the Oak Ridge plants. Both Hanford and Oak Ridge, as major industrial locations, remained crucial parts of the nuclear weapons complex for decades after World War II.

The scientific work was conducted at a third secret city, LOS ALAMOS, New Mexico, operated under contract with the University of California. There Oppenheimer assembled a group of leading physicists, chemists, and engineers. Oppenheimer, who had established a na-

tional and international reputation in the field of nuclear physics before the war, succeeded in attracting many physicists from the academic community to work on the weapon project. Many were refugees from Europe, and a few played double roles and spied for the Soviet Union while assisting in the development of the bomb.

Among scientists who worked either at Los Alamos or at other laboratories on aspects of the weapon were Luis ALVAREZ, Robert BACHER, Hans BETHE, Niels BOHR, James CHADWICK, James FRANCK, Earnest LAWRENCE, Enrico Fermi, Rudolf PEIERLS, Isidor RABI, Glenn SEABORG, Henry SMYTH, Leo SZILARD, Edward TELLER, and Eugene WIGNER.

The scientists focused on the issue of how the critical mass should be assembled instantaneously to set off the chain reaction that would release atomic energy in a single burst. Two designs evolved, based on the physical properties of the two fissionable materials. For the uranium weapon, a gun-design was employed, in which a subcritical mass of uranium was fired down a tube at a second subcritical mass to instantly bring together a mass larger than critical in which a chain reaction would immediately take place. When using plutonium, however, the reaction would occur even more rapidly, blowing apart some of the fissile material before it had fully fissioned. In order to achieve a critical mass even more quickly, a supercritical assembly of plutonium would be instantly imploded, using high explosives to crush it into a smaller sphere that would more thoroughly fission. Working on the two designs, the gun type and the implosion type, and conducting tests to ensure that each would work consumed the time of the scientists at Los Alamos.

In addition, contracts formerly administered by the OSRD at the University of CHICAGO, the University of Iowa, Columbia, and many other universities and private laboratories were taken over and run by the MED to work on various other aspects of the project. Bendix Corporation was recruited to produce many of the mechanical parts of the weapons. Groves also established a special group, ALSOS PROJECT, that worked through the Office of Special Services (OSS) to determine what progress had been made by the Germans in developing a nuclear weapon.

The MED worked closely with scientists in CANADA, particularly at McGill University, and with British scientists who had begun initial work toward a nuclear weapon even before the formation of the U.S. project, including John COCKROFT, Rudolf Peierls, and Klaus

FUCHS. Fuchs was German born, and he had escaped from Germany to study in Britain. Among a few others, Fuchs was instrumental in providing the Soviet Union with detailed information about the design of the weapons in the most famous breach of nuclear secrecy of the whole MED period.

At the University of Chicago, a theoretical group that included Eugene Wigner, Leo Szilard, and Enrico Fermi continued work on reactor designs. The scientists at Chicago also developed plans for the utilization of atomic energy in the postwar world, and they turned their attention to the difficult issue of nuclear arms control. Under the leadership of Leo Szilard and others, the Chicago scientists submitted several petitions through channels, urging that the weapon not be dropped on a civilian population but that it be demonstrated in some other fashion. The group at Chicago became the core of the postwar organization that published the *Bulletin of the Atomic Scientists*.

Altogether, the MED spent some $2 billion in developing the weapons, and employed upward of 100,000 people in construction, research and development, and production facilities.

The MED successfully met its objective by detonating a test weapon of the plutonium implosion design at the TRINITY test on July 16, 1945. President Franklin ROOSEVELT, who had authorized the original Manhattan Engineer District, died on April 12, 1945. His successor was Vice President Harry TRUMAN. On learning of the magnitude of the atomic weapon project being managed by General Groves, Truman urged that it be brought to fruition as quickly as possible. He asked that the test of plutonium weapon be scheduled as soon as possible, prior to his first meeting with Joseph STALIN.

When Truman was at the conference with Stalin at Potsdam, Germany, he received word that the Trinity test was successful. His eagerness to have the MED conduct the weapon test before Potsdam and the noticeable strengthening of his negotiating stance with the Soviets have been cited as evidence that Truman saw the long-term strategic value of the weapon in the competition for world power with the Soviets in the postwar era.

Meanwhile, plans for the use of the weapon went forward. The uranium-fueled weapon dropped on Hiroshima on August 6, 1945, had not been previously tested, as the design was simpler and the scientists were confident that it would be successful. A weapon following the implosion design was dropped on Nagasaki on August 9, 1945. A public explanation of the secret activities of the MED was made immediately after the two weapons were dropped by means of a technical report written by Henry Smyth and by public news releases prepared by William Laurence.

With the release of these rich sources of information, the whole development of the atomic weapon came to be known as the Manhattan Project. While the official name of the organization had been the Manhattan Engineer District, the name Manhattan Project entered the vocabulary of historians and the public. Many military men and scientists who had been unaware of the nature of the work concealed by the code-name Manhattan Engineer District learned for the first time why they had been unable to obtain strategic materials or key personnel over the previous three years.

Following the war, the Manhattan Engineer District organized the Joint Task Force that conducted the first postwar nuclear tests, OPERATION CROSSROADS, at BIKINI Atoll in the Pacific Ocean in 1946. With the creation of the ATOMIC ENERGY COMMISSION under the ATOMIC ENERGY ACT OF 1946, the MED turned over all its facilities, contracts, and materials to the commission.

See also TRUMAN'S DECISION.

Suggested Reading

Richard G. Hewlett and Oscar E. Anderson, *The New World* (Vol. 1 of *A History of the United States Atomic Energy Commission*). Washington, D.C.: Atomic Energy Commission, 1962.

Richard Rhodes, *The Making of the Atomic Bomb*. New York: Simon and Schuster, 1986.

Marshall Islanders

The sparsely populated Marshall Islands of the South Pacific, conquered from the Japanese by the United States during World War II, were chosen by the United States as the site for early atmospheric nuclear testing. The United States conducted over 60 nuclear tests on the atolls of BIKINI and ENEWETAK during the period 1946 to 1962, leaving the islands severely damaged. Physical rehabilitation of the atolls was not entirely successful in that Bikini was not judged habitable.

The Marshall Islanders resident on the islands were displaced, with those from Enewetak repatriated to their island only after extensive cleanup operations. Bikini, however, remained uninhabited at the end of the century, although the islanders have been able to arrange for tourist visits to the island for short stays.

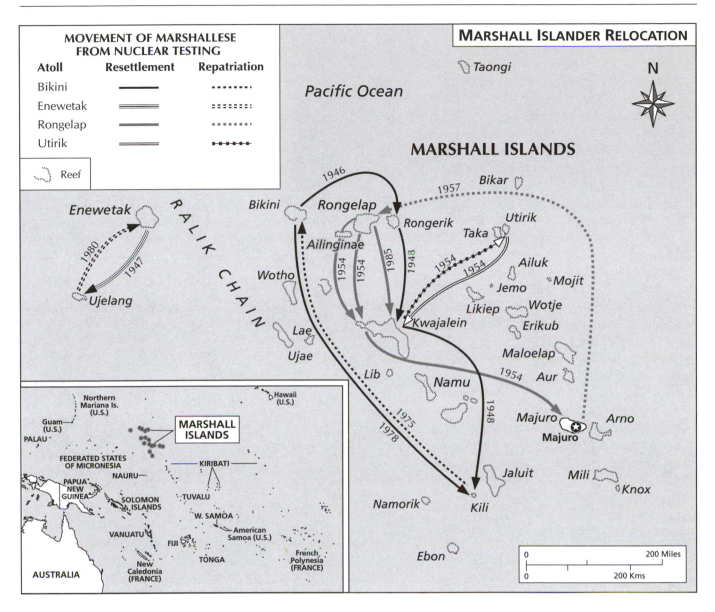

MARSHALL ISLANDER RELOCATION

MOVEMENT OF MARSHALLESE FROM NUCLEAR TESTING

Atoll	Resettlement	Repatriation
Bikini		
Enewetak		
Rongelap		
Utirik		

Reef

Residents of Bikini were moved to the island of Rongelap and provided housing there while their island was used for testing. However, during the Bravo Test in OPERATION CASTLE in 1954, some 236 Marshall Islanders were exposed to dangerous radiation as clouds from the test blew over Rongelap.

Following the test, Rongelap, about 100 miles from the test site at Bikini, suffered heavy FALLOUT. In the few days before islanders could be reevacuated, estimates of exposure ran as high as 110 Roentgen, at a time when test personnel were limited to 3 to 3.9 Roentgen for radiation safety reasons. Although the estimates of exposure were later reduced on the basis of further data, many of those evacuated showed signs of radiation poisoning, including depressed white blood-cell counts, hair loss, and skin lesions. In light of the simultaneous exposure of Japanese fishermen aboard the fishing vessel, LUCKY DRAGON (one of whom died), the exposure of the Marshall Islanders in this situation appeared extremely serious. Public concern about the plight of the islanders gradually became a minor focal point for antinuclear sentiment and protest.

In 1964, Congress voted $950,000 to compensate the islanders who had been exposed to high levels of fallout after the 1954 Bravo test in Operation Castle. Furthermore, any of the islanders who required thyroid surgery could receive payments up to $25,000 while relatives of any who died from what appeared to be a radiation-related disease could receive

$100,000. The United States admitted moral responsibility in these cases, without formally accepting legal liability.

The Marshall Islanders brought suit in U.S. courts for amounts up to $6 billion by the early 1980s. However, under the Compact of Free Association between the Republic of the Marshall Islands and the U.S. government, the United States set up a $150 million trust fund to compensate any injured or displaced islanders. In the compact, the Marshall Islands took on a relatively unique relationship with the United States under which its foreign relations and defense were handled by the United States and it obtained sovereignty for all other matters.

Under the compact, the islanders agreed to renounce claims on the United States arising from the testing. In the light of this compact, the U.S. Court of Claims dismissed three sets of cases: *Juda v. United States,* filed by the people of Bikini; *Peter v. United States,* filed by those from Enewetak; and *Nital et al. v. United States,* filed by downwind residents of other Marshall Islands.

The system of compensation without admission of legal liability that evolved in the Marshall Islander case was applied by the U.S. government is several other situations, including the Irene ALLEN V. UNITED STATES case, and cases of ATOMIC VETERANS. Rather than settling such claims through court actions, the government simply set up a financial system for compensating victims of radiation exposure without admitting responsibility or legal liability.

Suggested Reading

Barton Hacker, *Elements of Controversy: The Atomic Energy Commission and Radiation Safety in Nuclear Weapons Testing, 1947–1974.* Berkeley: University of California Press, 1994.

Massive Retaliation

During the early 1950s, as the United States began to develop a massive lead over the Soviet Union in the number of nuclear weapons produced, Eisenhower's secretary of state, John Foster DULLES, suggested that communist aggression by conventional force anywhere in the world might be met by a nuclear weapon response from the United States. He wrote in a 1952 article for *Life* magazine that the United States should "retaliate instantly" by "means of our own choosing." He reiterated the concept in a speech on January 12, 1954. The concept came to be called massive retalia-

tion in the press and dominated U.S. strategic thinking through the decade of the 1950s.

However, by 1960, many strategists had come to recognize that, with the growing Soviet nuclear arsenal and with the ability of the Soviets to launch INTERCONTINENTAL BALLISTIC MISSILES, such a policy could unleash a nuclear holocaust not only on the Soviets but also upon the United States. During the early 1960s, the doctrine of massive retaliation was replaced by a FLEXIBLE RESPONSE strategy, suggesting that the United States would develop sufficient conventional forces, including the army, navy, and marines, to respond with a wide range of military options in case of aggression.

Suggested Reading

Patrick Glynn, *Closing Pandora's Box: Arms Races, Arms Control, and the History of the Cold War.* New York: Basic Books, 1992.

Materials Testing Reactor

The Materials Testing Reactor (MTR) was planned in 1948 as part of the first reactor development proposals of the United States ATOMIC ENERGY COMMISSION (AEC). In 1949, when the AEC selected a site for its first field activity, taking over a Naval Proving Ground near Pocatello, Idaho, for the National Reactor Test Station, it planned to build the MTR there. Construction was guided by a team from OAK RIDGE NATIONAL LABORATORY.

The light-water cooled MTR went critical on March 31, 1952, operated under contract by Phillips Petroleum Company. The reactor was rated at 30,000 kilowatts-thermal, and by August 1952, it went into service testing the performance and durability under intense radiation of various substances and equipment parts for use in further reactors.

Maud Committee

The Maud Committee was a small group of British scientists formed in 1940. They explored the idea that a nuclear weapon could be developed using a fast CHAIN REACTION in URANIUM. The committee consisted of G. P. Thompson, the son of J. J. THOMPSON, James CHADWICK, and J. D. COCKROFT, and a few others. They met in April 1940 and again in June when they began experimentation with methods for separating uranium.

The term "Maud" was not an acronym but a cover name, apparently invented after Lise MEITNER sent a cable suggesting that information be passed to Cockroft and to "Maud Ray Kent." Cockroft decided that the three mysterious words were an anagram for "Radium Taken." Later, the scientists learned that Niels BOHR had a governess for his children named Maud Ray and that she was from Kent. Meitner had apparently hoped to signal that the information was so important and portentous that it could be best interpreted by Niels Bohr. In any case, the mysterious word seemed a good cover label, and the activities of the British scientists exploring the possibility of a nuclear weapon were cloaked under the name of the Maud Committee.

The Maud Committee issued a report in July 1941 and officially sent it to the U.S. government in October of that year. In the report, the committee concluded that it was possible to make an effective uranium bomb. They recommended that it was practical to build such a weapon, that work should begin and continue at the highest priority toward building one, and that Great Britain should collaborate with the United States on the project. British support for the idea came from Winston Churchill and from the British chiefs of staff. The report helped spur American developments in building a project that led from the OFFICE OF SCIENTIFIC RESEARCH AND DEVELOPMENT to the MANHATTAN ENGINEER DISTRICT.

Maxwell, James Clerk (1831–1879) *Scottish physicist who developed the concept that electromagnetic waves are responsible for light, magnetism, and electricity*

James Clerk Maxwell's theoretical work established the groundwork for the development of radio. He founded the laboratory at Cambridge that later hosted many developments in nuclear physics.

Maxwell was born in Edinburgh and educated there and at Cambridge. He taught natural philosophy at Aberdeen and astronomy in London. Following 1871, he taught experimental physics at Cambridge University. He was the founder of the Cavendish laboratory at Cambridge, the site of many 20th-century advances in nuclear physics.

May-Johnson Bill

In the weeks following Japan's surrender, the U.S. War Department drafted a hastily written bill to secure con-trol of the atomic weapons program for the military and enlisted the aid of two powerful congressional members. Senator Edwin C. Johnson of Colorado, the ranking member of the U.S. Senate Military Affairs Committee, and Representative Andrew Jackson May, chairman of the U.S. House Military Affairs Committee, introduced the War Department legislation on October 3, 1945.

The May-Johnson bill proposed the establishment of an atomic energy commission within the Department of Defense, permitted military control over all aspects of atomic energy, required strict secrecy and security regulations, and mandated heavy penalties for any security violations.

Despite the efforts of May-Johnson supporters to expedite the passage of the bill, opposition prevented its authorization. Johnson conducted a series of abbreviated hearings on the bill, designed to limit the input from critics. However, Manhattan Project scientists organized into associations to protest and lobby congressional members to halt the bill. The scientists objected to the bill's exclusive emphasis on the military applications of atomic energy. They believed the legislation's security regulations left little room for information exchanges between nations, discouraged international cooperation on peaceful uses of nuclear energy, and hindered the development of international control schemes.

Civilian atomic scientists felt nuclear energy needed to be placed under the authority of a civilian agency in order to convince the world that the United States truly wanted to promote the peaceful development of nuclear power and to avert its military use. They launched a lively and eventually successful public relations campaign against the May-Johnson bill.

See also ATOMIC ENERGY ACT OF 1946.

McCone, John (1902–1988) *American engineer and industrialist who served as chairman of the Atomic Energy Commission from July 14, 1958, to January 20, 1961*

John McCone was appointed by President Dwight EISENHOWER to follow Lewis STRAUSS as chairman of the ATOMIC ENERGY COMMISSION (AEC), where he was an advocate of continued atmospheric nuclear testing.

McCone was born in San Francisco on January 4, 1902. He graduated from the University of California at Berkeley in 1922 with a degree in engineering. After working in an iron and steel company in Los Angeles, he left in 1937 to form Bechtel-McCone Company, which became one of the largest defense contractors in the United States. Bechtel's early work included construction of petroleum refineries and power plants for the consortium of Texaco and Standard Oil of California, the forerunner of Aramco in Arabia.

During World War II, McCone headed California Shipbuilding Corporation, setting high goals for ship production. He also managed the Marinships firm in Marin County in California and the Oregon Shipbuilding Company.

President Harry TRUMAN appointed McCone to help develop air defense policies, working with Secretary of Defense James V. Forrestal. McCone continued to serve on governmental advisory boards while at the same time continuing his career as a business executive. In 1958, Eisenhower selected McCone to head the Atomic Energy Commission.

Well known as a moderate Republican, McCone was thought to be conservative but more flexible than Strauss on matters of policy. As chairman of the AEC, McCone argued against banning nuclear tests, arguing that further testing was necessary to develop a "clean" or fallout-free nuclear weapon. He accepted Eisenhower's decision to impose a moratorium on testing, but he disagreed with the president on the negotiating position that should be taken with the Soviet Union. McCone argued for continued testing so that both sides could develop techniques for detecting whether the other had conducted underground tests in excess of a low threshold. On those grounds, he supported a limited test ban treaty that would allow underground testing to continue. During his administration, the AEC began to work with the private sector in development of nuclear power.

See also LIMITED TEST BAN TREATY.

McMahon, Brien (1903–1952) *member of the U.S. Senate who was the lead author of the Atomic Energy Act of 1946*

James O'Brien ("Brien") McMahon was born on October 6, 1903, in Norwalk, Connecticut. He graduated from Fordham College in 1924, and he received a law degree from Yale in 1927. As senator from Connecticut, he took the lead in drafting the ATOMIC ENERGY ACT OF 1946. As member and chairman of the JOINT COMMITTEE ON ATOMIC ENERGY (JCAE), he helped shape atomic energy policy in the period 1946 to 1952.

Brien McMahon. Senator Brien McMahon took a key role in drafting the Atomic Energy Act of 1946 and served as chair of the Joint Committee on Atomic Energy, 1946 and 1949–1952. (Department of Energy)

McMahon served in Washington as assistant attorney general in 1935 and argued several cases before the Supreme Court. In 1939, he returned to Connecticut to practice law, and in 1944 he was nominated as the Democratic candidate for the Senate from Connecticut. In the Senate, he was a staunch supporter of Democratic policies and of Presidents Franklin ROOSEVELT and Harry TRUMAN.

With the detonation of the nuclear weapon over HIROSHIMA, McMahon immediately saw the need for civilian control of atomic energy. He proposed a special committee to deal with atomic matters, and he became chairman of that committee. When the Atomic Energy Act of 1946 was passed, it created a joint committee of the House and Senate on atomic energy. He became chairman of the JCAE in 1946. He served as a member of the committee during the period of Republican Party control, 1947–1948, and was again selected as chairman of the committee in 1949.

He advocated the buildup of the American nuclear stockpile and was a firm advocate of building the hydrogen bomb. Under his chairmanship, the Joint Committee played an active role in congressional oversight of the Atomic Energy Commission and its activities.

McMahon was reelected to the Senate in 1950, and he was considered as a possible candidate for the vice presidency in 1952. However, he died of cancer on July 28, 1952, during the Democratic national convention.

McNamara, Robert S. (1916–   ) *American businessman and secretary of defense in the administrations of John Kennedy and Lyndon Johnson*

Robert McNamara took the lead in the transformation of American nuclear policy from one of MASSIVE RETALIATION to one of FLEXIBLE RESPONSE.

McNamara was born on June 9, 1916, in San Francisco, California. A brilliant student, he graduated from the University of California at Berkeley with honors in 1937, and he finished a Masters of Business Administration at Harvard in 1939. He taught at the Business School at Harvard before World War II, and during the war served with the army air force in developing a method of statistical control of materiel, money, and personnel. His innovations in these techniques of operations management established his reputation as a pioneering and committed manager.

After the war, the air force group of managers, under former colonel Tex Thornton, established RAND, a private consulting firm to work with industry. McNamara worked with Ford Motor Company in restructuring its old management system to create a decentralized system of divisions with well-defined areas of responsibility. McNamara served from 1946 to 1949 as the manager of Ford's planning and financial analysis offices. He rose through positions of increasing responsibility to become, in 1960, the first president of Ford Motor Company who was not a member of the Ford family.

He was recommended to President John F. KENNEDY for appointment by Robert Lovett, who had known him during the war. Kennedy offered McNamara the choice of two cabinet positions, secretary of treasury or secretary of defense. McNamara chose defense, insisting that he be able to appoint his own staff. He selected Harold BROWN, director of the LAWRENCE LIVERMORE laboratory in California, to be director of defense research and engineering, and Charles Hitch, a senior executive at RAND Corporation, to be Pentagon comptroller. McNamara soon earned the enmity of many in the Defense Department for his reform of budgeting procedures and for seeking weapons system and weapons platforms, such as fighter aircraft, that could be used by more than one service. Among others, General Curtis LEMAY argued strongly that McNamara's policies endangered U.S. national security and prolonged the war in Vietnam unnecessarily.

McNamara was credited with pushing for the replacement of the doctrine of massive retaliation, developed under President Dwight EISENHOWER's secretary of state, John Foster DULLES. McNamara's doctrine of flexible response called for increasing troop strength and transport capability in order to create a strong mobile strike force that could meet conventional warfare or guerrilla warfare situations without relying on the threat of nuclear retaliation to prevent aggression. He worked with members of the NORTH ATLANTIC TREATY ORGANIZATION to try to get member-states to engage in a similar buildup of conventional forces.

McNamara pushed for the development of solid-fueled, rather than liquid-fueled, long-distance missiles as part of a strategy to build up a SECOND-STRIKE CAPABILITY. Since liquid-fueled INTERCONTINENTAL BALLISTIC MISSILES took a relatively long time to prepare for firing, and solid-fueled missiles could stand fueled at all times, the change would allow more rapid response in case of nuclear attack. His thinking along these lines contributed to the doctrine of MUTUALLY ASSURED DESTRUCTION in which both the United States and the Soviet Union would refrain from attack on each other, knowing that each possessed second-strike capability. For this reason, he opposed the development of ANTI-BALLISTIC MISSILES, and he was a strong supporter of the treaty which prohibited their wide use in both countries. Since each country was exposed to retaliatory attack, he reasoned, neither would launch a first strike.

McNamara's advisors at RAND developed the concept of COUNTERFORCE rather than COUNTERVALUE targeting strategy. Under counterforce doctrine, the United States would target military, rather than civilian, targets in the Soviet Union. Although the doctrine had been developed in secret over the period 1961–1962, McNamara revealed the outlines of the policy in a commencement address at the University of Michigan in Ann Arbor in 1962. Later called the "no-cities" speech and the no-cities doctrine, McNamara suggested that the United States would aim at principal military targets and give to the Soviets "the strongest possible incentive from striking our own cities." In this and other ways, McNamara regarded nuclear strategy as a means of communicating intent to the Soviets in hopes of working out with them an agreed scenario under which nuclear war would be fought in stages. The principle of communicating strategy and of an implied agreement about the conduct of a nuclear war was essential to the "mutual" side of the mutually assured destruction concept.

McNamara was closely associated with the means by which the Vietnam War was conducted, involving piecemeal increases in U.S. troop strength and selective bombing of targets in North Vietnam. As in his nuclear strategy, McNamara believed that each stage of escalation of the war would communicate intent and, if properly perceived, could avoid further slaughter. However, his method of evaluating the effectiveness of weapons by establishing a ratio between cost and numbers of enemy killed suggested to many that McNamara's accounting and civilian management methods were part of the difficulty in U.S. prosecution of the war. Despite his association with the principle of escalation, he urged a negotiated settlement on President Lyndon JOHNSON as early as 1967. In November 1967, President Johnson rejected McNamara's recommendation that the bombing of North Vietnam be halted and the war be turned over to South Vietnamese troops.

McNamara resigned from the Defense Department early in 1968 and took up the presidency of the International Bank for Reconstruction and Development (the World Bank) in April 1968. In his eight years as secretary of defense, McNamara had overseen the construction of the world's most extensive nuclear arsenal while the nation had conducted a limited war in Vietnam.

When the REAGAN administration began to develop the STRATEGIC DEFENSE INITIATIVE, McNamara opposed it. He remained committed to the idea that nuclear weapons should serve only to deter their use by others. Developing defenses against missiles, as proposed under the Reagan administration, would destabilize the balance of deterrence, McNamara argued.

Suggested Reading

Robert McNamara, *Blundering into Disaster: Surviving the First Century of the Nuclear Age.* New York: Pantheon, 1986.

———, *The Essence of Security: Reflections in Office.* London: Hodder and Stoughton, 1968.

Medvedev, Zhores   *See* KHYSTYM ACCIDENT.

Megaton

A megaton (Mt) is a measure of the yield of a nuclear device or weapon, equivalent to the explosive energy of one million tons of high explosive TNT or trinitrotoluene. One megaton is the equivalent of 1,000 KILOTONS. The yield of the bomb dropped over HIROSHIMA was estimated at less than 20 kilotons. Some hydrogen fusion or thermonuclear weapons had announced yields over 5 Mt, and one Soviet test was reputed to be in the range of 50 Mt.

Megawatt

A megawatt is equivalent to 1,000 kilowatts and is used as a measure of power rating of nuclear reactors. A megawatt-thermal, (MWth) measures the total energy output of a reactor, while a megawatt-electrical (MWe) measures the usable electrical output of a reactor-generator system. Depending on the efficiency of the system, the thermal rating may be about three times higher than the electrical rating. Thus a 1,000 MWth reactor might be rated at about 300 or 350 MWe. Most research reactors tend to be rated under 25MWth, while most modern power reactors are in the range of several hundred to over 1,000 MWe.

See also POWER REACTORS, U.S.

Meitner, Lise (1878–1968)   *Austrian physicist who was the first to describe nuclear fission*

Lise Meitner's contribution to the history of atomic energy was crucial, as she was the first researcher to identify atomic FISSION, offering an explanation for the splitting of the atom into elements that roughly equal in mass the original element together with a release of energy. Others following up on her work in a few years produced research that led to nuclear reactors and the atomic bomb.

Meitner was born in Vienna, Austria, on November 7, 1878, the daughter of a lawyer in that city. Although the family was Jewish, the children were raised as Protestants. She studied at the University of Vienna and then enrolled at the University of Berlin to study under physicist Max PLANCK. She and Otto HAHN developed a laboratory for radiation measurement, with Hahn focusing on the chemistry of new elements and Meitner working on their physical properties. During this period, prejudice against allowing women to work in German chemical laboratories prevented her from securing a paying position in her field.

In 1912, Meitner joined the Kaiser Wilhelm Institute for Chemistry in Berlin. During World War I, she served as a nurse in the Austrian army, with a specialty in X-rays. During her leaves, she and Hahn continued their work, and at the end of the war, their findings were published in a paper describing their discovery of the new element protactinium.

In 1917, Meitner was appointed head of her own physics section with the title of professor at the Kaiser Wilhelm Institute, and she kept her connection with the University of Berlin, where she sometimes gave lectures. Over the next years, she continued to manage the institute, encouraging younger scientists to make use of instrumentation, including the Wilson cloud chamber. In 1926 she became the first woman university professor of physics in Germany.

In the early 1930s, a series of exciting developments in physics brought a burst of new activity to the institute. Meitner resumed work with Otto Hahn to study the results of bombardment of URANIUM with neutrons. In particular, they studied the possibility that the results might produce new transuranic elements with atomic numbers higher than 92. Using chemical processes to separate the results of the bombardment, Hahn and Meitner were puzzled at the products. Hahn and Fritz STRASSMANN believed they had found radium as one of the products.

As this work progressed, Meitner was forced to leave Germany. In 1938, Germany took over Austria, which changed Meitner's status as a resident alien of Jewish ancestry. Under the Nazi regime, German Jews could not hold academic positions. Meitner went first to the Netherlands and then to Denmark, where she stayed in the home of Niels BOHR. Her nephew, O. R. FRISCH, worked in Copenhagen. Meitner considered staying there, but she was soon offered a position at the new Nobel Institute in Stockholm, Sweden. At the age of 60, she took up this new post, building a staff to work on a nuclear research with a cyclotron constructed there.

Her most important contribution to the advancement of nuclear science took place right after her arrival in Sweden. She wrote to Hahn and Strassmann asking them to confirm that the product of neutron bombardment of uranium was radium. Their experiments suggested it was closer to barium in nature. She

Lise Meitner. Lise Meitner, confronted with startling developments in the field of nuclear physics, was the first to define the process of nuclear fission in 1939, in a paper co-published with her nephew, Otto Frisch. (Library of Congress)

discussed this result with Frisch, and together they prepared a paper on the topic. With Frisch in Copenhagen and Meitner in Stockholm, they worked out the details of the paper over the telephone.

Their conclusion was startling: They proposed that the uranium atom had split, or fissioned, and that energy had been released. She also concluded that one of the products of neutron irradiation of uranium was a transuranic element—a speculation later demonstrated with the discovery of plutonium. The paper that she and her nephew published in 1939 in the scientific journal *Nature,* entitled "Disintegration of Uranium by Neutrons; a New Type of Nuclear Reaction," marks the first recognition and explanation of nuclear fission. In this way, Lise Meitner became the scientist who first identified the fission process that is the source of atomic energy in both nuclear reactors and atomic bombs.

A few years later, Meitner was invited to work on the atomic bomb project but she refused. In fact, she hoped, as did many nuclear scientists, that such bombs would be impossible to construct. She did no more work on nuclear fission, except for a brief paper on the nature of some fission fragments.

In the postwar years, she remained in Sweden where the Swedish scientific establishment recognized her work. First, the Swedish Atomic Energy Commission dedicated a small laboratory for her to work in, and later, the Royal Academy for Engineering Sciences provided her with a nuclear reactor. In 1960 she retired to Cambridge, England, and died there a few days short of her 90th birthday on October 27, 1968.

Suggested Reading

Deborah Crawford, *Lise Meitner, Atomic Pioneer.* New York: Crown, 1969.

George and Laurie Kauffman, "Lise Meitner (1878–1968)," *Chemical Heritage* (Summer 1998): 47–48.

Meltdown

Meltdown is a possible consequence of overheating in a nuclear power reactor such as might occur in a loss-of-coolant accident. Fuel cladding would be breached, and FISSION products would be released.

Mexico   *See* POWER REACTORS, WORLD.

Midgetman

The *Midgetman* missile was a small INTERCONTINENTAL BALLISTIC MISSILE that would be mobile, transportable by truck or railcar. It was planned during the administration of Ronald REAGAN. In the planning stages, the proposed weapon was sometimes designated the "Small ICBM." As part of the PRESIDENTIAL NUCLEAR INITIATIVE by President George BUSH in 1991 to reduce arms following the Strategic Arms Reduction Treaty (START I), development of the *Midgetman* was canceled.

Military Liaison Committee

Established with the ATOMIC ENERGY COMMISSION (AEC) in 1946, the Military Liaison Committee (MLC) was one of two advisory commissions working with the AEC, along with the GENERAL ADVISORY COMMITTEE. Designed to provide input from the military services, the MLC included representatives of the services and, after 1949, representatives of the Office of Assistant Secretary of Defense for Atomic Energy. The head of the Division of Military Applications of the AEC, a post usually filled by a flag officer from one of the services with experience in nuclear matters, served as the representative of the Atomic Energy Commission on the MLC.

The MLC served as the channel for communicating to the AEC and its technical and scientific personnel the concerns of the services regarding the types and numbers of weapons they wanted to see developed. The MLC served to help determine the military characteristics that would serve as specifications for new weapons to be developed, and the committee submitted to the president an annual memorandum spelling out the size, nature, and composition of the nuclear stockpile.

In 1986, following recommendations by a presidential blue-ribbon task group, the MLC was replaced by the Nuclear Weapons Council, which performed much the same function, serving as a liaison and planning group representing both the Department of Defense and the Department of Energy in matters pertaining to nuclear weapons.

General Leslie GROVES served on the MLC for a year, from February 1947 to February 1948. Although membership varied, through the 1950s there were usually five flag officers on the committee, that is, officers with the rank of admiral or general, with a senior scientist-administrator as chairman.

Minuteman

During the nuclear missile arms race between the United States and the Soviet Union, the *Minuteman* missile, in versions I, II, and III, came to be a mainstay of the U.S. INTERCONTINENTAL BALLISTIC MISSILE (ICBM) arsenal in the 1960s. The development by the Soviets of *SPUTNIK* in 1957 accelerated the program to develop a solid-fueled ICBM. During the supposed missile gap (1957–1960), the United States committed to build 1,000 *Minuteman* missiles.

Unlike the TITAN I missiles, the *Minuteman* missiles did not have to be fueled immediately before use; in effect, they were ready on a minute's notice because they were solid-fueled, hence the selection of their name. The solid fuel also made the missiles much safer than the earlier, liquid-fueled *Titan*. Accidents with the *Titan*, particularly one at DAMASCUS, ARKANSAS, in 1980, demonstrated how unsafe those missiles could be. The *Minuteman* was designed with three stages. The missile was 18 meters long and 1.8 meters in diameter. The range of the reentry vehicle was over 11,000 kilometers, that is, over 6,800 miles.

The major changes among *Minuteman* I, II, and III lay in increasing in power of the warheads mounted in them and growing improvement in range. Each *Minuteman* missile was mounted in an underground SILO, and the silos were grouped together in locations in Missouri, North and South Dakota, Wyoming, and Montana. At each location, the missile silos were several miles apart. Each silo was covered with a thick concrete lid that would be rolled back in order to fire the missile. The separation of the missiles and their heavy underground silos hardened them as targets against a possible enemy preemptive strike.

The *Minuteman* I was first deployed in 1962. Between 1965 and 1970 the United States deployed 450 *Minuteman* II missiles and, after 1970, began to replace the older *Minuteman* I with the *Minuteman* III missiles. A *Minuteman* IIIA missile had an upgraded warhead. Boeing Aerospace was the prime contractor for all models of the *Minuteman*.

Strategic analysts were very concerned with the accuracy of ICBMs, especially as they considered their use in a COUNTERFORCE strategy. That strategy would require that U.S. missiles hit very precise strategic targets, such as ICBM launch sites in the Soviet Union. The countervailing strategy developed during the CARTER administration and announced in PRESIDENTIAL DECISION DIRECTIVE 59 also required precise targeting of hardened command-and-control facilities. Much of the research and development focused both on increasing the payload or power of the weapons carried and on improving the missiles' accuracy by reducing the CIRCULAR ERROR PROBABLE.

Despite planning in the 1980s to replace the *Minuteman* with a new "MX" MISSILE, the *Minuteman* remained the major element of the ICBM leg of the TRIAD of strategic defense until the end of the cold war in the period from 1989 to 1991. The *Minuteman* III, configured with a single warhead, remained part of the U.S. nuclear arsenal under the START I and START II treaties.

Deployment of *Minuteman* missiles in 1980 to 1985 was as follows:

BASE	MISSILES	WARHEADS
Minot AFB, North Dakota	150	MMIII450
Grand Forks AFB, North Dakota	150	MMIII450
Ellsworth AFB, South Dakota	150	MMII150
Warren AFB, Wyoming	200	MMIII600
Malmstrom AFB, Montana	50	MMIII50
	150	MMII150
Whiteman AFB, Missouri	150	MMII150
Totals	1000	2000

The *Minuteman* III had MIRV warheads, with three weapons each. Thus the total number of warheads carried by the deployed *Minuteman* missiles during this period was 2,000.

In addition to these missiles sites, 54 of the older *Titan* missiles were deployed at three other sites in 1980, which were reduced to 30 by 1985. Each *Titan* carried a single warhead.

Published specifications of the *Minuteman* I, II, and III were as follows.

Minuteman I (LGM 30A and LGM 30B) Single warhead
   Range 10,000 kilometers
   Length 30A: 16.45 meters; 30B: 17.0 meters
   Diameter 1.88 meters
   Launch Weight 29,500 kilograms
   Deployment: 30A: 1962–1969; 30B: 1963–1974
Minuteman II (LGM 30F) Single warhead
   Range 12,500 kilometers
   Length 18.2 meters
   Diameter 1.8 meters
   Launch Weight 31,746
   Deployment: 1966–1998
Minuteman III (LGM 30G) Capable of 3 warheads
   Range 13,000 kilometers
   Length 18.2 meters
   Diameter 1.85 meters
   Launch Weight 34,467 kilograms
   Deployment: 1970–

Suggested Reading

E. M. Bottome, *The Missile Gap: A Study in the Formulation of Military and Political Policy.* Rutherford, N.J.: Fairleigh Dickinson University Press, 1971.

John M. Collins, *U.S.–Soviet Military Balance, Concepts and Capabilities, 1960–1980.* New York: McGraw-Hill, 1981.

John M. Collins, *U.S.–Soviet Military Balance, 1980–1985*. Washington, D.C.: Pergamon-Brassey's, 1985.

Herbert F. York, *Race to Oblivion: A Participant's View of the Arms Race*. New York: Simon and Schuster, 1970.

Missile

Any object thrown or propelled, such as a stone or arrow, can be regarded as a missile. In the world of nuclear weapons, however, the term has been used to refer to rocket-propelled or air-breathing, engine-propelled weapons that carry nuclear warheads, ranging from battlefield or tactical missiles (less than 20 mile range) through intermediate-range missiles (up to 1,500 or so miles) to intercontinental missiles.

In general, nuclear missiles fall into two classes—ballistic and guided. Ballistic missiles are aimed at the firing point at launch and fly in an arc to their target, much like an artillery shell. INTERCONTINENTAL BALLISTIC MISSILES are aimed at their targets on launching from ground bases, usually in protected underground SILOS, fly in a high arc out of the atmosphere, in "exo-atmospheric" flight, and come down on their targets. Similarly, SUBMARINE-LAUNCHED BALLISTIC MISSILES are launched under the water with a propellant or air-pressure charge and then ignite when above the water's surface to follow their predetermined course to their targets.

Among guided missiles, air-breathing propelled CRUISE MISSILES are the best known. Cruise missiles may be air-launched, ground-launched, or ship-launched, each requiring a somewhat different design. Some cruise missiles are equipped with a small on-board computer that operates a terrain-following system, allowing the missile to find its target very precisely by following a pre-programmed topographical map of the territory over which it flies. Others are guided remotely by a pilot who flies them directly into their target, using a television camera in the missile itself to identify and spot the target.

See also ANTI-BALLISTIC MISSILES; MULTIPLE INDEPENDENTLY TARGETED REENTRY VEHICLES.

Missile Gap

In the period 1957 to 1960, some defense experts and political leaders in the United States believed that the Soviet Union had developed a greater capability in INTERCONTINENTAL BALLISTIC MISSILES (ICBMs) than had the United States. Even before the launch of *SPUTNIK* in 1957 American intelligence had learned that the Soviets had tested an ICBM. In fact, during these years, the Soviets deployed only four ICBMs, but Western intelligence did not learn with certainty that the Soviet arsenal was so limited until 1961, when the information was gained by satellite photography.

During the late 1950s, the Soviets recognized that the United States had an incorrect estimate of the size and power of their ICBM forces. In 1956, Senator Henry JACKSON warned of "nuclear blackmail," and he became an outspoken critic of the Eisenhower administration for allowing the supposed missile gap to develop.

Premier Nikita KHRUSHCHEV made a number of speeches asserting that the strategic weaponry of the Soviets was superior to that of the United States. In 1958, 1959, and 1961, the Soviets created crises over the issue of Berlin, culminating in a confrontation between Soviet and American tanks at Checkpoint Charlie at the border between East and West Berlin. In August 1961, the East Germans erected a wall dividing the two sectors of Berlin, closing the route to the west previously taken by tens of thousands of refugees. Some observers attributed this aggressive stance of the Soviets to their belief that the United States was convinced of a missile gap and hesitated to take a firmer stand over the Berlin issues.

Aerial photography by the U-2 spy planes tentatively indicated that the Soviets had no massive ICBM force in 1960. However, after the shooting down of a U-2 piloted by Gary Powers in May 1960, the administration of President Dwight EISENHOWER discontinued the use of the U-2 in flights over the Soviet Union. A satellite (SAMOS) that could return photographs was launched early in 1961, confirming the actual state of Soviet ICBM development. Thus, during the American presidential election campaign in the summer and fall of 1960, the United States did not have direct access to photographic evidence about Soviet missiles.

Later intelligence revealed that the Soviets did not achieve initial operational capability with four SS-6 ICBM launchers until mid-1960. By 1962, the Soviets had 36 launchers, mostly of the next generation SS-7, in operation.

During the presidential campaign in 1960, the term "missile gap" became a shorthand term for the supposed lead held by the Soviets in ICBMs. John KENNEDY used the term to criticize the state of readiness of U.S. defenses under the Republican administration. Soon after Kennedy's inauguration, however, he admitted off the record that there had been no such missile gap or Soviet lead, and by the end of 1961 the Kennedy administration admitted publicly that there was not and never had been a significant missile gap.

The term was later revived in the years 1977 to 1979 to describe the fact that the Soviets had deployed intermediate-range ballistic missiles that could reach targets in Western Europe, while NORTH ATLANTIC TREATY ORGANIZATION missiles in Europe had much shorter range. Thus a European missile gap would lead to development of a strategy of deploying new American-made missiles to forward positions in Europe in the 1980s in a so-called DUAL TRACK STRATEGY.

Suggested Reading

E. M. Bottome, *The Missile Gap: A Study in the Formulation of Military and Political Policy.* Rutherford, N.J.: Fairleigh Dickinson University Press, 1971.

Richard Smoke, *National Security and the Nuclear Dilemma: An Introduction to the American Experience in the Cold War.* New York: McGraw Hill, 1993.

Donald P. Steury, *Intentions and Capabilities: Estimates on Soviet Strategic Forces, 1950–1983.* Washington, D.C.: Center for the Study of Intelligence, 1996.

Mixed Oxide Fuel (MOX)

Reactors can be designed to run on mixed oxide fuel (MOX), a combination of enriched URANIUM and PLUTONIUM. France has utilized MOX in some of its reactors. A program to utilize MOX in Japan began in the early 1990s, with the construction of a LIQUID METAL FAST BREEDER REACTOR and an associated reprocessing plant.

Due to the different physical properties of plutonium and uranium, most existing pressurized water reactors can only accept a small proportion of plutonium. Although MOX can be made in many combinations, the commonly used MOX represents a mix of 3% to 7% plutonium oxide, with the remainder uranium oxide. Reactors are limited to about one-third MOX and two-thirds regular enriched uranium fuel.

Some planners have suggested that reactors using MOX could be a means of "burning" plutonium to dispose of excess stocks resulting from arms control agreements.

In the United States, the NUCLEAR REGULATORY COMMISSION did not grant licenses to operate with MOX by the year 2000.

Suggested Reading

National Academy of Sciences, *Management and Disposition of Excess Weapons Plutonium.* Washington, D.C.: National Academy Press, 1994.

Mixed Waste

Mixed waste refers to waste from nuclear facilities that includes not only LOW-LEVEL WASTE but chemically or biologically toxic materials, such as petroleum, acids, or caustic materials.

Moderator

In a nuclear reactor, a light element is used to absorb kinetic energy to slow down naturally emitted neutrons from radioactive URANIUM. When the neutrons move at a "moderated" speed that increases chances of collision between the neutrons and other uranium nuclei, leading to FISSION and a CHAIN REACTION. The first atomic piles used graphite as a moderator. Later reactors used water, heavy water, sodium, beryllium, or other materials as moderators.

See also CHICAGO PILE-1; PILE.

Molotov, Vyacheslav Mikhaylovich (1890–1980)

commissar or minister of foreign affairs for the Soviet Union during and after the era of Joseph Stalin, serving in the period 1939 to 1949, and from 1953 to 1956

During World War II, Molotov helped establish the Soviet nuclear research project. During his second period of service as foreign minister, when the Soviets became a nuclear and thermonuclear power, Molotov regarded nuclear arms as the key to maintaining competition with the United States for world power.

V. M. Molotov was born in the village of Kukara in Russia and joined the Bolshevik Party in pre-revolutionary Russia about 1906. Molotov was born with the last name of Scriabin into a family of fairly prosperous shopkeepers. While in secondary school in Kazan, he joined the Bolshevik wing of the Russian Social Democratic Workers Party. In 1909 he was expelled from school for revolutionary activities and sent into exile to the town of Vologda. Two years later he enrolled in a polytechnic institute in St. Petersburg to study economics, where he remained a student until 1916. Dur-

V. M. Molotov. Molotov served as foreign minister of the Soviet Union at the height of the early cold war. Here, he signs the German-Soviet Non-Aggression Pact, August 23, 1939, that opened the way for the German invasion of Poland that launched World War II. Standing behind are Joachim Von Ribbentrop, German foreign minister, and Soviet premier Joseph Stalin. (National Archives and Records Administration)

ing this period he worked in the revolutionary underground, helping to found the newspaper *Pravda* and adopting the name "Molotov" derived from the Russian word for "hammer" (*molot*).

Although he was very junior in the party, since most of the Bolsheviks were in exile abroad and in Siberia, he became a member of the St. Petersburg central committee of the party in 1916. When the Bolsheviks seized power, Molotov began to follow precisely the party line as dictated by V. I. Lenin. By 1930 he rose to the position of chairman of the People's Commissars, and he continued to work closely with Joseph STALIN in the 1930s.

During World War II, Molotov asked the secret police for a list of reliable physicists in order to select one to head the nuclear research project. After meeting with Peter KAPITSA, A. F. IOFFE, and others, he selected Igor KURCHATOV to serve as the scientific director of Russia's nuclear weapon project. Molotov, who knew of the intelligence documents gathered from the espionage efforts of Klaus FUCHS, provided the material to Kurchatov in 1943. Kurchatov studied the reports in Molotov's office, becoming very impressed and realizing that the weapon could be constructed.

Immediately after HIROSHIMA, Kapitsa wrote an article that indicated that the atomic weapon's effect had been overestimated, partly because of the nature of the wood-and-paper construction of Japanese homes, and he asked Molotov for permission to publish. After consulting with Lavrenty BERIA, Molotov told Kapitsa he should not publish the material as it went against the emerging view in the Soviet Union that the nuclear weapon was crucial to establishing great-power status. Kapitsa later fell from favor with Beria.

Following the war, as the Soviet Union sought to develop its first nuclear weapon, Molotov announced to the world that the United States no longer had a monopoly on the atomic secret. Although American policymakers ignored this 1948 announcement, the Soviets proved it correct with the detonation of their first atomic device in 1949.

After Stalin's death and the development of the concept of peaceful coexistence between the Soviet Union and the United States during the regime of Georgy MALENKOV, Molotov found himself increasingly isolated from the center of power as a hard-line Stalinist. He was finally removed from his post on the Politburo by Nikita KHRUSHCHEV in 1957. He was expelled from the Communist Party in 1964, but he was reinstated in 1984. He died in 1986.

Suggested Reading

David Holloway. *Stalin and the Bomb.* New Haven: Yale University Press, 1994.

Albert Resis, ed. *Molotov Remembers: Inside Kremlin Politics.* Chicago: Ivan R. Dee, 1993.

Montebello Doctrine   *See* NORTH ATLANTIC TREATY ORGANIZATION.

Mossbauer Effect

In 1958, German physicist Rudolf Mossbauer discovered that under certain conditions, gamma rays can be bounced off atomic nuclei without the nuclei recoiling. Normally, when gamma rays strike an atomic nucleus, the nucleus recoils, absorbing energy and affecting the wavelength of the emitted ray. However, Mossbauer found that in low temperatures, crystals absorb gamma rays of a specific wavelength and resonate so that the whole crystal recoils, rather than individual nuclei. The wavelength of the emitted ray is virtually unaffected and can be measured to a high degree of accuracy. Using these observations, scientists were able to provide a verification of Einstein's general theory of relativity in 1960 by showing, as he had predicted, that gamma ray wavelengths became longer in a gravitational field.

Multiple Independently Targetable Reentry Vehicles (MIRVs)

The term, multiple independently targetable reentry vehicle (MIRV), has been used to describe the system employed in various U.S. and Soviet missiles that allows a single missile to carry several warheads that could separate as the missile approached the target area and fly to separate, pre-programmed targets. Thus a single missile could carry three to 10 or more separate nuclear weapons, greatly increasing the number of megatons of destructive force that could be delivered by a single INTERCONTINENTAL BALLISTIC MISSILE (ICBM) or SUBMARINE-LAUNCHED BALLISTIC MISSILE (SLBM). When a missile was designed or converted to carry several warheads, it was said to have been "mirved."

Two technical developments were necessary to make possible a MIRV missile. One was the reduction in size of the thermonuclear warhead. The other was the design of a missile vehicle that could make it possible to place several separately targetable missiles on the same rocket. Both developments came together in the 1960s.

Some of the mirved missiles in the U.S. and Soviet arsenals are listed below, with the number of warheads carried by each.

U.S. ICBM	
Minuteman III	3
U.S. SLBMs	
Poseidon C-3	10
Trident	8
Trident D-4	14

Soviet ICBMS	
SS-17 Mod 1	4
SS-18 Mod 2	8
SS-18 Mod 4	10
SS-19 Mod 3	6
SS-N-18	7
SS-20	3
SS-NX-20	12

A Soviet long-range missile, the SS-16, was solid-fueled and carried one warhead; it was not deployed. Under the Strategic Arms Limitation Treaty (SALT I), the Soviets agreed not to deploy it. The other Soviet ICBMs were liquid-fueled.

The early Polaris missile was modified to carry three warheads, but they could not be separately targeted. Thus the Polaris model was called a multiple reentry vehicle (MRV), in which all of the warheads would be directed at approximately the same target.

MIRVed missiles were controversial in that some observers believed they would stabilize the arms race between the Soviets and the United States by ensuring that each side had an enhanced destructive capability, enhancing MUTUALLY ASSURED DESTRUCTION. Furthermore, by matching the yield of particular warheads to specific targets, the amount of collateral damage could be reduced and the weapons could be targeted more efficiently, fitting in with a strong COUNTERFORCE targeting doctrine. Others believed that because of ever-increasing accuracy and megatonnage of warheads, the mirved missiles increased the possibility and the likelihood of a preemptive first strike by both sides.

Under the PRESIDENTIAL NUCLEAR INITIATIVE of 1991, President George H. W. BUSH suggested that both the United States and Russia agree to reduce the number of warheads on missiles to one warhead each, or to "de-mirv" the missiles. Although not formally part of the Strategic Arms Reduction Treaty II (START II), both sides proceeded to de-mirv unilaterally.

Suggested Reading

Dietrich Schroeer, *Science, Technology, and the Nuclear Arms Race.* New York: John Wiley, 1984.

Mutually Assured Destruction (MAD)

The term "mutually assured destruction" came to define the policy, beginning in the 1960s, held by both the United States and the Soviet Union to ensure that each had sufficient nuclear armaments to impose such destruction on the other in the event of nuclear attack that neither would initiate a first attack.

Secretary of Defense Robert MCNAMARA's policy of assured destruction, which he developed over the period 1962 to 1964, required that the United States be able to impose unacceptable damage upon the Soviet Union, even if the United States had been already attacked by nuclear weapons. Having such an ability would make clear to the Soviets that they should not make such an attack because the United States could "assure" their destruction even after being attacked. Hence, the policy required a SECOND-STRIKE CAPABILITY.

Robert McNamara developed the assured destruction policy to serve as a deterrent to prevent a Soviet first use of nuclear weapons against the United States. Unlike the earlier policy by Secretary of State John Foster DULLES, which had threatened nuclear retaliation in face of conventional attack, the plan of assured destruction was designed to prevent a nuclear war through the threat that both sides would face destruction.

Critics of McNamara and his assured destruction nuclear policy called the doctrine "mutually assured destruction," well aware that the initials "MAD" would imply that the policy reflected a "mad world." What bothered opponents of the policy was that it seemed to them to be based on a fundamental contradiction. McNamara claimed that the way to *reduce* the threat of nuclear war was to *increase* nuclear arsenals, not decrease them through arms reductions. Antinuclear advocates argued for arms reduction rather than for arms increases. To many, McNamara's logic did indeed seem "mad."

The MAD policy did not allow for a small arsenal of weapons targeted only at potential enemy strategic systems that was known as a COUNTERFORCE strategy nor for a defensive system of protecting American cities against a first strike from the Soviet Union using ANTI-BALLISTIC MISSILES or anti-aircraft sites. More and more nuclear weapons had to be built in increasing numbers to support a credible threat of assured destruction as retaliation for a possible first strike by the other side.

The U.S. side of the policy of mutually assured destruction relied on many options, ranging from retaliation against tactical nuclear strikes with a commensurate response through strategic counterforce attacks against Soviet weapons systems (a "no-cities" doctrine, which would serve as an early stage of a nuclear war) to the capability of city-destroying retaliation raids as well. Although presented to the public as

a simple policy of DETERRENCE, assured destruction required a SINGLE INTEGRATED OPERATIONAL PLAN (SIOP) that included a great variety of weapons and delivery systems and a thorough target list for each option.

After the resignation of Nikita KHRUSHCHEV as premier of the Soviet Union on October 15, 1964, and the announcement by CHINA of a successful nuclear test two days later, the new Soviet leadership decided to accelerate the deployment of strategic missiles. In contrast to weapons development during the late 1940s and the 1950s, the Soviet Union and the United States now entered an escalating arms race that focused on new types of delivery systems, such as vastly improved missiles and improved defensive systems, rather than on the nuclear weapons themselves. MAD was under way in earnest between 1964 and 1968.

Both sides came to believe that deterrence through MAD was a superior and safer system than attempts at defensive ANTI-BALLISTIC MISSILES (ABMs). As a consequence, in 1972, they signed the ANTI-BALLISTIC MISSILE TREATY.

Suggested Reading

Patrick Glynn, *Closing Pandora's Box: Arms Races, Arms Control, and the History of the Cold War.* New York: Basic Books, 1992.

Fred Kaplan, *The Wizards of Armageddon.* New York: Simon and Schuster, 1983.

MX Missile

The term "MX" stood for missile experimental and covered a variety of concepts debated in the United States in the early 1980s for a mobile missile or otherwise deceptively based missile. The air force maintained the U.S. arsenal of INTERCONTINENTAL BALLISTIC MISSILES and recognized that the MINUTEMAN missiles in SILOS were vulnerable to pinpoint preemptive attacks. A mobile basing mode of some sort could give the air force missiles a degree of protection similar to that of SUBMARINE-LAUNCHED BALLISTIC MISSILES.

The wide variety of basing modes discussed before silos had been developed in the 1950s included mounting on flat railway cars, tracked vehicles, river barges, ground-effect machines (that is, hovercraft), and aircraft. By the 1980s, eight separate mobile modes were considered for the MX missile: air-launched ballistic missiles, land-and-launch, shallow underwater missiles (to be based in the Great Lakes or on the continental shelf), covered trench, multiple protective structures, hardened open trenches, closed loop or "race track," and linear track. The covered trench mode would set up a covered trench 12 to 20 miles long, with the missile constantly moving beneath it. Studies revealed that a nuclear weapon that penetrated into the tunnel and burst within it would spread its blast and radiation effects through the tunnel, destroying equipment.

The various options all had some drawbacks. Shallow underwater missiles, in the Great Lakes or offshore, were regarded as too susceptible to underwater shock effects of nuclear attack. The idea of multiple protective structures, or a sort of "shell game" in which the missiles would be moved from one vertical launch site to another, was attractive. However, critics felt that it would be difficult to conceal or keep secret from possible Soviet targeters the exact location of the missile. Furthermore it would take several days to shift from one site to another. The idea of a trench, with the top left open in sections to release blast effects and

with missiles transported by rail, seemed most acceptable in the late 1970s.

On September 7, 1979, President Jimmy CARTER decided to deploy 200 road-mobile MX missiles on 200 closed loops that were each "race tracks" some 15 to 20 miles long. Each transport would rotate randomly among 23 launch sites along the route. The system would require 4,600 targeting points by the attacker. As sites were considered in Utah and Nevada, state officials considered both the environmental impact of the race tracks and the concept that their states would be likely targets for massive attacks. Alternative modes for the MX were considered through 1980, debated in the press and in specialized defense periodicals.

While the MX missile continued to be discussed during the administration of Ronald REAGAN, no plan acceptable to Congress and the administration was ever developed. The planning was overtaken by events as negotiations toward START I proceeded.

N

Nagasaki

Nagasaki was a large city located on the southern coast of Japan, and it was the target of the second nuclear weapon dropped in World War II by the United States on August 9, 1945. The destruction of Nagasaki by atomic attack represented the last use of a nuclear weapon in warfare in the 20th century. The city was located in a river valley nestled among mountains and was home to about 270,000 people. Industries in the city included the Mitsubishi Shipyards, the Electrical Equipment Works, and an arms plant. Ninety percent of the industrial workers in the city were employed at these plants. The city also housed a naval base and was a vital port for military shipments.

The United States Air Force B-29 *Bock's Car* dropped the nuclear bomb on Nagasaki on August 9, 1945, at about 11 A.M. (local time and date.) The weapon was the FAT MAN design of a PLUTONIUM-fueled weapon, identical to one that had been tested at the TRINITY test at Alamogordo, New Mexico, weighing about 10,000 pounds and measuring about five feet in diameter.

Due to a number of factors, the effect of the weapon was less than that at HIROSHIMA. Parts of the target city were partially protected by the mountainous terrain. Furthermore, a shift in winds helped limit the fires, and a firestorm did not occur as had happened at Hiroshima. The original plans called for visual bombing to ensure accuracy, but on the morning of August 9, much of Japan was obscured by rain clouds. The original target city for the mission was Kokura, but that city was so obscured by clouds that the pilot redirected the flight to the backup target of Nagasaki. Further delays occurred as the bomber awaited a photography plane at a rendezvous point.

When *Bock's Car* finally arrived over Nagasaki, the pilot found the city also obscured by clouds. However, with fuel running low, it would not have been possible to return to Okinawa carrying the bomb. Therefore, the bomb was dropped when a temporary opening in the clouds allowed a view of the city, but the drop point was two miles from the intended spot. The aircraft, low on fuel, barely made it back to Okinawa, with only seven gallons of fuel left in the tank.

Despite the errors, damage and destruction to Nagasaki was severe. Official estimates put the death toll at 23,753 with another 23,345 injured. Over 14,000 of the 52,000 residences in the city were destroyed. Later estimates of the total number killed from immediate and delayed effects varied widely, from about 60,000 to about 90,000. Several factors contributed to the uncertainty of the final count, including lack of precise in-

Nagasaki. After the bomb was dropped off target on Nagasaki, the crew of Bock's Car snapped this picture of the rising cloud. (Library of Congress)

formation as to the number of people in the city on the morning of August 9.

Among the controversies surrounding TRUMAN'S DECISION, the bombing of a second target city loomed large. Apparently President Harry Truman never endorsed or explicitly ordered a second bombing. General Leslie GROVES had originally scheduled a second bombing run for August 11, but predictions of rain on that day caused him to move the bombing run up two days. Upon hearing of the attack on Nagasaki, Truman ordered that no more atomic weapons be dropped to allow time for a surrender decision by the Japanese.

Suggested Reading

Donald Goldstein, Katherine Dillon, and J. M. Wenger, *Rain of Ruin*. Washington, D.C.: Brassey's, 1995.

The United States Strategic Bombing Survey, *The Effects of the Atomic Bombs on Hiroshima and Nagasaki*. Santa Fe, N.Mex.: W. Gannon, 1973.

National Technical Means

The term "National Technical Means" was introduced in arms control discussions to refer to various methods of verifying whether another country was adhering to its agreed limitation on nuclear testing. National Technical Means would not require on-site inspection but would consist of nonintrusive methods of verification, including satellite observation, air-sampling, and measurements of seismic shock from distant recorders. Radar, telemetry, and aircraft based optical and electronic systems also served to determine whether a nuclear test had taken place.

See also ARMS CONTROL; THRESHOLD TEST BAN TREATY.

Nautilus

The first nuclear powered submarine, *Nautilus* was launched on January 21, 1954. Admiral Hyman RICKOVER had directed that this submarine be powered by a pressurized water reactor. Construction on *Nautilus* began in 1950, and at the same time, construction went forward on *SEAWOLF*, powered by a sodium-cooled and moderated reactor. *Nautilus* was powered by a S2W reactor, the second-generation submarine reactor built by Westinghouse. The S1W, a prototype, had been tested at the Idaho Naval Reactor facility in 1953. *Seawolf* was powered by a S2G reactor, designating the

Nautilus. *The first nuclear-powered submarine underwent sea trials in 1954.* (Library of Congress)

second-generation submarine reactor built by General Electric.

Nautilus was commissioned in the U.S. Navy as SSN (Submarine Ship Nuclear) 571 in September 1954, and the vessel began its first action voyage on January 17, 1955. Commander Eugene Wilkinson sent the historic message, "Underway on Nuclear Power." The ship soon broke a number of distance underwater and speed records.

One of the more historic voyages of *Nautilus* was Operation Sunshine, the first crossing of the North Pole by any kind of ship. Commander William R. Anderson announced that the submarine reached the pole on August 3, 1958.

In May 1959, the first fuel core was replaced and the ship given her first overhaul. In August 1959, *Nautilus* took on a crew for refresher training and then joined the U.S. Sixth Fleet in the Mediterranean. There she participated in fleet exercises for the next six years.

By 1966, *Nautilus* had recorded over 300,000 miles underway. From 1966 to 1978, as other nuclear submarines joined the fleet, the *Nautilus* was engaged in developmental testing.

On May 26, 1979, *Nautilus* was decommissioned at the Mare Island Naval Shipyard in Vallejo, California. After conversion, the submarine was towed to Groton, Connecticut, where it was moored as part of a public display in 1985. The U.S. Navy operates the *Nautilus* as an historic ship museum and also runs a shoreside Submarine Force Museum at the same location.

Naval Research Laboratory

The Naval Research Laboratory (NRL) was the initial agency that began the U.S. Navy's exploration of using atomic energy for submarine propulsion. The Naval Research Laboratory's exploration of atomic energy for ship propulsion was the first atomic energy work funded by the U.S. government, well in advance of the funding that supported the ADVISORY COMMITTEE ON URANIUM (October 1939), the OFFICE OF SCIENTIFIC RESEARCH AND DEVELOPMENT (1941), and the MANHATTAN ENGINEER DISTRICT (1942).

Located on the Anacostia River in Washington, D.C., NRL had been established in 1922 in recognition of the navy's need for basic research in the sciences following World War I. The laboratory tended to focus on basic electronic and physics research in the interwar years, and the facility housed some of the best of the navy's scientific and technical personnel.

The navy's interest in using atomic energy for propulsion began on March 17, 1939, when Ross Gunn, technical advisor to the director of the NRL, and W. H. Sanders, also of the NRL, attended a meeting in which Enrico FERMI briefed navy scientists and commanders on Otto HAHN and Fritz STRASSMAN's 1938 splitting of URANIUM atoms. Participants in the meeting discussed the topic of using atomic energy for power production. Dr. Gunn immediately saw the potential of using atomic power in submarine propulsion.

On March 20, Gunn, eight NRL associates, and Captain Hollis Cooley, director of the NRL, approached Rear Admiral Harold Bowen, chief of the Bureau of Engineering, to request $2,000 for the NRL to begin experiments into nuclear propulsion. Admiral Bowen appropriated $1,500 for the project. They faced as their first hurdle how to obtain a plentiful source of uranium fuel enriched with ^{235}U.

Roman Miller of NRL's chemistry division and T. D. O'Brien from the University of Maryland began work on the uranium ISOTOPE problem. It was decided to synthesize a uranium-containing chemical compound that existed in a gaseous state. Miller and O'Brien found that uranium hexafluoride (UF_6) was the ideal substance. They were able to create gram-sized samples by January 10, 1940.

From there the samples were turned over to university laboratories to explore ways of enriching the samples' content of ^{235}U. The navy provided $13,000 to the University of Virginia for early phases of isotope separation using high-speed centrifuges. Columbia University was assigned $30,000 to study centrifugal fractionating columns. The Department of Terrestrial Magnetism of the Carnegie Institution in Washington was allotted $35,000 where Philip Abelson was studying the liquid thermal diffusion method of isotope separation.

The basic theory of liquid thermal diffusion was to place dissolved URANIUM hexafluoride into a column whose ends were kept at extremely different temperatures. The molecules containing the lighter ^{235}U atoms would diffuse slightly faster toward the higher temperature end of the column than those with heavier uranium isotopes (primarily ^{238}U). The lighter molecules would end up enriching on the warmer side of the column. The ^{235}U-enriched solution could then become the starting fluid for reiteration in a diffusion tube. The proportion of ^{235}U in each cycle (forming the center of uranium hexafluoride molecules) would continue to increase at the warmer end. Eventually technicians would remove the uranium hexafluoride and convert it into metallic uranium enriched in ^{235}U.

Abelson's work attracted Gunn's attention because of its practicality and its ability to be enlarged on a massive scale. Abelson's work was moved to the National Bureau of Standards (NBS) in October 1940. The first obstacle that Abelson had to overcome was the mass production of uranium hexafluoride, accomplished by the fluorination of UF_4 using a fluorine generator at the NRL. Facilities that could produce 800 grams of UF_6 were installed at the chemistry division of the NBS and later at the NRL. On July 1, 1941, Abelson became an employee of the NRL where he began constructing pilot plant columns at the NRL adjacent to the boiler house on the waterfront of the Anacostia River in Washington, D.C.

Abelson was joined by John I. Hoover in September 1941 as second in command of the experimental work. After a high-pressure boiler was obtained, a 36-foot column with a spacing of 0.053 cm was built and installed in January 1942. With the construction of each new column, Abelson and Hoover would change the spacing between the hot and cold walls of the tubes. The experiments showed that the composition of the columns was important.

By 1942 the NRL staff constructed a pilot plant of 12 columns, each 48 feet tall. The enriched material produced represented the first substantial amounts of enriched uranium. On December 10, 1942, the NRL pilot plant was unexpectedly visited by General Leslie R. GROVES to investigate the potential of the liquid thermal diffusion method for the work of the Manhattan Project.

After being examined by Groves's technical advisory body, the idea of using the NRL method for the production of fissionable material for atomic weapons was at first vetoed on the basis that it did not produce uranium enriched to weapons grade. However, MED personnel later decided that the concept appeared likely to produce partial enrichment and that it could provide feedstock for further enrichment at Oak Ridge.

The NRL continued to pursue the liquid thermal diffusion method for the purpose of developing fuel for propulsion reactors. By June 1943 the NRL was prepared to construct a 300-column production plant. The proposal was made to Vice Admiral Edward L. Cochran, chief of the Bureau of Ships. Once construction of the plant was approved, it was necessary to find a location that would be able to produce amounts of steam needed for the experiment.

After surveying naval facilities, the navy selected the Naval Boiler and Turbine Laboratory at the PHILADELPHIA NAVY YARD as the ideal location. Construction of the plant began on November 1943 and was completed by June 1944. The navy operated the Philadelphia Pilot Plant until early 1946. Abelson and the NRL's work on liquid thermal diffusion set the groundwork for the nuclear naval propulsion work headed by Admiral Hyman RICKOVER.

Suggested Reading

Ivan Amato, *Pushing the Horizon: Seventy-Five Years of High Stakes Science and Technology at the Naval Research Laboratory.* Washington, D.C.: Government Printing Office, 1998.

Richard G. Hewlett and Oscar E. Anderson Jr. *The New World* (Vol. 1 of *A History of the United States Atomic Energy Commission*). Washington, D.C.: Atomic Energy Commission, 1962.

Netherlands   *See* POWER REACTORS, WORLD.

NERVA   *See* PROJECT ROVER.

Neutron

The neutron is one of the two nucleons. The neutron is uncharged and has a rest mass of 1.008665 amu. Outside of the nucleus, the neutron decays to a proton and an electron with a half-life of approximately 12 minutes. The other nucleon is the proton. It carries a relative charge of +1, and it has a rest mass of 1.007276 amu. The proton does not undergo decay. The electron, with a mass of 0.000548 amu and a charge of -1, is an extranuclear, subatomic particle.

Neutron Activation Analysis (NAA)

Neutron activation analysis (NAA) is a technique for establishing the qualitative and quantitative composition of matter. NAA involves inducing radioactivity in the elements making up the material under investigation and selectively measuring the intensities of these induced radiations. NAA is sensitive and nondestructive. Among the applications of neutron activation analysis were the assessment of scalp hair from Napoleon I to determine if he was poisoned with arsenic and the evaluation of bullet fragments removed from the wrist of Governor John Connolly and from the body of President J. F. KENNEDY to determine if more than one gunman was involved in the shooting.

Neutron Bomb   *See* ENHANCED RADIATION.

Neutron Economy

Neutron economy is a measure of the degree to which neutrons in a reactor are used for their intended purpose instead of being lost by leakage or nonproductive absorption. The intended purpose may include: (1) propagation of the CHAIN REACTION, (2) conversion of fertile material to FISSILE MATERIAL, (3) production of radioisotopes, (4) neutron activation analysis, or (5) research. In some research reactors, neutron economy is increased with beryllium neutron reflectors.

Nevada Test Site (NTS)

Situated about 75 miles north of Las Vegas, Nevada, the Nevada Test Site (NTS) was the location of several series of atmospheric tests of nuclear devices through detonation and many more underground tests, from 1951 through 1992, when the United States conducted its last test.

The ATOMIC ENERGY COMMISSION had conducted one series of tests at ENEWETAK in 1948 but sought a site in the continental United States for another series. In December 1950, a special committee recommended to the commission that the Las Vegas bombing and gunnery range be utilized for the next series of tests. The commission agreed and took over the range as the Nevada Test Site. In January and February 1951, the AEC sponsored the OPERATION RANGER series of five tests of small-yield weapons that were air-dropped.

Troop exercise at NTS. During the 1950s, army and marine troops participated in exercises at the Nevada Test Site held to familiarize them with nuclear weapons and gauge their reaction. (Library of Congress)

Later in 1951, the AEC conducted the OPERATION BUSTER-JANGLE series of seven tests at the NTS, including the first underground test (Ranger) that was held on November 29, 1951. The OPERATION TUMBLER-SNAP-PER series included eight atmospheric tests in 1952.

Over the period 1953 to 1958, the AEC conducted some 99 more tests at the NTS. Following the LIMITED TEST BAN TREATY of 1963, the AEC and its successor agencies, the ENERGY RESEARCH AND DEVELOPMENT ADMINISTRATION and the DEPARTMENT OF ENERGY, continued to utilize the Nevada Test Site for underground tests of nuclear devices.

Underground tests were conducted either in shafts drilled deep into the earth and then plugged with concrete to contain the detonation or in tunnels, many of them hollowed out of Rainier Mesa at the NTS. The tunnels would allow vehicles to haul in equipment for the tests and could be sealed with concrete and rubble to prevent leakage of radioactive materials from the tests.

Over 900 announced tests were conducted at the NTS over the years as the United States developed new weapons, verified their designs and safety features, and also tested the effects of the weapons on materials and equipment emplaced in tunnels or at the ends of vertical or horizontal pipes that would allow radiation to irradiate sample materials.

See also ATMOSPHERIC NUCLEAR TESTING; FALLOUT; UNDERGROUND TESTING.

New Production Reactor

With the closing of the last PRODUCTION REACTORS in the United States in 1987 and 1988, the Department of Defense and the DEPARTMENT OF ENERGY specialists in nuclear weapons matters became extremely concerned that the weapons program would be hampered by the lack of PLUTONIUM and TRITIUM production. In particular, the lack of tritium, which has a short half-life of 12.26 years, would mean that the stockpile of tritium would decline by about 5.5% per year. Furthermore, without new plutonium production, it would be extremely difficult to add to the existing stockpile of nuclear weapons.

As a consequence, plans to build another production reactor were accelerated. However, the issue of where to locate the new production reactor, and what design it should follow needed to be resolved. Accordingly, an Office of New Production Reactors was established at the Department of Energy, which conducted close studies of candidate sites and candidate reactor designs. The three sites reviewed were HANFORD, Washington, the SAVANNAH RIVER SITE in South Carolina, and the IDAHO NATIONAL ENGINEERING LABORATORY. Three reactor designs were also studied, including a HEAVY-WATER REACTOR, a HIGH-TEMPERATURE GAS-COOLED REACTOR, and a lithium-deuteride target that could be placed in existing LIGHT-WATER REACTORS. A power reactor on the Hanford site, producing power for area utilities, appeared to be a likely candidate for the third alternative.

Competition between the potential sites delayed movement to immediate construction. Powerful senators and congressmen from the three states served on congressional committees that had reason to review the decision. Each sought the new reactor for the employment it would bring. Estimates of the cost of construction ran to several billion dollars and it was only natural for representatives from the three possible states to seek that level of expenditure in their own district. Furthermore, competition between the different designs aligned different corporations and research institutions as advocates of the different designs. Therefore, one of the most difficult challenges of the Office of New Production Reactors was to conduct the selection process with the utmost fairness and objectivity.

The Office of New Production Reactors did not consider the possibility of using a particle accelerator to produce tritium and plutonium but rather examined only reactor alternatives.

Meanwhile, arms control moved ahead, with the signing of the Strategic Arms Reduction Treaty (START I) on July 31, 1991. With that agreement and subsequent presidential initiatives that cut the nuclear stockpile deeply, the pressing need for a new source of plutonium and tritium suddenly declined. As a consequence, the Office of New Production Reactors cut back its activities and then disbanded in 1992. Thus, the new production reactor did not get past the planning stage.

In December 1998, the Department of Energy announced plans to produce tritium in power reactors located in the Tennessee Valley Authority. Sufficient plutonium from dismantled weapons existed to avoid a requirement to produce more of that element.

Suggested Reading

Rodney Carlisle, *Supplying the Nuclear Arsenal.* Baltimore, Md.: Johns Hopkins University Press, 1996.

New York City Civil Defense Protest Movement

Between 1955 and 1961, radical pacifists organized annual demonstrations in New York City against Operation Alert, rehearsals for World War III planned by civil defense officials, that simulated a nuclear attack on the United States. The protests, which can be collectively called the New York City Civil Defense Protest Movement, were co-sponsored by several pacifist organizations, including the religious pacifist Catholic Worker Movement (which initiated the protests), Fellowship of Reconciliation, Peacemakers, and the secular pacifist WAR RESISTERS LEAGUE.

The civil defense protests represented a pacifist critique of cold war policies, energized pacifists and non-pacifists, and evolved into a successful antinuclear movement. Following mass demonstrations in 1960 and 1961, officials canceled the annual civil defense drills.

The nationwide civil defense drills began in 1954 and ran until 1961, organized by the Federal Civil Defense Administration. On June 15, 1955, in a civil disobedience demonstration, 28 pacifists in New York City initiated the first major protest against Operation Alert. Remaining on their benches in City Hall Park, the pacifists ignored police orders and refused to take shelter when the sirens sounded. All 28 were arrested.

In 1955 and in subsequent years, pacifists condemned the drills as a form of "war preparation" that promoted the arms race, made World War III more likely, and "conditioned the public to accept war." Condemning civil defense as a "farce" promising a "false psychological shield," pacifists contended that the idea that civil defense and bomb shelters could protect the population from nuclear attack was an illusion. The fire, shock waves, and radiation produced by a single hydrogen bomb would obliterate any city and turn FALLOUT shelters into death traps, pacifists pointed out. "Civil defense today is a myth," a 1961 protest leaflet declared. Civil defense arrangements, which might have increased survival rates from an attack by 20-kiloton weapons such as those used against HIROSHIMA and NAGASAKI, had become suddenly outmoded by the development of thermonuclear weapons in the 1.5 to 5 megaton range.

After their June 1955 arrest, pacifists established the Provisional Defense Committee (PDC) to raise funds and coordinate their legal defense. During trial and appeal, the PDC emphasized civil liberties and conscience, including the right of conscientious objection against mandatory participation in quasi-military civil defense drills. The PDC claimed that the arrests violated the rights of free speech, press, and assembly; the freedom of conscience and religion; and the right to petition the government. The PDC also maintained that the Supreme Court's "clear and present danger" test established in 1917, which defined the conditions under which the state could curtail civil liberties, had not been met. Finally, the case raised the question of whether "conscience" should be defined in both religious and secular terms, an issue of special relevance to the nonreligious War Resisters League. The New York Court of Appeals affirmed the convictions

(1959), and the U.S. Supreme Court refused to hear the case (1961).

Each year from 1956 to 1959 a small number of pacifists protested the annual drills by refusing to take shelter. The demonstrations often attracted sympathetic media attention, generated publicity for the pacifist position on civil defense and nuclear testing, and prompted nonpacifists to join the civil defense protests and the emergent antinuclear peace movement. The PDC, which organized the demonstrations, sought to attract broader participation by offering both legal and illegal opportunities to challenge civil defense. The PDC moved from acts civil disobedience, including refusal to take shelter, to a strategy that encouraged legal public meetings and leafleting. In addition, participation by mothers and young children, whose role became even more significant in the 1960 and 1961 protests, tapped cultural sentiments in favor of motherhood, connected the peace action to ordinary families, and infused the movement with a new dynamism.

Conducted on May 3 in City Hall Park, the 1960 protest turned into a mass demonstration. This event was organized by the Civil Defense Protest Committee (CDPC), an ad hoc New York City–wide citizen's committee built around the PDC. One thousand protestors jammed City Hall Park. Although about half left when the drill alarm sounded, 500 people remained in the park, refused to take shelter, and thus committed civil disobedience to protest civil defense. For the first time, nonpacifists, including prominent New Yorkers, joined the civil defense protest.

Avoiding celebrities and CDPC leaders, police arrested 26 protestors. The demonstration, which received widespread media coverage, marked the transformation of civil defense from a small radical pacifist organization into a mass movement.

The April 28, 1961, demonstration exceeded even the 1960 turnout. Two thousand protestors, included both radical and nuclear pacifists, local celebrities, mothers, and students, assembled in City Hall Park to challenge civil defense. The police arrested 52.

Civil defense authorities canceled the 1962 Operation Alert drill, and protesters regarded the ending of the alerts as a major victory for their position.

Suggested Reading

Dee Garrison, "Our Skirts Gave Them Courage: The Civil Defense Protest Movement in New York City, 1955–1961," in Joanne Meyerowitz, ed., *Not June Cleaver: Women and Gender in Postwar America, 1945–1960*. Philadelphia: Temple University Press, 1994.

Ammon Hennacy, *The Book of Ammon: The Autobiography of a Unique American Rebel*. Salt Lake City: Ammon Hennacy Publications, 1970.

Lawrence S. Wittner, *Rebels against War: The American Peace Movement, 1933–1984*. Philadelphia: Temple University Press, 1984.

Nichols, Kenneth D. (1907–2000)   *U.S. Army officer who participated in the Manhattan Project, commanded the Armed Forces Special Weapons Project from 1948 to 1951, and served as general manager of the Atomic Energy Commission from 1953 to 1955*

General Kenneth Nichols participated in the MANHATTAN ENGINEER DISTRICT (MED) during World War II, concentrating on the development of OAK RIDGE and other facilities. In the postwar period he was the successor to General Leslie GROVES as head of the ARMED FORCES SPECIAL WEAPONS PROJECT (AFSWP) that took over the military aspects of the MED while the ATOMIC ENERGY COMMISSION (AEC) managed the civilian and production side of the work. He later served as general manager of the AEC during its period of great expansion from 1953 through 1955.

Nichols was born on November 13, 1907, in Cleveland, Ohio, and he entered the U.S. Military Academy at West Point in 1925. As an army engineer, he helped survey a possible canal across Nicaragua to link the Pacific and Atlantic Oceans, and he assisted in earthquake relief there in 1931. He continued his studies at Cornell University, receiving a bachelors degree in civil engineering in 1932 and a masters degree in 1933. Assignments in this period took him to the Waterways Experiment Station at Vicksburg, Mississippi. In 1937, he obtained a Ph.D. from the State University of Iowa in hydraulic engineering. He taught this subject at West Point, leaving in 1941 to lead the construction of the Rome Air Depot in New York and the Pennsylvania Ordnance Works at Williamsport.

With the formation of the Manhattan Engineer District, General Groves brought Nichols into the organization to oversee various construction projects, particularly the city and plants at Oak Ridge, Tennessee. Nichols also supervised the construction of HANFORD, on the Columbia River in Washington State, where the first PRODUCTION REACTORS were built by Du Pont Corporation. Altogether, Nichols oversaw more than 125,000 workers, engaged as direct employees and through construction contractors, universities, and industrial firms. Nichols was also in overall charge of the question of security, developing serious doubts about the reliability of key personnel, including J. Robert OPPENHEIMER. For Nichols's work on the Manhattan Project, he earned the Distinguished Service Medal and the Order of the British Empire.

Following the war, Nichols served as a consultant to the MILITARY LIAISON COMMITTEE established under the ATOMIC ENERGY ACT OF 1946, and he also acted as a consultant to Senator Bourke Hickenlooper, the first chairman of the JOINT COMMITTEE ON ATOMIC ENERGY. As the AEC took over the facilities and work of the Manhattan Engineer District, various military training and weapons-handling teams were placed under the command of the Armed Forces Special Weapons Project. General Groves commanded this project, retiring on February 29, 1948. Nichols took over the post and also became a member of the Military Liaison Committee (1948–1951).

Nichols worked to establish stockpile sites and managed the military participation in a deceptive plan that appeared to shift nuclear-armed aircraft from the United States to Great Britain during the Berlin Crisis of 1948–1949. Meanwhile, AFSWP teams made ready to assemble weapons in Britain should it become necessary. Nichols urged that nuclear weapons be placed in military custody, as the procedures for transfer from AEC jurisdiction to military control in time of emergency would be too slow and cumbersome. His recommendations were not implemented until much later.

His stand on other issues demonstrated that he was on the "conservative" side of nuclear issues through these years. He supported the development of the hydrogen bomb. He felt that Oppenheimer had never been a Soviet agent, but he still believed that he was a major security risk and should be denied a clearance. He had opposed Oppenheimer's clearance as early as 1942, and he supported the movement to strip him of it later. For these reasons, Lewis STRAUSS, AEC chairman, backed Nichols for appointment as general manager of the AEC to replace Marion Boyer in November 1953.

With his appointment as general manager, Nichols began to replace some of the AEC staff with former members of the MED program from the war years, particularly seeing to it that the more liberal and antimilitary members were replaced. By the end of Nichols's tenure, he had largely purged the group that had come

in under David LILIENTHAL and Caroll WILSON. Working with Strauss, Nichols ordered and managed expansion of the production facilities through the mid-1950s. A supporter of nuclear power development, he proposed a power demonstration program which supported nuclear power development by private firms and the construction of SHIPPINGPORT reactor. As controversies over FALLOUT developed as a consequence of nuclear testing, Nichols worked closely with Strauss and Willard LIBBY to develop a statement that would offer a factual rebuttal to public concerns about the dangers.

Nichols remained general manager of the AEC until June 1955 when he retired to start his own engineering consulting business.

Suggested Reading

Richard G. Hewlett and Francis Duncan, *Atomic Shield* (Vol. 2 of *A History of the United States Atomic Energy Commission*). Washington, D.C.: Atomic Energy Commission, 1972.

Richard Hewlett and Jack Holl, *Atoms for Peace and War, 1953–1961: Eisenhower and the Atomic Energy Commission*. Berkeley, University of California Press, 1989.

NIMBY: Not in My Backyard

During the 1970s, as protests developed against the construction of specific planned nuclear reactors, various local groups in California and then on Long Island, New York, had success in halting projects. Journalists began referring to the effective local protests as the NIMBY effect, standing for "Not in My Back Yard." Later, opposition to other hazardous facilities by local affected populations was also referred to as the NIMBY effect. Thus local protests against hazardous or radioactive waste disposal sites, chemical plants, and even ordinary garbage dumps or incinerator plants, as well as nuclear reactors, were sometimes called NIMBY protests.

The term itself implied that such protesters were concerned only with personal financial, health, and safety risks, rather than with larger issues of national or regional energy needs. Often, supporters of nuclear power used the term "NIMBY" to suggest that opposition to nuclear facilities sprang from uninformed, narrow self-interest rather than from a broader concern with national or general welfare.

The intensity of NIMBY protests was, of course, designed to magnify the political consequence of the protest; that is, a relatively small number of people directly affected by the presence of a facility, numbering in the hundreds or in the thousands, could be very effective through concerted efforts of letter writing, petitioning, demonstrations, and other forms of political action. In some cases, state political figures, including governors and senators, supported the position of such protestors, as in New Mexico and Nevada, or later in the cases of reactors at SEABROOK and SHOREHAM.

Partly because of the effectiveness of such political action, agencies concerned with nuclear and hazardous materials increased their vigilance and regulatory supervision. The Environmental Protection Agency and the NUCLEAR REGULATORY COMMISSION, at the national level, as well as many state regulatory bodies, represented governmental institutional responses to the NIMBY protests.

See also WASTE ISOLATION PILOT PLANT; YUCCA MOUNTAIN.

Nitze, Paul (1907–)   *U.S. government official and policy advisor, noted as the author of the National Security Council Memorandum 68 issued in 1950 that served as the basis for a strong military stand against possible Soviet aggression*

Paul Nitze served in the U.S. government in a wide variety of positions from 1944 to 1989 (with breaks during the 1950s and the 1970s) playing key roles in a number of policy decisions related to nuclear affairs. His authorship of National Security Council Memorandum 68 (NSC-68) in 1950, calling for a strengthened defense to offset possible Soviet advances around the world, constituted his most significant contribution.

Nitze was born on January 16, 1907, in Amherst, Massachusetts. He graduated from Harvard College in 1928 and joined the investment banking company of Dillon, Reed. During World War II, he served as vice chairman of the Strategic Bombing Survey. Following the war, he served as deputy director of the Office of International trade policy and deputy to the assistant secretary of state for economic affairs. In 1950, Truman appointed Nitze to replace George F. Kennan as director of the Policy Planning Staff. In that post, Nitze wrote NSC-68, agreeing with Secretary of State Dean ACHESON and James CONANT that a stronger line should be taken with the Soviet Union.

He left the government during the Eisenhower administration (1953–1961), but he served on an advisory committee in 1957 that warned that a "missile gap" had developed in which the Soviets led the United States in the ability to deliver nuclear weapons by INTERCONTINENTAL BALLISTIC MISSILES. In point of fact, the Soviet lead in such missiles was insignificant, but it became an issue in the 1960 presidential campaign. Under the Kennedy and Johnson administrations, Nitze served in several defense department positions, including secretary of the navy and deputy secretary of defense.

President Richard NIXON appointed Nitze to serve as head of the negotiating team that worked out the terms of the Strategic Arms Limitation Treaty (SALT I), signed in 1972. He began work on SALT II before resigning in 1974. He publicly criticized Secretary of State Henry KISSINGER regarding the Salt II negotiations.

Nitze helped form a reinvigorated COMMITTEE ON THE PRESENT DANGER, borrowing language from a similar committee created in 1950 by James CONANT. The 1978 Committee on the Present Danger attracted many Democrats like himself who disagreed with the policies of the Jimmy CARTER administration and who argued for an even stronger nuclear weapons policy toward the Soviets.

In 1981, President Ronald REAGAN selected Paul Nitze to head arms control negotiations, in which he took a strong stand requiring that the Soviets open their strategic weapons to inspection to verify compliance with agreements. He resigned from the government in 1989 to write his memoir *From Hiroshima to Glasnost: At the Center of Decision.*

Suggested Reading
David Callahan, *Dangerous Capabilities: Paul Nitze and the Cold War.* New York: HarperCollins, 1990.

Nixon, Richard (1913–1994)   *37th president of the United States who served in the period from January 20, 1969 to August 9, 1974*

During the presidency of Richard Nixon, nuclear diplomacy took a turn in the direction of DETENTE, an attempt to reduce the high tensions and the threat of nuclear war that had reached a peak during the confrontation between Soviet premier Nikita KHRUSHCHEV and U.S. president John F. KENNEDY in 1961.

Nixon was born on January 9, 1913, in Yorba Linda, California, and grew up in Whittier. He graduated from Whittier College and in 1937 from Duke University

*Richard Nixon. President of the United States (1969–1975),
Richard Nixon achieved the first major nuclear arms limitation
treaty in 1974.* (Library of Congress)

Law School. He served in the U.S. Navy during World
War II, and, on his return, he ran for Congress.

Nixon's political career was marked by controversy.
His abrasive and intense political style earned him the
animosity not only of opponents but also of much of
the press and television news media. He angered liberal Democrats by the nature of his campaigns against
opponents Jerry Voorhees and Helen Gahagen Douglas
in California, in which he accused them of sympathy
for communist-supported causes. In Congress, he
served on the House Un-American Activities Committee, investigating the case of State Department
employee Alger Hiss, accused of being a Soviet espionage agent. Nixon served two terms in Congress and
then was elected to the U.S. Senate in 1950.

In 1952, Nixon ran as the vice-presidential candidate under Dwight EISENHOWER and was elected, serving two terms. He was narrowly defeated for the
presidency in 1960 by Democratic candidate John
Kennedy. Nixon was elected to the presidency in 1968
and reelected in 1972. On August 9, 1974, during his
second term, he resigned the presidency over a scandal

involving his complicity in suppressing evidence
regarding a burglary of Democratic Party headquarters
in the Watergate building in Washington during the
1972 election.

Although renowned for his strong stand against
domestic communism throughout his political career,
his presidency was marked by a conciliatory foreign
policy toward the major communist powers. He inherited the Vietnam War from his predecessor, Lyndon
JOHNSON, and he worked to disentangle the United
States from that war by alternating heavy bombing of
the enemy with ongoing discussions toward a truce.
Secret negotiations from August 1969 to January 1972
finally produced an agreement in 1973. Nixon opened
relations with communist-dominated China, and he
negotiated major nuclear arms agreements with the
Soviet Union.

In all of these foreign policy matters, Nixon worked
closely with his national security advisor, Henry
KISSINGER. The two men shared elements of the same
political and negotiation style. Both believed in personal negotiation, covert arrangements, and the use of
powerful force. Both distrusted the formal structure of
government bureaucracy and resented interference
from Congress in the conduct of foreign policy. In
1973, Nixon replaced Secretary of State William
Rogers with Kissinger, and, during the rest of Nixon's
term, Kissinger served both as national security advisor and secretary of state. He was the only person to
hold both positions at the same time.

Nixon worked out a "rapprochement" or agreement
with the Soviet Union. Some observers believed that
the Soviet Union, under Leonid Brezhnev, was more
willing to cooperate with the United States because
Nixon had opened relations with China in February
1972. China was viewed as the archrival of the Soviet
Union for leadership of communist nations.

Over the period May 22–30, 1972, Nixon stayed in
Moscow to sign a series of agreements improving
U.S.–Soviet relations. The agreements comprised separate documents addressing many different issues,
including prevention of military incidents at sea; cooperation and exchange in science, technology, health,
environment, and space exploration; and improvement
of commercial relations.

The two crucial agreements for nuclear matters
were the SALT I treaty and the ANTI-BALLISTIC MISSILE
(ABM) TREATY. The Strategic Arms Limitation Treaty
was a complex treaty governing the balance of weapons
systems capable of delivering nuclear weapons, and it

had a five-year term. The ABM treaty, on the other hand, was permanent, and it limited both nations to installing no more than two anti-ballistic missile systems to protect potential targets from incoming INTER-CONTINENTAL BALLISTIC MISSILES.

The SALT I treaty was extremely complex and immediately became the subject of controversy in the United States. Nixon's successors—Gerald FORD, Jimmy CARTER, and Ronald REAGAN—found it difficult to build on the method of agreement that Kissinger and Nixon had worked out with Brezhnev. Nevertheless, the detente between the major powers toward which Lyndon Johnson had worked in the late 1960s appeared to reach fruition in the Nixon years.

SALT I had the effect of freezing U.S. and Soviet missile strength at the same level for the period from 1972 until 1979. It froze the number at those already deployed or in production at the time of the agreement signing, namely, about 2,300 missiles for the United States and about 2,500 for the Soviet Union. The United States retained a lead in strategic bombers. However, since the 1972 agreement did not limit the number of warheads per missile, it may have had the effect of stimulating the development of MULTIPLE INDE-PENDENTLY TARGETABLE REENTRY VEHICLES (MIRVs) by both sides. In terms of delivery systems, the nuclear arms race seemed to have been capped. Yet, when the number of deliverable warheads was considered, the race continued.

During his administration, the "great bandwagon market" for licensing and construction of nuclear power reactors continued. The number of power reactors in service increased from about 30 when he took office to 53 in 1974 and to more than 70 in the few years after he left office. At the same time, concern with the safety of the large nuclear reactors being installed led to criticisms of the ATOMIC ENERGY COM-MISSION (AEC) for its role as both promoter of and regulator of nuclear power. In 1970, the AEC proposed to use an abandoned salt mine in Lyons, Kansas, as a repository for nuclear waste but withdrew the plan two years later after environmental reviews. In 1972, the AEC created a Division of Waste Management, coordinating for the first time the commission's handling of radioactive waste. Electrical power shortages and early-1970s shortages of refined gasoline demonstrated that the United States did not have an overall coordinated energy policy. A fire in May 1969 at the AEC's PLUTONIUM processing plant at ROCKY FLATS, Colorado, contributed to public and con-

gressional concern that the AEC had insufficient concern for safety.

Nixon appointed James SCHLESINGER chairman of the AEC in 1971, and, in 1973, he appointed the only woman to chair the AEC, Dixy Lee RAY. Like their predecessors, Schlesinger and Ray were strong advocates of nuclear power. Ms. Ray worked to separate more clearly the commission's regulatory and development functions.

Nixon advocated the creation of a cabinet-level department to bring together the various government programs concerned with energy. He supported the Energy Reorganization Act of 1974, which abolished the ATOMIC ENERGY COMMISSION (AEC) and established the NUCLEAR REGULATORY COMMISSION to handle licensing and regulation of power reactors and the ENERGY RESEARCH AND DEVELOPMENT ADMINISTRATION to coordinate energy policy and continue the research and development work of the AEC in both nuclear weapons and nuclear power.

Although Nixon was discredited by the scandal surrounding the Watergate burglary and the impeachment hearings in Congress that forced his resignation, he continued to be highly regarded for his achievements in foreign policy. In retirement, he authored several books that added to that reputation. Nixon died on April 22, 1994.

Suggested Reading

Joan Hoff, *Nixon Reconsidered.* New York: Basic Books, 1994.

Franz Schurmann, *The Foreign Policies of Richard Nixon: The Grand Design.* Berkeley: University of California Press, 1987.

Nobel Prize

The Nobel Prize is an annual international prize, first awarded in 1901, with proceeds from the estate of Alfred Nobel, the Swedish inventor of dynamite. Separate prizes in physics, chemistry, medicine, and literature are awarded by academic committees based in Sweden.

A fifth Nobel Prize for contributions to the field of international peace is awarded by the Norwegian government, often the most controversial of the prizes. Selected Nobel Prizes in physics and chemistry are listed in the following table. Many other Nobel Prizes in physics and chemistry, not included here, have been awarded for research into other, non-nuclear topics. In

YEAR	WINNER	PHYSICS OR CHEMISTRY	WORK
1901	W. ROENTGEN	Physics	Discovery X-rays
1903	H. BECQUEREL	Physics	Discovery spontaneous radioactivity
1903	Pierre Curie		
	Marie CURIE	Physics	Radiation research
1906	J.J. THOMPSON	Physics	Work on electricity in gases
1908	E. RUTHERFORD	Chemistry	Chemistry of radioactive substances
1911	M. Curie	Chemistry	Discovery radium, polonium
1918	M. PLANCK	Physics	Quantum Theory
1921	A. EINSTEIN	Physics	Theoretical physics
1922	N. BOHR	Physics	Structure of atom
1923	J. FRANCK		
	G. Hertz	Physics	Discovery laws of impact of electron on nucleus
1927	A. COMPTON	Physics	Transfer energy from radiation to particle
1927	C. Wilson	Physics	Invention CLOUD CHAMBER
1932	W. HEISENBERG	Physics	Creation of quantum mechanics
1934	H. UREY	Chemistry	Discovery deuterium
1935	J. CHADWICK	Physics	Discovery of neutron
1938	E. FERMI	Physics	Use of neutrons to produce new elements
1939	E. LAWRENCE	Physics	Invention cyclotron
1944	O. HAHN	Chemistry	Discovery nuclear fission
1944	I. I. RABI	Physics	Resonance method of recording nuclei magnetic properties
1951	J. COCKROFT		
	E. Walton	Physics	Transmutation nuclei by accelerated particles
1951	H. McMillan		
	G. SEABORG	Chemistry	Work in transuranic elements
1958	P. CERENKOV		
	I. TAMM		
	I. Frank	Physics	Discovery Cerenkov radiation
1963	E. WIGNER	Physics	Discovery of symmetry
1967	H. BETHE	Physics	Theory nuclear reactions
1968	L. ALVAREZ	Physics	Work in elementary particles
1976	B. Richter and		
	S. Teng (Brookhaven)	Physics	Work in elementary particles
1978	P. KAPITSA	Physics	Invention low-temperature physics
1980	J. W. Cronin and		
	V. Fitch (Brookhaven)	Physics	Work in elementary particles
1988	L. Lederman,		
	M. Schwartz, and		
	J. Steinberger (Brookhaven)	Physics	Work in elementary particles

some years, the annual prize has been shared by more than one researcher, as in 1903.

The prizes include a large cash award, which has increased in size over the years as the endowment's value has grown.

In the above table, Igor Tamm and Peter Kapitsa are unique in that they received both the Nobel Prize and awards from the Soviet government as Heroes of Socialist Labor.

Andrey SAKHAROV, the father of the Soviet hydrogen bomb, received the Hero of Socialist Labor three times, and he also received the Nobel Peace Prize in 1975 after he had established himself as a dissident, urging expansion of human rights in the Soviet Union. He is the only Soviet scientist to have received both the Nobel Peace Prize and the Hero of Socialist Labor. In 1990 the Nobel Peace Prize, was awarded to Mikhail GORBACHEV.

A sixth prize, in the field of economics, has been awarded since 1969 by the Swedish National Bank.

Non-Proliferation Treaty (NPT)

The Treaty on the Non-Proliferation of Nuclear Weapons, called the Non-Proliferation Treaty (NPT) was signed on July 1, 1968, and came into force on March 5, 1970. The treaty attempted to freeze the number of countries that had developed nuclear weapons at the five nuclear-weapon states in the late 1960s: United States, Soviet Union, Great Britain, France, and China.

Under the treaty, those nations possessing nuclear weapons agreed not to export nuclear weapons or technology that could assist non-nuclear weapon states in developing the bomb. Countries that did not have nuclear weapons were asked to join, pledging not to develop nuclear weapons. By the mid-1980s, well over 120 nations had signed the treaty. Although France did not sign the treaty, its government agreed to abide by its terms.

The treaty also included provisions that supported the development of nuclear energy for peaceful purposes. Under the treaty, the countries with nuclear energy programs could export reactor technology to developing countries as long as there were adequate safeguards against the misuse of the technology and its direction toward weapons programs. In fact, French support of the nuclear power program in INDIA and Russian support of the reactor program in NORTH KOREA may have contributed to weapons programs in those countries. France sold reprocessing plants that were capable of separating PLUTONIUM from spent (used) power-reactor fuel rods to PAKISTAN and South Korea. Germany sold URANIUM enrichment and plutonium reprocessing plants to BRAZIL. China provided some training to nuclear experts in Pakistan. Such exports and information exchange, although not directly prohibited under the NPT, suggest that control on the spread of weapons-capable technology was less than absolute.

However, as individual nuclear technology exporting countries established requirements that the tools and equipment not be used for developing nuclear weapons, they increasingly required that the receiving countries accept inspection by the INTERNATIONAL ATOMIC ENERGY AGENCY (IAEA). Receiving countries that accepted the equipment agreed to allow IAEA inspectors to examine the equipment and conduct audits and inventory controls to ensure that nuclear material was not being diverted to weapons programs. These methods of the IAEA were called safeguards, and specific reactors and other equipment around the world became subject to IAEA safeguards.

Several countries without weapons programs refused to join the NPT, including India and Pakistan, which both developed nuclear weapons, and ARGENTINA and Brazil, both of which had the capability. After their commitment in the 1990s not to proceed with nuclear weaponry, Argentina and Brazil made arrangements for IAEA safeguards.

Despite weaknesses in the application of the treaty, the NPT may have slowed the spread of nuclear weapons to other nations.

See also PROLIFERATION.

Suggested Reading

Rodney W. Jones et al., *Tracking Nuclear Proliferation: A Guide in Maps and Charts, 1998.* Washington, D.C.: Carnegie Endowment for International Peace, 1998.

Milton Reiss and Robert S. Litwak, *Nuclear Proliferation after the Cold War.* Washington, D.C.: Woodrow Wilson Center Press, 1994.

Norsk-Hydro

Vemork, the hydroelectric plant of the Norsk-Hydro Power Company at Rjukan, Norway, provided the major source of HEAVY WATER or DEUTERIUM in Europe during World War II. With the German conquest of Norway, Germany acquired access to this facility in May 1940. Rjukan is located on the Hardanger Plateau, about 100 miles west of Oslo.

Allied intelligence organizations became concerned that reported German interest and protection of the facility indicated that Nazi Germany was intent on using the product of the plant to develop a heavy-water reactor, which could be used to produce PLUTONIUM for a nuclear weapon or to produce radioactive isotopes that themselves could be dispersed as a radiologic weapon.

The United States had decided to use graphite as a MODERATOR in reactors, but the Germans had focused instead on the use of heavy water. The reason for these different decisions apparently derived from the fact that Germany had not developed a synthetic graphite production industry, relying instead on natural graphite. Natural graphite contained impurities that would prevent its use as a moderator. The production of heavy water, a process requiring plentiful supplies of very pure natural water and also cheap and plentiful electricity, became possible for Germany with the conquest of Norway and the acquisition of the Norsk-Hydro electric plant and its heavy-water generating cells.

In 1941, the increased activity at the plant helped convince Allied analysts that the Germans were intent on developing a nuclear weapon and that they were making steady progress. In 1941, production at the plant was raised from a few kilograms of heavy water a month to about 100 kilograms per month. To intelligence agents in Great Britain and America, the Norsk Hydro plant became a tempting target to cripple the German nuclear weapons program.

As a consequence, the Allies planned raids on the plant aimed at bringing its production to a stop. A first effort to send in British commandos in November 1942 ended with the crash of the towed gliders containing the men and the loss of 38 personnel. On February 16, 1943, British-trained Norwegians parachuted into the area and worked with Norwegian underground resistance fighters to try to put the Norsk-Hydro plant out of operation. After setting off plastic explosives destroying 18 heavy-water production cells on February 27, the commandos escaped, some to Britain and some to continue working with the local underground. However, the Germans soon had the heavy-water plant repaired and back in operation.

An air raid by the U.S. Air Force on November 16, 1943, was more effective. Two waves of aircraft dropped 711 1,000-pound bombs and 295 500-pound bombs. Only a few of the bombs actually hit the plant. However, they were enough to damage the facility, and the Germans closed it, bringing production to a stop. On February 20, 1944, 39 drums of earlier-produced heavy water were shipped in railroad freight cars. The cars were being transported by the ferry barge *Hydro* across Lake Tinssjo, when the shipment was sunk by explosives that had been carefully placed in the bilge of the barge by Allied agents.

The four separate actions combined to prevent German access to heavy water for use in nuclear reactors, and they appeared to have seriously hampered any German effort to develop nuclear weapons during World War II.

See also ALSOS PROJECT; GERMAN ATOMIC BOMB PROJECT; HEISENBERG, WERNER.

Suggested Reading

David Irving, *The German Atomic Bomb.* New York: Simon and Schuster, 1967.

Thomas Powers, *Heisenberg's War.* New York: Knopf, 1993.

Richard Rhodes, *The Making of the Atomic Bomb.* New York: Simon and Schuster, 1986.

North Atlantic Treaty Organization (NATO)

The North Atlantic Treaty Organization (NATO) is a defensive treaty alliance incorporating the states of Western Europe, Canada, and the United States established in 1949. By committing the nuclear weaponry of the United States to the defense of Western Europe, the alliance helped assure the European powers that the U.S. nuclear deterrent would be effective in preventing aggression by the Soviet Union. For this reason, the nuclear weapons development and deployment decisions of the United States became heavily influenced by the concerns of its NATO partners.

The original signatories to the treaty were Belgium, Canada, Denmark, France, Greece, Iceland, Italy, Luxembourg, Netherlands, Norway, Portugal, Turkey, United Kingdom, and the United States. In 1955, the Federal Republic of Germany formally joined the alliance. In 1966 France withdrew from the joint military command system, although it continued to participate in the organization through the North Atlantic Council. In 1982, Spain joined the alliance on the same basis as France, without integrating its military forces into the alliance. Spain became the 16th member of the alliance.

In 1967, the Special Committee of NATO Defense Ministers, which had been formed in 1965, recommended the creation of two groups to deal with nuclear matters. A larger group, open to all member countries, constitutes the Nuclear Defense Affairs Committee. A group of seven countries forms a smaller Nuclear Planning Group (NPG). Between 1980 and 1982, the Nuclear Planning Group expanded to 14 countries and to 15 in 1987, including both France and Spain.

Following its formation, the Nuclear Planning Group met twice a year, with an agenda dealing with the strategic and tactical use of nuclear weapons in future conflicts and issues of arms control discussions with the Soviet Union. In 1979, the defense ministers of NATO agreed that the United States should withdraw 1,000 nuclear warheads from Europe, to be partially replaced by 572 ground-launched CRUISE MISSILES and PERSHING missiles. The withdrawal of the older 1,000 warheads was completed in 1981. This decision represented the initiation of what came to be called a double-track or DUAL-TRACK STRATEGY of simultaneously strengthening weapons systems and seeking arms control measures to limit those weapons.

As the NPG matured, the participation of NATO defense ministers in nuclear strategic planning appeared to establish positions later adopted or affirmed by the United States. For example, the NPG met October 27, 1983, in Montebello, Canada, and reaffirmed the policy of maintaining only a minimum number of nuclear weapons necessary to ensure a credible deterrent in Europe. The NPG announced a plan to withdraw another 1,400 nuclear warheads from Europe by 1988.

The Montebello policy and the simultaneous withdrawal of weapons with the planned installation of cruise missiles and Pershing missiles was later defended by the Bush administration in the United States. The INTERMEDIATE NUCLEAR FORCES (INF) treaty, agreed to in 1988, terminated the deployment of cruise missiles and *Pershing* missiles in Europe, suggesting that the NPG-ordered dual-track strategy had been effective.

After the collapse of the WARSAW TREATY ORGANIZATION and the dissolution of the Soviet Union, several states of the former Soviet bloc sought admission to NATO. On March 12, 1999, Poland, the Czech Republic, and HUNGARY were formally admitted to NATO.

See also PRESIDENTIAL NUCLEAR INITIATIVE 1991; SALT I.

Suggested Reading

NATO Information Service, *The North Atlantic Treaty Organisation: Facts and Figures*. Brussels, Belgium: NATO Information Service, 1989.

North Korea

The communist-ruled dictatorship of North Korea appeared in the 1990s to be one of very few nations attempting to build a nuclear weapon secretly in violation of its agreement to abstain from such development under the NON-PROLIFERATION TREATY (NPT). The crisis that developed there in the 1990s showed the close interrelationship of nuclear weapons issues and nuclear power issues.

Following World War II, the Japanese-held peninsula of Korea was divided into two occupation zones at the 38th parallel. The northern zone was occupied by the Soviet Union and the southern zone by the United States. In August and September 1948, the southern zone organized as a pro-Western regime, the Republic of Korea (ROK), and the Soviet zone was organized as the Democratic People's Republic of Korea.

The United States withdrew its troops, and on June 25, 1950, the North Korean army invaded, launching the KOREAN WAR. After a hard-fought war in which 20 nations of the United Nations, led by the United States, defended the ROK, the battle lines stabilized near the original boundary. An armistice was signed on July 27, 1953. Nearly 37,000 American service personnel, mostly soldiers and marines, died in this bitter and bloody war.

In the decades following, the regime in the North remained under the dictatorship of Kim Il Sung. Although highly militarized and oppressive, the regime signed the nuclear NPT on December 12, 1985. But North Korea did not fulfill its obligation under the treaty to permit inspection by the INTERNATIONAL ATOMIC ENERGY AGENCY (IAEA) until April 9, 1992. Even then, when inspectors sought to visit particular sites, North Korea blocked the inspections and threatened to withdraw from the NPT in 1993, bringing a major crisis to the nuclear arms control regime. North Korea was the first country ever to threaten withdrawal from the NPT. Discussions to resolve the issue were interrupted on July 9, 1994, with the sudden death of Kim Il Sung, after more than 35 years of one-man rule.

On August 12, 1994, North Korea reached an interim agreement with the United States, formalized on October 21, under which it pledged to freeze operations at nuclear facilities. Further, North Korea agreed to halt the production of new weapons-usable materials and to eventually dismantle a gas-cooled, graphite-moderated reactor suitable for PLUTONIUM production.

In exchange, under the "Agreed Framework," the United States, South Korea, and Japan promised to build two light-water reactors in North Korea and to deliver a half-million tons of fuel oil every year until the new reactor was completed. But in the absence of IAEA inspections, many observers and critics of the agreement believed the North Koreans were in the process of building one or more nuclear weapons per

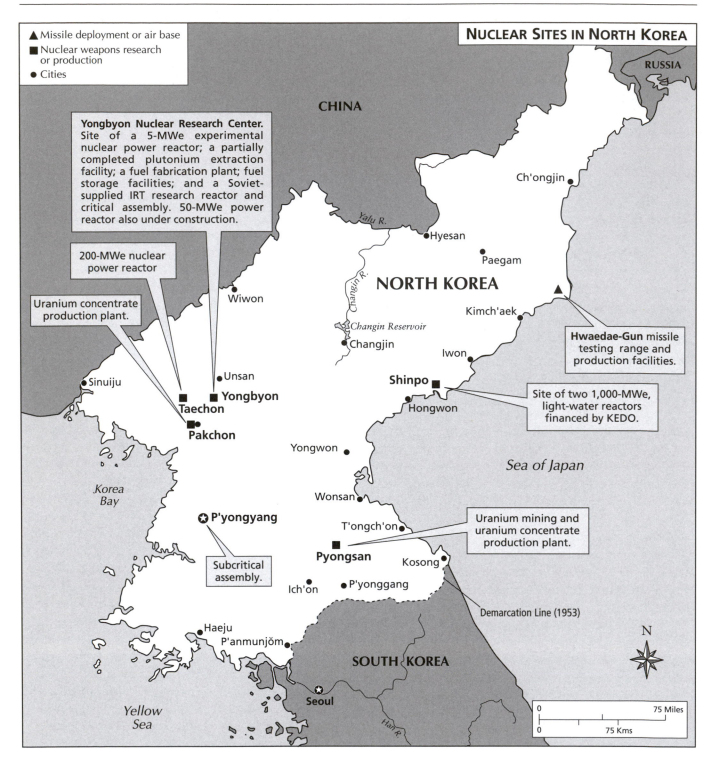

NUCLEAR SITES IN NORTH KOREA

▲ Missile deployment or air base
■ Nuclear weapons research or production
● Cities

Yongbyon Nuclear Research Center. Site of a 5-MWe experimental nuclear power reactor; a partially completed plutonium extraction facility; a fuel fabrication plant; fuel storage facilities; and a Soviet-supplied IRT research reactor and critical assembly. 50-MWe power reactor also under construction.

200-MWe nuclear power reactor

Uranium concentrate production plant.

Hwaedae-Gun missile testing range and production facilities.

Site of two 1,000-MWe, light-water reactors financed by KEDO.

Uranium mining and uranium concentrate production plant.

Subcritical assembly.

CHINA

RUSSIA

Ch'ongjin

Yalu R.

Hyesan

Paegam

NORTH KOREA

Changin R.

Kimch'aek

Changin Reservoir

Changjin

Iwon

Wiwon

Shinpo ■

Hongwon

Sinuiju

Unsan

Yongbyon ■

Taechon ■

Sea of Japan

■ **Pakchon**

Yongwon

Korea Bay

Wonsan

⊕ **P'yongyang**

T'ongch'on

Pyongsan ■

Kosong

Ich'on

P'yonggang

Demarcation Line (1953)

Haeju

P'anmunjŏm

SOUTH KOREA

Yellow Sea

N

⊕ **Seoul**

Han R.

0 — 75 Miles
0 — 75 Kms

year, and that they had no intention of abiding by the agreement.

At Yongbyon in North Korea, several key facilities appeared suspicious. In addition to an operational 5 megawatt-electric (MWe) experimental power reactor, the North Koreans had partially completed a large-scale reprocessing plant to extract plutonium from used fuel slugs and a 50 MWe power plant. They had also constructed a number of radiochemistry hot cells that could be used for plutonium extraction and a fuel fabrication plant. The 5 MWe reactor alone could have produced enough plutonium for one or two nuclear weapons before the agreement was signed in 1994. When unloaded again in 1994, the reactor could have yielded enough plutonium for another four or five weapons.

Other facilities included the 200 MWe nuclear power reactor at Taechon, where construction was halted in 1994 under the Agreed Framework with the United States. At Pakchon, the North Koreans maintained a uranium concentrate production plant that was supplied with ore from Sunchon-Wolbinson mine, some 50 kilometers to the south. At Pyongyang, the national capital, the North Koreans maintained a Soviet-supplied laboratory with hot cells that may have been used to extract small amounts of plutonium.

Following up on the Agreed Framework in 1995, the United States, South Korea, and Japan set up the Korean Peninsula Energy Development Organization (KEDO) to supply the two commercial power reactors promised. At first, North Korea refused to accept the South Korean-built reactors, but in June 1995 both sides agreed to accept a United States reactor design and an American contractor. The design accepted was a 1000 MWe South Korean model based on one developed by the United States firm, Asea Brown Boveri-Combustion Engineering. The construction firm selected was also a U.S. company, Duke Engineering and Services. Under the plan, South Korea would provide some 70% of the funding, Japan another 20% to 25%. The North Koreans would repay the funding over a 20-year period, without interest.

In 1996–1997, the IAEA began inspections of some of North Korea's nuclear facilities, but the regime continued to deny access to the reprocessing plant, the crucial facility for the manufacture of plutonium from spent reactor fuel. Despite the fact that the North Koreans' refusal to allow inspection was a violation of the Agreed Framework, negotiators continued to discuss the issues while construction plans went forward on the new light-water reactors. KEDO proposed to build them at the port city of Shinpo, on North Korea's east coast. Construction began there in August 1997.

Meanwhile, North Korea remained highly secretive about its nuclear program, its long-range missile development plans, and its chemical weapons program. Several border incidents with South Korea, a landing of a North Korean submarine in the South in 1996, defections of North Korean officials in 1997, North Korean famine, and financial difficulties of KEDO all suggested that the nuclear balance remained fragile at the end of the century.

Suggested Reading

Rodney W. Jones et al., *Tracking Nuclear Proliferation: A Guide in Maps and Charts, 1998*. Washington, D.C.: Carnegie Endowment for International Peace, 1998.

Leon Sigal, *Disarming Strangers: Nuclear Diplomacy with North Korea*. Princeton, N.J.: Princeton University Press, 1998.

Novaya Zemlya

The island group Novaya Zemlya (also transliterated as Novaia Zemlia) served as both a remote test site for Soviet nuclear weapons testing in the atmosphere in the period 1949 to 1962 and a dump site for hazardous nuclear waste. At least 87 of the 184 known nuclear tests conducted by the Soviets during that period were held at the icy, wind-swept archipelago.

The whole island group lies extremely far north, almost all of the group farther north than the most northerly point in Alaska, with winds over 100 miles per hour and the average temperature in March below -20 degrees Celsius, that is, below about -10 degrees Fahrenheit.

The nuclear weapons test site was established on the islands in 1954, and the first test was held there on September 21, 1955. The Soviet Union relocated about 300 individual natives from the islands to make way for the test site.

NOVAYA ZEMLYA NUCLEAR TESTS

Period	Atmospheric	Water	Under-ground	Total
1949–1958 Moratorium	31	3	0	34
1958–1961	0	0	0	0
Sept. 1961– Dec. 1962 Atmospheric Test Ban Period	56	0	0	56
1963–1990	0	0	42	42
Total	87	3	42	132

Source: Table information derived from Cochrane et al.

In 1958 alone there were some 26 nuclear weapons tests at Novaya Zemlya. After the test moratorium that began in 1958, the Soviets conducted an extensive test program beginning in September 1961. That program of more than 50 tests lasted for about 15 months, including the largest yield of any weapon ever tested. The test on October 30, 1961, had an estimated yield of 57 megatons.

To maintain the test site and to operate the weapons tests, a rotating population of about 10,000 lived at a settlement called Belyushy Guba (Whale Bay). At any time, about half of the population was military and half civilian.

The Soviet Union has used the seas near and around Novaya Zemlya to dump solid nuclear waste. One dump site is in the open sea to the east of Novaya Zemlya, and others are in fairly shallow water near the coasts of the islands. The types of radioactive waste that have been dumped include low- and medium-level waste, six reactors and one reactor screen assembly with spent nuclear fuel in them, and 10 reactors with the spent nuclear fuel removed. The majority of the radiation hazard has come from the reactors and reactor parts from nuclear-powered submarines and from nuclear-powered icebreaker ships.

The six entire reactors that were dumped came from four separate submarines. In one case, an entire damaged submarine containing two liquid metal-cooled reactors was scuttled at a depth of about 21 meters in Stepovy Bay. The screen assembly noted above consisted of 125 irradiated fuel assemblies from the reactor unit of the *Lenin* icebreaker, which were dumped in Tsivolka Bay at a depth of 49 meters in 1967. The 10 reactors with fuel removed consisted of the rest of three *Lenin* reactors and reactors from four other submarines. All of these reactors and assemblies were dumped in the Kara Sea near Novaya Zemlya in the period 1965 to 1988. The radioactivity in the waters near the archipelago from these and other dumped items has been estimated at more than 1.5 million Curies when dumped. Another 900,000 Curies of radioactivity are estimated at other dump sites in arctic waters around the former Soviet Union.

See also ATMOSPHERIC NUCLEAR TESTING; SEMI-PALATINSK; SOVIET WEAPONS TESTS.

Suggested Reading

Thomas B. Cochrane, Robert S. Norris, and Oleg A. Bukharin, *Making the Russian Bomb: From Stalin to Yeltsin.* Boulder, Colo.: Westview Press, 1995.

N-Reactor   *See* PRODUCTION REACTORS.

NSC-68   *See* NITZE, PAUL.

Nuclear Club   *See* PROLIFERATION.

Nuclear Fuel Cycle

The nuclear fuel cycle defines the flow of nuclear fuel from mine through reactor usage, through waste management. The stages of the cycle are as follows:

URANIUM MINING AND MILLING
enrichment
fuel fabrication
fuel burnup in reactor
spent fuel storage and decay
spent fuel reprocessing
RADIOACTIVE WASTE DISPOSAL

Those steps in the cycle prior to burnup in the reactor are sometimes referred to as the "front end of the fuel cycle," and those following removal from the reactor are called "back end of the fuel cycle." In the United States, very little attention was paid to the back end of the cycle until the 1980s, when pressure groups, journalists, Congress, and policymakers began to focus on the dangers inherent in the disposal of nuclear waste.

Opponents of nuclear power have pointed to several aspects of the nuclear fuel cycle that pose pollution and public health risks, including the radioactivity of mill tailings at uranium mills, extensive power requirements of the enrichment and fuel fabrication process, effect of thermal pollution from reactors to waterways, and most important, unresolved problems of radioactive waste disposal.

Advocates of nuclear power have pointed out that the nuclear fuel cycle, unlike the use of fossil fuels (oil or coal), produces neither greenhouse gases, such as CO_2, nor pollutants that cause acid rain, including NO and SO_2. Furthermore, in certain countries to which fossil fuels must be imported at high cost, such as France, the nuclear fuel cycle and power reactors have seemed an economical alternative to fossil fuels. When the total energy costs of light-water reactors (LWRs) are compared to those of oil-fired and coal-fired power plants, advocates argue, nuclear power is in the same general range. One estimate showed that oil-fired plants required 6.41 gigawatts (Gw) for every 24 Gw produced, LWRs required 6.81 Gw for 24 Gw produced, and coal required 7.82 Gw for 24 Gw produced. Most of the higher cost of coal derived from pollution control.

Uranium ore is mined and milled in several districts in the United States, mostly in Wyoming, New Mexico, Colorado, and Texas. Milling is required to extract uranium from the ore. The ore is pulverized, and then a solvent process produces YELLOWCAKE, a crude oxide of uranium with about 70% to 90% U_3O_8. The yellowcake is then further refined, and uranium hexafluoride gas is produced to send to the enrichment process.

Enrichment is required, as all PRESSURIZED WATER REACTORS and BOILING WATER REACTORS use enriched uranium, although CANDU heavy-water reactors and British-designed gas-cooled reactors (MAGNOX type) use natural, unenriched uranium. Gaseous diffusion and thermal diffusion plants increase the proportion of ^{235}U to ^{238}U from about 7/10 of 1% to 3% or more.

In fuel fabrication, enriched uranium is converted into a ceramic powder and compacted into metal tubes that are bundled together into fuel assemblies. Fuel burnup in the reactor may take several years.

The spent fuel is removed from reactor cores and stored in water pools at the reactor itself. Originally intended as a temporary holding point, most U.S. reactor waste has remained at the spent fuel storage facilities at the power plants.

The United States has not used a reprocessing stage for spent commercial fuel because one of the by-products of the process is PLUTONIUM, which can be utilized for nuclear weapons. Early plans for the U.S. power industry called for reprocessing plants and a possible breeder cycle, with reactors operating with plutonium or mixed plutonium-uranium oxide fuels (MOX). The United States abandoned both of these methods of dealing with the back end of the nuclear fuel cycle. However, other countries have utilized reprocessing, including countries of the former Soviet Union, INDIA, and CHINA, among others, while in the 1990s, Japan began to consider using MOX.

Radioactive waste disposal has become the most controversial aspect of the nuclear fuel cycle in the United States. A significant proportion of reactor waste will remain hazardous for thousands of years. A planned federal repository at YUCCA MOUNTAIN in Nevada has been opposed by residents and political leaders of that state.

See also POWER REACTORS, U.S.

Suggested Reading

James J. Duderstadt and Chiroro Kikuchi, *Nuclear Power: Technology on Trial*. Ann Arbor: University of Michigan Press, 1979.

Nuclear Posture Review

Approved by President Bill CLINTON in September 1994, Presidential Decision Directive-30 (PDD-30) established the Nuclear Posture Review, the primary nuclear weapon policy of the Clinton administration over the next seven years. The policy defined and integrated U.S. policy for nuclear DETERRENCE, ARMS CONTROL, and non-PROLIFERATION. Each of these policies had evolved in slightly different directions, and the intention the Nuclear Posture Review was to bring the three separate nuclear policies into closer harmony. The Nuclear Posture Review used the START II treaty as a starting point and basis for planning the American position regarding nuclear policy for the post–cold war era.

The announced policy assumed that the START II treaty would be fully implemented, but the Russian Parliament did not ratify the START II treaty until April 14, 2000. To deal with the uncertain situation in which the treaty had been signed and agreed to but not yet formally ratified nor entered into force, the policy embodied a principle of "lead and hedge," which meant that the United States would attempt to *lead* strategic arms control efforts toward lower force levels, but it would retain the ability to *hedge* by returning to START I levels of arms stockpile if the START II levels could not be agreed upon and achieved. In other words, until START II ratification and entry into force, the United States would draw down and maintain warhead levels consistent with START II. Under the START II agreement, the achievement of lower levels of warhead stockpiles would begin in the year 2003. In 1997, that implementation date was set back to the year 2007. In the meantime, the "hedge" strategy under the Nuclear Posture Review would allow the United States to reconstitute its warhead stockpile to the levels of START I.

Under the START II limits, the United States would reduce its nuclear strategic forces to one type of SUBMARINE-LAUNCHED BALLISTIC MISSILE (the TRIDENT), one type of INTERCONTINENTAL BALLISTIC MISSILE (the MINUTEMAN III) with a single warhead each, and two types of long-range bomber aircraft, the B-52 and the B-2.

Under the Nuclear Posture Review, the United States would need to keep both the *Trident* missiles and the *Minuteman* III missiles active into the indefinite future. As a consequence, the Department of Defense conducted extensive studies to develop means to keep the weapons well maintained, without a program of active testing. The debates over whether maintenance could be conducted without testing by detonation contributed to the rejection by the U.S. Senate in 1999 of the COMPREHENSIVE TEST BAN TREATY. Although the United States had ceased testing by detonation in 1992, it did so without a formal treaty prohibiting such tests. Some experts and members of Congress argued that the stockpile could not be trusted into the future without testing, whereas others believed that the safety and reliability of the weapons could be assured without testing. The debate in Congress was hampered by the fact that some of the information central to the question of reliability, safety, and testing by means other than detonation remained classified and could not be discussed in open session.

The Nuclear Posture Review required the DEPARTMENT OF ENERGY (DOE) to ensure confidence in the long-range, or "enduring," stockpile under very specific limitations and requirements. The DOE was to maintain the weapons capability without underground testing or the production of new FISSILE MATERIAL; it was to develop a stockpile surveillance engineering base; it was to demonstrate the capability to refabricate and certify the different weapons types in the enduring stockpile; it was to maintain the capability to design, fabricate, and certify new warheads; and it was to ensure the availability of TRITIUM. However, it was to achieve all these requirements without designing any new nuclear weapons.

The DOE developed a Stockpile Stewardship and Management Program to help assure confidence in the stockpile without testing and to meet the conditions and requirements of the Nuclear Posture Review. The Stockpile Stewardship and Management Program included enhanced surveillance of the stockpile, improved computers, the use of SIMULATORS, continued subcritical experiments with PLUTONIUM, maintenance of the ability to resume underground testing, and the assurance of a tritium production strategy.

The policy established under the Nuclear Posture Review defined the nuclear weapons stand of the United States for the duration of the Clinton administration.

Nuclear Propulsion

Scientists working on atomic energy during World War II immediately recognized that nuclear reactors could provide a source of power for propelling ships and submarines. In March 1939, Enrico FERMI explained the principles of nuclear physics to a group of naval officers and civilians, attracting the attention of civilian scientist Ross Gunn, who recognized that a power source that used no oxygen would be particularly useful for submarine propulsion.

The NAVAL RESEARCH LABORATORY (NRL) began a research program in 1941 into the possibility of nuclear propulsion of submarines completely independent of the Manhattan Project. Under the leadership of Gunn and Philip Abelson, the NRL recognized that a reactor small enough to power a ship or submarine would have to have enriched URANIUM. A reactor fueled with natural uranium would be too large.

The navy conducted experiments with a thermal diffusion plant to separate the uranium isotopes at the PHILADELPHIA NAVY YARD, utilizing steam from the Naval Boiler and Turbine Laboratory. The method developed there was utilized by the MANHATTAN ENGINEER DISTRICT to partially enrich uranium as staff replicated the facility at Clinch River, near the OAK RIDGE reservation.

Following the war, the navy conducted several experiments with alternate methods of propelling submarines. The traditional diesel-electric submarines had the disadvantage of needing to surface to run on the diesel engines and charge batteries. When running submerged, the subs would operate on batteries and electric power. As a consequence, submarines could operate submerged only for a few hours and at low speeds. Various experimental engines were reviewed at the navy's Engineering Experiment Station at Annapolis, Maryland, following experimental designs developed in Germany during World War II. The solution would be NUCLEAR-POWERED SUBMARINES.

Over the period 1954 to 1957, both Westinghouse and General Electric rapidly advanced the designs of ship-propulsion reactors. In addition, Bettis developed the A1W for aircraft-carrier propulsion and the C1W and F1W reactors for guided-missile cruisers and frigates.

Meanwhile, other nations worked on nuclear propulsion for ships as well. Over the period 1955 to 1994 the Soviet Union constructed some 256 nuclear-powered ships. These included 243 submarines, three cruisers, one communications/missile range ship, eight icebreakers, and one transport ship. Over 460 reactors propelled these vessels. The icebreaker *Lenin,* the first surface ship ever propelled by nuclear power, was put in operation in 1959 and was retired in 1989. The icebreakers and the transport ship built by the Soviets

U.S.S. Enterprise. *One of the major uses for nuclear propulsion of ships by the United States was to power such large aircraft carriers. The* Enterprise *saw action off Vietnam, launching the A-4 Skyhawk bombers parked on her bow.* (National Archives and Records Administration)

represent the largest nonmilitary nuclear-powered fleet in the world.

Other nonmilitary nuclear-powered ships included *Savannah,* built in the United States (1959), *Otto Hahn,* constructed in Germany (1969), and the Japanese *Mutsu* (1974), none of which led to follow-up ships of the type.

France and Britain have both constructed nuclear-powered submarines in much smaller numbers than the United States and the Soviet Union.

Nuclear Reactions

Nuclear reactions are either spontaneous or induced.

Radioactive decay is a spontaneous nuclear reaction in which an unstable arrangement of protons and neutrons emits energy to achieve greater stability. The energy is emitted as α, β, and γ nuclear radiations. Radioactive decay reactions demonstrate characteristic half-lives.

Induced nuclear reactions—those that require the input of energy—often involve neutrons. Neutrons can induce a variety of nuclear changes when added to nuclei. Types of induced nuclear reactions are n-alpha, n-proton, n-gamma, and n-fission, referring to the fact they are induced by neutrons and result in the emission of alpha particles, protons, gamma rays, or in FISSION.

For example, an n-alpha reaction would be as follows:

$$^{27}_{13}Al + ^{1}_{0}n \longrightarrow ^{24}_{11}Na + ^{4}_{2}He$$

An n-proton reaction would be as follows:

$$^{27}_{13}Al + ^{1}_{0}n \longrightarrow ^{27}_{12}Mg + ^{1}_{1}H$$

An n-gamma reaction would be as follows:

$$^{27}_{13}Al + ^{1}_{0}n \longrightarrow ^{28}_{13}Al + ^{0}_{0}\gamma$$

^{238}U and ^{239}Pu undergo n-fission reactions, resulting in asymmetrical fission products, particles, and energy release as radiation. The fact that the n-fission reactions of these elements release neutrons, which in turn generate further n-fission reactions, leads to propagation of the reaction, or a "chain reaction."

A fusion reaction occurs with DEUTERIUM and TRITIUM, called a d-n reaction. It can be described as:

$$^{3}_{1}H + ^{2}_{1}H \longrightarrow ^{4}_{2}He + ^{1}_{0}n$$

See also FISSION; FUSION POWER; RADIOACTIVITY.

Nuclear Regulatory Commission

The Nuclear Regulatory Commission (NRC) was established under the 1974 Energy Reorganization Act, beginning its operations in January 1975. The NRC inherited many practices, rules, and personnel from the ATOMIC ENERGY COMMISSION, which under the ATOMIC ENERGY ACT OF 1954, had held oversight over nuclear power plant licensing and regulation.

Also, the NRC acquired some new regulatory duties; the general plan was that the new agency would be less likely to override safety concerns in favor of development. The mandate of the NRC was more squarely focused on safety.

In its first months, the NRC concentrated on safeguards to prevent the theft or loss of nuclear fuels or the sabotage of nuclear plants. The rise in activities such as airplane hijacking and terrorist murder of civilians had created apprehension that terrorists would attempt to use nuclear materials if they could obtain them, perhaps to construct a bomb.

From its early days, the agency became embroiled in one public crisis or controversy after another. One of the first safety issues faced by the new agency was the fire at BROWNS FERRY on March 25, 1975. Another public debate grew out of the publication of the RASMUSSEN REPORT in October 1975. The NRC later announced that it did not support all of the language of the executive summary of the report, which had suggested that the risk of death from a reactor accident was minimal. In March 1979, the NRC was again propelled into public scrutiny after the accident at THREE MILE ISLAND.

The NRC responded to the episode at Three Mile Island with a reexamination of safety requirements and new emphasis on the human factors that had contributed to that accident. Working with industry, the NRC worked toward securing improvements in control room instrumentation and meeting the problem of small episodes that could compound into major accidents. The agency began to require PROBABILISTIC RISK ASSESSMENTS of proposed new reactors, and by 1995 agency personnel encouraged use of such assessments to supplement traditional safety methods.

Following the Three Mile Island accident, the NRC suspended the granting of operating licenses. The pause in licensing lasted through February 1980. In August 1980, the NRC issued a full-power operating license to the North Anna-2 plant in Virginia. Over the period 1980 to 1989, it issued more than 40 more licenses, most of which had been under construction from the mid-1970s.

Most of the licensing procedures went forward quietly, but two were highly controversial. The SEABROOK reactor in New Hampshire was delayed be opponents and state action until 1990, and the SHOREHAM reactor on Long Island, New York, was ultimately prevented from operating. In both cases, the primary cause for delay in the mid- and late 1980s was due to the problem of developing an evacuation plan for emergencies.

Another controversy faced by the NRC centered around the complex issue of safe levels of radiation exposure. In June 1990, the NRC issued a policy statement outlining plans to set up rules by which small quantities of extremely low-level radioactive materials would be exempt from regulation. This concept of "below regulatory concern" produced a wave of protest from the news media, Congress, antinuclear activists, and others.

As the first power reactors grew older, the NRC faced the issue of decommissioning them. Over the period 1984 to 1988, the commission developed a rule requiring reactor operators to specify how they planned to ensure funding to clean up sites and to reduce radioactivity at them to make them safe for other uses. The commission also developed a guideline that would limit a renewal of license beyond 40 years to a maximum of 20 additional years. In 1998, Baltimore Gas and Electric sought a renewal for its CALVERT CLIFFS reactor, and Duke Power asked to extend the license for its South Carolina Oconee reactors.

Controversies of one kind or another continued to haunt the NRC. In 1997, workers at the Millstone reactor in Connecticut complained that they had been intimidated and threatened with dismissal for pointing out safety issues. The commission found the safety issues either very minor or already corrected, or both. However, the commission also concluded that the utility had indeed intimidated "whistle-blowers" and fined the company $100,000. The issue of how to deal with worker complaints haunted the NRC through the 1990s, and it provided a basis for much criticism in the media of the commission.

In general, the commission was buffeted from two directions. On the one hand, it faced pressures from the industry with complaints that it was too prescriptive in its regulatory control. On the other hand, the NRC constantly dealt with complaints from various activists and the media that it was too lax and too sympathetic to the utility companies and companies engaged in the nuclear fuel cycle. Like other regulatory commissions with similar roles, and like the Atomic Energy Commission, the NRC has had to tread a difficult pathway between opposing constituencies.

Suggested Reading

J. Samuel Walker, *A Short History of Nuclear Regulation, 1946–1999*. Washington, D.C.: Nuclear Regulatory Commission, 2000.

Nuclear Submarines

When nuclear fission was first discovered, the U.S. Navy very soon recognized that it could become a source for powering submarines. With the development of microwave radar during World War II, aircraft could locate and destroy diesel-electric submarines that had surfaced to replenish their batteries. Microwave radar had destroyed the tactical advantage of submarines, and the navy needed a system to propel submarines underwater for extended periods of time. Nuclear power appeared to hold out promise.

In the United States, nuclear propulsion was under study in the immediate postwar period at the NAVAL RESEARCH LABORATORY, and it later received a strong advocate in the person of then captain Hyman RICKOVER.

During the period 1946 to 1948, Rickover worked to advance the concept of a small nuclear reactor that could be used to propel submarines. Rickover worked with the KNOLLS ATOMIC POWER LABORATORY near Schenectady, New York, operated by GENERAL ELECTRIC, WESTINGHOUSE Corporation, and ARGONNE NATIONAL LABORATORY, to develop a nuclear power plant.

By 1953, he had transferred most of the work to the BETTIS ATOMIC POWER LABORATORY, located near Pittsburgh and operated by Westinghouse. The Westinghouse laboratory at Bettis developed the Mark I reactor, and the General Electric Company at Knolls developed the Mark A reactor. The Mark I reactor was tested at the Naval Reactor Test Station in Idaho, and it proved successful.

Rickover had the Westinghouse Mark II reactor installed aboard *Nautilus*, launched in 1954. From 1954 through 1957, the navy began experimentation with a variety of reactor types.

During this experimental period, General Electric worked with the design of a sodium-cooled reactor, as well as a water-cooled plant, eventually settling on only a pressurized water-cooled model at Rickover's direction. Westinghouse developed at Bettis the S5W, which would become the standard propulsion plant for 20 attack submarines and for 29 Polaris missile submarines.

In May 1955, *Nautilus* cruised from New London, Connecticut, to San Juan, Puerto Rico, a distance of 1,300 miles, in 84 hours. In June 1955, the prototype for the *Seawolf* simulated a 2,000 mile continuous high-power run, and in July 1955 *Seawolf* was launched. *Seawolf* underwent initial sea trials in February 1957, and, at the same time, the first plans for a Polaris submarine were developed. The Polaris type was to be a submarine capable of launching long-range ballistic missiles.

At its first refueling in 1957, *Nautilus* had traveled 62,000 miles on the first reactor core, demonstrating the value of nuclear power for ships in a clear fashion. In 1958, *Nautilus* completed a trip from Hawaii, under the North Pole, to Great Britain. The next year, *Skate* surfaced at the North Pole. In June 1959, the first

Polaris submarine was commissioned. In 1960, *Triton* completed a trip around the world entirely submerged. In 1960, the first Polaris submarine launch of missiles was successful. Between 1955 and 1985, the U.S. Navy acquired 132 nuclear-powered submarines, of which 37 were missile-launching and 95 were attack or hunter-killer submarines.

See also SUBMARINE-LAUNCHED BALLISTIC MISSILES.

Nuclear Suppliers Group   *See* ZANGGER COMMITTEE.

Nuclear Test Limitation Treaties

Sometimes considered ARMS CONTROL treaties, a number of treaties between the major nuclear powers were devoted to limiting the testing of nuclear weapons.

The following table lists related nuclear test limiting and non-proliferation nuclear treaties. Although treaties limiting testing or pledging not to develop nuclear weapons are not, strictly speaking, arms control treaties, many publications include these related nuclear treaties under the general category of nuclear arms control.

See also ARMS CONTROL; BIG THREE CONFERENCES; ON-SITE INSPECTION AGENCY; SUMMIT MEETINGS.

Nuclear Waste Policy Act

In 1982, after the DEPARTMENT OF ENERGY failed to resolve where and how it planned to dispose of high-level nuclear waste generated from power reactors, Congress passed the Nuclear Waste Policy Act. Under the act, the secretary of energy was directed to name five geologic sites for initial study and then to narrow the choice to three, from which one was to be chosen as the first waste repository. These site-characterization studies were to generate a single site by March 31, 1987, which was to be subject to NUCLEAR REGULATORY COMMISSION (NRC) approval. Under the act, Congress also established a Nuclear Waste Fund, to be created by adding a 1/10 of a cent charge per kilowatt hour to electric rates. The goal was to create a repository by 1998.

The act was amended in 1987, designating YUCCA MOUNTAIN in Nevada as the waste site, and after several delays and disputes with the government of Nevada, the Department of Energy aimed to open the repository there by the year 2010.

Meanwhile, the Environmental Protection Agency (EPA) attempted to establish standards for a waste repository, and, after judicial action and further legislation, the National Academy of Sciences (NAS) was to recommend the nature of the safe limit on long-term radiation releases from the repository. The EPA was to set the magnitude of the limitation. Then, the DOE is to seek a license to operate Yucca Mountain from the Nuclear Regulatory Commission in accord with the standards evolved by the NAS and the EPA.

The resistance of the Nevada state government to the Yucca Mountain site, together with the involvement of NAS and three separate federal agencies (DOE, NRC, and EPA) appeared likely to delay the implementation of the original act beyond 2010, requiring further court and congressional action.

	TREATY	SIGNED	IN FORCE
M	Antarctic Treaty	Dec. 1, 1959	June 23, 1961
M	LIMITED TEST BAN TREATY	Aug. 5, 1963	Oct. 10, 1963
M	Outer Space Treaty	Jan. 27, 1967	Oct. 10, 1967
M	TREATY OF TLOTELOLCO	Feb. 14, 1967	country by country
M	NON-PROLIFERATION TREATY	Jul. 1, 1968	Mar. 5, 1970
M	Sea-Bed Treaty	Feb. 11, 1971	May 18, 1972
B	Nuclear Accidents Agrmt.	Sept. 30, 1971	Sept. 30, 1971
B	THRESHOLD TEST BAN TREATY	July 30, 1974	unratified pledge
B	Peaceful Nuclear Explosions	May 28, 1976	unratified

[Other nations adhered to this bilateral treaty, some with reservations.]

M	COMPREHENSIVE TEST BAN TREATY	July, 1994	unratified pledge

(M)=Multilateral; (B)=Bilateral between U.S. and U.S.S.R.

Suggested Reading

David Bodansky, *Nuclear Energy: Principles, Practices, and Prospects.* Woodbury, N.Y.: American Institute of Physics, 1996.

Nuclear Weapons Council   *See* MILITARY LIAISON COMMITTEE.

Nuclear Winter

Following the development of evidence by Luis W. ALVAREZ that the mass extinction of dinosaurs some 65 million years ago was due to the impact of a meteorite striking the earth and to the resulting smoke and dust clouds lowering the earth's temperature, a number of scientists developed, in 1983, the concept of a "nuclear winter." Under this scenario, a full-scale nuclear war would send up such a mass of smoke and dust into the high atmosphere that the sun would be blocked over much of the planet for a period of six weeks to six months, leading to a drop in temperature to the freezing point or below. The resulting damage to crops and food supply would add to the effects of the nuclear exchange, possibly extinguishing all human life on earth.

Astronomer Carl Sagan teamed with four other scientists to study the possible phenomenon and to arouse interest in the possibility that a nuclear exchange could result in worldwide freezing. Sagan joined with R. P. Turco, O. B. Toon, T. P. Ackerman, and J. B. Pollack, and their group was sometimes referred to by the acronym TTAPS. The group first presented the concept at a conference held from October 31 to November 1, 1983, in Washington, D.C. TTAPS then published their study, in which they used a computer model to evaluate the effect of the smoke that would result from a nuclear exchange, in the journal *Science* in December 1983.

The TTAPS study became extremely controversial. For one thing, it suggested that a nuclear war, already conceived as extremely destructive, could actually end the life of the human species on the planet through its environmental impact. In this regard, the TTAPS study combined the concerns of both antinuclear activists and those concerned to reduce the threat of nuclear war with the interests and motivations of those concerned with protection of the environment.

Soon the defense establishment commissioned studies to investigate the degree to which smoke would represent a previously little-studied weapons effect. Through 1984 to 1986 a number of more sophisticated computer models were applied to the question. Many variables entered into the calculation, not originally considered by the TTAPS group. Wind, temperatures at the time of the nuclear exchange, the moderating effect of ocean temperatures, and many other factors not originally included in the first computer model used by TTAPS suggested that the original calculation exaggerated the temperature effect that would result from various numbers of nuclear detonations.

Nevertheless, the defense community began to look closely at the effect of smoke from forest fires and destroyed cities in interfering not only with sunlight and heat but also with communications networks and intelligence derived from satellite optical equipment. The original nuclear winter concept, which received extensive public attention in the period 1984–1985, did not seem valid after more careful and more complex computer modeling. Nevertheless, the concept may have contributed to public pressure toward nuclear disarmament, and it certainly contributed to the thinking of nuclear war-fighting strategists as they considered the variety of weapons effects that could result from a large-scale exchange of weapons.

See also ARMS CONTROL.

Suggested Reading

Carl Sagan, "Nuclear War and Climatic Catastrophe: Some Policy Implications." *Foreign Affairs* 62 (Winter 1983–1984): 257–292.

Starley L. Thompson and Stephen H. Schneider, "Nuclear Winter Reappraised." *Foreign Affairs* 65 (Summer) 1986.

R. P. Turco, O. B. Toon, T. P. Ackerman, J. B. Pollack, and Carl Sagan, "Global Atmospheric Consequences of Nuclear War." *Science* 222 (December 23, 1983): 1283–1293.

Nunn-Lugar Program   *See* COOPERATIVE THREAT REDUCTION.

Oak Ridge National Laboratory

Constructed during World War II by the MANHATTAN ENGINEER DISTRICT, the Clinton site near Oak Ridge, Tennessee, had several distinct purposes. K-25 was a large GASEOUS DIFFUSION plant for the separation of $_{235}$U from ^{238}U. On the northern edge of the reservation, near the city of Oak Ridge itself lay the Y-12 plant, which housed the CALUTRONS that used an electromagnetic method of separation. About 10 miles from Y-12 lay the X-10 facility, a large air-cooled reactor used to produce sample amounts of PLUTONIUM. X-10 itself was also referred to as the Clinton Laboratory.

In 1948, with the creation of the ATOMIC ENERGY COMMISSION, the Clinton Laboratory was reorganized and renamed the Oak Ridge National Laboratory (ORNL). Over the next 50 years, ORNL expanded its role from research in nuclear weapons to investigations into a broad array of environmental, medical, and basic research and technology development areas.

Du Pont Corporation constructed the facilities and Monsanto Corporation operated them. The Clinton laboratory itself was organized in 1943, with facilities in chemistry, ISOTOPE separations, health, production, engineering, physics, and radiation biology. The staff

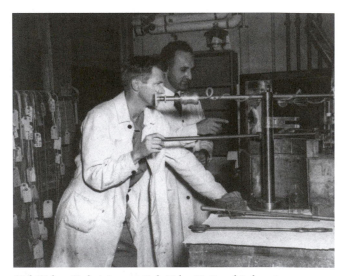

Oak Ridge. Technicians at Oak Ridge National Laboratory use an early remote-handling mechanism with radioactive materials. (U.S. Army Signal Corps-Library of Congress)

leveled off at about 1,500 during the last two years of the war.

In 1947, Union Carbide Corporation became the operating contractor, and the Clinton Laboratory became first Clinton National Laboratory in 1947 and then Oak Ridge National Laboratory in 1948. Eugene WIGNER was selected to head the laboratory's research and development division in 1946. Another development in 1946 saw the creation of the Oak Ridge Institute of Nuclear Studies (ORINS), a training institution to familiarize scientists and technicians with radiation and related topics. ORINS was a nonprofit corporation established by 14 universities in the southeastern part of the United States.

Over the following years, ORNL took over research work at Y-12, and the laboratory expanded its mandate into new areas, working on reactor design, isotope research, particle accelerators, radiation damage, and the biological effects of radiation. A research reactor was constructed and went into operation in 1958. An abortive plan for a gas-cooled reactor on the bank of the nearby Clinch River, started in 1959, was canceled in 1966.

Alvin Weinberg, who had served as associate director under Wigner, became director in 1955. Under Weinberg, the laboratory moved into new areas, including work on desalinization of seawater and the use of high-powered centrifuges for virus and other biological research. He brought Wigner back to head up a new 100 megawatt research reactor, a high-flux isotope reactor completed in 1965. In 1973 Weinberg resigned and Floyd Culler, a chemical engineer, served as acting director. In 1974, Herman Postma, a fusion energy specialist, took over as director. With the creation of the ENERGY RESEARCH AND DEVELOPMENT ADMINISTRATION and then the DEPARTMENT OF ENERGY, ORNL branched out more broadly again into a wide variety of energy and environmental fields.

In 1984, Martin Marietta Corporation was granted the contract to operate ORNL, and in 1988, Postma transferred to corporate headquarters. Martin Marietta, as distinct from Du Pont and Monsanto, drew from experience as a government contractor on technological systems rather than a chemical engineering firm. As a technology and defense firm, the new operating company was more focused on providing innovative technological solutions than on chemical research alone.

Alex Zucker served as acting director through 1988, to be replaced by Alvin Trivelpiece in early 1989. By the late 1980s and the 1990s, under Trivelpiece, the laboratory expanded its reputation for work into areas such as computer sciences, particle acceleration, and nuclear medicine, in addition to its traditional areas of focus.

Suggested Reading

Leland Johnson and Daniel Schaffer, *Oak Ridge National Laboratory, the First Fifty Years*. Knoxville: University of Tennessee Press, 1994.

Office of Scientific Research and Development (OSRD)

The Office of Scientific Research and Development (OSRD) was established in 1941 to take over a variety of research projects with military application, many of which had been sponsored under the National Defense Research Committee (NDRC) in the period 1939–1941. Vannevar BUSH headed both organizations. Early work under the ADVISORY COMMITTEE ON URANIUM (also known as the Briggs Committee, after its chair, Lyman Briggs) in the period 1939–1941 had established the feasibility of developing an atomic bomb, and the work had continued under the NDRC. Operating on a relatively small budget, the scientists had not only shown that a nuclear FISSION weapon was possible but had also worked out many of the basic calculations of fission CROSS SECTION and the principles of producing PLUTONIUM.

The atomic bomb work was organized in Section S-1 of the OSRD, and, for a period, the bomb was simply known as Project S-1, or "the S-1." Prior work under the Briggs Committee was confirmed by a report from the MAUD Committee in Great Britain.

In the period December 1941 to June 1942, work on plutonium, on URANIUM separation, and on the moderating properties of graphite that would be essential in PRODUCTION REACTORS continued under OSRD sponsorship. However, in order to build the industrial-scale facilities necessary to provide enough fissionable material for a weapon, President Franklin ROOSEVELT approved bringing in the U.S. Army Corps of Engineers. The MANHATTAN ENGINEER DISTRICT (MED) was formally established in June 1942. At first, the OSRD and the MED shared responsibility, with the MED focusing on working with land acquisition and with large corporations for industrial construction while the OSRD continued work with the scientists who had previously coordinated their work through the Briggs Committee and the NDRC.

The arrangement over the summer of 1942 proceeded slowly under Colonel James C. Marshall. One issue involved the problem of getting highest priorities assigned to the materials needed by the OSRD researchers. OSRD estimates of the expenses involved were woefully inadequate. Other difficulties arose as the scientists at the University of CHICAGO and elsewhere found it difficult to work with industrial engineers and military personnel. They were willing to continue under civilian control, but they feared they might be drafted and become subject to taking orders from officers less knowledgeable on technical matters than themselves. Yet their inexperience with large staffs, contract and budget matters, and security practices made it necessary to restructure the project. Colonel Marshall's inexperience with a project of this scale and his rank were further barriers to success.

The Army Services of Supply, under General Brehon Somervell, reorganized the work in September 1942. Somervell appointed Colonel Leslie GROVES, who had just completed the project to build the Pentagon office building, to head the Manhattan Engineer District. Somervell had Groves promoted to general, and he charged him with coordinating the whole project. Groves's personality and leadership transformed the project, and it began to move forward rapidly in the fall of 1942. Groves quickly closed the purchase on the land at OAK RIDGE, and he then selected J. Robert OPPENHEIMER to direct the scientific research.

Suggested Reading

Leslie Groves, *Now It Can Be Told.* New York: Harper and Row, 1962.

Richard Rhodes, *The Making of the Atomic Bomb.* New York: Simon and Schuster, 1986.

Oklo Mine

In 1972, French scientists analyzing URANIUM extracted from the Oklo uranium mine in Gabon, Africa, made a startling discovery. The natural uranium was depleted in concentration of ^{235}U, below the 0.07 normally found in natural uranium, a percentage that is fairly constant wherever the ore is found. Scientists suspected and then confirmed that this anomalous proportion of isotopes was due to a natural CHAIN REACTION that had occurred millions of years ago. Conclusive evidence that a chain reaction came with the discovery of rare earth FISSION products not normally found in abundance in nature. Some called the site the Oklo Natural Reactor.

At a point about 1.8 billion years ago, the enrichment of uranium, that is the proportion of ^{235}U, approached 3%, about the proportion in many modern reactors. Water intruded into the deposit, acting as a MODERATOR and apparently initiating a chain reaction that simmered for several hundred thousand years. Some experts have used the Oklo example to indicate that there is likely to be little migration of nuclear waste products from proposed underground waste emplacement sites.

On-Site Inspection Agency (OSIA)

In December 1987, a task force set up offices in the U.S. Coast Guard Headquarters in Washington, D.C., to develop a plan for carrying out the on-site inspection provisions of the INTERMEDIATE-RANGE NUCLEAR FORCES (INF) treaty that had been signed December 8 at the Washington summit. The resulting organization, the On-Site Inspection Agency (OSIA), was officially established in January 1988.

The first inspections under the treaty began in July 1988. On July 22, 1988, the Soviets conducted the first destruction of a missile under the treaty, with inspectors from OSIA observing the work. The United States followed up in September, with PERSHING as Soviet observers witnessed the destruction of the first missile under the treaty at Longhorn Army Ammunition Plant in Texas.

The agency took on more duties as new treaties required inspection groups made up of military experts. In 1989, the agency moved to new facilities near Dulles Airport outside Washington, D.C. The Conventional Forces in Europe (CFE) Treaty, signed in 1990, and the Strategic Arms Reduction Treaty (START I), signed in 1991, required inspection teams. OSIA took on responsibility for the United Nations in ensuring that no weapons of mass destruction were being hidden in Iraq. Over the decade 1988 to 1998, OSIA sent over 9,600 inspectors on hundreds of inspection tours.

All of the arms control treaties, including INF, CFE, and START I, involved the exchange of technical experts from the United States and the Soviet Union. The teams of experts, drawn from military and civilian backgrounds, would visit each other's territory. There they would oversee the destruction of missiles, missile SILOS, nuclear warheads, and other related emplacements. Detailed agreements provided for the exclusion of the foreign teams from extremely sensitive areas, but OSIA teams visited missile and weapons facilities, forts and bases, and manufacturing plants not only in the various republics of the former Soviet Union, but in locations within the Warsaw Pact countries of Eastern Europe. Corresponding Soviet experts visited U.S. locations to monitor American performance under the treaties.

With the dissolution of the Soviet Union and with U.S. funding of projects in the former Soviet countries to dismantle weapons, OSIA could not handle the large contracts required to do the work. Contracts involved not only specialized services but also procurement of special equipment, including video monitoring cameras, tamperproof seals and locks, and armored blankets to protect nuclear weapons in transit from small-arms fire.

In 1991, OSIA was assigned the task of supporting inspections of Iraqi chemical, biological, and nuclear facilities under United Nations Resolution 687. That resolution established the United Nations Special Commission (UNSCOM) on Iraq, and OSIA served the U.S. executive agency for UNSCOM. OSIA coordinated support, consisting of linguists, weapons experts, surveillance flights, and supply of staff.

In 1993, OSIA began inspections in the Czech Republic and HUNGARY, and in 1994, the agency worked in KAZAKHSTAN in a project to remove highly enriched uranium for safekeeping. In 1995, the OSIA set up continuous monitoring facilities in UKRAINE, similar to earlier facilities established in Russia at Votkinsk. In 1996, the agency took on inspection duties in Bosnia to assist in peacekeeping efforts there.

In 1998, the functions of OSIA and of the DEFENSE SPECIAL WEAPONS AGENCY were merged in a new DEFENSE THREAT REDUCTION AGENCY devoted to various functions, including inspection, funding of dismantling projects, and assessing American weapons systems for their survivability under nuclear warfare conditions.

See also ARMS CONTROL; COOPERATIVE THREAT REDUCTION.

Open Skies *See* EISENHOWER, DWIGHT DAVID.

Operation BUSTER-JANGLE
Operation BUSTER-JANGLE was the second nuclear weapon test series conducted at the NEVADA TEST SITE, with seven detonations over the period October–November 1951, and it was the first to include an underground shot.

Charlie shot, Operation Buster. This air-dropped device yielded 14 kilotons on October 30, 1951. (U.S. Army)

TEST	DATE	TYPE	YIELD
Able	Oct. 22, 1951	Tower	less than 1 kt
Baker	Oct. 28, 1951	Airdrop	3.5 kt
Charlie	Oct. 30, 1951	Airdrop	14 kt
Dog	Nov. 1, 1951	Airdrop	21 kt
Easy	Nov. 5, 1951	Airdrop	31 kt
Sugar	Nov. 19, 1951	Surface	1.2 kt
Uncle	Nov. 29, 1951	Undergr.	1.2 kt

The series had a double name because "BUSTER" had referred to a planned series of weapons-design tests, and "JANGLE" to a series of planned weapons-effects tests that would demonstrate nuclear effects, such as blast, radiation, and heat, and their impact on military equipment and civilian structures. The two series were meshed. Able, the first test of the series, was a misfire, with an extremely low yield.

The Sugar and Uncle shots allowed for the comparison of the effects of weapons detonated on the surface and underground and provided the military with some data regarding the "penetrating" weapons that would be detonated underground.

See also ATMOSPHERIC NUCLEAR TESTING.

Operation CASTLE
Operation CASTLE was a series of six weapons-related tests conducted in the period March–May 1954, five at BIKINI and one at ENEWETAK in the Marshall Islands of the Pacific.

Of all of the atmospheric nuclear tests conducted by the United States, the Bravo test held in 1954 was probably the most severe in its off-site consequences.

Test	Date	Yield
Bravo	March 1, 1954	15 mt
Romeo	March 24, 1954	11 mt
Koon	April 7, 1954	"fizzle"
Union	April 16, 1954	6+ mt
Yankee	May 5, 1954	13.5 mt
Nectar	May 14, 1954	1+ mt (at Enewetak)

A test of a thermonuclear weapon, Bravo's yield was over the 6 megatons anticipated, with preliminary after-shot estimates set as high as 15 megatons. Immediately after the detonation, radiation counters revealed higher than expected readings. As ships evacuated military and civilian test personnel from the area, they were instructed to begin to wash down immediately and to have all personnel stay below decks. As radiation declined over Bikini, indications came in that radioactive clouds had moved eastward toward inhabited islands. Amphibious aircraft went to Rongerik, some 133 nautical miles from Bikini, to evacuate military personnel at a monitoring station there. Later, destroyers were sent to evacuate native populations from other islands, including some closer to the test site than Rongerik. The USS *Philip* removed islanders from Rongelap and Ailinginae Atoll, while another destroyer, USS *Renshaw*, evacuated 154 islanders from Utirik on March 4.

Although the people from Utirik showed no signs of ill effects, those from Rongelap and Ailinginae had received much more FALLOUT. Calculations indicated that people on Utirik received 14 Roentgens, while those on Ailinginae had received 69 Roentgens, and the Rongelap islanders had received 175 Roentgens. Although these calculations were later revised somewhat downward, the islanders had received dangerous and excessive amounts of radiation from the explosion. It should be remembered that the approved standard dosage for test site workers ranged between 3 and 3.9 Roentgens during this period. Rongelap islanders suffered loss of hair, skin lesions, hemorrhages under the skin, and other ill-effects, including low blood counts. The Rongelap islanders were not permitted to return to their homeland until June 1957.

Meanwhile, fallout from Castle Bravo had contaminated a Japanese fishing vessel, the *Fukuryu Muru* (*LUCKY DRAGON*). This fact was discovered about two weeks after the detonation when the sailors arrived in Japan. Their ship had been closer to the detonation than any of the islanders but not within the exclusion zone established by the test managers.

In retrospect, it was clear that the exclusion zone had been based on the assumption that there would be much smaller fallout and that prevailing winds would carry any radioactive cloud away from the nearby islands. Rather than evacuate the islands for the duration of the test, the exclusion zone had been drawn close to Bikini.

Later, the MARSHALL ISLANDERS who had been contaminated filed suit against the U.S. government for damages, and, in a long-term settlement, the United States compensated the islanders. Both Bikini and Enewetak were rehabilitated, although Bikini atoll was never permanently resettled.

The long-range distribution of dangerous fallout demonstrated that if thermonuclear weapons of this magnitude were ever used operationally in a military situation over land, not only would a vast area be immediately destroyed but fatalities from radioactive fallout would occur in areas of thousands of square miles.

Almost all of the shots in this series designed to test the thermonuclear weapons had yields greater than anticipated, except for the third shot, Koon, that "fizzled," only partly detonating.

See also HYDROGEN BOMB DESIGN.

Suggested Reading

Barton Hacker, *Elements of Controversy: The Atomic Energy Commission and Radiation Safety in Nuclear Weapons Testing, 1947–1974.* Berkeley: University of California Press, 1994.

Richard Hewlett and Jack Holl, *Atoms for Peace and War, 1953–1961: Eisenhower and the Atomic Energy Commission.* Berkeley: University of California Press, 1989.

Operation CROSSROADS

Operation CROSSROADS was the first postwar nuclear test series conducted by the U.S. Government, designed to test the effect of nuclear weapons on naval ships. Conducted at BIKINI Atoll in the Marshall Islands, the series consisted of two shots: Able, detonated in the air on June 30, 1946, and Baker, detonated underwater on July 24, 1946.

Eighty-seven ships were arranged in the lagoon of the atoll, but in test Able, the bomb was dropped two miles off target, sinking only two ships immediately. Test Baker was more impressive. This time the target fleet of 92 ships was severely damaged. Several large

Baker shot, Operation CROSSROADS. The first underwater nuclear detonation took place in this test on July 24, 1946. Some of the target ships were heavily contaminated with radioactive material. In this photo, the old aircraft carrier Saratoga is lifted vertically on the central column of water from the lagoon. (Library of Congress)

ships sank immediately and a battleship was tossed into the air as a massive wave swept out from the detonation. The mushroom cloud sent up from the lagoon formed a cap three miles across. Much of the cloud fell back as radioactive rain, coating the remaining damaged ships.

All but nine of the target ships were either sunk, damaged, or very heavily contaminated with radioactivity. Experiments with sandblasting and decontamination demonstrated how difficult it would be to make the ships safe for further use.

See also ATMOSPHERIC NUCLEAR TESTING.

Operation DOMINIC

Operation DOMINIC was a series of nuclear tests conducted in 1962, after the Soviet Union broke its self-imposed moratorium on testing in September 1961. The Dominic I or Dominic-Phase I test series consisted of 36 shots, including about 20 weapons-development tests, several stockpile proof tests, and six weapons-effects tests. DOMINIC also included two tests of com-

plete weapons systems, the Polaris and the ASROC or antisubmarine rocket.

The tests in May through July were mostly conducted near Christmas Island; the tests in October and November were launched near JOHNSTON ISLAND. Most of the tests were of devices dropped from aircraft or launched on rockets, as noted in the accompanying table.

Several of the tests were particularly notable. The Starfish Prime test of July 9, 1962, was detonated over 200 miles high. The ELECTROMAGNETIC PULSE effect from this detonation was detected over a wide area, affecting street lights and burglar alarms in Hawaii, more than 800 miles from the detonation point. Frigate Bird was the first firing of a Polaris missile with a nuclear warhead, the first detonation of a nuclear warhead after reentry into the atmosphere, and the first and only operational test of a complete strategic nuclear ballistic missile weapon system. The flash from the high altitude Bluegill Triple Prime shot was seen in Hawaii.

Several tests of rocket-launched weapons during this series failed, and the rockets had to be detonated in midflight before the nuclear weapon reached its destination. Difficulties with the rockets and with cleanup of debris from their malfunction partially accounted for the delay in starting the Johnston Island series of tests.

TEST	DATE
Christmas Island Region	
Adobe	April 25
Aztec	April 27
Arkansas	May 2
Questa	May 4
Frigate Bird	May 6
Yukon	May 8
Mesilla	May 9
Muskegon	May 11
Swordfish	May 11
Encino	May 12
Swanee	May 14
Chetco	May 19
Tanana	May 25
Nambe	May 27
Aima	June 8
Truckee	June 9
Yeso	June 10
Harlem	June 12
Rinconada	June 15
Dulce	June 17
Petit	June 19
Otowi	June 22
Bighorn	June 27
Bluestone	June 30
Starfish Prime	July 9
Sunset	July 10
Pamlico	July 11
Johnston Island Area	
Androscoggin	Oct. 2
Bumping	Oct. 6
Chama	Oct. 18
Checkmate	Oct. 20
Bluegill Triple Prime	Oct. 26
Calamity	Oct. 27
Housatonic	Oct. 30
Kingfish	Nov. 1
	Launched by missile
Tightrope	Nov. 4
	Last U.S. atmospheric test

DOMINIC II was a series conducted underground at the NEVADA TEST SITE in the United States.

See also ATMOSPHERIC NUCLEAR TESTING.

Operation GREENHOUSE

Operation GREENHOUSE was a series of four tests conducted at the Pacific testing range at ENEWETAK in April and May 1951. It was the first effort by the United States to test thermonuclear principles.

TEST	DATE	TYPE	YIELD
Dog	April 7, 1951	Tower	
Easy	April 20, 1951	Tower	47 kt
George	May 9, 1951	Tower	thermonuclear
Item	May 24, 1951	Tower	45.5 kt-boosted

The operation was commanded by General Elwood Quesada of the U.S. Air Force, who oversaw Joint Task Force 3 from a control station on Parry Island in the Enewetak atoll. The George detonation not only destroyed the tower on which it had been placed, but also the concrete shelter housing experimental equipment, a cast iron structure, and much of the island on which it had been placed. The lagoon flowed into the crater left by the explosion.

The tests were carried out to examine design improvements, especially the George shot, which tested parts of a HYDROGEN BOMB DESIGN, and the Item shot, which tested the principle of a BOOSTED WEAPON. The devices were emplaced on 200- and 300-foot towers.

See also ATMOSPHERIC NUCLEAR TESTING.

Operation HARDTACK

Operation HARDTACK was a series of U.S. atmospheric nuclear and thermonuclear tests conducted at both BIKINI and ENEWETAK in the Pacific over the period April 1958–August 1958. In addition, two weapons were detonated high over the ocean, launched on missiles from JOHNSTON ISLAND. Altogether there were 37 tests, including the last of 23 tests at Bikini and the last of 43 tests at Enewetak. Of the 37 tests of Operation HARDTACK, 22 were detonated at or near the Enewetak atoll, 10 were on barges moored in lagoons or craters of the Bikini atoll, one was detonated from a balloon 98 miles northeast of Bikini, and two were the missile-launched weapons from Johnston Island. Dates are Pacific local time, one day earlier in the United States.

The shots from landing craft were detonated underwater; several of them were used to test weapons effects on moored ships and submarines.

Test	Date in 1958	Type	Comment
Bikini Series			
Yucca	April 28	Balloon	High altitude, over ocean
Fir	May 12	Barge	In Castle-Bravo crater
Nutmeg	May 22	Barge	
Sycamore	May 31	Barge	In Castle-Bravo crater
Maple	June 11	Barge	
Aspen	June 15	Barge	In Castle-Bravo crater
Redwood	June 28	Barge	
Hickory	June 29	Barge	
Cedar	July 3	Barge	In Castle-Bravo crater
Poplar	July 12	Barge	In Castle-Bravo crater
Juniper	July 22	Barge	Last test at Bikini
Enewetak Series			
Cactus	May 6	Surface	Crater later domed for waste
Butternut	May 12	Barge	
Koa	May 13	Surface	
Wahoo	May 16	Landing Craft	2 miles out in ocean
Holly	May 21	Barge	
Yellowwood	May 26	Barge	low yield
Magnolia	May 27	Barge	
Tobacco	May 30	Barge	
Rose	June 3	Barge	
Umbrella	June 9	Landing Craft	
Walnut	June 15	Barge	
Linden	June 18	Barge	
Elder	June 28	Barge	
Oak	June 29	Landing Craft	several mt yield
Sequoia	July 2	Landing Craft	
Dogwood	July 6	Landing Craft	
Scaveola	July 14	Barge	very low yield
Pisonia	July 18	Landing Craft	
Olive	July 23	Landing Craft	
Pine	July 27	Barge	
Quince	Aug. 6	Surface	
Fig	Aug. 18	Surface	Last test at Enewetak
Launched from Johnston Island			
Teak	July 31	Missile	High altitude burst
Orange	August 11	Missile	High altitude burst

The Teak and Orange shots were detonated at extremely high altitudes, causing spectacular effects. The Teak shot was visible at night in Hawaii, over 800 miles away, and blacked out shortwave transmission over the Pacific for several hours. In addition, it created a short-term aurora effect as the radiation spread through the earth's magnetic field. The aurora was visible over 2,000 miles away. The glow from the Teak fireball was estimated to have reached a diameter of 600 miles in a few minutes. The Orange shot was also visible from Hawaii.

Initial concerns that anyone looking directly at the high-altitude bursts might be blinded caused the atomic energy commission to decide not to locate the tests in the Marshall Islands, where native islanders might be within view. Instead, the more remote launch site of Johnston Island was selected.

As in other test series in the 1950s, HARDTACK combined diagnostic tests of new weapons and weapons effects testing, sometimes on the same shot.

Operation HARDTACK in the Pacific was often referred to as HARDTACK I because a later test series in 1958, HARDTACK II, was conducted at the NEVADA TEST SITE, comprising a series of 35 underground tests.

Operation RANGER

Operation RANGER was the first nuclear weapon test series conducted at the NEVADA TEST SITE in January and February 1951. The operation consisted of five tests of weapons, all dropped from aircraft.

TEST	DATE	TYPE	KILOTONS
Able	Jan. 27, 1951	Air	1
Baker	Jan. 28, 1951	Air	8
Easy	Feb. 1, 1951	Air	1
Baker-2	Feb. 2, 1951	Air	8
Fox	Feb. 6, 1951	Air	22

See also ATMOSPHERIC NUCLEAR TESTING.

Operation REDWING

Operation REDWING was a series of 17 nuclear atmospheric tests conducted at ENEWETAK and BIKINI in the period May–July 1956. In the following table, the nearest island to the detonation is shown, with the atoll indicated as "E" for Enewetak and "B" for Bikini. The REDWING test series contributed strongly to the radioactive legacy on the islands of both atolls.

Due to the crowded schedule of tests, the long supply lines from the United States, and several delays because of faulty equipment, the original test schedule

Navy Spectators. At many of the atmospheric tests conducted at Enewetak and Bikini, spectators witnessed the shot from ships more than 10 miles away, through smoked-glass lenses. This eerie photo was taken by the light of a pre-dawn detonation. (Library of Congress)

was altered several times. The listing provided shows the actual date of the test, local time. The dates would be one day earlier in U.S. local time.

TEST	DATE	TYPE	LOCATION	YIELD
Lacrosse	May 5, 1956	Ground	Runit, E.	20+kt
Cherokee	May 21, 1956	Air Drop	Namu, B.	3+ mt
Zuni	May 28, 1956	Ground	Eninman, B.	3+ mt
Yuma	May 28, 1956	Tower	Aomon, E.	>1 kt
Erie	May 31, 1956	Tower	Runit, E.	>20 kt
Seminole	June 6, 1956	Ground	Bogon, E.	13.7 kt
Flathead	June 12, 1956	Barge	Yurochi, B.	low
Blackfoot	June 12, 1956	Tower	Runit, E.	low
Inca	June 22, 1956	Tower	Rojoru, E.	15 kt
Dakota	June 26, 1956	Barge	Yorochi, B.	<100kt
Kickapoo	June 14, 1956	Tower	Aomon, E.	>1 kt
Osage	June 16, 1956	Air Drop	Runit, E.	>100kt
Mohawk	July 3, 1956	Tower	Ebireru, E.	<100kt
Apache	July 9, 1956	Barge	Engebi, E.	3+mt
Navajo	July 11, 1956	Barge	Yorochi, B.	4+mt
Tewa	July 21, 1956	Barge	Yorochi, B.	4+mt
Huron	July 22, 1956	Barge	Engebi, E.	<100kt

The announced purpose of the test series was to develop a variety of nuclear and thermonuclear weapons. Some of the larger tests demonstrated that the HYDROGEN BOMB DESIGNS were quite successful. As in other tests, military experts were able to evaluate weapons effects such as blast, heat, FALLOUT, and radiation on equipment and ground installations.

Operation SANDSTONE

Operation SANDSTONE was the second postwar series of atmospheric nuclear tests, conducted in April and May 1948 in the ENEWETAK atoll in the Pacific. It consisted of a series of three tests.

SHOT	DATE	TYPE	KILOTONS
X-ray	April 14, 1948	Tower Shot	37
Yoke	April 30, 1948	Tower Shot	49
Zebra	May 14, 1948	Tower Shot	18

SANDSTONE was conducted by Task Force 7 under the command of General John E. Hull, who operated from the command ship USS Mt. McKinley. The nuclear devices were detonated on 200-foot towers, and they were used to prove new design principles worked out at LOS ALAMOS. Air-sampling aircraft collected radioactive materials that were flown back to the United States for measurement.

See also ATMOSPHERIC NUCLEAR TESTING.

Operation TEAPOT

Operation TEAPOT was a series of 14 atmospheric nuclear tests conducted at the NEVADA TEST SITE over the period February–May, 1955. Nine of the tests had yields under 10 kilotons, and the higher yield shots were fired from towers 500 feet or more in height to minimize FALLOUT from dust picked up from the ground.

One of the major purposes of TEAPOT was to test small-diameter boosted nuclear weapons suitable for mounting in missiles.

TEST	DATE
Zucchini	May 15
Turk	March 7
Apple 1	March 29
Apple 2	May 5
Moth	n.a.
Tesla	n.a.
Post	n.a

n.a. = not available

Operation TUMBLER-SNAPPER

Operation TUMBLER-SNAPPER was a series of eight nuclear weapons tests conducted at the NEVADA TEST SITE in the period April–June 1952.

TEST	DATE	TYPE	YIELD
Able	April 1, 1952	Airdrop	1 kt
Baker	April 15, 1952	Airdrop	1 kt
Charlie	April 22, 1952	Airdrop	31 kt
Dog	May 1, 1952	Airdrop	19 kt
Easy	May 7, 1952	Tower	12 kt
Fox	May 25, 1952	Tower	11 kt
George	June 1, 1952	Tower	15 kt
How	June 5, 1952	Tower	14 kt

The test provided training for many of the personnel who would later participate in the Operation Ivy series, particularly including the air-sampling crews that would retrieve radioactive materials by aircraft.

Operation UPSHOT-KNOTHOLE

Operation UPSHOT-KNOTHOLE was a series of 11 atmospheric nuclear tests conducted at the NEVADA TEST SITE in the period March–June, 1953. As in the other test series with double names, some of the tests were for the purpose of testing designs and diagnostic equipment, while others yielded data about weapons effects. Some of the tests combined both weapons-effects and design evaluation.

TEST	DATE	TYPE	YIELD
Annie	March 17, 1953	Tower	16 kt
Nancy	March 24, 1953	Tower	24 kt
Ruth	March 31, 1953	Tower	0.2 kt
Dixie	April 6, 1953	Air Drop	11 kt
Ray	April 11, 1953	Tower	0.2 kt
Badger	April 18, 1953	Tower	23 kt
Simon	April 25, 1953	Tower	43 kt
Encore	May 8, 1953	Air Drop	27 kt
Harry	May 19, 1953	Tower	32 kt
Grable	May 25, 1953	Gun	15 kt
Climax	June 4, 1953	Air Drop	61 kt

The UPSHOT part of the series consisted of five shots by LOS ALAMOS, primarily related to diagnostic experiments, and two shots by LAWRENCE LIVERMORE NATIONAL LABORATORY to check new weapons designs. Three shots in the KNOTHOLE part of the series were primarily designed to evaluate weapons effects. The Grable test was an atomic artillery shell fired from a 280-millimeter cannon.

Grable shot, Operation UPSHOT-KNOTHOLE. In this test, on May 25, 1953, a nuclear artillery shell yielded 15 kilotons. (U.S. Army)

Among the weapons effects tested was the placement of 50 automobiles at various distances from the tower on the first shot (Annie) as well as the construction of ordinary frame houses with test dummies to provide evidence of the weapon's destructive force on structures and human beings. The automobiles that were located at a distance of 10 blocks from ground zero provided protection from radiation and could be driven away safely, as long as the windows had been slightly open to prevent the crushing of the car from differential pressure. The yield of the weapon in the Annie shot was higher than that at HIROSHIMA. Another conclusion from the tests was that basement fallout shelters provided protection from both blast and radiation effects.

Many of the results of Annie were filmed and became part of the effort over the next few years to enhance civil defense against possible nuclear attack.

Over 15,000 troops participated in Exercise Desert Rock V, including service personnel from the army, navy, marines, and air force. Troops were stationed in advanced positions during all of the shots in the series, and some volunteers occupied spots as close as 6,000 feet from ground zero in some of the tests. Most combat troops were stationed at distances about two miles from the detonation.

Oppenheimer, J. Robert (1904–1967)   *American physicist who led the American effort to build an atomic bomb during World War II*

J. Robert Oppenheimer was one of the central figures in the early history of the atomic age, often called "the father of the atomic bomb." The controversies sur-

J. Robert Oppenheimer. Father of the American atomic bomb, Oppenheimer lost his security clearance after he opposed the development of the hydrogen bomb. (National Archives and Records Administration)

rounding him made him the center of political issues in the mid-1950s, a full decade after the work that had produced the nuclear weapon.

Oppenheimer was born on April 22, 1904, in New York City, the son of a successful businessman. He was a child prodigy, learning Greek and giving a paper before the New York Mineralogical Club before he turned 12. He attended Harvard College, graduating with honors in three years, in 1925. Oppenheimer then went to Göttingen, Germany, a thriving center for the study of nuclear physics, where he completed his doctorate in 1927. He was fluent in both French and German.

After working in physics research in Leiden and Zurich for two years, Oppenheimer returned to the United States to accept two teaching positions. One was at the University of California at Berkeley and the other was at the California Institute of Technology in Pasadena. Between 1929 and 1942, he worked at both institutions, traveling by train between northern and southern California, teaching six months at one institution and six months at the other.

During the 1930s, Oppenheimer developed a strong reputation as a teacher, and, at the same time,

he continued to publish papers on the nature of the atomic nucleus, cosmic rays, the use of the cyclotron, and the nature of stars with neutron cores. As a teacher, he was regarded as brilliant, and he had a reputation as a charming and engaging host at informal gatherings at his home. His interests ranged far beyond physics, including the study of the Sanskrit language so that he could read Hindu religious materials in the original.

In his early years he had insulated himself from the world around him, learning of the stock market crash of 1929 several months after it occurred. He took up an intense interest in world affairs. He joined the teachers' union, became engaged in efforts to rescue Jews from Germany, and began to vote in elections. Like many American and British intellectuals of the 1930s, he supported the Loyalists in the Spanish Civil War against the fascist insurgents. He contributed $100 a month to the cause, a sum worth over $1,000 by the standards of the year 2000. This and other causes brought him in contact with many left-wing political activists and he supported many of their positions. He dated one woman who had belonged to the Communist Party and married another, Katherine (Kitty) Dallet, who had also belonged. His brother Frank was also a member of the party.

In October 1942, General Leslie GROVES asked Oppenheimer to assume the research direction of the effort to produce an atomic bomb, over the objections of army counterintelligence officers who believed his left-wing political background made him a risky choice. The project, established under the U.S. Army Corps of Engineers, was code-named the MANHATTAN ENGINEER DISTRICT (MED) and came to be known as the "Manhattan Project." Although Oppenheimer's politics continued to make him suspect in the eyes of some of the military officers engaged in the project, Groves warmly supported Oppenheimer as the best choice to help bring top scientists into the project.

Oppenheimer was influential in helping to select the site for the research at LOS ALAMOS, New Mexico. As a young man, he had taken vacations in New Mexico, and he knew of the location on the mesa above the Rio Grande north of Santa Fe from horseback trips. A boys' ranch school there formed the nucleus of the settlement. The setting had several things to recommend it: It was isolated and could be secured readily by placing a gate on the access road, had an awe-inspiring view of the Jemez and Sangre de Cristo Mountains, and had air that was clear and healthy. Oppenheimer had always enjoyed the desert country, and he saw the location as a chance to practice physics in a spot he loved. General Groves accepted advice from Oppenheimer on this point, agreeing that the scientists should be assembled at a single laboratory in a remote location to work on bomb design. By July 1945, over 4,000 people had formed the community that produced the first atomic weapons.

Although Oppenheimer had no experience as a laboratory administrator, his reputation throughout the physics community as a theoretician and his engaging personality proved assets in the post of scientific director. He soon built up a team that included many of the leading physicists in the nation, including many who had emigrated from Europe.

A major issue at the laboratory under Oppenheimer's administration was the problem of security. The site was fenced in, all phone calls and mail were monitored and censored, staff were followed by federal agents when they left the site, and many visiting scientists had to come under assumed names. A traditional means of maintaining secrecy in military projects was to compartmentalize information so that only a very few senior individuals knew all aspects of the work. Most researchers would concentrate in their own specialized and often narrow area, and they would not be familiar with progress in other areas.

Despite the military demand for compartmentalization, Oppenheimer insisted that information be shared between groups with frequent seminars discussing results and progress. The method helped spur creative work, particularly the solution to the problem of IMPLOSION required of a plutonium-fueled weapon. At the same time, however, the lack of compartmentalization made it easier for scientists who sought to spy for the Soviet government to gather details. Among those who were able to assemble information while participating in the research and to send it to the Soviets was Klaus FUCHS. Fuchs had emigrated from Germany to Great Britain, and he was then sent by the British to help on the project. Fuchs's espionage was not uncovered until 1950.

Oppenheimer sometimes returned to his home in Berkeley, and in one incident that later became the center of a controversy, he was approached by a friend, Haakon CHEVALIER. Chevalier suggested that Oppenheimer could relay information through a contact to the Soviets. Oppenheimer immediately rejected the idea and reprimanded Chevalier for suggesting it. Chevalier later claimed his comments were entirely misunderstood and that he had not intended to act as an espionage go-between.

In any case, Oppenheimer did not immediately report the approach to the security officers at Los Alamos, as operational security procedures required. He sought to protect Chevalier from the embarrassment of an investigation. When Oppenheimer did finally report the incident, Groves reprimanded him for the delay, but he accepted his explanation and the incident was apparently closed.

The bomb work was successful, and the first PLUTONIUM device was tested in southern New Mexico at the TRINITY test on July 16, 1945. Oppenheimer and many of the scientists from Los Alamos attended the demonstration. Oppenheimer was later quoted as remarking while the mushroom cloud ascended, "I am Shiva, destroyer of worlds." It was a line from the sacred Hindu text, the Bhagavad-Gita, that he had read in the original language. At the urging of President Harry TRUMAN, Oppenheimer hastened the production of the first weapon and its delivery to a target in Japan.

Oppenheimer participated in a panel to discuss how the weapon should be employed. Although some scientists had argued for a demonstration of the weapon over an uninhabited area of Japan before using it against a populated center, Oppenheimer and others on the panel opposed the idea. For one thing, only two weapons would be ready for use in early August. If the demonstration were unsuccessful, or if the Japanese were unimpressed with the result, the surprise effect of the weapon in bringing about a Japanese surrender might be mitigated. The morality of this decision has been much debated in the decades since 1945, and Oppenheimer's part in the decision appeared to have troubled him greatly in retrospect.

With the publication of the Smyth Report (by Henry D. SMYTH), the general public learned of the role of Oppenheimer. He soon became popularly regarded as "the father of the atom bomb." In the immediate postwar years, Oppenheimer participated in the drafting of the Acheson-Lilienthal Report, which advocated a system of international control of atomic weapons and atomic energy. After the establishment of the ATOMIC ENERGY COMMISSION in 1946, Oppenheimer served on the GENERAL ADVISORY COMMITTEE (GAC) as chairman until 1952. The GAC was charged with providing a scientific viewpoint on issues of nuclear policy, and, as the former scientific director of the Manhattan Project, his opinion was highly respected by other scientists in the field. In 1947, he moved to

Princeton, New Jersey, where he took an appointment as director of the Institute for Advanced Study.

An incessant cigarette smoker, Oppenheimer died in 1967 at the age of 63 from throat cancer.

See also OPPENHEIMER'S SECURITY HEARING.

Suggested Reading

Haakon Chevalier, *Oppenheimer, The Story of a Friendship.* New York: George Braziller, 1965.

Leslie Groves, *Now It Can Be Told.* New York: Harper and Row, 1962.

Richard Hewlett and Jack Holl, *Atoms for Peace and War, 1953–1961: Eisenhower and the Atomic Energy Commission.* Berkeley: University of California Press, 1989.

Oppenheimer's Security Hearing

J. Robert Oppenheimer became the center of a national and international controversy in the early 1950s. As the ATOMIC ENERGY COMMISSION (AEC) and the president worked with the decision whether to build a hydrogen bomb, which would be vastly more destructive than the atomic bomb, Oppenheimer, along with other scientists on the GENERAL ADVISORY COMMITTEE, advised against it.

This position angered President Harry TRUMAN and others who believed the weapon should be developed, especially after it became clear that the Soviet Union had developed an atomic bomb and tested it in August 1949. Among others, Edward TELLER, a Hungarian emigré scientist who had worked on the Manhattan Project, warmly advocated the construction of a thermonuclear weapon based on atomic fusion.

With the 1950 confession of Klaus FUCHS to his earlier espionage at LOS ALAMOS, Oppenheimer's actions with regard to security at the laboratory once again came under scrutiny. In December 1953, the AEC removed Oppenheimer's security clearance on the grounds that his loyalty to the United States was questionable. Removal of his clearance would mean that he could no longer have access to much of the research in his own field, particularly that conducted at the weapons laboratory that he himself had founded. Oppenheimer asked for a hearing to review the decision to withdraw his clearance.

The closed-door hearings over a period of three weeks in early 1954 took on the nature of a trial.

Oppenheimer defended himself against charges that his opposition to the thermonuclear weapon was based on divided loyalty: His associations during the 1930s demonstrated that he was sympathetic to the Communist Party, and his handling of the Haakon CHEVALIER case represented a serious violation of security procedures. Later the transcript of the hearings was published under the title "In the Matter of J. Robert Oppenheimer," and a play by the same title was widely performed and read.

The security review board, by a two-to-one vote, found Oppenheimer loyal, but members found his opposition to the hydrogen bomb questionable. The commissioners of the AEC reviewed the decision of the board, and they decided to continue to deny him a clearance on the grounds that he suffered from defects of character. Four of the commissioners voted to continue the denial of a clearance, and only one, Henry SMYTH, voted to reinstate the clearance. The final decision by the commissioners was dated June 28, 1954.

The fact that Oppenheimer had been punished, in effect, for his political views and his opposition to the hydrogen bomb made him seem to be a martyr in the eyes of many. Many supporters saw him as a man who stood for what he believed in, who suffered for that stand and for those beliefs. His opponents continued to doubt his loyalty and held that his rank as a leading scientist did not excuse him from the security rules that bound others. To some extent the division between supporters and opponents reflected the divisions between liberal opinion and conservative opinion in the United States in the 1950s and 1960s.

In 1963, Oppenheimer was awarded the Enrico FERMI prize for his work in nuclear physics, and the medal was bestowed by President Lyndon JOHNSON. The award of the prize seemed an attempt by the federal government (during a Democratic administration) to offer an apology for the 1953–1954 security proceedings and, at the same time, a recognition of his important work in bringing the nuclear weapon to completion.

See also OPPENHEIMER, J. ROBERT.

Osirak (Tammuz-1) Reactor   *See* IRAQ.

P

Paducah *See* WEAPONS PRODUCTION COMPLEX.

Pakistan

During the 1980s and 1990s, experts following the story of nuclear proliferation frequently ranked Pakistan as a "threshold" nuclear weapons state, a potential member of the nuclear club. After the tests by INDIA of nuclear devices early in May 1998, Pakistan conducted a series of underground nuclear tests on May 28 and May 30, 1998.

Ever since the partition of India following independence, Pakistan has been engaged in a series of conflicts, sometimes erupting into war with India. In 1971, after the defeat of Pakistan, the eastern section of the nation declared its independence as Bangladesh. Following that war, Pakistan began its nuclear weapons program in 1972, and after India detonated its first nuclear device in 1974, the Pakistani program moved ahead with new vigor.

In 1977 and 1979, the United States cut off military and economic aid to Pakistan in an effort to get that nation to terminate its nuclear weapons program. However, following the Soviet invasion of Af-ghanistan in 1979–1980, the United States lifted the sanctions against Pakistan. In 1985, the U.S. Congress passed the PRESSLER AMENDMENT, which required the U.S. president to certify, each year, that Pakistan had not acquired nuclear weapons in order for military and economic aid to continue to flow to the country.

By 1990, President George H.W. BUSH refused to issue the certification on the grounds that Pakistan had continued to work on assembling the cores for nuclear weapons. Through the mid-1990s, Pakistan did not produce weapons-grade uranium and continued to claim that it had not assembled weapons. Meanwhile, both President Bush and President Bill CLINTON refused to sell to Pakistan an order of F-16 aircraft, even though they had been partially paid for by Pakistan.

Studies by the U.S. Department of Defense in 1996 and 1997 included estimates that Pakistan had developed and had ready to assemble on short notice a number of nuclear weapons estimated between 10 and 25. Thus when the May 1998 tests occurred, they simply confirmed that Pakistan had moved ahead to assemble the weapons, apparently in response to the earlier tests by India that month.

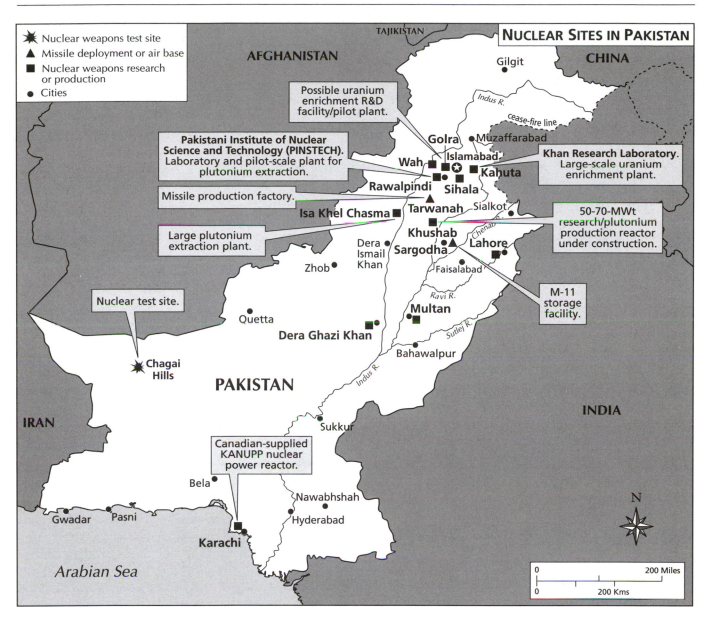

NUCLEAR SITES IN PAKISTAN

Legend:
- ✴ Nuclear weapons test site
- ▲ Missile deployment or air base
- ■ Nuclear weapons research or production
- ● Cities

Map labels:
- Possible uranium enrichment R&D facility/pilot plant.
- Pakistani Institute of Nuclear Science and Technology (PINSTECH). Laboratory and pilot-scale plant for plutonium extraction.
- Missile production factory.
- Large plutonium extraction plant.
- Nuclear test site.
- Khan Research Laboratory. Large-scale uranium enrichment plant.
- 50-70-MWt research/plutonium production reactor under construction.
- M-11 storage facility.
- Canadian-supplied KANUPP nuclear power reactor.

Countries/regions: TAJIKISTAN, AFGHANISTAN, CHINA, PAKISTAN, IRAN, INDIA, Arabian Sea

Cities and sites: Gilgit, Muzaffarabad, Golra, Islamabad, Wah, Kahuta, Rawalpindi, Sihala, Sialkot, Tarwanah, Isa Khel Chasma, Khushab, Lahore, Dera Ismail Khan, Sargodha, Zhob, Faisalabad, Quetta, Multan, Dera Ghazi Khan, Bahawalpur, Chagai Hills, Sukkur, Bela, Nawabhshah, Gwadar, Pasni, Hyderabad, Karachi

Rivers: Indus R., cease-fire line, Chenab, Ravi R., Sutlej R.

Scale: 0 — 200 Miles / 0 — 200 Kms

N (compass)

Pakistan's nuclear facilities, with the exception of three reactors, have not been subject to INTERNATIONAL ATOMIC ENERGY AGENCY (IAEA) safeguards. The three reactors include a power reactor KANUPP in Karachi, which is a heavy-water moderated, natural URANIUM 137 megawatt-electrical (MWe) reactor, and two research reactors, PARR-1 and PARR-2.

Among the other facilities maintained by Pakistan are the following that observers have claimed are related to the nuclear weapons program:

Possible weapons assembly plant
Pakistan Ordnance Factory
Wah

Reprocessing pilot facility
Pakistan Institute of Nuclear Science and Technology (PINSTECH)
Rawalpindi

Large scale centrifuge facility for Uranium enrichment
Weapons fabrication facility
Khan Research Laboratories
Kahuta

Plutonium production reactor, 50 megawatt-thermal
Khusab

Nuclear weapons test site
Chagai Hills (near Afghan border)

Unfinished plutonium reprocessing plant
Chasma

Heavy-water production plants
Multan
Karachi

In addition to the Canadian-supplied power reactor KANUPP, Pakistan has planned two other power reactors, CHASMA-1 and CHASMA-2. CHASMA-1 was scheduled to begin operations in 1998. These light-water, low-enriched power reactors, rated at 310 MWe, were supplied by china.

See also PRESSLER AMENDMENT; PROLIFERATION.

Palomares

On January 17, 1966, a B-52 bomber returning from a flight near the Soviet border in the Chrome Dome exercises collided with a KC-135 tanker during refueling over Spain. Both aircraft blew up high over Palomares, a small fishing village on Spain's southern Mediterranean coast. Four hydrogen bombs fell, automatically deploying safety parachutes. However, some of the parachutes did not fully open.

Three of the four bombs crashed among the fields and houses of the village. One of these broke open, and a high-explosive detonation scattered PLUTONIUM

KC 135 Tanker. An accident during a refueling similar to this one led to one of the most serious "Broken Arrow" incidents, in which four nuclear weapons fell near the village of Palomares in Spain. Pictured here is a modern KC135R tanker safely refueling a B1-B bomber. (U.S. Air Force)

from another. Within a few days, U.S. Air Force crews and specialists from the DEFENSE ATOMIC SUPPORT AGENCY found the three weapons and began decontamination and soil removal to prevent risk to the villagers. While the crews cut down plants and took away soil, the press began to focus on the fourth, lost weapon that had fallen into the sea. The villagers' economy was based on raising tomatoes for export and on fishing. About 650 acres of ground were seriously contaminated, according to the radiation survey.

The U.S. Navy brought in deep-diving submarines, including *Alvin* and *Aluminaut,* in the attempt to recover the fourth weapon over the next few months. After locating the bomb, it was difficult to bring it to the surface because of the hazard that the weapon would slip down into a deep undersea crevice. The navy finally succeeded in bringing up the missing bomb on April 7, 1966. In general, the U.S. Department of Defense did not discuss details of the procedure with the press. Some critics charged that that policy created more suspicion and public hysteria than would a more open sharing of information. On the other hand, the focus on the bomb lost at sea meant that journalists paid less attention to the more immediate danger from the plutonium that had been scattered from the bombs ashore.

For the Department of Defense, the public relations and diplomatic side of the cleanup were as difficult to manage as the recovery and the physical side of the accident. The U.S. government made cash payments to a number of individuals who submitted justified damage claims for their lost crops and or lost fishing income.

In later years, the mayor of the town, Antonia Flores, who had observed the accident as a child, began a vigorous campaign to gain access to medical and radiological records relating to the accident. In 1985, experts admitted that plutonium residue could still be detected in the community and among the population but that the levels were below those deemed dangerous. Other experts, including Dr. E. R. Farre at the Board of Scientific Research in Barcelona, disputed the claim that the plutonium residue was harmless.

The commander of the 16th Air Force, Major General Delmar Wilson, was responsible for coordinating the Palomares recovery efforts. He was later quoted as saying that the air force was at the time unprepared to provide adequate detection and monitoring, especially in a remote area of a foreign country.

See also BROKEN ARROW.

Suggested Reading

Defense Nuclear Agency, *Palomares Summary Report: Field Command, Defense Nuclear Agency,* Technology and Analysis Directorate, Kirtland Air Force Base, New Mexico 87115, Accession #NV0067458, Department of Energy, Nevada Coordination and Information Center.

F. Lewis, *One of H-Bombs Is Missing.* New York: McGraw-Hill, 1967.

Tad Szulc, *The Bombs of Palomares.* New York: Gollancz, 1967.

Pantex

About 20 miles northeast of Amarillo, Texas, near the center of the Texas Panhandle, is a large facility that once was the main plant for assembling nuclear weapons. In the 1990s, Pantex became the site devoted to the dismantling of the U.S. nuclear warheads, when the number of weapons held by the United States was drawn down as a consequence of arms control agreements with the Soviet Union. Under the INTERMEDIATE-RANGE NUCLEAR FORCES (INF) treaty and the START I agreement, the United States retired many weapons. Although the agreements only required that the delivery vehicles be dismantled, the United States proceeded to dismantle completely the warheads as well.

This factory traces its origins back to World War II. Between February and November 1942, the U.S. Army Corps of Engineers built a bomb factory near Amarillo. Within 10 months of the start of work, the assembly lines produced the first high-explosive bombs. The World War II plant was located on over 16,000 acres of land, had 13 administrative and manufacturing zones, and also contained a residential village with over 900 housing units complete with shopping center.

During World War II, the factory produced large numbers of 105–millimeter artillery shells, 500 pound bombs, and millions of pounds of high explosive. After the war, the factory was shut down. In the period 1945 to 1951, atomic weapons had been handmade at Los Alamos, New Mexico, and at the Sandia Laboratory in Albuquerque, New Mexico, but with stepped up production after the Soviets exploded their first nuclear device, the United States moved to mass production. Pantex would be the assembly point. In 1951, the ATOMIC ENERGY COMMISSION (AEC) took over one of the manufacturing zones built by the army corps during the war that had never been used. The AEC modified some buildings and built connecting ramps and access roads.

Crews began to move in during November 1951. Staff were sent to Los Alamos to be trained in handling the high-explosive components of the nuclear weapons. With the heightened arms race of the cold war, Pantex became a central part of the American nuclear weapons establishment. When the work of the AEC was transferred first to the ENERGY RESEARCH AND DEVELOPMENT ADMINISTRATION in 1974 and then to the United States DEPARTMENT OF ENERGY (DOE) in 1978, Pantex remained part of the nuclear weapons production complex.

During the cold war, Pantex served primarily as the assembly center for warheads, following designs developed at LOS ALAMOS and at Livermore National Laboratories. Production engineering drawings and detailed manufacturing plans for weapons and their modifications would be developed at Sandia National Laboratory and put into production at the Pantex plant. Parts manufactured elsewhere in the weapons complex, such as initiators and weapons casings, would be assembled together at the Texas location.

With the signing of mutual disarmament treaties between the United States and the Soviet Union, Pantex began to switch over to the work of disassembly of atomic and hydrogen bombs. The experienced staff and the safety facilities at the plant proved ideal for this new role. DOE put extra personnel on extra shifts to keep up with the flow of weapons out of the stockpile in 1992 and 1993.

Pauling, Linus (1901–1994)   *American Nobel Prize–winning chemist who was a leading opponent of the development and production of nuclear weapons*

Pauling was born in Portland, Oregon, on February 28, 1901, and won scholarships to Oregon State College at Corvallis, graduating in 1922. He earned a doctorate in chemistry at the California Institute of Technology, where he continued to teach and conduct research for more than three decades.

Pauling's specialty was organic chemistry, a field that he revolutionized in the 1920s through investigation of the nature of the chemical bond and through his application of quantum physics to the study of chemistry. He proposed a theory of "resonance" that explained how complex organic molecules would shift between different structures, laying the theoretical groundwork for the later creation of many drugs, dyes, plastics, and synthetic fibers. His work *The Nature of* the Chemical Bond and the Structure of Molecules and Crystals became an essential work of modern chemistry. He succeeded in making synthetic antibodies, and in 1949 he produced a major study of sickle-cell anemia. In 1951, he and his co-researcher, Robert Corey, described the atomic structure of proteins.

In the late 1940s, Pauling became convinced that nuclear testing and the nuclear arms race represented a major threat to the environment and human health. He began to speak out publicly on the topic, and he lost his teaching position. The U.S. State Department revoked his passport, but when he received the NOBEL PRIZE for chemistry in 1954 for his work on chemical bonding, the department relented so that he could travel abroad to receive the prize. In 1958, he published a book, *No More War*. In 1957–1958 he circulated a petition against nuclear testing, obtaining over 11,000 signatures from scientists around the world.

Pauling's campaign against nuclear testing may have contributed to the LIMITED TEST BAN TREATY signed in 1963. Pauling received a Nobel Peace Prize in 1962 for his efforts to ban nuclear testing, and he was one of very few Nobel laureates to win both the scientific award and the peace prize.

Pauling remained active in various antiwar movements, and he continued his scientific work as well. He won a large audience for his 1970 book *Vitamin C and the Common Cold*. He argued that vitamin C and other nutrients could play a part in preventing cancer, a view later accepted by many in the medical community.

He remained an active researcher and writer, continuing to publish popular works in the field of health and nutrition. He died on August 19, 1994 at the age of 93.

Peaceful Nuclear Explosions   *See* PLOWSHARE.

Peacekeeper

The *Peacekeeper*, or LGM 118, was a three-stage, solid-fueled INTERCONTINENTAL BALLISTIC MISSILE (ICBM), introduced into the American arsenal in 1986. It was capable of carrying up to 10 multiple independently targetable warheads. It had a low CIRCULAR ERROR PROBABLE. Published specifications of the missile were as follows:

Peacekeeper. *At the height of the cold war in the 1980s, the multiple warhead* Peacekeeper *missile represented a mainstay of the U.S. nuclear arsenal.* (U.S. Air Force)

Range: 9,600 kilometers
Length: 21.6 meters
Diameter: 2.34 meters
Launch Weight: 88,450 kilograms

Peierls, Rudolf Ernst (1907–1995)   *German-born physicist who worked in Great Britain and then in the United States and who played a central role in the development of the atomic bomb*

Rudolf Peierls was born in 1907 in Berlin and studied in both Germany and Switzerland. Like many German scientists, he left Germany when Hitler came to power and moved to Britain. In the period 1937 to 1940, he was a professor of physics at Birmingham University.

During this period, Otto FRISCH and Klaus FUCHS studied under him.

In 1940, Peierls devised the concept of a CRITICAL MASS of fissionable material. Together, he and Frisch estimated the energy that could be released in a nuclear CHAIN REACTION in URANIUM and suggested to the British government that a weapon utilizing FISSION energy could be constructed. Peierls was placed in charge of a small group studying the issue (the MAUD committee). In 1943, Peierls, Frisch, and others from Britain moved to the United States to assist on the MANHATTAN ENGINEER DISTRICT. Peierls served as the deputy head of the British mission at LOS ALAMOS under James CHADWICK.

After the war, Peierls returned to Birmingham University, where he taught until 1963. From 1963 to 1974 he taught at Oxford, and he was knighted in 1968. He died in 1995.

Suggested Reading

Richard Rhodes, *The Making of the Atomic Bomb.* New York: Simon and Schuster, 1988.

Pelindaba   *See* SOUTH AFRICA.

Permissive Action Link (PAL)

In 1960, technicians at Sandia developed the first Permissive Action Link (PAL), a device that was used to ensure that nuclear weapons could not be detonated unless a positive order with a coded key was officially put into the link. PALs were used not only on American weapons stored in the United States and overseas but also were offered to the Soviet Union, France, and Great Britain so that they could ensure that none of their weapons could be stolen or misused without proper authority. Later generations of PALs used systems such as those on automatic teller machines, requiring a multidigit number or code to be entered, with a shutdown after several incorrect tries.

Pershing I and II

The *Pershing* missiles developed by the United States were medium intermediate-range ballistic missiles, representing part of the intermediate nuclear forces deployed to Europe in defense of the NORTH ATLANTIC TREATY ORGANIZATION (NATO). The *Pershing* I was regarded as a medium-range, theater weapon with an announced range of 450 miles, and it was first deployed in August 1963. The announced yield of the warheads was 60 to 400 kt. The *Pershing* Ia began replacing the *Pershing* Is in 1969, with improved ease of maintenance, lower unit cost, and increased flexibility.

The *Pershing* II, under development beginning in 1974 and deployed to Germany as part of the announced theater nuclear force buildup endorsed by NATO in 1979, had an announced range of about 1,000 miles. It had an announced yield of 5–50 kt. The Soviets claimed the range of the *Pershing* II was much higher. Both *Pershing* Is and IIs had solid-fuel motors, and both systems were highly mobile, capable of being moved from site to site and launched by truck-mounted systems. The *Pershing* II had much improved accuracy and lower CIRCULAR ERROR PROBABLE than the *Pershing* I or Ia. With its increased range and accuracy, it represented a match for new Soviet missiles, the SS-20s, installed in Eastern Europe in the late 1970s.

The *Pershing* I, Ia, and II were all manufactured by Martin Company (after 1961, Martin-Marietta Corporation). Crews were trained at the U.S. Army Artillery and Missile School at Fort Sill, Oklahoma. In 1983, another training facility to assist in the transition from the *Pershing* Ia to the II was established.

Together with U.S. Air Force ground-launched CRUISE MISSILES deployed in Britain, Belgium, Italy, and the Netherlands, the army's *Pershing* IIs deployed in West Germany represented the "Euromissiles" that were the subject of intense public debate through the period 1981 to 1985.

As the *Pershing* IIs were first deployed to Germany in 1983, some *Pershing* Is were withdrawn. Under the INTERMEDIATE-RANGE NUCLEAR FORCES (INF) treaty signed on December 8, 1987 (ratified May 27, 1988), all the *Pershing* IIs and the remaining *Pershing* Is were withdrawn.

A total of 234 *Pershing* IIs and 169 *Pershing* Is were covered by the treaty. The last *Pershing* Is were eliminated in July 1989, and the last *Pershing* IIs eliminated in 1991. Most of the destroyed *Pershing* rocket engines were static fired at the Longhorn Army Ammunition Plant in Texas, and the casings were then crushed. The operation, which began in September and October 1988, was observed by inspectors from the Soviet Union and representatives of the United States ON-SITE INSPECTION AGENCY. Launchers and other equipment related to the *Pershings* were destroyed in Germany.

A few *Pershing* missiles that had been disabled were retained for display. *Pershing* IIs were put on exhibit at the Field Artillery Museum, Fort Sill, Oklahoma, with others at Cape Canaveral, Florida, White Sands, New Mexico, and Langley Air Force Base in Virginia, as well as at the Smithsonian Air and Space Museum in Washington, D.C. Both the Smithsonian and the Soviet Military Museum in Moscow mounted a joint display of a disabled *Pershing* II and a Soviet SS-20 missile in January 1990.

Philadelphia Navy Yard

In order to continue with the NAVAL RESEARCH LABORATORY'S (NRL) work with liquid thermal diffusion, the U.S. Navy had to identify a facility that would provide the means to construct a 300-column pilot plant. After surveying the naval shore establishments, planners determined that the Naval Boiler and Turbine Laboratory (NBTL) at the Philadelphia Navy Yard was an ideal location.

Rear Admiral Earle Mills, assistant chief of the Bureau of Ships, authorized construction of a 300-unit pilot plant at Philadelphia on November 17, 1943. He based his site selection on the availability of building space and cooling water and the considerable experience with both high-pressure steam and large-scale heavy construction of NBTL engineers.

Builders began construction of the facility on January 1, 1944. The NBTL oversaw the design, construction, and operation of equipment essential to supply steam and cooling water; the NRL held responsibility for the design of the columns and subsidiary equipment integral for their operation, in addition to the operation of the columns.

The NBTL housed the plant in half of a building originally designed to test turbines, located on the Navy Yard between First Street West and Second Street West, north of Rowan Avenue. The approximate dimensions of the plant were 164 feet by 81 feet, with one-half of the area at a level 10 feet below grade. All of the boilers and auxiliaries, with the exception of the condenser, were installed in the remaining space at ground level.

Given the experimental nature of the work, the navy staffed the plant mainly with technical personnel, most of whom were naval personnel. Philip H. Abelson and John I. Hoover of the NRL provided the technical direction. Captain T. A. Solberg from the Bureau

of Ships served as the project officer for the plant. Enlisted personnel from the NBTL operated the steam and water facilities.

As the plant neared completion in June 1944, the MANHATTAN ENGINEER DISTRICT (MED) decided to take a second look at liquid thermal diffusion as part of their enrichment of ^{235}U. The MED originally examined liquid thermal diffusion in December 1942 but had rejected its use on the basis that it did not produce URANIUM enriched to weapons grade. However, by 1944, the MED was behind schedule in uranium production and needed an additional method to aid the atomic bomb program.

J. Robert OPPENHEIMER brought the results of the NRL's experiments to the attention of General Leslie GROVES, as well as the potential worth of liquid thermal diffusion. General Groves sent a six-man reviewing committee to the Philadelphia plant on June 15, 1944. Their favorable report spurred the construction of a liquid thermal diffusion plant at OAK RIDGE, Tennessee.

General Groves visited the NRL on June 26 to obtain all available information. Officials at the Philadelphia plant turned over blueprints to him, and the MED issued orders to construct a 2,200 column plant, identical to the Philadelphia plant, in Oak Ridge.

The navy further assisted the MED by training four civilian and 10 enlisted army personnel from Oak Ridge in the operation of the Philadelphia plant. The soldiers arrived in Philadelphia in August 1944.

On September 2, the Philadelphia plant experienced an accident at 1:20 P.M. when a cylinder of uranium hexafluoride feed stock exploded in the transfer room, fracturing nearby steam pipes. When the steam mixed with the uranium hexafluoride, it created hydrogen fluoride, an extremely corrosive acid. The accident resulted in two deaths and eight injured personnel. After the accident, a navy judge advocate general investigation recommended improved safety procedures that were initiated in Oak Ridge.

After repairs to the Philadelphia plant, it continued to operate until 1946. Besides operating as a pilot plant, the Philadelphia installation sent more then 5,000 pounds of uranium hexafluoride containing 0.86% of ^{235}U to Oak Ridge. When the Philadelphia plant was shut down, the site was cleaned up, and all contaminated material was dumped at sea.

Suggested Reading

Philip H. Abelson, ed. *Liquid Thermal Diffusion*. Washington, D.C.: Naval Research Laboratory, 1958.

Ivan Amato, *Pushing the Horizon: Seventy-Five Years of High Stakes Science and Technology at the Naval Research Laboratory.* Washington, D.C.: Government Printing Office, 1998.

Vincent C. Jones, *Manhattan: The Army and the Atomic Bomb.* Washington, D.C.: Center for Military History, 1985.

Pike, Sumner (1891–1976)   *American financier who served on the Securities and Exchange Commission, the Office of Price Administration, and as a member of the U.S. Atomic Energy Commission*

Sumner Pike was a member of the ATOMIC ENERGY COMMISSION (AEC) from October 31, 1946, through December 15, 1951. When he left the commission, he had served the longest term among the first commissioners. Pike was born in a small fishing village in Maine, had been educated at Bowdoin College, and had made a fortune in Wall Street before retiring in 1939. He served as a member of the Securities and Exchange Commission and of the Office of Price Administration during World War II. He had retired again in 1946 before being nominated by President Harry TRUMAN to serve on the AEC.

Over time and as he became more familiar with the functions of the commission, he was noted for his independent positions. For example, he opposed the development of the hydrogen bomb, and he made up his own mind on many issues ranging from federal control of the town of OAK RIDGE to accepting requirements established by the Joint Chiefs of Staff for expansion of the nuclear weapons capacity following the Soviet development of an atomic bomb. From February 1950, when David LILIENTHAL resigned, until Gordon DEAN was appointed chairman in July 1950, Sumner Pike served as acting chairman of the Atomic Energy Commission.

Suggested Reading

Richard Hewlett and Francis Duncan, *Atomic Shield* (Vol. 2, *A History of the United States Atomic Energy Commission*), Washington, D.C.: U.S. Atomic Energy Commission, 1972.

Pile

The first nuclear reactors were built using graphite bricks. The standard industrial bricks served as refractory material to make structures in high-temperature ovens. When Enrico FERMI designed the first reactor at Chicago in 1942, the graphite served as a MODERATOR. Alternating solid bricks with hollowed-out bricks containing URANIUM in small spheres, the reactor was built by constructing a stack or "pile." In later years, as other materials, particularly water and heavy water, were used as moderators, the term "pile" was dropped in favor of the more generic term, nuclear reactor.

See also CHICAGO PILE-1.

Planck, Max Karl Ernst (1858–1947)   *German physicist who framed the quantum theory of atoms in 1900*

Max Planck postulated that energy is emitted in small indivisible amounts, which he called "quanta." He won the NOBEL PRIZE for this work in 1918. Albert EINSTEIN used Planck's concept to explain photoelectricity in 1905, and Niels BOHR applied Planck's concept to the atom itself in 1913.

Planck was born in Kiel in 1858 and studied in Munich. In 1888 he was appointed director of the Institute for Theoretical Physics in Berlin. He was president of the Kaiser Wilhelm Institute in 1930, but he resigned in 1937 in protest at Nazi treatment of Jewish scientists. In 1945, the Kaiser Wilhelm Institute was renamed the Max Planck Institute, and he was reappointed as president. He died in 1947.

Plowshare Program

"Plowshare" was the term applied by the ATOMIC ENERGY COMMISSION (AEC) to the use of nuclear explosives for peaceful purposes. These peaceful nuclear explosions (PNEs) were to be detonated underground for the purpose of heavy construction, for example, in the digging of canals. The term "plowshare" was derived from the biblical quote, "they shall beat their swords into plowshares" (Isaiah 2:4).

The canal concept would work as follows: A series of nuclear devices would be placed in deep shafts, as in an underground nuclear test. The shafts would be aligned so as to be under the pathway of the proposed canal. After detonation, the rock and earth surrounding the device would vaporize, causing the formation of a large underground chamber. Shortly after the detonation, the chamber would collapse, causing the earth above to fall, creating a subsidence crater at the surface. With the subsidence craters in a row, a deep channel would stretch along the route of the proposed canal. Then with earth-moving equipment, the canal could be shaped and later filled with water. In order to prevent radioactive release to the groundwater, devices with very low radioactive emission would be implanted, and the canals would be lined to prevent drainage down through the blast areas.

Other uses for PNEs included the concept of breaking up tight underground rock and sand formations in order to release natural gas. Other uses might be to shorten dangerous railroad curves and grades, removal of rapids to allow navigation in South American rivers, construction of dams for irrigation and power purposes, and excavation of harbors. One PNE plan that received considerable support during the administration of President Richard NIXON was the concept of a sea-level canal across Panama.

However, one of the difficulties with the concept was that even with very small nuclear devices with a very low level of radioactive emission, some FALLOUT was still likely. Even minute amounts of fallout beyond the borders of the nation conducting the activity would violate the terms of the LIMITED TEST BAN TREATY (LTBT) between the United States and the Soviet Union. Both the Soviets and some American officials regarded the LTBT as prohibiting all such fallout beyond the testing country, no matter how small.

A PNE in New Mexico in 1968, entitled Gasbuggy, had been designed to release natural gas, but the gas was too radioactive to market. Another PNE conducted at Rulison, Colorado, in 1969 was scheduled to be much deeper, but public opposition mounted, including a series of lawsuits. After the test, the gas released was also found to have increased radiation. Another gas-release test was conducted at Rio Blanco, Colorado, in 1973, but the underground fracture zones did not link up as planned. Popular opposition in Colorado was so severe that the state passed a constitutional amendment in 1974 prohibiting any future nuclear detonations for any purpose within the state.

The Rio Blanco test was the last under the Plowshare program in the United States. The Soviets continued using PNEs over the next years, not terminating their program until 1985.

See also UNDERGROUND NUCLEAR TESTS.

Pluto

Project Pluto was one of three efforts planned by the ATOMIC ENERGY COMMISSION to use nuclear power for propulsion of aircraft. The concept of using a reactor

to propel an airplane was designated AIRCRAFT NUCLEAR PROPULSION, and research and plans on this concept were developed over the period 1951 to 1961. A second plan, in the period 1955 to 1973, based on using nuclear rockets for propulsion of vehicles in outer space, was called PROJECT ROVER. Pluto was a scheme to use nuclear ramjets for propulsion of CRUISE MISSILES and unmanned bombers, developed over the period 1957 to 1964.

Ramjets had proven useful in World War II, achieving supersonic speeds with mechanically simple devices. Dubbed "flying stovepipes," ramjets worked by taking in air at the front of the missile, diffusing it over a heat source, and then funneling the expanded air through a nozzle to propel the machine forward. Ramjets only worked at high speeds and had to be boosted, usually with rockets, to the propulsion speed. The German *V-1* "buzz bombs" of World War II used ramjets, and U.S. researchers had developed several models in the postwar years. A nuclear ramjet would utilize a reactor to provide the heat.

In 1957 and 1958, planning studies of the nuclear ramjet principle projected a missile that could fly at three times the speed of sound, about 2,000 miles per hour, at low altitudes up to 1,000 feet. At that height, the missile could evade defensive radar. Plans called for a 600 megawatt-thermal, air-cooled reactor, shaped as a five-feet long, five-feet diameter cylinder. The reactor would only be fueled for a 10-hour life and would contain a core with thousands of ceramic fuel elements incorporating beryllium oxide and highly enriched URANIUM. Reactor temperatures would reach 2,500 degrees F.

LAWRENCE LIVERMORE NATIONAL LABORATORY constructed two test reactors for the Pluto program, designated Tory-II-A and Tory II-C. The first was designed to gather data on fuel, materials, and engineering and to test the system as a whole. The II-C reactor was designed to actually fit into a ramjet as an engine. To test the reactors at the NEVADA TEST SITE, a system to force the air through the stationary ramjet had to be developed, together with a heavily shielded structure in which to disassemble the reactors for study after testing.

The test sites for Rover and Pluto were built near each other on Jackass Flats at the test site. Pluto was highly classified at first, but even after it was publicly announced, the project received comparatively little publicity, whereas Rover and the aircraft project captured more attention. The first Tory reactor was tested in 1961, and Tory II-C, the ramjet reactor, was tested in May 1964. However, after a successful test of the ramjet engine, the Defense Department canceled further tests. Equipment from Pluto was locked away, and then some was loaned out to the Rover program. The site officially reverted to the Atomic Energy Commission in 1969. Altogether, about $133 million had been spent on the project.

The obscurity of the program and its having been bypassed despite the technical success of the testing have been attributed to a combination of secrecy surrounding the early project and the fact that the Defense Department did not develop an interest in cruise missiles at the time.

Suggested Reading

Barton Hacker, *Elements of Controversy: The Atomic Energy Commission and Radiation Safety in Nuclear Weapons Testing, 1947–1974.* Berkeley: University of California Press, 1994.

Plutonium

Plutonium, the element with atomic number 94, does not occur in nature except as a result of prehistoric nuclear excursions such as that proposed to explain the abnormal isotopic ratios of URANIUM at the OKLO MINE in Gabon. It has at least a dozen ISOTOPES ranging in mass number from 232 to 246. ^{239}Pu and ^{241}Pu undergo (n, fis) reactions with both thermal neutrons and fast neutrons. The thermal and fast fission CROSS SECTIONS for the former are 742 and 1.63 barns (b), and those for the latter are 1,009 and 1.80 b, respectively. The respective neutron releases are:

FISSILE MATERIAL	WITH THERMAL NEUTRON	WITH FAST NEUTRON
^{239}Pu	1.9	2.4
^{241}Pu	2.1	2.7

The fraction of delayed neutrons from plutonium FISSION is less than that from uranium fission. Hence, plutonium is superior for nuclear explosives and inferior for nuclear reactor fuel.

See also LIQUID METAL FAST BREEDER REACTOR.

Polaris Missiles   *See* SUBMARINE-LAUNCHED BALLISTIC MISSILES.

Polonium

Twenty-seven ISOTOPES of Polonium, with mass numbers ranging from 192 to 218, are known. All are radioactive. Most undergo alpha decay. Trace amounts of the isotopes of polonium, ^{210}Po, ^{211}Po, ^{216}Po, and ^{210}Po occur in nature. The half-life of ^{210}Po is 138.4 days. ^{210}Po is the penultimate member of the 13-step decay chain beginning with radioactive ^{230}U and ending with stable lead, ^{206}Pb. Polonium was discovered by Marie Sklodowska CURIE who named it after her native land, Poland. Early U.S. nuclear weapons used polonium as a neutron initiator. A drawback was that its short half-life required a constant supply of the material to keep the weapons ready for use.

Portsmouth   *See* WEAPONS PRODUCTION COMPLEX.

Poseidon Missiles   *See* SUBMARINE-LAUNCHED BALLISTIC MISSILES.

Potsdam Conference

On July 17–August 2, 1945, President Harry TRUMAN met with Premier Joseph STALIN of the Soviet Union and with Winston Churchill, prime minister of Great Britain in Potsdam, a suburb of Berlin. During the conference, Churchill was replaced by the new British prime minister, Clement Attlee. The subjects of the meeting were the occupation of Germany, plans for war reparations by Germany, and the proposed entry of the Soviet Union into the war against Japan, expected a few days after the conference ended.

President Truman had apparently delayed the beginning of the conference and asked that the weapon test at TRINITY be hurried so that he would have information as to its success or failure during the meeting. On July 21, Truman received a detailed report from Leslie GROVES regarding the successful Trinity test that had been held on July 16, 1945. During the conference, Truman mentioned to Stalin that the United States possessed a new and impressive weapon. Stalin replied that he hoped it would be put to good use against Japan. Stalin already knew of U.S. progress toward the nuclear weapon through the espionage efforts of several agents in the MANHATTAN ENGINEER DISTRICT, including Klaus FUCHS.

Potsdam, July 1945. British prime minister Clement Attlee, U.S. president Harry Truman, and Soviet premier Joseph Stalin pose at the Potsdam Conference. Truman knew of the successful test at Trinity when he met with the other leaders. (Library of Congress)

Four days after the end of the conference, the first atomic bomb was dropped on HIROSHIMA, and then, on August 7–8, the Soviets attacked Japanese troops in Manchuria and NORTH KOREA, as planned.

The timing of the conference and Truman's negotiating position during it have been examined closely by historians. Truman's knowledge of the success of the atomic device test at Trinity made him more willing to bargain forcefully with the Soviets, making the meeting the first case of "atomic diplomacy." In his memoirs, he admitted to being invigorated by the news and feeling able to "stand up to the Russians" with this new and fearsome weapon at his disposal.

In particular, Truman and his advisors took a firm stand, refusing to allow reparations for Soviet damage to be paid from the American occupation zone of Germany until all American claims had been settled. This issue was particularly important to the Soviets, as the most significant industrial equipment in Germany was in the Ruhr district, within the American zone of occupation.

Jimmy BYRNES, Truman's negotiator and advisor at the conference, also took a strong line with the Soviets, apparently as a result of the news from the Trinity test. Byrnes insisted that three proposals—one dealing with Poland, another with Italy, and the third with the reparations issue—be accepted as a package. If not, the U.S. delegation would walk out. Truman wrote to his wife that Stalin did not know it, but Truman had "an ace in the hole and another one showing."

In effect, Truman was able to use the bomb to strengthen his hand in refusing to allow Germany to be stripped of its economic strength. In the long run, the knowledge of the atomic bomb held by Truman and his advisors at the Potsdam Conference contributed to the strong industrial economic base of the western zone of Germany and helped Germany participate in European economic recovery after the war.

See also ARMS CONTROL; TRUMAN'S DECISION.

Suggested Reading

Gar Alperovitz, *Atomic Diplomacy: Hiroshima and Potsdam.* New York: Penguin, 1985.

————, *The Decision to Use the Atomic Bomb and the Architecture of an American Myth.* New York: Knopf, 1995.

Power Reactors Directory

By the end of the 20th century, the United States maintained 104 power reactors in operation, operated by 43 companies or public utilities, in 67 locations. Although early experiments with HIGH-TEMPERATURE GAS-COOLED REACTORS and with sodium-cooled reactors showed promise, by the 1990s all commercial power reactors in the United States were of two types, BOILING WATER REACTORS and PRESSURIZED WATER REACTORS.

Although many utility companies had only one or two reactors, several companies operated larger num-

bers. The largest operators, as can be seen in the following list, were Commonwealth Edison with 10 reactors and Duke Power with seven reactors. The Tennessee Valley Authority operated six reactors, with another three indefinitely postponed. A 40-year life expectancy was planned for most reactors. The oldest reactors operating in 1999 were Oyster Creek, in New Jersey, operated by GPU Nuclear Corporation, and Nine Mile Point 1, in New York, operated by Niagara Mohawk Power Corporation, both placed in service in 1969.

The following listing or directory was accurate in 1999, subject to changes in ownership and corporate organization. Transfers of licenses from one company to another were subject to approval by the NUCLEAR REGULATORY COMMISSION.

[Reactor status as of 1999/2000.]

Power Reactors, United States

In the United States, power reactor development began in earnest in the late 1950s and the early 1960s. The first reactor to produce power commercially was con-

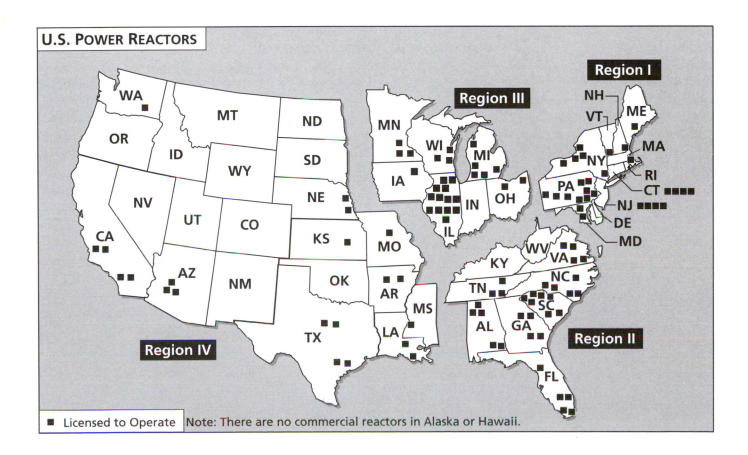

U.S. POWER REACTORS

Region I
Region III
Region IV
Region II

■ Licensed to Operate   Note: There are no commercial reactors in Alaska or Hawaii.

OWNING UTILITY

REACTOR NAME	LOCATION	MWE	TYPE	DATE OPEN	MFG.
AMEREN/UE					
Callaway	Fulton, Mo.	1235	PWR	Apr. 1985	W
AMERICAN ELECTRIC POWER					
Donald C. Cook 1		1020	PWR	Aug. 1975	W
Donald C. Cook 2		1090	PWR	Jul. 1978	W
	Bridgman, Mich.				
ARIZONA PUBLIC SERVICE COMPANY					
Palo Verde 1		1243	PWR	Jan. 1986	CE
Palo Verde 2		1243	PWR	Sep. 1986	CE
Palo Verde 3		1247	PWR	Jan. 1988	CE
	Wintersburg, Ariz.				
BALTIMORE GAS AND ELECTRIC					
Calvert Cliffs 1		825	PWR	May 1975	CE
Calvert Cliffs 2		825	PWR	Apr. 1977	CE
	Lusby, Md.				
BOSTON EDISON					
Pilgrim	Plymouth, Mass.	670	BWR	Dec. 1972	CE
CAROLINA POWER AND LIGHT COMPANY					
Brunswick 1	Southport, N.C.	767	BWR	Mar. 1977	GE
Brunswick 2	Southport, N.C.	754	BWR	Nov. 1975	GE
Robinson 2	Hartsville, S.C.	683	PWR	Mar. 1971	W
Shearon Harris	New Hill, N.C.	860	PWR	May 1987	W
COMMONWEALTH EDISON COMPANY					
Braidwood 1		1120	PWR	Jul. 1988	W
Braidwood 2		1120	PWR	Oct. 1988	W
	Braidwood, Ill.				
Byron 1		1105	PWR	Sep. 1985	W
Byron 2		1105	PWR	Aug. 1988	W
	Byron, Ill.				
Dresden 2		794	BWR	Jun. 1970	GE
Dresden 3		794	BWR	Nov. 1971	GE
	Morris, Ill.				
LaSalle County 1		1078	BWR	Jan. 1984	GE
LaSalle County 2		1078	BWR	Oct. 1984	GE
	Seneca, Ill.				
Quad Cities 1		789	BWR	Feb. 1973	GE
Quad Cities 2		789	BWR	Mar. 1973	GE
	Cordova, Ill.				
CONSOLIDATED EDISON COMPANY					
Indian Point 2	Buchanan, N. Y.	975	PWR	Aug. 1974	W
CONSUMERS ENERGY COMPANY					
Palisades	South Haven, Mich.	780	PWR	Dec. 1971	CE
DETROIT EDISON					
Fermi 2	Newport, Mich.	1139	BWR	Jan. 1988	GE

REACTOR NAME	LOCATION	MWe	TYPE	DATE OPEN	MFG.
DOMINION GENERATION					
North Anna 1		890	PWR	Jun. 1978	W
North Anna 2		890	PWR	Dec. 1980	W
	Mineral, Va.				
Surry 1		800	PWR	Dec. 1972	W
Surry 2		800	PWR	May 1973	W
	Gravel Neck, Va.				
DUKE POWER					
Catawba 1		1100	PWR	Jun. 1985	W
Catawba 2		1100	PWR	Aug. 1986	W
	Clover, S.C.				
McGuire 1		1100	PWR	Dec. 1981	W
McGuire 2		1100	PWR	Mar. 1984	W
	Cornelius, N.C.				
Oconee 1		846	PWR	Jul. 1973	B&W
Oconee 2		846	PWR	Sep. 1974	B&W
Oconee 3		846	PWR	Dec. 1974	B&W
	Seneca, S.C.				
DUQUESNE LIGHT COMPANY					
Beaver Valley 1		810	PWR	Oct. 1976	W
Beaver Valley 2		833	PWR	Nov. 1987	W
	Shippingport, Penn.				
ENTERGY OPERATIONS, INC.					
Arkansas Nuclear One 1		836	PWR	Dec. 1974	B&W
Arkansas Nuclear One 2		858	PWR	Mar. 1980	CE
	Russellville, Ark.				
Grand Gulf	Port Gibson, Miss.	1142	BWR	Jul. 1985	GE
River Bend	St. Francisville, La.	936	BWR	Jun. 1986	GE
Waterford 3	Taft, La.	1075	PWR	Sep. 1985	CE
FIRSTENERGY					
Davis-Besse	Oak Harbor, Ohio	877	PWR	Jul. 1978	B&W
Perry I	North Perry, Ohio	1205	BWR	Nov. 1987	GE
FLORIDA POWER AND LIGHT COMPANY					
St. Lucie 1		839	PWR	Dec. 1976	CE
St. Lucie 2		839	PWR	Aug. 1983	CE
	Hutchinson Island, Fla.				
Turkey Point 3		693	PWR	Dec. 1972	W
Turkey Point 4		693	PWR	Sep. 1973	W
	Florida City, Fla.				
FLORIDA POWER CORPORATION					
Crystal River 3	Red Level, Fla.	870	PWR	Mar. 1977	B&W
GPU NUCLEAR CORPORATION					
Oyster Creek	Forked River, N.J.	619	BWR	Dec. 1969	GE
Three Mile Island I		786	PWR	Sep. 1974	B&W
	Londonderry Township, Pa.				
IES UTILITIES, INCORPORATED					
Duane Arnold	Palo, Iowa	538	BWR	Feb. 1975	GE

REACTOR NAME	LOCATION	MWe	TYPE	DATE OPEN	MFG.
ILLINOIS POWER COMPANY					
Clinton	Clinton, Ill.	930	BWR	Feb. 1975	GE
NEBRASKA PUBLIC POWER DISTRICT					
Cooper	Brownville, Nebr.	764	BWR	Nov. 1987	GE
NEW YORK POWER AUTHORITY					
James A. FitzPatrick	Scriba, N.Y.	780	BWR	Jul. 1975	GE
Indian Point 3	Buchanan, N.Y.	965	PWR	Aug. 1976	W
NIAGARA MOHAWK POWER CORPORATION					
Nine Mile Point 1		610	BWR	Dec. 1969	GE
Nine Mile Point 2		1137	BWR	Apr. 1988	GE
	Scriba, N.Y.				
NORTH ATLANTIC ENERGY SERVICE CORPORATION					
Seabrook	Seabrook, N. H.	1162	PWR	Jul. 1990	W
NORTHEAST UTILITIES					
Millstone 2		875	PWR	Dec. 1975	CE
Millstone 3		1152	PWR	Apr. 1986	W
	Waterford, Conn.				
NORTHERN STATES POWER COMPANY					
Monticello	Monticello, Minn.	600	BWR	Jun. 1971	GE
Prairie Island 1	Red Wing, Minn.	535	PWR	Dec. 1973	W
Prairie Island 2	Red Wing, Minn.	535	PWR	Dec. 1974	W
OMAHA PUBLIC POWER DISTRICT					
Fort Calhoun	Fort Calhoun, Nebr.	478	PWR	Sep. 1973	CE
PACIFIC GAS AND ELECTRIC COMPANY					
Diablo Canyon 1	Avila Beach, Ca.	1130	PWR	May 1985	W
Diablo Canyon 1	Avila Beach, Ca.	1160	PWR	Mar. 1986	W
PECO ENERGY COMPANY					
Limerick 1	Pottstown, Pa.	1055	BWR	Feb. 1986	GE
Limerick 2	Pottstown, Pa.	1108	BWR	Jan. 1990	GE
Peach Bottom 2	Delta, Pa.	1100	BWR	Jul. 1974	GE
Peach Bottom 3	Delta, Pa.	1100	BWR	Dec. 1974	GE
PENNSYLVANIA POWER AND LIGHT, INC.					
Susquehanna 1	Berwick, Pa.	1100	BWR	Jun. 1983	GE
Susquehanna 1	Berwick, Pa.	1100	BWR	Feb. 1985	GE
PUBLIC SERVICE ELECTRIC AND GAS COMPANY (NEW JERSEY)					
Hope Creek	Salem, N. J.	1031	BWR	Dec. 1986	GE
Salem 1	Salem, N. J.	1106	PWR	Jun. 1977	W
Salem 2	Salem, N. J.	1106	PWR	Oct. 1981	W
ROCHESTER GAS AND ELECTRIC CORPORATION					
R.E. Ginna	Ontario, N. Y.	470	PWR	Jul. 1970	W
SOUTH CAROLINA ELECTRIC AND GAS COMPANY					
Virgil C. Summer	Parr, S.C.	885	PWR	Jan. 1984	W

REACTOR NAME	LOCATION	MWe	TYPE	DATE OPEN	MFG.
SOUTH TEXAS PROJECT NUCLEAR OPERATING COMPANY					
South Texas Project 1	Palacios, Tex.	1250	PWR	Aug. 1988	W
South Texas Project 2	Palacios, Tex.	1250	PWR	Jun. 1989	W
SOUTHERN CALIFORNIA EDISON COMPANY AND SAN DIEGO GAS & ELECTRIC					
San Onofre 2	San Clemente, Calif.	1070	PWR	Aug. 1983	CE
San Onofre 3	San Clemente, Calif.	1080	PWR	Apr. 1984	CE
SOUTHERN NUCLEAR OPERATING COMPANY					
Joseph M. Farley 1	Dothan, Ala.	847	PWR	Dec. 1977	W
Joseph M. Farley 2	Dothan, Ala.	852	PWR	Jul. 1981	W
Edwin I. Hatch 1	Baxley, Ga.	860	BWR	Dec. 1975	GE
Edwin I. Hatch 2	Baxley, Ga.	910	BWR	Sep. 1979	GE
Alvin W. Vogtle 1	Waynesboro, Ga.	1220	PWR	May 1987	W
Alvin W. Vogtle 2	Waynesboro, Ga.	1220	PWR	May 1989	W
TENNESSEE VALLEY AUTHORITY					
Bellefonte 1	Scottsboro, Ala.	1213	PWR	postponed	B&W
Bellefonte 2	Scottsboro, Ala.	1213	PWR	postponed	B&W
Browns Ferry 1	Decatur, Ala.	1065	BWR	Aug. 1974	GE
Browns Ferry 2	Decatur, Ala.	1065	BWR	Mar. 1975	GE
Browns Ferry 3	Decatur, Ala.	1065	BWR	Mar. 1977	GE
Sequoyah 1	Soddy-Daisy, Tenn.	1148	PWR	Jul. 1981	W
Sequoyah 2	Soddy-Daisy, Tenn.	1177	PWR	Jun. 1982	W
Watts Barr 1*	Spring City, Tenn.	1150	PWR	May 1986	W
Watts Barr 2	Spring City, Tenn.	1150	PWR	postponed	W
TU ELECTRIC AND GAS					
Comanche Peak 1	Glen Rose, Tex.	1150	PWR	Aug. 1990	W
Comanche Peak 2	Glen Rose, Tex.	1150	PWR	Aug. 1993	W
VERMONT YANKEE NUCLEAR POWER CORPORATION					
Vermont Yankee	Vernon, Vt.	510	BWR	Nov. 1972	GE
WASHINGTON PUBLIC POWER SUPPLY SYSTEM					
WNP-2	Richland, Wash.	1225	BWR	Dec. 1984	GE
WISCONSIN ELECTRIC POWER COMPANY					
Point Beach 1	Two Rivers, Wisc.	485	PWR	Dec. 1970	W
Point Beach 2	Two Rivers, Wisc.	485	PWR	Oct. 1972	W
WISCONSIN PUBLIC SERVICE CORPORATION					
Kewaunee	Carlton, Wisc.	510	PWR	Jun. 1974	W
WOLF CREEK NUCLEAR OPERATING CORPORATION					
Wolf Creek	Burlington, Kans.	1180	PWR	Sep. 1985	W

*Planned for production of tritium. See PRODUCTION REACTORS.
Abbreviations used in table:
Reactor Types:
BWR Boiling Water Reactor
PWR Pressurized Water Reactor

Manufacturers:
B&W Babcock and Wilcox
CE Combustion Engineering
GE General Electric
W Westinghouse

structed at SHIPPINGPORT, Pennsylvania, going into operation on December 23, 1957. That reactor was built following the design of the PRESSURIZED WATER REACTOR (PWR) used in the Naval Reactor Program.

After some experimentation with other types of reactors, including the Liquid Metal Fast Breeder Reactor constructed near Detroit (the Fermi Reactor), nearly all reactors for power in the United States have utilized water for both coolant and moderator. Reactors are designated by the types of coolant and moderator they use, and power reactors in the United States have employed either the boiling water or pressurized water system, whereas other countries have employed other moderator-coolant systems.

Most of the U.S. commercial reactors have followed two design patterns. The PWR, designed to fit into the small confines of a nuclear submarine, was a proven power plant. Beginning in the 1950s, ARGONNE NATIONAL LABORATORY developed the BOILING WATER REACTOR (BWR) type.

In the PWR type, pressurized water is circulated through the reactor and heated. It is then piped through a steam generator, where a separate water system is heated to produce steam to drive the turbine generators.

In the BWR, a single loop takes water through the reactor, raising it to steam temperature. The steam then proceeds through pipes and valves to the turbine, where it is condensed back to water to be pumped back into the reactor. In both systems, the steam is cooled by water circulated through a cooling tower.

On September 16, 1954, Lewis L. STRAUSS, chair of the ATOMIC ENERGY COMMISSION, gave a speech in which he stated that electricity would eventually become "too cheap to meter." In later years, as the costs of nuclear power mounted, this phrase came back to haunt nuclear power advocates. Costs were quite high when the whole cycle was included in the calculation, such as mining and manufacturing the fuel, constructing the plants, and handling the dangerous waste products of the reactors. In any case, the speech by Strauss reflected the early enthusiasm for the prospect of plentiful electrical power that could be derived from nuclear energy.

Connecticut Yankee–Haddam Neck. One of the early generation of power reactors, Haddam Neck stands decommissioned in the 1990s. (Victoria S. Harlow)

Among the first reactors to be built, following the Shippingport reactor, were these, rated in megawatt-electric (MWe) output.

EARLY U.S. POWER REACTORS

NAME AND LOCATION	MWE
Indian Point I, New York	265
Dresden I, Illinois	207
Yankee Rowe, Massachusetts	175

Another 11 reactors, some experimental, with ratings below 100 MWe, were constructed between 1953 and 1960. During the 1960s, a number of larger BWRs and PWRs were ordered and constructed. The two major firms competing for reactor business each concentrated on different designs, with GENERAL ELECTRIC focusing on boiling water reactors and WESTINGHOUSE concentrating on pressurized water reactors.

The total megawattage of power reactors in the United States exceeded the megawattage of weapons-material production reactors for the first time in 1970. Construction continued, bringing the total number in the United States to about 50 by the end of 1974. By 1974, the total megawattage of power reactors was over 30,000 or 30 gigawatts (GWe). Comparing the power output of nuclear reactors to other means of generating electricity, including hydroelectric and oil and coal-fired plants, 30 GWe represented about 6% of U.S. electrical power.

Following 1974, the rate of construction of new reactors declined, partly due to a slowing in the rate of growth of electric demand. Following the accident at THREE MILE ISLAND (TMI) in 1979, many reactor orders were canceled, and applications for new reactor licenses declined. Further reactors tended to be built only at locations that already had reactors rather than at entirely new sites.

By the late 1990s, there were about 100 reactors in the United States, with active plans to build several more. However, given the long lead time for reactor planning and licensing, most observers believed that the United States had achieved a plateau or leveling off in reactor construction by the 1990s.

In addition to arousing public concerns about nuclear safety, the accident at Three Mile Island also had the effect of increasing reactor operating company attention to safety. Many post–TMI improvements included new control room systems, new training, and more redundancy and backup systems. As a consequence, U.S. reactors since the early 1980s have been able to operate at higher capacity, that is, for a higher percentage of time, with few outages for repairs and maintenance.

Several reactors have been shut down in the United States for various reasons. These included the older reactors at Indian Point I (1974), Dresden I (1978), and Yankee Rowe (1979), along with all of the other 11 reactors constructed before 1960. The LMFBR Fermi Reactor near Detroit only operated briefly in 1963 before an accident led to its closure. Unit 2 at Three Mile Island was permanently closed after the accident there in 1979. Four reactors with histories of difficulties and low capacity were also closed, including the high-temperature gas-cooled reactor at Ft. St. Vrain in 1989, and three other light water reactors in 1991–1992. The SHOREHAM reactor in Long Island operated only briefly in 1985, but local opposition prevented the reactor from gaining a full-power license. Residents objected to the fact that if an accident occurred at the reactor, it would be extremely difficult to evacuate the area.

Following these closures, however, the remaining 104 reactors in the United States appeared to be likely to serve out their licensed operating period, usually set at about 40 years. Since about half of the reactors remaining went into operation before 1974, planners anticipated that the number of power reactors in the United States would decline by half by about 2014.

At the end of the century, 104 nuclear reactors operated at 67 sites, controlled by about 40 utility firms or government agencies. As utility firms sometimes consolidated or sold reactors to other firms, the number of owners changed slightly from year to year.

See also FERMI REACTOR ACCIDENT; NUCLEAR FUEL CYCLE.

Suggested Reading

David Bodansky, *Nuclear Energy: Principles, Practices, and Prospects.* Woodbury, N.Y.: American Institute of Physics, 1996.

Jack Holl, Roger Anders, and Alice Buck, *The United States Civilian Nuclear Power Policy, 1954–1984: A Summary History.* Washington, D.C.: DOE, 1986.

Power Reactors, World

The first power reactors were constructed in the Soviet Union, the United States, and Great Britain in the mid- and late 1950s. After a period of experimentation with different types of reactors, these three countries began to export reactor technology and completed "turn-key" reactors to other countries. By the 1970s, nuclear power began to represent a significant proportion of the electrical generating capacity of the world. In the United States, the proportion of electricity generated from nuclear reactors climbed rather rapidly in the early 1970s and then more gradually in the 1980s, approaching 20% to 25% of total U.S. power production by the 1990s. In other countries, notably France and Japan, nuclear power made up a greater proportion of the power resources of the nation. By the 1990s, nuclear power provided an estimated 75% to 79% of France's electricity and about 30% in Japan.

The exact proportion of a nation's electrical usage generated by nuclear reactors is difficult to calculate accurately for several reasons. Reactors are shut down periodically for maintenance, and many are troubled by unanticipated outages. Thus, the total megawattage or gigawattage (thousands of megawatts) of a nation's nuclear-generated power is usually an estimate based upon predicted efficiency. Advocates of nuclear power tend to present optimistic estimates, whereas opponents utilize lower figures. Some percentage calculations are based on electricity consumed, while others are based on total energy produced or consumed. All such factors account for wide variations between published statistics.

In general, the total number of nuclear power reactors in operation worldwide increased gradually to nearly 500 by the late 1990s. The precise figure constantly changed due to closures, shutdowns, new construction, canceled orders, and alterations in various countries' energy planning. Recognizing such variations in both gigawattage and in sheer number of reactors in operation, the following estimates are roughly accurate for the year 2000. In some cases, the figures include reactors planned, under construction, or expected to be in production within one or two years.

NUCLEAR POWER REACTORS, YEAR 2000

	Approx.#	Approx. Gigawattage
Nations with largest numbers of reactors		
United States	104	107
France	61	64
Japan	54	44
United Kingdom	35	13
Russia	29	23
Canada	22	15
Germany	19	23
Ukraine	20	18
India	16	4
Spain	15	13
Korea (South)	14	13
Nations with fewer reactors		
Argentina	3	2
Belgium	7	6
Brazil	3	3
Bulgaria	6	4
China	5	3
Cuba	2	1
Czech Republic	6	3
Finland	4	2
Hungary	4	2
Kazakhstan	1	—
Lithuania	2	3
Mexico	2	1
Netherlands	2	1
Pakistan	1	2
Philippines	1	1
Romania	1	1
Slovakia	8	3
Slovenia	1	1
South Africa	2	2
Sweden	12	10
Switzerland	5	3
Taiwan	6	5

[The totals shown include some reactors in planning stages.]

As can be seen from the table, the United States had over 23% of the power reactors in the world and about 36% of the total nuclear power–generating capacity. The number of reactors operating in any one year will continue to vary, but it is expected that by the year 2014, about 50 or more of the older reactors in the United States will be closed, while some other countries continue to expand their reactor programs. The proportion of the world's nuclear power generated in the United States is therefore expected to decline. The year-to-year changes in nuclear power reactors can be traced through *Nuclear News*, which publishes a listing annually in March, or in publications of the U.S. DEPARTMENT OF ENERGY and the INTERNATIONAL ATOMIC ENERGY AGENCY.

The 11 largest nuclear power states represent over 80% of the installed nuclear power in the world. However, among the countries with fewer nuclear reactors, several derive a very high proportion of their electrical energy from nuclear power. It should be noted that such estimates are only approximations, for the reasons suggested above.

ESTIMATED PERCENTAGE OF ELECTRICAL POWER DERIVED FROM NUCLEAR REACTORS

NATION	ESTIMATED PERCENTAGE
Lithuania	76%
France	75%
Belgium	56%
Sweden	51%
Slovakia	49%
Bulgaria	46%
Hungary	44%
Slovenia	38%
Switzerland	37%
Spain	35%
South Korea	35%
Ukraine	34%
Taiwan	32%
Finland	30%
Japan	30%
Czech Republic	28%

By the 1990s, all power reactors in the United States were light-water types. About two-thirds of the reactors were PRESSURIZED WATER REACTORS (PWRs), and about one-third were BOILING WATER REACTORS (BWRs). Britain built MAGNOX, or gas-cooled, graphite-moderated reactors, while Canada built pressurized heavy-water reactors (PHWRs), exported as CANDU reactors to INDIA, Romania, and elsewhere. The advantage of PHWRs is that they operate on natural, unenriched URANIUM. One disadvantage is that the HEAVY WATER utilized in the reactors may be diverted for use in reactors to produce weapons-grade PLUTONIUM.

The former Soviet Union developed three designs. The RBMK type was the *Reactory Bolshoi Moshchnosti Kanalynye* or "Channelized Large Power Reactor." The reactor is equivalent to a LWGR or light-water–cooled, graphite-moderated reactor, fairly similar to the first production reactors built in the United States at HANFORD. The CHERNOBYL reactor that suffered an accident was of this type. A second Soviet reactor was the VVER, or *Vodo-Vodyannoy Energeticheskiy Reactor,* which was a water-cooled and water-moderated reactor, equivalent to the western PWRs. The VVER-440, developed before 1970, was the most common; a later VVER-440 and a VVER-1000 developed in 1975 had added safety features. All of these types were constructed in the former Soviet Union, and the VVERs were exported to several Eastern European countries. In addition, the Soviets developed a third type, a fast

reactor designated "BN" in several designs, used in breeder reactor applications.

In nearly all countries that have built or planned nuclear power plants, public controversies have arisen that follow similar patterns. Those arguing for nuclear power point to the relatively low cost of the power compared to fossil-fuel (oil and coal) sources and to the fact that nuclear power does not pollute the atmosphere and can provide an important resource to meet expanding energy needs.

Opponents argue that the hidden costs of nuclear fuel fabrication and waste management, together with the risk to public health and safety from nuclear power plant accidents, make nuclear power a poor choice. In general, opposition to nuclear power plants is often quite localized, called in the United States the NIMBY effect, standing for "Not in My Back Yard." Local residents in the Ukraine and Poland have protested against proposed nuclear power plants in their neighborhoods, as have regional populations in France and Great Britain. Since the risk of exposure in case of a nuclear power reactor accident is greatest for those living near the plant, such opposition is quite understandable.

Episodes such as the THREE MILE ISLAND accident (March 28, 1979) and the Chernobyl accident (April 26, 1986) confirmed and heightened such concerns. The tendency of officials to conceal from the public information about accidents, when discovered, has also contributed to opposition. A release of radioactivity at WINDSCALE Reactor in Britain in 1957 was not immediately disclosed, and details of the Chernobyl accident were also temporarily suppressed.

More subtle is the association between nuclear power plants and nuclear weaponry. In the United States, a division was maintained between reactors that can be used for power production and those used to produce plutonium. However, in Britain, India, Russia, and France among other countries, more reactors are dual purpose; that is, they are used to produce plutonium and TRITIUM as well as power.

Even though power and weapons programs have been separated in the United States, there have been exceptions there. In the period 1964 to 1987, "N" reactor at Hanford was utilized both to produce plutonium and to generate electricity for the commercial network. In 1998, the U.S. Department of Energy announced plans to utilize two power reactors operated by the Tennessee Valley Authority to produce tritium.

Types of Reactors for Power	Countries
Boiling Water Reactor (BWR)	USA, France, South Korea, Former Soviet Union (VVER type)
Pressurized Water Reactor (PWR)	USA, Japan
Pressurized Heavy-Water Reactor (PHWR)	Canada, India, Romania, South Korea
Light-water Cooled, Graphite-Moderated (LGR)	RBMK type in Former Soviet Union
Gas-Cooled, Graphite-Moderated (GCR)	United Kingdom, Magnox type
High-Temperature Gas-Cooled (HTGR)	Ft. St. Vrain, USA (closed)
Liquid Metal Fast Breeder Reactor (LMFBR)	France, Russia, Kazakhstan, Japan
Heavy-Water Moderated, Light-Water Cooled (HWLWR)	Japan

Even without such direct connections between power reactors and weapons programs, some observers have pointed out that power reactors can serve as a psychological surrogate for nuclear weapons. Furthermore, public action groups opposed to nuclear armaments have sought to expand their political base by appealing to both environmental concerns and to NIMBY sentiments, allying the disarmament movement with the antinuclear power movement in organizations such as GREENPEACE and SANE.

See also FRANCE–NUCLEAR POWER; INDIA; JAPAN.

Suggested Reading

David Bodansky, *Nuclear Energy: Principles, Practices, and Prospects*. Woodbury, N.Y.: American Institute of Physics, 1996.

James J. Duderstadt and Chiroro Kikuchi, *Nuclear Power: Technology on Trial*. Ann Arbor: University of Michigan Press, 1979.

Presidential Decision Directive 59 (PDD 59)

On July 29, 1980 President Jimmy CARTER issued Presidential Decision Directive 59 (PDD 59), spelling out his nuclear weapons doctrine of countervailing power, which differed somewhat from the policy announced by Richard NIXON in 1974. Nixon's policy, as described in National Security Decision Memorandum-242, proposed to cripple Soviet recovery after a nuclear war between the two powers erupted. Carter's PDD 59 stressed the concept that the United States would place at risk assets that were highly valued by the Soviets at every stage, including military and political control. Thus the leadership would be targeted, in a policy sometimes called "decapitation."

PDD 59 required a range of weapons capable of penetrating accurately to the centers of Soviet power, including the TRIDENT II SUBMARINE-LAUNCHED BALLISTIC MISSILE, and the improved MINUTEMAN III missile. Since the details of the targeting changes were not made public, analysts had difficulty deciding whether PDD 59 represented a drastic change from Nixon's policies or simply a continuation and clarification of them. Some assumed that the policy was simply COUNTER-VALUE STRATEGY with a new name.

Some analysts, including Soviet authorities, took PDD 59 to represent a much more aggressive and possibly destabilizing nuclear weapon policy than that of Richard Nixon. Others saw it as designed to pressure the Soviets into further arms control discussions and to meet domestic political criticisms from Republicans that the United States was losing its strategic equivalence and falling behind the Soviet Union. Coupled with other moves during the late 1970s, such as modernization of the nuclear stockpile through the development of new weapons, the measure appeared to represent an attempt to strengthen the U.S. nuclear posture.

The Soviets invaded Afghanistan in December 1979, and in the same month, the NORTH ATLANTIC TREATY ORGANIZATION foreign ministers announced their DUAL-TRACK STRATEGY under which the United States would place modernized intermediate-range missiles in Europe to offset Soviet new missiles. When in January 1980, President Carter withdrew the Strategic Arms Limitation Treaty II (SALT II) from ratification hearings before the U.S. Senate and announced an embargo on grain sales to the Soviets, it was clear that the DETENTE policy of the 1960s and early 1970s was dead. PDD 59 appeared to represent a harsh new nuclear weapons targeting policy in accord with the tougher stand taken by the United States and its allies that characterized 1980. Taken together with the other measures, PDD 59 could be viewed as the turning point in American policy, heralding the intensified cold war of the last Carter years and the early years of the administration of Ronald REAGAN.

The second cold war, which would come to a head in the early 1980s under President Reagan, thus can trace its origins to the events and policies of the last years of the Carter administration, capped by PDD 59.

Suggested Reading

John M. Collins, *U.S.–Soviet Military Balance, 1980–1985.* Washington, D.C.: Pergamon-Brassey's, 1985.

L. Hagen, "PD-59 and the Countervailing Strategy: Continuity or Change?" Department of National Defense, Canada, Project Report No. PR 170, Ottawa, Canada, reprinted as "Presidential Decision-59, 1980" in Philip Cantelon and Robert Williams, eds., *The American Atom: A Documentary History of Nuclear Policies from the Discovery of Fission to the Present, 1939–1984.* Philadelphia: University of Pennsylvania Press, 1984.

Presidential Nuclear Initiative-91

On September 27, 1991, President George H. W. BUSH followed up on the Strategic Arms Reduction Treaty (START I) that had been signed on July 31, 1991, with a Presidential Nuclear Initiative (PNI-91), which was designed to provide confidence-building measures to supplement START. Bush's actions greatly reduced the U.S. posture of nuclear threat against the Soviet Union, and President Mikhail GORBACHEV responded with several similar unilateral reductions. With PNI-91, the United States and the Soviet Union moved away from negotiating every detail of arms reductions in treaties and international agreements and simply proceeded to make a variety of cuts that fit into the requirements of their own budgets and the needs of their own military services.

Under PNI-91 and Gorbachev's unilateral actions, all U.S. and Soviet ground-launched theater nuclear weapons would be eliminated, not only in Europe but also elsewhere. Theater nuclear weapons referred to weapons that were designed to be employed as tactical weapons in the event of a ground war in Europe. Furthermore, Bush announced that the United States would remove all theater nuclear weapons from ships, submarines, and land-based naval aircraft.

For the U.S. Navy, PNI-91 had the immediate effect of eliminating its nuclear role except for the nuclear weapons still carried on SUBMARINE-LAUNCHED BALLISTIC MISSILES (SLBMs). Nuclear-armed ship-to-shore missiles, such as the *Tomahawk,* were removed from all ships. Gorbachev ordered the elimination of half of all Soviet nuclear-armed surface-to-air missiles. Gorbachev's unilateral actions appeared to be one of the factors precipitating the abortive coup against him in August 1991.

As further measures, U.S. strategic bombers and MINUTEMAN II missiles were taken off alert. Bush also ordered the cancellation of several arms programs then in development, including the short-range attack missile and the rail-mobile basing system for the small INTERCONTINENTAL BALLISTIC MISSILE (ICBM). Bush also proposed the elimination of multiple independently targetable warheads.

President Bush followed up on his initiative in his State of the Union address on January 28, 1992. In this speech he announced further reductions in the U.S. nuclear modernization program, in steps that would be taken unilaterally and immediately. The construction of the B-2 bomber would be limited to 20 aircraft, and the small ICBM program was entirely canceled. Production of a warhead for the TRIDENT II SLBM was canceled. Further purchases of advanced cruise missiles were also halted.

Implementing the initiatives, on July 2, 1992, the United States notified its allies that it had completed the removal from Europe of all land-based nuclear artillery shells, LANCE warheads, and nuclear depth bombs, as well as all tactical nuclear missiles from surface ships and attack submarines.

Taken together, the reductions under the INTERMEDIATE NUCLEAR FORCES treaty, START I, PNI-91, and the unilateral steps announced in January 1992 represented the greatest cutback in nuclear forces since the beginning of the cold war. The cutbacks in nuclear weaponry meant that parts of the nuclear weapons production complex, which had encountered severe problems in meeting production goals in the late 1980s, could be shut down. Facilities at ROCKY FLATS, Colorado, HANFORD, Washington, Mound, Ohio, and Pinellas, Florida, were closed. Plans to build a NEW PRODUCTION REACTOR were terminated. The PANTEX weapons assembly plant in Amarillo, Texas, put on extra shifts to accommodate the need to dismantle retired weapons.

With the elimination of short-range and intermediate-range missiles operated by U.S. Army personnel, the army's nuclear role was terminated. By 1993, the only nuclear weapon delivery systems still deployed by the United States were air force strategic bombers and ICBMs and the navy's SLBMs. All tactical nuclear weapons and all nuclear weapons of the surface navy had been taken out of the active stockpile, and many were in the process of being dismantled.

Suggested Reading

NATO Office of Information and Press, *NATO Handbook*. Brussels, Belgium: NATO Office of Information and Press, 1995.

Pressler Amendment

The United States developed a very ambivalent attitude toward the government of PAKISTAN early in the 1980s. On the one hand, Pakistan provided a staging area for aid to the anticommunist rebels in Afghanistan. Thus, good relations and military assistance from the United States to Pakistan were essential to American foreign policy. On the other hand, the United States feared that Pakistan was in the process of developing a nuclear weapon, which ran counter to U.S. efforts to stop nuclear PROLIFERATION. These fears proved well grounded in 1998 when Pakistan held announced nuclear tests. The Pressler Amendment, which was passed in 1985, provided a solution to the dilemma of how to aid Pakistan while withholding assistance because of suspicions that the nation was building nuclear weapons.

The law stated that U.S. aid and government military sales to Pakistan would be cut off unless the president of the United States certified at the opening of each fiscal year that Pakistan did not have a nuclear explosive device and that the aid would reduce the risk that Pakistan would develop such a device. The act comprised an amendment to the Foreign Assistance Act of 1961, and it applied only to Pakistan. The intention was to deny assistance to Pakistan's nuclear program without threatening military aid during the Afghan crisis.

Pakistan regarded the Pressler Amendment as unfair, as INDIA was subject to no such restriction. An earlier Glenn-Symington Amendment in 1977 prohibited export of reprocessing technology, but India had already developed its domestic reprocessing facilities by that point.

In 1996, the Pressler Amendment was modified by the Brown Amendment, which deleted the provision that economic aid would be limited if the president could no longer certify Pakistan's non-nuclear status. Even so, export of reprocessing technology to Pakistan

was still prohibited under the Glenn-Symington Amendment. The president had been given authority to waive even this restriction as long as Pakistan's efforts to acquire nuclear weapons predated June 1994. However, between November 1994 and mid-1995, Pakistan imported crucial ring magnets from China. As a consequence, the United States could not provide aid to Pakistan, and its influence over the country's policy declined. Pakistan became an announced nuclear power in May 1998.

The Pressler Amendment and subsequent modifications and interpretations of the law had failed to allow the United States to use its foreign aid and support for Pakistan as a means to prevent it becoming a nuclear-armed nation.

Pressurized Water Reactor (PWR)

A pressurized water reactor is a type of nuclear power reactor utilizing ordinary water under pressure as the cooling and moderating material. In the primary loop of a pressurized water reactor, heat is transferred from the core to the heat exchanger by water kept under pressure sufficiently high to prevent it from boiling. The heat exchanger is part of the secondary loop where water at a lower pressure is converted to steam, which drives turbines for the generation of electricity. The primary loop through the 16-foot diameter × 40-foot high reactor vessel of a 500 MW PWR operates under a pressure of 2,250 psi at 600 degrees F. to produce steam at 500 degrees F. in the secondary loop. Of the nearly 500 nuclear reactors in operation worldwide, approximately half are PWRs.

Price-Anderson Act

In 1957 Congress passed and President Dwight EISENHOWER signed the Price-Anderson Act. The act was crucial to stimulating the development of nuclear power in the United States by providing federal backup in liability insurance in case of a nuclear power plant accident. Private power companies were reluctant to take on the risks that could result from a power reactor accident without insurance, even though such accidents appeared extremely unlikely. Private insurance companies were willing to provide insurance against liability for a single power plant accident up to a $60 million limit. The Price-Anderson Act provided further coverage by the federal government of $500 million up to a combined maximum of $560 million.

The act had a 10-year life, and it was renewed in 1967. It was renewed again in 1977, and in 1987 it was renewed for a 30-year period. The 1987 act raised the liability limit to $6 billion in constant dollars. In 1977, controversies over nuclear power surrounded the renewal of the act and the Rasmussen Report, which evaluated the safety of reactors, was criticized for being issued when the act was under consideration for renewal.

See also PROBABILISTIC RISK ASSESSMENT; RASMUSSEN REPORT.

Suggested Reading

George Mazuzan and J. Samuel Walker, *Controlling the Atom: The Beginnings of Nuclear Regulation, 1946–1962.* Berkeley: University of California Press, 1984.

Probabilistic Risk Assessment (PRA)

Probabilistic Risk Assessment (PRA) is a method of estimating the likelihood of a certain kind of accident to a system by multiplying estimates of various possible infrequent events together in chains of event trees or fault trees. For example, if the likelihood of a valve springing a leak is one time in a hundred years, and if failure of an automatic shutoff that would cut off the supply to the leak point was also one time in a hundred years, the combined chance of both failing would be 1/100 times 1/100 or one chance in 10,000 years. By calculating the probability of an event and expressing it as a number of chances within 100,000 or 10,000 years, the safety of two or more complete systems can be compared. In Great Britain and in other European countries, such studies are called "Probabilistic Safety Analyses." Such calculations are expressed as negative exponents, so that 1 in 10,000 is represented as 1×10^{-4} and 1 in 100,000 is shown as 1×10^{-5}

In the late 1960s, two landmark papers brought probabilistic thinking to the attention of nuclear engineers. One was F. R. Farmer's "Reactor Safety and Siting: A Proposed Risk Criterion," and the other was C. Starr's "Social Benefit versus Technological Risk." Farmer argued that risk could be measured by estimating the probability of a system's failure, and he made a distinction between acceptable and unacceptable risks. In the mid-1970s, Norman Rasmussen's study of reac-

tor safety popularized the idea of Probabilistic Risk Assessment and brought it to the attention of the policymakers, journalists, and general public.

Following the THREE MILE ISLAND accident in 1979, the NUCLEAR REGULATORY COMMISSION (NRC) required a Probabilistic Risk Assessment as part of the documentation in pending plant applications for licenses. The directive, spelled out in Title 10, Code of Federal Regulations, section 50.34(f), ordered that for all applications pending at the time, there should be a program of studies, including, at the head of the list, "a plant/site specific probabilistic risk assessment, the aim of which is to seek such improvements in the reliability of core and containment heat removal systems as are significant and practical. . . ."

After the Three Mile Island accident in 1979, the nuclear power industry and the NRC began research programs into reactor performance during a variety of hypothetical accidents. The earlier approach of studying only worst-case accidents, involving major pipe breaks, began to give way to the new approach of studying scenarios based on series of minor incidents and accidents that, as at TMI, might compound into a major problem. Small incidents were more probable and thus were more important as potential causes of major accidents. As PRA evolved in these studies, company engineers worked out a series of mathematical frameworks for evaluating the cause-effect linkages of system components.

The NRC announced the Severe Accident Policy Statement in 1985, which provided for "a systematic examination by industry of plants for risk contributors." In 1987 the NRC issued a preliminary draft of NUREG-1150, which gave PRAs for five existing nuclear power plants: Surry, Peach Bottom, Sequoyah, Grand Gulf, and Zion, each with a different containment system. The five PRAs, the NRC anticipated, would be used as models by companies to conduct further studies of risk contributors in order to implement the Severe Accident Policy.

A NATIONAL ACADEMY OF SCIENCES (NAS) group, the Committee to Assess Safety and Technical Issues at DEPARTMENT OF ENERGY (DOE) Reactors in the wake of the Chernobyl accident in 1986, criticized the Department of Energy for its late start on PRA. The NAS report, published in 1988, endorsed a modest use of PRA techniques.

Although, as shown in Table I, the use of PRA methods in the nuclear industry steadily gained ground, it is also clear that lots of variety in their

TABLE I
PROBABILISTIC RISK ASSESSMENT: EVOLUTION OF USE
IN NUCLEAR ENGINEERING

Year	Document	PRA used for:
1975	RASMUSSEN REPORT	Overall reactor safety assessment
1981	Monterey Conf.	*With older methods, component study
1982	10 CFR 50.34(f)	Pre-licensing requirement
1987	NUREG-1150	Systems evaluation; goal-setting
1988	NAS on DOE	SafetyTool for safety modification

TABLE II
CORE DAMAGE FREQUENCY (CDF) ESTIMATES BY PRA

Surry median CDF=	
(Rasmussen figures)	6.0 per 100,000/reactor-years
(NUREG-1150 figures)	2.3 per 100,000/reactor-years
Peach Bottom median CDF=	
(Rasmussen figures)	2.9 per 100,000/reactor-years
(NUREG-1150 figures)	1.9 per 100,000/reactor-years
Oconee Unit 3 mean CDF=	2.5 per 10,000/reactor-years
Seabrook mean CDF=	2.4 per 10,000 reactor-years
South Texas Project median CDF=	9.9 per 100,000/reactor-years
mean CDF=	1.7 per 10,000/reactor-years
Pressurized Water Reactors in general, mean CDF=	5.22 per 100,000/reactor-years
(Brookhaven figures)	

Conventionally, PRA figures are represented thus:
6.0 accidents in every 100,000 reactor years = 6×10^{-5}/RY
2.5 accidents in every 10,000 reactor years = 2.5×10^{-4}/RY

application continued. By the late 1980s, as shown in Table II, the range of predicted overall safety ranged from as low as 1 core-damaging event per 100,000 reactor years to as high as 2.5 such incidents in 10,000 years, that is, from 1×10^{-5}/RY to 2.5×10^{-4}/RY.

Even for the same reactors, estimates produced in the mid-1970s in the Rasmussen Report were soon superseded by figures that showed the reactors as much safer, produced by the NRC in the 1987 publication, NUREG-1150. For example, as shown in Table II, Rasmussen estimated the likelihood of a core-damaging event at Surry as 6.0×10^{-5}/RY and NUREG-1150 reassessed the frequency as 2.3×10^{-5}/RY, less than half as likely.

Although the Rasmussen Report had been criticized as an attempt to portray power reactors as safer than they were, within two to four years after the report Rasmussen's estimates of risk had been much higher than determined by the Nuclear Regulatory Commis-

sion. Through the following years, PRA methods in the United States (and PSA methods in Europe) were used to compare various reactor designs and sometimes to assist in the design of new reactors by pinpointing areas that required more backup or redundancy in safety.

See also DETERMINISTIC SAFETY ASSESSMENT.

Suggested Reading

Rodney Carlisle, "Probabilistic Risk Assessment: Engineering Success, Public Relations Failure," *Technology and Culture* (Fall 1997).

Production Reactors

Nuclear reactors that produce PLUTONIUM and/or TRITIUM for use in nuclear weapons are termed "production reactors." In the United States, the first production reactors were built during the work of the MANHATTAN

ENGINEER DISTRICT in the period 1943–1945 at HANFORD, Washington.

This first generation of three production reactors was constructed along the banks of the Columbia River to take advantage of the constant flow of cold water for cooling the reactors. The isolation of the site was also an advantage in case of a major reactor accident.

The reactors consisted of large (40 feet high) cores of graphite, pierced by horizontal tubes. The tubes were connected by piping to inlets from the river. In operation, slugs of natural URANIUM, encased in aluminum or tin, were inserted into the tubes. The slugs were smaller than the tube diameters, with fins to hold the slug in place. Thus, the cooling water could flow directly over the surface of the slugs. The reactors were moderated by graphite, controlled by cadmium rods, and cooled by river water.

As the CHAIN REACTION proceeded, heat would be carried off in the water to large ponds, where it was allowed to settle and cool before being pumped back into the river. The chain reactions split the ^{235}U atoms into FISSION products. In the natural uranium, 99% of the uranium was ^{238}U. When struck by neutrons, ^{238}U was transformed by a several-step reaction into plutonium.

After several weeks, the fuel slugs would be pushed out the back of the reactor and taken to a processing plant where the plutonium would be separated from the remaining uranium and fission products. In this procedure, small amounts of plutonium were obtained for use in the first nuclear device test at TRINITY, and amounts were also used to make FAT MAN, the weapon dropped on NAGASAKI.

Nuclear waste from the cooling ponds and from processing facilities at Hanford was stored in large metal underground tanks. Later seepage from these tanks remained a serious environmental concern, even years after the closing of the production reactors.

In response to the Soviet detonation of a nuclear weapon in August 1949 and in reaction to the outbreak of the KOREAN WAR in June 1950, Congress ordered the construction of a second production reactor complex. The United States built five more production reactors at SAVANNAH RIVER SITE, South Carolina. These reactors followed a different design from those built at Hanford. Using HEAVY WATER as a MODERATOR, that is, water that was based on the deuterium ISOTOPE of hydrogen, these reactors would produce tritium by the insertion of targets of lithium-deuteride

into the reactor along with the fuel slugs. The deuteride would be converted into tritium, later refined from the targets.

The tritium generated had a half-life of about 12.26 years, meaning that in order to provide tritium for the weapons stockpile, tritium needed to be continually produced.

All the nations that have produced nuclear weapons have also built reactors capable of producing plutonium and associated processing plants. Thus the Soviet facilities at CHELYABINSK-40 and later at KRASNOYARSK-26 and at TOMSK-7 housed production reactors, as did the British facility at CALDER HALL and the French at Marcoule. The Chelyabinsk-40 facilities released vast quantities of radioactive cooling water into the Techa-Iset-Tobol river system, exposing without warning 124,000 people. A dam to contain the most dangerous wastewater was built with slave labor.

Other nations planning to make nuclear weapons have built production reactors and separations plants. While reactors can be concealed by being built underground, the large separations plants can give evidence of a nuclear-capable nation's intention to develop nuclear weapons.

N reactor, built by the United States at Hanford, was a dual-purpose reactor, designed both to serve as a production reactor for making plutonium and to generate electricity. Some of the Soviet reactors at Tomsk-7 and Krasnoyarsk-26, the British plant at Calder Hall, and the French Marcoule facility were also dual-purpose reactors. In the United States, Congress debated the propriety of mixing the two purposes: weapons-material production and electrical power for the civilian power network. A similar controversy surrounded the Russian program at Tomsk-7.

All 14 production reactors in the United States operated at the same time briefly in 1964, but then the United States began to close the older reactors. A few reactors were kept open through the remainder of the cold war supplying plutonium and tritium until 1988.

With the closing of the last Savannah River reactors in 1988, the U.S. Department of Energy considered the construction of a new generation of production reactors, evaluating several different designs and locations. In order to keep the weapon stockpile operative, a supply of tritium would be required within a few years. However, with the signing of the START treaty, which drastically reduced the nuclear weapon stockpile of both the United States and the Soviet Union (later, Russia), the urgency declined.

D Reactor face. One of the first generation of production reactors at Hanford, the D reactor produced plutonium for nuclear weapons from 1944 through 1967. (Department of Energy)

Reactor	Year Opened	Year Closed
Hanford		
B	1944	1968
D	1945	1967
F	1945	1965
DR	1949	1964
H	1950	1965
C	1952	1969
KW	1955	1970
KE	1955	1971
N	1964	1987
Savannah		
R	1953	1964
P	1954	1988
L	1954	1968 (reopened 1985–1988)
K	1954	1988
C	1955	1988

By the late 1990s, the United States was considering alternative methods of producing tritium, either using electrical power reactors to irradiate lithium-deuteride targets or using a linear accelerator to produce tritium. In 1998, the Department of Energy settled on a plan to produce tritium using light-water power reactors in the Tennessee Valley Authority system.

In Russia, however, three production reactors remained in operation until the year 2000, including an underground graphite-moderated reactor at Krasnoyarsk-26 (renamed Zheleznogorsk) and two similar reactors at Tomsk-7 (renamed Seversk).

See also FRANCE—NUCLEAR ARMAMENTS; UNITED KINGDOM.

Suggested Reading

Rodney Carlisle, *Supplying the Nuclear Arsenal.* Baltimore: Johns Hopkins University Press, 1996.

Reactors at Hanford. In this rather idyllic view from the Columbia River, several of the production reactors at Hanford, Washington, are silhouetted against the hills and sky. All nine of the production reactors at Hanford were cooled by water brought directly from, and returned to, the river. (Department of Energy)

Thomas B. Cochrane, Robert S. Norris, and Oleg A. Bukharin, *Making the Russian Bomb: From Stalin to Yeltsin.* Boulder, Colo.: Westview Press, 1995.

David Holloway, *Stalin and the Bomb.* Hew Haven: Yale University Press, 1994.

Project Jennifer   *See* GLOMAR EXPLORER.

Project Rover

Rover was the name for a planned rocket design (1956–1973) that would be nuclear powered. Like the proposals for AIRCRAFT NUCLEAR PROPULSION and the plan for a nuclear ramjet engine in the PLUTO program, the technology was briefly experimented with and then abandoned as less risky, less expensive, and more conventional systems developed.

LOS ALAMOS had started designing Kiwi reactors that had cores that could reach high power levels in 1957. The name, Kiwi, was chosen because it was a flightless bird. The Kiwi reactors would be tested entirely on the ground, using liquid hydrogen.

The N division at Los Alamos took sole charge of the Rover project in 1957. While the laboratory at Livermore concentrated on Pluto, Los Alamos did the work on Rover. Los Alamos completed a test using an experimental Kiwi reactor on July 1, 1959, at Jackass Flats at the NEVADA TEST SITE. The test was successful, with a jet of hydrogen heated in the reactor core shooting hundreds of feet into the air from a nozzle.

Two later tests, using Kiwi reactors called Phoebus and Pewee, were conducted in the summer and fall of 1960. The Rover tests ran a high risk of radioactive particles spreading from the test site, although the first tests produced no visible cloud and only traces of radioactivity beyond the site.

Originally funded by the U.S. Air Force, Rover was transferred to the National Aeronautics and Space Administration (NASA) in 1958. Despite initial successes in 1959, tests of Kiwi-B led to delays as the rocket engine performed roughly in 1961, increasing concerns with possible off-site radioactive FALLOUT. Eventually, the nuclear rocket project was canceled entirely in 1973, partly due to increasing environmental awareness and concern that a rocket with a reactor engine would be extremely hazardous if it crashed. With successful rocket motors designed using solid and liquid fuel, the attractiveness of nuclear-powered space flight declined rapidly.

In the early 1960s, the concept of using nuclear power for space rockets was dubbed Nuclear Engine for Rocket Vehicle Application (NERVA), and the joint Atomic Energy Commission–NASA funded offices were designated Space Nuclear Propulsion Office (SNPO). In the 1960s, the Rover project with Kiwi engines and Kiwi-derived designs was administered by SNPO. SNPO was closed with the termination of the project in 1973.

Suggested Reading

Joseph A. Angelo and David Buden, *Space Nuclear Power.* Malibar, Fla.: Orbit Press, 1985.

Barton Hacker, *Elements of Controversy: The Atomic Energy Commission and Radiation Safety in Nuclear Weapons Testing, 1947–1974.* Berkeley: University of California Press, 1994.

Project Vela

During the negotiations over the LIMITED TEST BAN TREATY (LTBT) that would prohibit atmospheric nuclear tests, the United States began a series of experiments and tests to improve methods of detecting both high-altitude and underground nuclear tests. The code name Vela, for "verification" was adopted. As part of a series of SAFEGUARDS to ensure that the LTBT would not work against U.S. interests, methods of monitoring were tested.

Vela-Hotel satellites to detect high-altitude or outer space tests were developed, while Vela-Uniform tests pursued methods of verifying underground tests that were detonated in large excavated caverns and decoupled from the earth to reduce their seismic signatures. Together, Vela-Hotel and Vela-Uniform projects represented the fourth of four safeguards developed following the 1963 treaty.

See also DECOUPLING.

Proliferation

After the United States and the Soviet Union developed the nuclear arms race in the 1950s, both nations soon became concerned as other countries developed the capability to develop nuclear weapons.

JOINING THE NUCLEAR CLUB

United States	July 16, 1945
U.S.S.R.	Aug. 29, 1949
United Kingdom	Oct. 3, 1952
France	Feb. 13, 1960
Peoples Repub.	
CHINA	Oct. 16, 1964
INDIA	May 18, 1974
PAKISTAN	May 28, 1998

Soon Great Britain developed its own independent nuclear weapons industry, followed by France and China. By the mid-1960s, there were five announced nuclear powers, and it was clear that ISRAEL had begun to develop a nuclear capability. Although Britain, the U.S.S.R., and the United States, as announced nuclear powers, could agree on very little through the cold war period, they did agree that they did not want other nations to "join the nuclear club." The process of new nations developing a nuclear capacity came to be called "proliferation."

The three nuclear powers signed the Treaty on the Non-Proliferation of Nuclear Weapons (known as the NON-PROLIFERATION TREATY [NPT]) on July 1, 1968. The treaty came into force on March 5, 1970. China, France, and INDIA did not adhere to the treaty, although France agreed to adhere to the provisions not to export nuclear weapons technology. Over 120 nations signed the treaty, promising not to develop nuclear weapons.

On May 18, 1974, India detonated underground a PLUTONIUM nuclear device with an estimated yield of 10 to 15 kilotons, making it the sixth announced nuclear state, although it preferred to keep its status ambiguous, claiming the device was for peaceful purposes, not a weapon.

Pakistan also developed a capability but refrained from detonating a nuclear device. On May 11 and 13, 1998, India detonated nuclear weapons and announced that it had manufactured nuclear weapons. Pakistan responded with five tests on May 28 and 30, 1998. SOUTH AFRICA constructed six weapons but later dismantled them. Israel was reputed to have a stockpile of weapons exceeding 100 in number by the 1990s.

Plutonium for nuclear weapons can be manufactured by reprocessing spent fuel from power reactors. Thus one method of determining whether a nation has begun a nuclear weapons program is the identification of the large facilities needed for a reprocessing plant. An even more sure indication of a nation's intention to produce nuclear weapons can be revealed by its construction of a PRODUCTION REACTOR. Known production reactors outside of the United States and the Soviet Union are shown in the table on page 270.

Suggested Reading

Rodney Jones et al., *Tracking Nuclear Proliferation.* Washington: Carnegie Endowment for International Peace, 1998.

Gary Milhollin, "Heavy Water Cheaters," *Foreign Affairs* 69, (Winter 1987–1988).

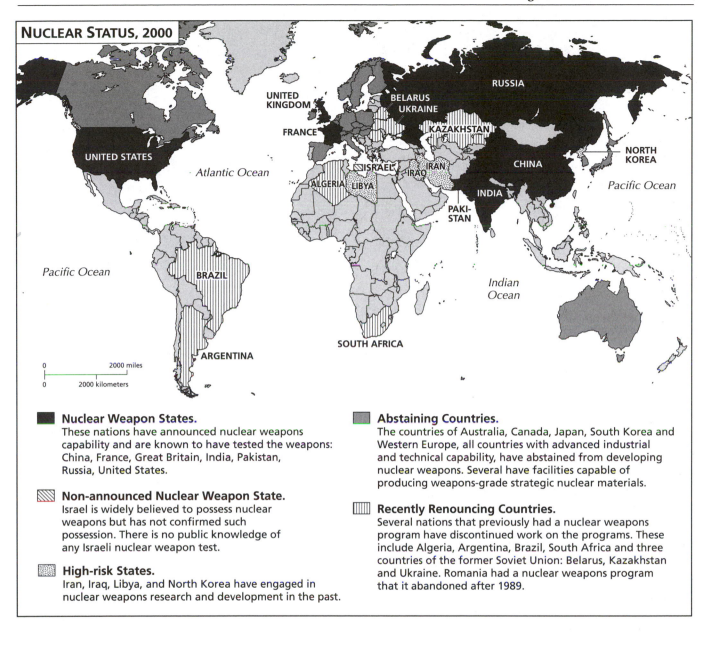

NUCLEAR STATUS, 2000

Nuclear Weapon States.
These nations have announced nuclear weapons capability and are known to have tested the weapons: China, France, Great Britain, India, Pakistan, Russia, United States.

Non-announced Nuclear Weapon State.
Israel is widely believed to possess nuclear weapons but has not confirmed such possession. There is no public knowledge of any Israeli nuclear weapon test.

High-risk States.
Iran, Iraq, Libya, and North Korea have engaged in nuclear weapons research and development in the past.

Abstaining Countries.
The countries of Australia, Canada, Japan, South Korea and Western Europe, all countries with advanced industrial and technical capability, have abstained from developing nuclear weapons. Several have facilities capable of producing weapons-grade strategic nuclear materials.

Recently Renouncing Countries.
Several nations that previously had a nuclear weapons program have discontinued work on the programs. These include Algeria, Argentina, Brazil, South Africa and three countries of the former Soviet Union: Belarus, Kazakhstan and Ukraine. Romania had a nuclear weapons program that it abandoned after 1989.

Tom Wilkie, "Old Age Can Kill the Bomb," *New Scientist* 139 (February 16, 1984).

Pugwash Conferences

Beginning in July 1957 and almost annually thereafter, nuclear scientists from the United States and the Soviet Union met to discuss various aspects of arms control. Named after the town of Pugwash in Nova Scotia, Canada, where the first meeting was held at the home of American industrialist Cyrus Eaton, these meetings were entirely nonofficial. However, the scientists could carry back to their governments informal suggestions from the other side, and together they could explore such questions as the NATIONAL TECHNICAL MEANS for verifying whether a nuclear explosion had occurred.

The first meeting was held in response to a suggestion in 1955 by a group including Bertrand Russell, Albert EINSTEIN, and nine other internationally respected scientists and scholars. Early on, the Pugwash conferences endorsed the concept of a comprehensive test ban. The first meeting included 22 scientists, with seven from the United States, three from the Soviet Union, three from Japan, two each from Britain and Canada, and single representatives from Australia, Austria, China, France, and Poland.

PROLIFERATION PRODUCTION REACTORS
(NON-SOVIET AND NON–U.S. WEAPONS-GRADE MATERIAL PRODUCTION REACTORS C. 1988)

NATION/LOCATION		MODERATOR/COOLANT	PRODUCT
BRITAIN			
Windscale		graphite/light water	PU
Calder Hall	4 reactors	graphite/light water	PU & Steam
Chapel Cross	4 reactors	graphite/light water	PU
	1 reactor	graphite/light water	Tritium
FRANCE			
Marcoule		graphite/gas	PU
Celestin I		heavy water/heavy water	Tritium
Celestin II		heavy water/heavy water	Tritium
CHINA			
Paotow	2 reactors	(info. not available)	PU
ISRAEL			
Dimona (100+MW)		heavy water/heavy water	PU and Tritium
INDIA			
Dhruva (220MW)		heavy water/heavy water	PU
Cirus	3 reactors	heavy water/light water	PU

Forty years later, as the group met in Lillehammer, Norway, the organization could look back on an impressive record of efforts to bring nuclear peace. The Pugwash organization had held over 220 meetings of experts in symposiums and workshops. Some of their findings were useful in the design of arms control inspection techniques. Soviet scientists appear to have been convinced at Pugwash meetings of the usefulness of a treaty against ANTI-BALLISTIC MISSILES, contributing to the Soviet willingness to agree to that treaty in 1972.

Among the organizers and supporters of the early Pugwash conference were Bernard Feld and Harrison Brown, both of whom had served as editors of the BULLETIN OF ATOMIC SCIENTISTS, and Joseph Rotblat, who had worked on the Manhattan Project until 1944. Eugene Rabinowitch, who had been one of the founders and first editor of the *Bulletin,* was also active in the group of scientists that founded the Pugwash movement. The Pugwash membership sought to control the total number of nuclear weapons, the testing of nuclear weapons, and their proliferation. Many of the elements of arms control agreements were discussed first at the Pugwash meetings.

The Pugwash meetings reflected some of the ideas about the dangers of nuclear weaponry put forward in World War II by such thinkers as Niels BOHR, Leo SZILARD, and James FRANCK.

See also ARMS CONTROL; UNIVERSITY OF CHICAGO.

Suggested Reading

Joseph Rotblat, *Scientists in the Quest for Peace.* Cambridge, Mass.: MIT Press, 1972.

Quantum Theory

The quantum theory of Max Planck maintains that energy is emitted or absorbed in distinct units or quanta. Energy is not emitted or absorbed continuously. A unit or quantum of radiant energy is equal to the mathematical product of its frequency and Planck's constant, 6.6256×10^{-34} Js. The carrier of a quantum of energy is the photon.

Max Karl Ernst PLANCK framed the quantum theory in 1900, winning the NOBEL PRIZE in physics for his work in 1918. Albert EINSTEIN applied Planck's theory to photoelectricity in 1905, and Niels BOHR successfully applied the theory to atomic structure in 1913.

R

Rabi, Isidor I. (1898–1988) *Austrian-born American Nobel Prize–winning physicist who worked as a consultant on the Manhattan Project and later served as an advisor on nuclear policy*

Isidor Rabi was a nuclear physicist specializing in subatomic particles, who received the NOBEL PRIZE for physics for his work in 1944. Born in Austria in 1898, he grew up in New York City and studied at Cornell University and Columbia University, receiving his doctorate from the latter in 1927. He taught at Columbia during the 1930s.

He took a leave from his academic position to serve as director of the Radiation Laboratory at the Massachusetts Institute of Technology during World War II. He was one of the first scientists approached by J. Robert OPPENHEIMER to work on the MANHATTAN ENGINEER DISTRICT. Rabi objected to the idea that the proposed development laboratory be under direct military control. After Oppenheimer was able to assure civilian scientists that they could retain their status, Rabi joined the project as a consultant. He was among those attending the first test of the atomic bomb at TRINITY on July 16, 1945.

With the establishment of the GENERAL ADVISORY COMMITTEE in 1946, Rabi served as one of the first appointees. He served on the committee until 1956.

With the resignation of Oppenheimer as chair of the committee, Rabi occupied that post from 1952 to 1956. As a member of the GAC, Rabi made many contributions. In 1948, he proposed that reactor safety be expressed in a formula, anticipating the development of PROBABILISTIC RISK ASSESSMENT by more than a decade. In 1952, he opposed the plans of Ernest LAWRENCE and Edward TELLER to develop a second weapons development laboratory in California. Like many others, he believed that a second laboratory would place a strain on the limited supply of talent in the field.

When the ATOMIC ENERGY COMMISSION reviewed Oppenheimer's security clearance and then refused to renew it, Rabi was an outspoken defender of Oppenheimer. He frequently praised Oppenheimer in later interviews, believing Oppenheimer to have been extremely creative and brilliant and the ideal person to have led the project during the war years.

Rabi was credited with originating the concept of the CERN international laboratory for high energy physics in Geneva, Switzerland, and he was one of the founders of the Brookhaven National Laboratory in Upton, New York. In 1957, he was appointed chairman of the President's Science Advisory Committee. Rabi died on January 11, 1988.

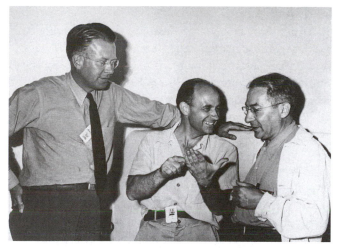

Lawrence, Fermi, and Rabi. E. O. Lawrence (left) listens intently as Enrico Fermi (center) jokes with Isidor Rabi (right) when the three nuclear scientists gather at a reunion of Manhattan Engineer District scientists at Los Alamos. (National Archives and Records Administration)

RAD

The RAD (Radiation Absorbed Dose) is a unit of radiation dosimetry equal to the absorption of 100 ergs of radiant energy by one gram of matter. The RAD has been replaced by the Gray (Gy), in which one Gy corresponds to the absorption of one joule of radiant energy by one kilogram of matter. 1 Gy = 100 RAD.

Radiation Shielding

Physical barriers are designed to provide protection from the effects of ionizing radiation. Nuclear reactors and nuclear materials processing facilities are usually shielded to protect workers from the indirect effect of X-rays, gamma-rays, and neutrons. Alpha and beta particles are not highly penetrating, and shielding requirements for these particles are minor.

Metal and concrete are often used as shielding materials, although both suffer damage or change in mechanical properties after extended exposure. Because of their CROSS SECTIONS, barium and lithium make excellent shields against gamma radiation.

In reactors, shielding often consists of two types: A thermal shield is designed to absorb most of the energy and to protect the reactor vessel from radiation damage, often made of steel; a biological shield is then added outside to provide protection for workers, reducing the external dose rate to an acceptable level.

Radioactive Waste

Radioactive waste has been classified into three categories: HIGH-LEVEL WASTE, TRANSURANIC WASTE, and LOW-LEVEL WASTE. High-level wastes are those that result from reprocessing of spent fuel or the spent fuel from defense reactors or commercial power reactors. When processed, the waste contains fission products and small amounts of PLUTONIUM. Although alternative schemes to dispose of the waste have been considered, deep geologic disposal is the current plan for U.S. high-level waste.

Transuranic wastes are those with ISOTOPES above URANIUM in the periodic table. They are by-products of fuel assembly and weapons production. Their radioactivity is low, but since there are long-lived isotopes in the waste, they must be handled separately. Isotopes with half-lives of over 20 years and with over 100 nanocuries per gram of waste material fall in this category. Common transuranic isotopes include neptunium-237, plutonium-239, americium-241, americium-243, curium-244, and curium-245.

Low-level waste is material with very little radioactivity and usually without transuranic elements. These include gloves, tools, garments, and equipment from the nuclear industry, hospitals, and research organizations.

Mixed wastes are low-level wastes that have some hazardous chemicals mixed with them. These might include heavy metals (such as lead or mercury), pesticides, dangerous compounds, corrosive acids, or explosives.

Uranium mill tailings represent a separate type of hazardous waste from the nuclear industry.

The handling of each of these categories of waste has presented special problems, especially at defense and commercial power reactor sites. During the 1970s, the American public began to become aware of the issue of radioactive waste generated by nuclear power reactors. All of the commercial power reactors and the government-owned production reactors used uranium fuel that, once used, had to be reprocessed or disposed of. The spent nuclear fuel was stored at the reactors, awaiting a national program for long-term disposal.

High-level waste and transuranic waste presented special problems because of the long-term radioactivity of the materials. Dumping high-level waste and transuranic waste in the ocean would pollute the water, and that practice was outlawed by Congress in 1970. Burial presented the danger that radioactive isotopes would seep into the water table and possibly pollute water used for drinking or for agriculture. The temporary solution of on-site storage at the reactors began to stretch into a semipermanent one.

In 1975, the ENERGY RESEARCH AND DEVELOPMENT ADMINISTRATION began study of a remote disposal facility that could handle transuranic wastes. The proposed WASTE ISOLATION PILOT PROJECT (WIPP) consisted of tunnels dug into a salt deposit near Carlsbad, New Mexico. However, New Mexico residents fought against the proposed WIPP site. A later plan to build a waste facility in granite deposits at YUCCA MOUNTAIN near the NEVADA TEST SITE also led to public and political opposition. In both New Mexico and Nevada, the governors demanded local participation in plans for long-term waste disposal of radioactive hazardous materials.

The federal government proceeded with plans for a long-term storage facility in Nevada for high-level waste generated by both defense and commercial rectors while states entered into compacts to share regionally the storage of low-level waste from commercial reactors and other facilities under a 1980 law.

The Low-Level Radioactive Waste Policy Act of 1980 stipulated that each state was responsible for providing the availability either within or outside of the state for disposal of low-level radioactive waste. The law called for interstate compacts to be formed and sites to be selected. By 1985, several compacts had been established, but disputes over sites and the failure of several states to affiliate with others in groupings made it clear the law would be not become effective. Congress then passed the Low-Level Radioactive Waste Policy Amendments Act (1985), keeping open commercial sites in Barnwell, South Carolina, Beatty, Nevada, and Richland, Washington, pending a future decision on low-level waste. The Waste Isolation Pilot Plant in New Mexico was to take transuranic waste, but court action delayed that operation until 1998.

Although legislative and judicial wrangling over these issues continued in the 1990s, Yucca Mountain and the Waste Isolation Pilot Plant in New Mexico appeared to be emerging as the final sites for long-term repositories of high-level waste and transuranic waste.

See also FALLOUT; NUCLEAR FUEL CYCLE; WEST VALLEY, NEW YORK.

Suggested Reading
Raymond L. Murray, *Understanding Radioactive Waste*, 4th ed. Columbus, Ohio: Battelle Memorial Institute, 1994.

Radioactivity

Radioactivity is the process by which radioactive nuclides spontaneously emit energy in order to achieve a more stable arrangement of nucleons. The energy is emitted as α and/or β and/or γ radiations, and the rate at which the process occurs is related to the half-life of the radioactive nuclide. Both the kinds of energy emitted and the rate of emission are characteristic of the radioactive nuclide.

The emission of an α particle, which consists of two protons and two neutrons, is α radiation. An α particle is identical to the nucleus of a helium atom. Compared to other forms of radiation, α particles can penetrate only a very small distance through matter. The most energetic α particles emitted from a radioactive substance are stopped after passing through less than 10 centimeters of air, or about 0.1 of a millimeter of water.

The emission of a β particle, which is an electron, is β radiation. β particles are more penetrating than α particles but less penetrating than γ radiation. The β particles emitted in natural radiation are negatively charged. In the 1930s, positively charged β particles were discovered, and they were called positrons. Although very rare in nature, they are more common among the radioactive nuclei produced in fission. They can travel a few meters in air.

γ rays are photons or quanta of radiation that have neither mass nor charge. They are the most penetrating form of the three types, and they are therefore the most dangerous.

See also NUCLEAR REACTIONS.

RAND Corporation

The RAND Corporation was established in 1948 by former Air Force General H. H. ("Hap" Arnold) to provide a setting for the new field of operations research that had developed during the World War II. The name of the firm stood for Research AND Development, although the company did not pursue development of equipment or hardware. In fact, although the company was staffed by many scientists and engineers, it soon developed a specialty in a new field of social science that came to be called national security affairs.

RAND was set up as a nonprofit corporation with its headquarters in Santa Monica, California, and many have regarded it as the first "think tank" in the United States. Although some of its early problems grew out of questions for the U.S. Air Force, it soon expanded its subject matter to larger questions of national policy regarding national security and nuclear weapons strategy.

Many specialists contributing to the debates surrounding the use of ANTI-BALLISTIC MISSILES, MULTIPLE INDEPENDENTLY TARGETABLE REENTRY VEHICLES, and the developing SINGLE INTEGRATED OPERATIONAL PLAN created through RAND in the 1950s and 1960s.

Rasmussen Report

The ATOMIC ENERGY COMMISSION (AEC) set up a panel to review the safety of nuclear reactors in 1971, appointing a team headed by Norman C. Rasmussen, an engineering professor at MIT. The panel began work in 1972, and in 1975 Rasmussen issued his panel's report, cited as the Rasmussen Report, the Reactor Safety Study, WASH 1400, or NUREG-75 014.

The report's first draft included an executive summary, disavowed later by the NUCLEAR REGULATORY COMMISSION (NRC). The summary stated that the risk of being killed by a nuclear reactor accident was about the same as the risk of being hit by a meteorite. Under the federal PRICE-ANDERSON ACT, passed in 1957 and reenacted in 1967 and 1977, the liability limit for a power reactor accident was set at $560 million. The Rasmussen Report was issued in time to become part of the debate over the 1977 renewal of the Price-Anderson Act. The report confirmed that the liability limit was adequate. The report's general conclusions about the relative safety of nuclear power reactors put it at the center of the pro- and antinuclear debates of the late 1970s.

The AEC had asked the Rasmussen panel to develop a credible means of assessing the likelihood of a large radioactive release from a reactor core and of evaluating the insurable risk. Rasmussen and his colleagues worked to find a nonpolitical and technically accurate means of estimating the risk of reactor operation. Critics charged that the report represented an effort to enlist science to make a policy decision seem more objective and palatable, which was partially true. Even so, the methods used in the report represented the best risk assessment techniques developed to that time.

Rasmussen approached the question of likelihood of failure of reactors by drawing on probabilistic methods, which studied event trees and fault trees to arrive at final probability scores or rankings. An event tree considers an event that starts off a chain of other events and their consequences. A fault tree is the reverse of an event tree. Presuming a machine shows poor performance or failure, what possible faults could have contributed to the failure? Rasmussen used event and fault trees and estimated probabilities at the branching points in the trees. By multiplying the fractional chances of failure, the likelihood of a very unlikely event could be mathematically estimated.

An unlikely event could have very serious consequences. Risk represented a combination of likely frequency and likely consequence.

In order to determine how the public would view such unlikely but very dangerous risks, the report compared nuclear reactor accidents to more socially accepted hazards, such as the failure of dams, catastrophic fires, and highway travel. The report quantified, measured, and spelled out the criteria of acceptable risk by showing that the public already accepted similar degrees of risk for other energy systems.

The panel studied the likelihood of a major failure resulting from infrequent events, including minor human errors or small power cutoffs or "transients," as well as major pipe or containment failures. Even some critics of the report would praise its attention to event chains or trees that showed how minor unlikely events could interact or happen in sequence, possibly leading to very serious accidents.

Even so, most critics of Rasmussen believed that the risk of reactors to the public should not be compared to the risk of driving in an automobile or riding on a railroad because such risks were matters of individual choice. But under nuclear reactor licensing and the Price-Anderson Act, policy decisions would impose reactor risk on people without their personal choice.

Although the executive summary of the Rasmussen Report left the impression that power reactors entailed minimal risks, the body of the report, endorsed by NRC, took a much more precise and more cautious tone. Considering all of the factors, the report concluded that the combined chance of a major failure at a reactor leading to more than 10 deaths could be estimated at about once in 1 million operating years. As the number of operating reactors in the United States climbed, the chance of serious accident at one of them would increase. On the other hand, as safety methods improved and designs were refined, a serious accident could become even less likely.

The overall conclusions of the Rasmussen Report and its method of using probability to assess risk were more widely accepted after the THREE MILE ISLAND accident in 1979.

See also DETERMINISTIC RISK ASSESSMENT; PROBABILISTIC RISK ASSESSMENT.

Suggested Reading

Rodney Carlisle, "Probabilistic Risk Assessment: Engineering Success, Public Relations Failure," *Technology and Culture* (Fall 1997).

Ray, Dixy Lee (1914–1994)   *American professor of biology who was the first woman appointed to a full five-year term on the Atomic Energy Commission (AEC), the only woman ever to serve as chair of the commission, and the governor of the state of Washington, 1977–1981*

Ray was born on September 14, 1914, in Tacoma, Washington. She was educated at Mills College, California, where she majored in zoology, and after a period of secondary school teaching, she earned a doctorate in biology at Stanford in 1945. She then took a position at the University of Washington, where she remained on the faculty until 1972. During this period, she served in a number of advisory and consulting positions, including special assistant to the director of the National Science Foundation and, in 1969, as a member of a presidential task force on oceanography.

President Richard NIXON appointed Ray as a member of the AEC in August 1972 and then as chair of the commission in February 1973. Although appointed to a five-year term on the commission, the commission was replaced by the ENERGY RESEARCH AND DEVELOPMENT ADMINISTRATION (ERDA) in January 1975, and with that change, her position terminated. Richard Seamans was appointed to serve as head of ERDA.

During her tenure with the AEC, Ray was a strong advocate of nuclear power and tried to correct misinformation regarding the impact of nuclear development on the environment. She also argued for the separation of the regulatory and advocacy functions of the AEC. That separation was realized by the creation of the Nuclear Regulatory Commission, which served to regulate nuclear power, and ERDA, which worked to assist in the research, development, and promotion of nuclear power.

In 1977, Ray won the Republican nomination for governor of Washington, and she served from 1977 to 1981. In retirement she resided at her family home on Fox Island in the Puget Sound in Washington. There she co-authored two works: *Trashing the Planet* (1990) and *Environmental Overkill* (1993). She died on January 2, 1994.

Reagan, Ronald (1911–)   *American movie actor who served as president of the United States from January 20, 1981, to January 20, 1989*

Although Ronald Reagan was known for his aggressive rhetoric directed at the Soviet Union and for his advocacy of a strong defense, during his administrations the United States negotiated significant arms reduction and arms control treaties. Furthermore, the United States deployed and then removed nuclear missiles from Europe, diminished and then stopped its production of nuclear materials for weapons, and developed programs of compensation for claimants for radiological injury as a result of prior weapons tests.

Reagan was born February 6, 1911, in Tampico, Illinois. He graduated from Eureka College in 1932, and he worked for a period as a radio sports announcer in Des Moines, Iowa. He began working as a movie actor in 1937, starring in numerous movies and appearing on television until the 1960s. He was president of the Screen Actors Guild (1947–1952) and entered politics by running for governor of California in 1966. He served as governor until 1974. In 1980, he was nominated for the presidency on the Republican ticket and defeated Jimmy CARTER. He was easily reelected in 1984.

During his first presidential campaign, he had advocated the elimination of the DEPARTMENT OF ENERGY, and his first secretary of energy, James B. EDWARDS, a former dentist, appeared committed to that goal. However, Reagan replaced Edwards with Donald HODEL and the department survived. The department studied the issue of supply of strategic nuclear materials needed to keep up with the demand generated by the production of missiles with MULTIPLE INDEPENDENTLY TARGETED REENTRY VEHICLES. Another program, to develop an enhanced-radiation weapon, or "neutron-bomb," also created needs for more production of TRITIUM and PLUTONIUM. As a consequence, L reactor at SAVANNAH RIVER

Ronald Reagan. As president of the United States from 1981 to 1989, Ronald Reagan took a strong rhetorical line with the Soviet leaders, but he also initiated arms control talks that eventually resulted in a reduction in nuclear arms. (Library of Congress)

SITE was reactivated in 1985. Studies of possible sites for a NEW PRODUCTION REACTOR, however, tended to result in political disputes between potential sites, and no decision was reached to build such a reactor. By the end of his second administration, all PRODUCTION REACTORS were closed, and the production of plutonium and tritium came to a halt.

In March 1983, Reagan announced his support for a system of space-based missile defenses, collectively known as the STRATEGIC DEFENSE INITIATIVE, or Star Wars. Discussions of this concept as well as discussions of a mobile missile system, the MX MISSILE, created a public impression of increased weaponry. At the same time, plans initiated during the administration of Jimmy Carter to develop and deploy intermediate-range ballistic missiles to be emplaced in Europe, particularly ground-launched CRUISE MISSILES and PERSHING II missiles went forward. Deployment of "Euromissiles" began in 1983, representing one prong of the DUAL-TRACK STRATEGY first announced by the NORTH ATLANTIC TREATY ORGANIZATION in 1979.

Reagan restated the other prong of the dual-track strategy by proposing the "ZERO OPTION" under which the United States and the Soviets would reduce their intermediate-range missiles to zero. Although attractive, the Soviets at first rejected this option because it

did not include British or French missiles nor missiles aboard U.S. ships and submarines. With the rejection of the zero option, deployment of *Pershings* and ground-launched cruise missiles began.

With these deployments and the breakdown of negotiations toward a SALT II treaty, as well as highly critical and hostile statements by Reagan and members of his administration toward the Soviets, it appeared that the nuclear weapons side of the cold war was entering a more serious and dangerous stage. Nevertheless, Reagan met with Mikhail GORBACHEV at REYKJAVIK, Iceland, in October 1986. At this SUMMIT meeting, the two leaders appeared to agree in principle that all nuclear weapons should be eliminated. Steps toward such a goal were initiated when Gorbachev embraced the zero option and agreed to the INTERMEDIATE-RANGE NUCLEAR FORCES TREATY signed in 1987, under which the Euromissiles were removed. Negotiations proceeded towards START I, originally proposed by Reagan as early as May 1982.

During his administration, public opposition to power reactors at both SEABROOK in New Hampshire and SHOREHAM on Long Island, New York, effectively stopped both projects. In both cases, Democratic governors worked strenuously with environmental groups to stop the reactor developments, while the DEPARTMENT OF ENERGY and the NUCLEAR REGULATORY COMMISSION sought to get the projects underway.

In 1985, Reagan appointed John HERRINGTON as secretary of energy. Herrington worked to advance programs to manage radioactive waste management, modernize the weapons complex, and plan a new production reactor. In 1988, Congress approved the administration-endorsed Radiation-Exposed Veterans Claims Act, in which the government agreed to compensate ATOMIC VETERANS who believed they had contracted cancer as a result of exposure during atmospheric nuclear testing in the 1950s.

Reentry Vehicle (RV)

A reentry vehicle (RV) is that part of a missile carrying the warhead. Reentry vehicles are released from the last stage of a missile that travels out of the atmosphere (in exo-atmospheric trajectory). RVs are shielded or insulated to survive the heating that results from friction with the air, and they are designed to protect the warhead and other components until detonation at or over the intended target. In order to protect the warhead against the weapons effects of ANTI-BALLISTIC MISSILES or against the FRATRICIDE effects of other weapons sent against the target, RVs have been hardened against radiation and other nuclear effects. When several RVs directed to separate targets are included in a single missile, it is described as a MULTIPLE INDEPENDENTLY TARGETABLE REENTRY VEHICLE (MIRV) missile.

See also INTERCONTINENTAL BALLISTIC MISSILE.

REM

The REM (Roentgen Equivalent Man) is a unit of radiation dosimetry that, when absorbed by the human body, produces the same biological effect as the absorption of one Roentgen of x or gamma radiation. The REM has been replaced by the Sievert (Sv), where one Sv is the biological damage caused by one joule of alpha or gamma radiation absorbed per kilogram of tissue. 1 Sv = 100 REM.

Reprocessing

When nuclear power plants were first licensed in the United States in the 1960s and early 1970s, the ATOMIC ENERGY COMMISSION (AEC) assumed that part of the cost of producing electric power from reactors would be offset by reprocessing the spent fuel from the reactors to gain PLUTONIUM from the fuel. The plutonium could be utilized in reactors designed to run on plutonium or on a plutonium-uranium mix.

Soon technical difficulties arose, however. The spent nuclear fuel contains uranium-236, which absorbs neutrons. A reprocessing plant was constructed at WEST VALLEY, NEW YORK, and operated for three years (1963–1966) before developing severe contamination. It was shut down permanently. Construction of another reprocessing plant began at Barnwell, South Carolina, but that was discontinued by 1984.

Because the raw material that goes into a reprocessing plant is highly radioactive, all operations have to be conducted in a shielded environment. The British established a reprocessing plant at WINDSCALE. There, the operation was conducted inside tanks containing a zinc bromide solution, using remote-controlled arms to put the spent fuel through a chemical organic solvent. The Windscale Head End Plant relied on chopping up the fuel elements and dissolving out the fuel from inside the cladding. The hazardous procedure

eventually led to an accident in September 1973 that resulted in closing the plant.

In the United States, the concept of putting spent reactor fuel through a reprocessing plant was abandoned after 1980 with the termination of the BREEDER REACTOR program.

Commercial reprocessing of fuels and production of plutonium began in the 1960s and 1970s at nine facilities:

NATION	FACILITY	YEAR STARTED
Belgium	Eurochemic-Mol	1966
France	Cap La Hague	1966
	Marcoule	1956
Germany	Karlsruhe	1969
Great Britain	Windscale	1964
India	Tarapur	1978
	Trombay	1964
Japan	Tokai Mura	1978
United States	West Valley	1963

In addition, military reprocessing plants operated in the United States, the Soviet Union, and France. Security surrounded presumed reprocessing plants in CHINA, ISRAEL, PAKISTAN, and NORTH KOREA. Other nations, such as ARGENTINA, developed laboratory-scale reprocessing facilities.

Suggested Reading

Patterson, Walter C. *The Plutonium Business*. San Francisco: The Sierra Club, 1984.

Reykjavik Summit Conference

On October 11–12, 1986, President Ronald REAGAN and the general secretary of the Soviet Communist Party, Mikhail GORBACHEV, met at the Hofdi House in Reykjavik, Iceland. This particular summit meeting was unusual in that both Reagan and Gorbachev first introduced the possibility of the total elimination of nuclear weapons and of the delivery systems involved. Apparently Gorbachev was willing to discuss the idea only if Reagan would agree to abandon the proposal for space-based defensive systems that had been introduced in 1983, the STRATEGIC DEFENSE INITIATIVE. Reagan refused, but even so, a tentative agreement to begin work toward total nuclear disarmament was hammered out. Later, neither side ratified the agreement.

Many U.S. arms control experts and nuclear strategists regarded the discussion at Reykjavik as irresponsible or uninformed, but the concepts introduced there received quite favorable responses among antinuclear activists and some journalists.

The concept of the ZERO OPTION later formed the basis of discussions leading to the Strategic Arms Reduction Treaty (START I) and to the intermediate nuclear forces agreements. Some commentators have compared the Reykjavik proposals to the original BARUCH PLAN developed in 1946, which would have required international inspection to verify that nations were not developing nuclear weapons.

Suggested Reading

Patrick Glynn, *Closing Pandora's Box: Arms Races, Arms Control, and the History of the Cold War.* New York: Basic Books, 1992.

Rickover, Hyman (1900–1986)   *a U.S. naval officer who advocated and promoted, then managed, the effort to bring nuclear propulsion first to submarines and then to surface ships*

Hyman Rickover was known for his demanding management style and his insistence on safety and quality. He built broad political and institutional support in order to stay in charge of the nuclear propulsion effort for more than 30 years, leaving an imprint on both the nuclear navy and the broader nuclear industry in the United States.

Born January 27, 1900, in Makow, Poland, he immigrated to the United States at age six. The family lived a few years in New York and then moved on to Chicago, where he attended public schools. In June 1918, he was admitted to the U.S. Naval Academy. He studied to make up for weakness in preparation, eventually graduating in 1922 with a standing of 107 in class of 540. As a Jewish student at the academy, he was not alone, and in fact the discrimination he experienced was not as serious as that suffered by some of his classmates. Nevertheless, he was known as an intense student, with his eye on academic achievement and a contemptuous disregard for naval traditions and protocol.

In 1929, he earned a master's degree in electrical engineering at Columbia University and sought to enlist in submarine duty. After studying at the New London submarine school, he was assigned as an executive officer on S-48, a diesel-electric submarine. In 1933, he was assigned a post as inspector of naval material at the PHILADELPHIA NAVAL SHIPYARD. While

Hyman Rickover. Admiral Hyman Rickover at the launching of nuclear submarine Dwight Eisenhower *with members of the former president's family. Rickover retained leadership of the nuclear submarine program for more than two decades.* (National Archives and Records Administration)

there, he translated from German to English a major treatise on submarine warfare, *Das Unterseeboot.* In the mid-1930s, he was assigned as assistant engineer officer on the battleship *New Mexico.* In this duty, Rickover insisted on maintaining peak efficiency, including conserving energy and improving the consumption of fuel oil. He literally unscrewed light bulbs and insisted that every dripping hot-water faucet be repaired, soon involving the whole crew in the competitive effort to improve energy efficiency. The ship earned the best rating in the navy on this score for a two-year period.

Rickover was promoted to lieutenant commander in 1937, and he took command of the minesweeper *Finch,* stationed in the China seas. During this period, he decided to apply for Engineering Duty Only, a designation that would keep him from ship command but would provide opportunities for advancement in ship design, construction, and maintenance.

In 1939 he reported to the Bureau of Ships in Washington under this designation, where he ran the electrical section of the bureau. As World War II started, his section of the Bureau of Ships began to contribute innovations and expand its authority to include infrared signaling and mine location. Under his leadership, the electrical section increased from a staff of 23 to over 300. During the war he was promoted to commander and then, in 1943, to captain.

With the end of the war, Rickover made a decisive career change. He took the opportunity to study, with other naval officers, the development of nuclear technology at OAK RIDGE. He arrived there in June 1946. Over the next few years, he emerged as the leader in the effort by the navy to develop reactors for nuclear propulsion. Chief of the Bureau of Ships, Admiral Earle Mills appointed Rickover to head Code 390 within the Research Division, the nuclear power branch.

As in many other developments in the navy, two alternative technologies were tried out: a pressurized water type reactor that was installed on *NAUTILUS* and a sodium-cooled reactor installed on *Seawolf*. In both cases, Rickover insisted on developing a land-based prototype and a reactor for the ship concurrently, thereby saving time. As difficulties in engineering were discovered in the prototype, they were solved and incorporated into the ship propulsion reactor immediately. Construction for *Nautilus* began in 1950 and for *Seawolf* in 1952.

Although Rickover was in charge of a major development effort, he was being passed over for promotion to admiral. Not only had he made many enemies along the way with his hard-driving and abrasive style, but the navy had only a limited number of slots for the admiral rank and had many deserving captains eligible for promotion. After the issue was publicly debated in the press and Congress, Rickover was promoted to rear admiral on July 1, 1953.

Rickover was able to secure a joint appointment as Director of Nuclear Reactor programs in the ATOMIC ENERGY COMMISSION as well as in the navy. He carefully built relations with the JOINT COMMITTEE ON ATOMIC ENERGY and with senators and congressmen serving on the armed services committees. Through such powerful legislators, he secured support for his programs and later was able to have Congress extend his tour of duty, delaying retirement 20 years beyond the normal retirement age of 62. He was reappointed every two years after 1962 by special congressional extensions. Congress forced his appointment to vice admiral in 1958 and full admiral in 1973.

Nautilus was commissioned on September 30, 1954, and went to sea on January 1, 1955. As more and more nuclear-propelled submarines were launched through the 1950s and 1960s, Rickover's reputation with Congress and the public further improved. His demanding management style and his concern for technical excellence became his hallmark, creating what has been dubbed the "Rickover effect." The officers who passed through his command in Naval Reactors took the same methods and style with them in operating the submarine fleet. Many who retired from the navy went on to serve in the commercial power sector, where Rickover's dedicated focus on safety, rigorous maintenance, and quality performance spread widely.

In working with those under his command in nuclear reactors or with the officers and crews of nuclear-propelled ships, Rickover constantly challenged personnel to demonstrate their knowledge and skills. Where they proved inadequate, he was very explicit in letting them know and in expecting them to come up to his standard.

Among the most famous of his management techniques were his interviews with prospective members of his team. He extended the practice to officers who would serve aboard nuclear ships. He would present those interviewed with problems and carefully watch their responses. Where they showed they were ill-prepared, he expected them to admit it, not to try to conceal their ignorance through evasion or persistence in error. Sometimes a candidate would be removed from the interview and told to reconsider his answer for an hour or two before the interview continued. Rickover remained suspicious of the navy's trust in "leadership" abilities, expecting officers to have excellent technical and scientific background and to be able to think for themselves.

Another management technique he employed was to work directly with individuals in his program rather than through extended chains of command. He put in extended hours and expected those working for him to do the same. He insisted that all persons working in the program or aboard nuclear ships and submarines be responsible for their own decisions and actions. Frequently, he would recruit naval reserve officers from good engineering schools, have them serve four or five years with the program, and then, on retirement from active duty, have them serve as civilians with the program, building a cadre of dedicated experts.

Rickover believed in what he called the "discipline of technology." By that he meant that technology knows no rank, would not yield to leadership, and would not obey an order. In all these ways, traditional naval values worked against the discipline of technology, which was rigid in its demands, based on the laws of nature. For these reasons, machines and products had to be extensively tested and analyzed so that the exact limitations of every component of a nuclear power system in a submarine or ship was thoroughly understood. A knowledge of the rules and limitations of technology based on such testing and analysis was essential to avoid a disaster with nuclear power.

During the period following the October 4, 1957, launching of the SPUTNIK satellite by the Soviet Union, Rickover increasingly emphasized the need for greater excellence in education in the United States, stressing the need for technical and scientific education and comparing the U.S. system to European schools with better records. He published several essays or short books on the topic: *Education and Freedom* (1959), *Report on Russian Education* (1960), *Education for All Children: What We Can Learn from England* (1962), *Swiss Schools and Ours—Why Theirs Are Better* (1962), and *American Education, A National Failure* (1963).

He made several contributions in the field of education: He was instrumental in setting up the Oak Ridge School of Reactor Technology, he worked with the Massachusetts Institute of Technology to establish a course in nuclear engineering, and he established a school at Bettis Atomic Power Laboratory and at the Naval Reactor Test Station in Idaho. In all of the programs, he expected students to gain a rigorous understanding of first principles and to be able to apply them to practical problems.

The nuclear propulsion program suffered two well-known accidents in the 1960s: the loss of THRESHER on April 10, 1963, and the loss of SCORPION on May 21, 1968. Various explanations have since been developed regarding the failure of these two submarines. A failure of piping on *Thresher*, when a seawater leak had sprayed electrical equipment, was the suspected cause of her loss. A torpedo accident was cited as one explanation for the loss of *Scorpion*. In neither case was the submarine reactor propulsion system blamed for the loss.

Rickover also played an important part in the origins of commercial nuclear power in the United States. In July 1953, the Atomic Energy Commission assigned the civilian power project to Rickover. In October 1953, Rickover authorized a contract with Westinghouse to design, fabricate, assemble, and test the reactor and the primary heat system. Ground was broken for the first plant by President Dwight EISENHOWER on September 6, 1954, at SHIPPINGPORT, Pennsylvania. The core of the reactor was installed on October 6, 1957, and the power station reached criticality for the first time on December 2, 1957. The reactor had a capacity of 60 megawatts-electrical and operated successfully until it was shut permanently on October 1, 1982.

Meanwhile, Rickover advocated and succeeded in establishing a program for nuclear propulsion of surface ships. By 1985, the navy had acquired nine nuclear-propelled cruisers and four nuclear-propelled aircraft carriers.

Shipyard	Period	Cruisers	Carriers
General Dynamics Quincy, Mass.	1961–1968	2	
Newport News, Va.	1958–1985	6	4
New York Shipbuilding Camden, N.J.	1960–1967	1	

In 1973, Rickover was promoted to full admiral. He received other honors in this period, including the naming of Rickover Hall at the U.S. Naval Academy in 1974 and the christening of a nuclear submarine, the *Hyman G. Rickover*, in 1983.

In 1982, Rickover retired from the navy a week before his 82nd birthday. Following his retirement, several controversies about his career surfaced. Rickover had charged Electric Boat and its holding company, General Dynamics, with excessive and unjustified cost overruns. P. Takis Veliotis, who had headed Electric Boat, left the United States to avoid prosecution on charges of taking kickbacks. From Greece, Veliotis released information accusing Rickover with having accepted personal gifts from Electric Boat. Although the gifts were minor items, such as tie-clasps, desk plaques, and a variety of ship and engine models, the press seized on the issue and gave it the dimensions of a scandal. More seriously, also included in the list of gifts were several jewelry items. Rickover, in his defense, pointed out that he had never let such gifts influence him in his dealings with contractors. Nevertheless, it was a violation of federal rules to have accepted any gifts whatsoever from contractors. Secretary of the Navy John Lehman issued a reprimand to Rickover and had it inserted in his personnel file.

Rickover supporters found the criticisms unfair and motivated by revenge on the part of Veliotis. Especially in view of the magnitude of expenses that Rickover sought to save the government in corporate price overruns, the gift issue was extremely minor and vindictive, they claimed. Rickover died on July 8, 1986.

See also NUCLEAR SUBMARINES.

Suggested Reading

Francis Duncan, *Rickover and the Nuclear Navy: The Discipline of Technology.* Annapolis, Md.: U.S. Naval Institute Press, 1990.

Richard G. Hewlett and Francis Duncan, *Nuclear Navy, 1946–1962.* Chicago: University of Chicago Press, 1974.

Norman Polmar, *Rickover.* New York: Simon and Schuster, 1982.

Theodore Rockwell, *The Rickover Effect: How One Man Made a Difference.* Annapolis, Md.: U.S. Naval Institute Press, 1992.

Risk

Risk is a measure of the likelihood of an event combined with the severity of the adverse effects of the event. For example, the risk of auto travel combines the fact that accidents are very likely to occur but, when they happen, they usually affect only a few individuals at a time. The risk of air travel is less in that fewer accidents occur; yet they affect more people at a time when they do occur, sometimes resulting in 100 deaths or more. Nuclear reactor accidents are even less common than airplane crashes, but, like the accident at CHERNOBYL they can expose millions of people to increased radiation and other possible ill effects. Because risk combines likelihood and severity, it is difficult to measure accurately.

Nuclear advocates claim that the risk of nuclear reactors is quite low and that the benefits to be derived from nuclear power outweigh the risks. This risk-benefit analysis is very difficult to calculate or to present in a convincing fashion to the general public. Opponents of nuclear power claim that the risk of an accident is so severe that the benefits of more plentiful electric power do not offset the risks. Supporters of nuclear power claim that such a line of criticism is not based on any calculation, but on an unreasonable appeal to fear or to a hostility to nuclear power based on its association with nuclear weaponry. In other words, some claim that the exaggerated sense of nuclear-power risk is a surrogate for fear of or opposition to nuclear weapons.

Engineers have tried to avoid the political side of the risk issue by developing methods of measuring risk that are based on mathematical or mechanical analyses. In PROBABILISTIC RISK ASSESSMENT, the likelihood of an accident is calculated based on the probability of various parts of a system failing. If the likelihood of a crucial subsystem failing is one out of 100, and the likelihood of a backup system failing at the same time is also one out of one hundred, the combined risk is 1 out of 10,000 or 1×10^{-4}. In DETERMINISTIC RISK ASSESSMENT, engineers make much simpler estimates based on traditional safety factors, making sure that essential components are several times stronger than needed for typical usage, ensuring that design is based on sound safety criteria.

For these reasons, the issue of risk is at the heart of the politicized debates over nuclear power and the safety of nuclear weapons–producing facilities. Different training and approaches among engineers over how to measure and assess risk have led to disagreements and compromises in which both probabilistic and deterministic methods are combined together in the effort to reduce risk.

See also NUCLEAR POWER, WORLD.

Rocky Flats

The primary mission of the nuclear weapons plant at Rocky Flats, near Boulder, Colorado, was to manufacture "pits," the core components of atomic bombs for 40 years, from 1952 through 1992.

Construction at the Rocky Flats site began in July 1951 during the KOREAN WAR. By April 1952, the first regular production of materials for weapons began and, by 1954, the 700,000-square foot plant was going at full pace. Employment at Rocky Flats increased from 131 people in 1951 to about 3,100 in 1963. During DETENTE with the Soviet Union in the late 1960s and the 1970s, employment dipped and then climbed again in the 1980s. At the end of the cold war, Rocky Flats employed between 5,000 and 6,000 workers.

When the United States began building large numbers of thermonuclear weapons in the 1960s, the new weapons required PLUTONIUM "primary" or "trigger" devices at their heart. Rocky Flat manufactured most of these plutonium triggers through the 1960s.

Hazardous waste disposal and potential accidents have been serious concerns since the beginning of Rocky Flats. On September 11, 1957, a fire began with plutonium in a protected area. The fire spread into an exhaust system and nearby rooms, damaging the air-exhaust system and duct work. It took over 24 hours to be sure the fire was extinguished.

A fire in 1965 received less public attention but may have spread more contamination through the vents of the plant. In this fire, 25 workers received dangerous levels of lung contamination. On May 11, 1969, another major fire in two buildings required management to close the buildings and move operations. The 1969 fire resulted in $45 million in damages. Both the 1957 and 1969 fires started in "glove boxes." Using a glove box, an operator would stand outside the box and work manually through gloves into the box to manipulate radioactive materials. The 1969 fire produced thick smoke and spread when plexiglass windows of the glove box caught fire.

An investigation of the 1969 fire led to the discovery of measurable amounts of plutonium in the soil around the plant. One of the problems with both fires was that workers could not use water to extinguish them as water might lead to a CHAIN REACTION and small nuclear explosion. However, as a last resort, fire fighters extinguished both fires with water.

Still another problem at Rocky Flats was the issue of liquid waste. Such waste was filtered and then solidified. The remaining fluid was channeled into ponds where it would evaporate or drained from holding ponds through a local creek into the Great Western Reservoir. Although the water from this reservoir was used for irrigation and not for drinking water, the drainage issue became one of concern in later years.

Some dangerous liquids were stored in buried steel drums, some of which were stacked on a concrete pad outdoors. When the tanks rusted, the drums started to leak, with radioactive seepage running into the ground. Traces of plutonium in the ground were traced to these leaking drums.

With increasing public concern about environmental issues in the 1970s, investigations by the Colorado Department of Health and the Environmental Protection Agency (EPA) made public many of the hazards of the plant.

In June 1989, in a much-publicized raid, the FBI and the EPA entered the plant with about 100 agents to collect records that the administrators had not withheld. As a result of the publicity, the DEPARTMENT OF ENERGY suspended plutonium processing at the plant. Governor Roy Romer of Colorado worked to obtain closer outside scrutiny of plant operations. The federal government shut the plant in December 1989 to bring it into compliance with environmental regulations. In 1992, however, the DOE canceled the plant's nuclear weapons role. After 1992, work at the plant focused on cleaning up the remaining hazardous waste there, and the plant ceased producing parts for nuclear weapons.

Suggested Reading

Office of Environmental Management, *Linking Legacies: Connecting the Cold War Nuclear Weapons Production Process to Their Environmental Consequences.* Washington, D.C.: U.S. Department of Energy, 1997.

Roentgen

The Roentgen is the quantity of x or gamma radiation producing one electrostatic unit of charge in one cubic centimeter of dry air at standard temperature and pressure. It is a measure of exposure to radiation equal to one Roentgen of x or gamma radiation. The Roentgen is named in honor of Wilhelm Roentgen who discovered X-rays in 1895.

Romania

For some years in the 1970s and 1980s, Romania was regarded as a potential nuclear weapon state. In 1989, the communist leader of Romania, Nicolae Ceausescu, announced that his country had the capability of building a nuclear weapon. When that regime was overthrown in December 1989, the new leader, Ion Iliescu, declared that the country had no intention of pursuing nuclear weaponry.

However, in 1992, investigation under Prime Minister Theodor Stolojan revealed that, as early as 1985, Romanian scientists at the Nuclear Research Institute at Pitesti had separated about 100 milligrams of PLUTONIUM in a laboratory experiment. Such a program could have been a first step toward producing weapons-grade fissionable material. Newspaper reports suggested that as early as the years from 1968 to 1970 Ceausescu had established an espionage network to gather nuclear information.

Ceausescu had poured resources into developing heavy-water manufacturing facilities on the border with Yugoslavia at Drobeta-Turnu Severin, and he had also started factories for the production of various components of nuclear reactors. Despite the massive effort, Romania had in operation only one 706 megawatt-electrical power reactor, a CANDU pressurized heavy-water reactor, Cernavoda-1. Plans to build a second reactor were stalled, as was construction on three more reactors. Checking of inventory from the heavy-water production plant suggested that some 175 metric tons were not accounted for. Some sources suggested the heavy water may have been exported to India.

Despite the heavy investment in nuclear technology, Romania lagged behind its Eastern European neighbors in the production of electrical power from nuclear energy.

See also POWER REACTORS, WORLD; PROLIFERATION.

Suggested Reading

Rodney W. Jones et al., *Tracking Nuclear Proliferation: A Guide in Maps and Charts, 1998*. Washington, D.C.: Carnegie Endowment for International Peace, 1998.

Roosevelt, Franklin (1882–1945)   *president of the United States from 1933 until his death in 1945, the longest-serving president in U.S. history*

Franklin Roosevelt made the crucial decisions during his administration that led to federal government development of the atomic weapon in the MANHATTAN ENGINEER DISTRICT. Since the project was cloaked in close secrecy during his administration, he made no public statements regarding the initiative, nor did he provide much in the way of guidance to those engaged in the work, leaving administrative details to Secretary of War Henry L. Stimson and to the head of the project, General Leslie GROVES. Roosevelt did not confide in Vice President Harry Truman regarding the weapon or his intentions regarding its use.

For these reasons, it has been a matter of some speculation whether or not Roosevelt would have decided to use the weapon against Japan, the path chosen in TRUMAN'S DECISION.

Roosevelt was born January 30, 1882, in Hyde Park, New York. He was educated at Harvard University and then attended Columbia University Law School. He was elected to the New York State Senate in 1910, and in 1913, he was appointed by President Woodrow Wilson to serve as assistant secretary of the navy. He held this post during World War I.

In 1920, Roosevelt ran for vice president on the Democratic ticket with James Cox and was defeated. He returned to private law practice in New York, and in August 1921, he contracted poliomyelitis, leaving his legs paralyzed. He underwent extensive physical therapy but was never able to walk more than a few steps with heavy leg braces. Nevertheless, he continued his political career, serving two terms as governor of New York (1929–1933). He was elected to the presidency in 1932.

His first two terms were characterized by a program dubbed the New Deal, in which he used a variety of government programs and agencies in an attempt to offset the economic hardships of the Great Depression. Late in 1939, he received a letter from Albert EINSTEIN, written at the suggestion of Leo SZILARD, urging that the government fund investigation of nuclear FISSION as a possible source for a new weapon.

Roosevelt authorized the program, and an ADVISORY COMMITTEE ON URANIUM was established to look into the matter. The research soon expanded and was supported by the National Defense Research Committee and then by the OFFICE OF SCIENTIFIC RESEARCH AND DEVELOPMENT (OSRD). The OSRD financed a series of contracts with academic and industrial laboratories to investigate the possibilities, and, under these contracts, Enrico FERMI began his work at the University of CHICAGO.

In mid-1942, the project began to require even larger industrial contracts and more concerted government management. Roosevelt approved the transfer of the research to the army to be administered by the U.S. Corps of Engineers. The Manhattan Engineer District (MED) was set up and took over the contracts and research already established under the OSRD. General Leslie Groves was appointed to head the MED, and he saw the project through to completion.

Despite efforts to maintain secrecy, the MED was penetrated successfully by Soviet espionage agents, most notably Klaus FUCHS. However, the German and Japanese governments and the American public did not learn the extent of American research into the project until after the detonation of the first atomic bomb over HIROSHIMA on August 6, 1945. The United States did share the information with the British and Canadian governments in the "ABC AGREEMENT" under which the British would have to approve the use of the weapon. Roosevelt had entered this agreement with British prime minister Winston Churchill at a conference in Quebec in August 1943.

Because of the extremely tight security surrounding the project, Roosevelt rarely discussed the project or his intentions regarding it. With Roosevelt's death in Warm Springs, Georgia, on April 12, 1945, the responsibility for further development and use of the nuclear weapon passed to his successor.

Suggested Reading

Richard Rhodes, *The Making of the Atomic Bomb.* New York: Simon and Schuster, 1986.

Martin Sherwin, *A World Destroyed.* New York: Vintage, 1987.

Rosenberg, Julius and Ethel (1918 and 1915–1953)   *a young Jewish-American couple convicted and executed for conspiracy to commit espionage during wartime for their roles in an atomic spy ring*

Julius and Ethel Rosenberg were convicted for their part in espionage into the MANHATTAN ENGINEER DISTRICT during World War II. In perhaps the most controversial espionage trial in American history, they were condemned to death by Judge Irving Kaufman. Despite numerous pleas for clemency from Americans and from abroad, the Rosenbergs were executed on June 19, 1953.

From the time of their arrest early in 1950 through their trial, appeal processes, and the execution, public interest in the case mounted and opinion divided, with many believing the couple were innocent or that, if guilty, the sentence was too severe. The nature of the evidence against them, based largely on the testimony of David Greenglass, cast doubts on their guilt. The fact that they had two young children and that their lives were quite ordinary won them wide sympathy. The U.S. government very rarely ordered the execution of a woman. Since Ethel Rosenberg was the mother of underage children, a lesser sentence seemed called for, even if they were both guilty as charged. The Rosenbergs were former members of the Communist Party and they were Jewish, factors that fed suspicions that the trial had been politically motivated. For many people on the political left in the United States, it became an article of faith that the Rosenbergs had been framed for crimes they had not committed.

However, later scholarship, based upon government files released under the Freedom of Information Act in the late 1970s, confirmed the involvement of the Rosenbergs in espionage. Later public release in the 1990s of decrypted VENONA messages between Moscow and the Soviet consulate in New York, which conducted espionage operations during the World War II years, presented further confirmation of the Rosenbergs' participation in the Soviet nuclear spy effort.

Julius and Ethel Rosenberg grew up on New York's Lower East Side. Born in 1918, Julius entered City College of New York at age 16 in 1934, becoming part

Julius and Ethel Rosenberg. Julius and Ethel Rosenberg were convicted and executed for conspiracy to commit treason during time of war for their part in espionage. The case remains controversial because of weaknesses in the prosecution case and the severity of their sentences. (National Archives and Records Administration)

of a generation of students who became highly political as a result of the Great Depression and the rising international crisis of the 1930s. He graduated with a degree in electrical engineering in 1935, and he remained active in left-wing causes. In the summer following his graduation, he met and married Ethel Greenglass.

During World War II, Julius Rosenberg worked for the U.S. Army Signal Corps, but he was dismissed in 1945 when it was discovered he had concealed his membership in the American Communist Party. Following the war, he set up a small machine shop with his brothers-in-law, including David Greenglass. Julius and Ethel had two sons, Michael, born in 1943, and Robert, born four years later. Their quiet lifestyle in the late 1940s hardly matched the public image of espionage agents, as they lived on a meager income struggling to meet their bills and raise their children.

In 1950, the confession of Klaus FUCHS to atomic espionage led the FBI to arrest Harry GOLD, who had served as messenger or courier to pick up detailed plans from Fuchs at LOS ALAMOS. Gold in turn provided information that helped identify David Greenglass as a corporal he had visited as part of Soviet efforts to collect information about the Manhattan Project. Gold had made one contact with Greenglass on a trip to Albuquerque during the war. When the FBI confronted Greenglass, he confessed and identified Julius Rosenberg as the person who had recruited him to conduct espionage and who operated a network of spies for the Soviets during and after the war.

When arrested, the Rosenbergs continued to deny their part in the espionage efforts described by Greenglass, and they refused to confess to any role whatsoever in espionage. The evidence that Julius Rosenberg in fact did operate a spy ring was convincing despite his refusal to admit it. Ethel's part in the conspiracy seems to have been limited to helping to recruit her brother and perhaps to typing some documents; no evidence has come to light indicating she was directly engaged in espionage. A balanced judgment regarding the Rosenbergs is that they indeed did participate in providing information to the Soviets and that they recruited Greenglass to help but that the information that Greenglass supplied was not crucial to the design of the nuclear weapon. Furthermore, the primary focus of the Rosenberg espionage effort was electronic technology obtained from the army signal corps, including design of a proximity fuse, not atomic weapon information from the Manhattan Project.

Greenglass provided, through Gold, a few amateurish sketches that may have been useful to the Soviets in helping to establish, through an independent channel, that the more detailed reports of Klaus Fuchs were valuable. Part of the Soviet espionage method was to establish at least two or three independent avenues to information to ensure that they were not being provided with false data by a single agent or source. At the Rosenberg's trial, however, the evidence focused on their part in atomic espionage, and Judge Kaufman appeared convinced they had been the leading atomic spies.

Apparently the FBI and the ATOMIC ENERGY COMMISSION wanted to keep the pressure on the Rosenbergs to the last minute, hoping that they would eventually seek clemency by confessing. In a confession, they would need to name the rest of the members of their ring, and, through such a process, the FBI could track and identify a much larger number of spies. The Rosenbergs were steadfast, and both went to their deaths without ever admitting to any crimes nor identifying any of the other participants in their network. Shortly after their death, their attorney placed the two sons with adoptive parents, Abel and Anne Meeropol.

Based on other evidence, the government secured convictions of others who had worked with the Rosenbergs. Harry Gold and Morton Sobell were each sentenced to 30 years; Greenglass was sentenced to 15 years in prison. In a related, but separate trial, Abraham Brothman (who had once employed Harry Gold) received a seven-year sentence, and Miriam Moskowitz got a two-year sentence.

The literature on the case runs from ardent defenses of the Rosenberg's innocence to heated condemnations of their guilt. Between these extremes lies the more balanced treatment presented by scholars who have reviewed the FBI files and the court records closely.

Suggested Reading

Robert and Michael Meeropol, *We Are Your Sons: The Legacy of Julius and Ethel Rosenberg, Written by Their Children.* Urbana: University of Illinois Press, 1986.

Ronald Radosh and Joyce Milton, *The Rosenberg File: A Search for the Truth.* New York: Vintage, 1984.

Walter Schneir, *Invitation to an Inquest: Reopening the Rosenberg "Atom Spy" Case.* New York: Penguin, 1973.

Russia

Russia was one of the 15 republics that made up the Union of Soviet Socialist Republics (U.S.S.R.) or the Soviet Union. During the period 1945 to 1991, the American press and public often referred to the Soviet Union as "Russia," since the dominant group and language of the Soviet Union were Russian.

Most of the leading Soviet scientists who contributed to the development of the nuclear weapon were Russian, including L. E. ARTSIMOVICH, P. KAPITSA, V. G. KHLOPIN, I. KURCHATOV, A. SAKHAROV, and I. TAMM. Some, like A. P. ALEKSANDROV and N. A. DOLLEZHAL', were from the UKRAINE or other republics in the Soviet Union.

SOVIET WEAPONS TESTS were conducted for the most part in the separate Soviet republic of KAZAKHSTAN; although some were conducted in the northern island territory of NOVAYA ZEMLYA. Some of the weapons development sites, such as ARZAMAS, CHELYABINSK, and KRASNOYARSK, were built on Russian territory. For these reasons, the Soviet nuclear weapon was often known

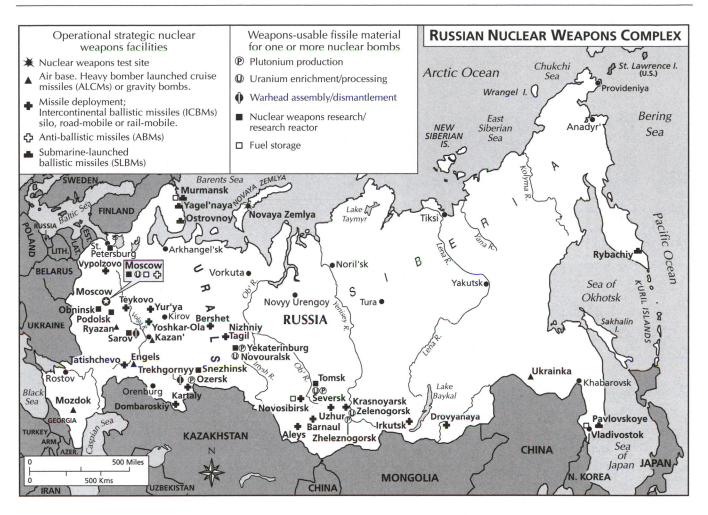

Operational strategic nuclear weapons facilities

✳ Nuclear weapons test site

▲ Air base. Heavy bomber launched cruise missiles (ALCMs) or gravity bombs.

✚ Missile deployment; Intercontinental ballistic missiles (ICBMs) silo, road-mobile or rail-mobile.

✥ Anti-ballistic missiles (ABMs)

▰ Submarine-launched ballistic missiles (SLBMs)

Weapons-usable fissile material for one or more nuclear bombs

Ⓟ Plutonium production

Ⓤ Uranium enrichment/processing

◉ Warhead assembly/dismantlement

■ Nuclear weapons research/ research reactor

□ Fuel storage

RUSSIAN NUCLEAR WEAPONS COMPLEX

in both the popular press and in scholarly publications as the "Russian bomb."

Russian and other Soviet scientists working in the field of nuclear physics suspected that American and British scientists were pursuing the development of a nuclear weapon as early as 1941. Espionage soon confirmed their suspicions. Using material provided by Klaus FUCHS and others, the Soviets began to coordinate work on nuclear weapons during World War II. Despite shortages of materials and resources, the secret project was organized under Igor Kurchatov as scientific director, and under the administrative control of the head of the Soviet secret police, Lavrenty BERIA. With the detonation of the American nuclear device at TRINITY and then the weapons at HIROSHIMA and NAGASAKI, Joseph STALIN ordered the Soviet project accelerated. Kurchatov and his team, utilizing the detailed plans obtained through Fuchs of the Alamogordo PLUTONIUM-fueled weapon, developed an identical weapon, first detonated on August 29, 1949.

The American press soon began to designate the Soviet tests as "Joe 1," "Joe 2," and so forth, using a tongue-in-cheek reference to Joseph Stalin.

EARLY SOVIET ATMOSPHERIC TESTS

Joe 1	August 29, 1949
Joe 2	October 3, 1951 (announced)
Joe 2	October 22, 1951 (announced)
Joe 4	August 12, 1953

The Joe 4 test was controversial, with the Soviets claiming it represented a thermonuclear weapon and the Americans identifying it as a boosted nuclear weapon similar to some tested earlier by the Americans. However, the Soviets soon began to develop hydrogen bomb designs that were similar to those of the Americans in the early 1950s.

The Soviet Union continued to test nuclear weapons in the atmosphere, conducting some 14 more tests, 12 of them at the test site at SEMIPALATINSK-21 in Kazakhstan. On November 22, 1955, the Soviets tested

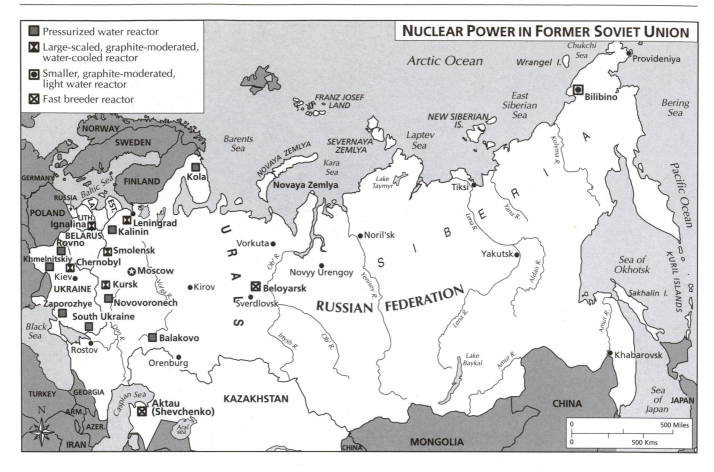

NUCLEAR POWER IN FORMER SOVIET UNION

- ■ Pressurized water reactor
- ⊠ Large-scaled, graphite-moderated, water-cooled reactor
- ⊡ Smaller, graphite-moderated, light water reactor
- ⊗ Fast breeder reactor

a true two-stage thermonuclear weapon with an estimated yield of 1.6 megatons (Mt) of TNT.

The Soviets stopped nuclear testing in 1958. The United States responded with a similar moratorium and both countries initiated negotiations toward a ban on atmospheric testing, but beginning in September 1961 the Soviets launched a new series of some 100 tests. They set off the largest atmospheric detonation at Novaya Zemlya, estimated at about 57 Mt on October 30, 1961.

Russian-American rivalry dominated the cold war, with the development of massive armaments on both sides and an emerging policy of MUTUALLY ASSURED DESTRUCTION. Both sides sought to end the arms race through negotiated ARMS CONTROL treaties, finally succeeding in the late 1980s with the INTERMEDIATE-RANGE NUCLEAR FORCES TREATY and START I. Russian-built nuclear-powered submarines, including the DELTA, TYPHOON, and YANKEE classes, matched American submarines in capabilities. Although the Russian submarines were generally regarded as more dangerous in radioactive releases to crew members

than were American submarines, the Russian fleet constituted a major component in the balance of power between the superpowers at the height of the cold war.

Meanwhile, Russia developed an intensive nuclear power industry. By the 1990s, Russia had 25 power reactors in operation (with at least four others planned) and had exported Russian-designed reactors to the Ukraine, Kazakhstan, Lithuania, HUNGARY, and Bulgaria. The *Reactory Bolshoi Moshchnosti Kanalynye* (RBMK), or "Channelized Large Power Reactor," attracted worldwide attention in 1986 with the accident in such a reactor at CHERNOBYL in the Ukraine. That reactor type is a light-water–cooled graphite-moderated reactor, similar to the PRODUCTION REACTORS built in the United States at HANFORD. A second Russian reactor that was built both domestically and exported was the *Vodo-Vodyannoy Energeticheskiy Reactor* (VVER) or water-cooled and water-moderated reactor, equivalent to the PRESSURIZED WATER REACTORS developed by WESTINGHOUSE in the United States and by other companies in Europe. The early VVER-440,

Location	Number and Megawattage	Type	Years Built
Balakovo	4 at 950MW	VVER	1986–1993
Beloyarskiy	1 at 560MW	LMFBR	1981
Kalinin	3 at 950MW	VVER	1985–1987
Kola	4 at 411MW	VVER	1973–1984
Kursk	4 at 925MW	RBMK	1977–1986
St. Petersburg	5 at 925MW	RBMK	1974–1981
Novoronezhskiy	2 at 385, 1 at 950	VVER	1972–1981
Smolensk	3 at 925	RBMK	1983–1990
Dimitrovgrad	1 at 50	VVER	1966

developed before 1970, was the most common type; the later VVER-440 and a VVER-1000 developed in 1975 had new safety features. A Liquid-Metal Fast Breeder Reactor (LMFBR) was built at one site with two planned at another.

At the end of the century, Russian power reactors were located at nine sites as shown in the table above.

Partially built or planned reactors were located at Kursk and two LMFBRs at Chelyabinsk.

With the end of the cold war and the collapse of the Soviet Union in 1991, only Russia emerged as the nuclear-weapon successor state to the Soviet Union. Kazakhstan, Ukraine, and Belarus cooperated in a denuclearization process, with American help, through the COOPERATIVE THREAT REDUCTION program. Russia inherited and agreed to the variety of arms control agreements that had been signed over the previous few years, including the INF and START I treaties. Russia also agreed to the terms of various arms control and antiproliferation efforts, such as the Nuclear Suppliers Group and the signed but unratified COMPREHENSIVE TEST BAN TREATY.

Despite drawdowns in stockpile and confidence-building measures taken in the early 1990s by both sides, the United States continued to regard the massive nuclear weapon capability of Russia with concern. Operational strategic nuclear weapons facilities and locations with weapons usable FISSILE MATERIAL were scattered around Russia. Concerns that such materials might be misused, sold, or stolen continued to haunt planners in both Russia and the United States.

Such locations included several research reactors and research institutes at locations including St. Petersburg, Moscow, Obninsk, Sarov, and Pdolsk; SUBMARINE-LAUNCHED BALLISTIC MISSILES at Rybachiy on the Kamchatka Peninsula, and at Yavel'naya and Ostrovnoy on the Berents Sea; heavy bomber bases with air-launched cruise missiles or nuclear bombs at Mozdok in the Caucasus Mountains, Ukrainka near the Chinese border, and Ryazan in central Russia; mobile ICBMs at several locations; and continued plutonium production and URANIUM enrichment plants in the Urals, at Krasnoyarsk, and in and around Moscow. Altogether, Western sources identified over 50 sites either housing nuclear weapons or housing fissile material that needed security against theft or misuse.

Suggested Reading

Thomas B. Cochrane, Robert S. Norris, and Oleg A. Bukharin, *Making the Russian Bomb: From Stalin to Yeltsin.* Boulder, Colo.: Westview Press, 1995.

David Holloway. *Stalin and the Bomb.* New Haven: Yale University Press, 1994.

Rodney W. Jones et al., *Tracking Nuclear Proliferation: A Guide in Maps and Charts, 1998.* Washington, D.C.: Carnegie Endowment for International Peace, 1998.

Rutherford, Ernest (1871–1937) *New Zealand-born physicist who worked both in Canada and Great Britain, establishing the basic types of radioactivity*

Ernest Rutherford is noted for developing the modern understanding of the atom, which identifies a nucleus surrounded by a field of orbiting electrons. For his early contributions, many regarded Rutherford as the founder of modern nuclear physics. He was born in New Zealand in 1871 and studied in Christchurch. In 1895, he went to Britain and became a research assistant under J. J. Thompson at the Cavendish Laboratory in Cambridge. He then accepted a position at McGill University in Montreal.

After the discovery of radioactivity by Antoine Becquerel in 1896, Rutherford identified three different types of radioactivity, naming them alpha, beta, and gamma. In 1903, Rutherford explained radioactivity as caused by the breakdown of atoms, identifying alpha particles as helium nuclei. In 1907, he left McGill to return to Britain, where he took a position at Manchester University.

He produced the nuclear model of the atom in 1911, suggesting the planetary model of electrons orbiting a nucleus. In 1914, he identified the proton, and he discovered that gamma rays are a form of radiation beyond X-rays in the electromagnetic spectrum. In 1919, he produced artificial atomic breakdown by bombarding nitrogen with alpha particles, producing hydrogen and oxygen.

In 1919, he became the director of the Cavendish Laboratory. In 1920, he suggested the name "proton" be given to the hydrogen nucleus and to that particle in atoms of other elements; he speculated that uncharged particles (neutrons) must also exist. Using equipment he developed at the Cavendish, he bombarded DEUTERIUM in HEAVY WATER with deuterons and, in 1934, produced TRITIUM, which could be regarded as the first controlled fusion reaction in a laboratory.

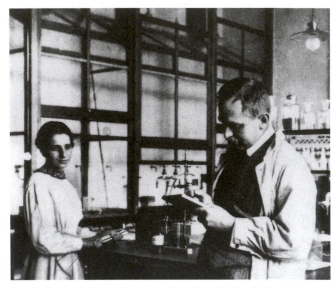

Ernest Rutherford (with assistant). *A New Zealand physicist, Rutherford established laboratories in Canada and Great Britain that made many contributions to the emerging field of nuclear physics in the 1930s and 1940s.* (National Archives and Records Administration)

Safeguards

Following the LIMITED TEST BAN TREATY (LTBT) of 1963, which prohibited atmospheric, underwater, and outer space testing of nuclear weapons, the United States nuclear weapons community established four "safeguards" to ensure that the test ban did not work to the disadvantage of U.S. national security. Safeguard A referred to continuing underground nuclear testing; Safeguard B referred to the maintenance of the weapons laboratories at Los Alamos and Lawrence Livermore; Safeguard C referred to maintaining the readiness to resume atmospheric testing; Safeguard D referred to improving methods to detect violations of the treaty through PROJECT VELA. Safeguard C was terminated in 1980 as the United States officially dropped the readiness-to-test principle.

As the Comprehensive Test Ban Treaty was being considered in the late 1990s, that treaty contained additional safeguards, including Safeguard F, a reservation that would allow any nation to announce withdrawal from that treaty on grounds of "supreme national interest."

The term "safeguard" is also used in a more general sense to refer to the variety of means used to ensure the safety and security of nuclear weapons, including use-control devices such as PERMISSIVE ACTION LINKS and DOUBLE-KEY SYSTEMS and safety systems that prevent accidental detonation during a fire or transportation accident.

Sakharov, Andrey Dmitrievich (1921–1989)

Russian physicist who developed the Soviet hydrogen bomb and became an advocate of disarmament, winning the Nobel Peace Prize

Andrey Sakharov is remembered as the father of the Soviet hydrogen bomb, an advocate of free thought for scientists and others within the Soviet Union, a defender of human rights in the Soviet Union, and an opponent of the Soviet intervention in Afghanistan. Toward the end of his life, he became internationally famous as an advocate of political change within the Soviet Union.

Sakharov was born in 1921, the son of a physics teacher. He graduated from Moscow State University in 1942 and worked during the World War II at an armaments factory in Ulianovsk on the Volga River. In 1945, he returned to Moscow to continue research work as a graduate student at the Institute of Physics of the Academy of Sciences under Igor TAMM.

He was recruited for the HYDROGEN BOMB DESIGN program in 1948, and he spent the period 1950 to 1968 working at ARZAMAS-16, the highly secret bomb development facility. Sakharov contributed the idea of adding lithium-deuteride to the weapon detonated by the Soviets in 1953. Although the Russians later claimed that this weapon was the world's first hydrogen bomb, American analysts continued to regard it as a boosted nuclear fission weapon.

A successful test of a new design, called "The Third Idea," was conducted on November 22, 1955, and yielded 1.6 megatons. Sakharov had made contributions to the development of this design, which resembled that worked out by Edward TELLER and Stanislaw ULAM in the United States. Together with Igor Tamm, Sakharov outlined the principle for isolation of a high-temperature plasma. Tamm and Sakharov worked toward the harnessing of fusion energy to serve as a source for a TRITIUM production reactor. For his work on these projects, Sakharov was named Hero of Socialist Labor three times.

Following 1955, Sakharov became increasingly concerned about the long-term effects of FALLOUT and began to campaign for the ending of atmospheric testing of nuclear weapons. Sakharov argued for a reduction in nuclear arms and for an increase in international cooperation, as well as for more recognition of human rights in the Soviet Union. His security clearance was revoked in 1968. In 1970, he was a founder of the Soviet Human Rights Committee, and he won the Nobel Peace Prize in 1975. He was the only scientist to win both that prize and the Soviet prize of Hero of Socialist Labor, although both Igor Tamm and Peter KAPITSA won the Hero of Socialist Labor and the NOBEL PRIZE for physics.

As Sakharov began to identify with the dissidents in the Soviet Union who opposed the suppression of human rights there, the Soviet security and intelligence service, the KGB, increasingly harassed him and his wife, Elena Bonner. In 1976, Yuri Andropov, then head of the KGB, branded Sakharov as "Public Enemy Number One."

In the period 1980 to 1986, Sakharov was kept in "internal exile" in the city of Gorky in the Soviet Union, not allowed to move about freely or to maintain free correspondence with other dissidents and foreigners. The internal exile for he and his wife was lifted suddenly on December 19, 1986, on orders from Mikhail GORBACHEV.

In 1989, Sakharov was elected to the Russian parliament. A popular weekly published a poll that showed that Sakharov was by far the most popular politician in the country, outpolling Gorbachev himself. Sakharov presented Gorbachev with thousands of telegrams calling for an end to the single-party rule of the Soviet Union. A few days later, he died of a heart attack in December 1989. Critics of the regime believed that Sakharov's death was at least partly due to the strain of his earlier persecution and to the lack of good medical treatment during his stay in Gorky.

In several ways, Sakharov's career seemed to parallel that of American scientist J. Robert OPPENHEIMER, the father of the U.S. atomic bomb, who was denied a security clearance for his political views and his opposition to the development of the thermonuclear weapon. Like Oppenheimer, Sakharov was briefly honored by the state that once shunned him prior to his death. Of course, the parallel is limited, in that Oppenheimer remained free to express his views and his years at Princeton University's Institute for Advanced Study after denial of his clearance were hardly the equivalent of Sakharov's internal exile.

Sakharov published several books outlining his ideas, including *Sakharov Speaks, My Country and the World,* and *Alarm and Hope.*

See also KURCHATOV, IGOR.

Suggested Reading

B. L. Altschuler et al. *Andrei Sakharov: Facets of a Life.* Gif-sur-Yvette, France: Editions Frontières, 1991.

Thomas B. Cochrane et al. *Making the Russian Bomb: From Stalin to Yeltsin.* Boulder, Colo.: Westview Press, 1995.

David Holloway, *Stalin and the Bomb.* New Haven: Yale University Press, 1994.

Richard Rhodes, *Dark Sun.* New York: Simon and Schuster, 1995.

SALT I

SALT I is the acronym for the Strategic Arms Limitation Treaty I, negotiated over the period 1968 to 1972 and signed by President Richard NIXON and Premier Leonid Brezhnev on May 26, 1972. When first proposed by Robert MCNAMARA in 1964 at a meeting at GLASSBORO, New Jersey, the Soviets did not agree to prohibiting ANTI-BALLISTIC MISSILE (ABM) systems. However, as the negotiations went on, a limitation on the ABM became most significant and permanent outcome of the discussions.

SALT I is sometimes referred to as the ABM treaty, although in fact there were two separate agreements negotiated and signed at the May 26 meeting: the ABM Treaty, and the Interim Agreement on Certain Measures with Respect to the Limitation of Strategic Offensive Arms.

The Interim Agreement was of a five-year length (1972–1977), setting limits of 1,054 INTERCONTINENTAL BALLISTIC MISSILES (ICBMs) for the United States and 1,618 ICBMs for the Soviet Union.

Since the Interim Agreement lasted only until 1977, that aspect of SALT I tended to be overlooked in some later historical treatments of the treaty, and SALT I was often referred to by some writers as the "Anti-ABM" treaty because the Anti-ABM Treaty signed at the same time was permanent. Strictly speaking, however, the SALT I limits were those imposed on long-range missiles through the Interim Agreement. The Treaty on the Limitation of Anti-Ballistic Missiles was a separate agreement signed at the same time as part of a package deal.

The negotiations went forward through an official or "front channel" by way of U.S. negotiator Gerald Smith, and at the same time, presidential national security advisor Henry Kissinger conducted "back-channel" or informal discussions to attempt to reach agreement. Meanwhile, the Soviets continued to deploy an ABM system around Moscow, and the United States responded by developing MULTIPLE INDEPENDENTLY TARGETABLE REENTRY VEHICLE (MIRV) systems for its strategic missiles. The MIRV systems allowed a single missile to carry six or more warheads; several "mirved" missiles could overwhelm an ABM system, it was believed.

The long deadlock over the treaty was finally broken when the two sides agreed to set the interim limits on strategic systems, continue discussion of longer term limits on strategic weapons, and accept the building of only two anti-ballistic systems in the United States and two in the Soviet Union, embodying these agreements in two separate documents.

In the Anti-ABM Treaty, each country could deploy one system around its capital and one around an intercontinental ballistic missile (ICBM) basing area. The Interim Agreement to limit strategic missiles set limits on total SILOS for ICBMs and tubes for SUBMARINE-LAUNCHED BALLISTIC MISSILES (SLBMs) as given in the table.

In the United States, there was some concern at the "lack of symmetry" between the allowed totals, but the U.S. lead in intercontinental bomber aircraft was presumed to make up for the difference in allowed total missiles.

	ICBM SILOS	TOTAL	SLBM TUBES
United States	old: 54, new: 1000	(1054)	950
Soviet Union	old: 210, new: 1408	(1618)	710

The U.S. Senate accepted the treaty, advising ratification by a vote of 88 to 2. Both the ABM Treaty and the Interim Agreement went into force on October 2, 1972.

Part of the understanding of the Interim Agreement was that negotiations toward more permanent limitations would continue. SALT II discussions began in November 1972, resulting in 1979 in a treaty that was never ratified.

See also ARMS CONTROL.

SALT II: Strategic Arms Limitation Treaty-II

The second Strategic Arms Limitation Treaty was signed in Vienna, Austria, on June 18, 1979. The interim agreement on strategic arms that had been signed as part of SALT I was due to expire in October 1977. As that date approached, both the United States and the U.S.S.R. announced that they would abide by the SALT I limitations as long as the process of negotiating the next treaty continued.

Another year and a half of discussions over the particular aspects of the new treaty began. The negotiations between the two countries were made difficult by disagreements between the two sides on how to deal with a new class of Soviet bomber, called in the West the "Backfire," and with the air-launched CRUISE MISSILES that the United States had developed.

During this period the two nations agreed on a three-tiered framework to treat different issues differently. One treaty would use the ceilings agreed to at VLADIVOSTOK as a basis and would set sublimits on certain kinds of forces. President Gerald FORD and Secretary Brezhnev had met in November 1974 at Vladivostok in the Soviet Union and agreed to work toward limits of 2,400 strategic launch vehicles for each side. SALT II accepted those limits in the main treaty and set up a short-term agreement about some of the issues, with guidelines for later reductions.

Under SALT II, the two nations agreed to limit themselves to 2,400 strategic launch vehicles each, until the end of 1981. This figure would include SUB-MARINE-LAUNCHED BALLISTIC MISSILES (SLBMs), intercontinental ballistic missiles (ICBMs), and heavy bombers. From then until the expiration of the treaty in December 1985, the two countries would agree to a limit of 2,250 launch vehicles each. Within the total figure, each country was to abide by sublimits on each category of missile.

Both sides agreed not to test or deploy a mobile ICBM system before 1981, and neither would deploy air-launched cruise missiles with ranges longer than about 375 miles. The various sublimits on the systems, the proposed cut in limits to 2,250, and the provision about cruise missiles were all the result of difficult and lengthy efforts to reach acceptable compromises.

President Jimmy CARTER submitted the treaty for ratification to the Senate in 1979. After the Soviet invasion of Afghanistan, the administration withdrew the treaty from the Senate early in 1980. During the 1980 presidential campaign, Carter promised to push for ratification of the treaty, but Ronald REAGAN announced he would not submit it for ratification and would open new negotiations.

During debates over the treaty, many U.S. specialists in arms control opposed it because they believed it did not offer essential equivalence between the nuclear forces of the United States and U.S.S.R., but rather erred in the Soviet's favor. President Carter announced that he would honor the terms of the agreement although not be bound by it if the Soviets continued to honor it. President Reagan also announced that the United States would honor the limits in the treaty.

However, in 1986, the United States announced that it was exceeding some of the treaty limits because, even if the treaty had been ratified, it would have expired in 1985. Events overtook the treaty as the Americans and the Soviets entered into new arms control negotiations in 1986–1987 (START I).

Suggested Reading

Dan Caldwell, *The Dynamics of Domestic Politics and Arms Control: The SALT II Treaty Ratification Debate.* Columbia: University of South Carolina Press, 1991.

Sandia

Sandia National Laboratory is located in Albuquerque, New Mexico, in a separately fenced section of the Kirt-

land Air Force Base near the Albuquerque International Airport.

During World War II, the laboratory base was first known as "Z Division" of the LOS ALAMOS laboratory. In late 1945, Los Alamos began to transfer its field testing and engineering organization, Z Division, to Sandia Base near Albuquerque.

Sandia Base was an army facility that included the Oxnard airfield that was an old municipal airport for Albuquerque and a cluster of ramshackle buildings all located near Kirtland Air Force Base. The army had used the Sandia facility to train aircraft mechanics, house wounded airmen, and to dismantle surplus military aircraft during and after World War II.

Z-Division staff at Sandia were joined from the U.S. Army Air Corps 509th Division, which included the *ENOLA GAY* and *Bock's Car,* the aircraft that bombed HIROSHIMA and NAGASAKI, respectively. Temporary buildings at Z Division housed activities of specialists in explosives, machinists, engineers, and technical workers. Non-nuclear parts for atomic weapons manufactured elsewhere were shipped to Z Division for storage.

In 1946, after the end of the war, Z-Division staff participated in OPERATION CROSSROADS. The U.S. Air Force built its own scientific testing laboratory near Sandia, which later evolved into the Phillips Laboratory.

Following World War II, Sandia Laboratory separated from Los Alamos administration, under the ATOMIC ENERGY COMMISSION (AEC). David LILIENTHAL, chairman of the AEC, sought to increase the production of atomic bombs, converting the laboratory processes of the war years into regular industrial operations. Sandia Laboratory played a crucial role in the period 1946–1947 in developing early weapon case designs, batteries, and other auxiliary parts for the first generations of bombs.

In 1949, on the urging of President Harry TRUMAN, the operation of the lab was taken over by Western Electric Company. Western Electric ran Sandia Corporation as a wholly owned subsidiary until 1993, when the Martin-Marietta Corporation took over the contract.

Managers and directors of the laboratory included many individuals with extensive scientific or industrial experience. In general, the general managers beginning in 1952 were assigned from Western Electric, while the president of the corporation was assigned from Bell Laboratories. Many of the senior administrative personnel had prior experience at Western Electric, while many of the senior researchers and technical people were drawn from Bell Laboratories. The administrative and senior technical personnel often served relatively short terms of office and then returned to other positions, often in New Jersey at the Western Electric and Bell Laboratory facilities.

1945–1949 Z-DIVISION

1945	Jerrold Zacharias
1945–46	Roger Warner
1946–47	Robert Henderson
1947–49	Paul Larsen

1949–1999 SANDIA CORPORATION

1949–1952	George Landry
1952–1953	Donald Quarles
1953–1958	James McRae
1958–1960	Julius Molnar
1960–1966	Siegmund Schwartz
1966–1972	John Hornbeck
1972–1981	Morgan Sparks
1981–1985	George Dacey
1985–1989	Irwin Welber
1989–1995	Albert Narath
1995–	C. Paul Robinson

Sandia's work focused on the engineering of parts of nuclear weapons and maintaining records and details of the many modifications to nuclear weapon designs and the many weapons components. Work at Sandia has included research, training, engineering, information storage and retrieval, and prototype development.

Under Donald Quarles as president, Sandia took a lead role in working out the 1953 agreement between the Atomic Energy Commission and the Department of Defense as to the division of responsibilities regarding nuclear weapons. Incorporated in the agreement was a fundamental model of the life cycle of the weapon. The life cycle included seven phases: conception, feasibility study, development, pilot production, initial production, quantity production and stockpile, and retirement. The role of the various agencies in each phase of the life cycle was clarified in the agreement.

Under the agreement, control of arming and fusing components of the weapons shifted from Sandia to the Department of Defense and its contractors, and, after 1953, Sandia worked on missile warhead arming and fusing only on special request.

One early development at Sandia was the management of the program to build "zippers," the neutron initiator that was designed to replace the early POLONIUM initiators that had a short half-life and had to be periodically replaced in the first atomic weapons. The zipper design included a miniature betatron that accelerated electrons into a BERYLLIUM target. These devices were eventually produced at a plant at Pinellas, Florida, that was established and operated under Sandia leadership before being turned over to General Electric as a contractor to operate it as part of the AEC's weapons production complex.

In 1956, during the administration of James McRae, Sandia opened a division in Livermore, California, to support the work at the LAWRENCE LIVERMORE NATIONAL LABORATORY on the new hydrogen bombs. Herbert York, the first director of the Livermore laboratory, insisted on having a separate engineering support facility there and warmly supported drawing personnel from Sandia.

Sandia technicians participated in developing test equipment used at many of the tests in the ATMOSPHERIC NUCLEAR TESTING program from the 1940s through the early 1960s for both the Los Alamos- and the Livermore-designed weapons. The division of Sandia at Livermore eventually employed about 1,000 staff members, while the main Sandia Laboratory in Albuquerque continued with about 4,000 staff employees.

In the period from 1963 to 1991, when the United States tested hundreds of nuclear weapons by exploding them in underground shafts and tunnels at the NEVADA TEST SITE, Sandia provided equipment and technical staff to assist in the experiments. Sandia technical personnel participated in key ways during the Project Plowshare projects, which included tests to utilize nuclear explosives to dig canals and to stimulate gas well production. Sandia engineers and scientists have worked on methods of making nuclear weapons safe from accidental use, such as PERMISSIVE ACTION LINKS, and have helped develop national technical means of detection of nuclear tests in other countries.

Suggested Reading

Leland Johnson, *Sandia National Laboratories: A History of Exceptional Service in the National Interest*. Albuquerque, N.Mex.: Sandia National Laboratory, 1997.

SANE

Meeting in June 1957 at the Overseas Press Club in New York City, 27 prominent clerics, business execu-

Three Mile Island Demonstration. The antinuclear movement developed in the 1950s received a new generation of protestors as shown in this rally in Harrisburg, Pennsylvania, after the March 28, 1979, accident at Three Mile Island. (National Archives and Records Administration)

tives, authors, scientists, labor representatives, and citizens formed the Committee for a Sane Nuclear Policy (SANE). Following a suggestion by psychoanalyst Erich Fromm that the fledgling group "bring the voice of sanity to the people," the founders adopted the name SANE in September 1957.

The idea for SANE had originated in an April 1957 meeting of pacifists and antiwar liberals who, motivated by growing nuclear anxiety and fear, including increasing evidence of radioactive FALLOUT, decided to create two ad hoc groups to lead a campaign to abolish nuclear testing and nuclear weapons: the liberal pacifist SANE and radical pacifist COMMITTEE FOR NONVIOLENT ACTION (CNVA). Unlike CNVA, whose membership was limited to radical pacifists who championed civil disobedience, SANE included nuclear pacifists and antiwar activists. SANE functioned as a broad liberal, conventional organization devoted to political education, and it quickly became the largest and most influential nuclear disarmament organization in America.

In November 1957, SANE published a full-page advertisement in *The New York Times.* "We Are Facing A Danger Unlike Any Danger That Has Ever Existed," SANE warned. "In our possession and in the possession of the Russians are more than enough nuclear explosives to put an end to the life of man on earth." SANE urged an end to nuclear testing in order to halt radioactive contamination and to initiate arms control negotiations. The advertisement sparked much support. Citizens reprinted the advertisement in 23 newspapers, and 25,000 reprints were distributed. The advertisement, which tapped into the national anxiety over nuclear weapons, radioactive fallout, and atomic war, "started a movement" and transformed SANE from a modest educational committee into a national mass membership grass-roots organization. By mid-1958, SANE had 130 chapters with a membership of 25,000.

Moreover, in numerous influential full-page newspaper advertisements, SANE highlighted the perils of nuclear weapons and nuclear testing. In 1959, the hazards of radioactive fallout were underscored by reports that radioactive strontium 90, released into the atmosphere during atmospheric tests the previous year, had polluted food and milk and from there entered children's teeth and bones. "No Contamination without Representation" proclaimed one SANE advertisement, which charged America with poisoning the world's atmosphere. "NUCLEAR BOMBS CAN DESTROY ALL LIFE IN WAR [and] NUCLEAR TESTS ARE ENDANGERING OUR HEALTH RIGHT NOW," another advertisement warned: "We must stop the contamination of the air, the milk children drink, the food we eat." Yet another advertisement that dramatized the danger that radioactivity posed to children declared: "$1\frac{1}{4}$ Million unborn children will be born dead or have some gross defect because of Nuclear Bomb testing."

Perhaps the most memorable SANE advertisement, a 1962 full-page message in *The New York Times*, featured famed pediatrician and SANE member Dr. Benjamin Spock. Under the caption "Dr. Spock is worried," the fatherly baby doctor pensively looked down on a small girl, his sober expression contemplating the fatal link between radioactive fallout and cancer. Seven hundred newspapers worldwide reprinted the Spock advertisement, 25,000 reprints were distributed throughout the nation, and 20,000 reprints were sent to President John KENNEDY at the White House.

Consistent with its moderate philosophy, SANE used a variety of political education methods to influence public opinion and shape public policy. In addition to serving as a clearing house for information on nuclear testing and disarmament issues, SANE wrote, reprinted, and distributed literature, prepared research reports, distributed films, and conducted press conferences. The organization issued public statements, organized conferences, arranged television and radio interviews, broadcast radio documentaries, arranged visits to policymakers, sponsored lawful demonstrations, and urged other groups to advocate disarmament.

In its first major victory, SANE worked with other organizations to rally public support for ratification of the American-Soviet LIMITED TEST BAN TREATY (banning atmospheric but not underground atomic testing), which the Senate approved in September 1963.

The anticommunist political climate of the 1950s and early 1960s weakened numerous social reform groups and also hurt SANE. In May 1960, Senator Thomas J. Dodd (D-Conn.), temporary chairman of the Senate Internal Security Subcommittee, charged that SANE contained communist members. Although refusing to submit names to or cooperate formally with Senator Dodd, SANE's board did adopt a resolution restricting membership to those who rejected "communist or other totalitarian doctrine[s]." Furthermore, SANE fired a top organizer and required local branches to apply for charters with national SANE, a policy aimed at eliminating metropolitan New York locals with communist members. About one-quarter of SANE's chapters refused to apply for new charters and were expelled. In addition, numerous members resigned to protest "McCarthyite" tactics within SANE.

From 1957 to 1963, SANE focused on nuclear weapons testing and nuclear disarmament; after the 1963 test ban treaty, however, SANE pursued a broader program with many other issues. Since the 1963 test ban treaty, SANE criticized U.S. military involvement in Vietnam, the Dominican Republic, Central America, and elsewhere; opposed and in several cases helped to defeat the ANTI-BALLISTIC MISSILE (ABM) and MX MISSILE systems, B-1 bomber, *Trident* submarine and missile, PERSHING II and CRUISE MISSILES, Neutron (ENHANCED RADIATION) bomb, and President Reagan's STRATEGIC DEFENSE INITIATIVE; mobilized support for the Strategic Arms Limitation Agreement (SALT I) and ratification of the SALT II Treaty. More generally, SANE promoted a demilitarized foreign policy, economic conversion of military to civilian needs, and amnesty for Vietnam-era draft resisters. SANE also emphasized the harmful effects of excessive military spending and the impact of the nuclear weapons budget on the federal deficit and unemployment. Highlighting the need for negotiation and peaceful conflict resolution, SANE took out a full-page advertisement in 1965 featuring a picture of a cockroach with the caption: "The winner of World War III." Reflecting these broader concerns, in 1969 SANE dropped "nuclear" from its name and became "SANE: A Citizen's Organization for a Sane World."

During the 1980s, SANE played a major role in the Nuclear Freeze Campaign, which sought a mutual, verifiable freeze on the testing, production, and deployment of nuclear weapons. SANE's membership, which following the Vietnam War had dropped to 6,000 in 1976, reached 100,000 by the end of 1984. By 1982, nuclear freeze resolutions had been adopted by 309 New England town meetings, 320 city councils nationwide, 56 county councils, one or both houses in 11 state legislatures, and 109 national and international organizations, including the UN General Assembly.

For over three decades, SANE played a leading role in the American antinuclear movement. SANE organized grass-roots citizen activism, legitimized antinuclear protest, and pressured the government to negotiate and limit nuclear weapons and testing.

Suggested Reading

Charles Chatfield, with the assistance of Robert Kleidman, *The American Peace Movement: Ideals and Activism.* New York: Twayne Publishers, 1992.

Milton S. Katz, *Ban the Bomb: A History of SANE, the Committee for a Sane Nuclear Policy, 1957–1985.* Westport, Conn.: Greenwood Press, 1986.

Lawrence S. Wittner, *Resisting the Bomb: A History of the World Nuclear Disarmament Movement, 1954–1970.* Stanford, Calif.: Stanford University Press, 1997.

Sarov Institute   *See* ARZAMAS-16.

Savannah, Nuclear Ship

The "N.S.," or Nuclear Ship, *Savannah* was launched on March 23, 1962, the first nuclear merchant ship. In 1972, after 10 years demonstrating the ability of the ship, she was laid up by the Maritime Administration as a cost-cutting measure. The ship required a subsidy from the government to operate, and it never ran at a profit. However, the original plan had been simply to demonstrate the feasibility of such a ship, not its profitability.

The ship had a sleek, yachtlike look. *Savannah* had 30 air-conditioned staterooms, a large dining

Nuclear Ship Savannah. *The nuclear–powered merchant ship* Savannah, *designed as a demonstration, was the only such ship built in the United States. Small craft welcomed her to San Francisco on her way to the World's Fair in Seattle. The ship could not compete on economic terms.* (National Archives and Records Administration)

room, and a movie theater, not the usual accommodations on a merchant ship for carrying cargo. The nuclear engines delivered 20,000 horsepower, and the ship's top speed was 23 knots, or over 27 miles per hour. Like nuclear-powered submarines, the ship could make many voyages without refueling. Because of the space for the nuclear engines and the guest accommodations, the ship had much less cargo space than comparable conventional diesel-powered cargo vessels.

The budget for the ship was high for a number of reasons. As a hybrid passenger/cargo ship, she was inefficient for either function. A special shore organization had to be maintained, along with a specialized shipyard for work. The crew was larger than those on comparable ships, with 67 rather than 50 personnel. The specially trained crew received higher pay than merchant sailors on conventional ships. Because of all these factors, the operating subsidy for the ship ran about $2 million more than for regular merchant ships subsidized by the U.S. Maritime Administration. Thus, in 1972, after only a few years operation, the ship was retired from service.

Savannah River Site

With the Soviet detonation of a nuclear weapon in August 1949, the ATOMIC ENERGY COMMISSION (AEC) decided it needed a second weapons material production center in addition to HANFORD. With only one such facility, a nuclear attack with a single weapon, it was presumed, could bring U.S. nuclear weapons production to a complete halt. Furthermore, as the United States began to move to the design of BOOSTED WEAPONS and HYDROGEN BOMB DESIGNS, the weapons program developed a requirement for the steady production of TRITIUM.

Part of the program to develop the hydrogen bomb relied on construction of the production facility at Savannah River Site (SRS) in Aiken and Barnwell counties, South Carolina, about 15 miles from Augusta, Georgia. The Savannah plant was constructed by Du Pont Company for the AEC, and Du Pont continued to operate the facility until 1989, when the contract was taken over by Westinghouse Corporation.

The site occupied approximately 250,000 acres. About 1,500 families had to be relocated from the remote and wooded area of the site in order to close off

R Area at Savannah River. The R Reactor at Savannah River was designed as a research reactor. It operated only briefly, from 1953 to 1964. Some parts from R were later stripped to keep other reactors in operation. (Department of Energy)

the area and make way for construction. Operations began in 1952 with the start up of a facility to extract heavy water from the Savannah River. Beginning in 1953, five PRODUCTION REACTORS were brought on line to produce both PLUTONIUM and tritium for the U.S. nuclear weapons arsenal. The reactors, like those at Hanford, were designated with letters.

SAVANNAH RIVER SITE PRODUCTION REACTORS

REACTOR	OPENED	CLOSED
R	1953	1964
P	1954	1988
L	1954	1968
		(reopened 1985–1988)
K	1954	1988
C	1955	1988

Eight of the nine original production reactors at Hanford were closed during the period from 1964 to 1971, as were two of the Savannah reactors due to the fact that the weapons program had a sufficient supply of plutonium. However, with new designs of weapons in the early 1980s, particularly the development of missiles with MULTIPLE INDEPENDENTLY TARGETABLE REENTRY VEHICLES and the development of PERSHING II and CRUISE MISSILES for deployment in Europe under the DUAL-TRACK STRATEGY, the need for more plutonium suddenly became urgent. The decay rate of the tritium ISOTOPE also meant that active reactors were needed to simply maintain the large weapons stockpile. For those reasons, L reactor at SRS was reopened and briefly went into production in the period 1985–1988, along with N reactor at Hanford and the three other operating reactors at Savannah River Site.

Du Pont Corporation remained very proud of its safety record, so the revelation in October to December 1988 that there had been a report of more than 30 safety violations at the facility came as a shock to corporate headquarters and provided arguments for critics of the DEPARTMENT OF ENERGY and the weapons program more generally. The department, under Secretary John HERRINGTON, took a stand of publicly discussing the issues quite frankly, and the press continued to criticize what had become perceived as a "culture of secrecy" surrounding the operation of the reactors.

In 1988, the four production reactors at SRS were closed for safety reasons. Although efforts were made to redesign them for restart, including the construction of a large cooling tower for K reactor, improving rela-

tions with the Soviet Union and the signing of the INTERMEDIATE NUCLEAR FORCES and START treaties meant that the SRS reactors would not be used. After refurbishing, K was briefly restarted to demonstrate that it could operate, and then it was shut down.

The declines in the stockpile under START I would allow the United States to maintain its weapons without a fresh supply of tritium for some years to come.

SRS, like many of the other facilities of the nuclear weapons production complex, became largely converted to a waste management and maintenance facility during the 1990s.

Suggested Reading

Rodney Carlisle, *Supplying the Nuclear Arsenal*. Baltimore, Md.: Johns Hopkins University Press, 1996.

Schlesinger, James (1929–)   *American government administrator who served as chairman of the Atomic Energy Commission (1971–1973), and later first secretary of energy (1977–1979)*

James Schlesinger held a variety of government posts in the administration of President Jimmy CARTER. He had briefly served as director of the CIA in 1973 and as secretary of defense in 1974–1975. Schlesinger was appointed secretary of energy August 5, 1977, and he held the post when the DEPARTMENT OF ENERGY (DOE) was officially activated on October 1, 1977. Schlesinger served as cabinet-level secretary of the department until August 24, 1979.

During his two-year term as secretary of energy, Schlesinger initiated several actions with long-term consequences. In September 1978, the DOE worked with the Department of the Interior and the Department of Defense in conducting an aerial survey of 11 atolls and two islands in the Marshall Islands to determine the extent of the hazards remaining from the nuclear testing that had taken place at ENEWETAK and BIKINI. Responding to the energy crisis of the 1970s, several conservation and alternative-energy policies were written into law during Schlesinger's term of office.

The Department of Energy's responsibility to promote the use of nuclear power was considerably hampered with the accident at THREE MILE ISLAND that occurred on March 28, 1979. The department dispatched response teams to monitor any release of radioactivity at Three Mile Island. Two days after the accident, Secretary Schlesinger cited the excellent historic record of the nuclear power industry, and he noted that the radiation exposures from the accident were very limited. Schlesinger said that, despite the accident, nuclear power had to remain an essential part of the drive for energy independence for the United States. A week later, on April 5, 1979, when President Jimmy CARTER addressed energy questions, he mentioned many other alternate solutions to the energy shortage without referring to nuclear power. Carter appointed an independent commission to review the causes of the accident.

During the remainder of Schlesinger's term of office, the DOE continued to emphasize solar power, gasohol-fueled vehicles, hybrid electric-gasoline power, and wind power generation of electricity. Schlesinger resigned as secretary of energy and was replaced on August 24, 1979, by Charles W. DUNCAN.

Under Schlesinger, it became clear that the new Department of Energy would be dealing with the environmental aspects of nuclear weaponry and nuclear power far more explicitly and with far more consciousness of public reaction than had its predecessor agencies, the ATOMIC ENERGY COMMISSION and the ENERGY RESEARCH AND DEVELOPMENT ADMINISTRATION. The Marshall Islands issue and the issue of nuclear power-plant safety would remain on the national agenda over the next decade.

See also MARSHALL ISLANDERS.

Scorpion

One of two nuclear submarines lost at sea by the United States, the USS *Scorpion* lost contact on May 21, 1968, while about 250 miles south of the Azores Islands in the Atlantic. The submarine was returning to base in Norfolk, Virginia, after a three-month cruise with the U.S. Sixth Fleet in the Mediterranean. In October, the navy announced that it had located the wreckage at a depth of some 10,000 feet on the seabed.

A naval court of inquiry looked into the accident. Reviewing records of minor mechanical problems turned up no known cause for the accident. Later speculation by newspaper reporters focused on the possibility that one of the torpedoes aboard the submarine had accidentally detonated, a theory supported by several experts in submarine design and performance.

Scorpion. *The U.S. nuclear powered submarine* Scorpion *made a call at Portsmouth, England, before her ill-fated voyage of May 1968.* (Library of Congress)

Aboard *Scorpion*, 99 U.S. servicemen perished. That same year, three other submarines, all diesel-powered, sank. They were the Israeli *Dakar* on January 22, the French *Minerve* on January 27, and a Soviet Golf-class submarine in April. Altogether about 300 submarine sailors from the four nations were killed in these accidents.

See also GLOMAR EXPLORER; THRESHER.

Suggested Reading

Sherry Sontag and Christopher Drew, *Blind Man's Bluff: The Untold Story of American Submarine Espionage*. New York: Public Affairs, 1998.

Scram

The word "scram" is used as both a noun and a verb, meaning either a nuclear reactor shutdown or the act of shutting down a reactor by inserting CONTROL RODS into it. The term is said to have originated from a joke associated with the first reactor, CHICAGO PILE-1, in which the red button that activated an electrically driven control rod was labeled "scram." If the reactor had a runaway reaction, the operators were to push the button and get out fast, or scram.

See also PILE.

Scud Missiles

Among the many classes of Soviet surface-to-surface (SS) missiles, the Scuds have become the most well known, particularly because the systems were employed with conventional high-explosive warheads by the Iraqis during the Gulf War of 1992 to attack targets in Israel and in Saudi Arabia. The SS-1b, Scud A was first deployed in 1957 and was capable of carrying a 40kt weapon a distance of 50 miles. The Scud A was liquid-fueled and could be hauled by a tracked or wheeled vehicle.

The Scud B, or SS-1c was introduced in 1965 and could carry a 1Kt warhead with a range of 185 miles. It was also liquid-fueled and was towed by a wheeled truck. The Scud was a ballistic missile rather than a cruise missile; that is, it was not air-breathing, and it was fired in a ballistic arc rather than lifting off and flying to its target like a pilotless aircraft, as did cruise missiles.

Seaborg, Glenn T. (1912–)   *American nuclear physicist who worked on the Manhattan Project during World War II and later became best known as the chairman of the Atomic Energy Commission from 1961 to 1971*

As chair of the ATOMIC ENERGY COMMISSION (AEC), Glenn Seaborg was a leader in promoting the use of nuclear reactors for the generation of electrical power.

Seaborg was born in Michigan in 1912 and studied at the University of California. During World War II, he shared in the identification of PLUTONIUM. He worked at the Metallurgical Laboratory at the University of CHICAGO, developing innovative methods for the separation of plutonium from the URANIUM slugs in the production reactors constructed at HANFORD. After the war he joined the faculty of the University of California. He was professor there from 1945 to 1961.

During this period he was involved in identification of a series of transuranic elements created by transmutation reactions. The new elements included americium, curium, berkelium, californium, einsteinium, fermium, mendelevium, and nobelium. He shared a NOBEL PRIZE with Edwin McMillan in 1951 for his discovery of plutonium and for his work in other transuranic elements.

Seaborg, in serving as chair of the AEC (1961–1971), was a convinced proponent of the advantages of the use of nuclear reactors to generate electricity,

Glenn Seaborg. Physicist and chair of the Atomic Energy Commission (1961–1971), Seaborg was a committed advocate of nuclear power, as the embroidery on his pocket handkerchief attests. (National Archives and Records Administration)

and he vigorously worked to advance the cause of nuclear power during his tenure.

His disputes and controversies with environmentalists and with various nuclear scientists who criticized the policies of the AEC, particularly concerning the safety of reactors, involved him in a series of public disputes. He fought to extend nuclear power and supported the concept of BREEDER REACTORS, although in retrospect, he admitted that there were serious intrinsic technical problems with the breeder approach.

He returned to the University of California in 1971. After his return to academic life, he worked on preparing a three-volume series of books documenting his life's work. In these books, his inside perspective on a number of issues, including ABM policy, nuclear accidents, and the supposed illegal diversion of enriched uranium to ISRAEL (which he denied occurred), made his works useful to historians of nuclear weapons.

Suggested Reading

Glenn T. Seaborg with Benjamin S. Loeb, *Kennedy Khrushchev and the Test Ban,* Berkeley: University of California Press, 1981; *Stemming the Tide: Arms Control in the Johnson Years,* Lexington, Mass.: Lexington Books, 1987; *The Atomic Energy Commission under Nixon: Adjusting to Troubled Times,* New York: St. Martin's, 1993.

Seabrook Power Reactor

The Seabrook Power Reactor is located in New Hampshire, less than five miles from the border with Massachusetts, on the edge of the tidal marshes of the Atlantic. The reactor is notable for its tortuous construction process, consuming 17 years, from first application for construction permit to the delivery of first commercial power.

The Public Service Company of New Hampshire (PENH) first applied for a construction permit with the ATOMIC ENERGY COMMISSION in 1973. Quite quickly, several different groups of opponents to the reactor formed. On the one hand, the Seacoast Anti-Pollution League and the New England Coalition on Nuclear Pollution began planning a series of challenges through hearing procedures and through the courts. In addition, a loose coalition of local protest groups formed in the Clamshell Alliance, committed to civil disobedience to stop the reactor from being built. The protesters in the Clamshell Alliance tended to be young people, many of whom were active in other causes as well.

In 1977, the Clamshell Alliance staged a major demonstration at the proposed site. The governor of New Hampshire, Meldrim Thomson, ordered the demonstrators stopped and arrested. Some 1,400 demonstrators were rounded up and jailed. When they refused to post bond, the financial burden of that number of prisoners on the resources of New Hampshire immediately caused a crisis, and the courts soon ordered the release of the protesters. They were never brought to trial. Meanwhile the hearings regarding the reactor construction permit proceeded with the permit issued in 1977.

A second major demonstration in 1978 by the Clamshell Alliance did not result in arrests, and its members appeared divided over whether to adopt different forms of direct action protests. The alliance members in 1977 and 1978 generally agreed they should not break any laws except those against trespass. After 1978, the alliance failed to mount any protests on the scale of those in 1977 and 1978.

Following the THREE MILE ISLAND accident in 1979, the Nuclear Regulatory Commission (NRC) required more detailed emergency evacuation plans for reactors under construction. The NRC suspended the Seabrook construction permit while evacuation plans were developed.

Meanwhile, the state legislature of New Hampshire passed a bill to prohibit the utility from raising its rates to cover the cost of the delays and the construction. Governor Thomson vetoed the bill, which appeared to contribute to his defeat for reelection by Democrat Hugh Gallen. Under Gallen, the bill was reintroduced and passed into law.

In the mid-1980s, Governor John Sununu of New Hampshire did support Seabrook, but the number of opponents, some conservative in their politics, continued to grow as the lack of an agreed emergency evacuation plan became an issue in both New Hampshire and Massachusetts.

By 1986, construction of the plant was complete, but, following the accident at CHERNOBYL in 1986, Governor Michael Dukakis of Massachusetts refused to cooperate in evacuation planning. The NRC had ruled that evacuation plans had to cover an area within a 10-mile radius, and a small slice of Massachusetts fell within that radius of the proposed Seabrook plant.

In 1988, the NRC adopted the "realism rule" in response to the delays in developing evacuation plans at both Seabrook and the SHOREHAM plant on Long Island, New York. The realism rule meant that even though states had not cooperated in evacuation emergency planning, they realistically would help in an emergency, and therefore the NRC could issue a license on the basis of an industry-developed plan submitted to NRC and the Federal Emergency Management Agency. Under this provision, the NRC issued an operating license for Seabrook, with all permissions in place by late 1989.

However, the delays in opening the plant had driven the utility company into bankruptcy, and the whole firm was bought by Northeast Utilities. The reactor went on line in July 1990.

By contrast to one of the oldest reactors, the 175 megawatt-electric (MWe) Yankee Rowe, which had cost $39 million to build and took only four years (1956–1960) from application for license to operation, Seabrook demonstrated how the changed political climate had affected nuclear reactor plans in the United

States. The 1,150 MWe Seabrook reactor had taken 17 years from first application to delivery of power, and it had cost between $6.3 and $6.4 billion.

Suggested Reading

Henry F. Bedford, *Seabrook Station: Citizen Politics and Nuclear Power.* Amherst: University of Massachusetts Press, 1990.

J. Samuel Walker, *A Short History of Nuclear Regulation, 1946–1999.* Washington, D.C.: Nuclear Regulatory Commission, 2000.

Second-Strike Capability

During the period of the development of the MUTUALLY ASSURED DESTRUCTION strategy, or "MAD," the necessity of each side having a "second-strike capability" was crucial. Particularly during the debates over whether or not to develop an ANTI-BALLISTIC MISSILE and whether or not to agree by treaty not to develop such a defense, the issue was raised.

A second-strike capability simply meant that each side should have sufficient nuclear weapon delivery systems so that, if they were to suffer from a devastating unannounced first strike, sufficient weapons could be delivered back in a second strike to wreak unacceptable damage on the country that attacked first. Thus the capability to deliver a strong second-strike, even after having been attacked, was at the heart of the mutually assured destruction strategy.

The need to maintain a strong second-strike capability accounts for the vast numbers of weapons developed by each side. Much of the public and especially disarmament advocates and groups criticized both the U.S. and Soviet Union governments for maintaining nuclear arsenals numbered in the tens of thousands of weapons. However, by the logic of MAD and from the strategic need to maintain a second-strike capability, a few hundred weapons were insufficient for the national security of the superpowers. If the locations of the ships, aircraft, and missile bases of the few hundred weapons were known, it was possible that they could all be destroyed in a preemptive first strike. If that was the case, then neither side was in a position to deter the other side from considering such a preemptive first strike.

With each side maintaining thousands of weapons, many of them mobile (on land, by air, or undersea), each side retained the capability of making a second strike even after being attacked first, and

hence each side believed it succeeded in deterring the other side.

By this line of thinking, second-strike capability was at the heart of the vast increase in nuclear arms and the development of ever-more sophisticated delivery systems in the form of missiles, submarines, and aircraft. Only by a comprehensive and verifiable agreement to reduce armaments mutually could the arms race cycle be stopped. START I and later START II agreements achieved that goal.

Semipalatinsk-21

One of the major nuclear test sites in the former Soviet Union, Semipalatinsk-21 was located in the northeast deserts of KAZAKHSTAN, some 160 kilometers west of the city of Semipalatinsk. Established on August 21, 1947, the site was first called Test Site Number 2, or N2. The first test, of a nuclear weapon designed and assembled at ARZAMAS-16, had a PLUTONIUM core constructed at CHELYABINSK-40. The weapon closely followed the design of the FAT MAN device the United States had tested at TRINITY and dropped on NAGASAKI. The Soviet test was held August 29, 1949. The U.S. press referred to this test as Joe 1.

The test site operated more or less continuously until 1991, when it was closed by the independent Kazakhstan government. Altogether, some 470 of the total 715 Soviet nuclear tests were held at Semipalatinsk. Of these tests, 348 were underground tests, and at least 117 were atmospheric. At Semipalatinsk, the Soviets, like the Americans, emplaced some devices in shafts and others in tunnels.

The 2,000-square mile reserve at Semipalatinsk had three distinct test sites: Shagan River, Degelen Mountain, and Konyastan. Workers lived at a secret city appropriately named after the father of the Soviet atomic bomb, Igor KURCHATOV.

See also ATMOSPHERIC NUCLEAR TESTING; SOVIET WEAPONS TESTS; UNDERGROUND WEAPONS TESTS.

Suggested Reading

Thomas B. Cochrane, Robert S. Norris, and Oleg A. Bukharin, *Making the Russian Bomb: From Stalin to Yeltsin.* Boulder, Colo.: Westview Press, 1995.

Sequoyah Fuels   See KERR-MCGEE.

Shell Model of the Nucleus

The nuclei of certain elements show higher than expected stability when compared with their near neighbors in the periodic table of elements. In particular, ^4_2He, $^{16}_8O$, and $^{40}_{20}Ca$ are particularly stable. These stabilities, coupled with observations such as large numbers of stable ISOTOPES (tin) and the terminus of natural decay series (such as lead), led to the idea of "filled" nuclear shells corresponding to 2, 8, 20, 28, 50, and 82 nucleons. In this model, unstable assemblies of protons and neutrons would undergo rearrangements to adjust the numbers of nucleons to match the nearest filled shell.

Shielding

Shielding refers to any material used to prevent or reduce the passage of radiation. Depending on the radiation, the shielding material varies. With X-rays, the effective shielding is lead; gamma rays require heavy concrete, iron, or lead shielding; beta radiation can be stopped by as little as 1/4 inch of plastic or wood.

Shippingport

The first nuclear power plant to provide electric power over the commercial network in the United States was built at Shippingport, Pennsylvania, by the ATOMIC ENERGY COMMISSION (AEC) for the Duquesne Power Company. Construction began in 1954, and the reactor went critical on December 2, 1957. Full power of 60 megawatts-electric (MWe) was achieved on December 23.

Although several other reactors, including X-1 at Oak Ridge and EBR-II in Idaho, had generated experimental amounts of electricity in 1955, the claim that Shippingport constituted the first commercial power reactor in the United States was accurate. The electricity from Shippingport was generated in a reactor operated by an established utility company, which sold the power over the regular commercial network. EBR-II was government owned and operated and only supplied the small town of Arco, Idaho. The earlier power at X-1 had simply lighted an array of light bulbs at the reactor building itself.

Even on the international level, Shippingport was something of a "first." The British had supplied power to the public grid in October 1956 from the dual-purpose production reactor and power reactor system at Calder Hall. The Russians had put a small power plant in operation in 1954 at Obninsk. But Shippingport was the first full-scale plant designed and operated solely for the purpose of advancing civilian reactor design.

The reactor was built with AEC funding by Westinghouse Corporation, following a design that had been worked out by the Naval Reactors Group under Hyman RICKOVER to propel a nuclear-powered aircraft carrier. Following the PRESSURIZED WATER REACTOR (PWR) design that had evolved for ship propulsion, the Shippingport reactor set the precedent for using PWRs with enriched URANIUM fuel as one of the major designs for power reactors in the United States. The core was later upgraded from 60 MWe to 150MWe.

One consideration that favored the PWR over HEAVY-WATER REACTORS for the early power reactors in the United States was the question of export of reactors under the ATOMS FOR PEACE plans of President Dwight EISENHOWER. If the United States were to export PWRs, it would also have to supply the fuel for the reactors, as most countries would not be in a position to develop uranium-enrichment processing plants. Thus, with PWRs that required enriched uranium fuel, the United States would control the supply of both the equipment and the fuel in any export program. Heavy-water reactors, like the CANDU developed in Canada, could operate on unenriched, or natural, uranium.

The AEC under Lewis STRAUSS hoped to stimulate private power rather than government-owned power projects. The Shippingport reactor, although operated by the private Duquesne Power Company, was in fact government financed and government built. The government retained ownership of the reactor itself, and the project did not have to be put through the commercial licensing procedure. Duquesne was willing to undertake the operation of the already-designed reactor for power purposes; the cost of developing a new design could be saved.

When in 1974–1975 Rickover decided that the Shippingport reactor core should be redesigned as a breeder core, he agreed that, although not required to do so, the plans should go through the regular NUCLEAR REGULATORY COMMISSION (NRC) licensing review. By July 1976 the NRC agreed that the reactor could be operated safely under the new design. The design also passed a review by the Commonwealth of Pennsylvania, and the breeder design went critical on August 26, 1977. It operated for several years quite safely. However, as Congress began looking into the breeder program in 1981 and 1982, budget constraints forced Rickover to settle on a closure date of October 1, 1982. Later analysis of the fuel cores determined that after five years of operation the FISSILE MATERIAL in the core had increased by a little over 1 percent.

Later advocates of HIGH-TEMPERATURE GAS-COOLED REACTORS and other designs argued that the United States should not have selected the PWR design. They pointed out that U.S. hesitation to develop public power, reliance on the proven ship reactor design, and export considerations all accounted for the choice of a design they contended was inferior, more difficult to operate safely, and less practical than other types.

Rickover's quiet demonstration of the breeder principle made less of an impact on the history of reactor development than did his proof that his disciplined approach to technology could be carried over to the civilian power community.

See also POWER REACTORS, U.S.

Suggested Reading

Francis Duncan, *Rickover and the Nuclear Navy: The Discipline of Technology.* Annapolis, Md.: U.S. Naval Institute Press, 1990.

Richard Hewlett and Jack Holl, *Atoms for Peace and War, 1953–1961: Eisenhower and the Atomic Energy Commission.* Berkeley: University of California Press, 1989.

Shoreham Power Reactor

The Shoreham Power Reactor was located on the north shore of Long Island, New York. The reactor was notable for the fact that, although its first construction permit was granted in 1973, it was built and completed but never operated. The NUCLEAR REGULATORY COMMISSION (NRC) granted Shoreham a low-power license, but the state of New York gave concessions to the owning utility, Long Island Lighting, to agree not to operate. The bitter controversy between the state of New York and the federal DEPARTMENT OF ENERGY over the Shoreham reactor led to several attempts in Congress to override the New York opposition and get the reactor opened.

When the NRC began to require detailed evacuation plans following the THREE MILE ISLAND accident in 1979 and the more serious accident at CHERNOBYL in the UKRAINE, New York governor Mario Cuomo argued that it would be impossible to evacuate Long Island if Shoreham suffered a major accident. The state refused to join in planning or in evacuation drills, even though utility company officials argued that the whole island would not need to be evacuated.

The opposition of New York State and its refusal to cooperate with evacuation planning, coupled with the refusal of Governor Michael Dukakis in Massachusetts to cooperate in evacuation planning for the SEABROOK reactor in New Hampshire, led the Nuclear Regulatory Commission (NRC) to issue a "realism rule" in 1988. A Federal Appeals Court in Boston upheld the NRC revision of its rules in September 1988. Under the revised rule, the NRC would accept as realistic the proposition that the states would probably help in the event of an accident and that, therefore, the plan developed by the utility company could be accepted. Following that decision, the state of New York negotiated with Long Island Lighting to prevent opening of the reactor, allowing for a rate increase if the company agreed not to operate the reactor even if granted an operating license.

The stockholders in the Long Island Lighting Company voted to accept the agreement, although the majority of residents of Long Island were opposed to the agreement because of the rate increases. In 1989, a new agreement transferred the Shoreham plant to the Long Island Power Authority for $1; the authority would arrange decommissioning. Without agreeing to a specific rate increase, the state agreed to make a good-faith effort to restore the Long Island Power Company to financial health.

Meanwhile, Secretary of Energy James WATKINS and members of the U.S. Senate were highly critical of the arrangement to prevent the opening of Shoreham. A committee of the House of Representatives approved an amendment to the Nuclear Regulatory Commission appropriation that would prohibit the transfer of the reactor to the Long Island Power Authority, and the U.S. Senate criticized the settlement as deeply flawed. President George H. W. BUSH also announced his opposition to the settlement. Despite these protests and pressures, New York State succeeded in stopping the plant from operating.

Suggested Reading

David P. McCaffrey, *The Politics of Nuclear Power: A History of the Shoreham Nuclear Power Plant.* Boston: Kluwer Academic Publishers, 1991.

J. Samuel Walker, *A Short History of Nuclear Regulation, 1946–1999.* Washington, D.C.: Nuclear Regulatory Commission, 2000.

Silkwood, Karen (1946–1974)   *American worker in a nuclear materials processing facility who complained of hazards and died under mysterious circumstances*

Karen Silkwood was an employee of KERR-MCGEE Company in Cimarron, Oklahoma, who raised questions about the radiological safety of the plant, where PLUTONIUM pellets were processed. Her mysterious death while she was engaged in delivering information to the press raised suspicions that she had been killed to quiet her complaints.

She was born in 1946 in Longview, Texas, and she graduated from high school as a National Honors Society student. She attended Lamar College in Texas and graduated with a degree in medical technology. She was married in 1965, had three children, and was divorced in 1972. In 1972 she took a job at the Kerr-McGee Metallography Laboratory in Cimarron, Oklahoma, where she joined the Oil, Chemical, and Atomic Worker's Union (OCAW). At union meetings, she raised the question of plant safety, and she began to secretly investigate conditions at the plant to prove her charges that the company's management was dishonest and unsafe.

On November 5, 1974, radiation monitoring discovered that she had been contaminated with plutonium-239. On investigation, it was discovered that the room in which she had worked and the gloves she had worn had not been contaminated. The next day, she was found to be still contaminated, and when her apartment was checked, high radiation levels were found in her bathroom and kitchen, and above-normal readings were taken in other parts of the apartment. She, her roommate, and her boyfriend were tested at Los Alamos on November 11, and the levels of radiation each showed were within acceptable limits.

On November 13, Silkwood drove to a planned meeting with a *New York Times* reporter, David Burnham, and an OCAW representative, Steve Wodka. On the way, her car ran off the road into a culvert and she was killed in the collision. An autopsy revealed both a sleep-inducing drug and high levels of plutonium in her intestinal tract.

The union, OCAW, hired an investigator, A. O. Pipkin, who reported that there was damage to the rear of Silkwood's car, suggesting she had been run off the road. Furthermore, she had been taking a manila envelope of information and a notebook to meet with the *Times* reporter, and those papers were missing.

The company contended that Silkwood had probably contaminated herself in order to dramatize her complaints about the safety of the facility and that her death was either an accident or suicide. After the formation of a support group by Kitty Tucker, the national legislative coordinator of the National Organization for Women, Silkwood's estate sued Kerr-McGee for wrongful death, and, after an initial jury award of $10.5 million, a final settlement of $1.38 million was agreed upon in 1986. The original decision marked the first time a jury awarded damages to a victim of radiation contamination from a nuclear facility. The Supreme Court upheld the authority of a lower court to hold a facility regulated by the NUCLEAR REGULATORY COMMISSION liable for negligence.

An AEC investigation into Silkwood's charges regarding plant safety turned up poor safety records and some falsified records. Kerr-McGee closed the plant a few months after Silkwood's death.

Suggested Reading

Los Alamos National Laboratory, "The Karen Silkwood Story," *Los Alamos Science* 23 (November 23, 1996).

Richard Rashke, *The Killing of Karen Silkwood*. New York: Houghton Mifflin, 1981.

C. Ware, "The Silkwood Coalition," *New West*, June 18, 1979.

Silo

In nuclear weaponry, the term "silo" is used to refer to the cylindrical shaped underground pits in which INTERCONTINENTAL BALLISTIC MISSILES (ICBMs) are stationed. In the United States, ICBMs were located in groups of silos located in North Dakota, Arkansas, Montana, and elsewhere. The silos would be clustered in small numbers around a central command post, connected by communication cables so that one launch control facility could manage several ICBM launches simultaneously.

Such silos were usually hardened with thick concrete lids and other protection against near misses by incoming nuclear weapons. During the height of the cold war, MISSILES would be kept armed, fueled, and pre-targeted so that they could be launched on short notice. Liquid-fueled missiles required longer preparation time in their silos than did solid-fueled missiles, and the technology of both types underwent rapid modification and modernization over the period from the 1960s through the 1980s.

It was hoped that under nuclear attack, one or more of a group of silos would survive to be able to launch a retaliatory strike. The principle of assured retaliation was at the heart of the strategy of MUTUALLY ASSURED DESTRUCTION that strategists believed deterred nuclear war between the major nuclear-armed nations.

Simulators

With the end of underground nuclear tests by the United States in 1992, the use of simulators to test the effects of nuclear weapons on machinery and other weapons became more important. Simulators send intense beams of radiation or other effects similar to the effect of a nuclear weapon detonation at a target to test the damage that would be caused by a nuclear weapon. Three SANDIA-operated simulators included Saturn, which hit targets with beams of X-rays, Hermes-III, which used gamma rays, and the Particle Beam Fusion Accelerator, which hit targets with ion beams.

The DEFENSE NUCLEAR AGENCY operated several other simulators. One that focused on nuclear survivability of weapons components was the Large Blast/Thermal Simulator (LB/TS) at White Sands, which became operational in 1995. The simulator provided airblast wave forms of pressures up to 35 pounds per square inch. The thermal simulator could be operated separately from the blast, or the two could be used together to show combined effects. The ability to combine thermal and blast effects similar to those of a nuclear weapon allowed somewhat realistic testing of newly developed military hardware long after testing through detonation of weapons had been discontinued.

A second simulator, DECADE, was operated by the Arnold Engineering Development Center, and it was designed to simulate realistic X-ray radiation of a nuclear detonation in space for testing the hardness of space systems and their components. In the 1990s, older simulators included BLACKJACK 5, DOUBLE EAGLE, PITHON, CASINO, PHENIX, and AURORA, all of which were fully booked with testing schedules. These simulators were used to test *Peacekeeper*, *Trident II*, *Milstar*, and other weapons and National Security Agency satellite components. By the late 1990s, simulators could duplicate a range of X-ray effects of nuclear weapons as well as other radiation, blast, and thermal effects, making it possible to harden new weapons against nuclear weapons effects without detonating a nuclear device.

Military communications and surveillance hardware for satellites, which had been developed after nuclear detonation testing had been discontinued, could be tested under realistic conditions. Simulators, it appeared in the 1990s, would be a permanent part of the research and development establishment as long as detonation was prohibited for political and diplomatic reasons.

Single Integrated Operational Plan (SIOP)

The United States developed a Single Integrated Operational Plan (SIOP) to coordinate the targeting of nuclear weapons from all branches of the TRIAD, each controlled by different services. The need for a SIOP became obvious to strategic planners in the 1960s, as each service developed different nuclear weapon delivery systems and coordination between the targeting lists of the various services became essential. The SIOP had to take into account whether the strategy employed was to be COUNTERFORCE or COUNTERVALUE and had to avoid wasting multiple weapons on the same intended target. The details of the SIOP, which continued to be updated into the 1990s, remained highly classified.

SL-1

On January 3, 1961, the first and most serious accident to happen at the ATOMIC ENERGY COMMISSION (AEC) experimental reactors took place at the National Reactor Testing Station (NRTS) in Idaho. The reactor was the Stationary Low-Power Reactor (SL-1), which had been started up in August 1958. It was the first reactor accident known to result directly in fatalities anywhere in the world.

SL-1 had been built to gain experience, develop plant performance tests, obtain data on the rate of core burnup, test components, and train military personnel in reactor operation and maintenance.

In late December 1960, the reactor was shut down for maintenance, new instruments had been installed, and the control rods had been disconnected from the driving mechanism that removed them from the reactor. A three-man crew, Richard Legg, Richard McKinley, and John Byrnes, came on at 4:00 P.M. on January 3, 1961, to reassemble the control rods. Exactly what happened during the accident is a matter of speculation, as all three men were killed.

Alarms went off at about 9:00 P.M. When fire and rescue crews arrived on the scene, they found radiation levels outside the reactor building high, and they could not locate the three operators. Inside, operator Legg was found on the floor alive, and he was taken to an ambulance, but he died before the ambulance could reach a hospital. Byrnes was dead on the floor, and McKinley had been impaled by a control rod in the ceiling of the reactor room. The bodies of all three victims were intensely radioactive, and crews had to work in shifts to limit their exposure while handling the bodies. The clothing on Legg when he was removed from the ambulance the next day was intensely radioactive, measured at over 300 Roentgen. Even though they worked in short shifts, those moving the bodies received heavy doses; 14 received over 5 Roentgens while six men received doses over 20 Roentgens.

The bodies of the three victims were buried in lead-lined coffins, surrounded by solid concrete vaults to limit the radiation, although their highly reactive heads and hands had to be removed and disposed of as high-level radioactive waste.

Decontamination of the reactor building took 18 months, and monitoring of the surrounding region continued in order to ensure that the off-site population, both on and beyond the boundaries of the NRTS, did not receive dangerous exposures. Monitoring of radiation levels downwind from the reactor found Iodine 131 in the air, vegetation, and milk. Over 99% of the radiation, however, was contained within the building.

Atomic Energy Commission investigators remained mystified by the accident. Apparently one of the reactor rods had been manually removed very quickly from the reactor, resulting in a short power surge that created a sudden volume of steam in the reactor core. The steam lifted the water above with such force that it blew the reactor lid off and drove the control rod through McKinley's body. The recording instruments had been turned off. The unusual and highly irregular procedure of manually removing the reactor control rod led some journalists and others to speculate that the accident may have been a suicide by one of the victims, perhaps because of a love triangle involving his wife and one of the other operators.

However, a later article in the journal *Nuclear Engineering* reported that there had been numerous problems with the reactor. Operators had frequently had to manually assist in the insertion and removal of the control rods.

The reactor vessel and core were taken out, and then the building was razed. The area was decontaminated and made ready for other use by July 1962.

See also IDAHO NATIONAL ENGINEERING LABORATORY.

Suggested Reading

Daniel Ford, *Cult of the Atom: The Secret Papers of the Atomic Energy Commission*. New York: Simon and Schuster, 1982.

Slotin, Louis (1911–1946) *young Canadian-born nuclear scientist in the Manhattan Project at Los Alamos during and after World War II, who was the second to die as a result of a tragic accident from acute radiation exposure*

Slotin had earned his bachelor's degree from the University of Manitoba, Canada, and his doctorate at the University of London just before the war. After working at the University of CHICAGO, he joined the MANHATTAN ENGINEER DISTRICT in 1944, moving to LOS ALAMOS. His research tasks involved running tests on nuclear assemblies that would be at the heart of atomic bombs.

In preparation for the Crossroads tests to be held in 1946 at Bikini in the Pacific, Slotin demonstrated one of the tests on the bomb core for Alvin Graves, who was to take over his position while Slotin went to BIKINI to be present at CROSSROADS.

In his maneuver, Slotin held up half of a PLUTONIUM sphere encased in BERYLLIUM metal, lowering it on to the second half, always maintaining at least a 1/8-inch distance between the two halves. With gamma and neutron counters running, he lowered the top sphere, ensuring that the neutron count would be sufficient for a CHAIN REACTION. Although there could be no nuclear explosion because the two halves were not compressed together with high explosive as in an IMPLOSION assembly, a chain reaction could be started and, in a primitive mechanical fashion, could be controlled.

Slotin kept the top half of the plutonium sphere from contacting the lower half with a screwdriver between the two halves, levering the two together. At 3:20 on the afternoon of May 21, 1946, the screwdriver slipped from his hand and the two halves fell together for an instant. A high burst of radiation, a flash of heat, and a blue glow indicated that the plutonium had initiated a runaway chain reaction. The heat of the reaction expanded the plutonium in an instant, preventing a nuclear detonation. But the intense radiation burst had occurred in less than a second. Slotin threw the top half to the floor and told everyone to evacuate the room.

He called an ambulance and while waiting for it, he assembled the group of lab technicians and witnesses and had them sketch exactly where each of them had stood so that medical workers would be able to make estimates of their exposure. As he was rushed to the hospital, he was nauseous.

Over the next few days, the fatal effects of the radiation led first to blistering and swelling of his hands and abdomen and eventually to the breakdown of his internal organs. Although he was conscious and coherent for the first few days, he died on May 30, nine days after the accident.

His quick reaction in separating the two hemispheres of plutonium and in shielding with his body others in the room made many regard him as a hero. Nevertheless, the procedure of holding the plutonium pit of a weapon apart with a screwdriver appeared, in the light of later methods, to have been a particularly risky and inappropriate procedure.

Slotin was the second individual to have died of acute radiation exposure on the American atomic weapon project. Harry DAGHLIAN had died in 1945 from a similar accident while working with the same plutonium hemispheres.

Suggested Reading
Richard Miller, *Under the Cloud.* New York: Free Press, 1986.

Slovakia   *See* POWER REACTORS, WORLD.

Slovenia   *See* POWER REACTORS, WORLD.

Smyth, Henry D. (1898–1986)   *an American nuclear physicist who served on the Manhattan Project and later on the Atomic Energy Commission*
Henry D. Smyth was best known for the "Smyth Report" published immediately after the detonation of the two weapons over Japan in August 1945, and later

for his support of J. Robert OPPENHEIMER. The formal title of the Smyth Report was *A General Account of the Development of Methods of Using Atomic Energy for Military Purposes under the Auspices of the United States Government, 1940–1945.* The work was controversial because it revealed a great deal about the nuclear project, including the locations of the so-called secret cities at HANFORD, Washington, LOS ALAMOS, New Mexico, and OAK RIDGE, Tennessee.

Smyth had been born in Princeton, New Jersey, the son of a professor at the university. He spent nearly his entire life at Princeton as a child, as a student at the university, and as a member of the faculty in the physics department before joining the MANHATTAN ENGINEER DISTRICT.

Commissioned by General Leslie GROVES to write a full report on the development of the atomic bomb without divulging any classified information, Smyth took his charge very literally. Although he did not divulge details of weapon design, his discussion of the methods used to solve various problems in connection with the production process and the weapons did prove useful to the Soviets as they sought to reproduce the American experience rapidly in their program in the years 1945 to 1949.

Smyth was appointed to serve on the ATOMIC ENERGY COMMISSION in May 1949 and left the commission in September 1954. When the five-member commission voted on whether to suspend Oppenheimer's clearance, Smyth cast the lone dissenting vote in support of Oppenheimer. He argued forcefully that Oppenheimer was loyal and that the issues surrounding his security record were either misunderstood or unimportant. On balance, he found that continuing Oppenheimer's clearance did not represent a threat to national security.

Suggested Reading
Richard G. Hewlett and Jack M. Holl, *Atoms for Peace and War: 1953–1961.* Berkeley: University of California Press, 1989.

SNAP Program
SNAP was the acronym used by the ATOMIC ENERGY COMMISSION (AEC) and its successor agencies and the National Aeronautics and Space Administration (NASA) for the term "Systems for Nuclear Auxiliary Power." The term covered both reactors and radioisotope heat source generators for space applications.

Launch of Transit-IV Satellite. *Communications and other satellites, such as the* Transit *launched here aboard a Thor-Able Star rocket, carried a SNAP nuclear generator to provide continuous electric power for radio transmitters.* (National Archives and Records Administration)

Announced in 1959 by President Dwight EISENHOWER, the first publicly displayed SNAP was a radio-isotope–fueled thermoelectric generator (RTG) that had been designated SNAP-3 by the AEC. The first RTGs had been developed secretly for U.S. Air Force reconnaissance satellites in the period 1955 to 1958.

The first RTG was fueled by the heat released from the radioactive decay of POLONIUM. The device, which weighed about five pounds, could generate five watts of electricity, enough to power low-wattage devices aboard satellites. An earlier SNAP-1 had used the decay heat from cerium to boil mercury that would then drive a small generator.

The SNAP-3 and later radioactive thermoelectric generators worked on the principle that two different metals, kept at different temperatures, generate a current. Discovered by the German physicist Thomas Seebeck (1770–1831), the so-called Seebeck effect allows for the direct but fairly inefficient conversion of heat into electricity.

Although publicly demonstrated in 1960, a SNAP-3 design using an RTG was not employed aboard a space vehicle until June 29, 1961. SNAP-3A used ^{238}Pu, that is, plutonium-238, permitting a power life of some five years, and two such generators were provided to the navy for use in *Transit* satellites in that year. Safety concerns focused on the danger from the radioactive ISOTOPES should a satellite crash to Earth. In particular, officials at the State Department raised the issue of a possible international incident if a satellite fell on a foreign country. With the June 1961 launching, the press began calling the RTGs "atomic batteries."

The second SNAP-3A was launched aboard a *Transit* navigational satellite on November 15, 1961. Over the next few years the military services and NASA launched rockets carrying a range of SNAP devices, with increasing power and longevity of service. By 1968, designers developed radioactive fuel elements in microcapsules that would limit dangerous release in case of crash. Later, more powerful RTGs were designated as multihundred watt (MHW) generators, with power for later designs projected in the range of 260 to 475 watts. Other improvements increased the efficiency from about 1% to 2% to between 5% and 6% and the electric wattage per pound from an initial 1.8 watts per pound to over 4 watts per pound.

RTG devices were particularly useful on long-range voyages into the outer solar system, where light from the sun is too weak to power solar-electric cells effectively.

Suggested Reading

Richard Engler, *Atomic Power in Space: A History.* Washington, D.C.: Department of Energy, 1987.

South Africa

The Republic of South Africa developed both a nuclear power production system and a weapons program in the 1970s and 1980s. With a network of research and development centers, the nation produced six nuclear weapons, later dismantling them and renouncing the weapons program. Nuclear work was centered at the Pelindaba Nuclear Research center, where a nuclear

WATTAGE AND LIFE

Type	
SNAP-3B	2.7w 5 year life
SNAP-9A	25 w 5 year life
SNAP-19	
Nimbus	49.4w microspheres of ^{238}Pu for safety
Pioneer	114–142w, using 4 RTGs, 1 year mission
Viking	35 w 90-day plus after 1 year voyage
SNAP-27	63.5 w at 16 volts for 1 year after moon landing
Transit RTG	30 w for five years
MHW	125–128w, up to 159.6 w, 30 volts, five years

EARLY SNAPS DEPLOYED 1961–1977

Power Source	Agency/Spacecraft	Mission	Date	Note
SNAP-3A	Navy/Transit 4A	Navigational	6/29/61	orbited
SNAP-3A	Navy/Transit 4b	Navigational	9/15/61	orbited
SNAP-9A	Navy/Transit 5BN1	Navigational	9/28/63	orbited
SNAP-9A	Navy/Transit 5BN2	Navigational	12/5/63	orbited
SNAP-9A	Navy/Transit 5BN3	Navigational	4/21/64	aborted
SNAP-19B2	NASA/Nimbus B1	Meteorological	5/18/68	aborted
SNAP-19B3	NASA/Nimbus III	Meteorological	4/14/69	orbited
SNAP-27	NASA/Apollo 12	Lunar	11/14/69	onto moon
SNAP-27	NASA/Apollo 13	Lunar	4/11/70	aborted
SNAP-27	NASA/Apollo 14	Lunar	1/31/71	onto moon
SNAP-27	NASA/Apollo 15	Lunar	7/26/71	onto moon
SNAP-19	NASA/Pioneer 10	Planetary	3/2/72	past Jupiter
SNAP-27	NASA/Apollo 16	Lunar	4/16/72	onto moon
TRANSIT RTG	NAVY/Transit	Navigational	9/2/72	orbited
SNAP-27	NASA/Apollo 17	Lunar	12/7/72	onto moon
SNAP-19	NASA/Pioneer 11	Planetary	4/5/73	past Saturn
SNAP-19	NASA/Viking 1	Mars	8/20/75	on Mars
SNAP-19	NASA/Viking 2	Mars	9/9/75	on Mars
MHW	Air Force/LES 8	Communications	3/14/76	orbited
MHW	Air Force/LES 9	Communications	3/14/76	orbited
MHW	NASA/Voyager 2	Planetary	8/20/77	past Saturn
MHW	NASA/Voyager 1*	Planetary	9/5/77	past Saturn

*Although launched after *Voyager 2*, *Voyager 1* reached Jupiter first and hence was designated "1."

weapon production facility was constructed. The Pelindaba center built South Africa's first weapon. A nearby center, the Circle Building at Adventa, constructed a second nuclear device and four others beginning in April 1982. The program was canceled in November 1989.

At Pelindaba, researchers operated a 20 megawatt (thermal) research reactor (SAFARI-I), a hot-cell complex for conducting work with radioactive materials, and a fuel fabrication plant.

At Upington, in the north of the country, the South African Defense Force maintained the Vastrap Range,

with two test shafts for the emplacement of weapons. Under pressure from the United States, South Africa refrained from testing a nuclear device in one of the shafts in 1977, and no nuclear test was ever conducted at Vastrap.

At Pelindaba East, formerly known as Valindaba, the nation maintained a pilot-scale uranium enrichment plant where weapons-grade uranium was made for nuclear weapons from 1979 to 1990. A semicommercial uranium enrichment plant, also at Pelindaba East, produced uranium for the nation's nuclear power program.

At Koeberg, west of Capetown, the nation maintains two large 920 megawatt (electrical) nuclear power plants. Both reactors are light-water cooled and moderated, operating on low-enriched uranium.

Following its renunciation of a nuclear weapons program, South Africa opened all its nuclear facilities in 1991 to inspection by the INTERNATIONAL ATOMIC ENERGY AGENCY (IAEA). The IAEA visited and verified the dismantlement of the facility at Pelindaba East for the production of weapons-grade uranium. The highly enriched uranium that had been produced for weapons was used in the SAFARI-I research reactor.

From the late 1970s through 1991, South Africa had been regarded as one of the major "threshold" states or "high-risk states" that might develop a nuclear weapon. The nation refused to join the NON-PROLIFERATION TREATY until 1991. An ambiguous flash in the South Atlantic Ocean on September 22, 1979, detected by satellites, appeared to result from a nuclear explosion. Experts speculated that the flash may have been evidence of a nuclear test by South Africa, ISRAEL, or the two nations in collaboration.

In light of the fact that South Africa maintained apartheid, a racialist policy of exclusion of the black majority from political participation and from social privileges, the nation was under international sanctions and threatened by insurrection. For these reasons, the development of a nuclear weapons program by the country was seen in the international community as extremely dangerous. If attacked by a neighboring nation, many believed, South Africa would not have hesitated to use a nuclear weapon. Prior to the ending of apartheid and the formation of a new constitution recognizing the political and social rights of the black majority, South Africa announced its plans to terminate the weapons program.

Suggested Reading

Rodney W. Jones et al., *Tracking Nuclear Proliferation: A Guide in Maps and Charts, 1998.* Washington, D.C.: Carnegie Endowment for International Peace, 1998.

Soviet Weapons Tests

Although the Soviet Union kept its weapons testing program secret, opened documents from RUSSIA, KAZAKHSTAN, and the United States have permitted a reconstruction of the number of Soviet tests. The table below gives the number of atmospheric tests and underground tests at various sites. The vast majority, over 80%, of the megatonnage of the tests were conducted in atmospheric tests in the period from 1949 to 1962.

The Soviets conducted an extensive program of peaceful nuclear explosions (PNEs), some of which may have also had a weapons purpose, although their primary and official purposes were to support oil, gas, and mining industries. The Soviet PNE program included 116 detonations from 1965 through 1988.

SOVIET PNES BY LOCATION

Location	
Russia	81
Kazakhstan	30
Ukraine	2
Uzbekistan	2
Turkmenistan	1
total	116

SOVIET NUCLEAR WEAPONS TESTS

LOCATION	ATMOSPHERIC	WATER	UNDERGROUND	TOTAL
Russia				
NOVAYA ZEMLYA	87	3	42	132
Other Russia			82	82
Kazakhstan				
SEMIPALATINSK	117		215 horizontal	
			133 vertical	
			5 empl.unk.	470
Other Kazakhstan			26	26
Other Republics			5	5
Total tests	204	3	508	715

Source: Estimates derived from Cochrane et al.

SOVIET PNES BY PURPOSE

seismic soundings	39
creation storage cavities	30
extraction of gas or oil	21
extinction oil well fires	5
excavation canals and reservoirs	21

The major tests sites included Semipalatinsk-21 in Kazakhstan, which consisted of three areas: the Shagan River area, the Degelen River, and Konyastan. The last test at Semipalatinsk-21 was in 1989, and the site was formally closed in 1991.

The first Soviet tests occurred in 1949, and American reporters developed the practice of naming the tests as "Joe 1," "Joe 2," and so forth, in a mocking reference to Joseph STALIN.

FIRST SOVIET ATMOSPHERIC TESTS

Joe 1	August 29, 1949
Joe 2	October 3, 1951 (announced)
Joe 3	October 22, 1951 (announced)
Joe 4	August 12, 1953

The Soviets claimed that Joe 4 was a thermonuclear device, and American testing of atmospheric samples at first seemed to confirm that claim. Later study of the question has shown that the weapon tested then more closely resembled what the Americans called a "boosted" weapon design, that is, an atomic fission weapon boosted with the addition of a small amount of tritium, with a yield of about 400 kt. The United States had conducted a similar test of the boosting principle during the Greenhouse series in 1951. Soviet records opened later suggested that there was an earlier test in August 1953 that the Americans did not detect, making Joe 4 actually the fifth Soviet test.

The Soviet Union continued nuclear testing in the atmosphere through 1954 and 1955, conducting further work on a thermonuclear weapon. Altogether, following the Joe 4 test, there were 14 more tests in the atmosphere by November 22, 1955. Most of the tests were conducted at the test site at Semipalatinsk-21, 140 kilometers from the town of Semipalatinsk in Kazakhstan. However, one test in 1954 took place at Totskoe in the southern Ural Mountains, and one in 1955 took place at Novaya Zemlya, the island archipelago north of Norway. Troops conducted an exercise during the Totskoe detonation. The November 22,

1955, test was of a true two-stage thermonuclear weapon, with an estimated yield of 1.6 Mt.

The Soviets imposed a unilateral moratorium in 1958, but they broke the moratorium with a series of over 100 tests beginning in September 1961. During this series, the largest atmospheric detonation in history took place at Novaya Zemlya, estimated at up to 57 Mt on October 30, 1961. The United States responded with OPERATION DOMINIC in 1962. The Novaya Zemlya test of 1961 demonstrated the principle that had been advanced by Edward TELLER, namely, that there was no practical upper limit to the force of a thermonuclear device.

The Soviet Union signed the LIMITED TEST BAN TREATY in 1963 and henceforth conducted all of its further tests underground. After the dissolution of the Soviet Union, Russia agreed with the United States to stop all underground testing in the COMPREHENSIVE TEST BAN TREATY, agreed to in 1993. Both abided by the terms of the treaty, suspending all testing by detonation.

See also ATMOSPHERIC NUCLEAR TESTING.

Suggested Reading

Thomas B. Cochrane, Robert S. Norris, and Oleg A. Bukharin, *Making the Russian Bomb: From Stalin to Yeltsin.* Boulder, Colo.: Westview Press, 1995.

Spain

Although Spain has not developed a nuclear weapons capability, in the 1980s the country increasingly relied upon nuclear reactors for the generation of electricity. By the end of the 20th century, Spain had nine power reactors in operation with several planned but at least temporarily suspended. An early Spanish reactor, at Vandellos, was a gas-cooled, graphite-moderated model imported from France. After going into operation in August 1972, the 480 megawatt-electric (MWe) reactor continued to provide power until October 1989, when it was closed.

The nine operating reactors at the end of the century were owned by seven separate utility companies, as shown in the table on the facing page. All nine were light-water reactors, including seven PRESSURIZED WATER REACTORS (PWRs) and two BOILING WATER REACTORS (BWRs). As in other parts of the world, Westinghouse and General Electric were major competitors for market share.

REACTOR/LOCATION	NET MWE	FIRST OPERATION	SUPPLIER
Asociation Nuclear (ASCO)			
ASCO 1 Tarragon	952	Dec. 1984 PWR	Westinghouse
ASCO 2 Tarragon	949	Mar. 1986 PWR	Westinghouse
Endesa			
Vandellos 2			
Tarragon	968	Mar. 1988 PWR	Westinghouse
Central de Trillo			
Trillo 1			
Guadalajara	1000	Aug. 1988 PWR	Kraftwerk U. Germany
Centrales Nuclear Del Norte			
Almaraz 1			
Caceres	942	Oct. 1981 PWR	Westinghouse/Siemans
Almaraz 2			
Caceres	951	Feb. 1984 PWR	Westinghouse/Siemans
Nuclenor			
Santa Maria de Garona			
Burgos	440	May 1971 BWR	General Electric
Iberdrola			
Cofrentes			
Valencia	984	Mar. 1985 BWR	General Electric
Union Electrica			
José Cabrera			
Guadalajara	153	Feb. 1969 PWR	Westinghouse

Work on six other reactors was either suspended or canceled in 1999, including a second reactor at Trillos, a reactor at Regodala, two at Valdecaballeros, and two at Lemoniz. Thus, many listings of reactors in Spain show a total of 15 reactors, including this group of six whose completion and operation remained in doubt at the turn of the century.

Although estimates were only approximate due to changes in reactor planning, rough calculations of electricity consumed, and varying reactor maintenance schedules, Spanish power reactors produced about 35% of the power consumed in the country. Thus Spain remained among the top 10 or 11 nations in proportion of power generated by nuclear reactors.

Spartan   *See* ANTI-BALLISTIC MISSILES.

Sprint   *See* ANTI-BALLISTIC MISSILES.

Sputnik

Sputnik is the name of the first artificial Earth-orbiting satellite. Launched on October 4, 1957, by the Soviet Union, the satellite was quite simple, emitting a radio signal that would help locate it. The satellite itself was spherical, nearly 23 inches in diameter, and weighed just over 184 pounds. The satellite demonstrated the Soviet ability in the area of rocketry and missiles, creating public concern in the United States that the Soviet Union was ahead in missile technology. Within a month, the Soviets successfully launched another satellite, *Sputnik* II. Despite some who claimed that launching a basketball-sized satellite was no great accomplishment, the fact was that the United States could not immediately match the feat.

Immediately following the launch, the main newspaper of the Soviet Communist Party, *Pravda,* provided the world with details.

The word *sputnik* in Russian means "fellow-traveler." The satellite traveled up to 900 kilometers above the surface of the Earth, revolving around the Earth every hour and 35 minutes. The satellite carried two radio transmitters, each giving off a beep one-third of a second long, followed by a pause of equal length. The radio frequency was set so that it could be picked up by radio amateurs around the world. The newspaper pointed out that space flight had originally been proposed by Russian scientist K. E. Tsiolkovskiy at the end of the 19th century. It was clear that the Soviets intended the satellite as a national accomplishment with high public relations or propaganda value. It soon achieved that purpose.

The Soviet Union had earlier launched and tested its first INTERCONTINENTAL BALLISTIC MISSILE (ICBM) on August 26, 1957, but world audiences and U.S. policymakers were much more impressed by the *Sputnik* satellites, with their "beeps" from outer space a few weeks later. For the administration of Dwight EISENHOWER, the development was not unexpected, but the massive world public reaction led to a change in defense priorities. In 1954, James R. KILLIAN had led a study that predicted the Soviets would pull ahead in missile systems by the end of the 1950s.

The United States pushed forward its missile efforts with the *ATLAS* missile in 1957, and it worked toward creating a satellite in the Discovery program, not achieving a successful satellite emplacement until January 31, 1958, with *Explorer 1*. By 1960, the United States had 18 *Atlas* ICBMs deployed, and production of the *TITAN* missile was getting underway.

The Soviet lead in satellites led many in the United States to believe that there was a "MISSILE GAP." That issue became politicized in the presidential campaign of 1960, in which Democrat John KENNEDY narrowly defeated Republican Richard NIXON, who had served as vice president under Eisenhower. Later intelligence information revealed that the ICBM forces of the two superpowers had not been strikingly different through the period.

Sputnik had broader consequences, causing the United States to attempt to increase the quantity and quality of science and technology training in universities and leading to improvements in all of the laboratories operated by the Defense Department and the ATOMIC ENERGY COMMISSION.

Suggested Reading

Robert A. Divine, *The Sputnik Challenge*. New York: Oxford University Press, 1993.

Walter McDougall, *The Heavens and the Earth: A Political History of the Space Age*. New York: Basic Books, 1985.

Stalin, Joseph (1879–1953)   *leader of the Soviet Union in the period from 1927 until his death in 1953, holding the positions of general secretary of the Communist Party and, during and after World War II, premier of the Soviet Union*

Under Joseph Stalin's dictatorial rule, the Soviet Union rapidly became a nuclear power, developing the atomic weapon between 1943 and 1949, and the country moved closer to the development of a thermonuclear or hydrogen bomb just before his death. Like President Harry TRUMAN of the United States, he viewed the possession of nuclear weapons as a key to international power.

Stalin was born on December 21, 1879, in Georgia, a country within the Russian Empire, and he was educated for the priesthood. He was expelled from seminary for revolutionary propaganda, and in the period 1903 to 1913 he was exiled to Siberia several times. After the revolution in RUSSIA, he rose rapidly through the party structure. Following the death of V. I. Lenin in 1924, Stalin and others struggled for power. By 1927, he had won out, supported by several key figures, including V. A. MOLOTOV.

During the 1930s, through a series of arrests, showtrials and executions, he was able to eliminate all serious competitors for power. Thousands of innocent people were executed and more were sent to harsh labor camps, where many died from disease, hunger, exposure to bitter cold, and brutal treatment.

During World War II, the Soviet espionage apparatus in Great Britain and the United States learned of the MANHATTAN ENGINEER DISTRICT and the beginnings of efforts to build a nuclear weapon. Stalin had Molotov select a Russian physicist to begin research into the possibility of construction of a weapon. Igor KURCHATOV began work on the project, and the administration was put under the administrative control of Lavrenty BERIA, the notorious head of Stalin's secret police.

With the successful demonstration of the U.S. nuclear weapons at TRINITY, HIROSHIMA, and NAGASAKI, Stalin ordered the effort to replicate the American weapon stepped up. Although Kurchatov and his colleagues had ideas of their own about bomb design, Stalin and Beria insisted that the first weapon exactly follow the U.S. IMPLOSION design used at Trinity and Nagasaki. The plans and details for this design had been obtained through the spying efforts of Klaus FUCHS and others in the American project.

With the successful test of the Soviet atomic bomb in August 1949, the Soviet Union was in a stronger

Stalin and Truman. Joseph Stalin of the Soviet Union and Harry S. Truman of the United States presided over the end of World War II and the beginning of the cold war. Both believed that a large nuclear arsenal was essential to defense of their own country from threats by the other. (Library of Congress)

position to challenge American policies in Europe. An early test of that power came with the Berlin blockade in GERMANY in 1948–1949 and then with the invasion by pro-Soviet NORTH KOREA of South Korea, launching the Korean War in 1950. Any consideration of the use of the atomic bomb in Korea by the United States was limited by the knowledge that the Soviet Union might retaliate with a similar weapon. The era of mutual deterrence had arrived.

Stalin's brutal and completely nondemocratic regime had caused many in the West who sympathized with the goals of the Russian Revolution to become disillusioned. Further, Stalin's decision in 1939 to sign a pact with Nazi Germany and to collaborate in the invasion and destruction of Poland in 1939–1940 showed his regime as ruthless. After Germany invaded the Soviet Union in June 1941, and after December 1941 when the United States entered the war against Germany, Italy, and Japan, the United States, Britain, and the Soviet Union became allies. The leaders of the two Western democracies, Franklin ROOSEVELT and Winston Churchill, met with Stalin at a number of "BIG THREE" MEETINGS during the war to settle strategy. However, both Churchill and Roosevelt agreed that the atomic research should not be shared with the Soviet dictator.

This uneasy alliance, in which two partners would not share a major secret technical advance with the third, represents a major source of the cold war in the

decades following World War II. Stalin died on March 5, 1953.

Suggested Reading

Thomas B. Cochrane, Robert S. Norris, and Oleg A. Bukharin, *Making the Russian Bomb: From Stalin to Yeltsin.* Boulder, Colo.: Westview Press, 1995.

David Holloway. *Stalin and the Bomb.* New Haven, Conn.: Yale University Press, 1994.

START I

On July 31, 1991, Presidents Mikhail GORBACHEV of the Soviet Union and George H. W. BUSH of the United States signed the Strategic Arms Reduction Treaty (START I) in Moscow. The treaty marked the continuing trend in improved U.S.–Soviet relations that had been underway for about five years. When President Ronald REAGAN first proposed deep cuts in nuclear arsenals in May of 1982, the concept had been called "SALT III," and negotiations toward the eventual Strategic Arms Reduction Treaty began in earnest in 1990–1991. (During the negotiations, the acronym "START" referred to the Strategic Arms Reduction Talks.)

The START agreement imposed equal "aggregate ceilings" or totals on megatonnage and warheads on each side. The treaty also limited the total number of delivery vehicles, including INTERCONTINENTAL BALLISTIC MISSILES (ICBMs), SUBMARINE-LAUNCHED BALLISTIC MISSILES (SLBMs), and heavy bombers. The reductions were to be carried out in three phases over a period of seven years after the treaty came into force. After that seven-year period of implementation, each country would be allowed 1,600 strategic nuclear delivery vehicles and no more than 6,000 accountable warheads. Even though the treaty was not ratified by the Soviet Union before its dissolution in December 1991, Russia and the other three republics of the former Soviet Union that held nuclear arms agreed to the terms of the agreement.

Under the Lisbon Accords signed in May 1992, Belarus, UKRAINE, and KAZAKHSTAN accepted the terms of START, and they pledged to join the Nuclear NONPROLIFERATION TREATY as non-nuclear states. The Kazakhstan Parliament ratified START I on July 2, 1992; the U.S. Senate approved START I on October 1, 1992; Belarus ratified START I on February 4, 1993; Ukraine approved the treaty with reservations on November

18, 1993, and without reservations on February 3, 1994. Russia confirmed its adherence to START I in several legal steps, confirmed in agreement between Presidents Bush and Yeltsin on June 16, 1992.

Immediately following the signing of the treaty, both the U.S. and Soviet governments and then the Russian government began confidence-building measures that conformed to the spirit of the agreement. The aggregate limits of START are as follows:

AGREED START CENTRAL TREATY LIMITS

Each country would be limited to the following totals:
- 1,600 deployed ICBMs, SLBMS, and heavy bombers
- 154 deployed heavy ICBMs
- 6,000 total accountable warheads
- 4,900 warheads on deployed ICBMs and deployed SLBMS
- 1,540 warheads on deployed heavy ICBMs
- 1,100 warheads on deployed mobile ICBMs
- 3,600 metric ton ceiling on throw weight

The complex formula had a purpose. Because of the principles of aggregate ceilings and sublimits, the START agreement allowed each country to make up its allowed total of 6,000 warheads by different combinations of weapons carried by bombers, ICBMs, and SLBMs. This arrangement allowed the Americans to take fuller advantage of its long-range aircraft and the Soviets to take fuller advantage of its heavy ICBMs.

Among the confidence-building measures put in place by both countries soon after the signing of the treaty were a series of efforts to increase transparency and provide early experience with verification techniques. For example, both countries opened ICBM SILO hatches and displayed submarine missiles so that they could be counted by satellite, and both displayed some of the electronic tools employed in launching and metering of ballistic missile launches.

See also PRESIDENTIAL NUCLEAR INITIATIVE 1991; SALT I; SALT II; START II.

START II

The Strategic Arms Reduction Treaty II (START II) was originally signed by Presidents George BUSH of the United States and Boris Yeltsin of Russia on January 3, 1993, as an extension of START I. Yeltsin submitted the treaty for ratification on June 22, 1995, but the treaty was not ratified by the Russian parliament until after he left office in April 2000. President Bill CLINTON

submitted the treaty for ratification to the U.S. Senate, and it was overwhelmingly voted up by 87 to 4 on January 26, 1996.

START II was originally written to take effect on January 1, 2003. However, in 1997 the treaty was renegotiated to take effect on December 31, 2007, and certain modifications were agreed to in order to make the treaty more acceptable to the Duma.

Under START II, the total number of active delivery vehicles with warheads held by Russia and the United States would be reduced to about 3,000 to 3,500 each. In the START II agreement, some of the complexities of the sublimit system set up under START I would be eliminated. The table below compares the limits in the two agreements.

SYSTEM	START I	START II
ICBM warheads	4,900	no limit specified
on MIRVed ICBMs	no limit	zero allowed
on Heavy ICBMs	1,540	zero allowed
SLBM warheads	no limit	1700–1750
bombers	not specific	not specific
Total	6,000	3,000–3,500

Under both treaties, neither side was required to destroy the actual warheads but only the delivery systems. Under START II, Russia would be obliged to dismantle all of its SS-18 missiles and some of its mobile missile carriers. Both sides would entirely eliminate MULTIPLE INDEPENDENTLY TARGETABLE REENTRY VEHICLE (MIRV) intercontinental ballistic missiles, reflecting actions already taken by both sides unilaterally. Arms control experts saw this feature as perhaps the most important because MIRVs were particularly destabilizing during the height of the cold war. Nevertheless, the United States announced that it would retain some 3,500 strategic warheads not mounted on delivery vehicles and also some 3,000 tactical weapons with less than intercontinental range. Critics pointed out that, despite the published totals, each side would be retaining some 10,000 warheads (including those not mounted on delivery systems) even if START II were fully implemented. Accounts in the media varied widely as to the numbers of weapons remaining in the stockpile after the implementation of the START I and START II limits, but the overall figure of at least 10,000 on each side, counting unmounted but ready weapons, appeared reliable.

The later renegotiation of START II with its starting dates set back to the year 2007 did not immediately result in ratification of the treaty by the Duma. The Duma voted to ratify on April 14, 2000.

Even though unratified, it appeared the two nations would implement the limits imposed by START II and perhaps even begin to move toward lower limits of about 1,500–2,000 warheads each in a so-called START III level. Following the precedent established by President Bush in PRESIDENTIAL NUCLEAR INITIATIVE-91, the Clinton administration implemented unilateral arms reductions in the spirit of Start II. If the START III limits were implemented, the reserved unmounted warheads would be eliminated. The Clinton policy of dealing with the uncertainty that derived from a negotiated but unratified arms control treaty was established in 1994 in the NUCLEAR POSTURE REVIEW.

See also CRUISE MISSILES; INTERCONTINENTAL BALLISTIC MISSILES; SALT I; SALT II.

Suggested Reading

Dunbar Lockwood, "Strategic Nuclear Forces under START II," *Arms Control Today* (December 1992).

———. "Stability and Symbolism: The Case for Start II," *Arms Control Today* (January–February 1992); START II Supplement 2–5.

Jack Mendelsohn, "The U.S. Russian Strategic Arms Control Agenda," *Arms Control Today* (November 1997).

Star Wars

See STRATEGIC DEFENSE INITIATIVE.

Stochastic

In the field of health effects of radiation, a stochastic effect impacts individuals on a random basis. The probability of any specific individual suffering an ill-effect, such as contracting cancer, depends on the absorbed DOSE. A stochastic effect is a random effect, and probability figures represent the likelihood of its effect on individuals.

Strassman, Fritz (1902–1980)   *German physical chemist who was the co-discoverer, with Otto Hahn, of the process of nuclear fission in uranium*

The joint paper authored by Fritz Strassman and Otto HAHN on neutron-induced fission, published in 1939, is often heralded as the opening of the atomic age.

Strassman was born on February 22, 1902, in Boppard, Germany. He received a doctorate from the Technical University in Hannover in 1929. Beginning in 1934 he worked with Hahn and Lise MEITNER in investigating the products formed when URANIUM is bombarded with neutrons. Strassman's use of analytic chemical methods contributed to the team's understanding that the lighter elements produced from neutron bombardment were FISSION FRAGMENTS, resulting from splitting the atom into two. Meitner and Otto Frisch developed the liquid drop model of the atom, and the ideas of Strassman, Hahn, Meitner, and Frisch were confirmed by scientists in laboratories in Great Britain, France, Russia, and the United States. The conclusions led scientists such as Leo SZILARD to conclude that an atomic bomb could soon be developed.

Strassman served on the staff of the Hannover and the Kaiser Wilhelm Institute during World War II, and in 1946, he became a professor of chemistry at the University of Mainz. From 1945 to 1953, he was director of the chemistry department of the Max Planck Institute for chemistry. Strassman died on April 22, 1980, in Mainz, Germany.

Strategic Bombers

During the height of the cold war, the United States and the Soviet Union developed and then improved several classes of strategic and medium-range bombers. As air defenses improved in both nations, with surface-to-air missiles (SAMs), they both moved to install air-launched CRUISE MISSILES (ALCMs) and short-range attack missiles (SRAMs) aboard their bomber aircraft so that they could attack from a standoff position several hundred miles from the intended target.

Strategic Bombers. *In the 1980s and 1990s, the strategic bombers remained an essential part of the nuclear deterrent system of the United States. Here three B-52s are lined up for take-off.* (U.S. Air Force)

	RANGE	PAYLOAD	SPEED	YEAR
United States				
Strategic				
B-52G	12000km	32 tons	0.95 Mach	1959
B-52 H	16000km	32 tons	0.95 Mach	
				1962
B-1B (stealth)	9800km		1.25 Mach	1986
Medium Range				
FB-111	4700km	19 tons	2.5 Mach	1969
Soviet				
Strategic				
Tu-95 Bear	12800km	18 tons	0.78 Mach	1955
Mya-4 Bison	11200km	9 tons	0.87 Mach	1956
Medium Range				
Tu-26 Backfire	8000km	9 tons	2.5 Mach	1974

Although the U.S. B-52 was first introduced in 1952, it was modified and modernized, with the G and H modifications still in operation in the 1980s. The H model remained in service into the 1990s, with exterior pylons for mounting SRAMs and internal racks for carrying ALCMs.

The following table presents the long-range and medium-range aircraft employed by both nations at the height of the cold war in the mid-1980s. The B-1 was designed and manufactured by 1970, but the reduced-radar signature stealth version, the B-1B, was not deployed until 1986. "Mach" is the speed of sound, about 1,070 feet per second or about 730 miles per hour at sea level. Thus a 2.5 Mach speed aircraft can travel about 1,800 miles per hour.

Speeds and payloads from International Institute of Strategic Studies, 1983. Maximum payloads shown probably could not be carried to maximum range.

Strategic Defense Initiative or "Star Wars"

On March 23, 1983, President Ronald REAGAN delivered a major address, soon referred to by the press as the "Star Wars" speech. He called for a technological effort to build a defense against strategic nuclear missiles that would render nuclear weapons impotent and obsolete. He asked the American scientific community to find ways to intercept and destroy strategic ballistic missiles before they reached their targets. Over the next year, two study groups examined the Strategic Defense Initiative (SDI) and concluded that several emerging technologies held promise. Funding for fiscal year 1985 was set at $1.74 billion to focus on five different technologies, with an estimated $24 billion to be spent over the period 1985 through 1989.

The five technological areas that were investigated were: (1) surveillance, tracking, and acquisition; (2) directed energy weapons; (3) kinetic energy weapons; (4) systems analysis and battle management; and (5) support programs. Most of the research money went into the first area. Directed energy weapons included possible space and ground-based chemical laser beam weapons, space-based particle beams, and directed energy from nuclear detonations. Kinetic energy projectiles referred to small projectiles sent at high velocity to intercept reentry vehicles.

SDI became extremely controversial and politicized. Even within advisory groups in the nuclear community, sharp argument centered around different views as to the feasibility of the idea and, if feasible, which technology should be pursued. Retired general Daniel Graham had advocated a defensive missile system he dubbed "High Frontier," and Graham's supporters believed that nuclear-tipped antimissile missiles represented the best pathway to pursue. Others, including followers of Edward TELLER and several research groups at LAWRENCE LIVERMORE NATIONAL LABORATORY, proposed the system of "nuclear pumped lasers" or directed energy from a nuclear detonation.

Among current and former scientific advisors on nuclear matters, many were opposed to the deployment of weapons to outer space. About one month after Reagan's speech, a number of well-known American scientists and other leaders sent an open letter in the form of a telegram to Yuri Andropov, general secretary of the Communist Party of the Soviet Union, opposing use of any weapons, defensive or offensive, in outer space. Among those signing the telegram were Hans BETHE and Isidor RABI, both winners of the NOBEL PRIZE, and Herbert YORK, former director of the Lawrence Livermore Laboratory.

During the 1986 presidential campaign, Democratic Party candidates charged that the program was both too expensive and impractical and that it might accelerate the arms race. Advocates of SDI claimed that it held out the promise of an end of the policy of assured destruction that required a threat of retaliation to serve as a deterrent. Some pointed out that even an imperfect SDI system would enhance the deterrent effect of American weapons by protecting a large number of them from a potential second strike, thereby strengthening the threat of retaliation.

During the period 1986 through 1989, the Strategic Defense Initiative Office (SDIO) continued to sponsor studies and research into particle beams and kinetic weapons. Many of the projects were channeled through the DEFENSE NUCLEAR AGENCY because that agency had worked with an extensive network of contractors and suppliers with expertise in high-energy effects because of the need to develop nuclear weapons SIMULATORS. Simulators had become necessary following the ending of atmospheric testing in 1963, the THRESHOLD TEST BAN TREATY limiting the size of underground detonations, and the potential for a complete ban on nuclear weapon testing through detonation in a COMPREHENSIVE TEST BAN TREATY. Such devices had been able to generate intense beams of radiation, similar to those emitted by nuclear weapons, in order to test their effects on materials, mechanical equipment, weapons, delivery systems, and electronics. Researchers with experience in such simulators could apply some of their concepts to potential new defensive weapons.

With the negotiation of the Strategic Arms Reduction Treaty and the decline in both nuclear weapons and delivery systems that followed in the early 1990s, the SDIO funding declined. Some of the research was turned to improvement of artillery weapons and to the hardening of satellite and missile systems against possible threats.

With the end of the cold war in 1989–1990 and the collapse of the Soviet Union in 1991, SDI advocates

Lewis Strauss. Chairman of the Atomic Energy Commission 1953–1958, Lewis Strauss was a committed advocate of the use of nuclear energy for the generation of electric power, as well as its central use in national defense. (Department of Energy)

claimed that the immense funding and high technology planned for the program contributed to the Soviet decisions to scale down the confrontation between the Soviet Union and the United States. However, critics of SDI continued to argue that the ideas had been impractical and that, if the plan had any effect in the Soviet Union, it was a case of "virtual" deployment or bluff. By merely threatening to spend billions on a new generation of technology, the United States may have had as much impact on Soviet policy as the actual deployment of the systems.

Strauss, Lewis (1896–1974)   *U.S. naval officer and government administrator who served as chairman of the Atomic Energy Commission in the years 1953 to 1958*

Lewis Strauss led the ATOMIC ENERGY COMMISSIONS (AEC) during a period that saw some of the agency's most controversial decisions and actions. Strauss (pronounced "straws") was born in 1897 in Richmond, Virginia. He had served under Herbert Hoover in the U.S. Food Administration and in Belgian relief during World War I. During World War II, he had served on the staff of James V. Forrestal and had retired with the rank of rear admiral. He served for three years as a member of the AEC (1947–1950) and then returned to a career in finance in New York.

Strauss was appointed by President Dwight EISEN-HOWER as chair of the AEC in June 1953. He immediately faced the issue of whether to seek the termination of the security clearance of J. Robert OPPENHEIMER, and he decided to do so. During his chairmanship, the AEC greatly expanded the weapons production complex, proceeded with the construction of the hydrogen bomb, and conducted a vigorous series of aboveground nuclear tests.

Following the emphasis by President Eisenhower on developing ATOMS FOR PEACE, the commission under the leadership of Strauss pushed for the development of nuclear power by private corporations.

Strauss was noted for his concern with operational security and with maintaining secrecy about the technology of nuclear weapons, manufacturing processes, and reactor design. His endorsement of the charges against Oppenheimer and his support for private rather than public ownership of nuclear power plants, as well as his tendency to view administration of the agency in political terms, all marked him as a strong conservative in the politics of the era.

Suggested Reading

Richard G. Hewlett and Jack M. Holl, *Atoms for Peace and War: 1953–1961.* Berkeley: University of California Press, 1989.

Strontium

Strontium is an element with the atomic weight of 87.63. There are 12 radioactive ISOTOPES of strontium, of which 11 can be produced as FISSION PRODUCTS of a reactor or nuclear weapon. Strontium-90, which emits beta radiation, has an effective half-life of 25 years. It can be extremely dangerous, as it is similar chemically to calcium and the human body absorbs some of it into the bones. It was named by its discoverer, Humphry Davy, after Strontian, a mining area in Scotland where it was first discovered in 1808. The isotope Strontium-89 has a half-life of 54 days.

See also FISSION PRODUCTS.

Submarine-Launched Ballistic Missiles (SLBMs)

The concept of marrying a long-distance rocket with a submarine had been proposed in Germany during World War II. A German plan, still on the drawing boards when the war ended, included a submarine capable of crossing the Atlantic, carrying one or more missiles that would be launched from the surfaced submarine toward American cities.

American engineers followed up on the concept with the development of the *Regulus* missile in the 1950s, outfitting a few Pacific long-range fleet diesel-electric submarines with this system. One such submarine, *Grayback,* was especially built to house a never-deployed *Regulus* II missile. *Grayback* was later converted to deploy swimmer delivery vehicles. The *Regulus* was carried in a housing on the deck of the submarine and would be launched when the submarine was surfaced. It would then be guided to its target by one or more other submarines at periscope depth. The obvious drawbacks of such a system included the fact that the launching submarine would lose one of its greatest assets, the protection from discovery while remaining submerged, in order to fire the missile. Another problem derived from the need for one or more "picket" submarines to guide the missile in its course.

In 1956, the Polaris program was begun in the United States, under the leadership of Captain (later Admiral) Levering Smith and Rear Admiral William (Red) Raborn. The objective of the Polaris program was to design a system that would include a specially designed submarine and a missile that would allow the missile to be launched while the submarine remained submerged. Further, the missile was to be ballistic, rather than guided so that the missile, once launched, was on its own.

Over the period 1956 to 1960, the system was developed, with the first ballistic missile submarine, the *George Washington,* launched in 1959 and the first Polaris missile tested from it in July 1960. The submarine remained stationary beneath the surface; the missile was propelled by compressed air from a vertical launching tube in the submarine to the surface and then ignited as it emerged from the water.

Working on the same principle, the Polaris missile immediately began to undergo improvements, with larger and more powerful rocket engines and therefore greater range. As a ballistic rather than a guided mis-

Polaris Submarine. Two officers, CDR Patrick Hanniker and CDR Landa Zech, confer at the construction of the Polaris submarine Lafayette *at the General Dynamics plant in 1962.* (Library of Congress)

sile, the weapon would arc up to the edge of outer space and fall on its target.

Accuracy always remained an issue with SLBMs, as very precise navigation would be required to ensure that the launch point in the ocean was exactly known and to aim the missile properly at its target. Consequently the CIRCULAR ERROR PROBABLE of SLBMs tended to be greater than that of ground-launched INTERCONTINENTAL BALLISTIC MISSILES (ICBMs) or various guided missiles such as air- and ground-launched CRUISE MISSILES.

Although the U.S. submarines carrying ballistic missiles are often designated by the type of missile they carry, the submarine classes were named for the lead ship of the class. Thus the George Washington class of ballistic missile submarines with numbers SSBN 598, 599, 600, 601, and 602 all followed the design of the first ship of the class, the *George Washington*. Two of the ships were taken out of service in 1980, and the remaining three were reclassified as attack submarines (SSNs) rather than ballistic missile submarines in 1981 and 1982.

The classes of U.S. SLBMs were as follows:

	Year Introduced		
Polaris A1	1960	500 nautical mile range	
Polaris A3	1966		
Poseidon C3	1971		
Trident C4	1981	First three-stage, mirv	
Trident D5	1989	Increased accuracy	

The classes of Soviet submarines carrying SLBMS were as follows:

Sub Class	Year Launched	Missile Type
Yankee I	1966	SS-6-4 liquid fuel
Yankee II		SS-N-17 solid
Delta I	1972	SS-N-8 2-stage
Delta II		SS-N-8 2-stage
Delta III		SS-N-18 MIRV
Delta IV		SS-N-23 3-stage
Typhoon	1981	SS-N-20 3-stage

SLBMs remained an essential part of the TRIAD of American strategic forces, along with ground-launched ICBMs and long-range bomber aircraft. After negotiation of the START I and START II treaties in the 1990s, the United States continued to rely on a fleet of ballistic missile submarines as a mainstay of its DETERRENCE.

Summit Meetings

Many meetings between world leaders were held during the cold war, following the pattern established during World War II with "BIG THREE" MEETINGS. At most of these meetings, questions of ARMS CONTROL and nuclear weapons were discussed.

The following are the most significant summit meetings pertinent to the maintenance of peace and nuclear arms control between the United States and the Soviet Union; usually the meetings were named for the city in which the meeting was held.

Geneva. July 18–23, 1955

Eisenhower met with Khrushchev, British prime minister Anthony Eden, and French premier Edgar Faure. Eisenhower proposed an Open Skies arrangement to allow reconnaissance of military installations.

Camp David (Maryland). September 15–27, 1959

Eisenhower and Khrushchev met to discuss future summits, the status of Berlin, and cultural exchanges.

Paris. May 16–17, 1960

Eisenhower met with Khrushchev, French president Charles De Gaulle, and British prime minister Harold MacMillan. Eisenhower refused to apologize for the U.S. incursion of Soviet airspace with a U-2 flight piloted by Gary Powers, shot down two weeks previously. The mission of the aircraft had been to gain information about Soviet ICBM and long-range bomber development. This summit meeting was canceled.

Vienna. June 3–4, 1961
Kennedy met with Khrushchev. The Soviets announced their intention to recognize East Germany as a sovereign state.

Glassboro (New Jersey). June 23, 25, 1967
Lyndon Johnson met with Aleksey Kosygin. The United States suggested limits be placed on anti-ballistic missile (ABM) systems. Kosygin rejected the proposal.

Moscow. May 22–30, 1972
Richard Nixon met with Leonid Brezhnev to sign the Strategic Arms Limitation Treaty I (SALT I) (May 26), and the limitation on ABM systems. Both sides agreed to basic principles of peaceful coexistence. The treaty was ratified by joint resolution of Congress on September 30, 1972.

Washington. June 18–25, 1973
Nixon and Brezhnev signed a protocol on the prevention of nuclear war (June 21), and they agreed to continue negotiations on limiting nuclear arms.

Moscow. June 28–July 3, 1974
Nixon and Brezhnev signed a protocol to the ABM treaty signed in 1972 to limit ANTI-BALLISTIC MISSILE sites to one in each country; they also signed the THRESHOLD TEST BAN TREATY, limiting test yields to 150 kilotons, on July 3.

Vladivostok (U.S.S.R.). November 23–24, 1974
Gerald Ford met with Brezhnev and agreed to the basic outline of the SALT II treaty; they indicated that its term would run from October 1977 to December 31, 1985.

Helsinki. July 30–August 2, 1975
Ford and Brezhnev discussed the SALT II negotiating process, but they were in disagreement about cruise missiles and the Soviet Backfire bomber. Following the summit, the Conference on Security and Cooperation in Europe agreed on August 1 to the Helsinki Final Act, establishing principles of negotiation.

Vienna. June 15–18, 1979
Jimmy Carter and Leonid Brezhnev signed SALT II on June 18, limiting U.S. and Soviet offensive strategic nuclear weapons; they also discussed a possible comprehensive nuclear test ban treaty, issues of nuclear proliferation, and general reduction of forces in Europe. Later, Carter withdrew the treaty from consideration for ratification by the U.S. Senate.

Geneva. November 19–21, 1985
Ronald Reagan met with Mikhail Gorbachev and agreed to seek early progress on an INTERMEDIATE NUCLEAR FORCES (INF) agreement, and they agreed to meet in 1986 and 1987.

Reykjavik (Iceland). October 10–12, 1986
Reagan met with Gorbachev and agreed on a framework for the START agreement, and they approved a framework for the INF agreement.

Washington. December 7–10, 1987
Reagan met with Gorbachev and signed the INF treaty (December 8). He instructed negotiators to work on START agreement.

Moscow. May 29–June 1, 1988
Reagan and Gorbachev exchanged ratifications of the INF treaty; they also signed agreements regarding nuclear test monitoring and agreed to give each other 24-hour notice of all ICBM and SLBM test launches.

New York. December 7, 1988
Gorbachev announced at the UN unilateral cuts in Soviet armed forces in Europe, and he called for progress on START.

Valleta (Malta). December 2–3, 1989
George Bush and Gorbachev announced their joint intention to conclude both a Conventional Forces in Europe (CFE) treaty and START by 1990.

Washington. May 30–June 3, 1990
Bush and Gorbachev agreed to accelerate discussions on START. They met again in Helsinki in September 1990 to advance discussions on START.

Paris. November 19–21, 1990
Together, the 22 leaders of NATO and Warsaw Pact countries signed the CFE treaty (November 19), agreeing to monitoring reduction of forces and destruction of weapons.

Moscow. July 31, 1991
Bush and Gorbachev signed START I, imposing limits on the nuclear stockpiles of the United States and U.S.S.R. and pledging to reduce the total number of weapons on each side.

Lisbon. May 1992
Ukraine, Kazakhstan, and Belarus agreed to abide by terms of START, signing the Lisbon Protocols.

Washington. January 3, 1993
Bush and Boris Yeltsin signed START II, pledging further reductions in nuclear weapons and delivery sys-

tems. The United States ratified on January 26, 1996; Russia ratified on April 14, 2000.

Several of the meetings held great promise for the future, sometimes not immediately fulfilled. In reference to the sense of optimism generated from the meetings, journalists recalled the "Spirit of GLASSBORO," the "Spirit of VLADIVOSTOK," or the "Spirit of REYKJAVIK," among others.

During the four decades of Big Three and summit meetings, conservative or hawkish critics in the West tended to believe that the Soviets used the agreements and treaties to delude American political leaders into complacency while the Soviets achieved military and political advantages. Liberal or dovish critics generally believed that arms control agreements provided excuses for continuing the arms race in managing rather than ending the arms race with complete nuclear disarmament. The outcome of the agreements by the early 1990s saw a sharp reduction in the number of weapons and delivery vehicles mounted by each side.

See also ARMS CONTROL; "BIG THREE" MEETINGS.

Surface-to-Air-Missiles *See* ANTI-BALLISTIC MISSILES.

Sverdlovsk

Two sites of the Soviet nuclear weapons complex were located at Sverdlovsk-44 and Sverdlovsk-45. Sverdlovsk-44 was the site of a gaseous diffusion enrichment plant that went on line in 1949, and Sverdlovsk-45 (with a closed city, Lesnoy) was a weapons-assembly site, the largest of four such plants in the Soviet Union. Sverdlovsk-45 has also been called the Electrochemical Instrument Combine. The city of Nizhnyaya Tura is located nearby.

Both sites are located in the Ural Mountains north of Yekaterinburg. Sverdlovsk-45 served as one of the largest weapons storage sites, and it included several separate factories.

Sverdlovsk-45, with its closed city of Lesnoy, had a population of 54,700 in 1991. Sverdlovsk-44, with the city of Novouralsk, had a population of 88,500 in the same year.

As with other facilities of the Soviet nuclear weapons program, often the exact location of the sites was kept secret and only with the end of the cold war have they been openly designated.

Suggested Reading

Thomas B. Cochrane, Robert S. Norris, and Oleg A. Bukharin, *Making the Russian Bomb: From Stalin to Yeltsin.* Boulder, Colo.: Westview Press, 1995.

Sweden

The Swedish nuclear power program consists of 12 nuclear reactors, producing slightly over 50% of the nation's electrical power at 10 gigawatts. However, the nation plans to phase out the nuclear power program, accelerating those plans after the 1986 CHERNOBYL accident.

The Swedish radioactive waste program for spent fuel from the power plants is quite sophisticated. The Swedish plan is to allow the depleted fuel to cool for a period of 40 years and then to place the waste in thick-walled canisters with a copper outer wall and a steel inner wall altogether about 10 centimeters thick. The canisters will be placed in vertical holes in an underground repository, surrounded with bentonite clay. Barring unforeseen shifting of the granite bedrock, the lifetime of the waste package is over 1 million years.

Swimming Pool Reactor

A swimming pool reactor is usually a light-water–moderated and cooled, low-power nuclear reactor designed for research purposes rather than power production. Although the design of many swimming pool reactors is unique, they have in common a core assembly submerged in a deep pool of water. The TRIGA (Training, Research and Isotopes–General Atomics) Reactor from Gulf General Atomics and the SLOWPOKE (Safe LOW-POwer Kritical Experiment) Reactor from Atomic Energy Canada, Ltd., are typical examples of swimming pool reactors. Both have found extensive use for NEUTRON ACTIVATION ANALYSIS. Some five dozen TRIGA Reactors are in operation at research facilities in 21 countries, and SLOWPOKE Reactors have been installed at a dozen research centers from Calgary to Colombo. The inherent safety of these reactors is due in part to their negative temperature coefficients. The ability of the water moderator/coolant to moderate neutrons decreases as its temperature increases. Hence, swimming pool reactors can be found in central locations on many university campuses.

Switzerland   *See* LUCENS; POWER REACTORS, WORLD.

Szilard, Leo (1898–1964)   *Hungarian-born American physicist who was co-inventor of the nuclear reactor and who foresaw the development of nuclear weapons*

Leo Szilard was among the most prominent of the emigré scientists from Europe who participated in the development of the atomic bomb in the United States for the MANHATTAN ENGINEER DISTRICT (MED). He was a co-inventor of the basic nuclear reactor and was a leader among MED scientists in the effort to conduct a demonstration of the weapon rather than drop it on a civilian target in Japan.

Szilard was born in Budapest, Hungary, on February 11, 1898. He was drafted into the Austro-Hungarian army during World War I, and he was still in officer's school when the war ended. He continued his studies at the Technical High School in Berlin and then transferred to the University of Berlin, where he earned a doctorate in physics in 1922. His work in the 1920s at the Kaiser Wilhelm Institute focused on X-ray crystallography, and he began to patent a number of devices that were later used extensively in nuclear physics research, including the basic principles behind a particle accelerator.

When the Nazis took power in Germany in 1933, Szilard left for Great Britain, where he developed the concept of a nuclear CHAIN REACTION. In 1938, he moved to the United States where he heard of the discovery of nuclear FISSION by Otto HAHN and Fritz STRASSMANN. He immediately recognized that fission could be the source of great power. He undertook research at Columbia University to measure the numbers of neutrons released in the fission process, a necessary step toward developing a reactor that could harness a fission chain reaction. At Columbia, he worked with Enrico FERMI in preliminary designs of an experimental graphite-moderated PILE that helped establish the moderating effect on neutrons emitted during a reaction.

He developed a draft letter that Albert EINSTEIN sent to President Franklin ROOSEVELT in 1939. In July of that year, he visited Einstein and urged him to write to Roosevelt outlining the possibility that nuclear fission could lead to the development of an extremely powerful weapon. Einstein's letter convinced Roosevelt to initiate the project that eventually evolved into the Manhattan Engineer District under army control and leadership.

During the war, Szilard provided assistance in the development of the earliest production reactor designs with the group assembled at the Chicago Metallurgical Laboratory. Szilard later worked with James Franck in attempting to convince President Truman to hold a nonlethal demonstration of the weapon rather than to drop it over Japanese cities. Their resultant FRANCK REPORT was rejected but was later recognized as an early voice of the conscience of the nuclear scientists. For this reason, and for his independent attitude, he was disliked and distrusted by General Leslie GROVES, who commanded the MED.

Following the war, Szilard turned his attention to problems of biology. He was a leader in the group lobbying for civilian control over nuclear energy, and he was an early participant in the PUGWASH CONFERENCES. He received several awards, including the Atoms for Peace Award in 1959. He died on May 30, 1964, in La Jolla, California.

Suggested Reading

Donald Fleming and Bernard Bailyn, eds., *The Intellectual Migration: Europe and America, 1930–1960*, Cambridge, Mass.: Harvard University Press, 1969.

Richard Rhodes, *The Making of the Atomic Bomb*. New York: Simon and Schuster, 1988.

Tailings

Tailings refer to the crushed rock remaining after particular ore minerals have been removed. Tailings are waste that impact environmental quality and public health. In the case of uranium mill tailings, the radioactivity of the material represents an additional hazard.

See also URANIUM MINES AND MILLS.

Taiwan   *See* POWER REACTORS, WORLD.

Tamm, Igor (1895–1971)   *Russian Nobel Prize–winning physicist who worked on the Soviet hydrogen bomb design*

Igor Evgenievich Tamm was born in 1895 in Vladivostok in the Russian Far East. He was most known for his work with Paul Cerenkov in discovering the explanation for the blue light emitted when radioactivity passes through water.

Tamm was the son of an engineer, and he was educated at the Universities of Edinburgh and Moscow, graduating from the latter in 1918. He taught first at Tauridian University in Simferopol from 1919 to 1920, and then at Moscow University from 1922 to 1941. He headed the Theoretical Physics Department at Moscow University from 1930 to 1941. In 1934, he accepted an appointment at the Physics Institute of the Academy of Sciences in Moscow, which he headed until his death in 1971.

In 1948, he began working with Igor KURCHATOV on the problem of the hydrogen bomb, recruiting Andrey SAKHAROV, one of his graduate students, to work with him on the project. In 1950, he and Sakharov proposed that a hot plasma in a magnetic field be used to obtain a controlled nuclear fusion or thermonuclear reaction. He worked at ARZAMAS-16, leaving there in 1954 to return to Moscow. He earned the Hero of Socialist Labor award for his work on thermonuclear weapons, and he later won the NOBEL PRIZE in physics in 1958 for his co-discovery of the CERENKOV effect. With Peter KAPITSA, he was one of two Soviet scientists to win both the Nobel Prize and the Hero of Socialist Labor.

See also HYDROGEN BOMB DESIGNS.

Suggested Reading

David Holloway. *Stalin and the Bomb*. New Haven, Conn.: Yale University Press, 1994.

Teller, Edward (1908–   ) *Hungarian-born American physicist, active in the Manhattan Engineer District who worked on the atomic bomb and on the design of the fusion or hydrogen bomb in the period 1946 to 1952*

Working with Stanislaw ULAM, Edward Teller was responsible for the basic idea that led to a successful HYDROGEN BOMB DESIGN. In the 1980s, he was closely associated with the STRATEGIC DEFENSE INITIATIVE.

Edward Teller was born in 1908 in Hungary and emigrated to the United States in 1935. Teller had studied in Hungary and in Germany before emigrating to the United States after the Nazis took over. He took a position as professor at George Washington University and then moved to the University of CHICAGO in 1942. When the MANHATTAN ENGINEER DISTRICT took over atomic bomb work, he moved to LOS ALAMOS, where he developed the concept of a fusion weapon.

In 1951, he worked to develop a preliminary fusion device that was successfully tested at ENEWETAK in 1952. This early device required a huge refrigeration machine to keep hydrogen in a liquid state, and it could not form the basis for a deliverable weapon. While that test was in preparation, Teller worked with Ulam in developing a different and smaller design that could be delivered by bombers or missiles. Within scientific circles closely associated with the work, many believed that Teller later tended to downplay the contributions of Ulam to the work in order that he himself would receive credit as the "inventor" of the hydrogen bomb.

In 1954, when the ATOMIC ENERGY COMMISSION held J. Robert OPPENHEIMER'S SECURITY HEARING, Teller testified. Although he spoke highly of Oppenheimer as a scientist and administrator, he indicated that he did not always respect Oppenheimer's judgment, particularly on the question of whether to proceed with the thermonuclear weapon. For the defenders of Oppenheimer, it appeared that Teller's testimony played a key part in the decision to strip Oppenheimer of his clearance and to deny him further participation in nuclear weapon work. For years afterward, many colleagues believed that Teller had betrayed his friendship with Oppenheimer. To an extent, he was shunned by the physics community, particularly those who felt Oppenheimer had been wrongly accused.

With Teller's strong advocacy of thermonuclear weaponry and his reputation for testifying against Oppenheimer, Teller seemed to many critics to be the embodiment of the cold war nuclear scientist. The media sometimes treated him as the real-life counterpart to the lead figure in Stanley Kubrick's 1974 film *Dr. Strangelove.*

Teller remained active, taking a position as director, then associate director, of the LAWRENCE LIVERMORE NATIONAL LABORATORY in California and as a professor at the University of California. Teller was instrumental in convincing President Ronald REAGAN of the possibility of space-based defenses against INTERCONTINENTAL BALLISTIC MISSILES. When Reagan developed the STRATEGIC DEFENSE INITIATIVE OR "STAR WARS" program, he based some of the approaches on ideas that Teller had advanced. Again, in this area, Teller's approach spurred controversy, as some scientists and policy analysts believed that his suggestion of using "nuclear-pumped lasers" would be both impractical and a violation of the 1972 treaty outlawing ANTI-BALLISTIC MISSILES.

Teller remained highly suspicious of Soviet motives and methods, opposing U.S. participation in test ban treaties. Throughout his career, he remained controversial, at least in part because his abrasive and outspoken manner offended colleagues and opponents.

Thermonuclear Reaction   *See* FUSION POWER.

Thorium

This element has the symbol Th and an atomic number 90. It is a heavy, slightly radioactive metallic element discovered by Jons Berzelius in 1828 and named by him after the Scandinavian god Thor. There are 13 radioactive isotopes of thorium, with mass numbers 223 through 235, although the most common ISOTOPE is thorium-232. Thorium is of interest as a possible source of uranium-233, a possible fuel element for power-producing nuclear reactors.

See also FISSILE MATERIAL.

Three Mile Island

One of the most widely publicized reactor accidents occurred beginning on March 28, 1979, at Unit 2 of the Three Mile Island (TMI) reactors located on the Susquehanna River below Harrisburg, Pennsylvania. The reactor was a 906 megawatt-electrical PRESSURIZED WATER REACTOR manufactured by Babcox and Wilcox. The reactor had been licensed a year before.

The accident began with a failure in the cooling system, resulting in an interruption in the flow of water to the steam generator. Pumps in an emergency line came on, but valves in the pipes leading from the emergency system to the steam generator were in the closed position. In the control room, operators did not notice the lights that indicated the closed position of the valves. With no flow of water to the steam generator, the pressure began to rise. A pressure relief valve opened but not fully. The reactor control rods were automatically inserted, but compounding of several minor mechanical faults and the failure of operators to read correctly the many conflicting (and sometimes erroneous) signal lights only made the problem more serious.

Operators feared that hydrogen produced by reaction of steam with the ZIRCALLOY cladding of the fuel elements at high temperatures would explode when mixed with oxygen resulting from the breakup of water under radiation. Experts disagreed over whether the hydrogen explosion was a real possibility, but word of a possible explosion was released to the public.

The governor of Pennsylvania ordered an evacuation of children and pregnant women from areas near the reactor. Voluntarily, tens of thousands of other nearby residents left the area over the weekend of March 31 and April 1.

When the reactor was finally brought under control and cooled, operators realized two conflicting facts. On the one hand, there had been very little radioactive release. On the other hand, the core damage was extremely high. The melting of part of the core had been contained by the concrete containment vessel, which performed very well. However, with the high degree of melting, experts had assumed that radioactive release would be higher than it had been.

There were no injuries or deaths as a result of the accident. However, Unit 2 had to be permanently shut down and entombed in concrete.

The reaction of the public and experts to the accident varied. The accident happened to coincide with the release of the motion picture *The China Syndrome,* which had centered around a dangerous reactor that threatened to melt down, producing a steam explosion as the melted core hit the water table, spewing radiation and making an area "the size of Pennsylvania" uninhabitable. Public concern with reactor hazards, already on the rise, was accelerated by the Three Mile Island accident. Opposition to new reactor construction mounted, and orders for new reactors and new reactor licensing applications by utilities both fell off.

Carter at TMI. President Jimmy Carter visited the Three Mile Island reactors near Harrisburg, Pennsylvania, to receive a first-hand account of the accident. (National Archives and Records Administration)

Meanwhile, the power reactor industry took several steps to increase training, improve safety practices, and generally improve performance. The industry formed the INSTITUTE FOR NUCLEAR POWER OPERATIONS to share information and training in safety measures.

Experts concluded that the accident demonstrated that some existing safety systems worked very well. However, the confusion surrounding the warning signals and the compounding of many minor problems into a major problem led to rethinking of control room design, operator training, and risk assessment. The very low release of radio nuclides, particularly cesium and radioactive iodine, led to many studies suggesting that the chance of release of dangerous radiation from a pressurized water reactor was much less than previously assumed.

Nevertheless, the heightened awareness of the possibility of reactor catastrophe as a result of the TMI accident reduced the political acceptability of reactors in the United States.

See also CHERNOBYL; INSTITUTE FOR NUCLEAR POWER OPERATIONS; PRESSURIZED WATER REACTORS; PROBABILISTIC RISK ASSESSMENT.

Suggested Reading

Philip Cantelon and Robert Williams, *Crisis Contained: The Department of Energy at Three Mile Island.* Carbondale: University of Southern Illinois Press, 1984.

John G. Kemeny, *Report of the President's Commission on the Accident at Three Mile Island.* New York: Pergamon Press, 1979.

Mitchell Ragovin, *Three Mile Island: A Report to the Commissioners and to the Public.* Washington, D.C.: Nuclear Regulatory Commission, 1980

Thresher

The first of two accidental losses of U.S. submarines occurred with the mysterious sinking of the USS *Thresher* on April 10, 1963. The two-year-old submarine was on routine patrol off the New England coast, accompanied by the USS *Skylark,* a surface vessel that maintained underwater telephone contact with the submarine. A short message came over the phone indicating that the submarine had minor difficulties and was attempting to blow ballast tanks in order to correct its angle. A few minutes later, another garbled message was received, and the submarine sank to the bottom, taking all 179 sailors aboard to their death.

After two weeks of searching, the underwater search vessel *Trieste* located the submarine in 8,500 feet of water on the seabed. The submarine was never recovered.

Various theories developed as to the cause of the accident, centering around a possible seawater leak or underwater turbulence. One commentator suggested that the seawater may have reached the control room, causing an automatic shutdown of the reactor, resulting in a loss of power needed to recover from a dive. The naval inquiry rejected any suggestion that the accident may have resulted from a failure of the nuclear power plant that drove the submarine.

See also SCORPION.

Suggested Reading

J. Bentley, *The Thresher Disaster: The Most Tragic Dive in Submarine History.* New York: Doubleday, 1975.

Normal Polmar, *The Death of the Thresher.* New York: Chilton Books, 1964.

Threshold Test Ban Treaty (TTBT)

The Threshold Test Ban Treaty (TTBT) was signed by the United States and the Soviet Union on July 3, 1974, but never ratified. Nevertheless, under international practice, both sides asserted that they were conforming to the terms of the treaty. The treaty pledged each country to not conduct nuclear tests with a yield in excess of 150 kilotons (kt) of TNT equivalent. From time to time over the next years, the United States accused the Soviet Union of conducting tests that were in excess of the limited yield. The treaty was superseded by the underground test bans undertaken unilaterally in 1992 and by the COMPREHENSIVE TEST BAN TREATY signed in 1994.

The formal name of the TTBT was the U.S.–U.S.S.R. Treaty on the Limitation of Underground Nuclear Weapon Tests. The parties also agreed to keep the number of weapons tests to a minimum and to exchange information on NATIONAL TECHNICAL MEANS of verifying the tests. In 1986, as part of the effort to strengthen the information-exchange provisions of the TTBT, President Ronald REAGAN invited Soviet scientists to observe the operation of CORRTEX, a technical system employed by the United States to measure the yield of underground nuclear tests.

See also ARMS CONTROL; UNDERGROUND NUCLEAR TESTING.

Suggested Reading

Julie Dahlitz, *Nuclear Arms Control with Effective International Agreements.* London: George Allen and Unwin, 1983.

Robert A. Divine, *Blowing on the Wind: The Nuclear Test Ban Debate, 1954–1960.* New York: Oxford, 1978.

Thule

At Thule, Greenland, one of the most well-known cases of a BROKEN ARROW occurred in 1968. Thule, also known as Qaanaaq, is at about 70 degrees west longitude and 75 degrees north latitude, very close to the geomagnetic North Pole.

The Chrome Dome exercises carried on in the mid-1960s required that U.S. Strategic Air Command bombers fly on courses near the Soviet Union with nuclear weapons aboard. One of the B-52s in this exercise caught fire over Greenland on January 21, 1968. The pilot rerouted the airplane to Thule where the United States maintained a key part of its North American early warning radar system and an airfield. The plane crashed seven miles short of the runway.

The crew parachuted and six of the seven airmen survived and were rescued. However, four 1.1 megaton bombs were lost or destroyed by fire. Over the next four months, decontamination teams removed one million tons of ice and snow. The material was taken to the PANTEX plant outside Amarillo, Texas, to recover the PLUTONIUM.

See also PALOMARES.

Tibbets, Paul (1915–) *U.S. Army Air Force pilot who led the unit that dropped nuclear weapons on Japan in 1945*

Paul Tibbets commanded the 509th Composite Group in the U.S. Army Air Force during World War II, the unit assigned to conduct the atomic bombing of Japan. He personally flew the ENOLA GAY, the B-29 that dropped the first atomic weapon over HIROSHIMA, on August 6, 1945.

Tibbets was born in Quincy, Illinois, on February 23, 1915. As a child in Florida, he participated in an airplane advertising stunt at the Hialeah racetrack near Miami. From that day, he wanted to be a pilot. He attended the University of Florida and the University of Cincinnati and studied pre-medicine, but he enlisted in the army air corps at age 22, and in 1938, he was commissioned as second lieutenant.

During World War II, Tibbets was first assigned as commander of the 340th Bomb Squadron, 97th Bombardment Group, from Great Britain. He flew B-17s, including the first raid by U.S. B-17s against occupied Europe. In November 1942, he led bombing missions in North Africa in support of the North African invasion.

In 1943, he returned to the United States to serve as a test pilot for the new B-29, or "Super Fortress." In September 1944, he was brought into the MANHATTAN ENGINEER DISTRICT, charged with the responsibility to organize and train a unit to deliver the nuclear weapons. At first, Tibbets was put in charge of a B-29 bombing squadron based at Wendover Air Base on the Utah/Nevada border. The group at Wendover provided support to LOS ALAMOS in testing bomb shapes and other components, conducting practice runs over the Salton Sea in southern California.

Tibbets was provided with a special requisitioning priority, "silverplate," that allowed him to obtain special equipment or to have personnel reassigned to his unit. Tibbets ordered 15 new B-29 aircraft and had them modified to achieve extreme high-altitude flight and to accommodate the heavy atomic bomb.

Without informing the aircraft crews of the eventual mission, Tibbets trained them to make a sharp banking turn immediately after dropping a single weapon, a maneuver that would allow them to escape at least 10 miles before the nuclear weapon would detonate.

The 509th Bomber Squadron was officially activated on December 17, 1944. With 1,542 enlisted men and 225 officers, all personally handpicked by Tibbets,

Colonel Paul Tibbets. Waving from the cockpit of the aircraft he named after his mother, Colonel Tibbets prepares to take off on his bombing raid to Hiroshima on August 6, 1945. (National Archives and Records Administration)

the unit moved to Tinian Island in the Mariana group in the Pacific. There the 509th conducted practices in extreme secrecy, earning the enmity of other army air force personnel on the island, who were not informed why the unit was provided special privileges and not assigned regular bombing raids over Japan.

Following TRUMAN'S DECISION to proceed with the atomic bomb attack on Hiroshima, Japan, Tibbets renamed the plane after his mother, whose maiden name was Enola Gay, and the name was painted on the plane the day before the raid. Tibbets insisted that he pilot the aircraft carrying the first weapon on August 6, 1945. The bomb was dropped precisely at 9:15 A.M. For the successful mission, Tibbets was awarded the Distinguished Service Cross.

Tibbets participated in OPERATION CROSSROADS in 1946 as a technical advisor. He later served as commander of two of the Strategic Air Command bomber organizations, and he served with the NORTH ATLANTIC TREATY ORGANIZATION in France. Tibbets retired from the air force on August 31, 1966. In retirement, he worked first in Geneva, Switzerland, and then in Columbus, Ohio, serving with Executive Jet Aviation, rising to become chairman of the board of the company. He retired from that company in 1985.

Titan

The United States deployed the *Titan* I and *Titan* II missiles in the 1950s and 1960s. The *Titan* I was deployed in 1962 and the *Titan* II in 1963. The disadvantage of the *Titan* I and the older ATLAS missile was that they were liquid-fueled and had to be made ready by an extensive fueling process.

The *Titan* II could be stored in an already-fueled state, with oxidizer and fuel aboard and with the missile in the SILO, ready to be fired on short notice. The *Titan* II carried a single, nine megaton-yield thermonuclear warhead. The missile had CIRCULAR ERROR PROBABLE of less than a mile.

Titan. *The earlier liquid-fueled* Titan *missiles were largely phased out in favor of solid-fueled* Minuteman *missiles in the 1980s.* (U.S. Air Force)

From 1963 through the mid 1980s, the *Titan* II represented the major INTERCONTINENTAL BALLISTIC MISSILE (ICBM) of the United States. Based at 54 sites in Arkansas, Nebraska, and Arizona, the numbers of *Titan* IIs were cut back to 30 by 1985 and all were retired by 1987. The single warhead *Titans* were supplemented by single-warhead *Minuteman* II missiles beginning in 1965 and the multiple-warhead *Minuteman* IIIs beginning in 1970. The *Minuteman* missiles were solid-fueled in contrast to the liquid-fueled *Titans*. Martin Marietta Corporation was the prime contractor for both models of the *Titan*.

Published specifications of the two *Titan* missiles were as follows:

Titan I (MGM 25A) single warhead
  Propulsion: two stage liquid, external fueling
  Range: 10,000 kilometers
  Length: 29.87 meters
  Diameter: 3.05 meters, tapered to 2.44 meters (second stage)
  Launch weight: 99,790 kilograms
  Deployment: 1962–1965
Titan II (MGM 25C) single warhead
  Propulsion: two stage liquid, pre-fueled
  Range: 15,000 kilometers
  Length: 31.3 meters
  Diameter: 3.05 meters
  Launch weight: 149,700 kilograms
  Deployment: 1963–1987

In 1980, the *Titan* II missiles were deployed as follows:

BASE	MISSILES
Davis-Monthan AFB, Arizona	18
Little Rock AFB, Arkansas	18
McConnell AFB, Kansas	18

By 1985, the number of Titans was reduced to 30, and the weapons were retired entirely by 1987.

Suggested Reading

E. M. Bottome, *The Missile Gap: A Study in the Formulation of Military and Political Policy.* Rutherford, N.J.: Fairleigh Dickinson University Press, 1971.

John M. Collins, *U.S.–Soviet Military Balance, Concepts and Capabilities, 1960–1980.* New York: McGraw-Hill, 1981.

John M. Collins, *U.S.–Soviet Military Balance, 1980–1985.* Washington, D.C.: Pergamon-Brassey's, 1985.

Tomsk-7

In 1949, the Soviet Union constructed its first PLUTONIUM production facilities at Tomsk Oblast on the Tom

River. The facility employed about 20,000 people and occupied an area of about 700 square kilometers. At Tomsk-7, there was constructed the Siberian Atomic Power Station, a chemical separation plant, together with plutonium processing and weapons pit manufacturing facilities. The power station was in fact a complex of five PRODUCTION REACTORS, some of them dual purpose, to produce both electric power and plutonium for weapons. The power output of the reactors ran in the 150–200 megawatt-electrical (MWe) range.

TOMSK-7 REACTORS

REACTOR	OPERATION	TYPE
Ivan 1	1955–1990	Pu production only
Ivan 2	1958–1998	Pu production, power, steam heat
ADE-3	1961–1992	Pu production, 150MWe power, steam heat
ADE-4	1965–2000*	Pu Production, 150MWe power, steam heat
ADE-5	1968–2000*	Pu production, 150MWe power, steam heat

*Under a U.S.–Russian agreement, the two reactors were scheduled to be closed in the year 2000.

All five reactors were graphite-moderated. Each of the four dual-purpose production-power reactors was fueled with natural URANIUM oxide at 98.5%. The fuel elements are clad in aluminum-tin alloy. The other 1.5% was made up of 90% ^{235}U highly enriched uranium-aluminum alloy pellets to "spike" the reactors and to bring up their reactivity. The 2,832 water channels of the production reactors are vertical.

The Soviet Union did not reveal the location of these reactors until 1990.

See also KRASNOYARSK-26.

Suggested Reading

Thomas B. Cochrane, Robert S. Norris, and Oleg A. Bukharin, *Making the Russian Bomb: From Stalin to Yeltsin.* Boulder, Colo.: Westview Press, 1995.

Totskoe

Totskoe is a small village that in 1955 was under the jurisdiction of the South Urals Military District in the province of Orenburg in the Soviet Union. Since the United States had already conducted several exercises in which ground troops were exposed to a nuclear detonation and then maneuvered across the target area, the Soviets decided to conduct a similar test. The function of such exercises on the part of both nations was to familiarize soldiers with nuclear explosions. Marshal G. K. Zhukov was in overall charge of the operation, and the local commander was General Ivan Petrov. Altogether 44,000 troops participated.

Different kinds of defenses were erected, ranging from ordinary field defenses to trenches and bunkers, dugouts, and weapons shelters. People living within seven kilometers of the target were evacuated.

On September 14, 1955, a plane took off some 680 kilometers away and flew with the weapon on a pathway carefully mapped out so as to avoid settled regions. At 9:33 A.M. the plane dropped the bomb, completely destroying an oak forest out to 1.5 kilometers from ground zero. After testing for radiation, troops advanced, but no closer than about a half kilometer to ground zero. Films were taken of the whole exercise and they were used for training purposes later.

As during the American exercises, some of the veterans later claimed to have developed serious illnesses from radiation received at the Totskoe exercise.

See also ATMOSPHERIC NUCLEAR TESTING; ATOMIC VETERANS; NUCLEAR TEST PERSONNEL REVIEW.

Suggested Reading

David Holloway, *Stalin and the Bomb.* New Haven, Conn.: Yale University Press, 1994.

Transuranic waste

Materials contaminated with elements higher in atomic weight than 235 are called transuranic wastes. Although these wastes do not generate heat, they contain long-lived isotopes that emit alpha particles, presenting a radiation hazard. Transuranic wastes are produced mostly in weapons-material production and in nuclear power reactor fuel work.

Transuranic elements are not only radioactive for long periods but are extremely toxic. Thus the materials need to be isolated from the environment for thousands of years to ensure that future generations are not exposed. In 1970, the ATOMIC ENERGY COMMISSION ruled that material containing 10 nanocuries of transuranic elements or more per gram would be regarded as transuranic waste. The DEPARTMENT OF ENERGY changed the definition to 100 nanocuries per gram for the transuranic wastes generated from the nuclear weapons programs.

Leakage of transuranic waste at a DOE facility at Maxey Flats, Kentucky, and the release of plutonium at the ROCKY FLATS, Colorado, facility contributed to decisions to close both of these facilities. Transuranic wastes were temporarily stored at several Department of Energy locations awaiting the development of a final repository. Those sites included Idaho Falls, Idaho; Sheffield, Illinois; Beatty, Nevada; LOS ALAMOS, New Mexico; WEST VALLEY, New York; SAVANNAH RIVER SITE, South Carolina; HANFORD, Washington; and smaller amounts at other locations.

Treaty of Tlatelolco

This treaty preceded the NON-PROLIFERATION TREATY (NPT) of 1968 by more than a year, being opened for signature on February 14, 1967, and entering into force in 1968. Like the later NPT, the Treaty of Tlatelolco was multilateral and designed to prohibit the spread of nuclear weapons. The treaty prohibited the possession, manufacture, or testing of nuclear weapons by the parties to the treaty. Nuclear devices used for propulsion or for peaceful purposes, including peaceful nuclear explosions, were not covered by the treaty. The formal name was the Treaty for the Prohibition of Nuclear Weapons in Latin America.

The treaty was eventually signed by all the countries of Latin America except Cuba. The treaty opened the countries to inspection by the INTERNATIONAL ATOMIC ENERGY AGENCY and to a special Latin American agency, the Agency for the Prohibition of Nuclear Weapons in Latin America (OPNAL).

When Chile and BRAZIL ratified the treaty, each proclaimed it would not go into effect until ratified by all other eligible countries. ARGENTINA delayed ratification until resolving a dispute with the International Atomic Energy Agency regarding inspections related to peaceful nuclear explosions. Transportation of nuclear weapons through the Panama Canal was not affected by the treaty.

The Treaty of Tlatelolco went further than the later NPT treaty since, under the Latin American treaty, the stationing of nuclear weapons in the signatory countries was prohibited. Under the NPT, the United States could station nuclear weapons in allied states of the NORTH ATLANTIC TREATY ORGANIZATION in Europe, and the Soviet Union could station nuclear weapons in WARSAW TREATY ORGANIZATION nations of Eastern Europe. The treaty made Latin America a nuclear-free zone. Furthermore, by creating OPNAL, the member states had established an international regional group to supervise enforcement of the nuclear-free zone.

Suggested Reading

Committee on International Security and Arms Control, National Academy of Sciences, *Nuclear Arms Control: Background and Issues.* Washington, D.C.: National Academy Press, 1985.

Triad

The term "triad" was introduced in the late 1960s to refer to the three elements of the U.S. nuclear deterrent delivery systems: land-based missiles, SUBMARINE-LAUNCHED BALLISTIC MISSILES, and aircraft-delivered bombs carried by intercontinental-range STRATEGIC BOMBERS.

See also INTERCONTINENTAL BALLISTIC MISSILES.

Trident

The *Trident* ballistic missile was the first American three-stage SUBMARINE-LAUNCHED BALLISTIC MISSILE (SLBM). As in other American SLBM systems, the missile and the various classes of nuclear armed sub-

The B-1 Bomber. The long-range strategic bomber, along with submarine-launched ballistic missiles and intercontinental ballistic missiles, made up the three legs of the U.S. deterrent "triad." (U.S. Air Force)

marines (SSBNS) that would carry it would be known by the same name. Thus Ohio class submarines were sometimes referred to as *Trident* submarines.

Despite controversy and cost overruns, the *Trident* missile was delivered and operational by the early 1980s, approximately the same time that the Soviet super SSBN TYPHOON was initially placed on active duty. Although in many ways *Trident* I was a disappointment, *Trident* II was funded and developed for a change in American nuclear weapons doctrine concerning submarines.

The *Trident* program was to an extent an ad hoc operation, but the end result, *Trident* II, was the most advanced ballistic missile system in the American navy to date.

The *Trident* missile was plagued with problems from the outset. After Admiral Hyman RICKOVER secured appropriations from Congress, the *Trident* system had many problems. Final delivery of *Trident* contractually was 1979, but only after six official extensions was the final missile and Ohio class ship to carry it delivered in 1981.

Trident was a missile designed to comply with the COUNTERVALUE doctrine, which had a role for missiles that could attack cities rather than precise, hardened targets. By the end of the development of the program, the navy leadership operated under a requirement for hard-target accuracy. President Richard NIXON, in National Decision Security Memorandum 242, changed American policy on nuclear strikes to COUNTERFORCE, hard-target precision attacks against military assets. In short, America wanted the ability to hit specific military installations with large nuclear weapons to surgically obliterate key enemy facilities. These more accurate targeting requirements created a design problem, but one that Rickover planned for.

In creating the *Trident* I submarine, Rickover and other designers allowed for excess room in the missile tubes. This followed an American tendency to limit new missile developments so that they could be deployed into earlier submarine designs. The *Trident* I missile was large and dynamic enough to warrant deployment in a new class of ship. During the design stage of the missile, however, restrictions were placed on the dimensions of the *Trident* I so it could be easily retrofitted into prior classes of submarines. Similarly, *Trident* II was designed to take no more room than that available in the enlarged tubes of the Ohio class.

This planning demonstrated the different approaches between Soviet and American missile development. Soviet missiles usually were deployed in a new class or a new modification on a class as in the DELTAS I through IV. American missile technology was usually designed to be retrofitted into the previous class of submarine, and submarines were designed to leave room for improvement in later designed missiles.

Trident II represented the newest wave of missile technology. It was highly accurate and had MULTIPLE INDEPENDENTLY TARGETABLE REENTRY VEHICLES (MIRVS) so that each missile could carry several large warheads. The Ohio class, designed to carry *Trident* II, was the largest submarine in the U.S. Navy, but not larger than the Soviet counterpart, *Typhoon*.

Suggested Reading

Graham Spinardi, *From Polaris to Trident: The Development of U.S. Fleet Ballistic Missile Technology.* Cambridge, U.K.: Cambridge University Press: 1994.

Triga   *See* GENERAL ATOMICS.

Trinity

The Trinity test was the first detonation of a nuclear device held by the scientists who had designed the weapon at the secret laboratory at LOS ALAMOS. Although they did not know how large the blast would be or how much radioactive FALLOUT the test would create, the MANHATTAN ENGINEER DISTRICT scientists wanted to be able to conduct the test in secrecy and, at the same time, keep the dangerous effects away from settled areas. At a remote location in the desert near Alamogordo in southern New Mexico, the scientists built a 120-foot tower on which to mount the plutonium-fueled heart of the atomic bomb.

The group that assembled on the morning of the test, July 16, 1945, included J. Robert OPPENHEIMER, the "father of the bomb," and Enrico FERMI. That morning, an unusual thunderstorm threatened to delay the test or to ignite the device accidentally with a blast of lightning. However, at about 5:30 A.M., the test went off as scheduled, with a yield estimated by Fermi to be equivalent to 13 kilotons of TNT. Later calculations showed that his figure was about right, although some estimates have been as high as 19 kilotons.

Much of the energy from the blast took the form of light, X-rays, and other radiation. The heat from the explosion raised a vast cloud of dust, vaporized the

Trinity. Early in the morning of July 16, 1945, the scientists who had worked at Los Alamos witnessed the first nuclear explosion on Earth and were awe-struck by its magnitude. (National Archives and Records Administration)

At Alamogordo, the area where the tower had stood was scarred, and the sand there had turned to green glass. The smudge of glass marked the spot where the age of atomic weapons began.

Suggested Reading

Gar Alperovitz, *The Decision to Use the Atomic Bomb and the Architecture of an American Myth.* New York: Knopf, 1995.
Leslie Groves, *Now It Can Be Told: The Story of the Manhattan Project.* New York: Harper, 1962.
Richard Rhodes, *The Making of the Atomic Bomb.* New York: Simon and Schuster, 1986.

Tritium

Tritium, ^{3}H or sometimes T, is a radioactive ISOTOPE of hydrogen. ^{3}H has a half-life of 12.262 years and decays by beta emission. It is three times as heavy as ordinary hydrogen, consisting of one proton and two neutrons. Tritium in the form of gas has been employed in nuclear weapons to boost the fission process. Tritium is produced for such purposes in nuclear reactors, through the exposure of lithium-deuteride targets in the reactor. It is also produced in HEAVY-WATER REACTORS as a dangerous waste product.

See also BOOSTED WEAPONS.

steel tower, and a huge boiling mass of flame and smoke rose to form a mushroom cloud. Radioactive dust from the detonation of the device settled over ranchlands, and later, scientists looked into the effects of the fallout on cattle. Some of the cattle were later shipped to OAK RIDGE, where they formed the nucleus of a herd to test the long-term genetic effects of radiation.

Oppenheimer, like many of the observers, was stunned at the power of what they had made. He was said to have quoted from the Bhagavad Gita, a Sanskrit religious text, saying the words: "I am Shiva, destroyer of worlds."

Notification of the successful test was radioed to President Harry TRUMAN, who was in a meeting with Joseph Stalin and Winston Churchill in POTSDAM, a suburb of Berlin, Germany. Truman had hoped to receive word of the outcome of Trinity during the conference, and he was immediately encouraged by the successful test. Not only would the test results mean that the United States could soon defeat Japan, but it also meant that America would have a great arms lead over its newly emerging rival, the Soviet Union. Some historians have interpreted the Trinity test as the opening shot of the cold war.

Truman, Harry S. (1884–1972) *president of the United States from 1945 to 1953, overseeing the nuclear bombing of Japan and the foreign policy of the early years of the cold war*

President Harry S. Truman was crucial to the development of the atomic age in several ways. He was most notable as the first and only world leader in the 20th century to authorize the operational use of a nuclear weapon.

Truman was born in Lamar, Missouri, in 1884. He had served as a corporal in the U.S. Army artillery in World War I and had operated an unsuccessful clothing business briefly before entering local politics in Missouri. He was elected a U.S. senator in 1934 and was selected as the vice president to serve under Franklin ROOSEVELT in his fourth term. On Roosevelt's death, he became president. He was reelected in 1948 and chose not to run for a third term in 1952, although under the constitution he could have done so. In retirement he published his memoirs and remained active as an elder statesman.

When he became president on the death of Franklin Roosevelt in April 1945, he knew nothing of the MANHATTAN ENGINEER DISTRICT. Upon learning of the secret development of the weapon, he realized he had an awesome responsibility. TRUMAN'S DECISION to use the atomic weapon on Japan to hasten the end of the war was later much debated.

Truman urged J. Robert OPPENHEIMER and Leslie GROVES to hasten the test of the first weapon at TRINITY, apparently hoping to have knowledge of the success of the test prior to his first meeting with Joseph STALIN at the POTSDAM CONFERENCE.

After the nuclear weapons had been dropped on HIROSHIMA and NAGASAKI, Truman continued to defend his decision on the grounds that dropping the weapons had brought a speedy end to the war and had saved many American and Japanese lives.

Under Truman, the nuclear research and development effort was converted from a military to a civilian endeavor, with the transfer of all the plants and research contracts from the Manhattan Engineer District to the civilian-administered ATOMIC ENERGY COMMISSION (AEC). Truman selected as the first chairman of the AEC David LILIENTHAL, former administrator of the Tennessee Valley Authority.

After an abortive effort to put nuclear research in the hands of the United Nations through the BARUCH PLAN, the United States continued to develop nuclear weapons under the AEC. During the period 1946 to 1949, the United States maintained a nuclear monopoly, and Truman took a strong stand against Soviet policies in Europe partly on the basis of that monopoly. During this period, the occupation zones of western Germany were united into a single state, against the protests of the Soviets.

When the Soviets responded with a blockade of the land routes to Berlin, Truman sent several B-29 aircraft that had been modified to carry large nuclear weapons to air bases in Great Britain, apparently as a signal of his willingness to employ the atomic bomb should it be needed.

However, at that time the United States had very few atomic bombs since no procedure had been established to mass produce them. The few in the stockpile had all been handmade by a limited number of scientists and technicians at LOS ALAMOS and SANDIA. Later revelations of details of Soviet espionage suggest that the size of the stockpile was known to Moscow at the time.

After the Soviet detonation of Joe 1 in August 1949, Truman received information from U.S. air-sampling

Harry S. Truman. President of the United States from 1945 to 1953, Truman was the only chief of state to order the operational use of nuclear weapons in the 20th century, and he ensured that nuclear weapons would become part of the American defense arsenal in the post–World War II period. (National Archives and Records Administration)

aircraft of the Russian test. Hesitating to reveal the source of U.S. information, Truman delayed announcing the Russian test for several weeks. With the confession of Klaus FUCHS in early 1950 and the later arrest of Julius and Ethel ROSENBERG, the Truman administration became open to criticism that it had not been sufficiently concerned with security of information regarding atomic weapons.

The invasion of South Korea by the pro-Soviet regime in NORTH KOREA in the summer of 1950 appeared to provide public confirmation that the breaking of the nuclear monopoly by the Soviet Union meant entry into a period of more dangerous relations between the superpowers.

All of these factors relating to nuclear politics made the second administration of Harry Truman a difficult one, which helped paved the way for the election of a Republican president, Dwight EISENHOWER, in 1952, after 20 years of Democratic control of the White House.

See also GERMANY IN INTERNATIONAL ATOMIC AFFAIRS.

Truman's Decision

Perhaps the most debated decision by a U.S. president in the 20th century has been the decision made by Harry TRUMAN to proceed with the atomic bombing of Japan. Those who have defended the decision, including Truman himself, argued that the two weapons dropped over Japan (HIROSHIMA on August 6, 1945, and

Moral Dilemma. Truman's decision to drop atomic weapons on Japan resulted in heavy civilian casualties and the leveling of cities that may not have been necessary to end the war. Here stunned survivors of the Nagasaki attack, a mother and son, stop to receive a small rice ration from Japanese troops sent in to provide aid. (National Archives and Records Administration)

NAGASAKI on August 9, 1945) brought World War II to a speedy conclusion and saved the lives of many American service personnel who would otherwise have been killed in the invasion of Japan. Those who have criticized the decision argue that Japan was ready to accept the terms of surrender that were offered after the bombs were dropped and that Truman knew of this position. Some have pointed out that a direct attack on civilian targets represented a violation of international law and treaty obligations of the United States.

Defenders of the decision counter that the Japanese had started the war with an unprovoked attack on the United States, they had been guilty of many violations of international law, and they had a record of atrocities against civilians prior to and during the war.

The estimates of the number of immediate and delayed casualties from the two weapons have varied a great deal, but most authorities agree that at least 100,000 civilians were killed at Hiroshima and another 70,000 died at Nagasaki at the time of the bombings. Thousands more died over the next weeks from radiation poisoning and from burns and injuries suffered during the bombings. Critics of the decision have questioned the morality of such a large-scale attack on a civilian population, especially if the attack was not needed to end the war.

Many of the facts and issues surrounding the decision have been examined closely. The most debated and most important specific issues in question have been these.

(1). What was the expected estimate of the number of American casualties that would result from an invasion of Japan? Although journalistic accounts and some public speeches suggested that American casualties might reach 500,000 to 1 million, careful review of documents from the time suggest that planners anticipated American casualties on the order of 200,000 to 300,000, including those injured. Defenders of Truman's decision have continued to insist that the bombing was justified for this reason alone. The employment by the Japanese of suicide attacks by pilots of aircraft loaded with high explosives had raised the casualty rate during the U.S. attacks on the island of Okinawa, and continued high casualties from such aircraft could be expected during an invasion of the Japanese main islands.

(2). What was the relationship of Truman's decision to his view of the Soviet Union? It has been argued that he delayed the meeting at POTSDAM in July 1945 and asked for the nuclear test at TRINITY to be held as soon as possible so that he would be certain of holding the nuclear weapon when entering negotiations with the Russians. Since the Soviets had agreed to enter the war against Japan in the early weeks of August 1945, Truman may have hoped to win Japanese defeat without Soviet participation and thereby prevent their making territorial gains at the conclusion of the war. Further, it has been argued that Truman wanted to demonstrate to the Soviets that the United States not only had the nuclear weapon but also had the will to use it, thereby creating a dominant position for the United States in the post–World War II period. The large size of the Soviet army, its control of much of Eastern Europe, and its harsh dictatorial regime under Joseph STALIN all posed threats that the United States could offset as a nation armed with nuclear weapons.

(3). Did the president and his advisors adequately consider alternatives, such as detonating a nuclear bomb over a deserted area as a demonstration to the Japanese of what they would face if they did not surrender? Such a demonstration had been advocated by a group of scientists at the Chicago Metallurgical Laboratory and submitted in a report by physicist James Franck. Several scholars have traced the fate of this recommendation, noting that it was ultimately opposed even by J. Robert OPPENHEIMER because the United States possessed only two weapons. Had the demonstration not been successful, the nation would have used up half its stockpile and lost the value of surprise.

(4). Was the president fully informed and aware of the Japanese indications that they were willing to accept a surrender in which their territorial integrity was preserved and in which they could retain the emperor? These terms, discussed in peace-feelers through the Soviet Union and Switzerland before the dropping of the atomic bombs, comprised the terms eventually agreed to in the final peace settlement. Were the peace-feelers in fact genuine, did they represent only the position of a faction within the Japanese government, or were they possibly intended only as a deception? Although information about the peace-feelers was known to some in the Truman administration, it is not clear that those making the bomb-targeting decision were aware of them.

(5). To what extent did the high cost of the Manhattan Project, some $2 billion, dictate that the weapon had to be used in order to justify the diversion of money and scarce resources of personnel and materials during the war to the project? To what extent did

Justification? Suicide attacks by Japanese pilots on American ships intensified in the last months of World War II, suggesting that an attempt to defeat Japan without the use of the nuclear weapon would lead to tens of thousands of American casualties. (U.S. Navy)

the institutional inertia of plans set in motion account for the dropping of the weapons? The decision to drop the second bomb was apparently not reviewed after the first weapon was detonated. General Leslie Groves explicitly dreaded that he would be subject to investigation and possible punishment for leading a project that spent valuable and scarce resources during the war without making a contribution to victory.

The historical literature on these and related issues is extensive. At the 50th anniversary of the use of the atomic weapon on Japan in 1995, public and academic discussion of the topic explored all sides of the issue.

See also ENOLA GAY.

Suggested Reading

Gar Alperovitz, *Atomic Diplomacy: Hiroshima and Potsdam*. New York: Penguin, 1985.

———. *The Decision to Use the Atomic Bomb and the Architecture of an American Myth*. New York: Knopf, 1995.

Herbert Feis, *The Atomic Bomb and the End of World War II*. Princeton, N.J.: Princeton University Press, 1966.

Gregg Herken, *The Winning Weapon: The Atomic Bomb in the Cold War, 1945–1950*. Santa Rosa, Calif.: Vintage, 1981.

Robert Jay Lifton and Greg Mitchell, *Hiroshima in America: A Half Century of Denial*. New York: Avon, 1996.

Douglas MacEachin, *The Final Months of the War with Japan: Signals Intelligence, U.S. Invasion Planning, and the A-Bomb Decision.* Washington, D.C.: Central Intelligence Agency Center for the Study of Intelligence, 1998.

Martin Sherwin, *A World Destroyed.* New York: Vintage, 1987.

Typhoon Class Submarines

The Typhoon Soviet nuclear submarine was the largest nuclear submarine ever constructed, and as a class of submarine, the Typhoon was also the most modern design of any of the Soviet submarines. All Typhoons carried SS-N-20 missiles, the first three-stage, solid-fueled, submarine-launched missile in the Soviet navy. The Typhoon was seen as a threat to the United States because not only could it target the continental United States from home ports but it was over one-half larger than the largest American submarine class, the Ohio.

The first Typhoon was laid down in 1975 and underwent sea trials in 1981. Unlike the DELTA class, which is a larger version of the YANKEE class (the first modern design), Typhoon was taken in a totally new direction. The Typhoon design dispensed with the noisy hump, which was the major visually distinguishing feature in both the Yankee and the Delta classes. Other unique characteristics of the Typhoons included three separate pressure hulls in keeping with Russian design but incorporating more hull protection than any other submarine. American submarines did not use multiple pressure hulls.

Typhoon also had its missile tubes in front of the conning tower instead of behind, which was common to most other ballistic missile submarines. The most unique and distinguishing feature about the Typhoon was its size. Despite the fact that the Soviet navy did not release much information regarding its submarine fleet, independent naval engineers estimated the Typhoon's displacement to be about 30,000 tons surfaced and 40,000 submerged, higher than published U.S. Navy estimates.

All Typhoon class submarines carried 20 SS-N-20 ballistic missiles. The SS-N-20 was touted to deliver more powerful nuclear warheads with greater accuracy than any other preceding SUBMARINE-LAUNCHED BALLISTIC MISSILE (SLBM). SS-N-20s are three-stage missiles carrying MULTIPLE INDEPENDENTLY TARGETABLE REENTRY VEHICLES (MIRVs). Each vehicle can be separately targeted and the missile may carry multiple nuclear warheads of various kilotonnage. Some sources claimed that the SS-N-20 had many problems in flight tests due to its solid-fuel propulsion system. By 1983 all problems were resolved with missile and ship design and the Typhoon class was placed on active duty.

Typhoon class submarines were a part of Russian submarine doctrine that was known as "bastioning." The Typhoon could target and launch its missile batteries from inside Russian territorial waters. Only the Deltas and the Yankees would patrol in forward positions. The design of the Typhoon perfectly fitted into this deployment strategy. Some sources believe that the Typhoon had a maximum speed of around 20–25 knots, whereas others estimated it to be as high as 30 knots. The lower estimate is consistent with the bastioning plan. Typhoon's primary role was to serve as a platform to launch its missiles, not requiring extremely high speeds. The immediate demands included the ability to move quietly in the water to avoid detection and targeting accuracy. Part of the advanced design cut down on the number of free-flooding holes, one of the features of the Yankee/Delta design that made the most noise.

In light of its intended mission, speed was not an issue for the Typhoon design. Even if the Typhoon could provide high speeds, its sheer size made maneuverability a real issue. The only real outside threat to the Typhoon would be hunter submarines infiltrating Russian waters. A hunter would be hard pressed to find the Typhoon if its silent design was successful. Soviet advances in quieting the Typhoon spurred on American submarine quieting efforts in the 1980s.

Only six Typhoons were ever built. Their size precluded the rapid output that previous classes enjoyed. The difference with Typhoon was quality, not quantity. The design advancements made in the Typhoon class gave the Soviet navy a powerful, highly survivable asset. Although there were few ships, each ship required a highly trained and professional crew. Typhoon was a force for Russian policy in the world arena through the last years of the cold war.

Suggested Reading

Jan Breemer, *Soviet Submarines Design Development and Tactics.* London: Janes Information Group, 1989.

U

U-2 Aircraft

The U-2 aircraft was designed in the United States to fly at high altitude and conduct aerial photography. The U-2 was successfully employed over the Soviet Union briefly in 1959 and 1960, and it was used elsewhere in the world through the early 1960s.

Early in the administration of Dwight EISENHOWER, the president sought advice from a secret scientific panel on the extent of the Soviet threat. Headed by James R. KILLIAN, president of the Massachusetts Institute of Technology, the 1954 panel reported that further Soviet missile advances would put the United States at risk by the late 1950s. Eisenhower proposed an Open Skies arrangement in which the Soviets and the United States would be able to photograph each other's installations to lessen the mutual risk. The Soviets rejected the proposal. With the successful launch of an earth-orbiting satellite, SPUTNIK, in 1957, the Killian report predictions seemed to come true.

Since information on Soviet nuclear facilities was extremely well guarded, the United States, under Eisenhower's direct order, began a series of overflights of the Soviet Union with specially designed high-altitude reconnaissance aircraft. Built at the secret Lock-heed "skunk works," or development shop, in southern California, the U-2 was capable of long-distance flights at extreme altitudes. The U-2, flying above 60,000 feet, would take off from bases in Turkey, PAKISTAN, or Western Europe, then fly over the Soviet Union, and take pictures in a 100-mile swath on both sides of the flight path. On return, the thousands of feet of film would be developed and analyzed yielding pictures of aircraft, missile emplacements, submarine bases, and other strategic facilities.

In effect, Eisenhower implemented a unilateral Open Skies program designed in fact as a form of espionage by aerial surveillance.

The Soviets were aware of these flights, but they were powerless to stop them until 1960. Eisenhower planned to meet with Premier Nikita Khrushchev on May 15, 1960, for a SUMMIT MEETING in Paris to ease tensions between the two countries. But to be well informed of the status of Soviet nuclear development and weapons delivery capabilities, Eisenhower ordered a last U-2 flight on May 1. This craft, piloted by Francis Gary Powers, was shot down by an improved Soviet high-altitude surface-to-air missile. Powers parachuted to the ground but was captured and put on trial.

341

Khrushchev proudly displayed the captured pilot and the remains of the aircraft. At the Paris summit meeting, when Eisenhower refused to apologize for the intrusion of Soviet airspace, Khrushchev walked out, bringing the meeting to an abrupt end. Eisenhower, however, did order that the U-2 flights over the Soviet Union be stopped.

Ukraine

One of the four Soviet republics that had nuclear weapons and nuclear weapon delivery systems when the Soviet Union dissolved in 1991, Ukraine appeared likely for a few years in the early 1990s to become a new nuclear weapons state. At the time of the breakup of the Soviet Union, the number of strategic and tactical nuclear weapons located within Ukrainian territory would have made it the third-largest nuclear power in the world after the United States and RUSSIA, with some 4,400 nuclear warheads. However, through a series of difficult negotiations, Ukraine agreed to transfer the nuclear weapons on its territory to Russia and to join the NON-PROLIFERATION TREATY as a non-nuclear state. Further, it agreed to INTERNATIONAL ATOMIC ENERGY AGENCY (IAEA) safeguards on its facilities and to cooperate in the destruction of missile systems.

In December 1991, when Ukraine declared its independence, the Ukrainian government announced its intention, along with KAZAKHSTAN and Belarus, to become a non-nuclear weapon state. However, the Ukraine parliament did not ratify this executive announcement, raising doubts about the country's future plans.

In May 1992, Ukraine, along with Russia, Kazakhstan, and Belarus, signed the Lisbon Accords, which committed those states to abide by the provisions of the Strategic Arms Reduction Treaty (START I) between the Soviet Union and the United States. Furthermore, Belarus, Kazakhstan, and Ukraine agreed that they would become non-nuclear weapon states. However, when the Ukraine parliament ratified the Lisbon Accords, they added provisions that would allow them to retain some strategic nuclear weapons.

The reason that the Ukraine parliament took these positions was that through the early 1990s, Ukraine was particularly concerned that Russia would dominate in the division of military assets of the Soviet Union, particularly the Black Sea fleet. Furthermore, Russia laid claim to the province of Crimea, which had a Russian ethnic majority, and to the naval base there, although both had been administratively part of Ukraine for decades.

After intensive negotiation involving the United States, Russia, and Ukraine, the three countries signed a trilateral statement on January 14, 1994, under which Ukraine agreed to ship all its nuclear weapons to Russia in exchange for assurances as to its national security and for a reduction in its debt to Russia for energy. In addition, some of the weapons-grade uranium in the weapons would be re-refined at a lower level of enrichment and returned to Ukraine for use in its power reactors.

The removal of all nuclear weapons from Ukraine territory was completed in June 1996. In the United States, legislation sponsored by Senators Sam Nunn and Richard Lugar established the COOPERATIVE THREAT REDUCTION program. This Nunn-Lugar program set aside some $350 million to assist Ukraine in dismantling and transporting weapons. In order to accelerate this program in 1997, the United States DEFENSE SPECIAL WEAPONS AGENCY began extensive funding, through contractors, to assist Ukraine in the process.

Ukraine has a nuclear power program as well as several nuclear research facilities. The power program consists of five generating stations, each with several reactors. The centers are located at Chernobyl/Pripyat, Neteshin, Kuznetsovsk, Kostantinovsk, and Energodar. The 1986 accident at the CHERNOBYL plant was the most serious in the 20th century.

The United States has been concerned that Ukrainian research and industrial facilities in the nuclear area could serve as the source of export of materials and know-how to potential nuclear weapons states, such as IRAN. Ukraine's agreement to allow IAEA safeguards and to impose export controls on nuclear technology mitigated that concern to an extent.

See also ARMS CONTROL.

Ulam, Stanislaw (1909–1984)   *Polish-born American physicist best known for his work in the design of the hydrogen bomb*

In 1950, Stanislaw Ulam demonstrated to Edward TELLER that previous calculations of the amount of TRITIUM required to initiate a fusion reaction had been far too small. Both were disappointed in a first design of the hydrogen bomb, called the "Classical Super." Ulam suggested a new approach, which Teller then developed. This concept, known as the Teller-Ulam design, proved workable.

In March 1951, Teller and Ulam published a classified paper describing the process that would eventually, after further invention and development, form the basis of U.S. thermonuclear weapons.

Ulam was born in 1909 in Poland and educated at Lvov University, now located in the Ukraine. He was invited to the United States in 1936 by the mathematician John Von Neumann, and he emigrated from Poland to work at the Institute for Advanced Study at Princeton. He joined the Manhattan Project during World War II.

See also FUSION.

Suggested Reading

Richard Rhodes, *The Making of the Atomic Bomb*. New York: Simon and Schuster, 1986.

Underground Testing

Before the 1962 LIMITED TEST BAN TREATY, very few nuclear tests had been conducted underground. However, following 1962, both the United States and the Soviet Union developed improved methods to test nuclear weapons underground, either in shafts or in tunnels. The Americans conducted most of their underground tests at the NEVADA TEST SITE; the Soviets conducted underground tests at their site in the island group of NOVAYA ZEMLYA and at facilities at SEMIPALATINSK in KAZAKHSTAN.

In shaft emplacement, a deep hole was drilled using well-drilling equipment that bores a hole six or more feet in diameter. At a suitable depth, a chamber was hollowed out for emplacement of the nuclear device to be tested, together with monitoring equipment. Cables from the effects monitoring equipment were run to the surface and from there to registering equipment located in remote buildings or in trailers.

The hole was then plugged with grout, that is, with a section of concrete, to ensure that radioactive gases and dust could not escape after the detonation. After the detonation, a large section of rock, soil, and sand would vaporize, leaving a cavity surrounding the original detonation point. Several minutes to several hours after the detonation, the roof of the cavity would begin to collapse, and the ground above would subside into the space. Thus the test sites became pockmarked with subsidence craters.

In an alternate method, a tunnel would be mined out at the base of a mountain or plateau. At the U.S. test site in Nevada, many such tunnels were drilled into the base of Rainier Mesa; the Soviets used a similar method at Degelen Mountain at Semipalatinsk-21. Tunnel emplacement allowed for bringing in much larger equipment because vehicles could be driven to the emplacement site.

With the detonation of a high-altitude burst at JOHNSTON ISLAND in the last atmospheric tests held by the United States in 1962, it became clear that ELECTROMAGNETIC PULSE (EMP) and other forms of radiation would be major weapons effects of nuclear detonations that were held at extremely high altitudes. As a consequence, the weapons-testing program began more extended use of simulators to test radiation effects. Designers also began constructing underground test systems with long pipes from which the air had been partially evacuated in order to test radiation effects from weapons that would simulate the effect of a high-altitude or exo-atmospheric burst. Both vertical line-of-sight pipes and horizontal line-of-sight pipes, mounted in tunnels that were then blocked with concrete and rubble, allowed for testing the effect of X-rays and EMP from underground detonations.

With the THRESHOLD TEST BAN TREATY signed on July 3, 1974, both the United States and the Soviet Union committed to detonating much smaller yield devices in their testing, with yields less than 150Kt, and to hold the number of tests to a minimum. As a result, many of the tests by both nations were quite small by the standards of an earlier era.

Both the United States and the Soviet Union ended their underground nuclear testing program in 1991–1992. The United States held over 900 announced underground tests, and the Soviets held over 500 such tests.

Union of Concerned Scientists

The Union of Concerned Scientists (UCS) was founded in 1969, beginning with a group of faculty members and students at the Massachusetts Institute of Technology (MIT), who were broadly concerned about the misuse of science and technology. Capturing the rising social concerns in the United States and Europe of the decade, the organization called for the redirection of scientific research to environmental and social problems. Among the co-founders of the organization was MIT physicist Victor Weisskopf, who had served as a group leader at LOS ALAMOS during the Manhattan Project, and Kurt Gottfried, professor of physics from Cornell University. Later members included scientists from other disciplines, including chemistry and biology, and from science-related policy fields.

Many of the organization's actions have been directed at questions of nuclear science and nuclear technology. In 1979, over 12,000 scientists signed a petition sponsored by the union entitled the "Scientists' Declaration on the Nuclear Arms Race." The petition urged a halt to the arms race and called for a moratorium on the testing and deployment of new nuclear weapons. Early in the same year, the UCS petitioned the NUCLEAR REGULATORY COMMISSION (NRC) to adopt stronger safety standards for nuclear plants. The organization called for the closure of 16 nuclear power plants because of the NRC's understatement of risk of accident at the plants. Following the accident at THREE MILE ISLAND, the union publicized information about the accident and reactor risk.

In 1980, the Union of Concerned Scientists published a report, "Energy Strategies: Toward a Solar Future," urging efforts to explore alternatives to both nuclear power and fossil fuels.

When President Ronald REAGAN proposed in March 1983 a system of space-based defenses against missiles known as the Strategic Defense Initiative, or Star Wars, the Union of Concerned Scientists mobilized swift opposition to the plan among scientists. The union marshalled analyses of the drawbacks and technical difficulties, providing arguments for the opponents of the proposal.

Other actions of the union through the 1980s focused on both the Nuclear Regulatory Commission and defense nuclear programs as well as upon broader environmental issues such as global warming. In 1987, the union sued the Nuclear Regulatory Commission to prevent cost considerations to offset public safety in enforcing safety standards at nuclear power reactors. The union also led a campaign to oppose the construction of the B-2 stealth bomber, resulting in a limitation on the number of that aircraft. In 1991, the union was able to sue successfully to force the closure of the Yankee Rowe nuclear plant in Massachusetts, at that time the oldest operating nuclear power reactor. This action set a precedent against allowing power companies to extend the licenses for nuclear reactors beyond the 40-year life expectancy built into the original licenses.

In the 1990s, the Union of Concerned Scientists turned its priorities to broader issues of environment, clean energy sources, air pollution, global warming, and the risks of genetic engineering.

United Kingdom

The United Kingdom, or Great Britain, emerged with the United States as a major nuclear power in the years following World War II. British scientists in 1939–1940, like their American counterparts, anticipated that a nuclear weapon would be possible once the energy of the atom was unleashed through fission.

Those who participated in the MAUD COMMITTEE reported in 1941 that an atomic bomb could be built and that it should be given the highest priority. Their report helped stimulate American work on the project. Several leading British scientists, including Rudolf PEIERLS, James CHADWICK, the German-born British citizen Klaus FUCHS, James Tuck, Geoffrey Taylor, and others contributed crucial research to the MANHATTAN ENGINEER DISTRICT, working in the United States at LOS ALAMOS, at the University of CHICAGO, and at other facilities.

Prime Minister Winston Churchill was kept informed of the progress of the atomic bomb project. Churchill attended the 1945 POTSDAM conference, where he was replaced by Clement Attlee, the new Labour prime minister. It was during this conference that the leaders, including President Harry TRUMAN, heard of the successful atomic test at TRINITY.

On March 5, 1946, at a commencement address in Fulton, Missouri, former prime minister Churchill introduced the term "iron curtain," referring to the Soviet domination of Eastern Europe and its division from the west.

Following the end of the war, most of the British scientists who had worked in the United States on the Manhattan Project returned to Britain, and several continued their work at the HARWELL RESEARCH ESTABLISHMENT. In 1947, the British cabinet, under Prime Minister Clement Attlee, secretly decided to begin work on a nuclear weapon, even concealing the extent of the budget.

The project culminated in the first test of a British-designed nuclear weapon on March 10, 1952, on Monte Bello Island off the coast of Australia. Altogether, technical teams detonated some 21 nuclear devices between 1952 and 1958 in a series of BRI-

POWER REACTORS IN THE UNITED KINGDOM

Legend:
- ⬛ Pressurized water reactor
- 🔺 Gas-cooled reactor
- 🔺 Advanced gas-cooled reactor
- ⊠ Fast breeder reactor

TISH ATMOSPHERIC NUCLEAR TESTS, at Monte Bello, at another site in Australia, and at Christmas Island in the South Pacific Ocean. The last seven of the tests were of thermonuclear weapons with megatonnage yields. Britain was the third nation to join the "nuclear club," after the United States (1945) and the Soviet Union (1949).

Meanwhile, the British began developing nuclear reactors. Their first power reactor went into operation at CALDER HALL, at Seascale, Cumbria, in 1956 at 50

POWER REACTORS, BRITAIN, OPERATING IN THE 1990S

NAME	LOCATION	NET MWE	TYPE	YEAR START
[British Energy—Nuclear Electric Limited]				
Dungeness B1	Lydd, Kent	220	AGR	1985
Dungeness B2	Lydd, Kent	220	AGR	1985
Sizewell B	Sizewell, Suffolk	1188	PWR	1995
Hinkley Pt.B1	Hinkley Point, Somerset	610	AGR	1978
Hinkley Pt.B2	Hinkley Point, Somerset	610	AGR	1976
Hartlepool 1	Hartlepool, Cleveland	605	AGR	1983
Hartlepool 2	Hartlepool, Cleveland	605	AGR	1984
Heysham A1	Heysham, Lancashire	575	AGR	1983
Heysham A2	Heysham, Lancashire	575	AGR	1984
Heysham B1	Heysham, Lancashire	625	AGR	1988
Heysham B2	Heysham, Lancashire	625	AGR	1988
[British Energy—Scottish Nuclear Limited]				
Hunterston B1	Hunterston, Ayrshire	625	AGR	1976
Hunterston B2	Hunterston, Ayrshire	625	AGR	1977
Torness 1	Dunbar, East Lothian	700	AGR	1988
Torness 2	Dunbar, East Lothian	700	AGR	1989
[British Nuclear Fuels]				
Calder Hall 1	Seascale, Cumbria	50	GCR	1956
Calder Hall 2	Seascale, Cumbria	50	GCR	1957
Calder Hall 3	Seascale, Cumbria	50	GCR	1959
Calder Hall 4	Seascale, Cumbria	50	GCR	1959
Chapelcross 1	Annan, Dumfriesshire	50	GCR	1959
Chapelcross 2	Annan, Dumfriesshire	50	GCR	1959
Chapelcross 3	Annan, Dumfriesshire	50	GCR	1959
Chapelcross 4	Annan, Dumfriesshire	50	GCR	1960
[Magnox Electric]				
Bradwell 1	Bradwell, Essex	123	GCR	1962
Bradwell 2	Bradwell, Essex	123	GCR	1962
Dungeness A1	Lydd, Kent	220	GCR	1965
Dungeness A2	Lydd, Kent	220	GCR	1965
Sizewell A1	Sizewell, Suffolk	210	GCR	1966
Sizewell A2	Sizewell, Suffolk	210	GCR	1966
Hinkley Pt. A1	Hinkley Point, Somerset	235	GCR	1965
Hinkley Pt. A2	Hinkley Point, Somerset	235	GCR	1965
Oldbury 1	Oldbury, Avon	217	GCR	1967
Oldbury 2	Oldbury, Avon	217	GCR	1968
Wyfla 1	Anglesey, Wales	475	GCR	1971
Wyfla 2	Anglesey, Wales	475	GCR	1972

megawatts-electric (MWe). The early British design was called the Magnox type and was a HIGH-TEMPERATURE GAS-COOLED REACTOR. Several of these gas-cooled reactors (GCRs) were exported to France, Italy, Japan, and Spain. The Magnox reactor used magnesium oxide as canning for the fuel slugs, and it was cooled with carbon dioxide. The Magnox design had been worked out at Harwell, and early models were constructed at both Calder Hall and Chapelcross.

The British pioneered in the mid-1950s the development of dual-use reactors that could serve as both PRODUCTION REACTORS to produce PLUTONIUM and electrical power-producing reactors for the commercial power system. The American ATOMIC ENERGY COMMIS-

SION did not develop a similar dual-use production and power reactor until 1964.

Over the decades, Britain built more than 30 power reactors, providing nearly 20 gigawatts of power by the 1990s (about 12.5 gigawatts net). All were of the Magnox GCR type, or the Advanced gas-cooled reactor (AGR) type, except for one PRESSURIZED WATER REACTOR (PWR) at Sizewell, developed in the 1990s.

Britain suffered one of the worst nuclear reactor accidents in the atomic age at the WINDSCALE production reactor facility near Sellafield, Cumbria, in 1957. However, due to the secret nature of the project at the time, the accident received very little publicity. Nevertheless, knowledge of the accident contributed to the British antinuclear movement.

Britain was a founding member of the NORTH ATLANTIC TREATY ORGANIZATION (NATO) in 1949, and its nuclear weapons became part of the alliance's balance of power against the WARSAW TREATY ORGANIZATION. As a nuclear weapon state within NATO, the United Kingdom was an active participant in the Nuclear Planning Group that worked out nuclear strategy.

As a member of the "nuclear club," the United Kingdom participated in the NON-PROLIFERATION TREATY as an original signatory on July 1, 1968, pledging not to assist non-nuclear weapon states in developing weapons. The United Kingdom participated in the ZANGGER COMMITTEE and in the Nuclear Suppliers Group, sometimes called the "London Club." Member nations agreed not to export technology that could be utilized to build nuclear weapons.

Britain imported Polaris missiles from the United States in 1962 and established a Polaris Sales Agreement in 1963. In 1973, Britain decided to develop its own warhead for its strategic ballistic missile submarines. The British Polaris fleet of four nuclear-powered submarines each carried 16 Polaris-type missiles. Britain also maintained a force of long-range bombers capable of carrying nuclear weapons, the Vulcans, and the newer multipurpose aircraft class, the Tornado, introduced in the 1990s. The Vulcan nuclear bomber force was assigned to NATO's Supreme Allied Command–Europe (SACEUR) in 1963. The later Tornado was a joint NATO design supported by Germany, Italy, and Britain.

When the United States and the Soviet Union discussed strategic arms reduction in the SALT II and in the START I negotiations, the Soviets at first insisted that the British nuclear forces be considered as part of the balance arrayed against them.

The British antinuclear movement took on a new focus in the mid-1980s. Protesters criticized the basing in Britain of American-built intermediate-range ground-launched cruise missiles (GLCMs) with nuclear warheads as part of NATO's DUAL-TRACK STRATEGY. The GLCM bases were at two facilities in Britain, at Greenham Common, Newbury, and Molesworth, Northampton. The Soviets insisted the intermediate-range missiles that could strike targets in the Soviet Union should be regarded as part of the strategic missile force to be reduced under the SALT negotiations.

However, by the late 1980s, the Soviets agreed that these missiles should be covered in a separate treaty.

BRITISH PRIME MINISTERS, 1937–2000

TERM BEGAN	PRIME MINISTER	PARTY
May 28, 1937	(Arthur) Neville Chamberlain	Conservative
May 10, 1940	Winston Churchill	Conservative
July 26, 1945	Clement Attlee	Labour
October 25, 1951	Winston Churchill	Conservative
April 6, 1955	Anthony Eden	Conservative
January 10, 1957	Harold Macmillan	Conservative
October 19, 1963	Alec Douglas-Home	Conservative
October 15, 1964	Harold Wilson	Labour
June 19, 1970	Edward Heath	Conservative
March 4, 1974	Harold Wilson	Labour
April 5, 1976	James Callaghan	Labour/Liberal
May 4, 1979	Margaret Thatcher	Conservative
November 28, 1990	John Major	Conservative
May 2, 1997	Anthony C.L. (Tony) Blair	Labour

Negotiations led to the INTERMEDIATE NUCLEAR FORCES TREATY between the United States and the Soviet Union in 1987–1988, in which both sides agreed to withdraw the intermediate-range missiles from their bases. Britain signed the treaty, allowing on-site inspection to verify the dismantling of the GLCM installations at Greenham Common and Molesworth on December 11, 1987, and removal began in 1988.

Although all British prime ministers from 1948 to the 1990s supported British membership in NATO, Conservative Party leaders tended to take a harder line against the Soviet Union than did Labour Party leaders. Harold Wilson (prime minister, 1964–1970 and 1974–1976) was noted for a much stronger willingness to compromise with the Soviets than his predecessors. During his second term, he was investigated by his own security services on suspicion of disloyal collaboration with the Soviets.

With the installation of the Labour government under Tony Blair in 1997, Britain undertook a full review of current nuclear policy. The review, presented to Parliament in July 1998, concluded that the United Kingdom needed a stockpile of less than 200 nuclear weapons. The plan called for the following policies: one British submarine to patrol at any given time, with a load of only 48 warheads, half the anticipated loading planned by the previous government. Furthermore, the submarines were to patrol on reduced alert. Britain would reduce its commitment to buy *Trident* D-5 missiles from the United States from 65 to 58 missiles.

Britain developed a modern ballistic submarine of the Vanguard class in the 1990s.

VANGUARD CLASS

Vanguard	December 1994
Victorious	December 1995
Vigilant	October 1995
Vengeance	September 1998

Each of the Vanguard class carried 16 U.S.–manufactured *Trident* II D-5 class submarine-launched ballistic missiles for a total of 48 missiles. Although Britain maintained title to 58 of these missiles, the missiles are kept at the Strategic Weapons Facility Atlantic of the U.S. Navy at Kings Bay Submarine Base in Georgia. Missiles deployed to Britain are returned to that base and may later be deployed on an American submarine.

In the late 1990s, the United Kingdom remained one of the largest producers of nuclear power in the world, ranked eighth after the United States, France, Japan, Germany, Russia, Ukraine, and Canada. Nuclear power made up slightly more than one-fourth of the electricity supplied in the United Kingdom.

Uranium

Uranium, the element with atomic number 92, exists in nature as three radioactive isotopes, ^{234}U(0.005%), ^{235}U (0.720%), and ^{238}U (99.275%). An additional dozen isotopes of uranium, with mass numbers ranging from 227 to 240, are known. The half-lives of the three naturally occurring uranium ISOTOPES are 2.47×10^5 years, 7.00×10^8 years, and 4.51×10^9 years, respectively. All three undergo alpha decay to initiate chains of decay products, usually terminating with stable isotopes of lead.

^{235}U is the only naturally occurring nuclide suitable for use as a nuclear fuel. ^{239}Plutonium can be bred from naturally occurring, fertile ^{238}U, and ^{233}U can be bred from naturally occurring, fertile ^{232}Thorium. Both ^{239}Pu and ^{232}Th have been used as nuclear fuels, the former quite commonly in nuclear weapons.

Uranium was discovered in 1789 by the German chemist Martin Klaproth, and he named it after the planet Uranus, which had just been identified in 1781 by astronomer William Herschel.

Uranium Mining and Milling

During the first development of the nuclear weapon in World War II, URANIUM was a scarce metal, available in only small quantities. Controlling the various international sources of uranium was regarded in the early days of the ATOMIC ENERGY COMMISSION as a means of regulating the spread of nuclear weapons to the Soviet Union and other countries. As a consequence, the United States bought up stocks of uranium in Africa and Europe. In 1947, the major sources of uranium for use in the United States were a mine in the Belgian Congo and another in Canada. In the years 1953 through 1968, the United States imported over 40,000 tons of uranium from South Africa.

In order to provide the uranium needed for both weapons and nuclear reactors, an extensive exploration program began in the United States during the period between 1948 and 1955. Discoveries in several

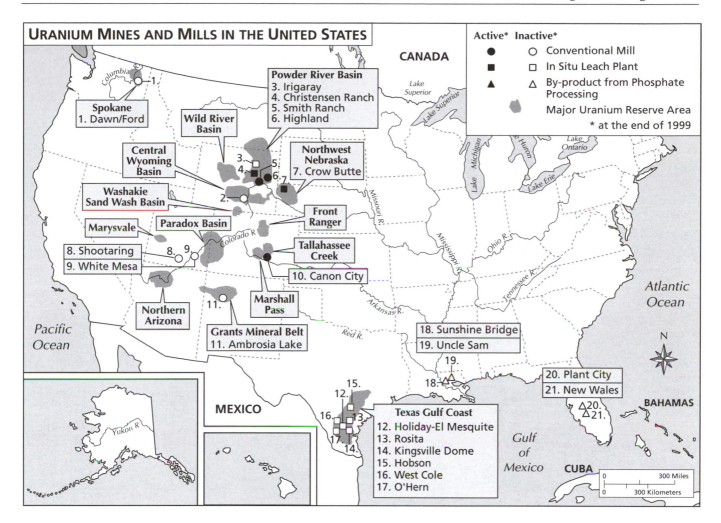

URANIUM MINES AND MILLS IN THE UNITED STATES

Active* Inactive*
- ● ○ Conventional Mill
- ■ □ In Situ Leach Plant
- ▲ △ By-product from Phosphate Processing

Major Uranium Reserve Area

* at the end of 1999

Spokane
1. Dawn/Ford

Powder River Basin
3. Irigaray
4. Christensen Ranch
5. Smith Ranch
6. Highland

Wild River Basin

Central Wyoming Basin

Washakie Sand Wash Basin

Northwest Nebraska
7. Crow Butte

Marysvale

Paradox Basin

Front Ranger

8. Shootaring
9. White Mesa

Tallahassee Creek
10. Canon City

Northern Arizona

Marshall Pass

Grants Mineral Belt
11. Ambrosia Lake

18. Sunshine Bridge
19. Uncle Sam

20. Plant City
21. New Wales

Texas Gulf Coast
12. Holiday-El Mesquite
13. Rosita
14. Kingsville Dome
15. Hobson
16. West Cole
17. O'Hern

300 Miles
300 Kilometers

regions, mostly in the Rocky Mountain states and Texas, increased the supply. By 1955, the United States was the world's largest producer of uranium.

In 1962, the United States produced some 17,000 tons of uranium oxide annually, and imported another 11,000 tons from Canada and Africa. By 1980, the United States had nine major uranium producing regions, mining some 21,000 tons annually. It should be recognized that to produce such a volume of uranium oxide required the processing of more than 10 to 20 million tons of ore annually.

The output of mines in these districts was processed by some 21 mills, operated by major energy companies, including United Nuclear, Anaconda, KERR-MCGEE, Exxon, and Gulf Oil. Most of the mills are located in or near the mining districts to minimize transport costs of the unprocessed ore. More than half of accessible mineral reserves at the high point of production in the 1980s were controlled by Gulf Oil and

Kerr-McGee, while Kerr-McGee controlled about one-quarter of the milling capacity.

U.S. URANIUM MINING DISTRICTS

Spokane, Washington
Powder River Basin, Wyoming
Shirley Basin, Wyoming
Crooks Gap, Wyoming
Gas Hills, Wyoming
Paradox Basin, Utah–Colorado border
Front Range, Colorado
Grants Mineral Belt, New Mexico
Texas Gulf Coast, Texas

One of the most noted and investigated public health hazards from the mining and milling process is the dry, powdery by-product known as mill TAILINGS. By the early 1980s, there were 35 large mill tailings mounds at active and inactive mill sites in the western states. In addition to the dry tailings, liquid chemical wastes from the milling process were also quite hazardous. This material was routinely released into waterways before 1959; after that time, it was stored in tailings ponds to evaporate.

The environmental impact and worker health hazards of the uranium mining industry have been the subject of several lawsuits. Most notable was a spill of radioactive mill tailings from a dam near CHURCH ROCK, New Mexico in 1979 and a suit launched on behalf of Navaho Uranium miners in 1983.

See also NUCLEAR FUEL CYCLE.

Suggested Readings

Donald Clark, *State of the Art: Uranium Mining, Milling and Refining Industry.* Corvallis, Ore.: Environmental Protection Agency, 1974.

Peter Metzger, *The Atomic Establishment.* New York: Simon and Schuster, 1972.

Union of Concerned Scientists, *The Nuclear Fuel Cycle: A Survey of the Public Health, Environmental, and National Security Effects of Nuclear Power.* Cambridge, Mass.: Union of Concerned Scientists, 1975.

Urey, Harold (1893–1981)   *American physicist who was the discoverer of deuterium, receiving the 1934 Nobel Prize in chemistry for this work*

Harold Urey worked with the MANHATTAN ENGINEER DISTRICT during World War II, and after the war he worked on methods of isolating TRITIUM for use in nuclear weapons.

Urey was born in 1893 in Indiana and was educated at Montana State University. He was appointed professor of chemistry at Columbia University in 1934, and worked at the University of CHICAGO during the Manhattan Project.

He suggested that HEAVY WATER could be used as a moderator in reactors. He visited Great Britain early in the war and reported to Vannevar BUSH regarding British progress and French ideas concerning possible future power reactors. He was put in charge of studying methods of separation of uranium isotopes and conducting investigations of heavy water as a possible moderator. In 1943, Leslie GROVES appointed Urey to direct the research at OAK RIDGE on gaseous diffusion, as well as on the production of heavy water. Even though production reactors were designed using graphite as a moderator during the war years, Urey continued to suggest a heavy-water design.

After the war, Urey was a strong advocate of civilian control of atomic research. During discussions of whether or not to proceed with a thermonuclear weapon, he disagreed with J. Robert OPPENHEIMER and was a spokesman, along with E.O. LAWRENCE and Lewis STRAUSS, for those scientists and administrators who favored building such a weapon in 1949 and 1950.

In the 1950s, he turned his attention to questions of the origin of life on Earth. He died in 1981.

Suggested Reading

Richard G. Hewlett and Oscar E. Anderson, *The New World* (Vol. 1 of *A History of the United States Atomic Energy Commission*). Washington, D.C.: Atomic Energy Commission, 1962.

Vemork *See* NORSK-HYDRO.

Venona Decrypts

"Venona" was the code word adopted by the Army Signals Security Agency (and its successors, the Army Security Agency and the National Security Agency) to refer to the body of secret telegraphic communication between Soviet embassy and consular offices in the United States and Moscow during and after World War II. The encrypted messages contained details of Soviet KGB espionage in the United States and Canada, eventually providing clues as to the degree of Soviet atomic espionage. The United States recorded the messages, but the encryption system was so difficult that American specialists could not at first crack the code.

Breakthroughs in cracking the coded messages came when specialists discovered that, due to a printing error in RUSSIA, pages of code numbers that should have been used only once had been used repeatedly. With careful comparison, eventually parts of many messages and a few complete messages could be read. The decoding teams found that even after they could

read parts of the messages, individual persons were identified only with code names. For these reasons, it took several years to make use of the information to track down individual spies in the United States, and eventually only a few of the several hundred Americans who had worked with the Soviets could be identified.

In the postwar years, specialists at the National Security Agency continued to work on the codes and ciphers, eventually uncovering pieces of the information. With the defection of Igor Gouzenko to Canada in 1945 and with the confession of several Soviet agents in the United States, the American intelligence community sought more information about Soviet espionage. Elizabeth Bentley and Whittaker Chambers explained to congressional committees that they had assisted the Soviet network, and interest in uncovering the extent of the spy operation increased throughout the U.S. security establishment.

The confessed spies could usually only identify very few individuals with whom they had worked because the Soviets had used a system of compartmentalization or cells to limit the agents' knowledge of each other and to thereby control any breakdown of the system.

Eventually, when the code was partially cracked, American specialists could read portions of more than 2,900 Soviet diplomatic telegrams sent between 1940 and 1948. The partially decrypted messages contained many revelations, particularly that the Communist Party of the United States (CPUSA) and its leaders had actively participated in espionage work for the Soviet Union. The messages showed that the Soviets had focused on learning information in four areas: Hitler's war plans in attacking Russia; any secret war aims of the British and Americans; any indications that the two Western Allies were seeking a separate peace with Germany; and American scientific progress, especially in developing an atomic weapon.

The National Security Agency gradually broke more and more of the messages, under the leadership of agent Meredith Gardner. At first the information Gardner and his team uncovered was very closely guarded and not even shared with the Central Intelligence Agency. Gardner and his associates learned that the Soviets had known of the MANHATTAN ENGINEER DISTRICT and the atomic bomb development work as early as 1942, code naming it "ENORMOUS." The messages showed that at LOS ALAMOS as many as four agents reported through couriers to the Soviet consulate in New York City. The messages showed that the four agents were: Klaus FUCHS, with the cover name CHARLES and then REST; David GREENGLASS, with the cover names BUMBLEBEE and CALIBRE; Theodore (Ted) Hall, with the cover name YOUNGSTER (in Russian, "*Mlad*"); and a fourth source with the cover name PERS, who was never identified with any certainty.

Several Soviet memoirs have confirmed all of this information in later years, although some Russian espionage agents remembered the name PERS as PERSEUS. Another agent with the cover names LIBERAL and ANTENNA was later identified as the brother-in-law of Greenglass, Julius ROSENBERG. Ethel Greenglass, David's sister, had married Julius Rosenberg. Several of the uncovered individuals, notably Rosenberg and Greenglass, had been members of the CPUSA.

By 1948, the National Security Agency began cooperating with the Federal Bureau of Investigation (FBI) in uncovering and providing evidence against some of the members of the network. The leader of the FBI effort was Special Agent Robert Lamphere. Lamphere used Venona information in 1949 and 1950 in identifying Klaus Fuchs. In Britain, Fuchs confessed and

eventually led the FBI to arrest Harry GOLD. After interrogating Gold, the FBI was able to identify David Greenglass as the enlisted man who had worked at Los Alamos and who was known as CALIBRE in the Venona material.

After questioning Greenglass on June 15, 1950, the FBI concluded that the code name LIBERAL referred to Rosenberg. The FBI followed Rosenberg and his wife for about a month and then arrested them. Although Ted Hall was interrogated, he was not arrested, as the only information against him had derived from the Venona messages (rather than through confessions, as in the case of Gold and Greenglass), and the U.S. intelligence agencies sought to keep secret the fact they had deciphered any of the messages.

The existence and details of Venona were released in 1995, and a detailed report and transcript of the messages were released to the public in 1996. With the release of the Venona materials, as well as the earlier release of information about the Rosenbergs through the Freedom of Information Act, historians and the public began to develop a more accurate understanding of the extent of Soviet espionage in the United States, the extent of the CPUSA cooperation with Soviet intelligence, and the degree of information the Soviets obtained about the nuclear weapon. That information had been crucial to the atomic weapon design efforts led by the KGB chief Lavrenty BERIA and scientist Igor KURCHATOV.

Suggested Reading

Robert Louis Benson and Michael Warner, *Venona: Soviet Espionage and the American Response, 1939–1957*. Washington, D.C.: National Security Agency and Central Intelligence Agency, 1996.

Vernadsky, Vladimir (1863–1945) *mineralogist and early leader in research into radioactive materials in Russia*

Vladimir Vernadsky led the effort to search for geologic sources of radioactive materials, and, under his prodding, the Russian Academy of Sciences sent expeditions to look for URANIUM deposits in the Ural and Caucasus Mountains and in Central Asia before World War I.

Vladimir Vernadsky (or Vernadskii) was born in 1863 in St. Petersburg, Russia. During the communist takeover of RUSSIA in the period 1919 to 1921, Vernadsky fled to the Ukraine. Despite his opposition to the

Bolshevik regime, he was allowed to return by Lenin. He helped establish the Russian Radium Institute in 1922. He defined the task of the institute very broadly, insisting that it should work toward harnessing atomic energy.

In 1938 he wrote a work, *Scientific Thought as a Planetary Phenomenon,* that could not be published in the Soviet Union because he claimed that the Soviet state was suppressing free scientific inquiry.

His son, George Vernadsky, emigrated to the United States and became a professor of history at Yale University. Young Vernadsky read an article in *The New York Times,* published in May 1940, by science writer William Laurence, describing the possibility of nuclear power and nuclear weapons. He sent a clipping of the story to his father, who was in a sanatorium near Moscow. Vernadsky immediately recognized the importance of the field, and, with fellow members of the Radium Institute, he pushed for the formation of a Uranium Commission. Although now 77 years old, his influence was such that his advocacy moved various members of the Russian scientific establishment to begin to coordinate their work, eventually leading to the development of the Soviet nuclear weapon. Vernadsky died in 1945 before the weapon project came to fruition.

See also KURCHATOV, IGOR.

Suggested Reading

David Holloway, *Stalin and the Bomb.* New Haven: Yale University Press, 1994.

Alexander Vucinich, *Science in Russian Culture.* Stanford, Calif.: Stanford University Press, 1970.

Vitrification

Vitrification is a process in which radioactive (or other hazardous) wastes are encapsulated in a glass-like material. The vitrification process begins with solidification of high-level liquid wastes (HLLW) from fuel processing by calcination. Solutions of the metal nitrates are thermally converted to the corresponding solid metal oxides. The oxides are then fixed in either a borosilicate or a phosphate glass. From a chemical stability standpoint, the glass can contain up to 30% fission product oxides, but 20% is a more usual value.

The HLLW is atomized into a fluidized bed calcinator where conversion to the solid oxides takes place. The calcined waste is continuously mixed with Borax

(30% B_2O_3) and silica (50% SiO_2) in a furnace at 1000–1200 degrees C. where a homogenous, molten glass is formed. The molten glass is poured into stainless steel cylinders for long-term storage. Each cylinder contains a half-ton of vitrified radioactive waste. The heat from radioactive decay can raise the temperature at the center of the cylinder to 700 degrees C. Consequently, the vitrified wastes are sometimes externally cooled with water or air during the early period of storage.

In another process, in situ vitrification, radioactive wastes that have leached into the ground have been vitrified by the application of 4,000 volts of electrical current. The target area is heated to 1,600 to 2,000 degrees C., and the molten mass grows downward. In test operations, individual melted areas as large as 1,400 tons and 22 feet deep have been successfully converted into a glasslike substance.

The virtue of both systems of vitrification is that, with radioactive or chemically dangerous particles immobilized in the glassy substance, they will not migrate with water.

Vladivostok Accord

President Gerald FORD met with Leonid Brezhnev, general secretary of the Central Committee of the Communist Party of the Soviet Union, in Vladivostok in the Soviet Far East in November 1974, where they signed a general agreement on relations between the two countries on November 24, 1974. Although the Vladivostok Accord did not have any specific nuclear arms control provisions, it outlined a commitment to work toward further strategic arms control. Critics claimed that Ford gave up too much, giving legitimacy to the communist regimes in Eastern Europe in exchange for hollow pledges to honor human rights.

The Strategic Arms Limitation Treaty (SALT I) had been signed in 1972 during the administration of Richard NIXON. In 1974, Nixon, one month before his resignation from the presidency, signed the treaty limiting the yield of underground nuclear tests, the THRESHOLD TEST BAN TREATY (TTBT). The Vladivostok Accord represented a commitment to proceed from these treaties to SALT II and outlined the general terms of the proposed further SALT Treaty. The formal name for the Vladivostok Accord was the "Joint US–USSR Statement on the Question of Further Limitations of Strategic Offensive Arms."

Ford and Brezhnev, in the general "spirit of Vladivostok," signed the Peaceful Nuclear Explosions (PNE) Treaty in 1976, limiting peaceful nuclear detonations to the same 150 kiloton yield that had been agreed to in July 1974 under the TTBT limiting underground testing of nuclear weapons. However, Ford did not submit the PNE treaty to the U.S. Senate for ratification, and both nations proceeded to follow the terms of the unratified treaty.

The Vladivostok Accord of 1974 may have represented the final high point of nuclear DETENTE, which began to break down by 1977 with Soviet deployment of new and more powerful nuclear missiles, particularly the SS-18 and SS-20. Negotiations toward SALT II, which was never ratified, and later, the final Strategic Arms Reduction Treaty (START) took more than 10 years.

See also ARMS CONTROL; PLOWSHARE PROGRAM.

War Resisters League

Founded in 1923 by Jessie Wallace Hughan, the War Resisters League (WRL) remained for decades the major pacifist organization in the United States. The WRL affiliated with the London-headquartered War Resisters' International (WRI), which in 1948 claimed 56 sections in 30 countries.

Since its creation, the WRL repudiated all wars, armed social revolutions, and militarism. Besides its original focus on war resistance, the league stood for a pacifist alternative both to the far left and the dominant political consensus. The WRL espoused an active, radical pacifism to challenge military aggression, political tyranny, and social injustice through nonviolent means, including mass strikes, boycotts, demonstrations, noncooperation, and civil disobedience. In addition, the WRL opposed the draft; championed civil rights, civil liberties, and the right of conscientious objection; and offered counseling and support to conscientious objectors (COs).

The WRL evolved from a single-issue educational forum and political pressure group devoted exclusively to war resistance into an organization advocating the use of nonviolent direct action and civil disobedience to promote an agenda on behalf of both peace and a wide range of social issues. With the religious pacifist Fellowship of Reconciliation, the WRL led the transformation of pacifism from simply repudiation of war into a nonviolent social movement to resist armed conflict and promote radical social reform.

During World War II, many COs were WRL members who opted for Civilian Public Service (CPS) camps and prison rather than military service. In CPS and prison, these COs staged nonviolent work and hunger strikes to protest racial segregation, prison censorship, and the entire Selective Service apparatus. Led by these COs, a militant faction gained control of the WRL after World War II and reorientated the league toward a wider agenda, using civil disobedience, nonregistration for the draft, and tax resistance. This radical group provided more than three decades of leadership, and included A. J. Muste, Bayard Rustin, and others.

During the cold war, the WRL challenged the dominant anti-Soviet policy in the United States, nourished an alternative radical pacifist vision, and sowed the seeds for social movements of the 1960s and 1970s. In addition, the WRL represented an international peace movement comprised of pacifists, nuclear scientists, and world government proponents whose view of the cold war remained critical of both the United States and the Soviet Union. Rejecting the United Nations as an imperial alliance of victor nations, the WRL advocated the transfer of sovereignty to a world government. The WRL opposed the draft, the Truman Doctrine, NATO, and sought a mediated settlement to the KOREAN WAR.

Following HIROSHIMA and the dawn of the atomic age, the WRL took a leadership role in the campaign to abolish atomic weapons and nuclear testing. The league condemned atomic warfare as a suicidal "crime against humanity," which even on practical grounds could neither thwart communist aggression nor protect the United States. No defense existed against the atomic bomb, the WRL warned; the only defense was the abolition of war. From the mid-1950s to the mid-1960s, the league devoted much of its antinuclear activism to the NEW YORK CITY CIVIL DEFENSE PROTEST MOVEMENT (1955–1961) and the antinuclear COMMITTEE FOR NONVIOLENT ACTION (CNVA; 1957–1967). In these and other campaigns, the league endorsed, promoted, and practiced direct action and civil disobedience.

In 1956, the WRL founded *Liberation* magazine, an influential pacifist journal and a voice of radical dissent that became a seedbed of the future New Left. Beginning in 1963, the WRL devoted most of its efforts to organizing resistance to the Vietnam War. WRL staffer David McReynolds emerged as an important antiwar leader. A key element of the broad antiwar movement, the WRL counseled war resisters, advocated draft refusal and desertion, blocked induction centers, sponsored draft-card-burning protests, and organized a campaign of war tax resistance.

After the Vietnam War, the WRL supported disarmament, environmental causes, and gender equality; reversed its immediate post-Hiroshima position and opposed nuclear power; and denounced American military intervention in Central America, Panama, the Persian Gulf, and Yugoslavia.

The WRL represented the central element of the secular, radical pacifist, American Left through much of the 20th century. In addition, the WRL proved instrumental in popularizing techniques of nonviolent direct action protest and resistance to advance its ideals.

Suggested Reading

Scott H. Bennett, "Pacifism Not Passivism": The War Resisters League and Radical Pacifism, Nonviolent Direct Action, and the Americanization of Gandhi, 1915–1963." Ph.D. Dissertation, Rutgers University, 1998.

Lawrence S. Wittner, *Rebels against War: The American Peace Movement, 1933–1983*. Philadelphia: Temple University Press, 1984.

Warsaw Treaty Organization (WTO)

The Warsaw Treaty Organization (WTO), sometimes referred to as the Warsaw Pact, was formed by the Soviet Union and its Communist-Party dominated European allies in 1955. The nuclear weapons policies of the United States and its allies in Western Europe were based on the assumption that a possible invasion of Western Europe by the Soviets would be supported by WTO member states and armed forces.

In response to the Paris Agreements, which admitted the Federal Republic of Germany (West Germany) as a member of the NORTH ATLANTIC TREATY ORGANIZATION (NATO) on May 5, 1955, the Soviets announced the conclusion of the Warsaw Treaty, or East European Defense Treaty, on May 14, 1955. The treaty had a 20-year life, and it was renewed in 1975 for 10 years. On April 26, 1985, it was renewed for another 20 years. However, it did not survive this third term.

In addition to the Soviet Union, the following nations became members of the original WTO: Albania, Bulgaria, Czechoslovakia, The German Democratic Republic (East Germany), HUNGARY, Poland, and ROMANIA. On December 30, 1955, the Soviets signed a treaty with East Germany, recognizing it as a sovereign state. Backing up the multilateral Warsaw Treaty, each of the satellite countries of Eastern Europe had one or more bilateral treaties with the Soviet Union regarding aid, cultural cooperation, and military matters.

In November 1956, the Soviets invaded Hungary to suppress an emerging democratic regime in that satellite nation. In August 1968, under the provisions of the Warsaw Treaty, the Soviet Union, Hungary, and Poland invaded Czechoslovakia to suppress liberal reforms instituted by Alexander Dubček in what had been called the "Prague Spring."

On September 12, 1968, Albania renounced its membership in the Warsaw Treaty Organization, having broken diplomatic relations with Moscow in 1961. This defection was attributed to the Stalinist orientation of Albania and its displeasure with the political changes brought about by Nikita KHRUSHCHEV and his successors, Aleksey Kosygin and Leonid Brezhnev. No doubt the willingness of the Warsaw Pact members to enforce their version of communism in Czechoslovakia contributed to the withdrawal of Albania. Over the next 10 years, Albania aligned itself with the government of CHINA in the Chinese-Soviet rivalry for domination of the world's communist parties and movements.

The WTO and NATO entered into a treaty in 1989–1990, the Conventional Forces in Europe (CFE) Treaty, under which heavy conventional weaponry, such as artillery and tanks, would be destroyed. On November 3, 1990, the WTO was superseded by the Budapest Group (Bulgaria, Czech Republic, Hungary, Poland, Romania, and Slovak Republic) with reference to the CFE treaty. The Budapest Group accepted the obligations of the CFE treaty that had been taken on by the WTO for their member states. The treaty was formally signed on November 19, 1990. In May 1992 eight nations of the former Soviet Union, including Armenia, Azerbaijan, Belarus, Georgia, KAZAKHSTAN, Moldova, RUSSIA, and UKRAINE, met in Tashkent, Uzbekistan, forming the "Tashkent Group," which accepted CFE treaty obligations of the former Soviet Union.

On June 26, 1990, the Hungarian National Assembly voted to begin negotiations for withdrawal from the WTO. In 1991, the WTO dissolved, and Czechoslovakia was reconstituted as two separate nations: the Czech Republic and the Slovak Republic or Slovakia.

The WTO members formally met on February 25, 1991, and disbanded the military side of the organization on March 31, with final and formal dissolution on July 1, 1991. Hungary, Poland, and the Czech Republic were admitted to NATO in 1999 while Bulgaria, Romania, and some of the former republics of Yugoslavia also sought membership in NATO.

During the period from 1955 to 1991, NATO and U.S. military strategists developed war planning around the concept that an attack by the Soviet Union on NATO would be supported by WTO members and forces. In much of the strategic literature from the period, authors assumed that the WTO was somewhat more monolithic than it appeared in historical perspective from later years.

Suggested Reading

NATO Information Service, *The North Atlantic Treaty Organisation: Facts and Figures*. Brussels, Belgium: NATO Information Service, 1989.

NATO Office of Information and Press, *NATO Handbook*. Brussels, Belgium: NATO Office of Information and Press, 1995.

Waste Isolation Pilot Plant (WIPP)

In 1979, the U.S. Congress approved a plan to construct a waste-isolation facility near Carlsbad, New Mexico, to house transuranic and low-level RADIOACTIVE WASTE from the nuclear weapons complex. Constructed in a natural salt deposit 2,150 feet beneath the desert floor, the facility comprised of an extensive network of tunnels into which the DEPARTMENT OF ENERGY (DOE) planned to deposit low-level waste. Low-level waste consisted of tools, clothing, gloves, and other equipment that had become contaminated in the course of weapons research and production throughout the weapons complex in the United States.

The facility was ready to receive shipments in the late 1980s, but various court cases and regulatory challenges prevented its being used. After many delays imposed by court action and political opposition in New Mexico, the first shipment was sent to the Waste Isolation Pilot Plant (WIPP) in March 1999. The waste was to be shipped in 10-foot-tall cylindrical casks containing 55-gallon drums full of contaminated items.

Under DOE plans, more than 37,700 truckloads of containers would be shipped to WIPP, with some 45% of the material coming from HANFORD, Washington.

Opponents of WIPP argued that the ceilings of the salt storage chambers were weak and could cave in, breaking open the waste containers. Westinghouse Corporation, which administered WIPP, responded by pointing out that state mining inspectors declared the chambers safe for use.

DOE planned to send high-level waste to another facility at YUCCA MOUNTAIN at the NEVADA TEST SITE.

See also NUCLEAR WASTE POLICY ACT.

Suggested Reading

Raymond L. Murray, *Understanding Radioactive Waste*, 4th ed. Columbus, Ohio: Battelle Memorial Institute, 1994.

Watkins, James (1927–)   *American naval officer who served as secretary of energy under President George H.W. Bush from 1989 to 1993*

James Watkins was appointed to serve as secretary of energy by President George BUSH in February 1989, serving through the Bush administration until January 1993. Watkins had formerly served as a naval officer and administrative assistant to Hyman RICKOVER. He was commissioned admiral in 1979, and he served as chief of naval operations (CNO) on the Joint Chiefs of

James Watkins. Admiral James Watkins served as U.S. secretary of energy during the administration of George H.W. Bush, 1989–1993, during a period of nuclear disarmament and efforts at environmental restoration at the nuclear weapons complex. (Department of Energy)

Staff from 1982 to 1986. He chaired a presidential commission on the AIDs virus (1987–1988) in the administration of Ronald REAGAN. Watkins brought many ideas regarding tighter management from his experience in the nuclear navy to his position in the Energy Department. As CNO, Watkins had sought to improve the navy's procurement system, ensuring competition and accountability among contractors. He oversaw the transformation of the navy to an all-volunteer force.

As secretary of energy, Watkins hoped to invigorate the DEPARTMENT OF ENERGY (DOE) and to bring about a change in the organization's "culture." Toward that end, he sought approval to increase salaries of top scientific and technical personnel. He also tried to change the rule that prohibited federal officials from moving to and from the private sector. In his selection of top assistants, he chose individuals with reputations for tightened management, some of whom were so contro-

versial that their nominations had to be withdrawn. He selected two former officials from the Environmental Protection Agency to serve as special assistants on environmental issues. He established a number of "Tiger Teams" to conduct environmental compliance assessments at each of the sites of the nuclear weapons complex. He proposed tying contractors' bonuses to environmental compliance.

He attempted a number of other reforms of the department dealing with the nuclear weapons production complex. He reset the department's priorities so that environmental, safety, and health issues were more important than production. He coordinated environmental compliance efforts with those of local and state authorities and set up a new management team in the Office of Defense Programs to give emphasis to safety over production. He ordered the establishment of a database containing health information on all past and current DOE employees. He also accelerated the cleanup of facilities by allocating $300 million to the task.

Watkins agreed to transfer long-term DOE employee health studies to the Department of Health and Human Services so that this independent agency would be responsible for monitoring potential safety hazards. He also created an internal Office of Environmental Restoration and Waste Management to oversee DOE activities in this area. In 1989, the department published a five-year plan for environmental restoration and waste management.

Collectively, these changes and others were intended to establish a new culture within the department. When he took office, the last of the PRODUCTION REACTORS operating at SAVANNAH RIVER and HANFORD had been closed, and, under his administration, plans to develop a new production reactor were investigated. However, with the end of the cold war in 1990–1991, the planning for a new generation of production reactors was terminated. The transformation of the department into an agency with a high priority on remediation of prior environmental damage had been advanced under Watkins. That mission would be continued by his successors in the 1990s.

Suggested Reading

Rodney Carlisle, *Supplying the Nuclear Arsenal.* Baltimore, Md.: Johns Hopkins University Press, 1996.
Jay Olshansky and R. G. Williams, "Culture Shock at the Weapons Complex," *Bulletin of Atomic Scientists* (September 1990): 29–33.

Weapons Effects

The term "weapons effects" refers to the consequences of a nuclear weapon detonation. When detonated in the atmosphere, much of the energy released from the nuclear reactions in the form of radiation is immediately transformed into heat and blast, with a wide range of radiation including X-rays, alpha, beta, and gamma radiation. The gamma and X-ray radiation in particular cause both immediate death and radiation sickness among exposed victims.

As of the end of the 20th century, only two nuclear weapons had ever been employed operationally, those detonated over HIROSHIMA and NAGASAKI, Japan, in August 1945. The widespread casualties (over 200,000 total from the two weapons), the gruesome burns and injuries, and the urban destruction from blast and firestorms induced by those two weapons have been widely perceived as the most dreaded weapons effects. However, extensive testing of nuclear weapons by the United States and other nuclear-armed nations in the atmosphere, at high altitudes, and underwater in the period 1946 to 1962 revealed many other effects that would result from more widespread employment of the weapons in warfare.

The total energy released from a nuclear detonation is referred to as the YIELD, measured in equivalent tonnages of TNT, in the kiloton or megaton range.

Nuclear weapons detonated in outer space or at very high altitudes deliver much more of their total yield in the form of radiation than those detonated nearer the surface of the Earth. X-rays travel in straight lines from the point of detonation, and the transfer of X-rays through the atmosphere generates a burst of radiation known as an ELECTROMAGNETIC PULSE (EMP). EMP is extremely destructive of electronic equipment. Thus a serious weapons effect of a burst in outer space or at very high altitude would be an EMP–induced destruction of electronic equipment over a wide territory. A single large weapon of several hundred kiloton equivalent power detonated high over the center of the United States could put out of operation computers, automobiles, aircraft, and power systems from California to New York and from North Dakota to Texas.

Weapons detonated underwater create a shock front through the water that is destructive to nearby shipping and also produce large quantities of radioactive FALLOUT in the form of rain or mist if detonated relatively close to the surface. Some of the ships exposed to radioactive fallout from test shots in the Pacific were so contaminated that they had to be scuttled at sea rather than brought to port for cleaning.

Secondary weapons effects from the blast and fires include great quantities of smoke and dust, carrying radioactive materials into a cloud that travels for many miles with the wind. Fallout of radioactive materials from the cloud may spread in a large footprint extending 100 miles or more downwind from the point of detonation. In particular, the Castle-Bravo nuclear test of 1954 demonstrated that fallout from a 10-megaton thermonuclear detonation could induce radiation sickness over a hundred miles from the point of explosion.

In a major exchange of nuclear weapons, some scientists have calculated that the total effect of smoke and dust might be so severe as to cause a worldwide drop in average temperature by shadowing the sun. Such an effect has been dubbed NUCLEAR WINTER. Preliminary calculations of the extent of this particular effect have been called into question by other experts.

In the United States, nuclear weapons tests have been of three basic types: weapons-related tests to determine the performance of a weapon and its modifications, safety tests to determine conditions under which a nuclear weapon might accidentally detonate, and weapons effects tests. The third category of tests determines how the various forms of energy released from a nuclear or thermonuclear detonation will affect structures, materials, equipment, organisms, and other weapons. Usually weapons-related tests and safety tests were conducted by the ATOMIC ENERGY COMMISSION and its successors, the ENERGY RESEARCH AND DEVELOPMENT ADMINISTRATION and the DEPARTMENT OF ENERGY. Weapons effects tests were generally conducted by the ARMED FORCES SPECIAL WEAPONS PROJECT and its successors: the DEFENSE ATOMIC SUPPORT AGENCY, the DEFENSE NUCLEAR AGENCY, the Defense Special Weapons Agency, and the DEFENSE THREAT REDUCTION AGENCY.

See also ATMOSPHERIC NUCLEAR TESTING; UNDERGROUND TESTING.

Suggested Reading

Samuel Glasstone, *The Effects of Nuclear Weapons*. Washington, D.C.: Department of Defense and Department of Energy, 1977.

Weapons Production Complex

The facilities for producing nuclear weapons were dispersed across the United States during the first years of the MANHATTAN ENGINEER DISTRICT. Mostly government-

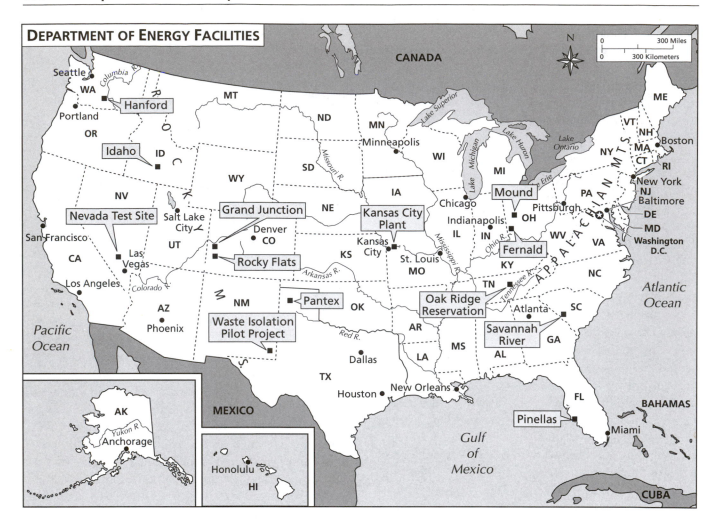

DEPARTMENT OF ENERGY FACILITIES

owned, contractor-operated (GOCO) facilities, the network of research and development laboratories, manufacturing plants, and assembly factories is referred to as the Weapons Production Complex.

By the 1970s, over 100,000 people were employed at the weapons complex GOCO facilities, with an operating budget exceeding $2 billion annually. Although largely devoted to the manufacture of weapons, the budget was included in the annual budget figures for the civilian agency, first the ATOMIC ENERGY COMMISSION, then the ENERGY RESEARCH AND DEVELOPMENT ADMINISTRATION, and, after 1977, the DEPARTMENT OF ENERGY (DOE).

The DOE defined the weapons complex as consisting of seven facilities directly involved in fabrication of nuclear weapons. A larger definition of the weapons complex would include URANIUM enrichment plants, materials processing plants, weapons research and development, testing of weapons, and the laboratories

devoted to naval nuclear propulsion. Altogether, there were more than 20 major sites involved in one or another aspect of the development of nuclear weapons, not including private-sector factories and laboratories that concentrated on aircraft, ships, and missile weapon delivery systems.

The seven weapons fabrication plants, at the height of the cold war were:

1. Kansas City Plant, Kansas City, Missouri. Contractor: Bendix. Product: Electronic, plastic, and mechanical weapons components.
2. Mound Facility, Miamisburg, Ohio. Contractor: Monsanto Research. Product: High explosive components and radioisotope batteries (using ^{238}U) for weapons.
3. Savannah River Weapons Facility, Aiken, South Carolina. Contractor: E.I. Du Pont (later, Westinghouse). Products: lithium deuteride and tritium for weapons.

4. Y-12 Plant, Oak Ridge, Tennessee. Contractor: Union Carbide (later Martin Marietta, then United Technologies—Battelle). Products: uranium weapons parts.

5. Pinellas Plant, St. Petersburg, Florida. Contractor: General Electric. Products: Neutron initiators.

6. Rocky Flats Plant, Golden, Colorado. Contractor: Rockwell International. Product: Plutonium parts.

7. Pantex Plant, Amarillo, Texas. Contractor: Mason and Hangar-Silas Mason. Product: completed weapons assembly and disassembly.

The parts and components made at the first six facilities would be transported to Pantex, where the final weapon assembly would bring together the parts. Components and some fully assembled weapons were tested at the NEVADA TEST SITE in underground detonations until testing ended in 1993. In the years 1974 to 1992, the THRESHOLD TEST BAN TREATY restricted the yield of such tests to less than 150 kilotons.

In addition to the seven facilities directly involved in the production of nuclear weapons, an additional dozen or so GOCO facilities, under DOE jurisdiction, engaged in other aspects of the utilization of nuclear energy for defense purposes.

Uranium Enrichment Plants. Concentrated ^{235}U, as uranium hexafluoride.
Oak Ridge, Tennessee
Paducah, Kentucky
Portsmouth, Ohio

Materials Processing Plants. Manufactured and processed fissile materials
Ashtabula Feed Materials Plant, Ashtabula, Ohio
Feed Materials Production Center, Fernald, Ohio
Idaho Chemical Processing Plant, Idaho Falls, Idaho
HANFORD Production Operations, Hanford, Washington
Savannah River Plant, Aiken, South Carolina

Weapons Research and Development. Developed and tested nuclear weapons.
LOS ALAMOS National Laboratory, Los Alamos, New Mexico.
LAWRENCE LIVERMORE NATIONAL LABORATORY, Livermore, California.
SANDIA Laboratories, Albuquerque, New Mexico.
NEVADA TEST SITE, north of Las Vegas, Nevada.

Naval Nuclear Propulsion. Reactor research and development.
BETTIS ATOMIC POWER LABORATORY, West Mifflin, Pennsylvania.
KNOLLS ATOMIC POWER LABORATORY, Schenectady, New York.

By the 1980s, many of the facilities within the complex had developed environmental or worker safety problems. Fernald was closed in 1989. The Rocky Flats site was subject to investigation, and it was finally raided by the Federal Bureau of Investigation in 1989 and closed by court order. Radiation release problems at Hanford, lost mercury at OAK RIDGE, and TRITIUM releases from reactors at SAVANNAH RIVER all attracted attention in the 1980s.

With the negotiation of START I in 1990–1991, Secretary of Energy James Watkins was able to order a reconfiguration of the weapons complex that would schedule closure of most facilities devoted to weapons production and the conversion of others to environmental remediation. ROCKY FLATS, Pinellas, Mound, and the Portsmouth Gaseous Diffusion Plant were permanently closed in 1994; all the reactors and processing facilities at Hanford were shut down, and the reactors at Savannah River had been closed by 1988. Abortive plans to restart K reactor at Savannah River Site were never implemented.

See also IDAHO NATIONAL ENGINEERING LABORATORY; PRODUCTION REACTORS; UNDERGROUND NUCLEAR TESTING.

Suggested Reading

Office of Environmental Management, *Linking Legacies: Connecting the Cold War Nuclear Weapons Production Process to Their Environmental Consequences*. Washington, D.C.: U.S. Department of Energy, 1997.

U.S. Department of Energy, *DOE Research and Development and Field Activities*. Washington, D.C.: 1979.

Westinghouse

Westinghouse was one of four companies in the United States to enter the nuclear reactor construction business in the mid-1950s. Along with BABCOCK AND WILCOX, GENERAL ELECTRIC, and COMBUSTION ENGINEERING, Westinghouse became a major supplier of nuclear reactors.

Westinghouse got its start in the nuclear reactor program through working on PROPULSION REACTORS for nuclear submarines. Hyman RICKOVER convinced the president of Westinghouse, Gwilym Price, that the company should compete with General Electric in the field. GE had already started operating the HANFORD plant and had established Knolls laboratory with AEC assistance. By 1948, Westinghouse established a similar laboratory, the BETTIS ATOMIC POWER LABORATORY near Pittsburgh, working on the navy's program to build a reactor for the first U.S. submarine to be powered by nuclear energy, the *Nautilus*.

The PRESSURIZED WATER REACTOR (PWR) designed by Westinghouse was successful, and the AEC, with support and influence from Rickover, selected the company to build the first power reactor at SHIPPINGPORT, Pennsylvania. Working from these experiences, Westinghouse soon sold power reactors to several utilities, including a consortium of New England companies organized as Yankee Atomic Electric Company. The consortium's first plant was at Rowe, Massachusetts, and it first began operating in 1960.

At the end of the century, Westinghouse had supplied 49 of the 104 operating power reactors in the United States, 14 more than its closest rival, General Electric.

Suggested Reading

George Mazuzan and J. Samuel Walker, *Controlling the Atom: The Beginnings of Nuclear Regulation, 1946–1962.* Berkeley: University of California Press, 1984.

West Valley, New York

West Valley was the site of the only reprocessing plant constructed in the United States. Its purpose was to refine the spent fuel from commercial power reactors. The plant was opened in 1966 but severe radioactive contamination of the plant required its closing in 1972. Attempts to repair the damage were unsuccessful. Technicians could only spend a few minutes in the radioactive environment even though wearing protective garments. As a consequence, it was not economically feasible to provide training in the work that needed to be done to a sufficient number of technicians to complete the repairs. Nuclear Fuel Services, Incorporated, operated the reprocessing plant.

When President Jimmy CARTER terminated plans for a BREEDER program in 1978, plans to utilize the reprocessing facilities at West Valley were suddenly made obsolete. The concept of reprocessing fuel to recover PLUTONIUM in the United States was abandoned.

Later, West Valley was selected as a commercial low-level waste disposal site, along with five other sites in the United States. The others were Sheffield, Illinois; Maxey Flats, Kentucky; Richland, Washington; Beatty, Nevada; and Barnwell, South Carolina. Low-level RADIOACTIVE WASTE included tools, garments, gloves, and other slightly contaminated equipment from nuclear industry or nuclear power plants.

At each of the sites, low-level radioactive waste was disposed of by digging a trench, depositing boxes and drums of waste, replacing the earth, compacting it, and then forming an earthen cap over the trench. Along with Sheffield and Maxey Flats, the West Valley trench system developed leaks and was closed.

Of the six sites, West Valley had the lowest volume of material stored, with about 2.72 million cubic feet. The Barnwell, South Carolina, site had over 23 million cubic feet of low-level waste, and the Richland Washington site had nearly 12 million cubic feet.

As at other sites, local residents objected to the designation of West Valley as a waste-repository system on NIMBY principles. The issue of West Valley as a possible repository became a rallying point for antinuclear and environmental activists in upstate New York in the 1980s.

Wiesner, Jerome (1915–1994)   *a physical scientist and science administrator who became influential in the area of nuclear policy during the administration of President John F. Kennedy*

Jerome Wiesner served as chairman of the President's Scientific Advisory Committee (PSAC) under Kennedy, and he was instrumental in arguing for the development of the LIMITED TEST BAN TREATY.

Wiesner was born in Detroit, Michigan, in 1915 and studied at the University of Michigan, where he earned a bachelor's and a master's degree before World War II. During the war he served on the staff of the Radiation Laboratory at the Massachusetts Institute of Technology (MIT). In 1945, he briefly worked at LOS ALAMOS on the electrical instrumentation to be used at OPERATION CROSSROADS. Following this work, he returned to teach at MIT. He earned his doctorate at the University of Michigan in 1950, and he remained on the staff of the Radiation Laboratory at MIT, serving as associate director (1949–1952) and director (1952–1961).

During the Eisenhower administration, Wiesner served on the PSAC, beginning in 1957, and he served as the staff director for the Geneva Conference of 1958. During the Kennedy administration he was selected as the president's special assistant for science and technology and chaired the PSAC, and he took a leave of absence from MIT to serve in these positions. As advisor, he helped convince the president that the Limited Test Ban Treaty should be signed and ratified. Wiesner helped establish the U.S. Arms Control and Disarmament Agency, and he argued against deployment of anti-ballistic missiles, a position taken in the 1972 Anti-Ballistic Missile Treaty. He was coauthor of *ABM: An Evaluation of the Decision to Deploy an Antiballistic Missile System.*

Following the death of Kennedy, Wiesner served briefly as science advisor to President Lyndon JOHNSON and then returned to MIT, where he held positions as dean of the School of Science and later as provost and president of MIT. He retired in 1980, although he continued to speak against the continuing arms race. He died of heart failure on October 21, 1994.

Wigner, Eugene Paul (1902–1995) *Hungarian-born American physicist who made crucial contributions to the development of the first nuclear reactors constructed as part of the Manhattan Project*

Eugene Wigner was born on November 17, 1902, in Budapest, HUNGARY. After earning a doctorate in chemical engineering in Berlin, he later joined the physics department at the University of Göttingen. In 1930, he moved to the United States and took a position at Princeton University.

During the 1930s he made a number of contributions to the understanding of the internal structure of the atom, particularly studying the binding energies that hold the atom together. Wigner earned a NOBEL PRIZE in 1936 for his contributions to the understanding of the symmetry of the atom. In 1939, he worked with Leo SZILARD and Edward TELLER in approaching Albert EINSTEIN, asking him to send a letter to Franklin ROOSEVELT urging him to develop an atomic weapon.

During World War II, Wigner worked at the Chicago Metallurgical Laboratory for the MANHATTAN ENGINEER DISTRICT. He worked on the design of the first reactors, heading a group that designed a water-cooled, graphite-moderated reactor, the design used for the PRODUCTION REACTORS constructed at HANFORD. He developed an understanding of the effect of neutrons on the lattice structure of graphite, leading to the

Eugene Wigner. Hungarian-born physicist Eugene Wigner worked at the Chicago Metallurgical Laboratory as part of the Manhattan Project and made contributions to reactor design and engineering principles. (Department of Energy)

expansion of the graphite. The expansion, in turn, could distort the reactor tubes and create mechanical difficulties in operation of the reactor. The graphite expansion came to be known as the "Wigner Effect," and the remedy for the problems it caused graphite-moderated reactors came to be called "Wigner Heating." After the war, he took the position of director of research and development at the Clinton Laboratories at Oak Ridge in 1946, and he remained director of the OAK RIDGE NATIONAL LABORATORY until 1955.

Wigner returned to Princeton, where he taught until 1971. He died in 1995.

See also MANHATTAN ENGINEER DISTRICT; PRODUCTION REACTORS; WIGNER EFFECT.

Suggested Reading

Eugene Wigner, *Symmetries and Reflections.* Indianapolis: Indiana University Press, 1967.

Wigner Effect

The bombardment of crystalline solids with nuclear radiation produces atomic dislocations. The dislocated atoms have higher energies than those in their normal lattice positions. The dislocations lead to energy storage in the crystal. This is the Wigner Effect. For graphite at 30 degrees exposed to neutron bombardment at a fluence of 2×10^{21} nfcm, the Wigner Effect can reach a value as high as 2,000 kJ/kg. This stored energy is released as the dislocated carbon atoms return to their normal lattice positions. If the release is too rapid, the graphite can be heated to temperatures above its ignition point. A fire at WINDSCALE Pile No. 1, a British graphite-moderated reactor, in early October of 1957 has been attributed to Wigner heating. Eugene WIGNER was a Hungarian-American who helped design the plutonium PRODUCTION REACTORS at HANFORD.

Wilson, Caroll (1910–1983)   *American science administrator who served as the first general manager of the U.S. Atomic Energy Commission from January 1, 1947 until 1950*

Caroll Wilson managed the affairs of the U.S. nuclear establishment, overseeing the transition from the Manhattan Project to the ATOMIC ENERGY COMMISSION (AEC). Wilson was born on September 21, 1910, in Rochester, New York, and received a B.S. degree from Massachusetts Institute of Technology (MIT) in 1932. After graduation, he remained at the institute, assisting President Karl T. COMPTON. In 1936, Wilson became assistant to Vannevar BUSH, at that time vice president and dean of engineering at MIT.

When Bush organized the National Defense Research Committee in 1940, Wilson joined the staff, and then followed Bush when he became director of the OFFICE OF SCIENTIFIC RESEARCH AND DEVELOPMENT. Following the war, Wilson assisted David LILIENTHAL in preparing the Lilienthal-Acheson Report calling for international control of atomic development.

When the Atomic Energy Commission was formed in 1946, Wilson served as consultant to the commission. When the commission took over the facilities built by the MANHATTAN ENGINEER DISTRICT in January 1947, Wilson was appointed general manager. His appointment, like those of Lilienthal and the commissioners, was controversial, and he was not confirmed by Congress until April 1947. The duties taken on by Wilson included the direct administration of the three secret cities built by the Manhattan District: LOS ALAMOS, HANFORD, and OAK RIDGE. Wilson worked on labor relations, revising the wartime contracts with the operators of the production facilities, developing reactors for both experimentation and for submarine propulsion and dealing with many crises in the first years of the AEC's operation.

When Wilson learned of the plans of Brien MCMAHON to replace Lilienthal with Gordon DEAN and to insist on more centralized management, Wilson decided to resign from the post of general manager, feeling that he lacked confidence in the new chairman of the AEC. His successor was Marion Boyer, who served from 1950 to 1953.

Suggested Reading

Richard G. Hewlett and Francis Duncan, *Atomic Shield* (Vol. 2 of *A History of the United States Atomic Energy Commission.* Washington, D.C.: Atomic Energy Commission, 1972.

Windscale

On October 7–10, 1957, the most serious nuclear accident up to that time occurred at the Windscale facility near Sellafield, in Cumbria, UNITED KINGDOM. Windscale had been built by Britain to continue its nuclear research program in 1946, after the wartime cooperation between the United States and Britain in the MANHATTAN ENGINEER DISTRICT came to an end.

At Sellafield, the British built two plutonium PRODUCTION REACTORS, naming the facility Windscale. The reactors were simple atomic piles, holding natural URANIUM fuel in a graphite moderator, along the lines of the CHICAGO PILE-1 (CP-1) experimental reactor at Chicago first built in 1942 by Enrico FERMI. Like CP-1, the Windscale reactors were air cooled.

Like the reactors at HANFORD, the Windscale reactors developed a change in the carbon positions in the graphite molecules as they stored energy. To release this so-called WIGNER EFFECT, the method developed was to allow the reactor to run at a hotter temperature briefly to release the energy spontaneously and to restore the graphite shape. This was done by shutting off the fans that provided the cooling air.

However, as the procedure for a Wigner energy release was started on October 7, 1957, in Pile No. 1, something went wrong. After initial heating did not appear to release all the energy, the reactors were put through a second heating cycle. However, when the fans were turned on, the temperature continued to rise. It was soon discovered that the temperature had risen so high that the graphite had ignited and that the fans only provided more oxygen to feed the fire. By October 10, radioactive meters registered over 10 times the normal activity. Finally, on October 11, the decision was taken to flood the reactor with water to douse the fire.

Part of the scandal surrounding the Windscale fire was the degree to which authorities decided to withhold information from the public about the accident. While a program was initiated to dispose of milk from dairies within an area of several hundred square miles because of contamination from Iodine 131, resulting in disposal of some two million liters of milk, the British government was not forthcoming about the other hazards that resulted from the accident.

In Pile No. 1, some 22 tons of melted and burned fuel could not be recovered. The pile was shut down and entombed in concrete. Soon thereafter, Pile No. 2 was also shut down. Estimates of the amount of RADIOACTIVITY released to the general public and the possible effect of the radiation on production of cancer and birth defects remained controversial. A full report on the episode was not released until 1982. That report suggested that as many as 260 cases of cancer, with about 13 fatal cases, could have resulted from the exposures. Critics of the report noted that it overlooked an important possible cause of further exposure, the release of radioactive POLONIUM. After consideration, the estimates of fatalities were increased to reflect contamination from this source.

Further controversy surrounded earlier releases of Strontium-90 from Windscale in 1957, as well as the issue of emission of radioactive waste into the water and air from Windscale over the period 1956 to 1960. Although the Windscale accident of October 1957 received far less publicity than later accidents at THREE MILE ISLAND in 1979 and CHERNOBYL in 1986, public reaction in Britain to this accident at the country's first production reactor facility became a key ingredient in the antinuclear movement in the United Kingdom.

Following 1957, both Pile 1 and 2 were closed, kept in a state of safe care and maintenance, and monitored to ensure that no radioactivity escaped. Decommissioning involved removal of the fuel in 1983, removal of the top of the pressure vessel in 1990–1992, and installation of a remote dismantling machine. Sealing the piles so that all air and water ducts were closed off was completed in 1999, bringing Phase I of the decommissioning project to a close. Contracts for a second phase of decommissioning, which involved the remote dismantling of the Pile 1 core, were awarded in 1997. The remote dismantling and removal of the radioactive waste is set to continue until 2007 at a cost of 54 million pounds.

Winfrith

Winfrith was a site in Dorset, in the United Kingdom, chosen in the mid-1950s by the British Atomic Energy Authority for the testing and development of different reactor types. The major facility there was the Steam Generating Heavy Water Reactor, closed in 1991. Other reactors included Dragon, Zebra, Nestor, and Dimple. Following the decline in nuclear power projects, the site was scheduled for decommissioning as a nuclear site, with the grounds set aside for industrial, scientific, computer software, and other business usages. The British Defence Evaluation and Research Agency located several of its facilities at Winfrith in the 1990s.

Xenon Poisoning

^{135}Xe is one of the neutron-absorbing fission products formed in the routine operation of a nuclear reactor. ^{235}Xe can reduce the multiplication factor, k. The half-life of ^{135}Xe is 9.1 hours, and its thermal neutron capture cross section is 2.6 X 10^6 barns, the largest thermal neutron capture CROSS SECTION known. In the routine operation of the nuclear reactor, the concentration of ^{135}Xe reaches a steady state that depends upon the rate of its formation by decay of ^{135}Xe, and the rate of its removal by (n, γ) reactions. The concentration of ^{135}Xe increases after shutdown of the reactor because it continues to be formed by decay of its parent, 6.6 h^{135}I, but it is no longer removed by (n, γ) reac-

tions. The concentration of ^{135}Xe reaches a maximum about 10 hours after shutdown and can reduce the multiplication factor by as much as 0.3 at this time. Few if any reactors have sufficient excess reactivity to overcome such a large reduction in the multiplication factor. Hence, criticality cannot be achieved until the sufficient time passes for the decay of ^{135}Xe.

Xenon poisoning with ^{135}Xe caused the delay in the first operation of the first PRODUCTION REACTOR at HANFORD. Enrico FERMI and the technicians at the site determined the cause of the problem and loaded extra fuel rods to achieve the excess reactivity to "push through" the Xenon poisoning.

Yalta Conference

Over the week of February 4–11, 1945, President Franklin D. ROOSEVELT, Prime Minister Winston Churchill, and Premier Joseph STALIN met in the Soviet Black Sea resort city of Yalta in the second of the "Big Three" conferences.

At the conference, the future of Poland, Germany, and Eastern Europe was discussed. Stalin agreed to allow the participation in the eventual government to be set up under Soviet occupation in Poland of members of a pro-Western Polish government in exile that had been established in London. Although such membership was granted, the eventual dismissal of those members from the government was seen in Britain and the United States as a betrayal of a commitment made at Yalta.

The three leaders agreed that the Soviets would enter into the war against Japan two to three months after the surrender of Germany. The Soviets reaffirmed this commitment at the POTSDAM conference held in July 1945. This schedule would allow time for the transport of troops and resources from Europe to the Soviet-Manchurian border. The Yalta timetable for Soviet participation against Japan three months after the German surrender probably contributed to TRUMAN'S DECISION to use the nuclear weapon in early

Yalta Conference. During World War II, the leaders of Great Britain, the United States, and the Soviet Union held several meetings to work out postwar plans. Here Winston Churchill, Franklin Roosevelt, and Joseph Stalin pose for photographers at their meeting at Yalta in February 1945. (National Archives and Records Administration)

August 1945. Germany surrendered on May 8, 1945, and the Soviet Union entered the war precisely three months after the German capitulation. The Soviets entered into the war against the Japanese on August 8, 1945, two days after the atomic bombing of HIROSHIMA.

See also ARMS CONTROL.

Yankee Class Submarine

The Yankee class nuclear submarine was the second class of ballistic missile submarines in the Soviet navy. Similar to the United States Polaris class, the Yankee class could launch its missiles while submerged. The invention of the Yankee moved the West and the Soviet Union toward a more equal ability to deliver a nuclear missile strike with no warning before launch.

Yankee was under design since the early 1950s and was first launched in 1966. The Yankee class followed the Hotel class, the first ballistic missile submarine in the world. Improvements over the Hotel class included a longer, wider, and faster ship. The missiles in Yankee were also improved. SS-N-6, the missile carried by the first Yankees, was the first liquid-fueled SUBMARINE-LAUNCHED BALLISTIC MISSILE (SLBM) and the first to be launched from underwater in the Soviet navy.

Later modifications in the Yankee class resulted in the Yankee II. The main modification in the Yankee II was the upgrade of its missiles to the SS-N-17. Upgrading the missile systems reduced Yankee's complement of missiles from 16 to 12. The SS-N-17 was the Soviet's first solid-fueled SLBM and was also the first to use a "Post-Boost Vehicle." This innovation aimed the SS-N-17's reentry vehicle, giving the missile greater accuracy. The SS-N-17 was deployed only in the Yankee II.

A third conversion of the Yankee class submarine was the Yankee Notch. The Yankee Notch was a guided missile nuclear submarine and was armed with the SS-N-21. The SS-N-21 was the Soviet version of the American *Tomahawk* cruise missile and could be launched through the torpedo tubes and launchers. Two units were converted to fire the SS-N-21, and accounted for the last modifications to the Yankee class.

The Yankee class submarine illustrates the speed at which technology changed. Growing from the inception of the underwater launching ballistic missiles to the first reentry vehicle missile, the Yankees represented almost the complete history of the nuclear ballistic missile. The modifications to the Yankee Notch displayed the versatility of submarines as a launch platform for all types of missiles through the use of CRUISE MISSILES launched from torpedo tubes to create the capability for many submarines to become stand-off nuclear missile launching platforms.

Looking at the Yankees as an attack group, one might use Yankee Notch as a guard ship allowing the others to maneuver into strategic positions to launch missiles.

A problem with the design of the Yankee class was that they were very noisy. A profile of the ship revealed the source of noise. Russian designers, to make room for missiles, designed the Yankee with a hunchback or hump on the deck. This design, along with the general bulky size, made lots of waterflow noise as the submarine moved, sounds that Western sonar could easily detect. Although a drastically disproportionate number of Yankees were built, the West had the advantage because the Yankee was widely thought of as the easiest ship to detect.

A brief history of the Yankee shows that, although the Soviet Union produced a large number of them, very few were ever on active duty patrolling in the Pacific or Atlantic Oceans. Their numbers were a concern for the U. S. Strategic Air Command on the theory that the bases of the B-2 bombers were the most likely targets for the Yankees.

The nuclear-missile launching submarines were added to the list of limited ships in the SALT treaty, although the treaty numbers were very high. SALT was probably the reason for the conversion of the Yankee Notch, since conversion to guided or cruise missile platforms was one of the acceptable outlets for either country to continue to make use of a former ballistic missile launching platform under the treaty. As later submarines were developed, the Yankee became a front-line weapon on the high seas. It took credit for the most ships on patrol in the Atlantic. In the event of a major conflict with the United States, only the older ships would be heavily lost, reserving the newer more powerful ships, the DELTA and TYPHOON classes, for a response after the initial exchange.

The Yankee class comprised an important part of the Soviet submarine fleet. It was the first modern ballistic missile design from which the more modern Delta was based, and it absorbed the brunt of patrol duty. Despite the design flaws and the age of the ships, Yankee formed a crucial part of the Soviet nuclear deterrent capability.

Suggested Reading

Jan Breemer, *Soviet Submarines Design Development and Tactics.* London: Janes Information Group, 1989.

Yellowcake

Yellowcake, impure ammonium diuranate, $(NH_4)_2U_2O_7$, is an intermediate material in the refining of URANIUM. It contains about 80% uranium oxide, or 65% to 70% uranium. Uranium ore typically contains only about 1/10 of 1% of uranium oxide. Yellowcake is heated to produce orange oxide, UO_3, which is another intermediate in the refining process.

To achieve enrichment to increase the ratio of the rare ^{235}U to the more plentiful ^{238}U, the yellowcake is converted to uranium hexafluoride gas. When preparing natural, unenriched uranium fuel for reactors, yellowcake is processed into purified uranium dioxide, UO_2.

See also NUCLEAR FUEL CYCLE.

Yeltsin, Boris (1931–) *the first democratically elected president of Russia, from 1991 to 2000, although he remained in power by manipulation of constitutional rules*

Boris Yeltsin's administration saw the end of the Soviet Union, the takeover of the former Soviet Union's nuclear arsenal by RUSSIA, and the signing of the START II treaty with the United States. In a period of political and economic readjustment, the former Soviet nuclear navy and weapons production complex fell into disrepair.

Yeltsin was born on February 1, 1931, in Butka in the Sverdlovsk region of Russia. When he was three, his father was imprisoned in a labor camp for anti-Soviet agitation. Yeltsin graduated from the Ural Polytechnic Institute in 1955 with a major in construction. On graduation, he worked in construction and engineering and headed up a large plant that developed housing. In 1961, he joined the Communist Party of the Soviet Union (CPSU).

Beginning in 1969, he changed his career, working in the Communist Party administrative structure of the Sverdlovsk region. In 1985, he moved to Moscow, where he served on the Central Committee of the CPSU. By 1987, he had emerged as a reformer within the party, advocating a faster pace of change. Because of his outspoken remarks, he was soon removed from his positions in the Moscow City Committee and the Politburo.

In 1989, he was elected to the Congress of People's Deputies of the Soviet Union from Moscow in a democratic and open multicandidate election. In the congress, he emerged as a leader of a group calling for expansion of human rights, democratic reforms, and reduced expenditures on the Soviet space program.

In May 1990, he was elected speaker of the Supreme Soviet of Russia and had emerged as the leading pro-reform critic of Mikhail GORBACHEV and an advocate of the transfer of power from the Soviet Union to the separate republics. On June 12, 1990, the Russian congress declared its independence from the Soviet Union. A year later, Yeltsin was elected president of Russia in the first open election for that post.

On August 18, 1991, an attempted coup, led by advocates for the preservation of the Soviet Union and those opposed to liberalizing reforms, resulted in the detention of Gorbachev in the Crimea. Yeltsin dramatically rallied unarmed citizens and several units of the Soviet military to resist the coup. Gorbachev was restored to his position. Over the next few months, agreements were reached to dissolve the Soviet Union, and on December 24, 1991, Russia took over the seat of the Soviet Union in the United Nations. On December 25, 1991, the Soviet Union was dissolved.

Yeltsin as president of Russia now emerged as a major world leader. His administration over the next eight years was characterized by one crisis after another. He survived an attempt to impeach him in the Congress of People's Deputies in March 1993. In October 1993, an attempted takeover by members of parliament led to the shelling of the parliament building and the death of over 100 people. Although Yeltsin was reelected in December 1993, antireform groups controlled parliament and granted amnesty to those participating in the coup attempts of 1991 and October 1993.

In December 1994, Yeltsin sent troops to Chechnya, a republic within the Russian Federation that had declared its independence, leading to thousands of casualties and hundreds of thousands of refugees.

Yeltsin suffered from severe health problems and frequently conducted government business from a hospital or from his bed at home. Accusations of bribery, corruption, secret financing of Yeltsin's reelection campaign, and outright theft of government funds continued to mar his administration. He voted for his own reelection in July 1996 from a sanitarium.

Meanwhile the Russian government took over the nuclear weapons and nuclear weapons complex of the Soviet Union and continued the process of arms reduction begun under START I. President Yeltsin met with President George BUSH of the United States and signed START II in January 1993, calling for arms reductions to be completed within a decade. Both nations began to implement planned reductions, even though neither side immediately ratified the treaty. Partly because Yeltsin had lost the confidence of a large section of his parliament, the treaty was voted down when he submitted it for ratification in June 1995.

In March 1997, Yeltsin and William CLINTON met in Helsinki, Finland, and reached several agreements. At that time, they agreed to an extension of the terms of START II, formally signed in September by Secretary of State Madeline Albright and Foreign Minister Yevgeny Primakov. Yeltsin again submitted the treaty to his parliament in April 1998. However, with the U.S. action against Iraq in December 1998, the Russian parliament (Duma) once again postponed action on START II, finally ratifying in April 2000.

The Russian government claimed it could not finance weapons security and weapons destruction called for under START I and START II. Under the COOPERATIVE THREAT REDUCTION plan, the United States provided funding and experts to assist in carrying out the weapons cutbacks.

Due to his failing health, Yeltsin resigned his office on January 3, 2000. Vladimir Putin took the office of president, later confirmed by election.

Yield

Yield is a measure of the total energy released in the detonation of a nuclear weapon in terms of the energy released in the detonation of trinitrotoluene (TNT), a chemical high explosive. Yield is expressed in kilotons or in megatons of TNT equivalent. The detonation of one ton of TNT releases approximately 4×10^9 joules.

Yucca Mountain

Yucca Mountain is located in southern Nevada, about 80 miles northwest of Las Vegas, adjacent to the NEVADA TEST SITE. The area is extremely dry, with nearly all of the light rainfall evaporating rather than sinking into the water table. This feature made the site particularly attractive as a possible repository for nuclear waste.

The original plans called for placing the repository underground about 225 meters above the water table and 350 meters below the ground surface. Plans called for the repository to take about 70,000 tons of spent fuel from reactors, including both power reactors and production reactors in the United States. This would be sufficient to take most of the waste-depleted fuel that would be produced by the year 2030.

Before the site can be started, further work is required to determine the flow of air and water, if any, through the ground surrounding the proposed site, and the drafting of a design that allows the handling of the heat generated by the decaying nuclear fuel.

The site has been surrounded by intense controversy and interagency issues. Although plans call for opening the site in 2010, observers believe that legal delays may prevent it. In particular, the state government of Nevada has opposed the site and may continue to do so.

See also NUCLEAR FUEL CYCLE; NUCLEAR WASTE POLICY ACT.

Suggested Reading

David Bodansky, *Nuclear Energy: Principles, Practices, and Prospects.* Woodbury, N.Y.: American Institute of Physics, 1996.

Zangger Committee

After the NON-PROLIFERATION TREATY (NPT) was signed in 1970, those countries that had developed advanced nuclear technology and exported it to developing nations sought means to prevent the diversion of nuclear technology from commercial uses to weapons uses. As various control schemes were considered, the nuclear technology–supplying countries entered into consultation to find a means that would guarantee that recipient countries accepted inspection by the INTERNATIONAL ATOMIC ENERGY AGENCY (IAEA).

In 1971, countries engaged in the export of nuclear technology, not including France, set up an expert committee chaired by Claude Zangger, a Swiss scientist. In 1974, committee developed, and the IAEA endorsed, a so-called trigger list. This was a list of hardware with nuclear applications, whose export would trigger the requirements of IAEA safeguards on the export.

Nuclear-exporting countries notified the IAEA that they intended to require IAEA safeguards on identical lists of technologies, the Zangger list. By 1997, the Zangger Committee included 33 countries.

The detonation of a nuclear device by India in 1974, the rising price of oil that increased underdevel-oped countries' interest in nuclear power, and the increasing interest in France and West Germany in exporting nuclear technology led the United States to seek a larger and more effective set of controls on nuclear exports. In 1975, the United States convened a meeting of nuclear-exporting countries that then used the basis of the Zangger trigger list to create a larger list of specific technology items. The new group included France and, after initial meetings, Belgium, Czechoslovakia, the German Democratic Republic, Italy, the Netherlands, Poland, SWEDEN, and Switzerland, in addition to the original group comprising the United States, U.S.S.R., Great Britain, Canada, France, JAPAN, and the Federal Republic of Germany. The group was called the Nuclear Suppliers Group (NSG), the London Suppliers' Group, and sometimes in the press, the London Club. The Nuclear Suppliers Group developed their own list of technologies to be safeguarded, including not only hardware but also engineering, design, and industrial process information. Like the Zangger Committee, the Nuclear Suppliers Group expanded, including 34 members by 1997.

The national memberships in the two control groups became nearly identical. CHINA belonged to the Zangger Committee but not the NSG, and BRAZIL and

New Zealand belonged to the NSG but not the Zangger Committee.

While the two groups appeared to be pursuing the same goal, they operated slightly differently. The Zangger Committee members continued to secure agreements from recipient countries to accept inspection from the IAEA, whereas the NSG enforced its restrictions by direct agreement. The Zangger Committee generated a list of technologies that the member countries pledged to export only after securing an agreement from the receiving country to accept IAEA safeguards and inspections. The NSG went further, not only in issuing an expanded list of technologies but also in securing specific pledges from recipient states designed to prevent theft and sabotage and prevent the conversion of the technology to weapons purposes. Further, under the NSG, the recipient countries agreed not to re-export technology except under similar restraints.

Suggested Reading

Rodney W. Jones et al., *Tracking Nuclear Proliferation: A Guide in Maps and Charts, 1998.* Washington, D.C. Carnegie Endowment for International Peace, 1998.

Zel'dovich, Yakov Borisovich (1914–1987)

Soviet physicist who was an important contributor to the development of the Soviet hydrogen bomb

Y. B. Zel'dovich was born in 1914 in Minsk, the son of a lawyer. He began his studies at the Institute for Chemical Physics in 1931. In 1939, he worked with Yuli Borisovich Khariton in describing the conditions under which nuclear CHAIN REACTIONS would take place, publishing two papers on the subject. They concluded that a chain reaction could not take place in ^{238}U. They developed calculations regarding the moderating effect of water and HEAVY WATER and considered the effect that enriching ^{238}U with ^{235}U would have on sustaining a chain reaction. Within a few years, the theoretical concepts they had worked out would form the basis for both reactors and nuclear bombs.

Zel'dovich was the first director of the theoretical department at ARZAMAS-16, in 1946, writing a paper on the topic of releasing nuclear energy from the light elements, focusing on the possibility of using DEUTERIUM. Along with other Soviet scientists, Zel'dovich concluded that a hydrogen fusion reaction could be initiated with an atomic bomb. At Arzamas-16, he headed

a group investigating the possibility of a hydrogen bomb. He earned the Hero of Socialist Labor award three times. He died in 1987.

See also SAKHAROV, ANDREY.

Zero Option

The concept that the United States and the Soviet Union would both work toward reducing their total nuclear weapons deployed to zero was introduced in May 1982 by President Ronald REAGAN. The idea had been developed by Richard PERLE, the assistant secretary of defense for international security, based on an idea that had been discussed in Germany and elsewhere in Europe, the concept of *Null Lösung,* or "zero solution." New Soviet SS-20 missiles were quite capable of destroying all of NATO military forces in one blow, and Perle argued for elimination of all such missiles to be matched by the elimination of similar intermediate nuclear force missiles by the West. Soon dubbed the "zero option," the position was rejected by the Soviet Union. Many observers believed that Reagan had proposed the reduction to zero only as a bluff or as a bargaining position.

However, the concept of the zero option was revived at the 1986 meeting in REYKJAVIK, Iceland, between Reagan and Mikhail GORBACHEV, where both leaders endorsed the concept of a "global zero-zero option" that would lead to elimination of all nuclear weapons in both the United States and the U.S.S.R.

Although global zero-zero was not implemented, the zero option concept was applied to intermediate nuclear forces in the INF treaty signed on December 8, 1987, and its logic lay behind the deep cuts initiated in Strategic Arms Reduction Treaty I (START I) and under START II. Incorporated in the INTERMEDIATE NUCLEAR FORCES (INF) treaty was a "double zero" proposal to reduce not only INF missiles, but also short-range missiles. The official title of the INF treaty was "Treaty on Intermediate and Shorter Range Nuclear Forces."

See also ARMS CONTROL.

Zinn, Walter (1906–2000)   *Canadian-born American physicist who served as director of the Argonne National Laboratory from 1946 to 1956*

After initial work with Leo SZILARD and Enrico FERMI under the MANHATTAN ENGINEER DISTRICT (MED) working on atomic piles, Walter Zinn established a reputation in reactor engineering. He had assisted Fermi in the construction of CHICAGO PILE No. 1.

Zinn was born in Canada in 1906 and studied mathematics at Queens University in Kingston, Ontario, earning his Ph.D. in physics from Columbia in 1934. ARGONNE NATIONAL LABORATORY, established in 1946, incorporated the work of the Chicago Metallurgical Laboratory of the University of CHICAGO, and Zinn oversaw the transition from military leadership under the MED to new arrangements under the ATOMIC ENERGY COMMISSION (AEC). In 1947, the AEC decided to make Argonne the national center for reactor development, and Zinn led the laboratory as it expanded into this area. However, he grew disappointed with the AEC when it established a separate organization to develop a major linear accelerator and when training of nuclear engineers was shifted from Argonne to Pennsylvania State University and the University of North Carolina. On his retirement in 1956, Zinn established his own nuclear engineering consulting company.

Suggested Reading

Jack Holl, *Argonne National Laboratory.* Urbana: University of Illinois Press, 1997.

Zircalloy

Zircalloy is a corrosion-resistant alloy of zirconium used for cladding nuclear fuel. The most commonly used Zircalloy is Zircalloy-2 that contains 1.5% tin and 0.3% chromium, nickel, and iron. The neutron capture CROSS SECTION of this alloy is 0.18 barns (b), lower than that for aluminum (0.23 b) and stainless steel (3 b).

CHRONOLOGY

September 1905 Albert Einstein publishes his special theory of relativity, which provides an understanding of the relationship of matter and energy. His work stimulates the advance of modern nuclear physics.

December 17, 1928 Leo Szilard files for a German patent on the concept of a linear accelerator.

February 27, 1932 James Chadwick identifies the neutron in an article in *Nature*.

March 12, 1934 Leo Szilard files for a British patent on the concept of a reactor based on a nuclear chain reaction. The idea had come to him on a London street corner in October 1933.

December 21, 1938 Otto Hahn and Fritz Strassman conclude work that shows the splitting of uranium atoms. The news is circulated by letter to other physicists over the next few weeks.

December 24, 1938 Lise Meitner and Otto Frisch describe the process of nuclear fission that had occurred in Hahn and Strassman's experiment.

March 17, 1939 Ross Gunn of the Naval Research Laboratory reviews with Enrico Fermi the work of Otto Hahn and Fritz Strassman, considering the possibility of atomic energy for submarine propulsion.

September 1, 1939 After concluding a non-aggression pact with the Soviet Union on August 23, Germany invades Poland, launching World War II.

October 1, 1939 Letter drafted by Albert Einstein and Leo Szilard on August 2, 1939, urging a research project to develop a weapon based on nuclear energy is delivered to President Franklin D. Roosevelt.

June 1940 Advisory Committee on Uranium is formed in the United States to study the possibility of a nuclear weapon. The Advisory Committee is part of the National Defense Research Committee (NDRC).

September 19, 1941 Werner Heisenberg and Niels Bohr meet in Copenhagen, Denmark, after an academic lecture. Heisenberg later claims he sought to discourage nuclear weapons work, although Bohr remembers the meeting differently.

December 7, 1941 The Japanese navy attacks the U.S. naval base at Pearl Harbor, Hawaii, bringing the United States into World War II.

December 18, 1941 NRDC work on nuclear weapons is transferred to Office of Scientific Research and Development (OSRD) as project S-1.

June 17, 1942 The U.S. Army Corps of Engineers takes over the construction phase of OSRD work on the nuclear weapon, organized under the Manhattan Engineer District (MED).

September 7, 1942 General Leslie Groves takes formal command of the MED and full charge of the nuclear weapon design and development project.

December 2, 1942 Beneath an abandoned football stadium at the University of Chicago, Enrico Fermi presides as the first nuclear reactor, Chicago-Pile 1, based on Szilard's concepts, goes critical. Some historians later regard this event as the birth of the "Atomic Age."

February 16, 1943 A joint British-Norwegian commando team damages the heavy-water production facility of Norsk Hydro, at Vemork, Norway. Later U.S. bombing raid on November 16, 1943, finally puts the plant out of service.

September 26, 1944 At the Hanford reservation in Washington State, the first production reactor to produce plutonium goes critical.

May 8, 1945 Following the defeat of German forces in Berlin and the suicide of Adolf Hitler, German Admiral Karl Dönitz signs unconditional surrender, ending World War II in Europe.

July 16, 1945 Manhattan Engineer District scientists detonate the world's first nuclear explosion, setting off the device called Fat Man at the Trinity test, held at Alamogordo, New Mexico.

July 17, 1945 U.S. president Harry Truman meets Soviet premier Joseph Stalin at Potsdam, Germany, to discuss postwar planning. Truman hints at the development of the U.S. nuclear weapon. Conference adjourns August 2.

August 6, 1945 U.S. aircraft *Enola Gay* drops uranium-pit atomic bomb over Hiroshima, Japan, killing an estimated 180,000 people.

August 6, 1945	Werner Heisenberg and other German scientists interned at Farm Hall in Britain discuss the news of an atomic bomb, revealing in secretly taped discussions their disbelief and shock.
August 9, 1945	U.S. aircraft *Bock's Car* drops plutonium-pit atomic bomb over Nagasaki, Japan, killing an estimated 70,000 people. (August 8 in the United States.)
August 14, 1945	Japanese agree to surrender.
August 20, 1945	Soviet Premier Joseph Stalin puts secret-police chief Lavrenty Beria in charge of the Soviet Union's nuclear weapon project to accelerate development in light of Hiroshima and Nagasaki.
August 21, 1945	Los Alamos researcher Harry Daghlian suffers fatal exposure to radiation while working with plutonium hemispheres.
September 2, 1945	The Japanese sign formal terms of surrender, ending World War II.
December 20, 1945	The Atomic Energy Act, sponsored by Brien McMahon, is signed into law, establishing the Atomic Energy Commission (AEC) and transferring MED facilities to the new civilian agency.
May 21, 1946	Louis Slotin suffers fatal exposure to radiation while working with the same plutonium hemispheres that had earlier killed Harry Daghlian.
June 14, 1946	Bernard Baruch presents the U.S. plan for international control of atomic weapons to the United Nations. His "Baruch Plan" supersedes an earlier draft plan by David Lilienthal and Dean Acheson.
July 24, 1946	In Operation Crossroads, the United States detonates a nuclear device underwater, destroying or damaging more than 80 ships of a target fleet in Bikini Atoll.
July 23,1948	Soviet authorities blockade access to Berlin, leading to a U.S.-sponsored airlift of supplies. Truman orders nuclear-ready aircraft flown to Britain. Blockade is lifted May 9, 1949.
April 4, 1949	The North Atlantic Treaty Organization (NATO) is formed by a treaty that comes into force August 24, 1949.
June 17, 1949	Soviet-backed communist officials seize power in Czechoslovakia. The country has the only known deposits of uranium in Europe at Joachimstahl.
August 29, 1949	The Soviet Union sets off its first nuclear detonation, which is known as "Joe 1" in the United States. U.S. president Harry Truman delays public announcement sev-
	eral weeks to conceal U.S. detection methods.
January 24, 1950	Klaus Fuchs confesses to nuclear espionage for the Soviet Union while working in the MED and for the British at the Harwell Nuclear Establishment.
June 25, 1950	North Korean forces invade South Korea, launching the Korean War. The fact that the United States no longer has a monopoly on the nuclear weapon is widely regarded as providing encouragement to the pro-Soviet North Korean government.
July 17, 1950	Julius Rosenberg is arrested on charges of conspiracy to commit espionage in time of war; his wife, Ethel, is arrested August 11.
October 7, 1950	In the worst nuclear reactor accident until that time, the Windscale reactor in Great Britain releases radioactive debris over the countryside.
March 10, 1952	Great Britain detonates its first nuclear device at Monte Bello Island, Australia, becoming the third country to join "the nuclear club."
October 26, 1952	In the Ivy-Mike test, the United States tests a thermonuclear device on Enewetak atoll. The large structure required by the device makes it impractical as a deliverable weapon.
June 19, 1953	Julius and Ethel Rosenberg, convicted of espionage, are executed.
July 27, 1953	United Nations and North Korean representatives sign an armistice ending the Korean War at Panmunjom, Korea.
August 12, 1953	In a nuclear detonation called "Joe 4" in America, the Soviet Union claims to have tested a thermonuclear weapon; American officials call it a boosted fission device.
December 8, 1953	President Dwight Eisenhower delivers his "Atoms for Peace" speech to the United Nations, pledging U.S. support for international peaceful uses of nuclear energy.
January 21, 1954	The world's first nuclear-powered ship, the United States submarine *Nautilus*, is launched.
March 1, 1954	Americans test first thermonuclear weapon with a yield of 15 megatons in the Bravo shot of Operation Castle. Marshall Islanders on distant islands and Japanese fishermen aboard *Lucky Dragon* are exposed to nuclear fallout.
August 30, 1954	President Dwight Eisenhower signs the Atomic Energy Act of 1954, which paves the way for private development of nuclear power.

June 28, 1954	A special personnel board denies renewal of a security clearance for J. Robert Oppenheimer, resulting from charges of his past association with communists and his opposition to the development of the hydrogen bomb.
May 5, 1955	NATO admits the Federal Republic of Germany (West Germany) as a member of the alliance.
May 14, 1955	Soviets announce the conclusion of the Warsaw Treaty or East European Defense Treaty. The Warsaw Treaty Organization is known as the Warsaw Pact.
October 4, 1957	The Soviet Union launches *Sputnik*, the first artificial Earth-orbiting satellite.
October 7, 1957	The International Atomic Energy Agency is established in Vienna, Austria.
December 2, 1957	First reactor to deliver commercial power to the net in the United States goes critical at Shippingport, Pennsylvania.
January 1, 1958	EURATOM (European Atomic Energy Committee) is formally organized in the Treaty of Rome.
October 31, 1958	United States enters a voluntary moratorium on the testing of nuclear weapons in the atmosphere. Soviet Union joins in a similar self-imposed moratorium in December.
February 13, 1960	France explodes its first nuclear device, yielding 60–70 kilotons, in the Algerian Sahara, becoming the fourth nuclear-armed nation.
May 1, 1960	The Soviet Union shoots down an American U-2 reconnaissance aircraft and captures its pilot, Francis Gary Powers.
January 3, 1961	The Stationary Low-power Reactor (SL-1) operated by the AEC at its test station in Idaho goes out of control, killing three operators. It is the most serious accident at a government-owned reactor in the United States in the 20th century.
April 28, 1961	More than 2,000 anti–civil defense protestors in New York City effectively bring an end to public civil defense exercises in the United States.
September 10, 1961	The Soviets end their atmospheric testing moratorium with a weapons test series at Novaya Zemlya. The thermonuclear detonation on October 30, 1961, at an estimated 57 megatons, is the largest in the 20th century.
April 25, 1962	The United States responds to the Soviet testing series by beginning Operation Dominic, with more than 30 atmospheric tests.
April 10, 1963	U.S. nuclear-powered submarine *Thresher* is lost at sea.
October 4, 1963	The Enrico Fermi liquid-sodium cooled power reactor outside of Detroit, Michigan, overheats and has to be shut down.
October 7, 1963	President John F. Kennedy signs the Limited Test Ban Treaty under which the United States and the Soviet Union agree not to conduct nuclear tests in the atmosphere, underwater, or in outer space.
January 13, 1964	A B-52 bomber carrying thermonuclear weapons crashes near Cumberland, Maryland.
August 7, 1964	U.S. Congress passes the Gulf of Tonkin Resolution, escalating U.S. involvement in the Vietnam War.
October 15, 1964	China detonates its first nuclear weapon, becoming the world's fifth nuclear-armed state.
January 17, 1966	American B-52 bomber returning from a flight near the Soviet border collides with a KC-135 tanker during refueling over Palomares, Spain. On April 7, navy and defense department teams recover the fourth thermonuclear weapon from the sea.
June 23, 1967	U.S. President Lyndon Johnson meets with Soviet Premier Aleksey Kosygin at Glassboro, New Jersey, to discuss nuclear arms limitation including a restriction on anti-ballistic missiles.
January 21, 1968	American B-52 bomber carrying thermonuclear weapons crashes near Thule, Greenland.
May 21, 1968	Nuclear-powered submarine *Scorpion* is lost at sea.
January 21, 1969	Reactor at Lucens, Switzerland, suffers a core-damaging accident and is permanently shut down and sealed in a cavern.
March 5, 1970	The Non-Proliferation Treaty, signed July 1, 1968, comes into force.
July 23, 1971	U.S. District Court of Appeals rules in the Calvert Cliffs case that the provisions of the National Environmental Protection Act of 1969 apply to power reactors licensed under the AEC.
May 26, 1972	U.S. president Richard Nixon and Soviet premier Leonid Brezhnev sign two basic arms control agreements. SALT I limits the number of nuclear delivery systems; the Anti-Ballistic Missile Treaty bars deployment of more than two anti-ballistic missile systems by either the United States or the Soviet Union.

January 27, 1973	A four-party treaty is signed in Paris, bringing the Vietnam War to an end.
May 18, 1974	India conducts an underground detonation of a nuclear device that it announces is not a weapon but a peaceful nuclear device.
August 9, 1974	President Richard Nixon resigns, and Gerald Ford is sworn in as president.
January 15, 1975	Under the 1974 Energy Reorganization Act, the nuclear weapons functions of the AEC are taken over by the Energy Research and Development Agency; the Nuclear Regulatory Commission takes over the licensing and regulation of nuclear power plants.
April 30, 1975	North Vietnamese troops seize control of Saigon, and the South Vietnamese government surrenders.
November 23, 1975	U.S. president Gerald Ford meets with Soviet premier Leonid Brezhnev in Vladivostok, and the two agree to a basic outline for a SALT II treaty.
October 1, 1977	The Department of Energy replaces the Energy Research and Development Agency, taking over the U.S. nuclear weapons complex.
March 28, 1979	Unit Two of the Three Mile Island reactor complex south of Harrisburg, Pennsylvania, suffers a criticality and partial meltdown accident.
June 18, 1979	U.S. President Jimmy Carter and Soviet Premier Leonid Brezhnev sign SALT II treaty. However, Carter withdraws the treaty from Senate approval process after Soviet military intervention in Afghanistan in December.
December 12, 1979	NATO foreign and defense ministers announce the dual-track strategy that calls for emplacement of nuclear weapons in Europe while simultaneously negotiating for arms control with the Soviet Union.
June 8, 1981	Israeli aircraft bomb Osiraq reactor in Iraq.
March 23, 1983	U.S. president Ronald Reagan delivers the "Star Wars" speech, calling for a space-based missile defense system.
October 27, 1983	Meeting in Montebello, Canada, the Nuclear Planning Group of NATO agrees to continue the dual track strategy and reaffirms installation of Ground-Launched Guided Missiles and Pershing II missiles in Europe over the next two years.
July 11, 1985	French agents sink Greenpeace ship *Rainbow Warrior* in waters off New Zealand.
April 26, 1986	Unit Four of the Chernobyl reactor complex near Kiev, Ukraine, catches fire, beginning the worst peacetime nuclear disaster of the 20th century.
October 11, 1986	U.S. president Ronald Reagan meets with premier Mikhail Gorbachev at Reykjavík, Iceland, and agrees on frameworks for the both the START and INF agreements.
December 8, 1987	Premier Mikhail Gorbachev and President Ronald Reagan sign the INF (Intermediate-Range Nuclear Forces) treaty in Washington.
November 1989	The Berlin Wall, erected in 1961, comes down, a symbol of the ending of the cold war.
July 1, 1991	Warsaw Treaty Organization, formed in 1955, is dissolved.
July 31, 1991	U.S. president George H. W. Bush and Soviet premier Mikhail Gorbachev sign START I, setting limits on the nuclear stockpiles of the United States and U.S.S.R., and pledging to reduce the total number of weapons on each side.
February 23, 1991	Coalition troops launch ground attack to drive Iraqi forces from Kuwait in the four-day Persian Gulf War.
December 26, 1991	The Soviet Union officially dissolves, one day after the resignation of Mikhail Gorbachev.
January 3, 1993	U.S. president George H. W. Bush and president Boris Yeltsin of Russia sign START II treaty.
January 26, 1996	U.S. Senate ratifies START II treaty.
September 24, 1996	United States, Great Britain, France, China, and Russia and many non-nuclear armed nations sign the Comprehensive Test Ban Treaty, agreeing not to test nuclear weapons. Forty-four specific ratifications are required before treaty is to come into force.
May 1998	India detonates a series of nuclear devices on May 11 and May 13. Pakistan responds with a series of nuclear detonations on May 28 and May 30.
October 13, 1999	The U.S. Senate votes *not* to ratify the Comprehensive Test Ban Treaty.
April 14, 2000	Russian Duma ratifies the START II treaty.
June 30, 2000	After an earlier vote in April, Russia ratifies the Comprehensive Test Ban Treaty.

BIBLIOGRAPHY

Abelson, Philip H. ed. *Liquid Thermal Diffusion*. Washington, D.C.: Naval Research Laboratory, 1958.

Alperovitz, Gar. *Atomic Diplomacy: Hiroshima and Potsdam*. New York: Penguin, 1985.

———. *The Decision to Use the Atomic Bomb and the Architecture of an American Myth*. New York: Knopf, 1995.

Altschuler, B.L., et al. *Andrei Sakharov: Facets of a Life*. Gif-sur-Yvette, France: Editions Frontières, 1991.

Alvarez, Luis. *Alvarez: Adventures of a Physicist*. New York: Basic Books, 1987.

Amato, Ivan. *Pushing the Horizon: Seventy-Five Years of High Stakes Science and Technology at the Naval Research Laboratory*. Washington, D.C.: Government Printing Office, 1998.

Angelo, Joseph A., and David Buden. *Space Nuclear Power*. Malabar, Fla.: Orbit Press, 1985.

Anspaugh, Lynn R., et al. "The Global Impact of the Chernobyl Accident," *Science* 242 (1988): 1513–1519.

Ball, Howard. *Justice Downwind: America's Atomic Testing Program in the 1950s*. New York: Oxford, 1986.

Balogh, Brian. *Chain Reaction: Expert Debate and Public Participation in American Commercial Power, 1945–1975*. New York: Cambridge University Press, 1991.

Bedford, Henry F. *Seabrook Station: Citizen Politics and Nuclear Power*. Amherst, Mass.: University of Massachusetts Press, 1990.

Bentley, J. *The Thresher Disaster: The Most Tragic Dive in Submarine History*. New York: Doubleday, 1975.

van Bentham van den Bergh, Godfried. *The Nuclear Revolution and the End of the Cold War*. London: Macmillan, 1992.

Bernstein, Barton. *The Atomic Bomb: The Critical Issues*. Boston: Little, Brown, 1976.

Bernstein, Jeremy. *Hitler's Uranium Club*. New York: American Institute of Physics, 1996.

Bethe, Hans. *The Road from Los Alamos*. New York: American Institute of Physics, 1991.

Betts, Richard K., ed. *Cruise Missiles: Technology, Strategy, Politics*. Washington, D.C.: The Brookings Institution, 1981.

Bhatia, Shyam. *India's Nuclear Bomb*. Ghazibad, India: Vikas, 1979.

Blakeway, Denys, and Sue Lloyd-Roberts. *Fields of Thunder: Testing Britain's Bomb*. London: Allen and Unwin, 1985.

Blumberg, Stanley, and Louis Panos. *Edward Teller: Giant of the Golden Age of Physics*. New York: Scribners, 1990.

Bodansky, David. *Nuclear Energy: Principles, Practices, and Prospects*. Woodbury, N.Y.: American Institute of Physics, 1996.

Bottome, E. M. *The Missile Gap: A Study in the Formulation of Military and Political Policy*. Rutherford, N.J.: Fairleigh Dickinson University Press, 1971.

Boyer, Paul. *By the Bomb's Early Light: American Thought and Culture at the Dawn of the Atomic Age*. New York: Pantheon, 1986.

Breemer, Jan. *Soviet Submarines: Design, Development, and Tactics*. London: Janes Information Group, 1989.

Brinkley, Douglas. *Dean Acheson: The Cold War Years, 1953–1971*. New Haven: Yale University Press, 1992.

Caldwell, Dan. *The Dynamics of Domestic Politics and Arms Control: The SALT II Treaty Ratification Debate*. Columbia: University of South Carolina Press, 1991.

Cantelon, Philip, and Robert Williams. *Crisis Contained: The Department of Energy at Three Mile Island*. Carbondale: University of Southern Illinois Press, 1984.

Carle, Rémy, *L'électricité nucléaire*. Paris: Presses Universitaires de France, 1994.

Carlisle, Rodney. *Supplying the Nuclear Arsenal*. Baltimore: Johns Hopkins University Press, 1996.

———. "Probabilistic Risk Assessment: Engineering Success, Public Relations Failure," *Technology and Culture* (Fall 1997).

Cassidy, David. *Uncertainty: The Life and Science of Werner Heisenberg*. New York: Freeman, 1992.

Chant, Christopher. *Air Defense Systems and Weapons: World AAA and SAM Systems in the 1990s*. London: Brassey's Defence Publishers, 1989.

Chatfield, Charles, with the assistance of Robert Kleidman. *The American Peace Movement: Ideals and Activism*. New York: Twayne Publishers, 1992.

Chevalier, Haakon. *Oppenheimer, The Story of a Friendship*. New York: George Braziller, 1965.

Clark, Donald. *State of the Art: Uranium Mining, Milling and Refining Industry*. Corvallis, Ore.: Environmental Protection Agency, 1974.

Cochrane, Thomas B., Robert S. Norris, and Oleg A. Bukharin. *Making the Russian Bomb: From Stalin to Yeltsin*. Boulder, Colo.: Westview Press, 1995.

Coffey, Thomas. *Iron Eagle: The Turbulent Life of General Curtis LeMay*. New York: Crown Publishers, 1986.

Collins, John M. *U.S.–Soviet Military Balance, Concepts and Capabilities, 1960–1980*. New York: McGraw-Hill, 1981.

———. *U.S.–Soviet Military Balance, 1980–1985*. Washington, D.C.: Pergamon-Brassey's, 1985.

Committee on International Security and Arms Control, National Academy of Sciences. *Nuclear Arms Control: Background and Issues*. Washington, D.C.: National Academy Press, 1985.

Compton, Arthur Holly. *Atomic Quest: A Personal Narrative*. New York: Oxford University Press, 1956.

Crawford, Deborah. *Lise Meitner, Atomic Pioneer*. New York: Crown, 1969.

Dahlitz, Julie. *Nuclear Arms Control*. London: George Allen and Unwin, 1983.

Defense Atomic Support Agency. *Cleanup of Bikini Atoll*. Washington, D.C.: DASA, 1971.

Defense Nuclear Agency. *Palomares Summary Report: Field Command, Defense Nuclear Agency*. Technology and Analysis Directorate, Kirtland Air Force Base, New Mexico 87115.

Divine, Robert A. *Blowing on the Wind: The Nuclear Test Ban Debate, 1954–1960*. New York: Oxford, 1978.

———. *The Sputnik Challenge*. New York: Oxford University Press, 1993.

Dower, John W. *War without Mercy: Race and Power in the Pacific War*. New York: Pantheon, 1986.

Duderstadt, James J., and Chiroro Kikuchi. *Nuclear Power: Technology on Trial*. Ann Arbor: University of Michigan Press, 1979.

Duffy, Robert J. *Nuclear Politics in America: A History and Theory of Government Regulation*. Lawrence: University Press of Kansas, 1997.

Dulles, John Foster. "Policy for Security and Peace," *Foreign Affairs* 36 (April 1954).

Duncan, Francis. *Rickover and the Nuclear Navy: The Discipline of Technology*. Annapolis, Md.: U.S. Naval Institute Press, 1990.

Engler, Richard. *Atomic Power in Space: A History*. Washington, D.C.: Department of Energy, 1987.

Federal Reporter Series: 449 F.2d 1109 (1971) (case report, Calvert Cliffs).

Feis, Herbert. *The Atomic Bomb and the End of World War II*. Princeton, N.J.: Princeton University Press, 1966.

Fermi, Laura. *Atoms in the Family: My Life with Enrico Fermi*. Chicago: University of Chicago Press, 1954.

Feynman, Richard P. *"Surely You're Joking, Mr. Feynman": The Adventures of a Curious Character*. New York: Norton, 1985.

Fleming, Donald, and Bernard Bailyn, eds. *The Intellectual Migration: Europe and America, 1930–1960*, Cambridge, Mass.: Harvard University Press, 1969.

Ford, Daniel F. *The Cult of the Atom: The Secret Papers of the Atomic Energy Commission*. New York: Simon and Schuster, 1982.

Frank, Charles, ed. *Operation Epsilon: The Farm Hall Transcripts*. Bristol, Pa.: Institute of Physics, 1993.

Fuller, John G. *We Almost Lost Detroit*. New York: Crowell, 1975.

Furman, Necah. *Sandia National Laboratories: The Postwar Decade*. Albuquerque, N.Mex.: University of New Mexico Press, 1990.

Garrison, Dee. "Our Skirts Gave Them Courage: The Civil Defense Protest Movement in New York City, 1955–1961." In Joanne Meyerowitz, ed., *Not June Cleaver: Women and Gender in Postwar America, 1945–1960*. Philadelphia: Temple University Press, 1994.

Garthoff, Raymond. *Detente and Confrontation: American-Soviet Relations from Nixon to Reagan*. Washington, D.C.: Brookings Institution, 1994.

Gerber, Michele Stenhejm. *On the Home Front: The Cold War Legacy of the Hanford Nuclear Site*. Lincoln: University of Nebraska Press, 1992.

Glasstone, S., and P. Dolan. *The Effects of Nuclear Weapons*. Washington, D.C.: U.S. Government Printing Office, 1977.

Glynn, Patrick. *Closing Pandora's Box: Arms Races, Arms Control, and the History of the Cold War*. New York: Basic Books, 1992.

Goldschmidt, Bertrand. *Atomic Adventure*. New York: Macmillan, 1964.

Goldstein, Donald, Katherine Dillon, and J. M. Wenger. *Rain of Ruin*. Washington, D.C.: Brassey's, 1995.

Goodchild, Peter. *J. Robert Oppenheimer: Shatterer of Worlds*. Boston: Houghton Mifflin, 1981.

Gorbachev, Mikhail. *At the Summit*. New York: Richardson, Steirman and Black, 1988.

Gottemoeller, Rose. *Strategic Arms Control in the Post–Start Era*. London: Brassey's, 1992.

Goudsmit, Samuel. *Alsos*. New York: Henry Schuman, 1947.

Gowing, Margaret. *Britain and Atomic Energy, 1939–1945*. New York: St. Martin's Press, 1964.

———. *Independence and Deterrence: Britain and Atomic Energy, 1945–1952*. London: St. Martin's Press, 1974.

Graetzer, Hans G., and David L. Anderson. *The Discovery of Nuclear Fission*. New York: Van Nostrand Reinhold, 1971.

Grahlff, F. Lincoln. *Voices from Ground Zero*. Lanham, Md.: University Press of America, 1991.

Grant, James. *Bernard M. Baruch: The Adventures of a Wall Street Legend*. New York: Simon and Schuster, 1983.

Gregory, Shaun. *The Hidden Cost of Deterrence: Nuclear Weapons Accidents*. London: Brassey's, 1990.

Groves, Leslie. *Now It Can Be Told: The Story of the Manhattan Project*. New York: Harper and Row, 1962.

Hacker, Barton. *The Dragon's Tail: Radiation Safety in the Manhattan Project, 1942–1946*. Berkeley: University of California Press, 1987.

———. *Elements of Controversy: The Atomic Energy Commission and Radiation Safety in Nuclear Weapons Testing, 1947–1974*. Berkeley: University of California Press, 1994.

Hennancy, Ammon. *The Book of Ammon: The Autobiography of a Unique American Rebel*. Salt Lake City: Ammon Hennacy Publications, 1970.

Herken, Gregg. *The Winning Weapon: The Atomic Bomb in the Cold War, 1945–1950*. New York: Alfred Knopf, 1980.

Hewlett, Richard G., and Oscar E. Anderson. *The New World*, Vol. 1 of *A History of the United States Atomic Energy Commission*. Washington, D.C.: Atomic Energy Commission, 1962.

Hewlett, Richard G., and Francis Duncan. *Atomic Shield*. Vol. 2 of *A History of the United States Atomic Energy Commission*. Washington, D.C.: Atomic Energy Commission, 1972.

———. *Nuclear Navy, 1946–1962*. Chicago: University of Chicago Press, 1974.

Hewlett, Richard G., and Jack Holl. *Atoms for Peace and War, 1953–1961: Eisenhower and the Atomic Energy Commission*. Berkeley: University of California Press, 1989.

Holl, Jack. *Argonne National Laboratory, 1946–1996*. Urbana: University of Illinois Press, 1997.

Holl, Jack, Roger Anders, and Alice Buck. *The United States Civilian Nuclear Power Policy, 1954–1984: A Summary History*. Washington, D.C.: DOE, 1986.

Holloway, David. *Stalin and the Bomb*. New Haven: Yale University Press, 1994.

Howorth, Jolyon, and Patricia Chilton, eds. *Defence and Dissent in Contemporary France*. London: Croom Helm, 1984.

Jones, Vincent. *Manhattan: The Army and the Atomic Bomb*. Washington, D.C.: Center for Military History, 1985.

International Atomic Energy Agency. *The International Chernobyl Project, An Overview*. Vienna: International Atomic Energy Agency, 1991.

Irving, David. *The German Atomic Bomb*. New York: Simon and Schuster, 1967.

Isserman, Maurice. *If I Had a Hammer: The Death of the Old Left and the Birth of the New Left*. Chicago: University of Illinois Press, 1993.

Jasper, James N. *Nuclear Politics: Energy and the State in the United States, Sweden, and France.* Princeton, N.J.: Princeton University Press, 1990.

Johnson, Leland. *Sandia National Laboratories: A History of Exceptional Service in the National Interest.* Albuquerque, N.Mex.: Sandia National Laboratory, 1997.

Johnson, Leland, and Daniel Schaffer. *Oak Ridge National Laboratory, the First Fifty Years.* Knoxville: University of Tennessee Press, 1994.

Jones, Rodney W., et al. *Tracking Nuclear Proliferation: A Guide in Maps and Charts, 1998.* Washington, D.C.: Carnegie Endowment for International Peace, 1998.

Jones, Vincent. *Manhattan: The Army and the Atomic Bomb.* Washington, D.C.: Center for Military History, 1985.

Kaplan, Fred. *The Wizards of Armageddon.* New York: Simon and Schuster, 1983.

Katz, Milton S. *Ban the Bomb: A History of SANE, the Committee for a Sane Nuclear Policy, 1957–1985.* Westport, Conn.: Greenwood Press, 1986.

Katz, Milton S., and Neil H. Katz. "Pragmatists and Visionaries in the Post–World War II American Peace Movement." In Solomon Wanks, ed., *Doves and Diplomats: Foreign Offices and Peace Movements in Europe and America in the Twentieth Century.* Westport, Conn.: Greenwood Press, 1978.

Kaufman, Luis, et al. *Moe Berg: Athlete, Scholar, Spy.* Boston: Little Brown, 1974.

Kegley, Charles W. Jr., and Euge R. Wittkopf. *The Nuclear Reader: Strategy, Weapons, War.* 2d ed. New York: St. Martin's, 1989.

Kemeny, John G. *Report of the President's Commission on the Accident at Three Mile Island.* New York: Pergamon Press, 1979.

Kevles, Daniel J. *The Physicists: The History of a Scientific Community in Modern America.* New York: Knopf, 1978.

Kramish, Arnold. *The Peaceful Atom in Foreign Policy.* New York: Dell, 1965.

Lanouette, William. *The Atom, Politics, and the Press.* Washington, D.C.: Woodrow Wilson International Center, 1992.

Lapp, Ralph. *The Voyage of the Lucky Dragon.* New York: Penguin, 1958.

Larkin, Bruce D. *Nuclear Designs: Great Britain, France, and China in the Global Governance of Nuclear Arms.* New Brunswick, N.J.: Transaction Publishers, 1996.

Laurence, William. *Dawn over Zero: The Story of the Atomic Bomb.* New York: Knopf, 1947.

LeMay, Curtis, with McKinlay Kantor. *Mission with LeMay: My Story.* Garden City, N.Y.: Doubleday, 1965.

Lewis, Flora. *One of Our H-Bombs Is Missing.* New York: McGraw Hill, 1967.

Lifton, Robert Jay, and Greg Mitchell. *Hiroshima in America: Fifty Years of Denial.* New York: Putnam, 1995.

Lin, Chong-Pin. *China's Nuclear Weapons Strategy: Tradition within Evolution.* Lexington, Mass.: D.C. Heath, 1988.

Lockwood, Dunbar. "Strategic Nuclear Forces Under START II." *Arms Control Today* (December 1992).

Los Alamos National Laboratory. "The Karen Silkwood Story." *Los Alamos Science* 23 (November 23, 1996).

MacEachin, Douglas. *The Final Months of the War with Japan: Signals Intelligence, U.S. Invasion Planning, and the A-Bomb Decision.* Washington, D.C.: Central Intelligence Agency Center for the Study of Intelligence, 1998.

Mazuzan, George, and J. Samuel Walker. *Controlling the Atom: The Beginnings of Nuclear Regulation, 1946–1962.* Berkeley: University of California Press, 1984.

McCaffrey, David P. *The Politics of Nuclear Power: A History of the Shoreham Nuclear Power Plant.* Boston: Kluwer Academic Publishers, 1991.

McLellan, David. *Dean Acheson: The State Department Years.* New York: Dodd, Mead, 1976.

McNamara, Robert. *Blundering into Disaster: Surviving the First Century of the Nuclear Age.* New York: Pantheon, 1986.

———. *The Essence of Security: Reflections in Office.* London: Hodder and Stoughton, 1968.

McPhee, John. *Curve of Binding Energy.* New York: Farrar, Straus and Giroux, 1974.

Medvedev, Zhores. *Nuclear Disaster in the Urals.* New York: Vintage, 1980.

Mendelsohn, Jack. "The U.S. Russian Strategic Arms Control Agenda," *Arms Control Today* (November 1997).

Metzger, Peter. *The Atomic Establishment.* New York: Simon and Schuster, 1972.

Milhollin, Gary. "Heavy Water Cheaters." *Foreign Affairs* 69 (Winter 1987–1988).

Miller, Richard. *Under the Cloud.* New York: Free Press, 1986.

Moss, Norman. *Klaus Fuchs, A Biography.* New York: St. Martin's, 1987.

Murray, Raymond L. *Understanding Radioactive Waste.* 4th ed. Columbus, Ohio: Battelle Memorial Institute, 1994.

National Academy of Sciences. *Management and Disposition of Excess Weapons Plutonium.* Washington, D.C.: National Academy Press, 1994.

National Research Council. *Film Badge Dosimetry in Atmospheric Nuclear Tests.* Washington, D.C.: National Academy Press, 1989.

NATO Information Service. *The North Atlantic Treaty Organisation: Facts and Figures.* Brussels, Belgium: NATO Information Service, 1989.

NATO Office of Information and Press. *NATO Handbook.* Brussels, Belgium: NATO Office of Information and Press, 1995.

Office of Environmental Management. *Linking Legacies: Connecting the Cold War Nuclear Weapons Production Process to Their Environmental Consequences.* Washington, D.C.: U.S. Department of Energy, 1997.

Patterson, Walter C. *The Plutonium Business.* San Francisco: The Sierra Club, 1984.

Polmar, Normal. *The Death of the Thresher.* New York: Chilton Books, 1964.

Potter, William. *Nuclear Profiles of the Soviet Successor States.* Monterey, Calif.: Monterey Institute of International Studies, 1993.

Powers, Thomas. *Heisenberg's War.* New York: Knopf, 1993.

Prochnav, William, and Richard Larsen. *A Certain Democrat: Senator Henry M. Jackson, A Political Biography.* Englewood Cliffs, N.J.: Prentice Hall, 1972.

Radosh, Ronald, and Joyce Milton. *The Rosenberg File: A Search for the Truth.* New York: Random House, 1984.

Ragovin, Mitchell. *Three Mile Island: A Report to the Commissioners and to the Public.* Washington, D.C.: Nuclear Regulatory Commission, 1980.

Rashke, Richard. *The Killing of Karen Silkwood.* New York: Houghton Mifflin, 1981.

Reiss, Milton, and Robert S. Litwak. *Nuclear Proliferation after the Cold War.* Washington, D.C.: Woodrow Wilson Center Press, 1994.

Report of the Secretary of Defense, Frank C. Carlucci, to the Congress on the FY 1990/FY 1991 Biennial Budget. Washington, D.C.: USGPO, 1989, 74–75.

Resis, Albert, ed. *Molotov Remembers: Inside Kremlin Politics.* Chicago: Ivan R. Dee, 1993.

Review of the Methods Used to Assign Radiation Doses to Service Personnel at Nuclear Weapons Tests. Committee on Dose Assignment and Reconstruction for Service Personnel at Nuclear Weapons Tests, NAS/NRC Washington, D.C.: National Academy Press, 1986.

Rhodes, Richard. *Dark Sun.* New York: Simon and Schuster, 1995.

———. *The Making of the Atomic Bomb.* New York: Simon and Schuster, 1986.

Richelson, Jeffrey, and Desmond Ball. *The Ties That Bind.* Winchester, Mass.: Allen and Unwyn, 1985.

Rockwell, Theodore. *Rickover Effect: How One Man Made a Difference.* Annapolis, Md.: U.S. Naval Institute Press, 1992.

Rotblat, J. *Scientists in the Quest for Peace.* Cambridge, Mass.: MIT Press, 1972.

Saffer, Thomas H., and Orville E. Kelly. *Countdown Zero.* New York: G.P. Putnam, 1982.

Sagan, Carl. "Nuclear War and Climatic Catastrophe: Some Policy Implications." *Foreign Affairs* 62 (Winter 1983–1984): 257–292.

Scheer, Robert. *With Enough Shovels: Reagan, Bush and Nuclear War.* New York: Random House, 1982.

Schroeer, Dietrich. *Science, Technology, and the Nuclear Arms Race.* New York: John Wiley, 1984.

Schwarz, Jordan. *The Speculator: Bernard Baruch in Washington, 1917–1965.* Chapel Hill: University of North Carolina Press, 1981.

Seaborg, Glenn T., and Benjamin S. Loeb. *Kennedy, Khrushchev and the Test Ban.* Berkeley: University of California Press, 1981.

———. *Stemming the Tide: Arms Control in the Johnson Years.* Lexington, Mass.: Lexington Books, 1987.

———. *The Atomic Energy Commission under Nixon: Adjusting to Troubled Times.* New York: St. Martin's, 1993.

Sherwin, Martin. *A World Destroyed.* New York: Vintage, 1987.

Sigal, Leon. *Disarming Strangers: Nuclear Diplomacy with North Korea.* Princeton, N.J.: Princeton University Press, 1998.

Smyth, Henry D. *Atomic Energy for Military Purposes.* Princeton, N.J.: Princeton University Press, 1945.

Sontag, Sherry, and Christopher Drew. *Blind Man's Bluff: The Untold Story of American Submarine Espionage.* New York: Public Affairs, 1998.

Spector, Leonard S. *The Undeclared Bomb.* Cambridge, Mass.: Ballinger Books, 1988.

Spinardi, Graham. *From Polaris to Trident: The Development of U.S. Fleet Ballistic Missile Technology.* New York: Cambridge University Press, 1994.

Steury, Donald P. *Intentions and Capabilities: Estimates on Soviet Strategic Forces, 1950–1983.* Washington, D.C.: Center for the Study of Intelligence, 1996.

Strauss, Lewis. *Men and Decisions.* Garden City, N.Y.: Doubleday, 1962.

Strickland, Donald. *Scientists in Politics: The Atomic Scientists Movement, 1945–1946.* West Lafayette, Ind.: Purdue University Press, 1968.

Szulc, Tad. *The Bombs of Palomares.* New York: Gollancz, 1967.

Teller, Edward. *Better a Shield than a Sword: Perspectives on Defense and Technology.* London: Free Press, 1987.

Thompson, Starley L., and Stephen H. Schneider. "Nuclear Winter Reappraised." *Foreign Affairs* 65 (Summer 1986).

Turco, R. P., O. B. Toon, T. P. Ackerman, J. B. Pollack, and Carl Sagan. "Global Atmospheric Consequences of Nuclear War." *Science* 122 (December 23, 1983): 1283–1293.

"Twenty Years Later: People of Three Mile Island exemplify Changes in Nuclear Industry," *The Nuclear Professional* 14, no. 1 (Atlanta, Georgia, 1999).

Union of Concerned Scientists. *The Nuclear Fuel Cycle: A Survey of the Public Health, Environmental, and National Security Effects of Nuclear Power.* Cambridge, Mass.: Union of Concerned Scientists, 1975.

United States Department of Energy. *DOE Research and Development and Field Activities.* Washington, D.C.: Department of Energy 1979.

United States Strategic Bombing Survey. *The Effects of the Atomic Bombs on Hiroshima and Nagasaki.* Santa Fe, N.M.: W. Gannon, 1973.

Vaisse, Maurice ed. *La France et l'atome: Études d'histoire nucleaire.* Brussels, Belgium: Bruyant, 1994.

Varner, R., and W. Collier. *A Matter of Risk.* London: Hodder and Stoughton, 1979.

Walker, J. Samuel. *Containing the Atom: Nuclear Regulation in a Changing Environment, 1963–1971.* Berkeley: University of California Press, 1992.

———. *A Short History of Nuclear Regulation, 1946–1999.* Washington, D.C.: Nuclear Regulatory Commission, 2000.

Walker, Mark. *Uranium Machines, Nuclear Explosives, and National Socialism: The German Quest for Nuclear Power, 1939–1949.* New York: Cambridge University Press, 1991.

Wang, Jessica. *American Science in an Age of Anxiety: Scientists, Anticommunism and the Cold War.* Chapel Hill: University of North Carolina Press, 1999.

Ware, C. "The Silkwood Coalition." *New West* (June 18, 1979).

Weart, Spencer. *Nuclear Fear: A History of Images.* Cambridge, Mass.: Harvard University Press, 1988.

Wilkie, Tom. "Old Age Can Kill the Bomb," *New Scientist* 139 (February 16, 1984).

Williams, Robert Chadwell. *Klaus Fuchs: Atom Spy.* Cambridge, Mass.: Harvard University Press, 1987.

Wittner, Lawrence S. *Rebels against War: The American Peace Movement, 1933–1984.* Philadelphia: Temple University Press, 1984.

———. *Resisting the Bomb: A History of the World Nuclear Disarmament Movement, 1954–1970.* Stanford, Calif.: Stanford University Press, 1997.

York, Herbert F. *The Advisors: Oppenheimer, Teller, and the Superbomb.* San Francisco: Freeman, 1976.

———. *Making Weapons, Talking Peace: A Physicist's Odyssey from Hiroshima to Geneva.* New York: Basic Books, 1987.

———. *Race to Oblivion: A Participant's View of the Arms Race.* New York: Simon and Schuster, 1970.

INDEX

Boldface page numbers denote main entries; *italic* page numbers denote illustrations.

SNAP program (systems for nuclear
    auxiliary power) 310–311, *311,*
    312
South Africa 311–313
    and Comprehensive Test Ban
        Treaty 66
    and Israel 152
    and proliferation 268, 269
South Korea 269
Soviet nuclear weapons tests 286,
    313–314
    Russia 286
    at Semipalatinsk-21 304
    at Totskoe 333
Soviet Union *See also* Russia
    and anti-ballistic missiles 10
    and Anti-Ballistic Missile
        Treaty 10–11
    and Armenia 15
    and Baruch Plan 31
    and "Big Three" Meetings 34
    and Niels Bohr 37
    and brinkmanship 40–41
    and Delta class submarines
        79–80
    and detente 82–83
    Mikhail Gorbachev and
        125–126
    Andrey Andreyevich Gromyko
        and 128
    Abram Fedorovich Ioffe and
        149
    Peter Leonidovich Kapitsa and
        159
    and Kazakhstan 160
    Vitali Khlopin and 162
    Nikita S. Khrushchev and
        162–164
    and Krasnoyarsk 167
    Igor Vasil'evich Kurchatov and
        167–168
    and Kyshtym accident
        168–169
    and Lithuania 177
    Vyacheslav Mikhaylovich
        Molotov and 195–196
    and proliferation 268
    and Russia 286
    Andrey Dmitrievich Sakharov
        and 292
    and SALT I 292
    and SALT II 293
    and *Sputnik* 315
    Joseph Stalin and 316–317
    and Sverdlovsk 325
    and Ukraine 342
    and Venona decrypts 351–352
    and Vladivostok Accord
        353–354
    and Warsaw Treaty Organiza-
        tion 356
    and Yalta Conference
        367–368
    Boris Yeltsin and 369
    Yakov Borisovich Zel'dovich
        and 372
    and zero option 372
Soviet weapons
    Anatoly Petrovich Aleksandrov
        6
    and Arzamas-16 16
    Lavrenty Beria and 32–33
    Delta class submarines as
        79–80

production at Sverdlovsk 325
production at Tomsk 332–333
Scud missiles as 302
submarines 323
Typhoon class submarines as
    340
Yankee class submarines as 368
space
    SNAP program 310–311
    Sputnik 315–316
Spain 37, 314–315
Spartan 10
spies *See* espionage
Sprint 10
Sputnik 315–316
    and Argonne National Labora-
        tory 12
    John Foster Dulles and 87
    Dwight David Eisenhower and
        92
    and France—nuclear arms
        108
    John F. Kennedy and 160
    Nikita Khrushchev and 163
    James R. Killian and 164
    and *Minuteman* missiles 192
    and missile gap 194
    Hyman Rickover and 281
    and U-2 Aircraft 341
Stalin, Joseph *250, 316–317, 317*
    and "Big Three" Meetings 34
    and Peter Leonidovich Kapitsa
        159
    and Nikita Khrushchev 163
    and Krasnoyarsk 167
    and Igor Vasil'evich Kurchatov
        168
    and Georgy M. Malenkov 181
    and Manhattan Engineer Dis-
        trict 184
    and Potsdam Conference 249
    and Russia 287
    and Soviet nuclear weapons
        tests 314
    and Harry S. Truman 337, 339
    and Yalta Conference 367
    at Yalta Conference 367
START (Strategic Arms Reduction)
    Treaties
    and Intermediate-Range
        Nuclear Forces Treaty 147
    and Savannah River Site 300
    and second-strike capability
        304
    and Vladivostok Accord 354
START I (Strategic Arms Reduction
    Treaty I) 317–318
    and arms control 15
    George Herbert Walker Bush
        and 45, 46
    and Cooperative Threat
        Reduction 68–69
    and dual-track strategy 86
    and France—nuclear arms
        108
    and Kazakhstan 160
    and *Minuteman* missiles 192
    and Nuclear Posture Review
        219
    and On-Site Inspection Agency
        228
    and Pantex 243
    and Presidential Nuclear Ini-
        tiative-91 261

Ronald Reagan and 277
and Reykjavik Summit Confer-
    ence 279
and Russia 288, 289
and SALT II 294
and Savannah River Site 300
and submarine-launched bal-
    listic missiles 323
and summit meetings 324
and Ukraine 342
and Weapons Production
    Complex 361
Boris Yeltsin and 370
and zero option 372
START II (Strategic Arms Reduction
    Treaty II) 318–319
    and arms control 15
    William Jefferson Clinton and
        62
    and Comprehensive Test Ban
        Treaty 66
    and *Minuteman* missiles 192
    and Nuclear Posture Review
        219
    and submarine-launched bal-
        listic missiles 323
    Boris Yeltsin and 369, 370
    and zero option 372
"Star Wars" *See* Strategic Defense
    Initiative (SDI)
Stationary Low-Power Reactor (SL-
    1) 308–309
stochastic 319
Strassman, Fritz 319
    and chain reaction 54
    and Lise Meitner 190
    and Naval Research Laboratory
        203
    and Leo Szilard 326
Strategic Arms Limitation Treaties
    See SALT (Strategic Arms Limita-
    tion) Treaties
strategic bombers *319, 319–320,*
    334
Strategic Defense Initiative (SDI)
    320–321
    Hans Bethe's criticism of 34
    Harold Brown and 44
    and Intermediate-Range
        Nuclear Forces Treaty 147
    and Lawrence Livermore
        National Laboratory 172
    Robert S. McNamara and 190
    Ronald Reagan and 277
    and Reykjavik Summit Confer-
        ence 278
    and SANE (Committee for a
        Sane Nuclear Policy) 297
    Edward Teller and 328
    and Union of Concerned Sci-
        entists 344
strategies
    counterforce strategy 70
    countervalue strategy 70
    decoupling 76
    dense-pack basing 80
    double-key system 85
    dual-track strategy 85–86
    fail-safe 98
    Single Integrated Operational
        Plan 308
    strategic bombers 319–320
    Strategic Defense Initiative
        320–321

triad 334
zero option 372
Strauss, Lewis *321, 321–322*
    and Atomic Energy Act of
        1954 22
    and William L. Borden 38
    and EURATOM 96
    and *Lucky Dragon (Fukuryu
        Maru)* 180
    and John McCone 187
    and Kenneth D. Nichols 208
    and power reactors of the
        United States 256
    and Shippingport 305
    and Harold Urey 350
strontium 322
submarine accidents
    Scorpion 301
    Thresher 330
submarine-launched ballistic mis-
    siles (SLBMs) 194, *322–323, 323*
    and cruise missiles 71
    and Delta class submarines 79
    double-key system on 85
    and multiple independently
        targetable reentry vehicles
        197
    and MX missiles 198
    and Nuclear Posture Review
        219
    and Presidential Decision
        Directive 59 260
    and Presidential Nuclear Ini-
        tiative-91 261
    and Russia 289
    and SALT I 293
    and SALT II 294
    and START I 317, 318
    and triad 334
    and *Trident* 334
    and Typhoon class submarines
        340
    and Yankee class submarines
        368
submarines *See* nuclear submarines
summit meetings 323–325
    and arms control 15
    "Big Three" Meetings 34
    James F. Byrnes and 47
    Glassboro Summit 121
    Nikita Khrushchev and 163
    Reykjavik Summit Conference
        278–279
    and U-2 Aircraft 341
    Vladivostok Accord 353–354
    Yalta Conference 367–368
Sverdlovsk 16, 325
Sweden 325
    boiling water reactor in 37
    in Zangger Committee 371
swimming pool reactors 325
    Cerenkov (Cherenkov) radia-
        tion in 53
    cladding in 62
Syria 60
Szilard, Leo 326
    and Advisory Committee on
        Uranium 4
    and Vannever Bush 46
    and chain reaction 54
    and University of Chicago 58,
        59
    and Albert Einstein 90
    and Enrico Fermi 103